Crete

THE ROUGH GUIDE

There are more than one hundred Rough Guide titles
covering destinations from Amsterdam to Zimbabwe

Forthcoming titles include
Bangkok • Barbados
Japan • Jordan • Syria

Rough Guide Reference Series
Classical Music • European Football • The Internet • Jazz
Opera • Reggae • Rock Music • World Music

Rough Guide Phrasebooks
Czech • French • German • Greek • Hindi & Urdu • Hungarian • Indonesian
Italian • Japanese • Mandarin Chinese • Mexican Spanish • Polish
Portuguese • Russian • Spanish • Thai • Turkish • Vietnamese

Rough Guides on the Internet
http://www.roughguides.com

ROUGH GUIDE CREDITS

Text editor: Helena Smith
Series editor: Mark Ellingham
Editorial: Martin Dunford, Jonathan Buckley, Samantha Cook, Jo Mead, Kate Berens, Amanda Tomlin, Ann-Marie Shaw, Paul Gray, Sarah Dallas, Chris Schüler, Caroline Osborne, Kieran Falconer, Judith Bamber, Olivia Eccleshall, Orla Duane (UK); Andrew Rosenberg (US)
Production: Susanne Hillen, Andy Hilliard, Judy Pang, Link Hall, Nicola Williamson, Helen Ostick, James Morris

Cartography: Melissa Flack, Maxine Burke, Nichola Goodliffe
Picture research: Eleanor Hill
Online editors: Alan Spicer, Kate Hands (UK); Geronimo Madrid (US)
Finance: John Fisher, Celia Crowley, Neeta Mistry
Marketing & Publicity: Richard Trillo, Simon Carloss, Niki Smith (UK); Jean-Marie Kelly, SoRelle Braun (US)
Administration: Tania Hummel, Alexander Mark Rogers

ACKNOWLEDGEMENTS

Our special thanks for their help with this new edition to Jackie Richardson in Sitía, Sharon Bowen in Mália, Carline Harber in Paleohóra, Professor Costis Davaras and Nikos Karellis, editor of *Stigmes* magazine. Valuable assistance was also rendered by Eftichios Botonakis, Stelios Manousakis, Kostas Kamaratakis, Yiorgos Margaritakis, Yiorgos Yeorgamlis, Stelios Tsirindanis, Froso Bora, Maria Picassi, Manolis Nikolodakis, Brian and Lynn Butterworth, Irene Michaelaki and María Kalaïtzaki at the Haniá Tourist Office, María Kafetzaki of the Sitía Development Organization, and Georgia Kanapitsa and the staff of the Greek Tourist Office in London. A fraternal *efharistó pára polí* also goes to Mark Dubin for help in updating the Basics section.

To all involved at Rough Guides go the usual plaudits for a great editorial and production job: thanks to the proofreader Jennifer Speake; James Morris, Eleanor Hill and Nichola Goodliffe in production; and especially to our editor Helena Smith who calmly kept her head when all about her were losing theirs.

John would like to thank Geoff and Julia for a great job, and, as always, A and the two little Js. Geoff says a big thank you to Han for copious help and support.

Finally, this edition would have been much the poorer without all the readers who sent in their comments, advice, criticisms and recommendations: the full roll of honour (barring those whose signatures defeated us) appears on p.v.

PUBLISHING INFORMATION

This fourth edition published May 1998 by Rough Guides Ltd, 1 Mercer St, London WC2H 9QJ.
    Previous editions 1988, 1991, 1995.
    Distributed by the Penguin Group:
Penguin Books Ltd, 27 Wrights Lane, London W8 5TZ
Penguin Books USA Inc., 375 Hudson Street, New York 10014, USA
Penguin Books Australia Ltd, 487 Maroondah Highway, PO Box 257, Ringwood, Victoria 3134, Australia
Penguin Books Canada Ltd, 10 Alcorn Avenue, Toronto, Ontario, Canada M4V 1E4
Penguin Books (NZ) Ltd, 182–190 Wairau Road, Auckland 10, New Zealand
Typeset in Linotron Univers and Century Old Style to an original design by Andrew Oliver.
Printed in England by Clays Ltd, St Ives PLC.
Illustrations in Part One and Part Three by Edward Briant.
Illustrations on p.1 by Simon Fell & p.331 by Henry Iles.

400pp – Includes index
A catalogue record for this book is available from the British Library
ISBN 1-85828-316-7

Crete

THE ROUGH GUIDE

written and researched by

John Fisher and Geoff Garvey

with additional research by

Julia Tweed

THE ROUGH GUIDES

THE ROUGH GUIDES

TRAVEL GUIDES • PHRASEBOOKS • MUSIC AND REFERENCE GUIDES

 We set out to do something different when the first Rough Guide was published in 1982. Mark Ellingham, just out of university, was travelling in Greece. He brought along the popular guides of the day, but found they were all lacking in some way. They were either strong on ruins and museums but went on for pages without mentioning a beach or taverna. Or they were so conscious of the need to save money that they lost sight of Greece's cultural and historical significance. Also, none of the books told him anything about Greece's contemporary life – its politics, its culture, its people, and how they lived.

So with no job in prospect, Mark decided to write his own guidebook, one which aimed to provide practical information that was second to none, detailing the best beaches and the hottest clubs and restaurants, while also giving hard-hitting accounts of every sight, both famous and obscure, and providing up-to-the-minute information on contemporary culture. It was a guide that encouraged independent travellers to find the best of Greece, and was a great success, getting shortlisted for the Thomas Cook travel guide award,

and encouraging Mark, along with three friends, to expand the series.

The Rough Guide list grew rapidly and the letters flooded in, indicating a much broader readership than had been anticipated, but one which uniformly appreciated the Rough Guide mix of practical detail and humour, irreverence and enthusiasm. Things haven't changed. The same four friends who began the series are still the caretakers of the Rough Guide mission today: to provide the most reliable, up-to-date and entertaining information to independent-minded travellers of all ages, on all budgets.

We now publish 100 titles and have offices in London and New York. The travel guides are written and researched by a dedicated team of more than 100 authors, based in Britain, Europe, the USA and Australia. We have also created a unique series of phrasebooks to accompany the travel series, along with an acclaimed series of music guides, and a best-selling pocket guide to the Internet and World Wide Web. We also publish comprehensive travel information on our Web site:

http://www.roughguides.com

HELP US UPDATE

We've gone to a lot of effort to ensure that this new edition of The Rough Guide to Crete is accurate and up-to-date. However, things change – places get "discovered", opening hours are notoriously fickle, restaurants and rooms raise prices or lower standards, extra buses are laid on or off. If you feel we've got it wrong or left something out, we'd like to know, and if you can remember the address, the price, the time, the phone number, so much the better.

We'll credit all contributions, and send a copy of the next edition (or any other Rough Guide if you prefer) for the best letters. Please mark letters: "Rough Guide Crete Update" and send to:
Rough Guides, 1 Mercer St, London WC2H 9QJ, or
Rough Guides, 375 Hudson St, 9th floor, New York NY 10014.
Or send email to: mail@roughguides.co.uk
Online updates about this book can be found on Rough Guides' Web site at http://www.roughguides.com

THE AUTHORS

John Fisher was one of the authors of the first ever Rough Guide – to Greece – in 1981, and has been inextricably involved with the series and with Crete ever since. The author of several other Rough Guide titles, John can normally be found at Rough Guide HQ in London, where work takes up far too much good island-hopping time. He lives in South London with his wife and two young sons.

Geoff Garvey first came to Crete as a student of ancient history and progressed from his study of the Minoans to develop a great affection both for the island and its people. His favourite activities when not working on the next update include checking out the bars in Iráklion and Réthimnon and searching for obscure Minoan sites and remote Byzantine chapels. A keen hiker, he also loves to go walking in the Psilorítis mountains, where he has been known to entertain bemused villagers with some truly dreadful renditions on the lyra. When away from the island he lives in London and is co-author of the Rough Guide to Andalucia.

READERS' LETTERS

We'd like to thank the readers of previous editions, who took the time to write in with comments and suggestions. For this edition, we were helped by letters from:

Stuart R.B. Johnston, Catherine & Ian Beaumont, J.M. Cooper, Professor Robin Higham, Simon D. Phillips, Jennifer Speake, Lucia Sanou, Fiona Daly, Dr Anne Tait, Stephen Foxcroft, Dini Hogenelst, Steve Henwood, Lorna Kellett, Gary Copper & Collette Bird, Simon Hutchence, Jill Singleton, Mike McKenna, Bud Evans, Julie Hopkins, Ian Laird, Thomas Buchendorfer, Mark Campbell & Susan Mulhall, Arlene Russo, John R.W. Thirlwell, Marilyn Miller, Bill Jones, Ben Jones, Sara Mathias, Alan Colling, Mark Talbot, Andrew Skinner, Zannie Fraser, Ann Simonsen, Peter Symon, Marjolein van de Rhoer & Budhy Wetters, Enney & Chanan Bernstein, Susan Wallis, Louie Tham, Emma Gervasio, D. Murray, David Brown, Joan & Paul Cardus, Andy Moffat, Tony Brennan, W.A. Francis, Elizabeth Read, Lance Chilton, James N. Scandalios, Ursula Nottnagel, Chris Bertram, Joachim Deisenhofer, Keith Goodchild, D.J. Authers, Peter de Leeuw & Monique Bosman, John Scott, Bea & Marc Perriéns-Hooghe, Mrs G.M. Smith, John & Cat Vlast, Celia Barden & Alan Gledhill, Kate Fearn, Teresa Read, Francoise Crabbé, Wim Hoogendijk, Ilias Perakis, Søren & Marie-Louise Pold, Greg & Di Veitch, Caroline Roberts, Peter & Dianne Barnes, Derrick & Vickie Neilson, Mrs M.E. Saxon, Eileen Scott, Simon Hunter, Lionel Crawford, Helen Orm, W J Francis, Ann Leonard, John Watt, A.A. Spittle, Sam Kenny, Brian Telford, Dana Winter, Chris Ellis, Kevin Tipton, Alison Gell & Neil Gardener, Eve Walter & Rinaldo Di Fabio, Steve Benterman, Peter Lentemans.

CONTENTS

Introduction x

● CHAPTER 3: RÉTHIMNON 195–239

● CHAPTER 4: HANIÁ 240–330

PART THREE CONTEXTS 331

LIST OF MAPS

MAP SYMBOLS

Major road		Church	
Minor road		Mosque	
Track		Cave	
Path		Mountain range	
Railway		Mountain peak	
Ferry route		Cutting	
Chapter division boundary		Gorge	
Provincial boundary		Information centre	
River		Post office	
Airport		Bus station	
Monastery or convent		Fortifications	
Castle		Built up area	
Refuge		Building	
Ancient monument		Cathedral	
Lighthouse		Park	
		Beach	

INTRODUCTION

Crete is a great deal more than just another Greek island. Much of the time, especially in the cities or along the developed north coast, it doesn't feel like an island at all, but a substantial land in its own right. Which of course it is – a mountainous, wealthy and at times surprisingly cosmopolitan one with a tremendous and unique history. There are two big cities, **Iráklion** and **Haniá**, a host of sizeable, historic towns, and an island culture which is uniquely Cretan: the Turks were in occupation less than a hundred years ago, and the Greek flag raised for the first time only in 1913.

Long before, Crete was distinguished as the home of Europe's earliest civilization. It was only at the beginning of this century that the legends of King Minos, and of a Cretan society which ruled the Greek world in prehistory, were confirmed by excavations at Knossós and Festós. Yet **the Minoans** had a remarkably advanced and cultured society, at the centre of a substantial maritime trading empire, as early as 2000 BC. The artworks produced on Crete at this time are unsurpassed anywhere in the ancient world, and it seems clear, wandering through the Minoan palaces and towns, that life on Crete in those days was good. The apparently peaceful Minoan culture survived a number of major disasters, following each of which the palaces were rebuilt on an even

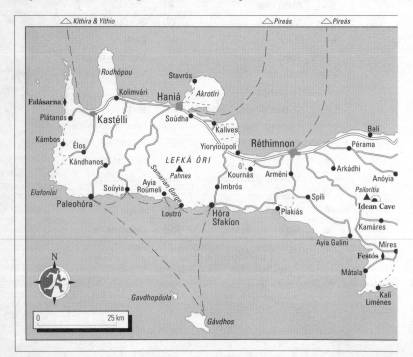

grander scale. It is only after a third catastrophe that significant numbers of weapons start to appear in the ruins, probably because Mycenaean Greeks had taken control of the island. Nevertheless, for nearly 500 years, by far the longest period of peace the island has seen, Crete was home to a civilization well ahead of its time.

The Minoans are believed to have come originally from Anatolia, and the island's position as meeting point – and strategic fulcrum – between east and west has played a crucial role in its **subsequent history**. Control passed from Greeks to Romans to Saracens, through the Byzantine Empire to Venice, and finally to Turkey for 200 years. During World War II Crete was occupied by the Germans, and gained the dubious distinction of being the first place to be successfully invaded by parachute. Each one of these diverse rulers has left some mark, and more importantly they have marked the islanders and forged for the land a personality toughened by endless struggles for independence.

Today, with a flourishing agricultural economy, Crete is one of the few Greek islands which could support itself without tourists. Nevertheless, tourism is heavily promoted, and is rapidly taking over parts of the island altogether. Along the populous **north coast**, Crete can be as sophisticated as you want it, and the northeast, in particular, can be depressingly overdeveloped. In the less known coastal reaches of the **south** it's still possible to find yourself alone, but even here places which have not yet been reached are getting harder and harder to find. By contrast, the high mountains of the interior are barely touched, and one

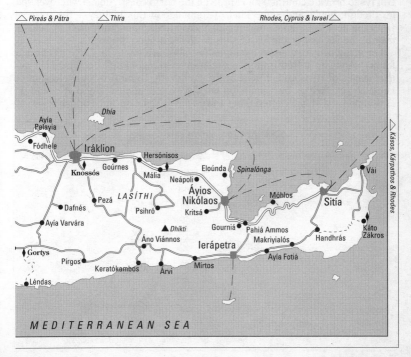

of the best things to do on Crete is to hire a Vespa and head for remoter villages, often only a few kilometres off some heavily beaten track.

The **mountains**, which dominate the view as you approach and make all but the shortest journey an expedition, are perhaps the most rewarding aspect of Crete. In the west, the White Mountains are snowcapped right into June, Psilorítis (Mount Ida) in the centre is higher still, and in the east the heights continue through the Dhíkti and Sitía ranges to form a continuous chain from one end of the island to the other. They make a relatively small place – Crete is about 260km long by 60km at its widest (roughly the size of Jamaica) – feel much larger. There are still many places where the roads cannot reach.

Where to go

Every part of Crete has its loyal devotees and it's hard to pick out highlights, but on the whole if you want to get away from it all you should head for the ends of the island – west, towards **Haniá** and the smaller, less well-connected places along the south and west coasts, or east to **Sitía**. Wherever you're staying though, you don't have to go far inland to escape the crowds.

Whatever you do, your first objective will probably be to leave behind the urban sprawl of **Iráklion** (Heraklion) as quickly as possible – having paid the obligatory, and rewarding, visits to the **archeological museum** and nearby **Knossós**. The **Minoan sites** are of course one of the major attractions of Crete: as well as Knossós itself there are many other grand remains scattered around the centre of the island – **Festós** and **Ayía Triádha** in the south (with Roman **Górtys** to provide contrast) and **Mália** on the north coast. Almost wherever you go though, you'll find some kind of reminder of this history – the town of **Gourniá** near the tourist enticements of **Áyios Nikólaos**, the palace of **Zákros** over in the far east or the lesser sites scattered around the west.

For many people, unexpected highlights also turn out to be Crete's **Venetian forts** – dominant at **Réthimnon**, magnificent at Frangokástello, and found in various stages of ruin around most of the island; the **Byzantine churches**, most famously at **Kritsá** but again to be discovered almost anywhere; and in Réthimnon and Haniá cluttered **old towns** full of Venetian and Turkish relics.

Month	Average daytime temperature		Average water temperature		Average rainy days
	°C	°F	°C	°F	
January	12	52	15	59	14
February	12	52	15	59	11
March	14	57	16	61	8
April	17	62	17	62	6
May	21	70	20	68	3
June	23	74	23	74	1
July	25	77	24	75	0
August	26	79	25	77	0
September	25	77	24	75	2
October	21	70	23	74	6
November	18	64	19	66	8
December	14	57	17	62	12

Readings taken from Iráklion, roughly in the centre of the island

The mountains and valleys of the interior also deserve far more attention than they get. Only the **Lasíthi** plateau in the east and the **Samarian gorge** in the west really see large numbers of visitors, but almost anywhere you can turn off the main roads and find agricultural villages going about their daily life, and often astonishingly beautiful scenery. This is especially true in the west, where the Lefká Óri – the **White Mountains** – dramatically dominate every view, and numerous lesser gorges run parallel to the Samarian one down to the Libyan Sea. But there's lovely country behind Iráklion too, in the foothills of the Psilorítis range, and especially on the other side of these mountains in the **Amári Valley**, easily reached from Réthimnon. The east also has its moments, in the Dhíkti range and in the spectacular cliff drive from Áyios Nikólaos to Sitía.

As for **beaches**, you'll find great ones almost anywhere on the north coast. From Iráklion to Áyios Nikólaos there's very heavy development, and most package tourists are aiming for the resort hotels here. These places can be fun if nightlife and crowds are what you're after – especially the biggest of them, like **Mália** and **Áyios Nikólaos**, which have the added advantage of being large enough to have plenty of cheap food and accommodation, plus good transport links. Mália also has sand as good as any on the island (if you can find it through the crowds), but Áyios Nikólaos really doesn't have much of a beach of its own. Further east things get quieter: **Sitía** is a place of real character, and beyond it on the east coast are a number of beautifully tranquil places – especially **Zákros** – and **Vái**, very busy with day-trippers. To the west there's another tranche of development around **Réthimnon**, but the town itself is relatively unscathed, and a rather lesser cluster of apartments and smaller hotels near **Haniá**, the most attractive of the big towns. Other places at this end of the island tend to be on a smaller scale.

Along the **south coast**, resorts are far more scattered, and the mountains come straight down to the sea much of the way along. Only a handful of places are really developed – **Ierápetra**, **Ayía Galíni**, **Mátala**, **Paleohóra** – and a few more, like **Plakiás** and **Makriyialós**, on their way. But lesser spots in between, not always easy to get to, are some of the most attractive in Crete.

When to go

As the southernmost of all Greek islands, Crete has by far the longest summers: you can get a decent tan here right into October and swim at least from April until early November. **Spring** is the prime time to come: in April and May the island is relatively empty of visitors, the weather clear and not overpoweringly hot, and every scene is brightened by a profusion of wild flowers.

By mid-June the rush is beginning. **July** and **August** are not only the hottest, the most crowded and most expensive months, they are also intermittently blighted by fierce winds and accompanying high seas, which make boat trips very uncomfortable, and at their worst can mean staying indoors for a day or more at a time. The south coast is particularly prone to these. In September the crowds gradually begin to thin out, and **autumn** can again be a great time to visit – but now the landscape looks parched and tired, and there's a feeling of things gradually winding down.

Winters are mild, but also vaguely depressing: many things are shut, it can rain sporadically, sometimes for days, and there's far less life in the streets. In the mountains it snows, even to the extent where villages can be cut off; on the south coast it's generally warmer, soothed by a breeze from Africa. You may get a week or more of really fine weather in the middle of winter, but equally you can have sudden viciously cold snaps right through into March.

> *Crete's mystery is extremely deep. Whoever sets foot on this island senses a mysterious force branching warmly and beneficiently through his veins, senses his soul begin to grow.*
>
> Níkos Kazantzakís, *Report to Greco*

PART ONE

THE

BASICS

GETTING THERE FROM BRITAIN

The vast majority of visitors to Crete are on some form of **package tour** which includes a charter flight direct to the island. This is certainly the simplest way of going about things, and even if you plan to travel independently, a seat on a charter to Iráklion or Haniá is the most straightforward way to start out. But charters – the only way of getting straight to Crete – do have their drawbacks, especially if your plans don't fit neatly into their two-week straitjacket. Anyone planning a longer visit will have to fly to Athens and take the ferry or a domestic flight from there; see p.16 for details of connections.

Overland alternatives take three to four days' of non-stop travel, but if you want to take your time over the journey then driving or taking the train can be enjoyable, while taking the bus remains the cheapest option of all.

BY PLANE

The only way to fly direct to Crete is with a **charter**. Be warned that, on the whole, there is a shortage of flights to Crete, especially to Haniá, and that if you try to book at the last minute you may be forced to fly to Athens instead; **student flights** operate only into Athens.

For details of **agents** and **operators** dealing in charter and discounted scheduled flights, check the list in the box on p.4. Other good sources of information are the ads in London's *Time Out* magazine, and the travel pages in the *Observer*, *Sunday Times* and other Sunday newspapers. *Teletext* is also worth a look, as is your local travel agent.

SCHEDULED FLIGHTS

The advantages of **scheduled flights** are that they can be pre-booked well in advance, and have longer ticket validities. However, many of the cheaper APEX and SuperAPEX fares have an advance-purchase requirement of between seven and fourteen days and/or a minimum-stay requirement, so check conditions carefully.

There are no direct scheduled flights to Crete from the UK. The best you can do is go with Olympic, changing planes in **Athens**: the cheapest official (SuperAPEX) fare is around £270 from London in the low season, rising to around £400 at summer peak times. All other airlines into Athens use a separate terminal some distance from the Olympic one, so be sure to leave plenty of time for the connection. Night flights on Olympic are a bargain possibility, costing between £160 and £390 depending on season; you'll need to get in early for these, however, as they go quickly. Otherwise, British Airways and Virgin have daily scheduled flights to Athens costing from £160 (low season) to £650 (high), with a whole range of fare options in between, with an average of £325 in summer; there is an add-on fare of around £100 to Iráklion. These depend on various restrictions, such as having to book a minimum period ahead and/or staying at least one Saturday night in Greece.

East European airways, such as ČSA, Balkan, Malev and LOT are often cheaper – around £120 one-way, £240 return to Athens for much of the year – but nearly always involve delays, with connections in (respectively) Prague, Sofia, Budapest and Warsaw. These airlines can also be relied on to provide a number of cheap seats to students or those under 26. It is not always possible to book discount fares direct from these airlines, and you'll often pay more by going through an agent (see over).

CHARTER AND DISCOUNTED FLIGHTS

From **London Gatwick** you can get a charter to Iráklion for about £170–200 for a low-season night flight, rising to around £230 at peak time;

AIRLINES

Balkan Airlines, 322 Regent St, London W1 (☎0171/637 7637).

British Airways, 156 Regent St, London W1 (☎0181/897 4000 and ☎0345/222111).

ČSA Czechoslovak Airlines, 72 Margaret St, London W1 (☎0171/255 1898).

LOT Polish Airlines, 313 Regent St, London W1R 7PE (☎0171/580 5037).

Malev Hungarian Airlines, 10 Vigo St, London W1X 1AJ (☎0171/439 0577).

Olympic Airways, 11 Conduit St, London W1 (☎0171/409 3400).

Virgin Airways, Virgin Megastore, 14–16 Oxford St, London W1 (☎01293/747747).

AGENTS AND OPERATORS

Air Travel Advisory Bureau, Charles House, 28 Charles Square, London N1 6HT (☎0171/636 5000). *Reliable agent for charter flights.*

Alecos Tours, 3a Camden Rd, London NW1 (☎0171/267 2092). *Regular Olympic Airways consolidator.*

Avro, 1 Weir Rd, London SW19 8UX (☎0181/715 0000). *Weekly summer charters to Iráklion from Gatwick and Manchester.*

Campus Travel, 52 Grosvenor Gardens, London SW1 (☎0171/730 3402); 541 Bristol Rd, Selly Oak, Birmingham (☎0121/414 1848); 39 Queen's Rd, Clifton, Bristol (☎0117/929 2494); 5 Emmanuel St, Cambridge (☎01223/324283); 53 Forest Rd, Edinburgh (☎0131/668 3303); 166 Deansgate, Manchester (☎0161/273 1721); 13 High St, Oxford (☎01865/242067). *Student/youth travel specialists, with branches also in YHA shops and on university campuses all over Britain. Campus usually has its own student/youth charter flights to Athens during the summer.*

Council Travel, 28a Poland St, London W1 (☎0171/287 3337). *Flights and student discounts.*

Eclipse Flights, First Choice House, Peel Cross Rd, Salford, Manchester M5 2AN (☎01293/554444). *Charter flights to Iráklion and Haniá from Gatwick and Manchester.*

Lupus Travel, 11 Vale Rd, Tunbridge Wells, Kent TN1 1BS (☎01892/553 500). *Reliable agent for all kinds of charter, discount and scheduled flights to Greece and Crete.*

South Coast Student Travel, 61 Ditchling Rd, Brighton (☎01273/570226). *Student experts, but plenty to offer non-students as well.*

Springway Travel, 258 Vauxhall Bridge Rd, London SW1 (☎0171/976 5833). *Reliable discount flight agent.*

STA Travel, 86 Old Brompton Rd, London W7 (☎0171/361 6161); 25 Queen's Rd, Bristol (☎0117/929 4399); 38 Sidney St, Cambridge (☎01223/66966); 75 Deansgate, Manchester (☎0161/834 0668); and personal callers at 117 Euston Rd, London NW1; 28 Vicar Lane, Leeds; 36 George St, Oxford; and offices at the universities of Birmingham, London, Kent and Loughborough. *Discount fares, with particularly good deals for students and young people.*

Travel Bug, 597 Cheetham Hill Rd, Manchester (☎0161/721 4000). *Large range of discounted tickets.*

Travel Cuts, 295 Regent St, London W1 (☎0171/255 1944). *Specialist in student and youth fares with a range of discount flights.*

flights to Haniá cost around the same, but seats are very much harder to come by. From **Manchester**, you can expect to pay around £190–200 (low) to £230 (high) to Iráklion, more like £250 to Haniá. Virtually no flights operate over the winter (Nov–April).

It's worth noting that **non-EU nationals** who buy charter tickets to Greece must buy a return ticket, of no fewer than three days and no more than four weeks, and must accompany it with an **accommodation voucher** for at least the first few nights of their stay – check that the ticket

satisfies these conditions or you could be refused entry. In practice, the "accommodation voucher" is a formality; it has to name an existing hotel but you're not expected to use it (and probably won't be able to if you try). Accommodation vouchers are not necessary when booking scheduled flights.

Student or **under-26** flights are available at fairly reasonable rates, starting at just under £100 for a low-season charter. Be warned, though, that you must be a legitimate student as you may well be required to prove your creden-tials on boarding, especially leaving Greece. People have been denied seats for not having valid ISIC cards. Campus Travel and STA have some of the best deals and also offer one-way tickets – by combining these you can stay much longer than a month.

Travelling **via Athens** may be your only option if you're booking at the last minute, since budget tickets to Athens are available long after all the Crete flights have gone. Prices for charter flights to Athens from London in midsummer start at around £125 (Manchester £190, Glasgow £195).

Finally, remember that **reconfirmation** of charter flights is vital and should be done at least 72 hours in advance.

PACKAGES AND TOURS

If you intend to do little more than stay in one place soaking up the sun, a **package holiday** can offer exceptional value. Especially if you buy one of these at a last-minute discount price, you may find it costs little more than a flight – and you can use the accommodation offered as much or as little as you want. Any high-street travel agent can sell you a standard package to the major resorts of eastern Crete, but for something a bit less predictable at the west end of the island, try one of the smaller, specialist operators listed below.

There are all kinds of deals available, depending on whether you opt for **hotel** or **apartment**

01784
492492

SPECIALIST TOUR OPERATORS

VILLA OR PACKAGE ACCOMMODATION

The Best of Greece, 23–24 Margaret St, London W1N 8LE (☎0171/255 2320). Limited number of exclusive villa and hotel arrangements from a long-established operator – offers packages to five-star and deluxe hotels along the whole north coast.

Direct Travel, Oxford House, 182 Upper Richmond Road, Putney, London SW15 2SH (☎0181/785 4000). Moderately priced studios and villas.

Freelance Holidays, 40b Grove Rd, Stratford upon Avon, Warks CV37 6PB (☎01789/297705). A wide variety of villas, apartments and hotel-based packages throughout the island, with some in tranquil, less-visited locations.

Kosmar Holidays, 358 Bowes Rd, Arnos Grove, London N11 1AN (☎0181/368 6833). Self-catering apartments throughout Crete, including Eloúnda and Áyios Nikólaos in the east, and Haniá and Paleohóra in the west.

Pure Crete, 79 George St, Croydon, Surrey CR0 1LD (☎0181/760 0879). Specializes in some rather pretty village houses and farms in western Crete and near Haniá.

Simply Crete, Chiswick Gate, 598–608 Chiswick High Rd, London W4 5RT (☎0181/994 4462 or 5226). Excellent selection of villas, small hotels and special-interest tours.

Sunvil Holidays, Sunvil House, Upper Square, Old Isleworth, Middlesex TW7 7BJ (☎0181/568 4499). Bigger company, with a good choice of self-catering villa packages in smaller resorts in the west and Haniá villages.

Travel Club of Upminster, 54 Station Rd, Upminster, Essex RM14 2TT (☎01708/225000). Better-than-average apartments and hotels in the Haniá area.

HIKING TOURS

Explore Worldwide (RGC), 1 Frederick St, Aldershot, Hampshire GU11 1LQ (☎01252/319448). Offers an organized rambling tour round the White Mountains, taking in the Samariá gorge.

Ramblers' Holidays, 2 Church Rd, Welwyn Garden City, Herts AL8 6PQ (☎01707/331133). Easy walking tours in western Crete, taking in the Samariá gorge and White Mountains.

Trekking Hellas, Filellínon 7, Athens (☎30/1/33 10 323). Greek specialists in walking tours with a programme devoted to western Crete.

Waymark Holidays, 44 Windsor Rd, Slough SL1 2EJ (☎01753/516477). Walks in the mountains and gorges of western Crete.

NATURE AND WILDLIFE

Marengo Guided Walks, 17 Bernard Crescent, Hunstanton, Norfolk PE36 6ER (☎01485/532710). Spring and autumn botanical outings around Yeoryioúpolis and Plakiás, led by a trained botanist.

Peregrine Holidays, 40–41 South Parade, Summertown, Oxford OX2 7JP (☎01865/511642). Natural history tours of the island, with the emphasis on wildlife, although some archeological sites are included.

accommodation and whether or not you include car rental as part of your holiday. Simply Crete, for example, offers a three-bedroom villa with pool in Haniá (sleeping six) for two weeks in high season at around £450 per person, including flights and transfers. Two-person deals in a self-catering one-bedroom apartment cost £450–520 per person per week in high season. There are considerable reductions on all these prices in low season. Crete is also a great place for **walking**, especially in spring, when lower temperatures combine with a profusion of wild flowers, and a number of companies offer guided rambling holidays. Ramblers' Holidays (see box on p.5), for example, provides a one-week package in May for around £440 per person, including flights, half-board accommodation and guided walks.

BY TRAIN

Travelling **by train** from Britain to Greece takes around three-and-a-half days, and fares are more expensive than flights. Obviously, trains will only take you as far as mainland Greece, from where you'll have to continue your journey by plane or ferry (see "Getting There from Mainland Greece", p.16). However, with a regular ticket, stopovers on the way are possible – in France, Switzerland and Italy – while with an InterRail (see below) or Eurail (p.13) train pass you can take in Greece as part of a wider rail trip around Europe.

One **route** from Britain takes in France, Switzerland and **Italy** before crossing on the ferry from Bari or Brindisi to Pátra (Patras). Rail Europe (see box above) has resumed the sale of through tickets to Greece, routed via the states of the former Yugoslavia. This has reduced demand for tickets on the Italian route which in previous years has put an extra burden on trains and ferries. Book seats on both well in advance, especially in summer (for further ferry information, see "Le Shuttle and the Ferries" below).

TICKETS AND PASSES

Regular **train tickets** from Britain to Greece are not good value. A standard second-class London to Athens return costs £380–400, depending on the route, though if you are **under 26**, you can get a **BIJ ticket**, discounting these fares by around 25 percent; these are available through Eurotrain and Wasteels (see box above). Both regular and BIJ tickets have two months' return validity, or can be purchased as one-ways, and the Italy

RAIL TICKET OFFICES
Eurotrain, 52 Grosvenor Gardens, London SW1 (☎0171/730 3402).
International Rail Centre (Rail Europe), Victoria Station, London SW1 (☎0990/848 848).
Wasteels, Victoria Station, London SW1 (☎0171/834 7066).

BUS TICKET OFFICES
National Express Eurolines, 52 Grosvenor Gardens, London SW1 (☎0171/730 0202).
Olympic Bus, 70 Brunswick Centre, London WC1 (☎0171/837 9141).

routes include the ferry crossing. The tickets also allow for stopovers, so long as you stick to the prescribed route.

Better value by far is to buy an **InterRail pass**, available to anyone resident in Europe for six months. You can buy it from Rail Europe (or any mainline station or accredited travel agent) and the pass offers unlimited travel on a zonal basis on up to 25 European rail networks. The only extras you pay are supplements on certain express and prestige trains, plus half-price fares in Britain (or the country of issue) and on the cross-Channel ferries. The pass includes the ferry from Brindisi in southern Italy to Pátra in Greece, but not travel on the Pireás–Crete ferries. To reach Greece from the UK you'll need a pass valid for at least two zones; Greece is zoned with Italy, Turkey and Slovenia. Once you reach Crete there are no trains at all, of course. Prices are currently £209 for a one-month pass if you're under 26, £279 for the over-26 version. You can't use this ticket for the overland route through the former Yugoslavia. Due to zonal restructuring following the break-up, you'll now need a Global Pass to get you through the four zones to Athens, which run to £259 for the under-26 and £349 for the over-26 versions, both valid for one month.

Finally, anyone over sixty and holding a British Rail Senior Citizen Railcard, can buy a **Rail Europe Senior Card** (£21 for 1 year). This gives up to fifty percent reductions on rail fares throughout Europe and thirty percent off sea crossings.

BY BUS

With charter flights at such competitive rates, it's hard to find good reasons for wanting to spend three or four days on a **bus** to Greece –particularly if your final destination is Crete. Just for the record, the main operators to Athens are Olympic Bus (£100–120 return) and the more reliable National Express Eurolines with better buses and higher prices (£200–220 return) – see the box on p.6 for booking numbers. Be wary of going for the lowest-price operator unless you've heard something positive about them; there have been a string of accidents in recent years with operators flouting the terms of their licence, and horror stories abound of drivers getting lost or their coaches being refused entry. The route is via France and Italy with a ferry across to Greece. Whoever you travel with it can be a gruelling ride; stops of about twenty minutes are made every five or six hours, with the odd longer break for roadside café meals.

BY CAR

If you have the time and inclination, **driving** to Greece can be a pleasant proposition. Realistically, though, it's really only worth considering if you have at least a month to spare, are going to travel in Greece for an extended period, or want to take advantage of various stopovers en route. If Crete is your main goal, you'd be better off flying, and renting a car once you're on the island.

It's important to plan ahead. The **Automobile Association** (AA) provides a comprehensive service offering general advice on all facets of driving to Greece; their European Route Service (contact AA on ☎01256/20123) can arrange a detailed printout of a route to follow. Driving licence, vehicle registration documents and insurance are essential; a Green Card is recommended. The most popular **route** is down through France and Italy to catch one of the Adriatic ferries. A much longer alternative through eastern Europe (Hungary, Romania and Bulgaria) is just about feasible, but driving through former Yugoslavia is unsafe; in any case, these eastern routes are less than convenient for ferries to Crete.

LE SHUTTLE AND THE FERRIES

The **shuttle** service through the Channel Tunnel doesn't significantly affect travel times for drivers to Greece, though it does of course speed up the cross-Channel section of the journey. Le Shuttle operates trains 24 hours a day, carrying cars, motorcycles, buses and their passengers, and taking 35 minutes

> ### CROSS-CHANNEL INFORMATION
> **Hoverspeed**, Dover (☎01304/240101); London (☎0181/5547061). *To Boulogne and Calais.*
> **Le Shuttle**, Customer Services Centre (☎01303/271100). *Information and ticket sales.*
> **P&O European Ferries**, Dover (☎01304/203388); Portsmouth (☎01705/772244); London (☎01705/772244). *To Calais.*
> **Sally Line**, Ramsgate (☎01843/595522); London (☎0181/858 1127). *To Dunkerque.*
> **Stena Sealink Line**, Ashford (☎01233/647047). *To Calais and Dieppe.*

between Folkestone and Calais. At peak times, services operate every fifteen minutes, making advance bookings unnecessary; during the night, services still run hourly. Full return fares from May to August cost £280–300 per vehicle (passengers included), but look out for special offers which can halve this, and for big discounts in the low season.

The alternative **cross-Channel** options for most travellers are the conventional **ferry** or **hovercraft** links between **Dover** and Calais or Boulogne (the quickest and cheapest routes), **Ramsgate** and Dunkerque, or **Newhaven** and Dieppe.

Ferry **prices** vary according to the time of year and, for motorists, the size of your car. The Dover–Calais/Boulogne runs, for example, start at about £180 return low season, £220 return high season for a car with up to five passengers. **Foot passengers** should be able to cross for about £50 return year round; taking a **motorbike** costs from £80 to £90 return.

ITALY–GREECE FERRIES

On the Italian run, there are regular **ferries** from Ancona, Bari, Brindisi and Otranto to **Pátra** (at the northwestern tip of the Peloponnese) or **Igoumenítsa** (the port for Epirus in northwestern Greece); both sail via the island of **Corfu**, but stopovers here are no longer allowed. It takes about nine hours from Brindisi – much the most common port of departure – to Corfu and from there it's two more hours to Igoumenítsa, ten to Pátra. The passenger fare in peak season is around £18–32/$30–53 to Corfu/Igoumenítsa, £30–32/$49–53 to Pátra, with a twenty-percent reduction for students on most of the lines. These figures normally include a small port tax and off-season should be at least thirty percent lower. Small cars are

THE ITALY–GREECE ROUTES

Note: all timings are approximate.

From **Ancona**: Marlines, Strintzis, ANEK and Minoan to Igoumenítsa (23–25hr) and Pátra (30hr); daily or nearly so year round. Minoan sails via Corfu, with separate lines for Pátra and Kefalloniá; Strintzis and ANEK via Corfu; Marlines has a summer extension from Pátra to Iráklion (Crete). Most sailings between 8pm and 10pm, but there are a number of afternoon departures.

From **Bari**: Ventouris to Pátra direct (20hr), nearly daily; to Corfu, Igoumenítsa (12hr) and Pátra (20hr) (all summer only); daily departures year round between 8pm and 9pm. To Pátra via Corfu and/or Igoumenítsa on Poseidon Lines who also have an extension to Çeşme (Turkey).

From **Brindisi**: Fragline and Adriatica to Corfu, Igoumenítsa (11hr) and Pátra (20hr). Hellenic Mediterranean Lines to Corfu and Pátra, three to seven a week depending on season; Igoumenítsa, Kefalloniá, Ithaki, Paxí and Zákinthos, served on separate sailings during summer. European Seaways to Corfu, Igoumenítsa and Pátra. Marlines to Igoumenítsa and Brindisi. Several ferries leave every day in season, most between 8pm and 10.30pm; at least one daily in winter.

From **Otranto**: R-Lines to Corfu and Igoumenítsa (9hr); five weekly, May–Oct only.

From **Trieste**: ANEK to Igoumenítsa, Corfu and Pátra (43hr). One weekly in summer, on Ancona service.

SAMPLE FARES

Prices below are one-way high/low-season fares; port taxes (£3–5 per person in each direction) are not included. Note that substantial reductions apply on most lines for both InterRail or Eurail pass-holders, and those under 26. Slight discounts are usually available on return fares.

Igoumenítsa from Bari or Brindisi: deck class £18–32 ($30–53)/£13–15 ($22–24); car £21–35 ($35–58)/£13–17 ($22–28).

Igoumenítsa from Ancona: deck class £40/50 ($60/75); car £65/£95 ($100/145).

Pátra: from Bari or Brindisi: deck class £30–£32 ($49–53)/£15–23 ($24–38); car £35–46 ($58–76)/£17–23 ($28–38).

UK FERRY AGENTS

For details of local agents in Greece, see the respective listings for Pátra and Igoumenítsa. The following are UK agents for advance bookings:

Serena Holidays, 40 Kenway Rd, London SW5 (☎0171/244 8422). *For Adriatica Lines.*

Viamare Travel Ltd, Graphic House, 2 Sumatra Rd, London NW6 (☎0171/431 4560). *For ANEK,*

Arkadia, Fragline, Marlines, Strintzis, Superfast, Ventouris. Also for Salamis and Poseidon Lines, which route Pireás–Rhodes or Crete–Limassol–Haifa.

---

charged about £13–17/$22–28 (Brindisi–Igoumenítsa), £17–23/$28–38 (Brindisi-Pátra); motorbikes around £25/$40. If you're taking a car over in mid-season it's essential to book in advance, otherwise you may face a two- or three-day wait.

Brindisi is in many ways the best place to leave from – if only because there are far more ferries from here – and it's a reasonably interesting place to wait around. On the other hand, embarkation is a chaotic nightmare. Less stressful departure points include Ancona, much further north hence less driving but a longer, more expensive ferry trip, and Bari. A new company, Superfast, is due to start operating with rapid new vessels (complete with pools, restaurants, discos and so on),

sailing between Ancona and Pátra in twenty hours (as against the normal 36) and Bari–Pátra in twelve hours; high season fares on the Ancona route are approximately £48 outbound and £38 inbound ($80/63) for a deck passenger, £58/38 ($96/63) ATS (aircraft seat) or about £68/48 ($113/80) for a dormitory bunk. Cabins start at about £98 ($163) per person one way, and cars go for around £68 outbound and £48 inbound ($113/80). Ring Viamare (see "UK Agents" in box above) for details of the Bari route (about twenty percent cheaper), not finalized at the time of writing.

Heading for Crete, **Pátra** is the obvious destination: from there you can avoid Athens altogether and continue down through the

Peloponnese to **Yíthio** (or less conveniently to Monemvassía or Neápoli) where you can pick up the twice-weekly ferry to Kastélli Kissámou in western Crete (see "Getting There from Mainland Greece", p.19). On the train, it's an easy run from Pátra to Athens.

For advance UK bookings for the Italy–Greece ferries, see the list of **UK ferry agents** on p.8.

GETTING THERE FROM IRELAND

Summer charter flights to Crete are easy to pick up from either Dublin or Belfast (around IR£200 return and upwards), while year-round scheduled flights operate daily to Athens with connections on to Iráklion.

Fares on **scheduled flights** with British Airways (routed via Heathrow) work out at around £420 from Belfast to Athens, with an add-on fare of around £100 to Iráklion. Aer Lingus don't have a direct scheduled service to Greece from Dublin, but for a comparable price will book you to Iráklion via Heathrow, where you change to another carrier. For youth and student discount fares, the best first stop is USIT (see box below for address).

For a typical two-week **package** in a self-catering apartment based on two people sharing,

FLIGHTS, PACKAGES AND TOURS

Aspro Holidays, 19 Donegal Place, Belfast BT1 5AB (☎01232/322550). *Self-catering apartments and studios and flight-only charters.*

Budget Travel, 134 Lower Baggot St, Dublin 2 (☎01/661 1866). *Self-catering apartments and studios; also sells flight-only charters.*

Falcon Holidays, Albany House, 73–75 Gt. Victoria St, Belfast BT2 7EF (☎01232/311366); Block 5, Westland Square, Pearse St, Dublin 2 (☎01/605 6500). *Operator specializing in self-catering and hotel packages along the central north coast of Crete.*

Joe Walsh Tours, 8–11 Baggot St, Dublin (☎01/676 0991). *General budget fares agent,*
selling charters and self-catering apartments on the north coast (May–Oct).

Thomas Cook, 118 Grafton St, Dublin (☎01/677 1721). *Mainstream package-holiday and flight agent, with occasional discount offers.*

Unijet, Unit 3, Lyndon Court, Queen St, Belfast BT1 5EF (☎01232/314656). *Self-catering studio packages based around the north coast.*

USIT. Branches at: Aston Quay, O'Connell Bridge, Dublin 2 (☎01/679 8833); 10–11 Market Parade, Cork (☎021/270 900); Fountain Centre, College St, Belfast (☎01232/324073). *Student and youth specialist.*

AIRLINES

Aer Lingus, 41 Upper O'Connell St, Dublin (☎01/844 4777); 46–48 Castle St, Belfast (☎01232/314844); 2 Academy St, Cork (☎021/274331).

British Airways, 9 Fountain Centre, College St, Belfast (☎0345/222111); in Dublin, contact Aer Lingus.

you can expect to pay from £200 per person low season to £500 high season (Belfast); from IR£260 to IR£450 (Dublin). For larger groups sharing, things can work out significantly cheaper. See the box on p.9 for travel agents' addresses.

Travelling to London in the first place to pick up a cheap charter from there may save you a little money, but on the whole it's rarely worth the time and effort. For the record, budget flights to London are offered by British Midland, BA, Aer Lingus and Ryan Air. Buying a Eurotrain boat and train ticket to London from USIT will slightly undercut plane fares but by this time you're starting to talk about a journey of days not hours to Greece, with the trip to Crete itself still to come.

GETTING THERE FROM NORTH AMERICA

Only a few carriers fly direct to Greece from North America, so most North Americans travel to a gateway European city, and pick up a connecting flight on from there with an associated airline. If you have time, you may well discover that it's cheaper to arrange the final Crete-bound leg of the journey yourself, in which case your only criterion will be finding a suitable and good-value North America–Europe flight; for details of onward flights from the UK, see "Getting There from Britain", pp.3–5.

In general there just isn't enough traffic on the US–Greece routes to make for very cheap fares. The Greek national airline, Olympic Airways, is the only carrier to fly "direct" to Crete from North America, landing briefly in Athens; these flights serve New York (JFK) only. From Boston, Montréal and Toronto, Olympic fly to Athens, offering reasonably priced add-on flights to Crete (either Iráklion or Haniá), leaving from the same Athens terminal that you will fly into.

AIRLINES IN NORTH AMERICA

Air Canada (in Canada, call directory enquiries, ☎1-800/555-1212, for local toll-free number; US toll-free number is ☎1-800/776-3000).

Air France (☎1-800/237-2747; in Canada, ☎1-800/667-2747).

Alitalia (☎1-800/223-5730).

British Airways (in US, ☎1-800/247-9297; in Canada ☎1-800/668-1059).

Canadian Airlines (in Canada, ☎1-800/665-1177; in US, ☎1-800/426-7000).

Czech Airlines (in US ☎1-800/223-2365; in Canada ☎1-800/641-0641).

Delta Airlines (☎1-800/241-4141).

Iberia (in US, ☎1-800/772-4642; in Canada, ☎1-800/423-7421).

KLM (in US, ☎1-800/374-7747; in Canada, ☎1-800/361-5073).

LOT Polish Airlines (☎1-800/223-0593).

Lufthansa (☎1-800/645-3880).

Olympic Airways (☎1-800/223-1226).

Sabena (☎1-800/955-2000).

Swissair (☎1-800/221-4750).

TAP Air Portugal (☎1-800/221-7370).

TWA (☎1-800/892-4141).

United Airlines (☎1-800/538-2929).

SHOPPING FOR TICKETS

Discount ticket outlets – advertised in the Sunday travel sections of major newspapers – come in several forms. **Consolidators** buy up blocks of tickets that airlines don't think they'll be able to sell at their published fares, and unload them at a discount. Many advertise fares on a one-way basis, enabling you to fly into one city and out from another without penalty. Consolidators normally don't impose advance purchase requirements (although in busy times you should book ahead just to be sure of getting a ticket), but they do often charge very stiff fees for date changes.

EUROPEAN CONNECTIONS

There are direct flights to **Iráklion** from Amsterdam, Rome and Vienna.

Discount agents also deal in blocks of tickets offloaded by the airlines, but they typically offer a range of other travel-related services like insurance, rail passes, youth and student ID cards, car rentals and tours. These agencies tend to be most worthwhile for students and under-26s, who can benefit from special fares and deals. **Travel clubs** are another option – most charge an annual membership fee, which may be worth it for

DISCOUNT TRAVEL COMPANIES

Air Brokers International 323 Geary St, Suite 411, San Francisco, CA 94102 (☎1-800/883-3273). *Consolidator.*

Air Courier Association 191 University Blvd, Suite 300, Denver, CO 80206 (☎303/278-8810). *Courier flight broker.*

Airhitch 2472 Broadway, Suite 200, New York, NY 10025 (☎212/864-2000). *Standby-seat broker: for a set price, they guarantee to get you on a flight as close to your preferred destination as possible, within a week.*

Council Travel Head Office: 205 E 42nd St, New York, NY 10017 (☎1-800/226-8624; 1-888 COUNCIL; 212/822-2700). *Student travel organization with branches in many US cities. A sister company, Council Charter (☎1-800/223-7402), specializes in charter flights.*

Educational Travel Center 438 N Frances St, Madison, WI 53703 (☎1-800/747-5551). *Student/youth discount agent.*

Encore Travel Club 4501 Forbes Blvd, Lanham, MD 20706 (☎1-800/444-9800).*Discount travel club.*

Interworld Travel 800 Douglass Rd, Miami, FL 33134 (☎305/443-4929). *Consolidator.*

Last Minute Travel Club 132 Brookline Ave, Boston, MA 02215 (☎1-800/LAST MIN). *Travel club specializing in standby deals.*

Moment's Notice 425 Madison Ave, New York, NY 10017 (☎212/486-0503). *Discount travel club.*

New Frontiers/Nouvelles Frontières Head offices: 12 E 33rd St, New York, NY 10016 (☎1-800/366-6387); 1001 Sherbrook E, Suite 720, Montréal, H2L 1L3 (☎514/526-8444). *French discount travel firm. Other branches in LA, San Francisco and Québec City.*

Now Voyager 74 Varick St, Suite 307, New York, NY 10013 (☎212/431-1616). *Courier flight broker.*

STA Travel Head office: 48 E 11th St, New York, NY 10003 (☎1-800/777-0112; nationwide). *Worldwide specialist in independent travel with branches in the Los Angeles, San Francisco and Boston areas.*

TFI Tours International Head office: 34 W 32nd St, New York, NY 10001 (☎1-800/745-8000). *Consolidator; other offices in Las Vegas, San Francisco, Los Angeles.*

Travac Head office: 989 Sixth Ave, New York NY 10018 (☎1-800/872-8800). *Consolidator and charter broker; has another branch in Orlando.*

Travel Avenue 10 S Riverside, Suite 1404, Chicago, IL 60606 (☎1-800/333-3335). *Discount travel agent.*

Travel Cuts Head office: 187 College St, Toronto, ON M5T 1P7 (☎1-800/667-2887; 1-888/238-2887; 416/979-2406). *Canadian student travel organization with branches all over the country.*

Travelers Advantage 3033 S Parker Rd, Suite 900, Aurora, CO 80014 (☎1-800/548-1116). *Discount travel club.*

UniTravel 1177 N Warson Rd, St Louis, MO 63132 (☎1-800/325-2222). *Consolidator.*

Worldtek Travel 111 Water St, New Haven, CT 06511 (☎1-800/243-1723). *Discount travel agency.*

Worldwide Discount Travel Club 1674 Meridian Ave, Miami Beach, FL 33139 (☎305/534-2082). *Discount travel club.*

their discounts on air tickets and car rental. Some agencies specialize in **charter flights**, which may be even cheaper than anything available on a scheduled flight, but again there's a trade-off: departure dates are fixed, and the withdrawal penalties are high (check the refund policy). Student/youth fares can sometimes save you money, though again the best deals are usually those offered by seat consolidators advertising in Sunday newspaper travel sections.

Don't automatically assume that tickets purchased through a travel specialist will be cheapest; once you get a quote, check with the airlines and you may turn up an even better deal. In addition, exercise caution and never deal with a company that demands cash up front or refuses to accept payment by credit card.

For destinations not handled by discounters – which applies to most regional airports – you'll have to deal with airlines' published fares. The

SPECIALIST TOUR OPERATORS

USA

Archeological Tours, 271 Madison Ave, New York, NY 10016 (☎212/986-3054). *Specialist archeological tours.*

Astro Tours, 2359 East Main St, Columbus, OH 43209 (☎1-800/543-7717; 614/237-7798). *Cruise packages to the Greek islands.*

Classic Adventures, PO Box 153, Hamlin, NY 14464-0153 (☎1-800/777-8090). *Hiking, biking and walking tours in June and September, covering archeological sites and coastal trips.*

Cloud Tours Inc., 645 Fifth Ave, New York, NY 10022 (☎1-800/223-7880 or 212/753-6104). *Six- or nine-day tours combining Crete with other islands, such as Santorini, Mikonos, Kos and Rhodes.*

Different Strokes Tours, 1841 Broadway, New York, NY 10023 (☎1-800/668 3301). *Customized tours for gay and lesbian travellers.*

Educational Tours and Cruises, 9 Irving St, Medford, MA 02155 (☎1-800/275-4109). *Custom-designed tours to Greece and the islands, specializing in art, history, food and wine, ancient drama, painting, birdwatching, etc.*

Elderhostel, 75 Federal St, Boston, MA 02110 (☎617/426-8056). *Educational and activity programs for senior travellers (companions may be younger).*

Epirotiki Lines, 551 Fifth Ave, New York, NY 10176 (☎212/949-7273). *Greek cruise specialist.*

Globus and Cosmos Tours, 5301 South Federal Circle, Littleton, CO 80123 (☎1-800/221-0090). *Offers a variety of city and island packages, including a cruise that calls at Santorini, Crete (tour of Knossós), Rhodes, Patmos and Míkonos.*

Guaranteed Travel, 83 S St, Box 269, Morristown, NJ 07963 (☎201/540-1770). *Specializes in "Greece-Your-Way" independent travel.*

Hellenic Adventures, 4150 Harriet Ave South, Minneapolis, MN 55409 (☎1-800/851-6349; 612/827-0937). *A vast range of small group and independent tours: cultural, historical, horseback-riding, hiking, wilderness, culinary and family-oriented.*

Homeric Tours, 55 E 59th St, New York, NY 10017 (☎1-800/223-5570). *All-inclusive tours from 9 to 23 days, as well as cruises and charter flights.*

Insight International Tours, 745 Atlantic Ave, Suite 720, Boston, MA 02111 (☎1-800/582-8380). *General Greek vacations.*

ST Cultural Tours, 225 W 34th St, New York, NY 10122 (☎1-800/833-2111; 212/563-1202). *A wide range of package and independent educational tours.*

Triaena Travel, 850 Seventh Ave, New York, NY 10019 (☎1-800/223-1273; 212/245-3700). *Packages, cruises, apartments and villas.*

Valef Yachts, Box 391, Ambler, PA 19002 (☎1-800/223-3845; 215/641-1624). *Yachting trips and charters.*

CANADA

Adventures Abroad, 20800 Westminster Highway, Suite 2148, Richmond, BC V6V 2W3 (☎1-800/665-3998; 604/303-1099). *General operator, offering group and individual tours and cruises.*

Auratours, 1470 Peel St, Suite 252, Montréal, Québec H3A 1TL (☎1-800/363-0323). *General operator, offering group and individual tours and cruises.*

Worldwide Adventures, 36 Finch Ave West, Toronto, Ontario M2N 2G9 (☎1-800/387-1483; 416/221-3000). *General operator, offering group and individual tours and cruises.*

cheapest way to go is with an **APEX** (Advance Purchase Excursion) ticket. This carries certain restrictions: you have to book – and pay – at least 21 days before departure and spend at least seven days abroad (maximum stay three months), and you're liable to penalties if you change your schedule. On transatlantic routes there are also winter **Super APEX** tickets, sometimes known as "Eurosavers" – slightly cheaper than an ordinary APEX, but limiting your stay to between seven and 21 days. Some airlines also issue **Special APEX** tickets to those under 24, often extending the maximum stay to a year.

Note that fares are heavily dependent on **season**, and are highest from June to September; they drop either side of this, and you'll get the best deals during the low season, November–February (excluding Christmas). Flying on weekends ordinarily adds $50 or so to the return fare; price ranges quoted in the sections below assume midweek travel.

FLIGHTS FROM THE USA

New York–Crete prices with Olympic range from about $760 return in winter, rising to $1080 for a maximum thirty-day stay with seven-day advance purchase. Delta has a daily direct service from New York to Athens for the same APEX fare; likewise United, Swissair, Sabena and Iberia, although their flights are via European gateway cities. And United also flies to Athens from Washington DC for a high/low season rate of around $1140/$820.

Non-stop Olympic flights to **Athens** from New York are similarly priced, ranging from $700 to $1100, with **add-on flights** to Iráklion or Haniá available for around $60 each way. Olympic also flies out of **Boston** once a week in winter, twice a week in summer, at much the same rates. Delta and TWA have daily services from New York to Athens via Frankfurt, and while fares cost around $300 more than with Olympic, a consolidator or agent might be able to get you a flight for around half the cost the airlines themselves quote: return trips run from around $600 in winter, and $900 in summer. High/low season fares on Olympic, Delta, United, Iberia and so on start at $1180/$860 from **Chicago**. One particularly good deal is on LOT Polish Airlines, which flies out of New York and Chicago to Athens several times a week via Warsaw. Fares run from around $700 return. At the time of writing this airline also have

a special deal on their round-trip low season APEX fares from the US to Athens via Warsaw ($596 from New York, $656 from Chicago, $846 from LA). Since it's possible that similar offers may be made in the future (including comparable reductions on their high season fares), it's certainly worth contacting them.

As with the service from the eastern cities, the stiff competition between the different airlines dictates that fares to Athens from the mid-west or west coast are virtually identical: high/low season fares on Olympic, Delta, United, Iberia and so on start at $1330/$1010 from LA, San Francisco or Seattle. With little else to choose between the major carriers, you might look into the stopover times at the different European gateway cities, as these can sometimes be overnight; check with your ticket agent.

Otherwise, **charter** flights will probably be the best and cheapest way of getting direct to Crete – check with your travel agent and scan the Sunday papers to see what's on offer.

FLIGHTS FROM CANADA

One of the best-value scheduled fares is on Olympic, who fly non-stop to Athens out of Montréal and Toronto twice a week in winter for CDN$1268 return, and in summer for CDN$1751.

KLM operates several flights a week to Athens via Amsterdam, from Toronto, Montréal, Vancouver and Edmonton; from Toronto, expect to pay around CDN$1050 in winter, CDN$1750 in high season; and from Vancouver, CDN$1470 (low) or CDN$2170 (high). Travellers from Montréal can also try the European carriers Air France, Alitalia, British Airways, Iberia, Lufthansa, Sabena, Swissair and TAP Air Portugal, all of which operate several flights a week to Athens via major European cities. One unlikely source for good deals is Czech Airlines, which flies out of Montréal to Athens via Prague for a fare of around CDN$840 (low) or CDN$1240 (high).

Finally, Air Canada, flying in conjunction with European carriers, quote the following low/high season fares to Athens: from Toronto/Montréal around CDN$1150/CDN$1485 and from Vancouver around CDN$1570/CDN$1860.

RAIL PASSES

Buying a rail pass, you should bear in mind that Crete itself has no railway. A **Eurail pass** is not likely to pay for itself if you're planning to stick to

RAIL CONTACTS IN NORTH AMERICA

CIT Tours, 9501 West Devon Ave, Suite 502, Rosemont IL 60018 (☎1-800/223-7987).

DER Tours/GermanRail, 9501 W Divon Ave, Suite 400, Rosemont, IL 60018 (☎1-800/421-2929).

Rail Europe, 226 Westchester Ave, White Plains, NY 10604 (☎1-800/438 7245).

ScanTours, 1535 6th St, Suite 205, Santa Monica, CA 90401 (☎1-800/223-7226).

Greece and will only take you as far as the mainland, so it's only worth considering if you plan to travel to Greece from elsewhere in Europe. The pass, which must be purchased before arrival in Europe, allows unlimited free train travel in Greece and sixteen other countries. The **Eurail Youthpass** (for under-26s) costs $365 for 15 days, $587 for one month or

$832 for two months; if you're 26 or over you'll have to buy a **first-class pass**, available in 15-day ($522), 21-day ($678), one-month ($838), two-month ($1188) and three-month ($1468) increments.

You stand a better chance of getting your money's worth out of a **Eurail Flexipass**, which is good for a certain number of travel days in a two-month period. This, too, comes in under-26/first-class versions: 5 days cost $255/$348; 10 days $431/$616; and fifteen days $568/$812. If you're travelling in a group of two or more, you might also want to consider the **Eurail Saverpass**. This costs $444 for 15 consecutive days; $576 for 21; $712 for a month; $1010 for two months; and $1248 for three. And there's also a **Flexi Saverpass** at $524 for 10 days or $690 for 15.

North Americans are also eligible to purchase more specific passes valid for travel in Greece only, for details of which see "Getting around".

GETTING THERE FROM AUSTRALIA & NEW ZEALAND

Thanks to the number of Greeks who've adopted the country, connections between Australia and Greece are good, though from New Zealand things are less promising. Given the prices and most people's travel plans, you'll probably do better looking for some kind of Round-the-World ticket that includes Greece.

Note that the **prices** given on pp.14–15 are in Australian/New Zealand dollars for published mid-season return fares; the specialist travel agents listed opposite should be able to get at least ten percent off these. **Students** and anyone **under 26** should try STA Travel in the first instance which has a wide range of discounted fares on offer.

FLIGHTS FROM AUSTRALIA

Cheapest fares to Athens **from Australia** are with Olympic Airways from $1700 low season; **add-on fares** to Iráklion or Haniá from Athens with Olympic run to around another $125–133 including airport taxes. Alitalia via Rome, Aeroflot via Moscow and Thai Airways via Bangkok all start at around $1850. In addition, Singapore Airlines have a good connecting service to Athens from $1899. Quantas and British Airways offer a free return flight within Europe for $2499–3099 which differs only slightly from their "Global Explorer" Pass $2599–3199, a **Round-the-World** fare that allows six stopovers worldwide wherever these two airlines fly to (except South America). Also worth considering is Garuda's $1550 fare from Sydney, Brisbane or Cairns via Jakarta or Denpasar to various European cities, from where you could pick up a cheap onward flight or continue **overland** to Athens.

AGENTS AND AIRLINES

AIRLINES

☎008 numbers are toll free, but only apply if dialled outside the city in the address.

Aeroflot, 24/44 Market St, Sydney (☎02/9262 2233). No NZ office. Twice-weekly flights from Sydney to Athens via transfers in Moscow and Bangkok.

Alitalia, Orient Overseas Building, 32 Bridge St, Sydney (☎02/9247 1308); Floor 6, Trust Bank Building, 229 Queen St, Auckland (☎09/379 4457).

British Airways, 26/201 Kent St, Sydney (☎02/9258 3300); Dilworth Building, corner of Queen and Customs streets, Auckland (☎09/356 8690). Daily flights to London from major Australasian cities; BA code share with Quantas to offer their "Global Explorer" RTW fare.

Garuda, 55 Hunter St, Sydney (☎02/9334 9944 or 1800/800 873); 120 Albert St, Auckland (☎09/366 1855). Several flights weekly from Australian and New Zealand cities to London, Frankfurt and Amsterdam via either a transfer or stopover in Denpasar/Jakarta.

KLM 5 Elizabeth St, Sydney (☎02/9231 6333 or 1800/505 747). No NZ office.

Lufthansa/Air Lauda, 143 Macquarie St, Sydney (☎02/9367 3888); 36 Kitchener St, Auckland (☎09/303 1529).

Olympic Airways, S.A. Floor 3, 37–49 Pitt St, Sydney (☎02/9251 2044). No NZ office. Twice-weekly flights to Athens from Sydney and Melbourne, with onward connections to Crete.

Qantas, 70 Hunter St, Sydney (☎13 1211); 154 Queen St, Auckland (☎09/357 8900 or 0800/808 767). Daily flights to London from major Australasian cities; Qantas code share with British Airways to offer their "Global Explorer" RTW fare.

Singapore Airlines, 17 Bridge St, Sydney (☎13 1011); Lower Ground Floor, West Plaza Building, corner of Customs and Albert streets, Auckland (☎09/379 3209). Daily flights to Athens from Brisbane, Sydney, Melbourne, Perth and Auckland via Singapore.

Thai 75–77 Pitt St, Sydney (☎13 1960); Kensington Swan Building, 22 Fanshawe St, Auckland (☎09/377 3886). Three flights a week to Athens via either a transfer or stopover in Bangkok from Brisbane, Sydney, Melbourne, Perth and Auckland.

United 10 Barrack St, Sydney (☎13 1777); 7 City Rd, Auckland (☎09/379 3800).

TRAVEL AGENTS

Adventure World, 73 Walker St, N Sydney (☎02/956 7766); 8 Victoria Ave, Perth (☎09/221 2300). Agents for a vast array of international adventure travel companies that operate trips to mainland Greece and the islands, including Crete.

Flight Centres, 82 Elizabeth St, Sydney, plus branches nationwide (☎13 1600); 205 Queen St, Auckland (☎09/309 6171), plus branches nationwide. Good discounts on fares.

Grecian Mediterranean Holidays, 49 Ventnor Ave, West Perth (☎09/321 3930). Good selection of mainland and island holidays, including Crete.

Grecian Tours Travel, 237a Lonsdale St, Melbourne (☎03/9663 3711). Offers a variety of accommodation, and sight-seeing tours.

House of Holidays, 298 Clayton Rd, Clayton, Victoria (☎03/543 5800). Greek specialist with wide selection of holidays.

STA Travel, Australia: 702 Harris St, Ultimo, Sydney; 256 Flinders St, Melbourne; other offices in state capitals and major universities (nearest branch ☎13 1776, fastfare telesales ☎1300/360 960). New Zealand: 10 High St, Auckland (☎09/309 0458, fastfare telesales ☎09/366 6673), plus branches in Wellington, Christchurch, Dunedin, Palmerston North, Hamilton and at major universities. Web site: www.statravelaus.com.au Email: traveller@statravelaus.com.au

FLIGHTS FROM NEW ZEALAND

From New Zealand, best deals to Athens are with Thai ($2399 via Bangkok) or Singapore Airlines ($2499 via Singapore), and a very versatile offer with Lufthansa ($2899), who can route you through anywhere that Air New Zealand or Qantas fly – including Los Angeles, Singapore, Sydney, Hong Kong or Tokyo – for a stopover. British Airways/Qantas can get you to Europe, but not Athens, for $2699, so again you're better off with their Global Explorer Pass (see above) at $3099. Surprisingly expensive at $3974 are Alitalia (via Rome) and United (Los Angeles, Washington, Paris).

GETTING THERE FROM MAINLAND GREECE

Not everyone flies direct to Crete. Cheap charter flights to Athens abound, while many people choose to see more of Greece on the way – either travelling by train, using InterRail and Eurail tickets, or even driving across Europe. For how to reach Athens and the mainland in the first place, see the relevant "Getting There" sections above, and read on for details of how to move on to Crete.

BY PLANE

Olympic operates at least five flights a day from **Athens** to **Iráklion** in peak season – fewer through the winter – and three or four daily to **Haniá**; journey time is less than an hour. This may seem a lot, but in summer they are all booked well in advance. The flights are probably good value when weighed against a twelve-hour ferry trip: one-way prices are around £45/$75 to Haniá, £48/$80 to Iráklion. There's also a twice-weekly service (Tues and Sat) to **Sitía** for a one-way price of £50/$83. Flights leave from the west terminal, for details of which see p.17.

Fully booked or not, it can be worth trying for a **stand-by** ticket, especially if you arrive at the airport in the middle of the night and can be first in the queue next morning. You have to purchase a ticket (credit card will do) in order to get on the stand-by list: if, in the end, you don't manage to fly they should give you a full refund. Once you're on the list the system works pretty well, despite appearances – just make sure you are by the departure gate when they call out the names of the lucky few for each flight.

There are four flights a week from **Rhodes** to **Iráklion**, and three a week from **Thessaloníki**, as well as regular flights from some of the smaller islands. All of these, again, tend to be heavily booked, and the short hops are relatively expensive.

BY FERRY

The vast majority of ferry traffic to Crete goes **from Pireás** (the port of Athens), though there are also services from the Peloponnese and from many of the Cycladic and Dodecanese islands.

The cheapest class of ticket is **deck class**, variously called *tríti* or *gámma*. This gives you the run of most boats except for the upper-class restaurant and bar. Seats and cabins (see below) are also available on all lines sailing between Pireás and Iráklion. The service to Crete is daily throughout the year, with additional sailings in summer; most leave in the evening (see below) but you can check current schedules with the ferry agents in Pireás, listed in the box below.

FROM PIREÁS

The **ferries for Crete** leave from the heart of the port, not far to the south of the metro station – simply turn left and follow the harbour round. If you've arrived by bus get someone to point you in the right direction, basically down the hill from Platía Koraí.

Two major lines operate on this route, Minoan and ANEK, each with a daily ferry to Iráklion, with the ANEK service also sailing daily to Haniá. In

---

TRAVELLING VIA ATHENS AND PIREÁS

You may well find yourself travelling to Crete via **Athens**, which is not necessarily a hardship. The Greek capital is, admittedly, not much of a holiday resort, with its concrete architecture, dire traffic and air pollution, but it has modern excitements of its own, as well as its superlative ancient sites. A couple of nights' stopover will allow you to take in the Acropolis, ancient Agora and major museums, wander around the old quarter of Pláka and the bazaar area, and sample some of the country's best restaurants and clubs. Even a morning flight into Athens allows you enough time to take a look at the Acropolis and Pláka, before heading down to the port of **Pireás** (Piraeus) to catch one of the early evening ferries on to Crete.

What follows is a brief guide to getting in and out of the city, and some pointers on what to do while you're there. For a full treatment of the city, see the *Rough Guide to Greece*.

ARRIVING

Athens **airport** – Ellinikón – has two separate terminals: west (*dhitikó*) which is used by Olympic Airways (both national and international), and east (*anatolkó*) which is used by all the other airlines. The terminals are on opposite sides of the runway, so you have to drive halfway round the perimeter fence to get from one to the other. Olympic buses connect the two regularly from around 6am to midnight; taxis are available, too, and should cost no more than 2000dr. Both terminals have money exchange facilities, open 24 hours at the east terminal, 7am to 11pm at the west one; the west terminal also has automatic teller machines that accept Visa, Mastercard, Cirrus and Plus cards. Insist on some small denomination notes for paying for your bus ticket or taxi-ride.

It's about 9km to central Athens or to the ferry port of Pireás (Piraeus). The easiest way to travel is by **taxi**, which should cost around 1500–2000dr, depending on traffic. Make sure that the meter is switched on, as new arrivals are often charged over the odds. You may find that you have fellow passengers in the cab: this is permitted, and each drop-off will pay the full fare.

If you're happy to carry your bags around, you could use the **bus**. Bus #091 connects both terminals with the centre of Athens (Omónia and Síndagma squares). In theory, the bus runs every thirty minutes from 5.30am to 11.30pm, and every hour from 11.30pm to 5.30am. Tickets cost 170dr; 200dr between 1.30 and 5.30am. Bus #19 runs

from both airport terminals to Pireás, allowing you to get straight to the ferries. It runs about every hour between 6am and 9.20pm. Tickets again cost 170dr (200dr from midnight to 5.30am). Take the bus to the end of the route, Platía Karaïskáki, which fronts the main harbour, and a line of ferry agencies.

All international **trains** arrive at the Stathmós Laríssis, just to the northwest of the city centre. There are hotels in this area or you can take yellow trolley bus (#1) immediately outside to reach Síndagma square.

If you are just spending the day in Athens, and want to **store your baggage**, you can do so for 200dr per piece at Pacific Ltd, Nikis 26 – just off Síndagma (Mon–Sat 7am–8pm, Sun 7am–2pm).

ACCOMMODATION

Finding **accommodation** in Athens is unlikely to be a major problem except at the very height of summer – though it's best to phone ahead. A small selection of places are listed below, or you can book more upmarket rooms through the main EOT tourist office (Mon–Fri 9am–7pm, Sat 9am–2pm; ☎33 10 437 or 33 10 562 or 33 10 565) at Ameríkas 2, just up from Stadíou, which can also supply you with maps of the city.

If you're only in town for a quick stay, **Pláka**, the oldest quarter of the city, is the best area. It spreads south of Síndagma Square, is in easy walking range of the Acropolis, and has lots of outdoor restaurants and cafés. It's possible to stay in the port of **Pireás**, too, though since most Crete ferries leave late in the evening, and arrive at Pireás early morning, there's no real need, and you might as well make the most of your time in Athens.

All the listings below are in the Pláka; price categories are for a double room in high season:

4000–6000dr
George's Guest House, Níkis 46 (☎32 26 474).
John's Place, Patróou 5 (☎32 29 719).
Thisseus Hostel, Thisséos 10 (☎32 45 960).

6000–8000dr
Dioskouri, Pittákou 6 (☎32 48 165).
Kouros, Kódhrou 11 (☎32 27 431).
Phaedra, Herefóndos 16 (☎32 27 795).

8000–16000dr
Acropolis House, Kódhrou 6 (☎32 22 344).
Adonis, Kódhrou 3 (☎32 49 737).
Nefeli, Iperídhou 16 (☎32 28 044).

continues over

EATING AND DRINKING

Pláka is bursting with touristy restaurants, most very pleasantly situated but poor value. Three with nice sites and good food are *Kouklis* (Tripíodhon 14), *O Platanos* (Dhioyénous 4) and *Iy Klimataria* (Klepsídhras 5). *Eden* (Iiossíou 12) is a decent vegetarian restaurant.

THE CITY AND SIGHTS

Central Athens is a compact, easily walkable area. Its hub is **Síndagma Square** (Platía Sintágmatos), flanked by the Parliament, banks and airline offices, and the National Bank. Pretty much everything you'll want to see in a fleeting visit – the Acropolis, Pláka, the major museums – is within 20–30 minutes' walk of here. Just east of the square, too, are the **National Gardens** – the nicest spot in town for a siesta.

Walk south from Síndagma, along Níkis or Filellínon streets, and you'll find yourself in Pláka, the surviving area of the nineteenth-century, pre-Independence village. Largely pedestrianized, it is a delightful area just to wander around – and it is the approach to the Acropolis.

For a bit of focus to your walk, take in the fourth-century BC **Monument of Lysikrates**, used as a study by Byron, to the east, and the Roman-era **Tower of the Winds** (Aéridhes), to the west. The latter adjoins the Roman forum. Climb north from the Tower of the Winds and you reach **Anafiótika**, with its whitewashed Cycladic-style cottages (built by workers from the island of Anáfi) and the eclectic **Kanellópoulos Museum** (Tues–Sun 8.30am–3pm; 500dr).

Head north from the Roman Forum, along Athinás or Eólou streets, and you come to an equally characterful part of the city – the **bazaar** area. The best bit is the old Central Market Building, on the corner of Athinás and Evripídhou. **Monastiráki Square** is worth a look, too, with its Turkish mosque. On Sundays a genuine **Flea Market** sprawls to its west, out beyond the tourist shops promoted as the "Athens Flea Market".

Even with a few hours to spare between flight and ferry, you can take in a visit to the **Acropolis** (April–Sept daily 8am–6.30pm; Oct–March Mon–Fri 8am–4.30pm, Sat & Sun 8am–2.30pm; 2000dr, students free). The complex of temples, rebuilt by Pericles in the Golden Age of the fifth century BC, is focused on the famed Parthenon. This and the smaller Athena Nike and Erechtheion temples are given context by a small museum housing some of the original statuary left behind by Lord Elgin.

If you have more time, make your way down to the **Theatre of Dionysos**, on the south slope (daily 8.30am–2.45pm; 500dr), and/or to the **Ancient Agora**, northwest of the Acropolis hill (Tues–Sun 8.30am–2.45pm; 1200dr); presided over by the Doric **Thiseion**, or Temple of Hephaestus.

As a preparation for Crete's ancient sites, two of Athens's museums are especially worth visiting. Most importantly, the **National Archeological Museum** (Patissíon 28; Mon 12.30–7pm, Tues–Fri 8am–7pm, Sat & Sun 8.30am–7pm; 2000dr, students 1000dr) contains, upstairs, the brilliant Minoan frescoes from Thíra (Santoríni). Even more spectacular than anything surviving on Crete itself, these were also important evidence in the earthquake theory of the Minoan destruction. The Mycenaean treasures downstairs are also relevant to Crete, besides being great in their own right.

Two other superb museums are the **Benáki** (scheduled to re-open in 1998), a fascinating personal collection of ancient and folk treasures, and the **Goulandris Museum of Cycladic and Ancient Greek Art** (Mon, Wed–Fri 10am–4pm, Sat 10am–3pm; 600dr, free Sat), with its wonderful display of figurines from the Cycladic island civilization of the third millennium BC.

PIREÁS

Pireás (Piraeus), the port of Athens, is the last stop on the single-line **metro**, which you can board at Omónia or Monastiráki squares. The journey takes about 25 minutes – trains run from 6am to midnight – and there's a flat fare of 100dr. If you're travelling by rail from Pátra, the train continues through Athens down to Pireás. **Taxis** cost around 1500dr from the city centre or the airport.

You can buy **ferry tickets** from agencies at the harbour in Pireás, or in central Athens (there are several outlets on Lefóros Amalías, which runs south of Síndagma Square). Wherever you buy from, make sure you get a ticket on one of the main lines (ANEK, Minoan or Rethymnaki), which are fast, efficient and direct.

The ferries for Crete leave from the **main harbour**, just south of the metro station (see p.16). You can get a meal, or buy **provisions** for the trip, all around the port; prices tend to be lower if you head inland a block or two.

theory the Iráklion-bound Minoan ferries leave at 7.15pm and the ANEK ones fifteen minutes later, but in practice they race to be first out of the harbour and continue jostling for position all the way to Crete, where they arrive around twelve hours later (sooner in good weather). There's virtually nothing to choose between the two: both charge around £12/$20 for a deck-class passenger, £40/$66 for a small car. Rethymniaki also offers a daily (8pm) service from Pireás to Réthimnon. Beware of tickets offered on any other line – these will almost certainly involve a roundabout route through the Cyclades, and take twice as long.

It's a matter of opinion whether it's worth paying extra for a berth or cabin on the overnight journey. The older ferries' sleeping quarters tend to be airless and thoroughly unpleasant on an Aegean summer night, while the newer ones are efficiently air-conditioned and far more comfortable. Travelling on deck (or in the seats available to deck-class passengers) can be fine – even idyllic in the right conditions – but it can also be crowded, noisy and cold. If you do go this way, embark early to claim some space. The Aegean is usually calm and comfortable, but high winds (especially in August) sometimes make for a very queasy crossing.

FROM THE PELOPONNESE AND OTHER ROUTES

Much the most useful of the other services is that from the **Peloponnese** to **Kastélli Kissámou**, on the *Candia*, a boat operated by ANEK Lines. On its high summer schedule (mid-Aug to end Sept) it runs twice weekly on Tuesday and Saturday at 4pm (arriving 11pm) from Yíthio. Departure days and times change outside this period, although most weeks the Tuesday departure leaves at the same time. Contact Rozakis Shipping Agency (☎0733/22-207) in Yíthio for details; they will also have details of the less frequent winter service.

You can get to Iráklion from the larger of the **Cycladic** islands (daily from Thíra) and from **Rhodes**, and to Sitía and Áyios Nikólaos from Rhodes and the Dodecanese. There's also a weekly service to Iráklion from **Israel** and **Cyprus**. All of these ferries are included in the "Travel Details" at the end of each regional chapter.

It's worth knowing that boats to Crete from or via the Greek islands are invariably behind schedule (4hr late is normal), as Crete is the last stop. For up-to-date sailing times, check with the shipping agents or port police in Pireás. The tourist office in Athens publishes a regularly updated schedule of sailings from Pireás.

TRAVELLERS WITH DISABILITIES

It is all too easy to wax lyrical over the attractions of Crete: the stepped, narrow alleys, the thrill of clambering around the great archeological sites. It is almost impossible, on the other hand, for the able-bodied travel writer to see these attractions as potential hazards for anyone who has some difficulty in walking, is wheelchair-bound or suffers from some other disability.

However, don't be discouraged. It is possible to enjoy an inexpensive and trauma-free holiday on the island, if some time is devoted to gathering **information** before arrival. However, much existing or readily available information is out of date – you should always try to double-check. A list of contact organizations is published on p.20. The Greek National Tourist Office is a good first step as long as you have specific questions to put to them; they publish a useful questionnaire which you could send to hotels or owners of apartment/villa accommodation.

PLANNING A HOLIDAY

There are **organized tours** and **holidays** specifically for people with disabilities – both Thomsons and Horizon in Britain will advise on the suitability of holidays advertised in their brochures. If you want to be more independent it's perfectly possible, provided that you do not leave home with the vague hope that things will turn out all right, and that "people will help out" when you need assistance. This cannot be relied on. You must either be completely confident that you can manage alone, or travel with an able-bodied friend (or two).

It's important to become an authority on where you must be self-reliant and where you may

USEFUL CONTACTS

National Tourist Organization of Greece (EOT): See p.29 for addresses. *Offers general advice on terrain and climate. They have nothing specific for disabled visitors except a brief list of hotels which may be suitable.*

GREECE

Association Hermes, Patriarchou 13, Grigouiou E, 16542, Argyroúpolis (☎01/99-61-887). *Can advise disabled visitors to Greece.*

Lavinia Tours, Egnatía 101, 541 10 Thessaloníki (☎031/240-041). *Evyenia Stravropoulou will advise disabled visitors and has tested many parts of Greece in her wheelchair. She also organizes tours within Greece.*

UK

Access Travel, 16 Haweswater Ave, Astley, Lancashire M29 7BL (☎01942/888844, fax 891811). *Tour operator that can arrange flights, transfer and accommodation. This is a small business, personally checking out places before recommendation.*

Holiday Care Service, 2nd floor, Imperial Building, Victoria Rd, Horley, Surrey RH6 7PZ (☎01293/774535, fax 784647; Minicom ☎01293/776943). *Publishes a fact sheet, and also runs a useful "Holiday Helpers" service for disabled travellers.*

Opus 23, Sourdock Hill, Barkisland, Halifax, West Yorkshire HX4 0AG (☎01422/375999). *Part of Grecofile; will advise on and arrange independent holidays, or for those with carers.*

RADAR, 12 City Forum, 250 City Rd, London EC1V 8AF (☎0171/250 3222; Minicom ☎0171/250 4119). *Publishes fact sheets and an annual guide to international travel for the disabled.*

Tripscope, Evelyn Rd, London W4 5JL (☎0181/994 9294). *Transport advice to most countries for all disabilities.*

NORTH AMERICA

Directions Unlimited, 720 N Bedford Rd, Bedford Hills, NY 10507 (☎1-800/533-5343). *Tour operator specializing in custom tours for people with disabilities.*

Information Center for People with Disabilities, Fort Point Place, 27-43 Wormwood St, Boston, MA 02210 (☎617/727-5540; TDD ☎617/345-9743). *Clearing house for information, including travel, primarily in Massachusetts.*

Jewish Rehabilitation Hospital, 3205 Place Alton Goldbloom, Montréal, PQ H7V 1R2 (☎514/688-9550, ext 226). *Guidebooks and travel information.*

Kéroul, 4545 Ave Pierre de Coubertin, CP 1000, Station M, Montréal, PQ H1V 3R2 (☎514/252-3104). *Organization promoting and facilitating travel for mobility-impaired people, primarily in Québec.*

Mobility International USA, PO Box 10767, Eugene, OR 97440 (Voice and TDD: ☎503/343-1284). *Information and referral services, access guides, tours and exchange programmes.*

Society for the Advancement of Travel for the Handicapped (SATH), 347 Fifth Ave, New York, NY 10016 (☎212/447-7284). *Non-profit travel-industry referral service that passes queries on to its members as appropriate; allow plenty of time for a response.*

Travel Information Service, Moss Rehabilitation Hospital, 1200 West Tabor Rd, Philadelphia, PA 19141 (☎215/456-9600). *Telephone information and referral service.*

Twin Peaks Press, Box 129, Vancouver, WA 98666; ☎206/694-2462 or 1-800/637-2256). *Publisher of the Directory of Travel Agencies for the Disabled ($19.95), listing more than 370 agencies worldwide; Travel for the Disabled ($14.95); and the Directory of Accessible Van Rentals and Wheelchair Vagabond ($9.95), loaded with personal tips.*

AUSTRALIA

ACROD, PO Box 60, Curtain, ACT 2605 (☎02/6282 4333).

NEW ZEALAND

Disabled Persons Assembly, 173–175 Victoria St, Wellington (☎04/811 9100).

---

expect help, especially regarding **transport** and **accommodation**. For example, to get between the terminals at Athens airport, you will have to fight for a taxi; it is not the duty of the airline staff to find you one, and there is no trace of an organized queue.

It is also vital to be honest – with travel agencies, insurance companies, companions and, above all, with yourself. Know your limitations and make sure others know them. If you do not use a wheelchair all the time but your walking capabilities are limited, remember that you are likely to need to cover greater distances while travelling (often over tougher terrain and in hotter weather than you are used to). If you use one, take a wheelchair with you: have it serviced before you go, and carry a repair kit.

Read your travel **insurance** small print carefully to make sure that people with a pre-existing medical condition are not excluded. And use your travel agent to make your journey simpler: **airlines** or bus companies can cope better if they are expecting you, with a wheelchair provided at airports and staff primed to help. A **medical certificate** of your fitness to travel, provided by your doctor, is also extremely useful; some airlines or insurance companies may insist on it.

Make a list of all the **facilities** that will make your life easier while you are away. You may want a ground-floor room or access to a large elevator; you may have special dietary requirements; or need level ground to enable you to reach stores, beaches, bars and places of interest. You should also keep track of all your other special needs, making sure, for example, that you have extra supplies of drugs – carried with you if you fly – and a prescription including the generic name in case of emergency. Carry spares of any kind of drug, clothing or equipment that might be hard to find in Crete; if there's an association representing people with your disability, contact them early in the planning process.

VISAS AND RED TAPE

GREEK EMBASSIES ABROAD

Australia 9 Turrana St, Yarralumla, Canberra, ACT 2600 (☎02/6273-3011).
Britain 1a Holland Park, London W11 3TP (☎0171/221 6467).
Canada 80 Maclaren St, Ottawa, ON K2P 0K6 (☎613/238-6271).
Ireland 1 Upper Pembroke St, Dublin 2 (☎01/767254).
New Zealand 5-7 Willis St, PO Box 27157, Wellington (☎04/473 7775).
USA 2221 Massachusetts Ave NW, Washington, DC 20008 (☎202/939-5800).

UK and all other EU nationals need only a valid passport for entry to Greece; you are no longer stamped in on arrival or out upon departure, and in theory at least enjoy uniform civil rights with Greek citizens. US, Australian, New Zealand and Canadian citizens, and most other Europeans, receive entry and exit stamps in their passports and can stay, as tourists, for ninety days.

If you are planning to **travel overland**, you should check current visa requirements for France and Italy, or Hungary, Romania and Bulgaria; transit visas for most of these territories are at present issued at the borders, though at a higher price than if obtained in advance at a local consulate.

VISA EXTENSIONS

If you wish to stay in Crete (or elsewhere in Greece) for longer than three months, you should officially apply for an **extension**. This can be done through the Ipiresía Allodhapón (Aliens' Bureau) in Iráklion; prepare yourself for concerted bureaucracy. Elsewhere you visit the local police station, where staff are apt to be more cooperative.

Visitors from **non-EU countries**, unless of Greek descent, are currently allowed only one six-month extension to a tourist visa, which costs 11,000dr. In theory, **EU nationals** are allowed to stay indefinitely but, at the time of writing, must still present themselves every six months or year, according to whether they have a non-employment resident visa or a work permit; the first extension is free, but you will be charged for subsequent extensions.

In all cases, the procedure should be set in motion a couple of weeks before your time runs out – and, if you don't have a work permit, you will be required to present pink, personalized bank **exchange receipts** (see "Costs, Money and Banks", p.27) totalling at least 500,000dr for the preceding three months, as proof that you have sufficient funds to support yourself without working.

Some individuals get around the law by leaving Greece every three months and re-entering a few days later for a new tourist stamp. However, with the recent flood of Albanian and ex-Yugoslavian refugees into the country, and a smaller influx of east Europeans looking for work, security and immigration personnel don't always look very kindly on this practice.

Several countries maintain **consulates** in Iráklion – British at Papalexándrou 16 (☎224-012), Dutch at 25-Avgóustou 23 (☎246-202), German at Zografóu 7 (☎226-288), Norwegian at Platía Ay. Dimítriou 24 (☎220-536). For other nationalities, refer to the embassy in Athens.

If you **overstay** your time and then leave voluntarily, you'll be given a 22,000dr spot fine upon departure, effectively a double-priced retroactive visa extension – no excuses will be entertained except perhaps a doctor's certificate stating you were immobilized in hospital. It cannot be over-emphasized how exigent Greek immigration officials often are on this issue.

CUSTOMS REGULATIONS

For anyone travelling between EU countries, limits on goods which have been already taxed have been relaxed enormously. However, **duty-free** allowances are as follows: two hundred cigarettes or fifty cigars, two litres of still table wine, one litre of spirits and 50ml of perfume. When leaving Greece for your home country, your normal domestic customs and excise regulations apply.

Exporting **antiquities** without a permit is a serious offence; **drug smuggling**, it goes without saying, incurs severe penalties. Note that codeine is banned in Greece; see opposite.

HEALTH

No inoculations are required for Greece, though it's wise to have a typhoid-cholera booster, and to ensure that you are up to date on tetanus and polio. Don't forget to take out travel insurance (see "Insurance", p.24), so that you're covered in case of serious illness or accidents.

The **water** is safe pretty much everywhere, despite the fact that everyone drinks the bottled stuff instead. Crete has few of the **water shortages** which bedevil smaller islands – it's only in isolated villages or resorts that have grown faster than the plumbing can cope with that you're likely to have a problem.

MEDICAL ATTENTION

For **minor complaints** it's enough to go to the local *farmakío*. Greek **pharmacists** are highly trained and dispense a number of medicines which in other countries can only be prescribed by a doctor. In the larger towns there'll usually be one who speaks good English. If you regularly use any **prescription drug** you should bring along a copy of the prescription together with the generic name of the drug – this will help should you need to replace it and also avoid possible problems with customs officials. It's also worth being aware that **codeine** is banned in Greece; if you import any – and it is fairly common in headache drugs including Panadeine, Veganin, Solpadeine, Codis and Empirin Codeine, to name just a few common compounds – you just might find yourself in serious trouble. So check labels carefully.

Homeopathic and **herbal** remedies are also widely available: there are homeopathic pharmacies in Iráklion and Haniá, and probably elsewhere too.

DOCTORS AND HOSPITALS

For serious medical attention you'll find English-speaking **doctors** in any of the bigger towns or resorts: the tourist police or your consulate should be able to come up with some names if you have any difficulty.

British and other EU nationals are officially entitled to **free medical care** in Greece, by virtue of the E111 form, available from post offices – but "free" means admittance to only the lowest grade of **state hospital** (known as a *yenikó nosokomeío*). In practice, however, hospital staff tend to greet E111s with uncomprehending looks, and you may have to request reimbursement by the NHS upon your return (so make sure to obtain **receipts** for all drugs and treatments paid for). Basic treatment for cuts, broken bones and emergencies is given, but extended care and nursing will be virtually non-existent; Greek families take food and bedding into hospitals for relatives so as a tourist you'll face difficulties.

Rather better are the ordinary **state out patient clinics** (*yatría*) attached to most hospitals and also found in rural locales; these operate on a first-come-first-served basis, so go early – usual hours are 8am–noon. Again, EU citizens are eligible for free treatment; if you don't have an E111, outpatient clinics make a small charge.

SPECIFIC HEALTH PROBLEMS

The main **health problems** experienced by most visitors have to do with overexposure to the sun, and the odd nasty creature from the sea. To combat the former, wear a hat and drink plenty of fluids in the hot months to avoid any danger of **sunstroke**, and don't underestimate the power of even a hazy sun to burn. **Hayfever** sufferers should be prepared for an earlier season than at home. For protection against perils at sea, a pair of goggles for swimming and footwear for walking over wet rocks are useful.

HAZARDS OF THE SEA

You may just have the bad luck to meet an armada of **jellyfish**, especially in late summer; they come in various colours and sizes including invisible and minute. Various over-the-counter remedies are sold in resort pharmacies; baking soda or ammonia also help to lessen the sting.

Less vicious but more common are **sea urchins**, which infest rocky shorelines year round; if you are unlucky enough to step on, or graze one, a needle (you can crudely sterilize it with heat from a cigarette lighter) and olive oil are effective for removing spines from your anatomy. The worst maritime danger – fortunately very rare – seems to be the **weever fish** (*dhrakéna*), which buries itself in tidal zone sand with just its poisonous dorsal and gill spines protruding. If you tread on one the sudden pain is unmistakably excruciating, and the venom is exceptionally potent. Consequences can range up to permanent paralysis of the affected area, so the imperative first aid is to immerse your foot in water as hot as you can stand. This degrades the toxin and relieves the swelling of joints and attendant pain. Another more common hazard are **stingrays** (Greek names include *platí*, *selakhí*, *vátos* or *trígona*), which mainly frequent bays with sandy bottoms where they can camouflage themselves. Though shy, they can give you a nasty lash with their tail if trodden on, so shuffle your feet a bit when entering the water.

MOSQUITOES AND SANDFLIES

While **mosquitoes** (*kounóupia*) don't carry anything worse than a vicious bite, they can be infuriating in places. The best solution is to burn pyrethrum incense coils (*spíres* or *fidhákia* in Greek), widely and cheaply available on Crete. If you're going to be staying in hotels you can also use an electrical device, called a Vape-Nat in Greece, which activates a chemical tablet. These are widely available from pharmacies, for much less than they cost at home. A recently developed refinement of this contraption uses a 40-day fluid cartridge rather than tablets; it sells on the island under the name Baygon. Whilst eating or drinking outdoors, a rub-on stick such as Autan, is equally effective.

If you are sleeping on or near a beach, it's wise to use an insect repellent, either lotion or wrist/ankle bands, and/or a tent with a screen to guard against **sandflies**. Their bites are potentially dangerous, carrying visceral leishmaniasis, a rare parasitic infection characterized by chronic fever, listlessness and weight loss.

INSURANCE

British and other EU nationals are officially entitled to free medical care in Greece upon presentation of an E111 form (see "Health" p.23). "Free", however, means admittance only to the lowest grade of state hospital (known as *yenikó nosokomeío*) and does not include nursing care or the cost of medications. In practice, hospitals tend to greet E111s with uncomprehending looks, and you may have to request reimbursement by the NHS when you return home. If you need prolonged medical care, you'll prefer to make use of private treatment, which is expensive.

Some form of **travel insurance**, therefore, is advisable – and essential for **North Americans** and **Australasians**, whose countries have no formal health-care agreements with Greece (other than allowing for free emergency trauma treatment).

For **medical claims**, keep receipts, including those from pharmacies. You will have to pay for all private medical care on the spot (insurance claims can be processed if you have hospital treatment) but it can all be (eventually) claimed back. Travel insurance usually provides cover for the **loss of baggage**, **money** and **tickets**, too. If you're thinking of renting a **moped** or motorbike in Greece, make sure the policy covers motorbike accidents, which most don't without a supplemental payment.

In all cases of loss or theft of goods, you will have to contact the local police to have a **report** made out so that your insurer can process the claim. This can occasionally be a tricky business in Greece, since many officials simply won't accept that anything could be stolen on their turf, or at least don't want to take responsibility for it.

INSURANCE COMPANIES

BRITAIN

Endsleigh, 97–107 Southampton Row, London WC1 (☎0171/436 4451).

Campus Travel, 52 Grosvenor Gardens, London SW1 (☎0171/730 3402).

Columbus, 17 Devonshire Square, London EC2 (☎0171/375 0111).

Frizzell Insurance, Frizzell House, County Gates, Bournemouth, Dorset BH1 2NF (☎01202/292333).

NORTH AMERICA

Access America, PO Box 90310, Richmond, VA 23230 (☎1-800/284-8300).

Carefree Travel Insurance, PO Box 9366, 100 Garden City Plaza, Garden City NY 11530 (☎1-800/323-3149).

Travel Assistance International, 1133 15th St NW, Suite 400, Washington, DC 20005 (☎1-800/821-2828).

Travel Guard, 1145 Clark St, Stevens Point, WI 54481 (☎1-800/826-1300).

Travel Insurance Services, 2930 Camino Diablo, Suite 300, Walnut Creek, CA 94596 (☎1-800/937-1387).

AUSTRALIA & NEW ZEALAND

Cover More, 9/32 Walker St, North Sydney (☎02/9202 8000 & 1800/251 881).

Ready Plan, 141 Walker St, Dandenong, Melbourne (☎03/9791 5077 & 1800/337 462); 10/63 Albert St, Auckland (☎09/379 3208).

Be persistent and if necessary enlist the support of the local tourist police or tourist office.

EUROPEAN COVER

In Britain, there are a number of low-cost specialist insurance companies (see box above). At all of these you can buy two weeks' basic cover in Greece for around £20, or £30 for a month. If you travel abroad more than twice a year it's also worth considering an **annual cover** policy which allows unlimited trips (of no longer than 90 days' duration) and costs between £55 and £65 depending on the company and the type of cover required.

Most **banks** and **credit card** issuers also offer some sort of vacation insurance, often automatic if you pay for the holiday with a card. In these circumstances, it's vital to check what the policy actually covers.

NORTH AMERICAN COVER

Before buying an insurance policy, check that you're not already covered. **Canadians** are usually covered for medical mishaps overseas by their provincial health plans. Holders of official student/teacher/youth cards are entitled to accident coverage and hospital in-patient benefits. **Students** will often find that their student health coverage extends during the vacations and for one term beyond the date of last enrolment. Bank and credit cards (particularly American Express) often have levels of medical or other insurance

included, and travel insurance may also be included if you use a major credit or charge card to pay for your trip. **Homeowners'** or **renters'** insurance often covers theft or loss of documents, money and valuables while overseas, although conditions and maximum amounts vary from company to company.

After exhausting the possibilities above, you might want to contact a specialist **travel insurance** company; your travel agent can usually recommend one, or see the box above. Policies are comprehensive (accidents, illnesses, delayed or lost luggage, cancelled flights and so on), but maximum payouts tend to be meagre. Premiums vary, so shop around. The best deals are usually to be had through student/youth travel agencies; the policy offered by STA, for instance, comes with or without medical cover. Rates are $110/85 for one month, $165/120 for two, and rise by $55/35 for each extra month.

Most **North American** travel policies apply only to items lost, stolen or damaged while in the custody of an identifiable, responsible third party – hotel porter, airline or left luggage, for example. Even in these cases you will have to contact the local police within a certain time limit to have a complete report made out so that your insurer can process the claim. Note also that very few insurers will arrange on-the-spot payments in the event of a major expense or loss; you will usually be **reimbursed** only after going home.

Travel insurance is available from most **travel agents** (see p.15) or direct from **insurance companies**, for periods ranging from a few days to a year or even longer. Most policies are similar in premium and coverage – but if you plan to indulge in **high-risk activities** such as mountaineering, bungy jumping or scuba diving, check the policy carefully to make sure you'll be covered. A typical policy for Greece will cost: $100/NZ$110 for two weeks, $170/NZ$190 for one month, $250/NZ$275 for two months.

COSTS, MONEY AND BANKS

Although Crete is no longer really cheap, it remains inexpensive in comparison with anywhere else in Europe, barring perhaps Portugal. Travelling around is reasonably cheap too, as are the costs of restaurant meals, accommodation and public transport, and if you're willing to cut a few corners and avoid the more overtly developed areas, you can still get by on relatively little.

Prices depend on where and when you go. The cities and tourist resorts are usually more expensive and costs increase in July, August and at Easter. **Solo travellers** invariably spend more than if they were sharing food and rooms. An additional frustration is the relative lack of single rooms. **Students** with an International Student Identity Card (ISIC) can get free – or fifty-percent discount off – admission fees at most archeological sites and museums. These, and other occasional discounts, tend to be more readily available to EU nationals. A FIYTO card (available to non-students under 26) has fewer benefits, though is still worth having – both cards are available from student/youth travel agencies.

SOME BASIC COSTS

In most places, and keeping costs to the bare minimum, it should be possible to manage on around £12–15/US$20–25 a day, assuming you're prepared to camp and rough it a little; whilst on £15–20/$25–33 a day you can start to enjoy some comfort, providing you're sharing room costs. A budget of £20–25/$33–41 will get you a share of a double room with bath or shower, breakfast, a picnic or simple taverna lunch, bus ride, museum tickets, a couple of beers and a restaurant evening meal. On £25–30/$41–50 a day you could live quite well and even run to sharing a motorbike or small car.

Buses on Crete are efficient and still fairly cheap, although fares are rising. Travelling the length of the island, from Haniá to Sitía, costs around £12/$20 one way. You should always be able to find a basic **room** for two for around £10/$15 a night, although popular tourist venues like Áyios Nikólaos or Haniá are more expensive in high season, and the coast is generally pricier than the inland areas and the mountains. **Single accommodation**, too, is rare and much poorer value (you'll often have to pay the full double price in the resorts or haggle for around a third off). **Campsites** cost about £2/$3.25 a person or less and, with discretion, you can camp on your own near the beaches for free, although you should be sensitive to increasing local concerns about squalor and rubbish. A solid **taverna meal**, even with considerable quantities of local wine, should rarely work out much above £6/$10 a head. Adding a better bottle of wine, going for classier place with an "international" menu or eating seafood in a touristy place could easily mean you'll pay more than double that.

CURRENCY AND EXCHANGE

Greek currency is the **drachma** (*Dhrahmí*), with the **exchange rate** at present around 450 to the pound, or 260 to the US dollar.

The most common **notes** in circulation are those of 100, 200, 500, 1000, 5000 and 10,000 drachmas (*dhrahmés*); while **coins** come in denominations of 5, 10, 20, 50, and 100; you might come across 1dr and 2dr coins, though they're rarely used these days. In practice shopkeepers rarely bother with differences of under 10dr – whether in your favour or theirs. The airports at Haniá and Iráklion should always have an **exchange booth** operating for passengers on incoming international flights, but it's well worth taking some local currency to tide you over the first few hours.

Since 1994, Greek currency restrictions no longer apply to Greek nationals and other EU member citizens, and the drachma is now freely convertible. Arcane rules may still apply to arrivals from North America, Australia or non-EU European countries, but you'd have to be exceptionally unlucky to fall foul of them. If, however, you have any reason to believe that you'll be acquiring large quantities of drachmas – from work or sale of goods – declare everything on arrival, then request, and keep, the pink, personalized **receipts** for each exchange transaction. (These receipts are also essential for obtaining a visa extension; see p.22.) Otherwise you may find that you can only re-exchange a limited sum of drachmas on departure. Even at the best of times many banks stock a limited range of foreign notes – your best bet is often the exchange booth in airport arrivals.

CHANGING MONEY

Travellers' cheques are the safest and easiest way to carry money, and are obtainable from banks (even if you don't have an account) or from offices of Thomas Cook or American Express. You'll pay a commission of between one and two percent although it's worth shopping around for the best deals; for example in the UK, American Express are currently charging one percent commission on purchase with no commission charged on exchange at their offices and affiliated agencies and banks worldwide. Besides being accepted at all banks, when these are closed travellers' cheques are also accepted at quite a number of hotels, agencies and tourist stores. If you intend to spend much time away from the bigger centres in Crete, though, you should plan to have a fair amount of currency to hand. **Eurocheques** supported by a Eurocheque card are also honoured at Greek banks and post offices but they're not widely accepted by stores.

Banks on Crete are normally open Mon–Thurs 8.30am–2pm, Fri 8.30am–1.30pm. Certain branches in the tourist centres open extra hours in the evenings and Saturday mornings to change money, while outside these hours larger hotels and travel agencies can often provide this service, albeit sometimes with hefty commissions. When using a bank, always take your passport with you as proof of identity and be prepared for at least one long queue – often you have to line up once to have the transaction approved and again to pick up the cash. **Commissions** can vary considerably (400–800dr per transaction is typical), even between branches of the same bank, so ask first. Remember, though, that both commission and rate will usually (though not always) be worse if you change money at a hotel or travel agent.

Alternatives to banks are **travel agents**, **bureaux** and **official tourist offices**. The travel agents often serve as general purpose information centres in smaller resorts and will change travellers' cheques and banknotes. Although they're likely to be trustworthy, you should have a rough idea in your mind of what the official exchange rate is. Since the freeing up of all remaining currency controls in 1994, a number of authorized bureaux for exchanging foreign cash and travellers' cheques have emerged in the major tourist centres in the north of the island. When changing small amounts, choose those that charge a percentage commission (usually one percent) rather than a high flat minimum. The government and local government tourist offices are to be found in most of the major centres and usually stay open until quite late in the evening; they offer exchange facilities at a rate similar to (and sometimes better than) the banks.

Exchanging money at the **post office** also has considerable advantages in Greece. You miss out on the queues at banks and have access to exchange almost anywhere you go. Many out-of-the-way places will have a post office but no bank. Commissions levied for both travellers' cheques and cash tend, at about 300dr per transaction, to be lower than at the banks. If you have a UK-based post office **Girobank** account you will be able to draw money out at almost any post office in Crete.

CREDIT CARDS, CASH DISPENSERS AND EMERGENCY MONEY

Major **credit cards** are widely accepted, but only by the more expensive stores, hotels and restaurants: they're useful for renting cars, for example, but no good in the cheaper tavernas or rooms places. If you run short of money, you can also get a **cash advance** on a credit card, though there's a minimum limit of around 15,000dr (about £33/$55): the Emborikí Trápeza (Commercial Bank), Trápeza Písteos (Credit Bank) and Ioniki Trápeza (Ionican Bank) handle Visa and American Express; whilst the Ethnikí Trápeza (National Bank) acts for Mastercard. However, there is usually a two percent credit card charge, often unfavourable rates and always interminable delays while transaction approval is sought by telex. Some private exchange places will also give advances on credit cards, with a lower minimum, but they may charge more.

It's much easier to use the small but growing network of 24-hour **cash dispensers**, although these are presently confined to the major towns along the north coast and Ierápetra in the south; due to the frequency of power and computer failures and eccentric machines telling you to come back later, you'd be wise not to rely solely on this means of getting hold of cash. Check with your bank whether your card offers this facility (for which you will need a PIN number) before relying on it. The most useful and well-distributed cash dispensers are those for the Ethnikí Trápeza (National Bank), which take Cirrus and Mastercard; the Emborikí Trápeza (Commercial Bank) which accepts Plus and Visa; and the Trápeza Písteos (Credit Bank) which accepts Visa and American Express.

Failing this, you'll have to arrange to have **money wired** from home in an emergency. Though this is theoretically very quick, you should in practice count on delays of three to six days for receipt of telexed funds. You can pick up the sum in foreign currency, or even travellers' cheques, but there tend to be heavy commissions.

INFORMATION AND MAPS

The National Tourist Organization of Greece (Ellinikós Organismós Tourismóu, EOT) is the obvious first stop for information on Crete, even though few of their glossy pamphlets apply exclusively to the island. Go armed with specific questions, or you'll simply be given the general leaflet on Crete, which has plenty of pictures, a very small-scale map, and hardly any hard information at all. They may also have up-to-date bus and ferry timetables and prices.

The National Tourist Organization maintains **offices** in most European capitals (though not Dublin), Australia and North America; see the box on p.29 for addresses.

TOURIST INFORMATION

On the island, there are EOT offices in Iráklion (see p.66), Haniá (see p.245) and Réthimnon (see p.198). Where there is no EOT office, you can get information (and often a range of leaflets) from municipal **tourist offices** or from the **tourist police**. The latter are basically a branch (often just a single delegate) of the local police and deal with complaints about restaurants, taxis, hotels and all things tourist-related; call ☎104 for information and help, and see individual towns for local addresses. They can also sometimes provide you with lists of rooms to rent, which they regulate. In addition, local **travel agencies** are always helpful.

EOT OFFICES ABROAD

Australia 51 Pitt St, Sydney, NSW 2000 (☎02/9241-1663).

Britain 4 Conduit St, London W1R 0DJ (☎0171/734 5997).

Canada 1300 Bay St, Main Level, Toronto, ON M5R 3K8 (☎416/968-2220); 1223 rue de la Montagne, QCH 3G, Montréal (☎514/871-1535).

Denmark Copenhagen Vester Farimagsgade 1,2 DK 1606-Kobenhavn V (☎325-332).

Netherlands Leidsestraat 13, NS 1017 Amsterdam (☎20/254-212).

Norway Ovre Stottsgate 15B, 0157 Oslo 1 (☎2/426-501).

Sweden Grev Turigatan 2, PO Box 5298, 10246 Stockholm (☎8/679 6480).

USA 645 Fifth Ave, New York, NY 10022 (☎212/421-5777); 168 North Michigan Ave, Chicago, IL (☎312/782-1084); 611 West 6th St, Los Angeles, CA(☎213/626-6696).

If your home country isn't listed here, apply to the embassy. Note that there are no Greek tourist offices in Ireland or New Zealand.

MAPS

Island **maps** are available locally, but you'll almost certainly find a better one at home. None seems to be particularly accurate when it comes to minor roads and footpaths: the best of the bunch for **driving** and **general use** are the Harms-Verlag maps (see below) and the Nelles and Freytag & Berndt (this, in Crete, under the Efstathiadis Group imprint) offerings are also satisfactory.

Until recently, more detailed **hiking/topographical maps** were virtually non-existent,

making life in Crete a trial for walkers and climbers. This is historically due to Greece's (and Crete's) geographical position, flanked by Turkey to the east and its Balkan neighbours to north; government paranoia about maps falling into the wrong hands (usually Turkish ones) severely restricted the accuracy of what could be published. The continuing unsettled situation in the Balkans, allied to new tensions with Turkey have now resulted in plans for more openness being shelved indefinitely. The 1:200,000 maps of the National Statistical Service (Ethnikí Statistikí Ipiresía), occasionally

CRETE ONLINE

www.interkriti.org
Extraordinarily comprehensive site including maps, aerial photography, lists of hotels, local travel agents and car rental outlets, as well as details of all the major towns, sites, museums and personalities of the island. There's even a Cretan recipe or two.

www.hellasweb.com
General Greek site with useful info and the excellent online version of Cretan magazine *Stigmes*, which has interesting articles and cartoons as well as some useful links to other Cretan sites including an online book store.

www.dilos.com/region/crete/
Travel operator with substantial site, general and cultural info and pics.

www.odysseas.com
General interest site with brief tourist guides to

most places of interest and some accommodation and other practical information.

www.yahoo.com/Regional/Countries/Greece/ Islands/Crete/
Search site for most things Cretan.

http://www.usatoday.com/weather/basemaps/n w167540.htm
Five-day Iráklion forecast; you'll find much the same at *http://www.weatherpost. com/cities/Igir.htm*

www.forthnet.gr/intercity
Forthnet is a Greek server which hosts a number of Crete-related sites, including a mirror of *Stigmes* magazine. The intercity section promises information on transport and accommodation in all the main towns, but at the time of writing didn't actually deliver much, while the server was very slow.

available in specialist shops, are so out of date as to be almost entirely worthless.

The best available maps until recently were the Harms-Verlag 1:80,000 five-map set covering the whole of the island, now sadly superseded by a new **two-map edition** (*Crete Touring Map*) covering the eastern and western sectors at 1:100,000. Despite the downgrading in scale many footpaths are still marked (including the pan-European E4 Footpath which crosses Crete) and the maps detail many topographical features

missing from other publications. The five-map edition is still to be found at shops on the island until supplies run out. A new publication, the *Crete Trekking and Road Map* produced by Iráklion publisher Petrákis, is a worthy attempt to improve the situation for walkers. Using a scale of 1:100,000, the island is covered in four provincial maps (Haniá 1, Réthimnon 2 and so on), and is the first series to contain most of the walking trails, tracks and walkable gorges on the island (including the E4 European Footpath). This is still far

MAP OUTLETS

UK

London National Map Centre, 22–24 Caxton St, SW1H 0QU (☎0171/222 2466); Stanfords, 12–14 Long Acre, WC2E 9LP (☎0171/836 1321); Daunt Books, 83 Marylebone High Street, London W1M 3DE (☎0171/224 2295); The Travel Bookshop,

13–15 Blenheim Crescent, London W11 2EE (☎0171/229 5260).
Glasgow John Smith and Sons, 57–61 St Vincent St (☎0141/221 7472).

Maps by **mail** or **phone order** are available from Stanfords.

USA

Chicago Rand McNally, 444 N Michigan Ave, IL 60611 (☎312/321-1751).
New York The Complete Traveler Bookstore, 199 Madison Ave, NY 10016 (☎212/685-9007); Rand McNally, 150 E 52nd St, NY 10022 (☎212/758-7488); Traveler's Bookstore, 22 W 52nd St, NY 10019 (☎212/664-0995).
San Francisco The Complete Traveler Bookstore, 3207 Fillmore St, CA 92123 (☎415/923-1511); Rand McNally, 595 Market St, CA 94105 (☎415/777-3131).

Santa Barbara Map Link Inc., 30 S La Patera Lane, Unit 5, Santa Barbara CA 93107 (☎805/692 6777 or fax 962 0884).
Seattle Elliot Bay Book Company, 101 S Main St, WA 98104 (☎206/624-6600).
Washington DC The Map Store Inc., 1636 1st NW, Washington, DC 20006 (☎202/628-2608); Rand McNally, 1201 Connecticut Ave NW, Washington, DC 20036 (☎202/223-6751).

Note: Rand McNally now has more than twenty stores across the US; call ☎1-800/333-0136 (ext 2111) for the address of your nearest store, or for **direct mail** maps.

CANADA

Montréal Ulysses Travel Bookshop, 4176 St-Denis (☎514/843-9447).
Toronto Open Air Books and Maps, 25 Toronto St, M5R 2C1 (☎416/363-0719).

Vancouver World Wide Books and Maps, 736A Granville St V6Z 1G3 (☎604/687-3320).

AUSTRALIA

Adelaide The Map Shop, 16a Peel St, Adelaide, SA 5000 (☎08/8231 2033).
Brisbane Worldwide Maps and Guides 187 George St, Brisbane (☎07/3221 4330).
Melbourne Bowyangs, 372 Little Bourke St,

Melbourne, VIC 3000 (☎03/9670 4383).
Perth Perth Map Centre, 891 Hay St, Perth, WA 6000 (☎08/9322 5733).
Sydney Travel Bookshop, 20 Bridge St, Sydney, NSW 2000 (☎02/9241 3554).

NEW ZEALAND

Auckland: Specialty Maps, 58 Albert St (☎09/307 2217).

from ideal, but the same publisher does hope to bring out 1:50,000 and 1:25,000 maps in the near future. The Petrákis maps are currently available only from bookshops on the island but you can obtain them by post from Planet International Bookstore, Hándhakos and Kidonias (☎081/281-558, fax 287-142), in Iráklion.

Both the Harms-Verlag and Petrákis maps seem to have been based on the Military Geographical Service maps (see below), and the two-map set is available from bookshops in Iráklion, Réthimnon and Haniá, or Stanfords in London (see box on p.30) by mail order. Mountainous zones are also covered by the Greek mountaineering magazine Korfés (Platía Kentrikí 16, Arhanés, Athens; ☎246-1528) which covers Crete in its 1:50,000 series of alpine areas. More than thirty now exist and a new one is issued every other month as a centre-fold in the magazine, which is sold at many news-

stands. Recently production of Roman-lettered maps began, but you have to go out to the Aharnés office to get these.

Whilst these maps are extremely accurate for natural features and village positions, based as they are on the generally unavailable maps of the **Hellenic Military Geographical Service**, they are less reliable in the matter of trails and new roads. If you want to try your luck at obtaining these, visit the HMGS at Evelpídhon 4, north of Areos Park in Athens, Monday, Wednesday or Friday from 8am to noon only. All foreigners must leave their passport with the gate guard; EU citizens may proceed directly to the sales hall, where efficient computerized transactions take just a few minutes. Other nationals will probably have to go upstairs for an interview; if you don't speak reasonably good Greek it's best to have a Greek friend get them for you.

GETTING AROUND

By Greek standards Crete is pretty well served for roads and transport, and the main towns and resorts along the north coast are linked by an excellent road served by a fast and frequent bus service. To get away from the crowds, though, and see a little of the real Crete, you'll want to get off the main roads – for at least some of your time you should think about renting some transport or, better still, setting out on foot.

The main public transport **routes** and **timings** are detailed at the end of each chapter in "Travel Details".

BUSES

Buses are the standard – indeed the only – form of public transport on Crete, covering the island remarkably comprehensively; modern, fast and efficient buses run along the main north-coast road every hour or so. Off the major routes services vary: the ones used primarily by tourists (to Omalós and Hóra Sfakíon for the Samariá gorge, or Festós and Mátala) tend also to be modern and convenient; those that cater mainly for locals are generally older buses which run once daily as transport to market or school – into the provincial capital very early in the morning and back out to the village around lunchtime. This means that for day-trips they are of little use. If you are determined, though, there are few places not accessible by bus, and if you combine the services with some walking you'll get about exceptionally cheaply, if not always especially quickly.

Buses on Crete are a turquoise-green colour, and are run by a consortium of companies jointly known as **KTEL** (Kratikó Tamío Ellinikón

Leoforíon). That this is not one single company is most obvious in Iráklion where there are three separate termini, each serving different directions. On the whole, buses serving a given village will run from the provincial capital – Iráklion, Réthimnon, Haniá or, in the case of Lasíthi, Áyios Nikólaos or Sitía – but there are also a number of small-scale services which cross inter-provincial borders. A **timetable** of island-wide services is produced each year, and is available from bus stations and tourist offices.

TAXIS AND TOURS

Local **taxis** are exceptionally cheap, at least as long as the meter is running or you've fixed a price in advance. A good proportion of their business is long-distance, taking people to and from the villages around the main towns (in some places, including the airports; there's a printed list of prices to the most common destinations). If you want to visit somewhere where there's only one bus, or hike somewhere and get a ride back, it's well worth arranging for a taxi to pick you up: for four people this generally costs little more than the bus.

It's also quite easy to negotiate a day's or half-day's **sightseeing** trip, although this does require a certain ability in Greek and faith in the driver, and over long distances can become expensive.

A simpler alternative for a one-off visit is to take a **bus tour**. Travel agents everywhere offer the obvious ones – the Samariá gorge, Vái beach, a local "Cretan night" – and a few offer much more adventurous alternatives; some of the best of these are detailed in the guide. They're worth at least considering as a relatively cheap and easy way to see things you might otherwise be unable to get to – a day-trip to the Minoan sites or the gorge, for example; you can always escape from the rest of the group once there.

DRIVING

Cars have obvious advantages for getting to the more inaccessible areas, but this is one of the more expensive countries in Europe to **rent a car**. If you drive **your own vehicle** to and through Greece (not really an option on a short visit to Crete), you'll need international third-party insurance, the so-called **Green Card**, as well as an International Driving Licence and the registration documents. Upon arrival your passport will get a **carnet stamp**; this normally allows you to keep a

vehicle in Greece for up to six months, exempt from road tax.

CAR RENTAL

Car rental in Greece starts at £180/$298 a week in high season for the smallest model, including unlimited mileage, tax and insurance. Outside peak season, at the smaller local outfits, you can sometimes get terms of about £25/$40 per day, all inclusive, but three days is the preferred minimum duration. Open jeeps, an increasingly popular extravagance, begin at about £35/$58 per day, rising to £55/$90 at busy times.

You may get a better price from one of the **foreign companies** that deal with local firms than if you negotiate for rental in Crete itself. One of the most competitive, which can arrange for cars to be picked up at both Iráklion and Haniá airports, is Holiday Autos (see box for phone number). Most travel agents can also offer car rental in Greece, though their rates are generally higher than the specialist rental agents. In Greece, Payless, Thrifty and Just are reliable medium-sized companies with branches in many towns; all are considerably cheaper than (and just as reputable as) the biggest international operators, Budget, Europcar, Hertz and Avis. A reliable and competitively priced **local operator** in Crete is Clubcars (see box for phone number) who have offices in all the provincial capitals as well as Sitía.

All agencies will want either a credit card or a large cash **deposit** up front; minimum age requirements vary from 21 to 25. In theory an **International Driving Licence** is also needed, but in practice European, Australasian and American ones are honoured.

Note that initial rental prices quoted in Greece almost never include tax, collision damage waiver fees and personal insurance. These are absolutely vital; the coverage included by law in the basic rental fee is generally inadequate, and not covering yourself could land you with a bill of thousands of pounds or dollars should you damage the vehicle. It is extremely important to check the fine print on your contract. Be careful of the hammering that cars get on minor roads and tracks; tyres and the underside of the vehicle are often excluded from insurance policies, especially when hired locally.

In terms of available **models**, the more competitive companies tend to offer the Subaru M80 or Vivio, the Fiat Cinquecento and the Suzuki Alto

CAR RENTAL AGENCIES

BRITAIN

Avis	☎0990/900 500
Budget	☎0800/181 181
Europcar/InterRent	☎01345/222 525
Hertz	☎0990/996 699
Holiday Autos	☎0990/300 400
Transhire	☎0171/978 1922
Thrifty	☎0990/168238

NORTH AMERICA

Alamo	☎1-800/522 9696
Auto Europe	☎1-800/223-5555
Avis	☎1-800/331-1084
Budget	☎1-800/527-0700

Camwell Holiday Autos	☎1-800/422-7737
Dollar	☎1-800/800-6000
Europe by Car	☎1-800/223-1516
Hertz	☎1-800/654-3001;
in Canada	☎1-800/263-0600
National	☎1-800/CAR RENT
Thrifty	☎1-800/367-2277

CRETE

Athenscars ☎081/220-680; Iráklion main office
Bestrent ☎0841/23-405; Áyios Nikólaos
Clubcars ☎0841/25-868; Áyios Nikólaos main office
Ritz ☎223-638; Iráklion

800 as A-group cars, and Opel (Vauxhall) Corsa, Nissan Micra or Fiat Uno/Punto in the B-group. The Suzuki Alto 600, Fiat Panda or Seat Marbella should be avoided if at all possible unless you intend sticking to the coast; they're just not built for the Cretan terrain. Be aware also that hire cars tend to come in the most basic model; unless you are hiring from a top-name international company (where of course you pay considerably more) your car will normally not have a radio and never a cassette deck.

DRIVING IN GREECE

Greece has the highest **accident rate** in Europe after Portugal, and many of the roads can be quite perilous – asphalt can turn into a dirt track without any warning on the smaller routes. Uphill drivers insist on their right of way, as do those first to approach a one-lane bridge – headlights flashed at you mean the opposite of what they mean in the UK or North America, signifying that the driver is coming through. Wearing a **seatbelt** is compulsory and children under ten are not allowed to sit in the front seats. If you are involved in any kind of accident it's illegal to drive away, and you can be held at a police station for up to 24 hours. If this happens, ring your consulate immediately, in order to get a lawyer (you have this right). Don't make a statement to anyone who doesn't speak, and write, very good English.

Tourists with proof of membership of official motoring associations are given free **road assistance** from **ELPA**, the Greek equivalent, which runs breakdown services – there's an office based in Crete. The information number is ☎174. In an **emergency** ring their road assistance service on ☎104, anywhere in the country. Many car rental companies have an agreement with ELPA's competitors, Hellas Service and Express Service, but they're prohibitively expensive to summon on your own – over 25,000 drachmas to enrol you as an "instant member" in their scheme.

Petrol/gasoline currently costs around 225-240dr a litre for unleaded (*amólivdhi*) or super. It's easy to run out of fuel after dark or at weekends, especially in the extreme east and west of the island; most rural stations close at 7 or 8pm and some shut at weekends; when touring in these areas it's wise to maintain a full tank, especially when a weekend or national holiday is approaching. Filling stations normally take credit cards, although some of the more rural places may not have the facilities.

BIKES, MOPEDS, SCOOTERS AND CYCLES

Motorbikes, mopeds and Vespas are also widely available in Crete, at prices starting at around £8/$13 a day, £45/$75 per week for a 50cc moped, to about £17/$28 a day, £100/$165 a week for a 175cc trail bike.

The smaller bikes and scooters – known in Greek as *papákia* (little ducks) after their characteristic noise – are ideal for pottering around for a day or two, but don't regard them as serious transport: Crete is very mountainous and the mopeds simply won't go up some of the steeper hills, even with only one person aboard. Be sure not to run beyond the range of your petrol tank either, as they're not designed for long-distance travel and there are few filling stations outside the towns. For serious exploration, or to venture into the mountains, you really need a motorbike or a powerful Vespa – the latter is cheaper but much more dangerous. Whatever you rent, make sure you check it thoroughly before riding off, since many are only cosmetically repaired and if you break down it's often your responsibility to return the machine. It's worth taking the phone number of the rental company in case they do give out miles from anywhere, or you lose the ignition key.

Although motorbikes are enormous fun to ride around, you need to take more than usual care: there's an alarming number of **accidents** each year (many fatal) among visitors and locals because simple safety procedures are not followed. It's only too easy to come to grief on a potholed road or steep dirt track – especially at night. Two tips: never rent a bike which you feel you can't handle, and use a **helmet**. The latter is now required by Greek law (which is rarely enforced), but more crucially it will probably be the one item that saves your life in a spill. All operators should have helmets (*kránio* in Greek), but only a few will supply them unless you ask, and only one or two insist that you wear them; for reasons of comfort and hygiene some people now bring their own helmet with them. Quite apart from your own injuries you're likely to be charged a criminally high price for any repairs needed for the bike, so make sure that you are adequately **insured**, both in the rental agreement (which you should read carefully) and by your own travel insurance – many of these schemes specifically exclude injuries sustained while riding/driving a rented vehicle.

If you are thinking of touring Crete by motorbike then it's worth getting hold of a copy of *Unexplored Crete* (see Contexts, p.369) which covers the island from a biker's viewpoint with suggested itineraries and details of many off-road tracks along, with helpful hints.

CYCLING

Cycling isn't greatly popular in Crete, not surprisingly, perhaps, in view of the mountainous terrain and fierce summer heat, but again the seat of a bike offers an incomparable view of the island and guarantees contact with locals the average visitor could never meet – provided you are a hardy hill-climber. You can bring your own bike in

by plane (it's normally free within your ordinary baggage allowance) or train (in which case it should go free on the ferry). On the island you may have difficulty with bus conductors, always protective of their luggage compartments, but if you stick to older buses you can always throw it on top.

The popularity of **mountain bikes** has resulted in a proliferation of rental outlets in all the major tourist centres, and these are detailed throughout the guide.

WALKING AND HITCHING

The idea of **walking** for pleasure is one that has yet to catch on widely in Crete, but if you have the time and stamina it is probably the single best way to see the island. There are suggestions for hikes – from easy strolls to serious climbing – throughout the guide, and further tips for hikers in the Contexts section. The two Cretan books in the *Landscapes* series (*Landscapes of Eastern Crete* and *Landscapes of Western Crete*, both by Jonnie Godfrey and Elizabeth Karslake, Sunflower Books) make excellent further reading. See "Information and Maps", p.29, for details of walkers' maps of Crete. If you're planning on doing some serious walking – such as any of the various gorges – stout shoes or trainers are essential and walking boots with firm ankle support recommended, along with protection against the sun and adequate water supplies.

It's worth noting that Crete also offers some exciting possibilities for **climbers**: contacts for the local mountaineering clubs (EOS) in Iráklion, Réthimnon and Haniá are given in their respective listings.

When you get tired of walking, or you're stuck in a place after the last bus back has gone, **hitching** usually recommends itself. This, of course, carries the usual risks and dangers, and is inadvisable for women travelling alone. At its best, though, it's a wonderful way to get to know the island and to pick up some Greek. Your luck hitching in Crete will very much depend on where you are. The main road along the north coast is very fast if you want to travel some distance in a hurry, though drivers are less inclined to stop. In rural areas, hitching is great as long as you're not too pushed for time – most people will stop (the more obscure the road, the better your chance) but there may be little traffic and locals are rarely going further than the next village.

FERRIES

Around the island there are numerous **local ferry services** to offshore islets and isolated beaches; these are detailed throughout the guide. Where there is no ferry service you can often arrange a trip by **kaïki** with local fishermen. An enquiry at the bar in the nearest fishing village will usually turn up someone willing to make the trip – it's always worth trying to knock a bit off the first price quoted. To give some idea of prices, a kaïki from Móhlos, near Áyios Nikólaos, to Psíra would cost about 12,000dr return, which includes a couple of hours on the island.

ACCOMMODATION

There are vast numbers of beds available for tourists in Crete, and most of the year you can rely on turning up pretty much anywhere and finding something. In July and August, however, you can run into problems without an advance reservation, especially in the bigger resorts and in Iráklion, Haniá and Áyios Nikólaos. The only real solution is to turn up at each new place early in the day, and to take whatever is on offer in the hope that you will be able to exchange it for something better later.

HOTELS AND ROOMS

Hotels are categorized by the tourist police from "Luxury" down to the almost extinct "E" class, and all except the top category have to keep within set price limits. Letter ratings are supposed to correspond to facilities available, though in practice categorization can depend on such factors as location within a resort and "influence" with tourism authorities. "D" class places usually come with en-suite bath and WC, whilst in "C" class this is mandatory, along with a bar or break-fast area. The additional presence of a pool and/or tennis court, will attract a B-class rating, while A-class hotels must have a bar, restaurant and extensive common areas. Away from the cities, often they and the deluxe outfits (essentially self-contained complexes) back onto a beach. C- and D-class places tend to be very reasonable, costing £9–18/$15–30 for a double room with bath and £7–10/$12–17 for single rooms (where available – in practice they are rare). More luxurious establishments and quite a few of the more "charming" smaller hotels, except perhaps in the centres of larger towns, are often fully booked in advance by foreign tour operators.

Far more often, you'll be staying in **"rooms"** (*dhomátia* – but usually spotted by a *Rooms for Rent* or *Zimmer Frei* sign), which once again are officially controlled and divided into three classes ("A" down to "C"). At the bottom end these are cheaper, and generally cleaner and much more congenial, than hotels of a similar price. These days, most rooms places are in new purpose-built apartment buildings, but some are still, literally, rooms in people's homes – where you'll often be treated with disarming hospitality. At its most basic, a room might consist of a bare concrete space with a bed and a hook on the back of the door, and toilet facilities (cold water only) outside in the courtyard but this is now (and thankfully) becoming rare; at its fanciest it could be a fully furnished place with en-suite marble bathroom. Between these extremes you will probably find that there's a choice of rooms at various prices (they'll always offer you the most expensive first) and that price and quality are not necessarily directly linked; always ask to see the room first. A double room could cost anything from £6/$9 for a

ACCOMMODATION PRICES

All accommodation establishments in this book have been **price-coded** according to the scale outlined below. The rates quoted represent the cheapest available **double room** in high season. For rented apartments and villas, the price code refers to the price of the whole apartment, not just to a double room within the apartment. Out of season, room rates can drop by up to fifty percent, especially if you negotiate rates for a stay of three or more nights. Single rooms, where available, cost around seventy percent of the price of a double.

Rented private rooms usually fall into the ② or ③ categories, depending on their location, facilities, and the season; a few in the ④ category are more like plush self-catering apartments. They are not generally available from late October through the beginning of April, when only hotels tend to remain open.

① up to 4000dr	④ 8000–12,000dr	⑦ 20,000dr upwards
② 4000–6000dr	⑤ 12,000–16,000dr	
③ 6000–8000dr	⑥ 16,000–20,000dr	

very basic place out of season, to £20/$30-plus for high-season luxury in a resort.

As often as not, rooms find you: owners descend on ferry or bus arrivals to fill any space they have. In smaller places, simply ask in a taverna or kafeníon – even if there are no official places around there is very often someone prepared to earn extra money from putting you up. In the larger places there are now signs posted by the tourist police warning against going with people who offer rooms. Some caution is sensible – make sure that you at least know where you're being taken. It's also wise to be aware of the "airport taxi scam" when you pick up a cab at Iráklion or Haniá airports: a driver will frequently attempt to persuade you to go to a "good" hotel (perhaps after rubbishing the one you have in mind) with which, of course, he has an arrangement.

It has become standard practice for rooms proprietors to ask to keep your **passport**; ostensibly "for the tourist police", but in reality to prevent you leaving with an unpaid bill. Some owners may be satisfied with just taking down the details, as in hotels, and they'll almost always return the documents once you get to know them, or if you need them for another purpose (to change money, for example). In the larger resorts, bitter experience has made proprietors wary, and the only way to keep hold of your passport may be to pay in advance.

Prices, for rooms and hotels, should be displayed on the back of the door: if you feel you're being overcharged at a place which is officially registered, it should be enough to threaten to go to the tourist police (who really are very helpful in such cases), although small amounts over the odds may be legitimately explained by tax or out-of-date forms. In recent years there has been more bed capacity than visitors, which has led to proprietors vigorously undercutting their competitors in the quest for business. For much of the time (away from the coast) you will probably find that you are paying less than the official price and occasionally in the towns, too, you may find that you have bargained so well, or arrived so far out of season, that you are actually paying less than you're supposed to. And it's worth remembering that, as the Greeks and Cretans are born traders, there's nothing at all wrong with trying to haggle for a better price providing you're not seen as being unreasonable.

APARTMENTS AND VILLAS

Another of the great traditions of Greek travel is finding that perfect villa and renting it for virtually nothing for a whole month. In the Cretan summer, forget it. All the best **villas** on the coast are contracted out to one agent or other, and let through foreign operators. Even if you do find one empty for a week or two, you'll discover that renting it in Crete costs far more than it would have done to arrange from home. See the addresses of specialist operators listed under the "Getting There" sections if you're interested.

Having said that, all hope is not lost if you arrive and decide you want to drop roots for a while. If you don't mind avoiding the coast altogether, then the old cliché might just come true. Pick an untouristy inland village – in the Amári valley, for example, up behind Paleohóra or inland from Haniá – get yourself known and ask about; you might still pick up some fairly wonderful deals. Out of season your chances are again much better – you'd undoubtedly be able to bargain a very good rate even in touristy areas if you wanted to stay any time between October and March, especially for a month or more. Travel agents are another good source of information on what's available locally, and many rooms places have an apartment on the side or may know of friend or relative with one to rent. Likely villa renting possibilities are suggested throughout the guide.

One other alternative is to rent a regular **apartment** in one of the larger towns. Most renters would be expecting longer-term tenants, but you might be able to strike a deal: look for a sign saying *Enoikhiázete*, or check classifieds in the local papers.

YOUTH HOSTELS

If even rooms are beyond your budget, then an alternative can usually be found. There are six official and semi-official **youth hostels** (*ksenón neótitas*) on Crete, all of which must be among the least strictly run in the world. However the official hostel movement in Greece is in a state of upheaval, largely connected with grave funding problems; as a result many hostels on the island have closed down and others have been left to fend for themselves. This has resulted in higher prices, and whilst the better establishments are still good places to meet people, you may well be paying prices comparable to the cheaper rooms places. Crete's surviving hostels are in Iráklion, Hersónisos, Réthimnon, Sitía, Mírthios and Plakiás; the last four are particularly good. Facilities are basic – you pay around £3–5/$5–8 a night for a dormitory bed on which to spread your sleeping bag – but they usually offer cheap meals and/or kitchen facilities, a good social life and an excellent grapevine for finding work, travelling companions or whatever. They rarely ask to see a membership card, though if you want to be on the safe side, join your home country's hostelling association (see addresses in box below) before you go.

A few of the cheaper hotels, especially in Iráklion and Haniá, are run on similar lines as unofficial hostels: here or from a sympathetic rooms or taverna proprietor, you may be able to negotiate **roof space**. Sleeping on the tiles is better than it sounds – most Cretan buildings have flat concrete roofs on which will be provided a mattress for you to lay a sleeping bag on; there's also often an awning for shade. The nights are generally warm and the stars are stunning, though as this practice is now officially illegal and contraveners face losing their licence, it's becoming increasingly rare.

CAMPING

Official **campsites** are surprisingly rare – they're mentioned in the guide where they exist – and are not, on the whole, very good. They tend to be either very large and elaborate or else nothing more than a staked-out field. Although prices start at around £1.50/$2.50 a night per person at the latter (and count on at least double this at the more elaborate places), they begin to mount up once you've added a charge for a tent (about £2.50/$4), a vehicle (£1.50/$2.25) and everyone in the party. When it's all added up you may feel that a basic room represents better value. A leaflet detailing Crete's seventeen official campsites and seven mountain refuges is widely available from tourist offices on the island.

"**Freelance camping**" – outside authorized campsites – has always been the cheapest and in many ways most pleasant means of travel around the Greek islands. In modern Crete, however, it's a dying tradition. For a start, it's officially forbidden – there's been a law since 1977 which once in a while gets enforced – and, much more significantly, the best sites are gradually being developed, which inevitably means turfing off the "undesirables" (and unfortunately some campers have been undesirable, leaving otherwise scenic sites filthy). Nevertheless, with discretion and sensitivity it can still be done, and

just occasionally you may find yourself with nowhere to sleep but the beach. Obviously the police crack down on people camping rough on (and littering) popular mainstream tourist beaches, especially when a large community of campers is developing: elsewhere nobody is really bothered. The ideal is to find a sympathetic taverna near which to sleep out: if you take most of your meals there they'll often be prepared to guard your gear during the day and let you take showers. If you do camp like this, however, take your rubbish away with you.

It's warm enough to sleep out in just a sleeping bag from May until early September, so you don't even need to drag round a tent. A waterproof bag (available from camping shops) or groundsheet is, however, useful to keep out the late summer damp: so too is a foam pad, which lets you sleep in relative comfort almost anywhere. You will always need a sleeping bag, since even in midsummer the nights get cool, but this can be as lightweight as you can find.

EATING AND DRINKING

Greek food has a poor reputation which is not entirely deserved. No one would argue that this was one of the world's great cuisines, but at its best it can be delicious – fresh, simple and flavoured with the herbs that scent the countryside. The most common complaint is that food is often luke-

warm and always oily. Both are deliberate, and any local will be happy to lecture you on the dangers of consuming too-hot food and on the essential, life-enhancing properties of good olive oil.

This has some justification as the island's diet, based on the ancient triad of wheat, olive and grapes (the so-called Mediterranean diet) has led to its having one of the longest-lived and least diseased populations in the world.

BREAKFAST, FAST FOOD AND SNACKS

Breakfast is not a meal normally served in Greek restaurants. In the major resorts there are now plenty of places offering a choice of English or Continental starts to your day, but mostly these are poor and overpriced. Try to search out instead a *galaktopoleío* (milk bar), which serve puddings and yoghurt (many kafenía also serve yoghurt with honey), or a **zaharoplasteío** (patisserie) for gorgeously sweet and syrupy cakes and pastries. A combination *galaktozaharopoleío* (quite a mouthful in every sense) is not uncommon.

At **bakeries**, you'll find oven-warm flaky pies filled with *féta* cheese (*tirópita*), with spinach (*spanakópita*), sausage (*louhanikópita*), or better still *bougátsa*, filled with creamy cheese and sprinkled with sugar. In the tourist areas you will also find that many of the bakeries are now catering for northern European palates by turning out croissants, donuts and even wholemeal (*olikís*) and rye (*sikalísio*) breads. Kafenía normally make no objections if you eat these at an outdoor table, but politeness demands that you order at least a coffee.

Ubiquitous **fast-food snacks** include *souvláki* – small kebabs most commonly in the form of the doner-kebab type *yíros píta* or chunks of *píta-souvláki*, stuffed into a doughy bread (more like Indian nan than pita bread) along with salad and yoghurt, and quite superb. These are all cheap, and are at their best and most varied in the larger towns. You'll also find places serving varieties of *tost* – bland toasted sandwiches – and pizza; but avoid Cretan hamburgers at all costs.

TAVERNAS AND RESTAURANTS

You can get a meal at a **taverna**, an **estiatório** or a **psistariá**. Regular tavernas are by far the most common, *estiatória* are very similar but tend to be cheaper and simpler, perhaps more "Greek". *Psistariés* are restaurants that specialize in fresh prepared plates – predominantly grilled meat but often good vegetables too. A *psarótaverna* is a taverna which specializes in fish. Chic appearance is not a good guide to quality; often the most basic place will turn out to be the best, and in swankier restaurants you may well be paying for the linen and stemmed wine glasses.

Often at traditional tavernas and *estiatória* there are no menus and you're taken into the kitchen to inspect what's on offer: uncooked cuts of meat and fish, simmering pots of stew or vegetables, trays of baked foods. This is a good time to fix prices, since they always seem to turn out higher if you wait until after you've eaten. Even where there is a **menu** in Greek and English it will probably be a standard printed form and bear little relation to what is actually on offer: again, check the kitchen or display case. Where prices are printed you'll be paying the right-hand (higher) set (inclusive of taxes and, usually, service) and often a number of unexpected extras, too. Unless you're feeling overwhelmingly expensive, a **tip** of five percent will suffice.

Cretans generally eat late: **lunch** is served at 2–3pm, **dinner** at 9–11pm. You can eat earlier than this, but you're likely to get indifferent service at a tourist establishment or find yourself eating alone everywhere else. If you find that you can't wait that long, do what the locals do: take an aperitif along with a few *mezédhes* (see "Vegetarians" below).

DISHES AND CRETAN SPECIALITIES

A typical Greek **meal** consists of appetizers and main course (only the tourist restaurants serve desserts though there's sometimes fresh yoghurt) – the Greek practice is to visit a zaharoplasteío (see p.38) for pastries, coffee and liqueurs once the main meal is over.

In tavernas, the courses will often be served at the same time – if you want the main course later, stagger your ordering. The **main course** of meat or fish comes on its own except for maybe a piece of lemon or half a dozen chips/fries; salads and vegetables are served as separate dishes and usually shared. **Vegetable** dishes (usually cooked in a tomato sauce) are often very good in themselves and, if you order a few between several people, can make a satisfying meal. Some of them, like the tomatoes, peppers or aubergines/eggplants stuffed with rice and minced meat (*yemistés*) are basically a main course. And if you're really pushed for money you can always fall back on pasta – *pastítsio* (macaroni pie) and *makarónia* (spaghetti) are usually available – or soup, which can be filling and delicious.

The **baked dishes** – generally a mixture of meat and vegetables like *moussaká* or *yemistés* – and **stews** – usually some form of lamb with potatoes – are cheaper in general than straight meat or fish dishes. **Meat** usually means lamb, or sometimes pork; which can be pretty tough but excellent in its various spit-roasted forms.

Fish is varied and delicious, but can be expensive, though it's still a bargain compared with typical northern European restaurant prices. And if the prices on the menu seem phenomenally high, that's generally because they are per kilo; most tavernas will encourage you to go into the kitchen to see what's available and when you've selected your fish they'll weigh it to determine the actual price (don't leave it to the waiter, or you'll get the biggest). Some Cretan favourites are *sargós* (white bream), *skorpídi* (scorpion fish), *barbounía* (red mullet), *fagrí* (common sea bream) and *skáros* (parrotfish), a tasty white fish which is eaten whole. The island's bouillabaise, *kakaviá*, a fish soup flavoured with lemon, wild onions and herbs can be a fabulous treat.

Crete makes its own unique contribution to the Greek cuisine – among dozens of typical dishes *salingária stifádo* (snail stew) and *kalitsounia* (savoury stuffed pastries) are two favourites that you should try at least once. Another speciality you also shouldn't miss if you get a chance is *hórta* – the wild greens that grow in abundance on the Cretan hills. These are gathered and boiled to be served up lukewarm (or sometimes cold), dressed with olive oil and vinegar, and are invariably delicious. Although you can eat them all year round, spring and autumn – when they grow vigorously in the damper climate – are the best times.

VEGETARIANS

If you are **vegetarian**, you may be in for a dull time but you are unlikely to starve, as many dishes in the Cretan cuisine are vegetable based. However, you will often have to assemble a meal from various appetizers or *mezédhes* (small snacks) on offer at most tavernas and many bars. These include *tzatzíki* (yoghurt, garlic and cucumber dip), *melitzanosaláta* (aubergine/eggplant dip), *yígandes* (white haricot beans in vinaigrette), *mavromátika* (black-eyed peas), *tyropitákia* or *spanakópites* (small cheese and spinach pies). Eventually even these and the excellent standbys of yoghurt and honey, and Greek salad begin to pall, and you should be aware that many of the "vegetable" dishes on the menu are cooked in meat stock or have small pieces of meat added to liven them up. Restaurants catering for vegetarians, especially in areas which see a lot of younger travellers, are on the increase but still need ferreting out. Many of these are listed throughout the guide.

BUYING YOUR OWN FOOD

Stores and markets open very early and yoghurt, bread, eggs or fruit, as well as picnic foods like cheese, salami, olives and tomatoes are always easy to buy. Remember that Greek cheese isn't all *féta* (salty white sheep's cheese) and, if you ask, there are some remarkably tasty local Cretan varieties: try *mitizíthra*, *káskavali*, *kritiko* and *graviéra*, the latter a peppery, mature full-fat sheep's cheese. All, though, are surprisingly expensive. Beach picnics can be further supplemented by tinned foods such as stuffed vine leaves (*dolmádhes*) or baby squid (*kalamarákia*).

Fruit is wonderful, and seasonal fruits exceptionally cheap – look out for what's on offer in the markets or by the roadside: cherries in spring, melons, watermelons, plums and apricots in summer, pears and apples in autumn, oranges and grapes most of the time. They even grow small bananas on Crete – an endeavour heavily subsidized by the EU.

DRINKING

For ordinary drinking you go to a **kafeníon** – simple places filled with old men arguing and playing *távli* (backgammon), a national obsession. Most places will lend you a set if you ask. They start the day selling coffee (*kafé*) until this is gradually replaced by óuzo (an aniseed-flavoured spirit, drunk neat or mixed with water) and, later still, brandy (which is usually Metaxa or Botrys and graded with 3, 5 or 7 stars) or *raki*, a burningly strong, flavourless spirit also known in Crete as *tsípouro* or *tsikoudhiá*. Raki is also Greece's great ice-breaker and the symbol of the hand of friendship being extended: when you're offered one – inside or outside a bar – you are being honoured and it's polite to accept even if you have to force it down. Outside the major towns, most of the *raki* you'll encounter will be home made – stills are everywhere in the countryside and especially the mountains – and Cretans pride themselves on being able to detect the most subtle distinctions in taste and quality of one brew against another. They have nothing but contempt for the commercial brands on the market and everyone thinks his own concoction to be the nectar of the gods.

The miniature Greek **coffee** is what most Westerners would call "Turkish" and is usually medium sweet or *métrio*. If you want more sugar ask for *glikó* (sickeningly sweet); if none at all *skéto*. Ordinary coffee is also usually available – ask for "Nescafé", which is what it generally is (*Nes me gála* is Nescafé with milk). Iced coffee is known as *frappé*, and is an excellent refresher. Óuzo and other drinks are traditionally served with small snacks – **mezédhes** (see above) – but nowadays you generally have to order and pay for these. **Tea**, *tsái*, is often available too, usually served black with a tin of milk to add. It often tastes better with lemon, *me lemóni*, instead. In the towns, many of the new-style kafenía are starting to serve a whole range of herbal teas, including Cretan **dittany** (*díktamos*), an infusion made from the leaves of this plant which is unique to the island and was used by the ancients as a medicinal panacea.

Real **bars** are rare in traditional Crete, though occasionally you'll find an ouzerí, which differs little from a kafeníon. Bars for the younger set now proliferate in the major towns and cities and mostly follow the northern European design with fancy furniture and drinks, and prices to match. Tourist bars in the resorts tend to be either be staid affairs where you can sit outside in cushioned armchairs sipping exotic, expensive cocktails, or hectic, tumultuous disco-bars serving less exotic but even more expensive concoctions.

WINE

Wine (*krasí*) on the island comes in many varieties; the hot, dry summers are more suited to producing dry red wines – dark and powerful – than whites. There are four appellation wine-growing areas: Pezá, Dafnés, Sitía and Arhánes, the last still using vineyards cultivated by the Minoans almost four thousand years ago. The house wine offered in most tavernas will normally be the brown and cloudy rosé-style Cretan *kókkino* (red), especially good around Kastélli in the west or Sitía in the east, or the white which often has a sherry tang. This will not be resinated (if you want to specify this to make sure, ask for *aretsínato*) and restaurants, especially rural ones, will often have a barrel from which jugs are filled. These locally made brews can vary enormously in quality due to the vagaries of the production process, but they're always worth a try. If you want to test a brew before committing yourself to a *karáfa* (which come in kilo or half-kilo measures), most places will be only too pleased to let you try a glass first.

Although not as popular here as on the mainland (it was largely unknown in Crete before World War II), **retsína** is now produced on the island and most commonly comes in half-litre bottles: you may also find it served from the barrel in quarter, half or kilo metal mugs. This resinated wine is an acquired taste, but once you like it you'll start finding some varieties are extremely good. Acquiring the taste is helped by the fact that it is exceptionally cheap: a litre can cost under £1/$1.50, often less than a litre of beer. The *retsína* produced by the Central Union of Haniá Wine Producers is recommended, but stay well

clear of the same cooperative's red variety which is quite awful.

Cretan **bottled wine** is rather more expensive – Pezá brands like Minos red and white, which you can get everywhere, are fine if rather boring, although the more mature vintages such as Minos Sant Antonio and Palace VDQS (red and white) are getting much better. Minoiko and Mantiko, also from the Pezá district (located to the south of Iráklion) are full-bodied reds with a bit more character, and Logado is another red worth trying. The Arhánes wine region (to the west of Pezá and based on the town of the same name) also produces some pretty good red and white vintages and has a cooperative which sells its wines under the Arhánes brand name. The Sitian wines Topiko (medium-dry with a hint of sherry) and Myrtos, are both good everyday whites to drink with seafood. In the west, Kissamos red is another good bet.

One of the great marketing hits of recent years has been the blended Vin de Crete (widely available on the island), produced by the Kourtakis company from the mainland who have created a blended French-style wine using Cretan grapes. Though it has proved a great success in northern European supermarkets, it is rather bland. Keep an eye out too for the wines of Santorini (Thíra), the volcanic island to the north, which are becoming noted; any of the Santo vineyard's output are worth a try, particularly the white Asyrtiko. Whichever wines you try, you should be aware that irregular production processes can often lead to wines of the same vintage tasting quite different from each other (even when the bottle label is identical), and duff bottles are a frequent hazard. If you suspect any wine call the waiter over for a second opinion; you'll usually get another bottle and an apology.

The best mainland brands of unresinated wine are by Boutari – especially the Lac des Roches and Rotonda whites and the justifiably famous Naoussa red. Marko, Cambas and the excellent Afelia red are also drinkable.

BEER

Beer is standard European lager served in half-litre bottles or smaller cans. The locally brewed Amstel and Henninger are fairly bland versions of their north European counterparts, and imported Heineken (known locally as *prásino* – the green one, after its green bottle) and Lowenbrau are worth the extra few drachmas. After the demise of Fix beer, fondly remem-

A FOOD AND DRINK GLOSSARY

BASICS AND TERMS

Neró	Water	*Fitofágos/Hortofágos*	Vegetarian
Psomí	Bread	*Avgá*	Eggs
Sitarénio psomí	Wholemeal bread	*Tirí*	Cheese
Siskalísio psomí	Rye bread	*(Horís) ládhi*	(Without) oil
Aláti	Salt	*Katálogo/lísta*	Menu
Yiaoúrti	Yoghurt	*O logariasmós*	The bill
Méli	Honey	*Sto foúrno*	Baked
Kréas	Meat	*Psitó*	Roasted
Psári(a)	Fish	*Sti soúvla*	Spit roasted
Lahaniká	Vegetables	*Tis óras*	Grilled/fried to order

SOUPS AND STARTERS

Soúpa	Soup	*Taramósalata*	Fish roe paté
Avgolémono	Egg and lemon soup	*Tzatzíki*	Yoghurt and cucumber
Dolmádhes	Stuffed vine leaves		dip
Fasoládha	Bean soup	*Melitzanosaláta*	Aubergine/eggplant dip

VEGETABLES

Patátes	Potatoes	*Kolokithákia*	Courgette/zucchini
Hórta	Greens (usually wild)	*Spanáki*	Spinach
Radhíkia	Wild chicory	*Fakés*	Lentils
Piperiés	Peppers	*Rízi/piláfi*	Rice (usually with *sáltsa –*
Domátes	Tomatoes		sauce)
Fasolákia	String beans	*Saláta*	Salad
Angoúri	Cucumber	*Horiátiki (saláta)*	Greek salad (with olives,
Angináres	Artichokes		*féta* etc)
Yígantes	White haricot beans	*Yemistés*	Stuffed vegetables
Koukiá	Broad beans	*Papoutsákia*	Stuffed aubergine/eggplant
Melitzána	Aubergine/eggplant	*Bouréki*	Courgette/zucchini, potato or
			cheese pie

MEAT AND MEAT-BASED DISHES

Kotópoulo	Chicken	*Kleftiko*	Meat, potatoes and veg
Arní	Lamb		cooked together in a pot
Hirinó	Pork		or foil; a Cretan speciality
Vodhinó	Beef		traditionally carried to
Moskhári	Veal		bandits in hiding
Sikóti	Liver	*Pastítsio*	Macaroni baked with meat
Patsás	Tripe soup	*Païdhákia*	Lamb chops
Nefrá	Kidneys	*Brizóla*	Pork or beef chop
Biftéki	Hamburger	*Keftédhes*	Meatballs
Moussaká	Aubergine/eggplant, potato	*Loukánika*	Spicy sausages
	and mince pie	*Kokorétsi*	Liver/offal kebab
Stifádho	Meat stew with tomato and onion	*Tsalingária*	Garden snails

FISH AND SEAFOOD

Garídhes	Prawns	*Xifías*	Swordfish
Okhtapódhi	Octopus	*Sinagrídha*	Cuttlefish
Astakós	Lobster	*Gópa*	Bogue
Kalamária	Squid	*Soupiá*	Anchovy
Kalamarákia	Baby squid	*Marídhes*	Whitebait
Glóssa	Sole	*Gávros*	Bogue (cheap!)
Barbóuni	Red mullet	*Fagrí*	Sea bream

SWEETS, FRUIT AND CHEESE

Karidhópita	Walnut cake	Fráoules	Strawberries
Baklavá	Honey and nuts pastry	Kerásia	Cherries
		Stafília	Grapes
Rizógalo	Rice pudding	Portokália	Oranges
Galaktobóuriko	Custard pie	Pepóni	Melon
Pagotó	Ice cream	Karpoúzi	Watermelon
Pastéli	Sesame and honey bar	Míla	Apples
Kasséri	Hard cheese	Síka	(Dried) figs
Graviéra	Gruyère-type cheese	Fistíkia	Pistachio nuts

DRINKS

Neró Enfialoméno	Mineral water	Gálakakáo	Chocolate milk
Bíra	Beer	Portokaládha	Orangeade
Krasí	Wine	Limonádha	Lemonade
Mávro	Red	Gazóza	Generic fizzy drink
Áspro	White	Boukáli	Bottle
Rosé/Kokkinéli	Rosé	Potíri	Glass
Tsáï	Tea	Stiniyássas!	Cheers!
Kafés	Coffee	Yiásou!	Cheers!

bered by those with Sixties and Seventies memories of Greek travels, a new domestic label, Mythos, has emerged to carry the national flag and compares well with the foreign beers. Beware of exotic brands or gold-trimmed bottles served by bars in tourist areas (especially if you leave it to the waiter) – the mark-up is usually outrageous.

COMMUNICATIONS

POST

Local **post offices** are open from about 7.30am to 2.30pm, Monday to Friday; in big towns and important tourist centres, hours may extend into the evening and weekends. Bigger post offices will change money as well as handle mail. **Airmail** letters take three to six days to reach the rest of Europe, five to eight days to get to North America, and a bit more for Australia and New Zealand. **Aerograms** are faster and surer, and postcards can be inexplicably slow, although things are gradually improving: up to ten days for Europe, three weeks to the Americas or the Pacific. For a modest fee (about 500dr) you can use the **express service** (*katepígonda*), which cuts letter delivery time to two days for the UK and three days for the Americas.

For a simple letter or card, **stamps** (*grammatósima*) can also be purchased at a *períptero* (corner kiosk). However, the proprietors are entitled to a ten-percent commission and never seem to know the current international rates. **Post boxes** are bright yellow: if you are confronted by two slots, make sure to use *Esoterikó* for Greek mail and *Exoterikó* for overseas.

If you are sending large purchases home, note that **parcels** should and often can only be handled in sizeable towns, preferably a provincial capital. This way your package will be in Athens and on an international flight within a day or two. **Registered** (*sistiméno*) delivery is also available, but it is extremely slow.

RECEIVING MAIL

For **receiving mail**, the *poste restante* system is reasonably efficient, especially at the big town post offices. Mail should be clearly addressed and marked *poste restante*, with your surname capitalized and underlined, to the main post office of whichever town you choose. It will be held for a month and you'll need your passport to collect it. Alternatively, **American Express** cheque- or card-holders can use the office in Iráklion as a mail drop: c/o Creta Travel Bureau, Epimenídhou 20–22.

PHONES

Making local calls is relatively straightforward, though the state-run telephone company **OTE** (Organismós Tiliepikinoníon tis Elládhos) provides some of the worst service in the EU – at about the highest rates. Calls will cost, very approximately, £2 for three minutes to all EU countries and most of the rest of Europe, or $5 for the same time to North America or Australia. **Cheap rates**, such as they are, apply from 3pm to 5pm and 9pm to 8am daily, plus all weekend, for calls within Greece; overseas off-peak periods vary, but for Europe fall between 10pm and 8am. **Call boxes**, invariably sited at the noisiest street corner or where there is zero shade, are now all **cardphones** taking no coins at all and functioning only with **phone cards** (*tiliekarta*) sold in 100, 500 or 1000dr units. The largest ones are the best value, and it's worth getting hold of one as soon as you arrive if you think you're going to be doing a lot of phoning for such things as booking rooms. They can be bought from kiosks, OTE offices and newsstands. In many hotel lobbies or cafés you'll find **counter coin phones**; these take 10, 20, 50 and 100dr coins and, unlike the street phone boxes, can be rung back. Most of them are made in northern Europe and bear instructions in English. If you won't be around long enough to use up a phone card, it's probably easier to make local calls from a *períptero* (**street kiosk**). Here the phone is connected to a meter, and you pay after you have made the call. Local calls cost just 20dr for a six-minute call, but **long-distance** ones add up quickly to some of the most expensive rates in Europe – and utilize some of the worst connections.

PHONING GREECE FROM ABROAD

Dial the international access code (given below)
+ 30 (country code) + area code (minus initial 0) + number

Australia	☎0011
Canada	☎011
Ireland	☎010
New Zealand	☎00
UK	☎00
USA	☎011

PHONING ABROAD FROM GREECE

Dial the country code (given below) + area code (minus initial 0) + number

Australia	☎0061
Canada	☎001
Ireland	☎00353
New Zealand	☎0064
UK	☎0044
USA	☎001

USEFUL TELEPHONE NUMBERS

Operator (domestic)	☎131	Speaking clock	☎141
Operator (international)	☎161	Tourist police	☎171
Medical emergencies	☎166	Fire brigade	☎199
Police/emergency	☎100	Road assistance	☎104

For **international** (*exoterikó*) calls, it's better to either use card phones or visit the nearest **OTE** office, where there may be a digital booth reserved for overseas calls; make your call, then pay afterwards. **Reverse-charge (collect) calls** can also be made here, though connections are not always immediate. Be prepared to wait; late evening is usually a quieter time. In Iráklion and Haniá there are OTE branches open 24 hours; in smaller towns, the OTE can close as early as 3pm, though in a few resorts there are OTE Portakabin booths. Outgoing **faxes** can also be sent from OTE offices, post offices and some travel agencies – at a price. Receiving a fax may also incur a small charge.

Another option for calls – and possibly the only one in remoter areas – is from a kafeníon or bar, but make sure the phones are metered: look for a sign saying *Tiléfono me metrití*. Avoid making long-distance calls from a hotel, as they

slap a fifty percent surcharge onto the already exorbitant rates. If you have access to a private phone you can dial the international operator on ☎161 to get a reversed-charge call put through, or dial direct: ☎00, followed by the country code (see box) and the local number without its initial zero.

British Telecom, as well as North American long-distance companies such as AT&T, MCI and Sprint all enable their customers to make long distance **credit-card calls** from Greece, but only back to the home country. There are now a few local-dial numbers with some providers, such as BT, which enable you to connect to the international network for the price of a one-unit call, and then charge the call to your home number – usually cheaper than the alternatives. **Mobile** users should note that only GSM phones will work in Greece, over one of two networks.

MEDIA

NEWSPAPERS

British newspapers are fairly widely available in Crete for 450–600dr, 800–900dr for Sunday editions. You'll find day-old copies in all the resorts as well as in Haniá and Iráklion. **American** and international alternatives are represented by the turgid *USA Today* and the more readable *International Herald Tribune*; *Time* and *Newsweek* can also be found.

Cheaper and more up-to-date, though heavily biased in favour of US press agency reports, the daily *Athens News* and weekly *Kriti News* are also on sale anywhere there might be a market for them: they have selections from the Greek press. *This Month Crete* is a monthly bi-lingual English-German publication which, as well as feature articles on Crete, also carries useful bits of information on food and entertainment. It's free, and available from tourist shops and bars in all the major towns.

Much of the **Greek national press** is funded by political groups, which tends to decrease the already low quality of Greek dailies. Among these, only the centrist *Kathemerini* – whose former proprietor Helen Vlakhos attained heroic status for her defiance of the junta – approaches the standards of a major European newspaper. *Eleftherotypia*, once a PASOK mouthpiece, now aspires to more independence and has links with the UK's *Guardian*; *Avriani* has taken its place in the PASOK claque. *Ta Nea* is mostly known for its extensive small ads. On the **Left**, *Avyi* is the Eurocommunist forum with literary leanings, while *Rizopastis* is the organ for the KKE (unreconstructed Communists). *Ethnos* became notorious some years back by receiving covert KGB funding to act as a disinformation bulletin. At the opposite end of the political spectrum, *Apoyevmatini* generally supports the centre-right Néa Dhimokratía party, while *Estia*'s no-photo format and reactionary politics are both stuck somewhere at the turn of the century. The **ultra-nationalist** lunatic fringe is staked out by *Stokhos* ("Our Goal: Greater Greece. Our Capital: Constantinople").

Crete's **main newspapers** are, like much else on the island, divided along regional lines. Iráklion's main dailies are the socialist-slanted *Allaghi* and the centrist *Patrias*, the latter with the biggest circulation due to its small ads. In the east, Lasíthi's *Anatoli* is a politically neutral organ with another good small ads section. Réthimnon's *Rethemiotika Nea* is another paper which gets its sales from small ads, easily beating the PASOK-supporting daily *Kritiki Epitheorisi* into second place. *Hamiotika Nea*, with more classifieds, is the main Haniá paper, followed by *Kiryx*, owned by the prominent Néa Dhimokratía politician and ex-Greek premier Constantine Mitsotákis.

RADIO

If you have a **radio** you may pick up something more interesting. As well as the BBC World Service, there are also regular news bulletins and bouts of tourist information in English on local Greek stations. American Forces' Radio can be picked up through most of the island, too, while on the extreme eastern end of the island you can receive BBC domestic radio programmes on the FM frequency, disseminated from the British base on Cyprus. As regards the **Greek stations**, playing dial roulette can be rewarding. Greek music programmes are always accessible (if variable in quality) and, despite the language barrier, and with recent challenges to the government's former monopoly of wavelengths, regional stations have mushroomed; the airwaves are now positively cluttered, as every town sets up its own studio and transmitter. Crete's stations are particularly good for hearing some of the island's best exponents of traditional music, particularly *lyra*.

TV

Greece's two central, government-controlled **TV stations**, ET1 and ET2, now lag behind the private channels – Mega Channel, New Channel, Antenna, Star and Seven-X – in the ratings. Programming on all stations tends to be a mix of soaps (especially Italian, Spanish and Latin American), gameshows, westerns, B-movies, and sports. All foreign films and serials are broadcast in their original language, with Greek subtitles. Numerous **cable** and **satellite channels** are received, including Sky, CNN, MTV, Super Channel, and French Canal Cinque and Italian Rai Due. The range largely depends on which hotel you happen to be staying in, although in most Cretan budget hotels you'll be lucky to have a TV at all.

POLICE, TROUBLE AND HARASSMENT

As in the past, Crete, along with Greece as a whole, remains one of Europe's safest regions, with a low crime rate and a deserved reputation for honesty. If you leave a bag or wallet at a café, you'll most likely find it scrupulously looked after, pending your return. Similarly, Greeks are relaxed about leaving possessions unlocked or unattended on the beach, in rooms or on campsites.

However, in recent years there has been an increase in **thefts** and **crimes** on the mainland (perpetrated largely by Albanian refugees) mainly in cities and resorts. Whilst Crete is still generally unaffected by this, it would be wise not to take chances and to make sure to lock your car, cycle or other property. The police on the island tend to be laid back in the extreme (policewomen are often to be seen wearing high heels and make-up), which can sometimes result in catastrophic underreaction: a few years ago a riot involving hundreds of violent and drunken young tourists in Mália continued for most of the night because only two police officers were on duty. But this is a long way from the norm, and the most common causes of a brush with authority for visitors – all of them technically illegal – are nude bathing or sunbathing, camping outside an authorized site and (a major crime in the Greek book) taking or possessing cannabis products or any other drug.

Below are a few pointers to offences that might get you into trouble locally, and some advice on **sexual harassment** – all too much a fact of life given the classically Mediterranean machismo of the culture.

SPECIFIC OFFENCES

Nude bathing is currently legal on only a very few beaches, and is deeply offensive to many more traditional Cretans: exercise considerable sensitivity to local feeling and the kind of place you're in. As a general rule, stay away from families with children, the main entrance of a beach and any tavernas – it's also considered very bad etiquette to swim or sunbathe nude within sight of a church. If a beach has become fairly established for nudity, or is secluded, it's highly unlikely that the police are going to come charging in. Where they do get bothered is if they feel a place is turning into a "hippy beach" or if nudity is getting too overt on mainstream tourist stretches. But there are no hard and fast rules; it all depends on the local cops. Mostly the only action would be a warning, but you can officially be arrested straight off – facing as much as three days in jail and a stiff fine. Topless (sun) bathing for women is now technically legal nationwide, but specific locales often opt out of the "liberation" by posting signs to that effect, which should be heeded.

Very similar guidelines exist for **camping rough** (see p.38) – though for this you're still less likely to incur anything more than a warning to move on. The only real risk of arrest is if you are told to move on and fail to do so. In either of the above cases, even if the police do take any action against you, at worst it's more likely to be a brief spell in their cells to speed you on your way than any official prosecution.

Drug offences are a far more serious matter and are treated as major crimes, particularly since there's a growing local use and addiction problem. The maximum penalty for "causing the use of drugs by someone under 18", for example, is life imprisonment and a ten million drachma fine. Theory is by no means practice, but foreigners caught in possession of quite small amounts of hash and grass do get jail sentences of up to a year – much more if there's any suggestion they're supplying others. Greek prisons are not to be recommended.

If you get arrested for any offence you have an automatic right to contact your country's **consul**, who will arrange a lawyer for your defence. Beyond this, there is little they can, or in most cases will, do.

CONSUMER PROTECTION ON HOLIDAY

In a tourist industry as developed as in Greece there are inevitably a number of cowboys and shady characters amongst the taxi-drivers, hoteliers and car rental agencies. EKPIZO, the **Greek Consumers' Association**, has established a "Legal Information and Assistance for Tourists" programme, to be run yearly from June to September. Their main branch is in Athens (☎01/330-4444), but there is also an office in Iráklion at Milatou 1 (☎081/240-666), slightly east of Platía Venizélou ("Fountain Square"). EKPIZO issues a pamphlet about holidaymakers' rights, available in airports and tourist offices. They are always prepared to pursue serious cases, by friendly persuasion, or by court action if necessary.

SEXUAL HARASSMENT

Many women travel about Greece on their own without feeling intimidated or harassed – but some undoubtedly are. This has little to do with the way individuals look or behave, and only indirectly relates to the way Greek women themselves are treated. What is important is that different assumptions are made about you as a foreign woman depending on where you are.

In most of the **rural areas**, you'll be treated first and foremost as a *ksénos* – a word which means both stranger and guest – in much the same way as a foreign man. You can sit and drink óuzo in the exclusively male kafenía (there's often nowhere else) without always suspecting the hospitality and friendliness that's offered.

In the large **resorts** and **towns**, however, where tourism has for a long time determined the local culture, things can be very different. Here the myths and fantasies of the "liberated" and "available" woman are widespread: not perhaps to the extent of other Mediterranean countries but oppressive nonetheless. The Greek version of **machismo** is strong; most of the hassle you are likely to get is from Greek *kamákia* (fish harpoons)

who migrate to the main resorts and towns in summer in pursuit of foreign females. The locals, who become increasingly protective of you as you become more of a fixture, treat these outsiders (particularly if they're Athenians) with contempt. Their obvious stake-outs are beach bars and discos. Without a good control of the language it can be hard to deal with: words worth remembering as an unambiguous response are "*stamáta*" or "*pápsteh*" (stop it), "*afísteme*" (leave me alone) and "*fíyete*" (go away), the latter intensified by "*dhrómo*" (road, as in "Hit the road!").

Hitching in Crete is normally safe but probably not advisable for lone women travellers. **Camping** is generally not a problem, though away from recognized sites it is often wise to attach yourself to a local family by making arrangements to use nearby private land. In the more remote areas you may feel more uncomfortable about travelling alone. The intensely traditional Greeks may have trouble understanding why you are unaccompanied, and might not welcome your presence in their exclusively male kafenía – often the only place where you can get a drink. Travelling with a man, you're more likely to be treated as a *ksénos*, a word meaning both stranger and guest.

OPENING HOURS AND PUBLIC HOLIDAYS

It is virtually impossible to generalize about Cretan opening hours, except to say that they change constantly. The traditional timetable starts early – stores open at 7am or 8am – and runs through till lunchtime, when there is a long break for the hottest part of the day; things may then reopen in the mid- to late afternoon. In tourist areas, though, stores and offices may stay open right through the day: certainly the most important archeological sites and museums do so.

Matters are further confused by Crete's **public holidays**, during which almost everything will be closed; there's a list of the most important ones in the box below. It's worth bearing in mind, too, that either side of major **festivals** (see p.50) many public buildings and banks tend to close, possibly leaving you stranded for days without cash. Keep an eye on the calendar and plan accordingly.

STORES AND BUSINESSES

Store hours are theoretically Monday, Wednesday and Saturday from approximately 8am to 2pm, and Tuesday, Thursday, Friday from 8am to 1pm and 5 to 8.30pm. There are so many exceptions to the rule though, by virtue of holidays and professional idiosyncrasy that you can't count on getting anything done, except from Monday to Friday between 9.30am and 1pm or so. Closed pharmacies are supposed to have a sign on their door referring you to the nearest open one. Most **government agencies** are open to the public from 8am to 2pm. In general, however, you'd be optimistic to show up after 1pm expecting to be served on the same day.

ARCHEOLOGICAL SITES

Opening hours vary from site to site: as far as possible, individual times are quoted in the guide, but bear in mind that these change with exasperating frequency and, at smaller sites, can be subject to the whim of a local keeper who may decide to close early, or even leave the gate open after the official closing time or on the official closing day (usually Monday). The times given are generally summer hours, which operate from around April to the end of September. Reckon on similar days but later opening and earlier closing in winter. A list of current **opening hours** is available from the tourist offices in Iráklion and Haniá.

Smaller archeological sites generally close for a long lunch and siesta (even where they're not meant to), as do **monasteries**. Most monasteries are fairly strict on dress, too, especially for women: they don't like shorts and often expect women to cover their arms and wear skirts. They are generally open from about 9am to 1pm and 5 to 7pm.

PUBLIC HOLIDAYS

January 1	May 1
January 6	Whit Monday (fifty days after Easter;
March 25	see below)
First Monday of Lent (Feb or March; see below)	August 15
Easter weekend (according to the Orthodox calendar, see below)	October 28
	December 25 and 26

VARIABLE RELIGIOUS FEASTS

	Lent Monday	Easter Sunday	Whit Monday
1998	March 2	April 19	June 8
1999	Feb 22	April 11	May 31

FESTIVALS AND ENTERTAINMENT

Most of the big Greek popular festivals have a religious base so they're observed in accordance with the Orthodox calendar: this means that Easter, for example, can fall as much as three weeks to either side of the Western festival.

On top of the main religious festivals, there are literally scores of local festivals, or **paniyíria**, celebrating the patron saint of the village church, and with some 330-odd possible saints' days you're unlikely to travel round for long without stumbling on something. Local tourist offices should be able to fill you in on events in their area.

EASTER

Easter is by far the most important festival of the Greek year – infinitely more so than

THE FESTIVAL YEAR

Epiphany (Jan 6) The hobgoblins who run riot on earth during the twelve days of Christmas are rebanished to the nether world by various rites of the Church. Most important of these is the blessing of baptismal founts and all outdoor bodies of water. At lake or seashore locales the priests cast a crucifix into the deep to be recovered by crowds of young men. There used to be a substantial cash prize for the winner, but this custom is now honoured more in the breach owing to recent, serious violence between contenders.

Pre-Lenten carnivals These span three weeks, climaxing over the seventh weekend before Easter.

Clean Monday (*Kathará Dheftéra*) The beginning of Lent, a traditional time to fly kites and to feast on all the things which will be forbidden over the coming weeks.

Independence Day and the feast of the **Annunciation (March 25)** Parades and dancing to celebrate the beginning of the revolt against Turkish rule in 1821 combined with church services to honour the news being given to Mary that she was to become the mother of Christ. Special celebrations in Paleohóra.

The Feast of St George (April 23). Áyios Yeóryios is the patron saint of shepherds, and big

rural celebrations are held throughout Crete with much feasting and dancing. Major celebration in Asigonía (near Réthimnon).

May Day The great urban holiday – most people make for the countryside to picnic. In the towns demonstrations by the left claim the day, *Ergatikí Protomayiá* (Working-Class First of May), as their own.

Battle of Crete (May 20–27) The anniversary of the battle is celebrated in Haniá and a different local village each year: sporting events, folk dancing and ceremonies with veterans of the battle.

Áyios Konstandínos (May 21). The feast of St Constantine and his mother, Ayía Eléni (St Helen) celebrates the first Byzantine Orthodox ruler and his mother. Services and celebrations at churches and monasteries named after the saint, especially Arkádhi.

Summer Solstice/John the Baptist (June 24) Bonfires and widespread celebrations.

Naval Week (late June) Naval celebrations culminate in fireworks – especially big at Soúdha.

Réthimnon Wine Festival (July) A week of wine tasting and traditional dancing.

Iráklion Festival (July and Aug) A wide variety of cultural events – from drama and film to

Christmas – and taken much more seriously than anywhere in the West apart from, perhaps, southern Spain. From Wednesday of Holy Week, the radio and TV networks are given over solely to religious programmes until the following Monday. It is an excellent time to be in Crete, both for the beautiful and moving religious ceremonies and for the days of feasting and celebration which follow. If you make for a smallish village, you may well find yourself an honorary member for the period of the festival.

The first great ceremony takes place on **Good Friday** evening as the Descent from the Cross is lamented in church. At dusk, the *Epitáfios*, Christ's funeral bier, lavishly decorated by the women of the parish, leaves the sanctuary and is paraded solemnly through the streets. Late **Saturday** evening sees the climax in a majestic mass to celebrate Christ's triumphant return. At the stroke of midnight all lights in each crowded church are extinguished and the congregation plunged into the darkness which envelopes Christ as He passes through the underworld. Then there's a faint glimmer of light behind the altar screen before the priest appears, holding aloft a lighted taper and chanting "*Avtó to fos . . .*" (This is the Light of the World). Stepping down to the level of the parishioners he touches his flame to the unlit candle of the nearest worshipper – intoning "*Devthe, levethe fos*" (Come take the light) to be greeted by the response "*Hristós Anésti*" (Christ is risen). And so it goes round, this affirmation of the miracle, until the entire church is ablaze with burning candles. Later, as the church bells ring, the celebrations begin with fireworks and the burning of effigies of Judas.

Even solidly rational atheists are likely to find this moving, as worshippers leave the church carefully attempting to preserve their flickering candles alight, to symbolically carry the "Light of the World" into their own homes. The successful achievement of this is regarded as a sign of good

traditional dance and jazz – at scattered sites through most of the summer.

Metamórfosi/Transfiguration (Aug 6) Another excuse for feasting. Specially celebrated in Voukoliés (Haniá), Máles (Ierápetra) and Zákros.

Áyios Matthaíos (Aug 12) The feast of St Matthew, with special celebrations in Kastélli Kissámou.

Sitía Sultana Festival (mid-Aug) Enjoyable, week-long celebration of the local harvest, with plenty of wine.

Assumption of the Virgin (Aug 15) Celebrated in towns and villages throughout Crete, the great feast of the *Apokímisis tís Panayías* is a day when people traditionally return to their home village, often creating problems for unsuspecting visitors who find there is no accommodation to be had anywhere. Services in churches begin at dawn, but latecomers usually arrive for the *psomí*, *arní*, and *krasí* (bread, lamb and wine), served in the churchyard at the end of the service around lunchtime. A main centre for this feast is the town of Neápoli, though the great event is the pilgrimage to the island of Tínos.

Áyios Eftíhios (Aug 24) Celebrations of this saint's day are especially fervent in the southwest corner of the island, where many infants are given his name; there are special festivities at Kambanós (Haniá).

Áyios Títos (Aug 25) Patron saint of the island – celebrated all across the island and with a big procession in Iráklion.

Cretan Wedding (late Aug) A "traditional" wedding laid on in Kritsá for the tourists – quite a spectacle nonetheless.

Áyios Ioánnis (Aug 29) Massive name-day pilgrimage to the church of Áyios Ioánnis Giónis on the Rodhópou peninsula in Haniá.

Áyios Stavrós/Holy Cross (Sept 14) Special festivities at Tzermiádho and Kalamáfka.

Mihaíl Arhángelos (Oct 11) The feast of the archangel is especially popular at Potamiés (Lasíthi).

Chestnut Festival (mid-Oct) Celebrated in Élos and other villages of the southwest where chestnuts are grown.

Óhi Day (Oct 28) Lively national holiday – parades, folk dancing – commemorating Prime Minister Metaxas' one-word reply ("No") to Mussolini's ultimatum in 1940.

Arkádhi (Nov 7–9) One of Crete's biggest gatherings celebrates the anniversary of the explosion at the monastery of Arkádhi.

Áyios Nikólaos (Dec 6). The feast of the patron saint of seafarers. Many chapels are dedicated to him around the island's coastline, including the one at the resort named after him, where processions and festivities mark the day.

fortune and the sign of the cross is made on the lintel with the flame, leaving a black smudge, visible for the rest of the year. The traditional greeting, as firecrackers explode all around you in the streets, is *Hristós Anésti* and the reply *Alithos Anésti* (He is risen indeed). In the week leading up to Easter Sunday, you should wish acquaintances "*Kaló Páskha*" (Happy Easter); on or after the day, you say "*Khrónia Pollá*" (Many Happy Returns). The Lenten fast is traditionally broken early Sunday morning with a meal of *mayirítsa* (a soup based on lamb tripe, rice and lemon), and later the rest of the lamb will be roasted.

The Greek equivalent of **Easter eggs** are hard-boiled eggs (painted red on Holy Thursday and signifying the rebirth and blood of Christ), which are baked into twisted, sweet bread-loaves (*tsouréki* or *lambrópsomo*) or distributed on Easter Sunday. People rap their eggs against their friends' eggs, and the owner of the last uncracked egg is considered lucky.

LOCAL ENTERTAINMENT

The events of the various festivals aside (and Iráklion's last for much of the summer), Crete can offer little in the way of cultural diversion. **Dancing** is of course a tradition here as throughout Greece, but for the real thing you have to go to a *paniyíri*, or else be exceptionally lucky in falling into the right company. Which is not to say that the stuff put on for the tourists isn't enjoyable – it is – simply that it may not be entirely authentic. With regard to **music** it's worth keeping an eye out in the villages for posters advertising *lyra* and *laoúto* (lute or Cretan *bouzoúki*) concerts. The *lyra* is Crete's "national" instrument: a three-stringed violin made from mulberry or maple which is propped on the knee and played with a small bow. These events can be highly entertaining and you will often find that you're the only foreigners present, thus ensuring a warm Cretan welcome.

WORK

It's not easy to find work in Crete, and in recent years it has been getting harder, with more people chasing fewer possibilities. Add to this the influx into Greece of over 300,000 Albanians, Poles, Yugoslavs, Russian Greeks and other assorted refugees from the upper Balkans, and it's easy to understand the resulting surplus of unskilled labour and severely depressed wages. That said, it is still possible with determination and a little initiative to turn up something, especially agricultural labouring jobs at harvest times, and there are a few other possibilities as well. Any form of short-term work, however, will always be on an unofficial basis, the EU freeing-up of employment restrictions notwithstanding, and for this reason it will generally be badly paid and subject, possibly, to police harassment.

TOURISM-RELATED WORK

Casual work in **bars** or **restaurants** around the main tourist resorts is one of the easiest options, though very much more so for women than for men. If you're waiting/serving, most of your wages will come from tips, but you may well be able to negotiate a deal that includes free food and lodging; evening-only hours can leave a lot of freedom, too. The main drawback may be the machismo and/or chauvinist attitudes of your employer. In particular in Haniá, and to a lesser extent elsewhere, many of the bars like to hire young foreign women as decoys, to lure men in and persuade them to drink. This can occasionally lead to confrontation with irate clients, and more frequently to harassment by the bar owner, who expects his employees also to be his harem. A common tactic is to threaten to report you to the police, whom the bar is usually paying off. With this in mind, ads in the local press for "girl bar staff" are certainly best ignored.

On the whole, you should be moderately pleased with landing a washing-up job. Trained chefs or cooks will do better. Start looking, if you can, in April or May: you'll get better rates if you're taken on for a whole season, when you will also have a better chance of finding somewhere affordable to live.

You might be able to get a job touting/selling for **tourist stores** or, if you've got the expertise helping to supervise one of the burgeoning **wind-surfing** "schools" or acting as a translator or even a guide for a local travel agent. If you're tempted to set yourself up as a tour guide you should be aware that you won't be allowed to escort groups around archeological sites or muse-ums, for which you will need an official registra-tion and fluent Greek. **Yacht marinas** can prove good hunting grounds for work, though less for the romantic business of crewing than for scrub-bing down and repainting. Again, the earlier in the year you arrive, the better your chances. One new possibility, if you can handle it, is touting for **time share**, at the new developments along the north coast, but it has to be said that this is a pretty seedy way to try and get by.

For a full season's work, relatively slim creden-tials might also get you a job as a courier/greeter/group courier for a **package holiday company**. Some firms are willing to take on peo-ple waiting to go to university or, more promising-ly, having just finished. The nominal pay will be appalling but you'll get a place to live and you can make extra money in tips from grateful clients. Scour the brochures as early in the year as possi-ble and turn up at the companies' offices or enquire at travel agents in the resorts for infor-mation on British companies operating locally. Some of the many companies renting villas to for-eign visitors may also be a source of odd-job work. The more luxurious **hotels** with a large anglophone clientele are another possibility for all kinds of odd jobs, ranging from pool and beach cleaning to portering and table waiting, but you

will need to be reasonably presentable and may be required to provide a reference.

Preparations for the tourist season also often require temporary labour, especially if you have a relevant skill: **building**, **painting** or **signwriting**, for example. Many jobs are advertised in the **local press** (see p.46) immediately prior to, or early in, the current summer season, and it's worth buying the local Greek paper to check these. Some ads actually appear in English, but even those that don't are easy enough to decipher with the aid of a pocket dictionary or perhaps, with the help of a friendly English-speaking barman.

AGRICULTURE

Another possible source of income is from casual, unskilled **agricultural** labour (but see opposite regarding the influx of cheap labour from the north); it is invariably low-paid and usually more so for women, who tend to be paid at a lower rate. Incidentally, the fields are quite a rough scene, and single women labourers are in a dis-tinct minority. Incidents of violence, non-payment or underpayment, abuse by employers and police harassment are commonplace. If you're still intent on doing it, hang around hostels in the appropri-ate geographical areas (such as Ierápetra) and ask other travellers about the current situation; tourist offices and even vegetable and fruit markets can be good sources of information about work possi-bilities. Something is being harvested somewhere in Crete through most of the year, and there are various well-known centres where the farmers come if they need labour. The best time for work is the massive **olive harvest** which takes place between October and December, when it's all hands to the pumps as everyone heads for the groves. The **citrus-harvesting** season runs from November to February (sometimes continuing until April), and is concentrated in the area known as the Portokalahória ("the orange villages"), an extensive orange-growing district near Alikianós in Haniá.

TEACHING ENGLISH

Long-term work is very unlikely, unless you've fixed it up in advance. The main opportunity is **teaching English** at one of the many private lan-guage schools or crammers (*frontistíria*) around the island where Greek parents send their kids for additional after-hours schooling. To get a job in all state schools and many private ones you will need to have a university degree (preferably in English). A **TEFL** (Teaching English as a Foreign Language) certificate is not essential, but will certainly improve your chances of a better job. The same applies to speaking Greek; a basic knowledge is helpful and greater fluency opens even more doors. The simplest way to get a teaching job is to apply before leaving – preferably in Britain. There are ads published weekly, particularly from June to September in the UK's *Guardian* (Tuesday) and *Times Educational Supplement* (Friday). Once accepted, you should get a one-way air fare from London paid (usually), accommodation found for you and a contract of employment. The other big advantage of arranging work abroad is that some of the red tape will be cleared up for you before you set off. A work permit isn't necessary for EU nationals, but a residence permit and teacher's licence are. You'll always be asked for a translated copy of your degree or TEFL certificate. You will also be required to present a medical certificate of good health.

For non-EU citizens, it is now very difficult to obtain a work permit to teach English legally in Greece. However, those of Greek descent will find it easier (and in fact qualify to operate their own schools). In practice, however, schools don't always follow the letter of the law, and if they like your qualifications, and you happen to be around at the right time, you're likely to find a place.

If you're already in Crete and want teaching work, one technique is to approach *frontistíria* directly – dozens are listed in the phone book for all larger towns, and many are jointly owned and will send you to an affiliate if they don't have a vacancy. Try in late August/early September, or again in January – some teachers don't last the isolation of a Greek winter.

Teaching is essentially a winter exercise – the schools close down from the end of May until mid-September, operating only a few special courses in June and July – so it's general practice to supplement your income by giving **private lessons**. For this the going rate is around 2500 and 4000dr an hour. Some teachers finance themselves exclusively on private lessons and, although you still officially need a teaching permit for this, few people experience any problems over it. *Teaching English Abroad* by Susan Griffiths (Vacation Work) provides much more useful detail on this.

AU PAIR WORK

The popularity and scale of private English-language teaching also means that English-speaking women may be able to find work as **au pairs**. As ever, positions tend to be exploitative and low-paid, but if you can use them to your own ends – living reasonably well and learning Greek – there can be mutual benefits. It's unwise to arrange anything until you arrive, so you can at least meet and talk terms with your prospective family. There are a number of specialist agencies in Athens which cater for women looking for long-term employment. Try Pioneer Tours, Níkis 11 (☎01/32 24 321) or Greek YWCA (XEN) Amerikís 11 (☎36 26 180).

DIRECTORY

ADDRESSES in Greek are usually written with just the street name followed by the number (Sífaka 11); numbers outside the city centres usually represent a whole block so you may get an individual building number added in brackets. *Odhós* means street; *leofóros*, avenue; *platía*, square. In a multistorey building, the ground floor is the *isóyeio*; there may be a mezzanine (*imiórofos*) before the first floor (*prótos órofos*).

ADMISSION CHARGES All the major ancient sites are now fenced off and, like museums, most charge admission. This ranges from a token 100dr to a hefty 1500dr at the five-star sites such as Knossós, but with an ISIC or FIYTO youth card you can get up to fifty-percent reductions or even free admission, so it's always worth asking. Current students of archeology, classics or history of art qualify for a free admission permit – write (well in advance) to the Ministry of Science and Culture (Museums Section), Aristídhou 14, Athens. Over-sixties can also get a small reduction. It's worth remembering that entrance to all state-run sites and museums is free to EU nationals on Sundays and public holidays.

BARGAINING is not a regular feature of life, though you'll find it possible with "rooms" and some off-season hotels. A nice line is always to offer to use your sleeping bag, saving the washing of the sheets. Similarly, you may be able to negotiate discounted rates for vehicle and motorbike and scooter rental, especially for longer periods.

BRING . . . film which is expensive in Greece, an alarm clock for early buses and ferries, as well as a torch for camping out, coping with power cuts, visiting caves and churches or finding your way to a midnight swim. A pair of binoculars will enhance enjoyment of the plentiful birdlife.

CHILDREN Travelling with children presents few problems in Crete, since kids, on the whole, are worshipped and indulged, perhaps to excess. For young children, heat and sun are the worst hazards. Baby foods and nappies are widely available and under-eights travel free on the buses (but over-eights pay full fare). A "rooms" establishment is more likely to offer some kind of babysitting service than the more impersonal hotels.

CINEMA You're unlikely to see any very inspiring films in a Cretan cinema, but most English-language titles are subtitled rather than dubbed, and the open-air screens which can be found in all the major towns in summer are wonderful.

CONTRACEPTIVES Condoms (*kapótes*) are available from city kiosks or *farmakía*; the pill, too, can be obtained from a *farmakío* – you shouldn't need a prescription.

ELECTRICITY is 220 volt AC (British appliances should work, US ones need a transformer); plugs are usually the standard European pattern of two round pins. Power cuts are a common feature in Crete, particularly in summer, when generating capacity is stretched to breaking point. Bank computers and cash machines going down, nonfunctioning fuel pumps at garages and warm beer and wine in restaurants are some of the hassles which affect visitors; many places (especially cinemas) have their own back-up generators.

GAY LIFE There are no overtly gay resorts on Crete but, as throughout Greece, attitudes are relaxed. Homosexuality is legal over the age of 17 and (generally, male) bisexuality quite widely accepted.

LAUNDRIES These are rare, with service laundries (about 2000dr for a big wash and dry) more common in the big towns; they appear in the relevant "Listings" and "Practicalities" sections of the guide. Off the beaten track, hotels and rooms places almost always have somewhere to wash your own clothes. Ask to use the laundry trough (*skáfi*) rather than risk destroying your room's plumbing.

NAME DAYS In common with other parts of the Mediterranean, Greeks get two birthdays a year – one is the anniversary of their actual birth whilst the other (and more important one) celebrates the feast day of the saint he or she is named after; it is unusual for any Greek not to be named after a saint. Popular names on Crete such as Ioánnis and Yeóryios mean that the celebrations on these saints' days make for an island-wide holiday.

PERÍPTERO A *períptero* is a street-corner kiosk. They sell everything – pens, combs, razors, stationery, postcards, soap, sweets, nuts, condoms, *kombolói* ("worry" beads) – double as phone booths, and stay open long after everything else has closed.

SKIING Believe it or not, it is possible to ski in Crete in winter, and there's even a tiny ski lift on the Nídha Plain above Anóyia, while the Kalleryi Lodge in the White Mountains may also open for ski parties. Don't come specially.

SPECTATOR SPORTS Soccer and basketball are, along with the rest of Greece, Crete's major sports. OFI, from Iráklion, is Crete's leading first-division football team and, in season, matches – normally played on Sundays – against many of the mainland's other major sides are easy enough to catch at the ground near to the Martinengo Bastion. Warm-up games for the new season in late August often feature visits by foreign teams.

TIME Greek summertime begins on the last Sunday in March, when the clocks go ahead one hour, and ends on the last Sunday in September when they fall back. Be alert to this, as scores of visitors miss planes and ferries every year; the change is not well publicized. Greek time is two hours ahead of the UK, and three hours when the respective changes to summertime fail to coincide. For North America, the standard time difference is seven hours for Eastern Standard Time, ten hours for Pacific Standard Time, with again an extra hour for those weeks in April and October. A recorded time message (in Greek) is available by dialling ☎141.

TOILETS Public ones, generally foul, are usually in parks or squares, often subterranean. Otherwise try a bus station. Throughout Greece (and to the horror of most first-time visitors) you're urged to toss paper in adjacent wastebaskets, not in the bowl: learn this habit, or you'll block the pipes. It's worth carrying toilet paper with you; though it's provided by the attendants at public facilities, there may be none in tavernas or cafés.

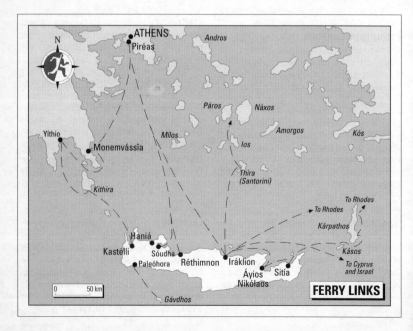

FERRY LINKS

PART TWO

THE

GUIDE

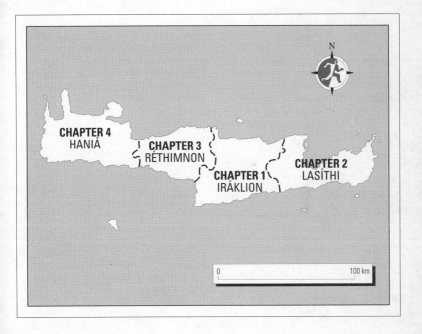

CHAPTER 4
HANIÁ

CHAPTER 3
RÉTHIMNON

CHAPTER 1
IRÁKLION

CHAPTER 2
LASÍTHI

N

0   100 km

CHAPTER ONE

IRÁKLION

The **province of Iráklion** sees more tourists than any other in Crete. They come for two simple reasons: the string of big **resorts** which lies to the east of the city, only an hour or so from the airport, and the great **Minoan sites**, almost all of which are concentrated in the centre of the island. **Knossós**, **Mália** and **Festós** are in easy reach of almost anywhere in the province and there are excellent beaches all along the north coast. The price you pay is crowds: **Iráklion** is a big, hustling city, the development to the east is continuous and huge, and in summer the great sites are constantly awash with people.

There seems little here of the old Crete, ramshackle and rural, and yet, by taking the less obvious turn, it is still possible to escape. **West** and **south** of Iráklion the beaches are smaller and the coastline is less amenable to hotel builders. The south coast in particular is far less peopled: beaches are accessible only in a handful of places (of which only **Mátala** is at all exploited), whilst the interior remains traditional farming country, the Crete of simple hamlets and ancient churches.

IRÁKLION AND THE NORTH COAST

Iráklion itself can at first seem a nightmare, particularly if you arrive expecting a quaint little island town. You find yourself instead in the fifth largest city in Greece; it's ugly and modern, a maelstrom of traffic, building work, concrete and dust. Penetrate behind this façade and – as with Athens – you can discover a vibrant working metropolis with myriad attractive features which do much to temper initial impressions. Stay long enough and you can even begin to like the place – but it would take a determined visitor to stay that course. You're perhaps better off taking the city for what it has – **Knossós** and the **Archeological Museum** most famously, but also snatched visions of another city, of magnificent fortifications, a wonderful market, the occasional ancient alley, curious smaller museums – before moving on to more immediately inviting places.

Knossós apart, the immediate **surrounds of Iráklion** offer little compensation. If you are based in the city with time on your hands then the Minoan remains at **Arhánes** or the views from **Mount Yioúhtas** are worth taking in, and transport to local beaches is excellent. But this is hardly getting the most the island offers.

East of Iráklion, the startling pace of tourist development is all too plain to see. The merest hint of a beach is an excuse to build at least one hotel, and these are outnumbered by the concrete shells of rivals-to-be. It can be hard to find a room in the peak season in this monument to the package tour, and expensive if you do. Some of the resorts, most notably **Mália** and **Hersónisos**, do at least have good beaches and lively nightlife. They wouldn't be at all bad if you were on a package deal – providing you like crowds, noise and commercialism. But turn

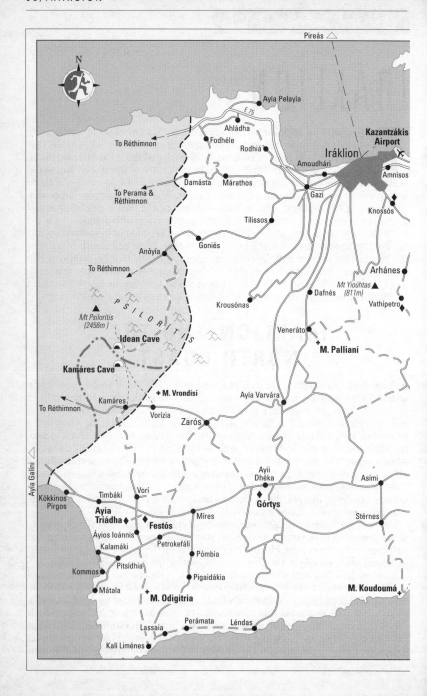

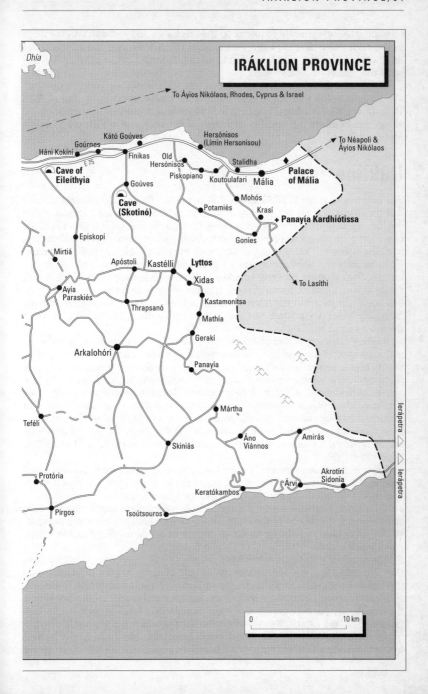

IRÁKLION PROVINCE

Dhía

To Áyios Nikólaos, Rhodes, Cyprus & Israel

Kató Goúves

Hersónisos
(Límin Hersonísou)

Goúrnes

Háni Kokíni

To Néapoli &
Áyios Nikólaos

Fínikas

Old
Hersónisos

Stalídha

E 75

**Cave of
Eileíthyia**

Piskopiano

Koutoulafari

Goúves

Mália

**Palace
of Mália**

**Cave
(Skotinó)**

Mohós

Potamiés

Krasí

+ Panayía Kardhiótissa

Epískopí

Goníes

Mirtiá

Apóstoli

Kastélli

Lyttos

Xidas

Ayía
Paraskiés

To Lasíthi

Thrapsanó

Kastamonítsa

Mathía

Gerakí

Arkalohóri

Panayía

Mártha

Teféli

Áno
Viánnos

Amirás

Skiniás

Akrotíri
Sidonía

Protória

Árvi

Keratókambos

Pírgos

Tsoútsouros

0   10 km

Ierápetra

Ierápetra

up hoping to find somewhere to stay on the off-chance and you won't regard them as the most welcoming of places. As a general rule, the further you go, the better things get: where the road veers briefly inland, the real Crete – olive groves and stark mountains – reveals itself.

To the **west** there's much less to detain you, with mountains which drop virtually straight to the sea. There is just one small, classy resort in the bay at **Ayía Pelayía**, a few isolated hotels and, in the hills behind, a number of interesting old villages: at **Fódhele** the possible birthplace of El Greco, and at **Tílissos** a famous Minoan villa.

Iráklion

The best way to arrive in **IRÁKLION** is from the sea, the traditional approach and still the one which shows the city in its best light, with Mount Yioúhtas rising behind, the heights of the Psilorítis range to the west and, as you get closer, the city walls encircling and dominating the oldest part of town. As you sail in, you run the gauntlet of the great fortress guarding the harbour entrance. Unfortunately the old harbour can't handle ships of ferry size, and the ferries actually dock at great concrete wharves alongside – a juxtaposition which seems neatly to sum up much about modern Iráklion. What little remains of the old city has been heavily restored, often from the bottom up, but the slick renovations invariably look fake, pristine and polished alongside the grime which coats even the most recent buildings.

Iráklion's name is of Roman origin, taken from a port which stood hereabouts, and readopted at the beginning of this century. The present city was founded by the Saracens who held Crete from 827 to 961. In those days it was known, after the great ditch which surrounded it, as El Khandak, later corrupted by the Venetians to Candia, or Candy, a name applied also to the island as a whole. This Venetian capital was in its day one of the strongest and most spectacular cities in Europe: a trading centre, a staging-point for the Crusades and, as time wore on, itself the front line of Christendom. When the Turks finally conquered the city it was only after 21 years of war, culminating in a bitter siege from May 1667 to September 1669.

Under its new rulers the city's importance declined in relation to Haniá's, but it remained a major port and the second city in Crete. It was here, too, that the incident occurred which finally put an end to Turkish occupation of the island. In 1898 fourteen British soldiers and the British consul were murdered, the final straw – which the deaths of thousands of Cretans had not been – which persuaded the great powers to insist on the departure of the remaining Turkish troops and administrators.

Finally united with Greece, Iráklion's prosperity was assured by its central position. Almost all that you see, though, dates only from the last few decades, partly through the reconstruction after the heavy bombing it suffered during World War II but also through a boom in agriculture, industry and tourism – the city is now the wealthiest in Greece per head of population. In 1971 Iráklion regained the official title of island capital. Its growth continues, as you'll see if you venture to the fringes of town where the concrete spreads inexorably, but it can hardly be said to add to the attraction. In recent years Iráklion's administrators have been giving belated attention to dealing with some of the city's image problems and large tracts of the walled city are currently undergoing costly landscaping and refurbishment schemes designed to present a less daunting prospect to the visitor. Whilst Iráklion will never be one of the jewels of the Mediterranean, the ebullient friendliness of the people and an infectious cosmopolitan atmosphere may tempt you into giving it more than the customary one-night transit.

Orientation, arrival and information

Virtually everything you're likely to want to see in Iráklion lies within the walled city, and even here the majority of the interest falls into a relatively small sector, the northeastern corner. The most vital thoroughfare, **Odhós 25-Avgoústou**, links the harbour with the commercial city centre. At the bottom it is lined with shipping and travel agencies, car and motorbike rental outfits, but as you climb these give way to banks, restaurants and city-centre shops. **Platía Venizélou** (Fountain Square), off to the right, is thronged with cafés and restaurants favoured by Iráklion's youth; behind Venizélou is **El Greco Park**, with the OTE office and more bars which, with nearby Hándhakos, comprises one of the town's main nightlife zones. On the opposite side of 25-Avgoústou from the park are some of the more interesting of Iráklion's older buildings.

Further up 25-Avgoústou, **Kalokerinoú** leads down to Haniá Gate and westwards out of the city; straight ahead, Odhós 1821 – a fashionable shopping street – goes nowhere very much, but adjacent 1866 is given over to the animated **market**. To the left another major shopping street, Dhikeosínis, heads for the newly revamped **Platía Eleftherías** (Liberty Square), paralleled by the touristy pedestrian alley Dedhálou, the direct link between the two squares. Eleftherías is very much the traditional centre of the city, both for traffic, which swirls around it constantly, and for life in general; it is ringed by more expensive tourist cafés and restaurants, and in the evening is alive with strolling locals.

Points of arrival

Iráklion **airport**, four kilometres east of the city, lies right on the coast – you come in to land low over some of the better local beaches. The #1 bus leaves for Platía Eleftherías every few minutes from the car park in front of the terminal; buy your ticket (150dr) at the booth before boarding. There are also plenty of **taxis** outside (which you'll need to use if you miss the last bus at 10.30pm) and prices to major destinations are posted; it's about 1200dr to the centre of town. Get an agreement on the fare before taking the cab and beware if the driver extols the virtues of a particular place to stay – he may be motivated by the prospect of a kick-back from the proprietors, rather than your best interests.

From the wharves where the **ferries** dock, the city rises directly ahead in steep tiers. If you're heading for the centre, for the archeological museum or the tourist office, cut straight up the stepped alleys behind the bus station onto Doúkos Bófor and to Platía Eleftherías (this will take about fifteen minutes). For accommodation, though, and to get a better idea of the layout of Iráklion's main attractions, it's simplest to follow the main roads: head west along the coast, past the

The phone code for Iráklion is ☎081.

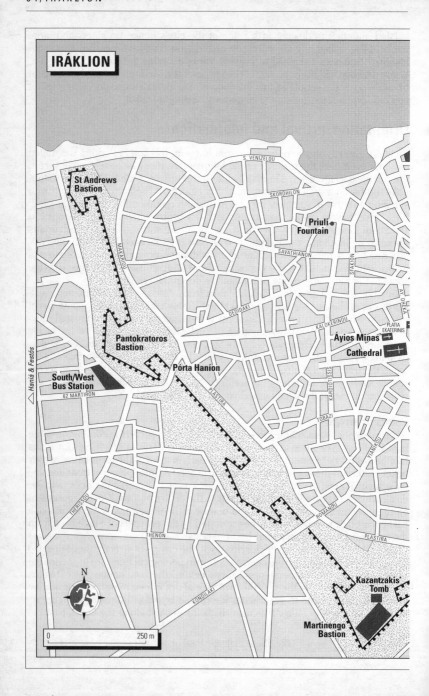

IRÁKLION

St Andrews Bastion

Priuli Fountain

S. VENIZELOU

SKORDHILON

SAVATHIANON

ISAKON

AV. DHEKA

MAKARIOU

DEDIDAKI

KALOKERINOU

PLATIA EKATERINIS

Áyios Minas

Cathedral

Pantokratoros Bastion

Pórta Hanion

△ Haniá & Festós

South/West Bus Station

62 MARTIRON

PLASTIRA

KARDIOTISSIS

ITOBAZI

TIANVKOU

ROMANOU

THERISSOU

PLASTIRA

THENON

Kazantzakis' Tomb

N

KONDILAKI

Martinengo Bastion

0   250 m

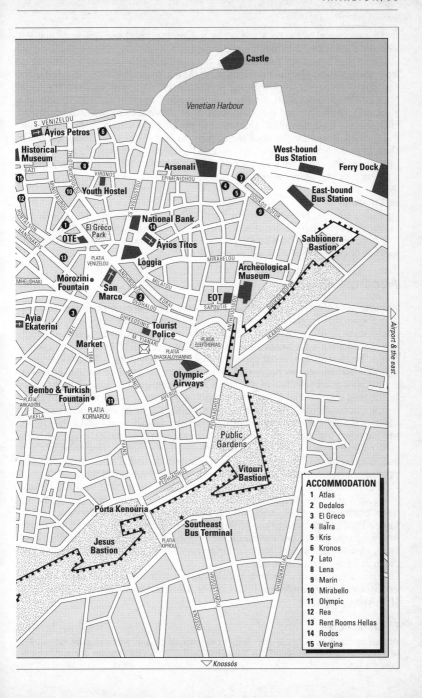

major east-bound bus station and on by the Venetian harbour before cutting left towards the centre on Odhós 25-Avgoústou.

There are three main **bus stations**. Services along the coastal highway to or from the **east** and **southeast** (Hersónisos, Mália, Áyios Nikólaos, Sitía, Ierápetra and points en route) use the terminal just off the main road between the ferry dock and the Venetian harbour; the #2 local bus to Knossós runs from the city bus stop, adjacent to the east bus station. Main road services **west** (Réthimnon and Haniá) leave from a terminal right next to the east bus station on the other side of the road. Buses for the **southwest** (Festós, Mátala or Ayía Galíni) and along the inland roads west (Tílissos, Anóyia and Fódhele) operate out of a terminal just outside Haniá Gate, a very long walk from the centre up Kalokerinoú (or jump on any bus heading up this street).

Information

Iráklion's **tourist office** (Mon–Fri 8am–2.30pm; ☎228-225, fax 226-020) is just below Platía Eleftherías, opposite the Archeological Museum at Zanthoudhídhou 1. The **tourist police** (☎283-190) – more helpful than most – are on Dhikeosínos, halfway between Platía Eleftherías and the market.

Accommodation

Iráklion has a distinct lack of decent, reasonably priced **accommodation**, especially in the height of summer. If possible, arrange to arrive early in the day; rolling up after 8pm or so without a reservation, you'd be lucky to find anything at all – though the hostels are always worth a try. In general, if you do find a room – any room – take it. You can always set out early next day to find something better. Noise can be a problem wherever you stay; we've indicated some of the more tranquil locations.

There's a good selection of mid-range **hotels** conveniently located in the areas to the east and west of Odhós 25-Avgoústou and we've listed the best of these below. For hotels of C class and above, it's usually simplest to approach the tourist office first – they should know where there are available rooms and if they're not too harassed will make the phone calls for you. At quieter times, if you have the time and patience (or just happen to be passing), it's worth trying some of the B and C class hotels "on spec". During slack periods they'll often make you surprising offers – sometimes reducing prices by fifty percent and more.

The greatest concentration of **cheaper rooms** is to be found near Platía Venizélou, around Hándhakos and in the vicinities of the bus stations. There are a few central, but rather noisy and marginally more expensive places around El Greco Park and by the bottom of the market; and another small enclave of generally less pleasant places towards the bottom of Kalokerinoú, near the Haniá Gate. Few of the cheaper places offer private bathrooms, but they should all be clean and have (some) hot water.

There are no **campsites** near to Iráklion; the nearest sites are both to the east of the city – *Creta Camping* at Káto Goúves, 16km away, and *Caravan Camping* at Hersónisos, 28km away.

El Greco Park

Atlas, Kandanoléon 11 (☎288-989). Rather rundown old pension with a pleasant roof garden in a convenient alley between Platía Venizélou and El Greco Park. Freshly squeezed orange juice for breakfast. ②.

ACCOMMODATION PRICE CODES

All accommodation establishments in this book have been **price-coded** according to the scale outlined below. The rates quoted represent the cheapest available **double room** in high season. For rented apartments and villas, the price code refers to the price of the whole apartment, not just to a double room within the apartment. Out of season, room rates can drop by up to fifty percent, especially if you negotiate rates for a stay of three or more nights. Single rooms, where available, cost around seventy percent of the price of a double.

Rented private rooms usually fall into the ② or ③ categories, depending on their location and facilities, and the season; a few in the ④ category are more like plush self-catering apartments. They are not generally available from late October through the beginning of April, when only hotels tend to remain open.

① up to 4000dr	⑤ 12,000–16,000dr
② 4000–6000dr	⑥ 16,000–20,000dr
③ 6000–8000dr	⑦ 20,000dr upwards
④ 8000–12,000dr	

For more accommodation details, see p.35.

Rent Rooms Hellas, Hándhakos 24 (☎280-858, fax 284-442). Occupies the small but spruced-up original youth hostel building, and has the usual facilities including roof garden and snack bar; some private rooms. ①.

Hotel Kronos, Agarathou 2, west of 25-Avgoústou (☎282-240, fax 285-853). Pleasant, modern hotel with sea-view balconies and baths in all rooms. ③.

Hotel Lena, Lahana 10 (☎223-280). Around the corner from the youth hostel on Vironos, this quiet small hotel has clean rooms with and without bath; the second floor has more air. ③.

Hotel Mirabello, Theotokopoúlou 20 (☎285-052, fax 225-852). Good-value, family-run place just north of El Greco Park in a quiet street. Rooms with and without bath. ③.

Rea, Kalimeráki 1 (☎223-638, fax 242-189). A friendly, comfortable and clean pension in a quiet street. Some rooms with washbasin, others with own shower. ③.

Pension Rodos, Platía Áyios Títos, next to the *Pagopoleion* bar (☎228-519). Homely no-frills doubles and triples on a picturesque square with a great breakfast bar next door. ②.

Vergina, Hortátson 32 (☎242-739). Basic but pleasant rooms, with washbasins, set around a courtyard which boasts an enormous banana tree. ②.

Youth Hostel, Vironos 5 (☎286-281). This used to be Iráklion's official youth hostel, but was stripped of its IYH status. It is in fact a good place to stay; it is family run and very friendly and helpful, with plenty of space and beds (albeit illegal) on the roof if you fancy sleeping out under the stars. Private rooms as well as dormitories, hot showers, breakfast and other meals available. ①.

Port and Venetian Harbour

Hotel Ilaïra, Ariadnis 1 (☎227-103, fax 227-666). Tastefully furnished modern hotel with character; all rooms with balcony sea views, the higher the better. ④.

Kris, Doúkos Bófor 2 (☎223-944). Apartment-style rooms with kitchenette, fridge and balconies overlooking the harbour. Very friendly. ④.

Hotel Lato, Epimenidou 15 (☎228-103, fax 240-350). Stylish and luxurious hotel where air-conditioned rooms come with mini bar, TV and fine balcony views over the old Venetian port. Easily the best of the upmarket places. ⑥.

Hotel Marin, Doúkos Bófor 12 (☎224-736, fax 224-730). Pleasant balcony rooms here all have showers and most have fine harbour views. Very convenient for bus stations and the Archeological Museum. ③.

Platía Eleftherías and around

Hotel Daedalos, Dedhálou 15 (☎244-812, fax 224-391). Very centrally placed on the pedestrianized alley between Venizélou and Eleftherías. Balcony rooms with bath. ④.

Hotel El Greco, Odhós 1821 4 (☎ & fax 281-071). One of Iráklion's best-known hotels, but with little to distinguish it from any of the others in its price range. ⑤.

Hotel Olympic, Platía Kornárou (☎288-861, fax 222-512). Refurbished 1960s hotel overlooking a busy square and the famous Bembo and Turkish fountains. ⑤.

The City

By far the most striking aspect of Iráklion is its massive Venetian walls; though well preserved and restored in parts, access is difficult. The obvious starting point for your explorations is the fortress, which stands guard over the harbour.

The fortress and the walls

Built between 1523 and 1540, the **Fort** (Mon–Sat 8am–6pm, Sun 10am–3pm; 500dr, students 200dr, explanatory video 1000dr) was known to the Venetians as the Rocca al Mare, to the Turks as Koule. Painstakingly refurbished, it now often houses temporary exhibitions which may disrupt the standard opening hours. Taken simply as a structure, it is undeniably impressive: massively sturdy walls command superb views over harbour and town and protect a series of chambers (many still piled with cannonballs) in which the defenders must have enjoyed an overwhelming sense of security. It is easy to see here how Venetian Iráklion managed to resist the Turks for so long.

On the other hand there is something unsatisfying about the way the fort has been so thoroughly scrubbed, polished and cosseted, losing any hint of atmosphere in the process. While you may know that the fort is the genuine sixteenth-century article from the lions of St Mark adorning the exterior and the simple solidity of the stone, it feels as if it were built yesterday for some swashbuckling Hollywood production. At night, when the fortress is floodlit, the causeway leading to it is the haunt of courting couples, while the niches in the walls provide temporary accommodation for people awaiting ferries or for fishermen: it's a fine place to watch the ships coming and going.

The only other survivors of the Venetian harbour installations, the vaulted **Arsenali**, are now lost in a sea of concrete and traffic. Here, ships were built or dragged ashore to be overhauled and repaired – close up, you may still find bits of broken boat lying about.

The **walls** themselves are rather harder to penetrate. Perhaps the easiest approach is to follow Odhós Pedhiádhos south from the back of Platía Eleftherías and find your way up one of the dusty tracks which lead to the top of the rampart. With luck and a little scrambling you can walk all the way around from here, clockwise, to Áyios Andréas Bastion overlooking the sea in the west. There are some curious views as you walk around, often looking down onto the rooftops, but the fabric of the walls themselves is rarely visible – it's simply like walking on a dusty path raised above the level of its surrounds. A word of warning though: usually completely safe in daytime, the walls tend to attract less desirable types from dusk onwards.

On the Martinengo Bastion, facing south, is the **tomb of Níkos Kazantzákis** (1883–1957, see p.90), Crete's greatest writer. Although his works were banned for their unorthodox views, Kazantzákis' burial rites were performed at Áyios

Mínos Cathedral, although no priests officially escorted his body up here. His simple grave is adorned only with an inscription from his own writings: "I hope for nothing, I fear nothing, I am free". At the weekend Iraklians gather to pay their respects – and to enjoy a grandstand view of the matches played by the city's crack first-division football team, OFI Crete, in the stadium below.

For more impressive views of the defences, from the outside, stroll out through one of the elaborate **gates** – the Pórta Haníon at the bottom of Kalokerinoú or the Pórta Kenoúria at the top of Evans. Both of these date from the second half of the sixteenth century when the majority of the surviving defences were completed. Originally thrown up in the fifteenth century, the walls were constantly improved thereafter as Crete became increasingly isolated in the path of Turkish westward expansion: their final shape owes much to Michele Sanmicheli who arrived here in 1538 having previously designed the fortifications of Padua and Verona. In its day this was the strongest bastion in the Mediterranean, as evidenced at the Kenoúria Gate, where the walls are over 40m thick.

If you want to follow the walls in the other direction, from the sea up, simply head west along the coastal road from the harbour – a considerable walk – until you reach them. Not far along the way you pass the recently extended **Historical Museum** (Mon–Sat 9am–2pm; 500dr). The collection does help fill the gap which, for most people, yawns between Knossós and the present day, and since it's always virtually deserted, wandering around is a pleasure. The basement, if you're working chronologically, is where you start; it contains sculptures and architectural fragments from the Byzantine, Venetian and Turkish periods. There are some beautiful pieces, most especially a fifteenth- or sixteenth-century tiered fountain from a Venetian palace. The ground floor has religious art, wall paintings and documents from the same periods, a reconstruction of a typically domed Cretan church and a work by the Cretan artist El Greco – a view of Mount Sinai painted around 1570. Upper floors bring things to the present with reconstructions of the studies of Níkos Kazantzákis and of the Cretan statesman (and Greek prime minister) Emanuel Tsouderós; photos and documents relating to the occupation of Crete by the Germans plus the odd helmet and parachute harness; and a substantial selection of folk art – particularly textiles. The new extension has also given the museum the space to re-create the interior of a Cretan farmhouse. On your way out, take a look at the charming Venetian **fountain of Idomeneus** (mentioned by Kazantzákis in his novel *Freedom or Death*) opposite the entrance and partly obscured by bushes.

From the harbour to the market

Heading inland from the harbour, Odhós 25-Avgoústou offers a less strenuous walk past more obvious attractions. On the left as you approach Platía Venizélou, the church of **Áyios Títos** commands a lovely little plaza. Originally Byzantine, but wholly rebuilt by the Venetians in the sixteenth century, it was adapted by the Turks as a mosque and rebuilt by them after a major earthquake in 1856. The Orthodox Church renovated the building after the Turkish population left Iráklion, and it was reconsecrated in 1925. A reliquary inside contains the skull of St Titus, which came here originally from his tomb in Górtys (the rest of the body was never found) and was later taken to Venice, where it stayed from the time of the Turkish invasion until 1966: in the Middle Ages the head was regularly and ceremonially exhibited to the people of Iráklion.

On the top side of this square, abutting 25-Avgoústou, stands the Venetian **City Hall** with its famous *loggia*, reconstructed after the work of earthquakes was compounded by the rigours of World War II. Just past here on the left is **San Marco**, a church very much in the Venetian style which, also restored, is used for exhibitions and occasional lectures or meetings. Under the Venetians it was the cathedral and under the Turks a mosque: nowadays the church steps make a handy overflow for the cafés in **Platía Venizélou**. In the square, the **Morosini Fountain** (hence "Fountain Square") dates from the final years of Venetian rule. On first sight it's a rather disappointing little monument, but a recent cleaning and restoration job now allows the fine marine decoration on the basins to be appreciated close up; the lions on guard, which replaced an original statue of Neptune and are two to three hundred years older than the rest of the structure, are wonderful.

Straight across the main crossroads, Odhós 1866 is packed throughout the day with the stalls and customers of Iráklion's **market**. This is one of the few living reminders of an older city, with an atmosphere reminiscent of an eastern bazaar. There are luscious fruit and vegetables, as well as bloody butchers' stalls and others selling a bewildering variety of herbs and spices, cheese and yoghurt, leather goods, souvenirs, an amazing array of cheap kitchen utensils, pocket knives and just about anything else you might conceivably need. At the far end you emerge in a quiet square, **Platía Kornárou**, the focal point of which is a beautiful **Turkish pumphouse**. Heavily restored, this hexagonal building houses a café which serves as a lively meeting place for the male octogenarians of this quarter who converse at the tables under the trees. A small Venetian drinking fountain – the **Bembo Fountain** – incorporating a headless Roman torso imported from Ierápetra – stands beside the café.

Churches and icons

Turning right before the market leads you down Kalokerinoú towards the Haniá gate and the main road west. Veer left after about 100m, up Áyii Dhéka or one of the streets immediately after, and you'll reach a large open space beside the **Cathedral of Áyios Mínas**. The cathedral, a rather undistinguished nineteenth-century building, is notable mainly for its size. Just in front, however, stands the tiny original medieval church of Áyios Mínas: the interior is worth a look and contains some interesting icons (if it's closed, ask at the cathedral).

Far more worthwhile, and just at the bottom of the same square, is the church of **Ayía Ekateríni** (Mon–Sat 10am–1pm, plus Tues, Thurs & Fri 4–6pm; 500dr) which houses a **Museum of Religious Art**. This is the finest collection of Cretan icons anywhere, and some Cretan icons are very fine indeed. Built in the fifteenth century, the church was part of a monastic school which in the following centuries – up to the end of Venetian rule – was one of the centres of the "Cretan Renaissance", a last flourish of Eastern Christian art following the fall of Byzantium. Among the school's students were Vitzéntzos Kornáros, author of the Cretan classic *Erotókritos*, and many leading Orthodox theologians; most importantly, however, it served as an art school where Byzantine tradition came face to face with the influences of the Venetian Renaissance. Among the greatest of the pupils was Miháilis Dhamaskinós; six of his works form the centre of the collection. It was the much-imitated Dhamaskinós who introduced perspective and depth to Byzantine art, while never straying far from the strict traditions of icon painting; in his later works he reverts to a much purer, archaic style. The most famous Cretan painter of them all, El Greco, took the opposite course – wholeheartedly embracing Italian styles to which he brought the influence of his Byzantine training. Although there is little evidence, it's generally accepted that these two – Dhamaskinós and El Greco – were near contemporaries at the school. Two further icons now attributed to Dhamaskinós are in the fourteenth-century church of Áyios Mathéos, now sitting below street level on Odhós Taxiárhou Markopoúlou as it leads southwest from the cathedral.

Alongside Ayía Ekateríni is the church of Áyii Dhéka, a seventeenth-century building which acted as a chapel to the larger church. Turning left from the cathedral before the market brings you quickly up to the recently face-lifted **Platía Eleftherías**, a mass of pavement cafés and whirling traffic, but still the city's most popular venue for walking, talking and sitting out. There's a small bust of Níkos Kazantzákis and a larger-than-life statue of Eleftheríos Venizélos (leading figure in the struggle for union with Greece), staring out over the harbour from the ramparts and looking remarkably like Lenin. Beyond the statue you reach the entrance to the **Public Gardens**, as often as not half taken over by a funfair, but otherwise relatively peaceful. Above all, however, Platía Eleftherías offers access to the Archeological Museum and the new Battle of Crete and Resistance Museum on the corner of Doúkos Bófor and Hatzidaki.

The Archeological Museum

Iráklion's **Archeological Museum** (April–Sept Mon 12.30–6pm, Tues–Sun 8am–6pm; Oct–March daily 8am–5pm; 1500dr, free on Sun; students free) on Zanthoudhídhou, just off Platía Eleftherías, is one of the major reasons to visit the city. The museum houses far and away the most important collection of Minoan art and artefacts anywhere in the world, and there's no doubt that the enjoyment and meaning of a visit to Knossós or the other sites will be greatly heightened if you've been here first. Despite being old-fashioned, poorly displayed and sparsely labelled, it's always crowded (at least in summer) and at times quite overwhelmed by the stampede of coach parties thundering through. Try to see it early, late or during everyone else's lunch break. The collection is large and will prove a lot more rewarding in small doses: take in the highlights first time around and go back later for whatever you feel you've missed – tickets are valid for re-entry the same day.

Several good museum guides are on sale (the best is probably the glossy one by J. A. Sakellarakis), but the following should give you some idea of what to expect. Basically, the galleries on the ground floor, which you have little choice but to walk through in order, follow a chronological pattern: they run from the Neolithic era right through to Roman times, with the more important Minoan periods also divided according to where the items on display were discovered. Upstairs, larger rooms show the fabulous Minoan frescoes. Due to ongoing renovation and reorganization (partly to move the most popular items to places where crowds cause less of an obstruction), some items may not be precisely where stated below, but they should still be in the same room.

Prehistory to the early Minoans

Room I covers several thousand years, from the earliest signs of human settlement around 6000 BC to the beginnings of Minoan civilization in the Pre-Palatial period. There's a bit of everything here, of interest mainly because it is so very old: statuettes, including a Neolithic "fertility goddess"; pottery, among which the blotchy **Vasilikí ware** (Case 6) with elegant elongated spouts points to the great things to come; and stone jars from the island of Móhlos (Case 7), displaying an early mastery of the lapidary's craft. Among the miniature sculpture don't miss a **clay bull**, in Case 12, with tiny acrobats clinging to its horns: an early sign of the popularity of bull sports. In the central cases, and typical of what is to be seen later, is a display of some sophisticated early **jewellery** alongside some intricately engraved **seal stones** – among the latter, one from ancient Mesopotamia (no.1098), suggesting early contact between the island and its Near Eastern neighbours.

Room II contains objects from the earliest period of occupation of Knossós and Mália (2000–1700 BC), along with items found in various peak sanctuaries of the same era. Archeologically most significant is the **Kamáres ware** pottery, with often-elaborate white and red decoration on a dark ground. For casual visitors, however, the miniature figures are of far more immediate interest, in particular the famous "**Town Mosaic**" from Knossós in Case 25. This consists of a series of glazed plaques depicting multistorey Minoan houses, beautiful pieces which probably fitted together to form a decorative scene. There are also some lovely figurines and tiny animals, mostly offerings found in the peak sanctuaries: look out for the three-columned shrine with a dove perched on the top of each column, thought to represent the epiphany, or a manifestation, of the goddess worshipped there. Finally, note the **clay statuettes** (Cases 21 and 24) of sanctuary worshippers – their arms crossed or placed on the chest in reverential attitudes – as well as the *taxímata* (ex votos) representing parts of the human body the deity was requested to heal, a custom still followed in churches all over Greece today.

Room III is devoted to the same period at Festós. Here the **Kamáres ware** is even more elaborate, and it was at Festós that this art reached its peak – exemplified by a magnificent vase with sculpted white flowers in high relief. In Case 30 you'll find the original pieces, retrieved from the cave at Kamáres, that gave the style its name. Nearby in Case 33a there is a unique portrayal of lively dolphins plunging among cockles and seaweed. The celebrated **Festós Disc** in Case 41, is a circular slab of clay upon which hieroglyphic characters have been inscribed in a spiral pattern. The disc is frequently described as the earliest-known example of printing, since the impressions of hieroglyphs were made with stamps before it was fired; the various signs are divided up into groups, believed to be words. Interestingly, some of these "words" are repeated, leading scholars to suggest that what is represented on the disc may be some form of prayer or hymn. Despite a plethora of theories – and claims in several books on sale around the island to "reveal the secret" of the disc – this earliest Minoan script remains undeciphered.

New Palace period

Room IV represents the New Palace period (1700–1450 BC) in which the great sites reached their peak of creativity, rebuilt after the first destruction. Kamáres pottery is now replaced by new styles with patterns painted in dark colours on a light background, and themes drawn from nature (in particular marine life) rather than abstract patterns. The **Jug of Reeds** in Case 49 is a brilliant example of this stylistic development. Other objects are more immediately striking: above all in Case 51 the renowned **bull's head rhyton**, a sacred vessel used in religious ceremonies and found in the Little Palace at Knossós. Carved from black stone (steatite) with inlaid eyes and nostrils (the wooden horns are new), the bull is magnificently naturalistic. There are other animal heads here too, including another rhyton in the form of a lioness's head crafted from white limestone, and the stunning leopard's-head axe (Case 47) from Mália. In Case 46 are a number of vessels connected with the snake cult; some of them may have been snake containers. These are pertinent to Case 50, where two representations of the **snake goddess** – both wearing tight-waisted, breast-baring dresses and decorated aprons, each with snakes coiling around their hands – may equally be priestesses engaged in sacred rituals. A delicate ivory acrobat (Case 56), generally accepted to be a bull-leaper, and a faience relief of a *kri-kri*, or wild goat, suckling her kid (Case 55), also stand out. The **gaming board**, in Case 57 from the Corridor of the Draughtsboard at Knossós, is beautiful too – made of ivory, blue paste, crystal and gold and silver leaf, with ivory pieces – and a further reminder of the luxurious life which some Minoans at least could enjoy. Room IV also contains a collection of tools and weapons (especially a giant sword from Mália), almost all bronze with decorative work in ivory, gold and semiprecious stones. Finally, in Case 44, two small clay cups may hold important clues to the history of Minoan writing, of which so little survives. These vessels bear inscriptions written in Linear A script – developed from the cumbersome hieroglyphic – using cuttlefish ink. This use of ink suggests the existence of other suitable writing materials (possibly imported papyrus or even domestically produced palm-leaf paper) which have since perished in the Cretan climate.

Room V is devoted to the last period of the palace culture (1450–1400 BC), mainly at Knossós; the objects are considerably less exciting. In pottery, similar decorative themes continue to be used, but with a new formalism and on new types of vessel, which has been taken as a sign that Mycenaean influences were beginning to take hold – such influences are clear on the giant amphorae which stand against the walls. The numerous **Egyptian objects** found at Knossós are interesting too: fine in themselves and providing important evidence of the extent of trade between the two civilizations – and for archeologists, vital ammunition in the war over dates. In Case 70a is a clay model of a modest **Minoan dwelling** from Arhánes: with small rooms and tiny windows to keep out the bright Cretan sun and fierce winds, it has a small court in one corner which must have served to let in light. The roof terrace above, with typical tapered columns, is similar to those seen on village houses throughout Crete today. Side by side in Case 69, you can also see examples of both Linear A and Linear B scripts. A recent addition here is a fine "marine style" vase found in a tomb at Poros, near Iráklion.

Room VI covers finds from cemeteries at Knossós, Festós and Arhánes of approximately the same period. First come some small groups of clay figures from a tomb near Festós, in particular one of a ritual dance inside a circle decorated with horns of consecration – very crude work but wonderfully effective. In Case 75a (against the wall) is the curious horse burial found in a fourteenth-century *thólos* tomb at Arhánes, and now believed to be a sacrifice in honour of the possibly royal personage buried in the same tomb. After slaughter, the beast had been systematically dismembered and its parts carefully placed in the position in which they are now displayed. In the centre of the room is some of the museum's finest **jewellery**: gold signet rings, necklaces of gold and beads, and other gold work demonstrating the fine granulation typical of Minoan style. The martial arts are represented by some fine gold sword hilts and two fabulous **helmets**, one of boar's tusks (reconstructed), the other of bronze with long cheek-pieces. The boar's tusk helmet also makes an appearance on a ceramic amphora in Case 82. Taken with the other weapons displayed here, these items can be seen as further proof of the subordination of Minoan culture to the more warlike Mycenaean in this period.

Minor sites and jewellery

Room VII backtracks slightly in time to include objects from minor sites – mostly small villas and sacred caves, though including the larger complex of Ayía Triádha – throughout the main palace period and beyond (1700–1300 BC). As you enter you'll see great bronze double axes, erected on wooden poles, stone horns of consecration and bronze cauldrons set about the room. In the cases themselves are some very famous pieces, above all the three **stone** (steatite) **vases** from Ayía Triádha and the **gold jewellery** from a grave near Mália. The "Harvesters Vase" is the finest of the three vases, depicting with vivid realism a procession returning home from the fields; the harvesters are led by a strangely dressed character with long hair and a big stick, possibly a priest, and accompanied by musicians. The other two show scenes from boxing and wrestling matches and a chieftain receiving a report from an official.

The Mália jewellery is to be found in a single case (101) in the centre of the room – worth seeing above all is the stunningly intricate **pendant of two bees** around a golden disc (the latter supposedly a drop of honey which they are storing in a comb). Beside it are a number of other gold animal pendants, as well as necklaces and rings. Some **bronze figurines** in Case 89 depict worshippers making the ritual "salute" gesture to the deity whilst leaning backwards, and there's also a rare depiction of an older man released from the constriction of the usual tight belt, demonstrating that not all Minoans had such sylph-like figures as their art would lead you to believe. The enormous bronze cauldrons are worth a closer look; superbly crafted from sheets of metal riveted with nails, their discovery at Tílissos led to the excavation of the villas there. More mundane items in Case 99 include large copper ingots, almost certainly used as a form of currency.

Zákros and the eastern sites

Room VIII is given over to finds from the palace at Zákros (1700–1450 BC) and again includes several superlative items. There's a magnificent **rhyton of rock crystal** with a handle of beads and a collar that hides a join between two pieces encased in gold (Case 109). Its beauty aside, this exhibit is always singled out by guides as an example of the painstaking reconstruction undertaken by the museum – when discovered, it was broken into more than three hundred fragments. Also striking, in Case 111, is the **Peak Sanctuary Rhyton**, a green stone vessel on which a low-relief scene depicts a peak sanctuary with horns of consecration decorated with birds and wild goats. Originally covered in gold leaf, this discovery provided valuable information on Minoan religion. In the case parallel to this is a bull's head rhyton, smaller than but otherwise similar to that in Room IV. Room VIII also has a fine display of pottery from both palace and town, mostly from the zenith of the **marine and floral periods**. Finally, there are some outstanding stone and ceramic miniatures – shells and a butterfly in particular – and an assortment of the craftsmen's raw materials: a giant elephant's tusk, burnt in the fire which destroyed the palace, and unused ingots of bronze from the storerooms.

Room IX contains discoveries of the same period from lesser sites in the east. As usual there is an assortment of pottery and everyday objects, the most important of which are a series of **terracotta figurines** from a peak sanctuary at Piskoképhalo (Case 123). These naturalistic figures are fascinating in that they show what ordinary Minoans must have looked like and how they dressed – albeit for worship. Beside them are some charming miniature animals and models of sanctuaries. In Case 127 you can see a collection of bronze tools and weapons from the workers' village at Gourniá: hammers, picks, cutters and even "razor blades". Also in this room (Case 128) is the museum's largest collection of **seal stones**. Two things stand out about these. First, the intricacy of the carving, superbly executed in tiny detail on the hardest of stones, and second, the abundance of different themes (for obvious reasons, no two seals are the same) relating to almost every aspect of Minoan life, from rare portraits of individuals to religious ceremonies, hunting scenes and, most commonly, scenes from nature. The seals were used to fasten parcels or clay amphorae and for signing correspondence – a number of impressions of seals in clay have survived from Minoan times, mostly baked hard in accidental fires. Some of the larger seals, especially those in precious stones or with non-natural designs, may also have seen use as charms or amulets.

The post-Minoan age

Room X begins the museum's post-Minoan collection, covering a period (1400–1100 BC) when Crete was dominated by Mycenaean influences. The stylization and repetition of the themes employed in pottery decoration, coupled with a near-abandonment of the highly skilled craft of stoneworking, are obvious indications of artistic decline. Figurines from the sanctuaries are also far less naturalistically executed; there are many examples of a stereotyped goddess, both hands raised perhaps in blessing. However, an evocative clay sculpture of a **dancing group** with a lyre player from Palékastro (Case 132) does seem to echo past achievements, but even here Mycenaean influences are apparent.

Room XI continues the theme into the period of the arrival of Dorian Greeks (1100–900 BC). Among the Minoans, the goddess with raised hands remained important. The anguished features of the example from Mount Karfí (Case 148) – a remote mountain above the Lasíthi Plateau to where many Minoans fled from the vulnerable coastal areas – seem to foreshadow the end. The newcomers introduced stylistic changes: the **clay cart** drawn by curiously portrayed bodyless oxen is a new form of ritual vessel. The passing of the Bronze Age is reflected in Case 153: the metal of the new age was iron, which came to be used for the vast majority of weapons and tools. But some Minoan beliefs and traditions survived, such as worship at the cave sanctuary of the Minoan goddess of childbirth, Eileíthyia, to the east of Iráklion; Cases 149 and 158 display votive offerings from the cave dating from Hellenistic and Roman times. Some clay figurines portray couples engaged in sexual intercourse, pregnant women or women giving birth – leaving the goddess in little doubt as to what was required of her.

Room XII takes the collection up to about 650 BC. The early part of the period simply shows a development of the art of the previous era; later exhibits betray eastern, notably Egyptian, influences. This is most evident in the pottery, which is decorated with griffins, and with figures who would look at home in Tutankhamun's tomb. An interesting jug in Case 163 is typical of this era: on the vessel's neck two lovers – thought by some to be Theseus and Ariadne – embrace fondly. There are also some fine pottery and bronze figures, and a small treasure of gold jewellery.

Room XIII may well come as a relief, simply because there is nothing tiny or intricate to look at. Instead it contains a collection of **lárnakes** (clay coffins) from various periods, their painted decoration reflecting the prevailing pottery style. The Minoan burial position of knees drawn up to the chest explains the small size of the coffins – and also suggests that the bodies would have been placed in them soon after death, before the onset of rigor mortis. They come in two basic shapes: chests with lids and "bathtubs" (which may well have been used as such during their owners' lifetimes). From here stairs lead to the rooms on the second floor.

The palace frescoes

Room XIV upstairs, the **Hall of the Frescoes**, is perhaps the most exciting in the museum – and warrants another visit if by now you're too weary to appreciate it. Only tiny fragments of actual frescoes survived, but they have been almost miraculously reconstituted, and mounted on backgrounds which continue the design to give as true an impression of the entire fresco as possible. Frescoes are among the greatest achievements of Minoan art: they were originally painted directly onto wet plaster, using mostly plant dyes but also colours from mineral sources and even shellfish – a technique which has ensured their relatively unfaded survival. The job of the restorers was helped to an extent by knowledge of the various conventions, which matched Egyptian practice: men's skin, for example, was red, women's white; gold is shown as yellow, silver as blue and bronze, red.

Most of the frescoes shown in the museum come originally from Knossós, and date from the New Palace period (1600–1400 BC). Along the left-hand wall are four large panels from the enormous fresco which led all the way along the Corridor of the Procession at Knossós; an artist's impression shows how the whole might originally have looked. Two groups of youths are shown processing towards a female figure, presumably a priestess or goddess. Between the doors there's the **fresco of griffins** from the Throne Room at Knossós, and then on the far side a series from the villa at Ayía Triádha, some blackened by fire. Among these, the animation of the wild cat is especially striking; a floor painting of a seascape is also shown here. The opposite wall signals a return to Knossós, with some of the most famous of the works found there: the shields which adorned the Grand Staircase; the elegant **priest-king**, or Lily Prince; the great relief of a bull's head; a heavily restored fresco depicting elegantly attired ladies of the court; a beautifully simple fresco of dolphins from the queen's apartment; and the famous depiction of athletes leaping over a bull. Finally, there are two simple pictures of lilies from the walls of a villa at Amnísos (see p.83).

In some ways more striking than the frescoes themselves – because nothing has been restored or reconstructed – is the **Ayía Triádha sarcophagus**, decorated in the same manner, which stands in the centre of the room. The only stone sarcophagus to have been found in Crete, its unique and elaborate painted-plaster ornamentation has led archeologists to assume that it was made originally for a royal burial and later re-used. On one side is an animal sacrifice, with a bull already dead on the altar and two goats tied up awaiting their fates. On the other are two scenes, perhaps of relatives making offerings for the safe passage of the deceased. The ends feature a scene of goddesses riding in a chariot drawn by griffins, and of two women in a chariot pulled by goats above a procession of men. Also in this room is a wonderful wooden model of the **Palace of Knossós**.

Room XV has more **frescoes** of the same period. The most famous of them is **"La Parisienne"**, so dubbed for her bright red lips, huge eyes, long hair and fancy dress, but in reality almost certainly a priestess or a goddess if her twin image on the next panel has been interpreted correctly.

Room XVI exhibits yet more frescoes, the most interesting being the first, the **"Saffron Gatherer"**. Originally reconstructed as a boy, it has since been decided that this in fact represented a blue monkey; the two versions are shown side by side. Here too is the **"Captain of the Blacks"**, a work from the troubled end of the New Palace period. It apparently shows a Minoan officer leading a troop of African soldiers, probably Sudanese mercenaries – a sign of the period's increasing militarism.

Yiamalakis Collection and sculpture

Room XVII breaks off from the chronological approach to display the accumulations of an Iráklion doctor, the **Yiamalakis Collection**. This covers the entire remit of the museum in a single room, and it has some very fine pieces indeed. Of particular note is a steatopygous ("fat-buttocked" in plain English) Neolithic figurine – perhaps a fertility goddess – from near Ierápetra. There are also stunning gold jewels, especially the bull's head and two other pieces of the "Zákros Treasure"; some fine miniatures, bronze and ceramic; and from later periods, huge Roman figures and a mosaic relaid on the floor. For the whole of 1998 this room will be closed to house a special exhibition on the eastern Aegean, but the Yiamalakis collection will return in 1999.

Room XVIII continues the chronological collection right through from the Archaic period to the division of the Roman empire (c.650 BC–400 AD). There's an enormous variety of styles and objects here, including a collection of Roman **oil lamps** (Case 202) upon which – if you strain your eyes — are featured some fairly saucy erotic images. Among the larger items, a striking terracotta figurine of a spear-bearing **Athena** and a sensitively worked bronze of a youth in toga and sandals from Roman Ierápetra stand out – but the period was not one of Crete's artistic high points.

Downstairs, **Room XIX** backtracks a little to display larger pieces from the early years of this final period, the Archaic (650–500 BC), in particular three large **bronze figurines** of Apollo and Artemis with their mother Leto from the early sanctuary of Apollo Delphinios at Dréros. These are impressive in their simplicity, and significant as early examples of works made from sheets of hammered bronze, riveted together.

Room XX is devoted to Classical Greek and Greco-Roman sculpture which, as happens frequently in Crete, is not given the attention it deserves due to the overwhelming interest in Minoan civilization. Most of the items on view – some of them extremely fine and which would stand out in any other museum – do not carry any provenance or details, which lessens their impact. That said, look out for a magnificent **statue of Apollo** (or Athena) plus a superbly carved Roman sarcophagus, as well as a number of other outstanding examples of the sculptor's craft. There are also a few good Roman copies of Greek Classical works, and some stern portrait busts of members of Rome's imperial families, all deserving of a better standard of presentation.

Eating

Big city as it is, Iráklion disappoints when it comes to **eating** – and even more when it comes to going out after you have eaten. The cafés and tavernas of the main squares – **Venizélou** and **Elefthérias** – are quintessential places to sit and watch the world pass, but their food is on the whole expensive and mediocre. The cafés and tavernas on **Dedhálou** itself, the pedestrian alley linking the two main squares, are popular with tourists too, but again are not particularly good value.

For better quality and reasonably priced food, you need to get away from the more obvious tourist haunts, although you don't always have to travel very far. A more atmospheric option is to head for the little alley, Fotiou Theodosaki, which runs through from the **market** to Odhós Evans, and is entirely lined with the tables of rival taverna owners, who cater for market traders and their customers as well as tourists.

At the basic end of the scale, **takeaways** are not in short supply. There's a whole group of *souvláki* stalls, for instance, clustering around 25-Avgoústou at the entrance to El Greco Park; the park itself is handy if you need somewhere to sit and eat. For cheese or spinach pies or some other pastry, sweet or savoury, try the *Samaria* zakharoplasteío next to the Harley Davidson shop.

Restaurants

There are good restaurants scattered across town. Just off Eleftherías at **Platía Dhaskaloyiánnis** (where the post office is) are some cheaper, if not exceptional tavernas. The platía – which each summer hosts a fair of ceramics made by prisoners at a local jail – is a pleasant and relaxing venue and a good place to break your tour of the nearby Archeological Museum; nearby are a couple of authentic ouzerí (try *Ta Asteria*) serving up tasty mezédhes. Nearer Venizélou, try exploring some of the back streets to the east, off Dedhálou and behind the *loggia*.

Down around the harbour, you'll find a number of slightly more expensive restaurants, many specializing in fish. Far more promising just to the south is a line of ouzerí, plying fish mezédhes, along the narrow Marineli (passage leading into Platía Áyios Dimítrios, with a pint-sized church of the same name). On the unpromising coastal outskirts west of town is a trio of fish tavernas worth seeking out.

Chiao, Platía Venizélou facing the Morosini fountain. Good fast food restaurant open day and night if you need sustenance outside normal feeding times.

Geroplatanos, in the leafy square fronting the church of Ay. Títos. Taking its name from the great old plane tree beneath which its tables are set out, this is one of the most tranquil lunch spots in town.

Giovanni, on the alley Koraí, parallel to Dedhálou. One of the better tavernas in Iráklion, this friendly place uses fresh, good-quality ingredients to produce a varied menu, including vegetarian dishes, while Giovanni's pet parrot, cockatoo and mynah bird entertain the clientele.

Ionia, corner of Evans and Yiánari. This taverna has been operating since 1923 and is the sort of place to come for substantial, no-nonsense Greek dishes.

Ippokampos, Sófokli Venizélou, west of 25-Avgoústou, close to the *Kronos* hotel. The best and least-expensive fish to be had in Iráklion, served in unpretentious surroundings. Deservedly popular with locals, this place is often crowded late into the evening, and you may have to queue or turn up earlier than the Greeks eat. Even if you see no space it is worth asking as the owner may suddenly disappear inside the taverna and emerge with yet another table to carry further down the pavement.

Kapetanios, Marineli 1, opposite the tiny church of Ay. Dimítrios. The first in a row of ouzerí that line this alley off Vironos, sloping down to the harbour. Good fish dishes and mezédhes.

Katsina, Marineli 12. A simple and friendly ouzerí at the opposite (seaward) end of the alley from *Kapetanios*. Tasty and economical seafood mezédhes served at outdoor tables.

Loukoulos, on the alley Koraí, parallel to Dedhálou. Rather snooty garden restaurant with an Italian slant to its international menu; Iráklion's smart set come here to be pampered by over-fussy service and prices to match.

O Miltos, Linoperamata, 5km west of the centre (☎821-584). Excellent and friendly fish tav-erna with a terrace overlooking the sea. This is one of a cluster of economical fish tavernas owned by three competing brothers. *Taverna Delfini*, which has the best reputation, and *I Kalouba* are the others here, but unlike *O Miltos*, open evenings only. You'll need your own transport or a taxi to get there; they are located on the sea 1km beyond the city's power sta-tion with its distinctive red and white chimney stacks, and close to the Aget Iraklis cement factory, but don't let this put you off.

New China Restaurant, on the alley Koraí, parallel to Dedhálou. Chinese cuisine served in a leafy courtyard.

Rizes, Hándhakos 54. Economical option with a pleasant, quiet courtyard setting.

Taberneio, Idomeneos 4, near to the Arsenali. Good little neighbourhood taverna offering a wide selection of mezédhes and traditional meat-based dishes.

Tartuffo, Dhimokratías 83, near the *Galaxy* hotel. The ten-minute walk out along the road to Knossós is worth it for excellent pizzas.

Cafés

Several places in Venizélou and at the top of Dhikeosínis specialize in luscious pastries to accompany a strong mid-morning coffee; local treats include *bougátsa* and *loukoumades*.

Bougátsa Kirkor, by the fountain in Venizélou. The place to sample authentic *bougátsa*, a creamy cheese pie served warm and sprinkled with sugar and cinnamon.

Ta Leontaria, next door to *Kirkor*. Another classic *bougátsa* place, with tables on the square.

Onar, Hándhakos 36b, north of Venizélou. Café with a small terrace, where a wide variety of teas are served.

Rigas, Kandanoléon 2. A good breakfast place on the southwestern side of El Greco Park – with a wide range of mouthwatering cakes and pastries as well as the usual standards such as *tirópita* and *spanakópita*.

Themeneopoulos, N. Foká 5, the alleyway between Dhikeosínis and Dedhálou. This café specializes in *loukoumades*: you can watch the yeasty dough bubbling away before it is dropped to cook in the hot oil, then served with honey syrup, sesame seeds and crushed nuts. These confections are traditionally taken with a glass of cold water.

Drinking and nightlife

As for **nightlife**, Iráklion is a bit of a damp squib when compared to many other towns on the island. Much of what does happen takes place in the suburbs or out along the hotel strip to the west. If you're determined, however, there are a cou-ple of city-centre possibilities – and plenty of options if all you want to do is sit and drink. Indeed there is a new breed of kafeníon emerging in Iráklion, aimed at younger people: the drinks are cocktails rather than *raki*, the music is western or modern Greek, and there are prices to match.

There are also a number of **cinemas** scattered about: check the posters at the tourist police office for programme details. Most enjoyable is the open-air cinema on the beach to the west of the city.

Bars

Bars congregate in the same areas as the restaurants. Perhaps the most animat-ed are in Platía Koraí, a quiet square behind Dedhálou, while slightly more touristy alternatives are centred around Platía Venizélou and around the fringes of El Greco Park. After ten at night, a lively bar scene also fans out into the streets around Hándhakos and you'll stumble on many places by following the crowds.

Iráklion looks a great deal better than you'd expect from above, and most of the fancier hotels have rooftop bars; the *Ilaira* hotel, just above the harbour, has particularly stunning views.

To Avgo, Platía Koraí. Trendy little bar frequented by students, on a pleasant square just to the north of Dedhálou.

El Azteca, Psaromilíngon 32, west of Hándhakos. Lively Mexican bar serving tacos and fancy beers, with a garden at the back.

Café Flou, Platía Dhaskaloyiánnis. This laid-back café-bar casts off its daytime serenity after ten when locals gather to sink into the canvas chairs on the square, listen to soft rock and sip long drinks.

De Facto, Platía Venizélou. One of the most popular of the fashionable bars in this area, especially for people-watching early evening.

Flash, Platía Koraí. This bar has outdoor tables and serves a wide variety of exotic (and expensive) beers and cocktails. Those on a tight budget can nurse a *frappé* for hours.

Idaean Andron, Perdhíkari 1, just east of Platía Venizélou. A good example of the new-style kafeníon, with a nice, easy atmosphere.

Jasmin, Ayiostefanitón 6, tucked in an alley on the left midway down Hándhakos. Another good night-time rendezvous, with jazz, soul and latin music and an outdoor terrace. Also serves 45 different types of tea, including herbal.

To Mílon tis Eridos, Platía Korai, facing the place above. This café-bar serves everything from twelve types of coffee to cocktails and herb teas including *diktamo* or Cretan dittany, used by the ancients as a panacea.

Odysseia, Hándhakos 63. Popular meeting place for Iráklion's younger set, with music and an outdoor terrace.

Pagopoleion (ice-factory), Platía Áyios Títos. Stunning new bar created by photographic artist Chryssy Karelli inside Iráklion's former ice factory. She has preserved much of the old building including a lift for hauling the ice from the basement freezer and a fascistic call to duty in German Gothic script on one wall – a remnant of Nazi occupation of the factory in World War II. Make sure to visit the toilets which are in an artistic league of their own. *Pagopoleion* often puts on live music and is a good breakfast place.

Piano Bar/Ladies Café Loggia, Platía Venizélou. Pleasant rooftop bar.

Rebels, Perdhíkari 3. A stylish new bar which also claims to be Iráklion's first Internet café.

Clubs and discos

For **discos** proper, there is a greater selection – even if they all play techno interspersed with Greek music. **Nightclubs** are clustered in two areas: down around the harbour and on Ikarou, downhill from Platía Eleftherías, around twenty minutes' walk apart.

Babel, junction of Odhós Ay. Títos and Idomeneos, slightly east of Áyios Títos church. Three bars and cinema screens round the dance floor project films and video clips.

Makao, on the opposite side of the street to *Trápeza*. Has a loyal following, as does the *Genesis* next door.

Trápeza. The most popular of the clubs down towards the harbour at the bottom of Doúkos Bófor, below the Archeological Museum.

Listings

Airlines Olympic, on Platía Eleftherías (☎229-191), is the only airline with a permanent office in Iráklion. Charter airlines flying into Iráklion mostly use local travel agents as their representatives. For airport information call ☎245-644.

Airport buses Bus #1 runs from Platía Eleftherías to the airport every few minutes; buy a ticket from the booth on the square first.

Banks The main branches are on 25-Avgoústou, many of which have 24hr cash machines (not always working); there's also a Visa machine at Ergo Bank on Dhikeosínis.

Beaches For city beaches take a #7 bus east to Amnísos or a #6 west to Amoudhári: both leave from Platía Eleftherías. The ticket booth is outside the *Astoria Hotel*; see "Buses" section below for details.

Bike and car rental 25-Avgoústou is lined with rental companies, but you'll find cheaper rates on the backstreets and it is always worth asking for discounts. Good places to start include Athens Cars, Koraí 23, behind the *Astoria* hotel (☎220-680); Blue Sea, Kosma Zotou 7 near the bottom of 25-Avgoústou (☎241-097) for bikes; Eurocreta, Sapotie 2 (☎226-700); Ritz in the *Hotel Rea*, Kalimeráki 1 (☎223-638); and Sun Rise, 25-Avgoústou 46 (☎221-609) for cars. All offer free delivery to hotels and airport.

Buses See p.66 for locations of bus stations – and p.134 for a timetable.

Cinema Check details of what's on at the hoardings along Dhikeosínis near the tourist police office or by the main entrance to the Public Gardens. There's an open-air cinema in the west of the city.

Consulates See Basics p.22.

Festivals The Iráklion Summer Festival runs from July to mid-September. It includes exhibitions, concerts and plays by groups from around the world, some of which are top-notch: details from the tourist office. August 25 is St Titus' Day, marked by a major procession from the church of Áyios Títos.

Hospitals There are three hospitals. The one on Apollónion southwest of Platía Kornárou, between Alber and Moussoúrou is reasonably central. The others are out of town, including a new modern one, Periferiako Panenistemiako Veniko Nosokomeio Irakleio (PAYNE; ☎269-111) – not one to get your lips around when you're feeling under the weather.

Laundry Washsalon, Hándhakos 18 (Mon–Sat 8am–8pm; ☎280-858) is reliable and also does service washes. There's another place at Mirabelou 25 just behind the Archeological Museum (Mon–Sat 9am–3.30pm & 6–8pm). Take plenty of change.

Left luggage There's a left luggage office in the east-bound (A) and southwest (B) bus stations (daily 6am–8pm; 300dr per bag per day) but not at the west-bound one. There is also a commercial agency at 25-Avgoústou (daily 7am–11pm; 450dr per bag per day) and another at Hándhakos 18 (open daily 24 hours; 400dr per locker per day). You can also leave bags at the youth hostel (even if you don't stay there) for 200–300dr per bag per day. If you want to leave your bag while you go off on a bike for a day or two, the rental company should be prepared to store it.

Mountaineering The local EOS is at Dhikeosínis 53 (☎227-609).

Newspapers and books English-language and other foreign newspapers are sold throughout the city centre – the best bet is up Dedhálou where at Bibliopoleio (no. 6) you'll find a selection of Jackie Collins novels as well as local guides and maps. For a more comprehensive selection of English-language titles including education books, there is the Planet International Bookstore at the corner of Hándhakos and Kidonias (☎281-558) behind Platía Venizélou.

Parking Bringing a vehicle into the centre of town can mean a tedious search for a parking place. All-day parking is available at a guarded park on the east side of Platía Eleftherías, for around 600dr per day.

Pharmacies Plentiful on the main shopping streets. At least one will be open 24hr on a rota basis; check the list on the door of any pharmacist for the nearest one. There are traditional herbalists in the market.

Post office Main office in Platía Dhaskaloyiánnis, off Eleftherías: open Mon–Fri 7.30am–8pm. There's also a temporary office (a van) at the entrance to El Greco Park (daily 7.30am–7pm), handy for changing money.

Shopping The market is best for food as well as for cheap practical goods and for leather-ware and most standard tourist items. Herbs make an unusual souvenir from Crete – one of the best places to buy is at the stall belonging to Kostas Stathakis along Odhós 1866, about 50m from the junction with Dhikeosínis, on the right. Saffron is a bargain here, but get the strands and not the powdered stuff. More upmarket tourist shops – jewellery and fabrics especially – can be found down Dedhálou. Everyday shops and embroidered textiles down Kalokerinoú and clothes and shoe shops around Averof are good value in late July sales. Small mini-markets in tourist areas are open every day, and the Continent hypermarket has recently opened out towards Amoudhári. CDs and cassettes of Cretan and Greek music including *lyra* and *rembétika,* can be purchased at Aerakis, Dedhálou 35.

Taxis Major taxi ranks in Platía Eleftherías and El Greco Park or call ☎210-102 or 210-168. Prices displayed on boards at ranks.

Telephones The OTE head office is in El Greco Park, with long queues but an efficient 24-hour service. Most destinations abroad can now be phoned from street booths by using a phone card obtainable from a *períptero* (kiosk).

Toilets In El Greco Park and the Public Gardens and near the cathedral, at the bus stations and the Archeological Museum (no need to pay entrance charge to use them).

Tourist office The EOT is opposite the Archeological Museum at Zanthoudhídhou 1 (Mon–Fri 8am–2.30pm; ☎228-825). Friendly, but often very crowded in high summer.

Tourist police On Dhikeosínis 10 (☎283-130). Better informed and more helpful than most.

Travel agencies 25-Avgoústou is crammed with shipping and general travel agents. Cheap/student specialists include the extremely helpful Blavakis Travel, Platía Kallergon 8, just off 25-Avgoústou by the entrance to El Greco Park (☎282-541) or Prince Travel, 25-Avgoústou 30 (☎282-706). Ferry tickets also from Minoan Lines, 25-Avgoústou 78 (☎224-303) or Kavi Club near to the tourist office (☎221-166). For excursions around the island, villa rentals and so on, the bigger operators are probably easier: try Irman Travel, Dedhálou 26 (☎242-527); Creta Travel Bureau, Epiménidhou 20–22 (☎227-002); or Adamis Tours, 25-Avgoústou 23 (☎246-202). The latter two are the local American Express agents.

Amnísos and other local beaches

If all you want to do is escape Iráklion to lie on a beach for a few hours, the simplest course is to head **east**, beyond the airport, to the municipal beach, Amnísos or to the marginally quieter Tobrúok beach. All are easily reached by public transport: the #7 bus runs every fifteen minutes or so from the tree-shaded stop opposite the *Hotel Astoria* in Platía Eleftherías.

Leaving the city through its sprawling eastern suburbs and the town of Néa Alikarnassós into which they merge, the bus follows the old road as it skirts around the airport. Even in spring this manages to be a wasted and dusty-looking landscape – an impression not helped by the ill-camouflaged bunkers of the Greek air force base which shares the runway. Once past the airport, however, the road swings down to the coast and a narrow patch of level ground between the sea and the hills. First stop is at the **municipal beach**: fenced off (you pay to get in) and provided with showers and changing rooms. There seems little point in paying unless you want to study the undercarriages of incoming planes in intimate detail – this beach tends to be crowded and only marginally cleaner than the free sections.

The next halt is **AMNÍSOS**, where there are a couple of tavernas and food stalls immediately behind the beach, and even a huddle of hotels. Although you're unlikely to want to stay here, it's not a bad beach to find so close to the city. The main drawback is the stream of planes coming in to land: on peak weekends there seems to be one every few minutes, while during the week quiet periods are enlivened by fighters on low-level runs.

The last of these beaches, **Tobróuk**, is perhaps the best, with more tavernas and drink stalls, slightly fewer people, and relative peace to be found if you walk a little way along the sand.

Amnísos and Eileíthyia: two minor sites

Amnísos is also a famous name in Minoan archeology, although today the site is not particularly impressive, and the remains – right by the road down to Amnísos beach, on the low hill to the left – can only be glimpsed through a fence. There was a small settlement here, apparently a port for Knossós, from which the Cretan forces engaged in the Trojan War are said to have set sail, and it was here, in a villa, that the unusual Fresco of the Lilies was found – now on display in the Iráklion Archeological Museum (see p.76). The site is also noted for excavations by Marinatos in the 1930s, when the archeologist's discovery of pumice fragments amongst the ruins prompted him to develop his theory attributing the destruction of Minoan palaces to an eruption of the volcanic island of Thíra (see p.336). The scorch marks on many of the remaining stones testify to the intense fire which destroyed the villa during this period. On the west side of the rocky outcrop behind the villa, new excavations have unearthed the remains of a harbour, possibly verifying the link with the world of Homer.

On the eastern edge of Amnísos, a sign points inland from the main road towards the hills (the turnoff to Episkopí) indicating another significant ancient site, the **Cave of Eileíthyia**, which gets a mention in the *Odyssey* as one of Odysseus's stopovers on his way home from Troy. Just over 1km up the steep road from the junction, the cave's entrance is signed on the left (although only the pole was visible at the time of writing) and lies below the road on the left next to a fig tree. Eileíthyia was a goddess, primarily of childbirth, of very ancient origin and this cave was a cult centre from Neolithic times. Inside are two large walled stalagmites which were almost certainly regarded as fertility totems. One of these has been worn smooth by the touch of countless worshippers, who conducted rituals here from Neolithic times until the fifth century AD. The cave itself is now fenced and locked and if you are intent on making a survey (it's about 50m deep), you'll need to get a key from the guardian 7km away at Nírou Háni (see p.98).

Beaches to the west

The **beaches** to the west of the city are less noisy but also less atmospheric and more touristy than the eastern ones. If you take a #6 bus from immediately in front of the *Hotel Astoria*, it will head out through the Haniá Gate and into Iráklion's more prosperous western extremities. Eventually you'll end up on the road which runs behind the hotel strip, past the Continent hypermarket (and a small Marks and Spencer department store) and on eventually to the luxury *Creta Beach* hotel complex, unappealingly sited immediately before the power station and cement works (see p.79 for some excellent fish tavernas here). You can get off almost anywhere in this area, and attempt to get to **Amoudhári Beach**, though this is not always easy. Although the beach itself is public, there are very few access roads to it, and the hotels and campsite try hard to prevent any non-residents walking through their grounds: you just have to ignore the people shouting at you, or take one of the roads down and put up with the crowds who tend to congregate at these access points.

Knossós

> *. . . a dancing place*
> *All full of turnings, that was like the admirable maze*
> *For fair hair'd Ariadne made, by cunning Daedalus*

Homer, *The Odyssey*

KNOSSÓS (April–Sept Mon–Fri 8am–6pm, Sat & Sun 8.30am–6pm; Oct–March daily 8.30am–3pm; 1500dr, students free; free on Sun) lies some 5km south of Iráklion on a low, largely man-made hill. No matter when you come, you won't get the place to yourself – but exploring on your own does give you the opportunity to appreciate individual parts of the palace in the brief lulls between groups. The best time of day to avoid the crowds in summer is two hours before closing time, which also has the advantage of being cooler. If you get the opportunity to come back a second time, it will all begin to make a great deal more sense.

By far the largest of the Minoan palaces, it thrived over three thousand years ago at the heart of a highly sophisticated island-wide civilization. Long after

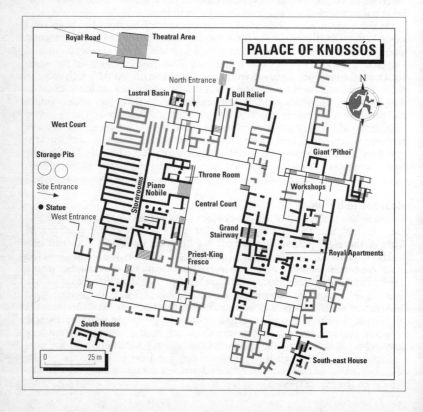

Minoan culture had collapsed, a town on this site remained powerful, rivalling Górtys right into the Roman era. Although only the palace itself is much visited, the hills all around are rich in lesser remains dating from the twentieth century BC through to the second or third century AD.

Yet less than a hundred years ago this was a place thought to have existed only in mythology. Here it was in legend that King Minos ruled and that his wife Pasiphae bore the Minotaur – half-bull and half-man. Here the labyrinth was constructed by Daedalus to contain the monster, and youths were brought from Athens as human sacrifice, until finally Theseus arrived to slay the beast and, with Ariadne's help, escape its lair. Imprisoned in his own maze, Daedalus later constructed the wings that bore him away to safety – and Icarus to his untimely death.

The excavation of the palace, and the clothing of these legends with fact, is among the most amazing tales of modern archeology. Today's Knossós, whose fame rivals any such site in the world, is associated above all with Sir Arthur Evans, who excavated the palace at the turn of the century and whose bust is one of the first things to greet you at the site. The autocratic control he exerted, his working standards and procedures, and, above all, the restorations he claimed were necessary to preserve the building have been a source of furious controversy among archeologists ever since. It has become clear that much of Evans's upper level, the *Piano Nobile* – is pure conjecture. Even so, his guess as to what the palace might have looked like is certainly as good as anyone else's, and it makes the other sites infinitely more meaningful if you have seen Knossós first. Without the restorations, it would be hard to visualize the ceremonial stairways, strange top-heavy pillars and brightly frescoed walls that distinguish Knossós – and almost impossible to imagine the grandeur of the multistorey palace. To get an idea of the size and complexity of the palace in its original state, take a look at the cutaway drawings on sale outside – they may seem somewhat fantastic, but are probably not too far from reality.

The palace

When you enter the **Palace of Knossós** through its West Court – the ancient ceremonial entrance – you soon discover how the legends of the labyrinth grew up around it. Even with a detailed plan, it's almost impossible to find your way around: the trick is not to try too hard. Wander around for long enough and you'll eventually stumble onto everything; if you're worried about missing the highlights, you can always tag onto one of the guided tours for a while, catch the patter and then hang back to take in the detail when the crowd has moved on.

The remains you see are mostly those of the second palace, which was rebuilt after the destruction of around 1700 BC and was occupied (with increasing Mycenaean influence) through to about 1450 BC. At the time it was surrounded by a town of considerable size. The palace itself, though, must have looked almost as much a mess then as it does now – a vast bulk, with more than a thousand rooms on five floors, which had spread across the hill more as an organic growth than a planned building, incorporating or burying earlier structures as it went. In this the palace simply followed the pattern of Minoan architecture generally, with extra rooms being added as the need arose. It is the style of building still most common on Crete, where finished buildings are far outnumbered by those waiting to have an extra floor or room added when need and finance dictate.

The West Court and first frescoes

The **West Court**, across which you approach the palace, was perhaps a market-place or at any rate the scene of public meetings. Across it run slightly raised walkways, leading from the palace's West Entrance to the Theatral Area, and once presumably onto the Royal Road. There are also three large, circular pits, originally grain silos or perhaps depositories for sacred offerings, but used as rubbish tips by the end of the Minoan era. If you follow the walkway towards the West Entrance nowadays, you arrive at a typically muddled part of the palace, not at all easy to interpret. First there's a line of stones marking the original wall of an earlier incarnation of the palace, then the facade of the palace proper, and beyond that a series of small rooms of which only the foundations survive. When the palace was still standing, you would have passed through a guardroom and then followed the **Corridor of the Procession**, flanked by frescoes depicting a procession, around towards the south side of the palace. This is still the best way to go, though it can be hard to fathom which is the corridor.

Around on the south side of the Central Court, you can climb a flight of stairs to admire the reproduction of the **Priest-King Fresco** (also known as the Prince of the Lilies) and look down over the palace. Apparently a whole series of large and airy frescoed chambers, perhaps reception rooms, once stood up here.

The Central Court, Throne Room and Piano Nobile

You can climb from this side of the courtyard to the *Piano Nobile*, the upper floor on the west side, but this is best left till later. Instead, proceed straight into the **Central Court**, the heart of the palace. Aligned almost exactly north–south, the courtyard paving covers the oldest remains found on the site, going back to Neolithic times. Some say this was the scene of the famous bull-leaping, but that seems rather unlikely; although the court measures almost 60m by 30m, it would hardly be spacious enough to accommodate the sort of intricate acrobatics shown in surviving pictures, let alone for an audience to watch. In Minoan times the courtyard would have had a very different atmosphere from the open, shadeless space which survives, with high walls hemming it in on every side.

The entrance to one of Knossós's most atmospheric survivals, the **Throne Room**, is in the northwestern corner of the courtyard. Here a worn stone throne sits against the wall of a surprisingly small chamber: along the walls around it are ranged stone benches and behind there's a copy of a fresco depicting two griffins. In all probability, this was the seat of a priestess rather than a ruler – there's nothing like it in any other Minoan palace – but it may just have been an innovation wrought by the Mycenaeans, since it appears that this room dates only from the final period of the palace's occupation. Overexposure has meant that the Throne Room itself is now closed off with a wooden gate, but you can lean over this for a good view, and in the antechamber there's a wooden copy of the throne on which everyone perches to have their photo taken. Opposite the real throne, steps lead down to a lustral basin: a sunken "bath", probably for ritual purification rather than actual bathing, with no drain.

Alongside the Throne Room, a stairway climbs to the first floor and Evans's reconstructed **Piano Nobile**. Perhaps the most interesting feature of this part of the palace is the view it offers of the palace storerooms, with their rows of *pithoi* (storage jars) often still in place. There's an amazing amount of storage space here, in the jars – which would mostly have held oil or wine – and in spaces sunk into the ground for other goods. The rooms of the *Piano Nobile* itself are again rather confusing, though you should be able to pick out the Sanctuary Hall from stumps that remain of its six large columns. Opposite this is a small concrete room (complete with roof) which Evans "reconstructed" directly above the Throne Room. It feels entirely out of place: inside there's a small display on the reconstruction of the frescoes, and through to the other side you get another good view over the Central Court. Returning through this room, you could climb down the very narrow staircase on your right to arrive at the entrance to the corridor of storerooms (now fenced off) or head back to the left towards the area where you entered the palace.

The Royal Apartments

Returning to the courtyard allows you to cross to the east side, where the **Grand Staircase** leads into the **Royal Apartments** (currently undergoing restoration), plainly the finest of the rooms at Knossós. The staircase itself is a masterpiece of design: not only a fitting approach to these sumptuously appointed chambers, but also an integral part of the whole design, its large well allowing light into the lower storeys. Light wells such as these, usually with a courtyard at the bottom, are a common feature of Knossós and a reminder of just how important creature comforts were to the Minoans, and how skilled they were at providing them.

For more evidence of this luxurious lifestyle you need look no further than the **Queen's Suite**, off the grand **Hall of the Colonnades** at the bottom of the staircase. The main living room is decorated with the celebrated dolphin fresco and with running friezes of flowers and (earlier) spirals. On two sides it opens to courtyards which let in light and air – the smaller one would probably have been planted with flowers. In use, the room would probably have been scattered with cushions and hung with rich drapes, while doors and curtains between the pillars allowed for privacy, and for cool shade in the heat of the day. Plausible as it all is, this is largely speculation – and some pure con. The dolphin fresco, for example, was found in the courtyard, not the room itself, and would have been viewed from inside as a sort of *trompe l'oeil*, like looking out of a glass-bottomed boat. There are also some who argue, convincingly, that grand as these rooms are, they are not really large or fine enough to have been royal quarters. Those would more likely have been in the lighter and airier rooms that must have existed in the upper reaches of the palace, while these lower apartments were inhabited by resident nobles or priests.

The truth hardly matters, for whether or not you accept Evans's names and attributions, the rooms remain an impressive example of the sophistication of Minoan architecture – all the more so when you follow the dark passage round to the **Queen's Bathroom**, its clay tub protected behind a low wall (and probably screened by curtains when in use), and to the famous "flushing" lavatory (a hole in the ground with drains to take the waste away – it was flushed by a bucket of water).

On the floor above the queen's domain, the Grand Staircase passes through a set of rooms which are generally described as the **King's Quarters**. These are chambers in a considerably sterner vein: the staircase opens into a grandiose reception area known as the **Hall of the Royal Guard**, its walls decorated in repeated shield motifs. Opening off it is the ruler's personal chamber, the **Hall of the Double Axes** – a room which could be divided to allow for privacy while audiences were held in the more public section, or the whole opened out for larger functions. Its name comes from the double axe symbol, so common throughout Knossós, which here is carved into every block of masonry.

The palace fringes

From the back of the queen's chambers you can emerge into the fringes of the palace where it spreads down the lower slopes of the hill. This is a good point at which to consider the famous **drainage system** at Knossós, some of the most complete sections of which are visible under grilles. The snugly interconnecting terracotta pipes ran underneath most of the palace (here they have come more or less direct from the Queen's Bathroom) and site guides never fail to point them out as evidence of the advanced state of Minoan civilization. They are indeed quite an achievement – in particular the system of baffles and overflows (most clearly seen down by the external walls), designed to slow down the run-off and avoid flooding. Just how much running water there would have been, however, is another matter: the water supply is at the bottom of the hill, and even the combined efforts of rainwater catchment and water physically carried up to the palace can hardly have been sufficient to supply the needs of more than a small elite.

From the bottom of the slope you get a fine impression of the scale of the whole palace complex and can circle around towards the north, climbing back inside the palace limits to see the area known as the **Palace Workshops**. Here potters, lapidaries and smiths appear to have plied their trades, and here also are the spectacular **giant píthoi**; people queue to have their photograph taken with the jars towering over them. There's also a good view of the bull-relief fresco set up by the north entrance.

Outside the main palace, just beyond the North Entrance, is the **Theatral Area**, one of the more important enigmas of this and other Minoan palaces. An open space resembling a stepped amphitheatre, it may have been used for ritual performances or dances, but there's no real evidence of this, and again there would have been very little room for an audience if that was its function.

Beyond it the **Royal Road** sets out: originally this ran to the Little Palace (see below), and beyond that probably on across the island, but nowadays it ends after about 100m in a brick wall beneath the modern road. Alongside are assorted structures variously interpreted as stores, workshops or grandstands for viewing parades, all of them covered in undergrowth. Back down the Royal Road, you can re-enter the palace by its **North Entrance**. Beside the entry is a well-preserved **lustral basin**, and beyond that a guardroom. Heading back to the central courtyard, a flight of stairs doubles back to allow you to examine the copy of the **Bull Relief** close to.

Of the lesser structures which crowd around the palace, a number of houses on the south side are particularly worth noting, although they aren't open to the public. The one known simply as the **South House**, reconstructed to its original three floors, seems amazingly modern, but actually dates from the late Minoan period (c.1550 BC). The dwelling is believed to have belonged to some important official or noble, since it encroaches on the palace domain. In the **Southeast House**, of the same period, a cult room with a sacred pillar was discovered, as well as stands for double axes and a libation table. Across a little valley from here, outside the fenced site, was the **Caravanserai** where travellers would rest and water their animals; the restored building contains two elegant rooms, as well as a large stone footbath still running with water from an ancient spring.

Among the other important outlying buildings are the **Little Palace**, on a site which also contains a mansion and many Roman remains (just up the narrow alley which veers off to the left as you head back towards Iráklion), and the

Royal Villa, facing the palace from the slope to the northeast. Both are occasionally open for special visits.

About 100m along the road to Iráklion from the site entrance lies the **Villa Ariadne**, an Edwardian villa constructed by Evans where he lived while conducting excavations. Later the house served as a military hospital during the German siege of Iráklion and, following the city's fall, as the residence of the German commander of Crete. It was where General Kreipe was based when he was kidnapped by Paddy Leigh Fermor and others (see p.343). The villa's dining room was also where the German army signed the surrender on May 9, 1945. Although not open to the public, nobody seems to mind if you walk up the drive past the gatehouse to have a look at the house's exterior and gardens.

Practicalities

Getting to Knossós from Iráklion could hardly be easier. The #2 and #4 buses set out every ten minutes from the city bus stands adjacent to the east-bound bus station, run up 25-Avgoústou (with a stop just below Platía Venizélou) and out of town on Odhós 1821 and Evans. Taxis run from the city and cost about 700dr (see p.82). If you're driving you can take this route, through Evans Gate, or follow the signs from Platía Eleftherías; from anywhere other than Iráklion turn directly off the bypass onto the badly signed Knossós road.

On arrival, you're confronted first by a string of rather pricey tavernas and tacky souvenir stands. There are several **rooms** places here too, and if you're really into Minoan culture there's a lot to be said for staying out this way to steal an early start. Be warned, though, that the site area is expensive and unashamedly commercial. At the end of all the development, on the other side of the road, is the free official car park – although it tends to be inadequate at peak times. This is where the bus drops you, and it's through the car park that you enter the site proper, having first run the gauntlet of map salesmen and tour guides and bought your ticket at the turnstiles. To catch the bus back, you have to walk a short way back up the road; a ruse no doubt designed to force you once again past all those souvenir shops.

South to Mount Yioúhtas

The countryside south of Knossós is dominated by the bulk of **Mount Yioúhtas** (811m), which rises alone from a landscape otherwise characterized by gently undulating agricultural country. Seen from the north, and especially the northwest, the mountain has an unmistakeably human profile, identified with Zeus in the post-Minoan period. The ancient Cretans claimed that Zeus lay buried underneath the mountain: given that the god is immortal, this furnished proof for other Greeks of the assertion that "All Cretans are liars" – it may even have been the original basis of this reputation.

Beyond Knossós the nature of the journey is transformed almost immediately – the road gradually empties and the country becomes greener. Almost any of these roads south makes a beautiful drive, past vineyards draped across low hills and through flourishing farming communities. Just a couple of kilometres from the site, at the head of the valley, there's an extraordinary **aqueduct** arching along beside the road. This looks medieval and was built on the line of an earlier Roman aqueduct, but is in fact barely 150 years old, having been constructed during the brief period of Egyptian rule (1832–40) to provide Iráklion with water; it has now been taken over by a colony of noisy rooks. Just beyond are a couple of tavernas/cafés beside the road – a convenient escape from the Knossós crowds – and just past them is a turning on the left, clearly signposted to Mirtiá.

Mirtiá and the Kazantzákis Museum

The main reason to visit **MIRTIÁ** is for the Kazantzákis Museum in the village, but you don't need to be a fan of the writer to find the trip worthwhile. Only enthusiasts are likely to spend long over the exhibits, but it's an enjoyable collection to look over quickly and a lovely drive there on almost deserted roads. Mirtiá itself is larger than you'd expect – as indeed are many of these villages – and bright with flowers planted in old olive-oil cans.

The **museum** (Mon, Wed, Sat 9am–1pm & 4–8pm; Tues & Fri 9am–1pm; Thurs & Sun closed; 500dr) is on the central platía (well beyond the multi-coloured, multilingual signs on the main street at either end of the village), along with three pleasant kafenía where you can stop for a drink. Occupying a house where Kazantzákis's parents once lived – a fine bourgeois mansion – the collection includes a vast quantity of ephemera relating to the great author: diaries, photos, manuscripts, first editions, translations into every conceivable language, playbills, stills from films of his works, costumes and more. There's also a video documentary in Greek.

Briefly, **Níkos Kazantzákis** was born in Iráklion in 1883, and his early life was shadowed by the struggle against the Turks and for union with Greece. Educated in Athens and Paris, he travelled widely throughout his life working for the Greek government on more than one occasion (serving briefly as minister for education in 1945) and for UNESCO, but above all writing. He produced a vast range of works including philosophical essays, epic poetry, travel books, translations of classics (such as Dante's *Divine Comedy*) into Greek and, of course, the novels on which his fame in the West mostly rests. *Zorba the Greek* (1946) was the first and most celebrated novel, but his output remained prolific to the end of his life. Particularly relevant to Cretan travels are *Freedom or Death* (1950), set amid the struggle against the Turks, and the autobiographical *Report to Greco*, published posthumously in 1961 (Kazantzákis died in Freiburg, West Germany, in 1957 after contracting hepatitis from an unsterilized vaccination needle during a visit to China). Kazantzákis is widely accepted as the leading Greek writer of the century, and Cretans are extremely proud of him, despite the fact that most of his later life was spent abroad, that he was banned from entering Greece for long periods and was excommunicated by the Orthodox Church for his vigorously expressed doubts about Christianity; the latter gained him more recent notoriety when *The Last Temptation of Christ* was filmed by Martin Scorsese. The church was also instrumental in working behind the scenes to deny him the Nobel Prize, which he lost by one vote to Albert Camus in 1957. Plenty of people now regard his writing as overblown and pretentious, but even they admit that the best parts are where the Cretan in Kazantzákis shows through, in the tremendous gusto and vitality of books like *Zorba* and *Freedom or Death*. He himself was always conscious, and proud, of his Cretan heritage.

Arhánes and its Minoan sites

Back at the turning to Mirtiá, it's a further 2km through the vineyards on the main road to the junction where you turn right for Arhánes. It was here, at what seem a singularly unthreatening spot on a summer afternoon, that General Kreipe was kidnapped on April 26, 1944 (see p.343).

The fork leads for another 2km through Patsídhes and Káto Arhánes to the large agricultural centre of **ARHÁNES** – a town substantial enough to have a one-way traffic system. Arhánes is also served by hourly buses from Iráklion. The centre, with a small square by a restored church and a couple of large, dozy kafenía, is on the north-bound side: drive through and double back. The church has an incongruous whitewashed clock tower and a fine collection of icons; elsewhere there are Byzantine frescoes in the church of Ayía Triádha on the fringes of town and, much more importantly, at the church of **Asómatos** to the east, where the superb fourteenth-century works include a horrific *Crucifixion* and a depiction of the fall of Jericho with Joshua in full medieval armour. Before setting out, you'll need to get the key from the *Miriófiton Snack Bar* on the square, leaving a passport with them as a deposit. To get there, follow the road through the town, and then the signs east for a couple of kilometres.

Arhánes was a sizeable centre of **Minoan civilization**, and there are a number of sites roundabout. All of them are relatively recent discoveries, having been excavated in the last 25 years or so, and not all of the excavations are yet fully published. Consequently they are neither particularly famous nor especially welcoming to visitors, but many of the finds have been important. The largest of the structures is the **Palace**, in reality more likely a large villa, which lies right in the heart of the modern town, signed just off the main road. Through the chain-link fence you can see evidence of a substantial walled mansion, representing only a small part of what once stood here. Piecemeal excavation is still going on at other sites in the centre too, but much is hidden beneath more modern buildings. The museum (see below) will direct you to where these excavations can be viewed.

Archeological Museum

Arhánes has an excellent new **Archeological Museum** (8.30am–2.30pm, closed Tues; free) which displays finds from the town and the sites surrounding it. To get there follow the Vathípetro road from the main square for 100m; the museum is signed up a narrow street on the left.

The museum is superbly laid out in a single room and gives you an idea of how much more stimulating Iráklion's museum could be if the same principles were applied. Near the entrance are some well-preserved Minoan **larnakes** (clay coffins) from Foúrni (see below) dating from around 1800 BC, suggesting (because the knees needed to be drawn up to the chest to squeeze the corpses in) that the deceased would have been placed into these before the onset of rigor mortis. Case 4 has an interesting and unique **sistrum** found in the same cemetery at Foúrni. Dating from around 2000 BC (and probably borrowed from Egypt), this musical instrument was used much like a tambourine, emitting a maracas-type sound when the clay discs suspended on wooden rods were vigorously rattled; it may well be the oldest surviving musical instrument in Europe. There's a photo nearby of the famous "Harvesters Vase" in the Iráklion museum, depicting a sistrum in use.

Case 7 has fascinating finds from **Anemospília** (see below) where human sacrifice appears to have taken place in the temple there. The **dagger** found lying on the sacrificial victim is displayed here with its curious motif of a hybrid animal – resembling a deformed boar – carved on the blade. There's also a copy of the seal stone (now in Iráklion) which the priest was wearing on his left wrist as well as the terracotta feet of a wooden statue which was destroyed in a fire caused by the many oil lamps used to light the shrine. Further evidence of the fire comes from two giant pithoi, the smaller of which was deformed by the intense blaze which consumed the temple. On the top of nearby Case 19 can be seen the terracotta "horns of consecration" also found in the shrine. Case 9 displays small terracotta cups which contained ochres used to paint the frescoes on the walls in the palaces and villas, whilst an imaginative display of **pottery shards** (Case 13) evidences five thousand years of human occupation in this town: crude works of the third millennium BC are succeeded by the various Minoan periods, then Greek, Roman, Byzantine, Venetian, Turkish pieces, down to broken pots of the present. Case 16 has fragments of Minoan wall painting which underline the mastery of this medium and convey some idea of how brilliant the colours must have been when newly painted.

Foúrni

The second of the sites is **Foúrni** (daily 8.30am–3pm; free) off to the right as you enter the town (immediately before the school) and about ten minutes' walk up a ferociously rocky, steep trail. The size of Foúrni is evidence of the scale of the Minoan community that once thrived around Arhánes; what has been unearthed here is a burial ground used throughout the Minoan period, with its earliest tombs dating from around 2500 BC (before the construction of the great palaces), and the latest from the very end of the Minoan era. The structures include a number of early *thólos* tombs – round stone buildings reminiscent of beehives – each of which contained multiple burials in sarcophagi and *píthoi*. Since many simpler graves and a circle of seven Mycenaean-style shaft graves were also revealed at Foúrni, it is by far the most extensive Minoan cemetery known. Its significance was increased by some of the finds made here: most importantly, within "Thólos A", where a side chamber was found which revealed the undisturbed tomb of a woman who, judging by the jewellery and other goods buried with her, was of royal descent and perhaps a priestess. Another recent suggestion is that she was a princess buried here shortly before the final destruction of Knossós Palace. Her jewellery and rings are now on display at the Iráklion Archeological Museum, as is the skeleton of a horse apparently sacrificed in her honour.

Anemospília

As sites go, **Anemospília**, 2km northwest of Arhánes, is considerably more worthwhile than other sites in the vicinity, enlivened by a spectacular setting and a controversial story. The approach road heads north from Arhánes: coming from Iráklion you enter the one-way street and turn sharp right, back on yourself, almost straight away, just past a small chapel. Following the best of the roads, you begin to climb across the northern face of Mount Yioúhtas, winding around craggy rocks weirdly carved by the wind (Anemospília means "Caves of the Wind") until you reach the fenced site held in a steep curve of the road.

What stood here was a temple, and its interpretation has been the source of outraged controversy among Minoan scholars since its excavation at the beginning of the 1980s. The building is a simple one, consisting of three rooms connected by a north-facing portico, but its contents are not so easily described. The temple was apparently destroyed by an earthquake, which struck during a ceremony that appears to have involved **human sacrifice** – the only evidence of such a ritual found in Minoan Crete. This came as a severe shock to those who liked to portray the Minoans as the perfect peaceable society, but the evidence is hard to refute. Three skeletons were found in the western room: one had rich jewellery, indicative of a priest; another was a woman, presumably a priestess or assistant; the third was curled up on an altar-like structure, and, according to scientists, was already dead when the building collapsed and killed the others. A large bronze knife lay on top of this third skeleton. Outside the western room, another man was crushed in the corridor, apparently carrying some kind of ritual vase. These events have been dated to around 1700 BC, roughly the time of the earthquakes that destroyed the first palaces and, in the circumstances, it seems easy to believe that the priests might have resorted to desperate measures in a final attempt to appease the gods who were destroying their civilization.

The summit of Mount Yioúhtas and Vathípetro

Continuing beyond Arhánes you'll see a sign after a couple of kilometres for the summit of **Mount Yioúhtas**, up a track which is a relatively easy drive. You can also climb to the top in little over an hour from Arhánes along the same route, but it seems rather unsatisfying to do this only to discover other people rolling up on their motorbikes or in taxis. The panoramic views are the main lure, back across Iráklion especially, but also west to Psilorítis and east to Dhíkti. On the summit is a small and fairly ordinary chapel, and the trappings of the annual *Paniyíri* (festival), which is celebrated on August 15 and attracts villagers from all around. There was once a Minoan peak sanctuary too, but no significant trace of it remains; on the shoulders of the mountain, not easily accessible, are caves associated with the local Zeus cult.

The main road running beneath Mount Yioúhtas continues south toward **VATHÍPETRO**, which is well signposted along the way. Here, at last, is a site which can be examined close to: a large Minoan **villa** (Mon–Sat 8.30am–2pm; free), which once controlled the rich farmland south of Arhánes. Inside a remarkable collection of everyday items was found – equipment for making wine and oil and other tools and simple requisites of rural life. Still surrounded by a vineyard, the house was originally a substantial building of several storeys, with a courtyard enclosing a shrine, and fine large rooms – especially on the east. The basement workrooms, however, were the scene of the most interesting discoveries, agricultural equipment and a superb **wine press**, which can still be seen *in situ*; when the doors are locked, you can see something of what remains through the barred windows – which you may be forced to do anyway as the site often closes early on the whim of the guardian (if he turns up at all).

West of Iráklion

Heading west from Iráklion the modern E75 highway, cut into the cliffs, is as fast and efficient a road as you could hope to find. In simple scenic terms it's a spectacular drive, but with very little in the way of habitation – only a couple of developed beach resorts and the "birthplace of El Greco" at Fódhele until the final, flat stretch just before Réthimnon. If you go this way, the point where you join the bypass offers perhaps the best view of Zeus's profile on Mount Yioúhtas – open mouth, prominent nose and chin.

If you're in no hurry, forget the highway and try the older roads west, curling up amid stunning mountain scenery. The only specific site on these back roads is the Minoan one at Tílissos (see p.96), but they have the advantage of taking you through archetypal rural Crete, with tracks tramped solely by herds of sheep or goats, isolated chapels or farmsteads beside the road, and occasionally a village. City buses will take you as far as the *Creta Beach* hotel (see p.83), but to travel any further west you'll need either your own transport or a KTEL bus from one of the west-bound stations.

The new road

Once past the city beaches, the highway heads north, climbing into the foothills of the Psilorítis range as they plunge straight to the sea. As you ascend, keep an eye out for the immaculately crafted medieval fortress of **Paleókastro**, built into the cliff right beside the road; it's easy to miss, so completely do the crumbling fortifications blend in against the rocks. Just beyond, the road crosses a bridge over the modern village of Paleókastro, nestling in a little gully which leads down to the sea: a beautiful setting, with wealthy suburban homes and restaurants popular for weekend outings.

Ayía Pelayía

As you round the headland, **AYÍA PELAYÍA** is laid out below, a sprinkling of white cubes around a deep blue bay, unbelievably inviting from this distance. Closer to, the attraction is slightly diminished: continuing development is rapidly outpacing the capacity of the narrow, taverna-lined beach, and is beginning to take its toll on the village. Meanwhile, the water is clear and calm, and the swimming excellent; water-skiing, parasailing and motorboats are all available if you're prepared to pay. There's a superb view, too, of all the ships which pass the end of the bay as they steam into Iráklion – spectacular at night when the brightly lit ferries pass. Although the beach can get very crowded with day-trippers from Iráklion at weekends, the resort clings to its exclusivity in the shape of two of the best-looking luxury hotels on the island – the *Capsis Beach* (☎081/811-112, fax 811-076; ⑦), on a promontory overlooking the town, and the *Peninsula* (☎081/811-313, fax 811-219; ⑥), over on the headland beyond, which is almost a village in itself. If you feel in need of a little more space, you can always head for the nearby beach to the east – **Ligaria**, which is much more welcoming with three tavernas fronting the beach but has fewer facilities.

Buses run between the *Capsis Beach* hotel and the *Astoria* in Platía Eleftherías, Iráklion, six times a day. If you take a long-distance bus bound for Réthimnon or Haniá, you face a steep three-kilometre descent from the main road where you'll be dropped – and it's even worse walking back up.

Food is an easier proposition: if you tire of or can't afford the beachfront restaurants, head into the village where there are some more basic takeaways and small supermarkets for the makings of a picnic on the beach. **Accommodation** tends to consist of hotels and studios or apartments with cooking facilities, rather than straightforward rooms. Out of season, these can be excellent value if you're prepared to bargain hard, but through the summer they're mostly block-booked. If you do want to stay, it's a question of wandering around asking at every door with a sign – the owners will usually know who (if anyone) has a room free. Otherwise, try one of the travel bureaux, such as Pagasimo (☎081/811-042, fax 811-424), just past the Vasilis Supermarket behind the beach at the western end. For late-night **entertainment**, there are plenty of bars lining the beach, including loud disco bars such as *Banana* and more subdued cocktail bars, like the nautically themed *Bloom*. Up the hill heading out of town, *Tam-Tam* and *Manu Paradise* are other popular and noisy nightspots.

Fódhele

Turning **inland from the main road** opposite Ayía Pelayía, an old stretch of paved road runs from Ahládha to Fódhele, connected by rutted, unpaved sections with other old roads inland. Ahládha's spectacular hilltop setting serves to detract from the lack of attractions in the village itself. If you're simply heading for Fódhele, you can get there more efficiently by taking the later turnoff about 3km west, but if you can afford the time to travel at a more leisurely pace, the old route is a great deal more diverting.

FÓDHELE is firmly established on the tourist circuit as the birthplace of El Greco, although there's virtually no hard evidence to substantiate this and most academic opinion now believes that he was born in Iráklion. The excursion is a pleasant one, in any case: Fódhele lies in a richly fertile valley, surrounded by orange and lime groves. On the far side of the river as you drive up are a couple of small Byzantine chapels, and there's an ancient church in the village. Despite the craft and souvenir shops that line the main street, selling local embroidery, and the café tables ranged along the river bank, Fódhele most of the time is almost preternaturally sleepy – you can sit at one of these shady tables for half an hour before anyone emerges to take your order, and wait as long again before the order has any effect. Meanwhile, take a few minutes to study the plaque in the village square: made of stone from Toledo (where Domenico Theotokópoulos settled to produce the bulk of his most famous works and earn the name El Greco), it was presented to Fódhele in 1934 by the University of Valladolid – an authentication of the locale's claim to fame, which must be responsible in some measure for its current prosperity, whatever the scholars may say.

To get to **El Greco's House** you cross the bridge over the river, pass the church (which has copies of many of his works) and follow the clearly signed road (right) which heads northwards out of town among orange groves, fragrant with blossom at Easter. Now heavily restored, the building does not look old enough to have been around when the painter was, but having got this far you might as well see it – although the house itself and its spurious display relating the artist's life is rarely open. A better reason for making the journey is the charming, mainly fourteenth-century **church of the Panayía** (Mon-Fri 9.30am–5pm; free), sited opposite the path leading to the house. This exquisite drum-domed church was built over an eighth-century basilica – the central nave and the interesting baptismal font in the floor beside the church (deep enough for total immersion) date from the earlier building. Recently restored, the thirteenth and fourteenth-century frescoes (partially visible through windows in the apse when the church is closed) were uncovered beneath later works; the jarring glass windows in the dome spoil the overall impression. Beneath the orange groves surrounding the church are the remains of the medieval village it once served.

A couple of **buses** a day run direct to Fódhele from the Haniá Gate terminal in Iráklion, but the timings aren't really conducive to a quick visit. On the other hand, it's not too far to walk back to the junction, 3km away, so you could catch the direct afternoon bus up (2.30pm; Mon–Fri only) and then try flagging down a long-distance bus on the main road. There are also occasional tours from Iráklion.

The old roads

Ignoring the benefits of the modern coastal road and taking the slower, mountain route you run at first through villages, like Gazí, which are mostly industrial and lacklustre. Once under the raised highway, however, you immediately start to climb into the hills. Almost straightaway there's a right turn signed to Rodhiá, a sizeable village looking back down over the city. This is the quieter way to Ayía Pelayía and Fódhele, but to get there you face more than 9km of atrocious road between here and Ahládha.

From Rodhiá a signed detour climbs 5km northwest into the hills to the famous **convent of Savathianá** (8am–1pm & 4–7pm), set in a rock cleft and surrounded by lofty cypresses. Founded in the Venetian period, the settlement has been transformed by its diligent nuns into a flower-festooned oasis; a quince orchard behind the convent is the source of homemade jams sold to visitors. The convent gained further celebrity in 1991 when an eighteenth-century icon entitled *Lord Thou Art Great*, and identical to the one at Tóplou (see p.172), was discovered; both were painted by Ioánnis Kornáros.

As you apparently start to leave development behind, you promptly come across it again in the form of **Arolíthos**, a brand new "traditional village", which represents a surprisingly successful attempt to create the atmosphere of traditional Crete in a tourist development. There are craftsmen – potters, weavers, artists, a smith – at work using traditional methods, stores where you can buy their products, a restaurant with wood-fired ovens, and events such as Greek dancing evenings. There are also some upmarket rooms, though no very good reason to stay. For the moment the place seems half empty except when a bus tour calls by, but it's worth a look as you pass.

A little way beyond Arolíthos, the way divides: the road that used to be the main route from Iráklion to Réthimnon is the one which runs through **MÁRATHOS**, 9km beyond Arolíthos. Famous for the honey that seems to be on sale at every house, Márathos is an attractive place with a couple of kafenía if you feel like breaking the journey (this road runs through very few other villages of any size). Not far beyond the village, it's possible to cut down by unpaved but reasonable track to Fódhele (see above).

These days more people travel by the furthest inland of the roads, the one that climbs up through Tílissos and on via **Anóyia** (see p.218). It's a pleasant ride through the Malevísi, a district of fertile valleys filled with olive groves and vineyards renowned from Venetian times for the strong sweet **Malmsey wine** much favoured in western Europe.

Tílissos

The big attraction of the first part of the trip along this inland route is **TÍLISSOS**, a name famous in the annals of Minoan archeology as among the first sites to be excavated. Local archeologist Hatzidákis, working at the beginning of the century, revealed evidence of occupation from the early Pre-Palace period (c.2000 BC), but interest focuses primarily on three large villas (known as Houses A, B and C) from the New Palace era, contemporary with the great periods at Knossós, Festós and elsewhere. They were probably not as isolated in the country-house sense as they seem today, but may well have been part of a thriving community, or even a staging-post on the route west towards as yet undiscovered centres there. The existence of a rather simpler villa at Sklavókambos, on the road halfway from here to Anóyia, may lend weight to this latter theory. The site shared in the destruction of the palaces about 1450 BC, but new buildings then arose, among which was the cistern in the northeast corner. Following the arrival of the Dorians Tílissos developed into a Greek city of the Classical period, issuing its own coinage. This later construction tends to makes it a bit harder to get a clear picture of what's there.

The archeological **site** (daily 8.30am–3pm; 500dr, students free) is signed to the left at the foot of the main street of the modern village. While it's not always the easiest of sites to interpret, it is a lovely place to wander round: it gets few

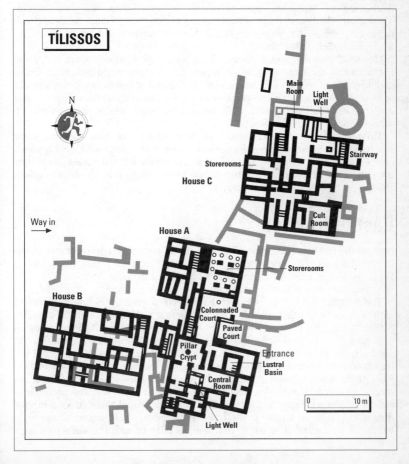

visitors, has pine trees for shade, and boasts some evocative remains including staircases and walls still standing almost 2m tall – alongside some unsubtle restoration. Immediately beyond the fence, vineyards and rich agricultural land suggest a seductive, but probably illusory, continuity of rural life.

Houses A and C are of extremely fine construction and design (C is the more impressive), while little remains of House B apart from its ground plan, although it does contain some of the oldest relics here. A building of finely dressed ashlar stone, **House A** has a **colonnaded court** at its heart with a window lighting the staircase to the west side of this. In **storerooms** on the north side, some of the large reconstructed *píthoi* can be seen with holes near their bases for tapping the contents (probably oil); a number of Linear A tablets also came to light in this area. In the south wing, the main rooms open onto a light well with the **central room** having a **lustral basin** – in this case more of a sunken bath – just off it. A stand for a double axe, similar to finds from Knossós, was found in the **pillar crypt**, along with the three enormous bronze cauldrons (now in the Iráklion Archeological Museum) that originally prompted the site's excavation. Throughout the house, fragments of painted stucco were found, leading archeologists to postulate the existence of a luxurious second storey to this dwelling, which had fallen in over time.

House C contains a **cult room** with a central pillar, **storerooms** and, at its northern end, the living area, where a paved main room would have been illuminated by a light well on its eastern side. At the end of one of many corridors (a Minoan speciality), a staircase would once have led to an upper floor. There is also evidence of a drainage system, while outside the house, beside the **cistern**, is a **stone altar** from the Classical period.

Tílissos village, a pleasant enough place, provides food, drink and even a few **rooms** for its visitors. For a delicious Cretan omelette, made with local *tirozoúli* cheese, stop at the *Estiatorio Akropolis*, 150m up on the left of the main street after the site turnoff. **Buses** run five times daily to the village from the Haniá Gate in Iráklion, and continue towards Anóyia.

East of Iráklion

Beyond the city beach at Amnísos there's almost continuous development all the way to Mália, as what little remains of the coastal landscape is torn apart to build yet more hotels, apartments and beach complexes flanking the main E75 highway; you'll need to turn off to reach the places below.

The first distinct centre is **HÁNI KOKKÍNI**, a grubbily nondescript resort with a long but rather pebbly beach. There's a **Minoan villa** (Tues–Sun 8.30am–3pm; free) here – known as Nírou Háni – which must have been beautifully sited when it stood alone. With the road immediately outside and traffic roaring by, however, it is harder to appreciate. Excavations of the villa revealed the foundations of a two-storey building dating from the New Palace period (c.1550 BC). All the usual Minoan architectural features are present – light well, storage rooms, connecting corridors, decorative paving – and the site was particularly rich in religious paraphernalia, including tripod altars and some striking bronze double axes now on display in the Iráklion Archeological Museum. These finds led the excavators to name it the "House of the High Priest". The site is now open on a regular basis but the guardian is often available after this – enquire at the nearby cafés if he's not immediately apparent; the guardian also holds the key to the Cave of Eileíthyia (see p.83).

Through **GOÚRNES** and **GOÚVES** things get even worse. At Goúrnes a giant US air force base has now closed; the Greek government have not yet decided what to do with the base, and it may be their own planes that buzz the coast in the future. The beach stretches unbroken for several kilometres, but for the most part it's a narrow strip of dirty pebbles, windy and exposed. The picture is completed by giant radar dishes overlooking it all from the hills. At Káto Goúves, just east of Fínikas, there's a campsite, *Camping Creta* (☎0897/41-400) which shares a boundary with the base; some shelter is provided by the small tamarisk trees. Apart from the beach there is little here to warrant a special stop, although it is the nearest site to Iráklion.

About 6km inland by car from the junction with the E75 up the turning to Goúves proper, is the **Skotinó Cave**, one of the largest and most spectacular on the island. You can walk here from Goúves along 3km of unsigned tracks (marked on the *Harms Verlag* map) if you're feeling adventurous. It's a pleasant walk of some 45 minutes from the coast road, passing through Goúves village, which makes an encouragingly complete contrast to the coastal strip. You can stop here for refreshment – there are a couple of decent tavernas – and to check directions before continuing to the signed turnoff, on the right, for Skotinó (which means "dark"). Driving, head through Goúves, then take a right turn to Skotinó village. About a kilometre out of the village on the main road heading south, take a road (signed "Cave of Ayía Paraskeví") downhill on your right after a hairpin bend marked by a taverna; the road eventually degenerates into a track, and the cave entrance is a further kilometre below a whitewashed chapel which you will see on the horizon. Divided into four levels with an awesomely huge main chamber, the cave is 160m deep. It was first investigated by Evans and more scientifically explored in the 1960s by French and Greek archeologists. A considerable number of bronze and ceramic votive offerings were found here (the earliest dating back to early Minoan times), suggesting that this was an important sacred shrine. The cave remained in use well into the Greek and Roman eras, when the fertility goddess Artemis was worshipped in what is thought to have been a substitution for an earlier Minoan female fertility deity, possibly Brytomartis. In the chapel above, *taxímata* (ex votos) left by pilgrims continue a tradition of supplication to the (now Christian) deity which has persisted on this same spot for well over four thousand years.

Hersónisos (Límin Hersonísou)

Continuing east along the main coast road, the turning for the direct route up to the **Lasíthi Plateau** is signed 3km beyond the bridge over the Apsolémis winter torrent. Shortly after this, you roll into the first of the really big resorts, **HERSÓNISOS** (or, more correctly, Límin Hersonísou; Hersónisos is the village in the hills just behind). A brash, sprawling and rather seedy resort, Hersónisos is replete with all the trappings of mass tourism. If you're looking for tranquillity and Cretan tradition, forget it; this is the world of concrete high-rise hotels, video bars, English breakfasts and Eurodisco nightlife. That said, there are enough restaurants to keep prices down, and plenty of sand to escape the crowds – the one thing you won't find in high season is a room.

Along the modern seafront, a solid line of restaurants and bars is broken only by the occasional souvenir shop: in their midst you'll find a small pyramidal fountain with broken mosaics of fishing scenes. This dates from Roman times and is the only real relic of the ancient town of **Chersonesos**, a thriving port from Classical Greek through to Byzantine times, handling trade from Lyttos, which once lay inland near Kastélli. Around the headland above the harbour and in odd places along the seafront you can see remains of Roman harbour installations, mostly submerged, and on the headland above the more modern church is the fenced and locked site where an early Christian basilica (probably the seat of a bishop) has been excavated. But in the main the new port covers the old.

There is little more of historic interest to keep you occupied in the town, although thé newly opened **Lychnostatis Open-air Museum** of folk culture (Tues–Sun 9.30am–2pm; 1000dr), just past the campsite on the eastern fringes of the resort, is worth a visit, particularly if you haven't had a chance to see the "real thing" inland. A reasonably authentic-looking recreation of a traditional Cretan village in a pleasant location next to the sea, the lifestyle on display within the museum couldn't be more different to the resort centre. There are orchards and herb gardens, live displays of local crafts such as ceramics and weaving, as well as collections of lace, embroidery and traditional costumes within the main house. Concerts of traditional music and dance are frequent and they occasionally mount more elaborate "dance spectaculars" in the evening.

A short distance inland are the three **hill villages** of Koutoulafári, Piskopianó and "Old" Hersónisos – worth searching out for accommodation and for their good selection of tavernas. Despite restoration and their increasing use by tour operators, the villages still maintain a reasonably traditional atmosphere. Piskopianó has a **Museum of Rural Life** (10am–1pm & 4–8.30pm; 500dr), situated in one of the narrow streets, which makes for a welcome break from the hustle and bustle of Hersónisos below. The olive press and the *raki* still in the courtyard outside act as reminders to search out the village kafeníon afterwards.

If you begin to get withdrawal symptoms from a lack of contact with water, try the **Star Water Park** on the beach to the eastern side of the resort; admission is free, but you pay to indulge in the range of water sports on offer, which includes scuba-diving lessons – also available at Scubakreta at the *Nana Beach Hotel* (☎0897/22-950).

Practicalities

Every thirty minutes from 6.30am to 10am **buses** run between Hersónisos and both Iráklion and Áyios Nikoláos. For shorter hops around town, **taxis** gather next to the *Aria* disco and the *Creta Maris* hotel, or can be called on ☎0897/22-098. The **OTE** office (Mon–Sat 7.30am–10pm; Sun 9am–2pm & 5–10pm) is just north of Elefthériou Venizélou (the main road through town) on the road leading up to Piskopianó, while the clearly signed post office (Mon–Fri 7.30am–8pm; Sat 7.30am–2pm) is nearby on Digeni Akriti. There is a very helpful **tourist office** which is usually housed on Giaboúdaki down towards the harbour, but at the time of writing has been temporarily evicted to a small kiosk next to the news-stand in front of the church on Elefthériou Venizélou. This makes a good starting-point for information, and can offer guidance in the search for somewhere to stay.

ACCOMMODATION

Although you should have little problem finding somewhere to stay outside the peak season of July and August, much **accommodation** is allocated to package-tour operators and what remains is not cheap – you are unlikely to find anything less than 6000–8000dr per night for a double room. Your best option is to call in at the **tourist office** (see opposite), or at one of the travel companies on the main street, such as Zakros Tours (☎0897/22-317). A word of warning: hotels in the centre are subject to a fair amount of noise; for more peaceful surroundings, head inland or towards Sarandáris. If you don't mind a short taxi-ride or twenty-minute walk, the pleasant hill villages of Piskopianó or Koutouloufári are useful options – as is "Old" Hersónisos, although this is not within walking distance. There are few pensions in the villages, but plenty of private rooms, studios and apartments, many of the latter taken up by the tour operators – try asking on spec or at travel agencies on the coast. A typical place in this category is *Elgoni Apartments* (☎0897/21-237; ③), high above Piskopianó with great views over the coast and a pool. There are also simple rooms (②) above Supermarket Anna in the village centre below.

Caravan Camping (☎0897/22-025), by the beach at the eastern end of Hersónisos, has ample places to camp in the shade, although the pitches can be extremely close to one another. If you crave more comfort, reed-roofed bungalows (①) with sea views are also available. Just outside the western end of town is *Camping Hersónisos* (☎0897/22-902).

Creta Maris (☎0897/22-115, fax 22-130). One of the ritziest places in the resort, with a good range of facilities. ⑤.

Crystal, Giaboúdaki (☎0897/22-546). Reasonable, centrally located hotel. ③.

Nancy, Ayía Paraskevís (☎0897/22-212). Decent hotel, also in the town centre. ④.

Selena Apartments, Maragáki 13 (☎0897/22-412). Clean, family-run establishment on a quiet street. ②.

Virginia, Machis Critis 18 (☎ & fax 0897/22-455). Eclectic little place above an ouzerí at the quieter end of the port road. Basic but clean. ③.

Youth Hostel, Elefthériou Venizélou (☎0897/23-674). Situated across from *Caravan Camping*, this hostel is well run by a helpful and friendly American-born Greek; meals and laundry facilities available. ①.

EATING

Despite the abundance of **places to eat**, there are few worth recommending in the resort itself, with the vast majority being merely average; the tavernas down on the harbour front are generally best avoided. The hill villages have the greatest selection and a more relaxed atmosphere – particularly Koutoulafári where, among others, there's a nameless, unpretentious family-run taverna with a small garden courtyard in the centre of the village near *Koutoulafari Apartments*. Restaurants also cluster around the main square of "Old" Hersónisos, while Piskopianó has a good kafenío and a number of tavernas.

Chicken Georges, 2km out, on the road to Lasíthi. Worth visiting for tasty and cheap chicken, although it can be rather quiet on some nights, presumably because of the extra distance involved.

Copper Kettle, Elefthériou Venizélou. Take your pick from a fairly standard international menu.

Taverna Emmanuel, central square of Koutoulafári. Pleasant and popular with reasonably authentic cooking including lamb and potatoes baked in a traditional clay oven.

Fegari Taverna, on the Piskopianó road near the junction to Koutoulafári. Friendly taverna serving good Greek food at reasonable prices. Entertainment is provided by the steady stream of clubbers heading down the hill to the bars and nightclubs of Hersónisos.

Kavouri, Arhéou Théatro. A good but pricey traditional taverna, whose decor boasts a diverting mural of inebriated crab, octopus and other seafood; the house speciality is lamb with garlic and lemon wrapped in paper.

Pithari, in the central square of Koutoulafári. Popular, but a little on the expensive side.

Tria Adelphi, just off the square in "Old" Hersónisos. This stands out as a more authentic taverna among the mass of more touristy places in the vicinity.

NIGHTLIFE

Hersónisos is renowned for its **nightlife** and there's certainly no shortage of it. A night's partying kicks off around the bars ringing the harbour, which is packed with strollers and the overspill from countless noisy bars from 10pm through to the early hours. Later on, the larger disco-pubs and clubs in the streets leading up to and along Elefthériou Venizélou are the places to be seen. If you fancy a quiet drink, you've come to the wrong resort, but you could seek refuge at the open-air cinema attached to the *Creta Maris* hotel, or try the cocktails at the Hawaii-style *Kahlua Beach Bar*, at the east end of the port road. Amateurish, sing and dance-along Cretan evenings are held in the *Dorian Garden Restaurant* in Elefthériou Venizélou, but for something closer to the real thing enquire about the frequent performances at the **Lychnostatis Open-air Museum** (see p.100). Travel agencies also run evening trips to tourist-orientated "cultural" evenings in the inland villages such as Kósari and Anópoli where noted dancers and musicians often appear.

Aria, on the main road to the west of town. Perennially popular glass-fronted disco – reputedly the biggest on Crete.

Hard Rock Café, at the east end of Elefthériou Venizélou. Live music daily.

La Luna Elefthériou Venizélou. A lively venue, with up-to-date music.

Legend. Smaller, more intimate upmarket club at the east end of town.

New York, at the entrance to the harbour. This beach bar and pleasant breakfast venue metamorphoses into deafening disco-pub by night.

Pirates. Dancing by the beach at the east end of town.

Stalídha

STALÍDHA is something of a Cinderella, sandwiched in between the two louder, brasher and, some would say, uglier sisters of Mália and Hersónisos. This rapidly expanding beach resort can offer the best of both worlds: a friendlier and more relaxed setting, a better beach with the usual array of water sports, and easy access to its two livelier neighbours. Don't be misled, though – Stalídha itself is not exactly quiet and undeveloped.

Finding **accommodation** can be difficult as most rooms are block-booked by package companies. Out of season, however, you may well be able to negotiate a very reasonable price for a studio or apartment complete with pool; ask at the central travel agencies first as they will know what's available, usually in category ③–④ of our accommodation scale. **Eating** is less likely to be a problem, but don't expect anything particularly special. *Maria's* and the *Hellas Taverna* are both at the western end of town, an area which comes closest to feeling like a resort centre. The **post office** (Mon–Sat 9am–1pm) is also here, and there are a couple of **banks** along the main beach road. The **nightlife** scene in Stalídha is low-key – compared to its neighbours, anyway. There are a few discos, including *Bells* on the main coast road, and *Rhythm* on the beach, while *Sea Wolf Cocktail Bar* and *Akti Bar*, near each other along the beach, play music to accompany your drink.

Mália

Large enough to be a substantial town in its own right, **MÁLIA** is undeniably commercial, and its beach, long and sandy as it is, becomes grotesquely crowded at times. If you're prepared to enter into the holiday spirit, however – party all night and sleep all day – it can be very enjoyable. And, of course, there's a Minoan palace just down the road.

The town consists of two distinct parts, fanning out to the north and south of a T-junction where the main **bus** from Iráklion or Áyios Nikólaos drops you. The more raucous side of town lies along the **beach road**, which snakes for a good kilometre towards the sea. Here you'll find supermarkets, souvenir shops, tour agents, cafés, restaurants, video bars and nightclubs. To walk the length of this will take you about fifteen minutes – longer if you allow yourself to be enticed by the sales patter along the way. At the end there's a car park, a small harbour and a couple of beaches to the west. The **main beach**, however, stretches away to the east; in summer, you'll need to walk through the mass of bodies for about another fifteen minutes before you find somewhere to spread out. At this eastern end of the beach is a small church backed by dunes and patches of marshy ground alive with frogs. For entertainment, you can swim out to a tiny **offshore islet**: the rocks here are sharp for barefoot exploring, but your efforts will be rewarded by a (perpetually locked) white chapel and rockpools alive with crabs, shellfish and sea urchins – on the islet's seaward side. To find a trace of real Cretan life in all of this, turn inland to the south of the main road. Here in the **old town**, with its narrow, twisting alleyways and whitewashed walls, old Mália determinedly clings to what remains of its self-respect.

In terms of both action and accommodation, Mália has a great deal more to offer than any of its rivals along the north coast, and practical matters are easily attended to, with a **post office** (Mon–Sat 7.30am–2pm), a couple of banks and an **OTE** right in the centre; good exchange rates can also be had at the three-storey tourist emporium called Mália Maria Market, a little way down the beach road. The best place for **bike rental** is Moto Euro Tours (☎0897/31-636), back along the main road going west, where the owner, Pit Frankoulis, will tell you of his lifetime love affair with the motorcycle if you give him the chance. Or **rent a car** from Athena (☎0897/31-705) nearby, who do special offers. And, if you're shopping for food, look out for bananas: chances are they'll have been grown under plastic sheets in the fields around the town.

Accommodation

As in Hersónisos, many rooms are taken up by the package industry and in the peak season finding somewhere to stay is not always easy, although, unlike its near neighbours, Mália has a good range of small hotels and pensions in addition to apartment blocks and large resort hotels. Your best bet if you want any sleep is to try one of the numerous **rooms** signed in the old town; *Esperia* (☎0897/31-086; ③) is a good bet. Most of the cheaper hotels around the T-junction are invariably full. Backtracking from here along the main Iráklion road there are a number of reasonably priced **pensions** on the left, including *Argo* (☎0897/31-636; ④). A central place if you're determined to be in the thick of the action is *Kostas* (☎0897/31-485; ③), a family-run pension incongruously located behind the mini-golf at the end of the beach road.

To save time, you could call in at one of the travel and tourist companies, such as Foreign Office on the main road, which, in addition to giving information on bus excursions and car rental, can also give details of accommodation availability.

Restaurants

Restaurant owners jostle for your custom at every step in Mália, especially along the beach road; none is particularly good, but they know their clientele – *moussaká* and pie and chips abound. Incidentally, the beach road also has a reputation for poisonous *souvláki*. One way of avoiding this would be British-style fish and chips, authentically wrapped in newspaper, from the *Electra Café* at the bottom of the beach road near the sea; they're at least as good as the real thing – and cheaper.

But the best places to eat are in the **old town**, to the inland side of the main road: wander up to Platía Áyios Dhimítri, a pleasant square beside the church. Here you can choose from a variety of welcoming tavernas in and around the square including *Yiannis, Kalimera, Kalesma, Petros* – and the *Romantic Raphael Restaurant* which proudly proclaims that all their dishes (including Thai, Chinese and Indonesian) are prepared in butter and not oil. For an aperitif, try the excellent local wine from the barrel at *Ouzeri Kapilla*, facing the church.

Nightlife

The beach road is transformed during the hours either side of midnight when the profusion of bars, discos and **clubs** erupt into a pulsating cacophony. The aptly named *Zoo* is a popular new club where, after midnight, great excitement is generated as one of the internal walls parts to reveal an even larger dance area. The club's newest (and dubious) attraction is a body-piercing studio which opens at 2am, presumably when the clients are sufficiently anaesthetized by alcohol. Other popular venues nearby include *Corkers, Takis* and *Highway*, and of course plenty of "English pubs" with names like *Newcastle* and *Camden*. Unfortunately, good nights out are frequently spoilt by gangs of drunken youths pouring out of the bars: a great battle a few years back between hundreds of drunken English, German and Dutch visitors resulted in deaths and mayhem. To avoid the seafront brawls, stick to the old village.

If all you want is a **quiet beer**, try *Bar Epsilon* on the main road near the bus stop, or the *Stone House* café-bar in the old town. Both also have good live music some nights, but of a gentler variety with acoustic guitars.

For *après*-club refuelling, *Kipouli Bar* is the place: situated in the old town, it proudly advertises the fact that it opens from "5.50 o'clock in the morning", and is instantly recognizable from the spectacle of a red plastic panda, halfway up a tree, clutching a case of Heineken while astride a brightly painted and fairy-lit mountain bike – only in Mália.

The Palace of Mália

The **Palace of Mália** (Tues–Sun 8.30am–3pm; 800dr, Sun & students free) lies forty minutes' walk east of the town, just off the main road. Any bus bound for Áyios Nikólaos will stop; or rent a bicycle – it's a pleasant, flat ride. Much less imposing than either Knossós or Festós, Mália in some ways surpasses both. For a start, it's a great deal emptier and you can wander among the remains in relative peace. And while no reconstruction has been attempted, the palace was never reoccupied after its second destruction, so the ground plan is virtually intact.

It's a great deal easier to comprehend than Knossós, and if you've already seen the reconstructions there it's easy to envisage this seaside palace in its days of glory. Basking on the rich agricultural plain between the Lasíthi mountains and the sea, it retains a real flavour of an ancient civilization with a taste for the good life.

From this site came the famous gold pendant of two bees which can be seen in the Iráklion Archeological Museum or on any local postcard stand. It was allegedly part of a horde which was plundered and the rest of which now resides (as the "Aegina Treasure") in the British Museum. The beautiful leopard's-head axe, also in the museum at Iráklion, was another of the treasures found at Mália. Of the ruins, virtually nothing stands above ground level apart from the giant *píthoi* which have been pieced together and left about the palace like sentinels: the palace itself is worn and brown, blending almost imperceptibly into the landscape. With the mountains behind, it's a thoroughly atmospheric setting.

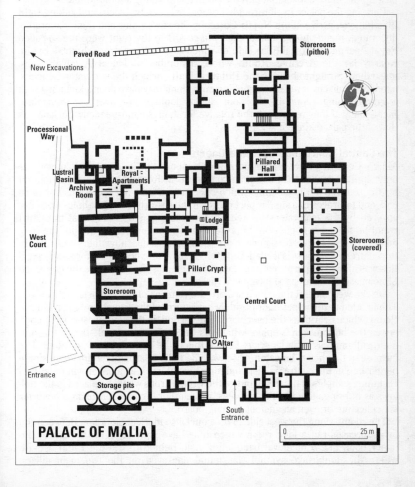

PALACE OF MÁLIA

First discovered by Joseph Hatzidákis early this century, in 1922 the site passed to the French School at Athens. As at Knossós and Festós, there was an earlier palace dating from around 1900 BC, which was devastated by the earthquake of about 1700 BC. The remains you see today are those of the palace built to replace this, and which functioned until about 1450 BC, when it was destroyed for the last time in the wave of violence which swept across the island (see p.336).

Entering the palace: the West Court

You enter the site through the **West Court**. As at the other palaces, there are raised pathways leading across this, with the main one heading south towards the area of the eight circular **storage pits**. These probably held grain – the pillars in the middle of some would once have supported a protective roof. In the other direction the raised walkway takes you to the building's north side, where you can pick up the more substantial paved road that apparently led to the sea.

Entering the palace itself through a "door" between two rocks and jinking right then left, you arrive in the **North Court** by the storerooms and their elaborately decorated, much-photographed giant *píthoi*. Off to the right were the so-called Royal Apartments, on the far side of which is a well-preserved **lustral basin**. Nearby lay the **Archive Room** where a number of Linear A tablets were unearthed. Straight ahead is the **Pillared Hall** – which the excavators, encouraged by the discovery of some cooking pots, think may have been a kitchen – with a grand dining room on the floor above, looking out over the courtyard. Incidentally, if they're correct, the relative location is almost exactly the same as that of the palace kitchen at Zákros.

The Central Court and Royal Apartments

Mália's **Central Court**, a long, narrow area, about 48m in length by 22m wide, is only slightly smaller than the main courtyards at Knossós and Festós. Look out for the remains of the columns which once supported a portico at this northern end, and for traces of a similar portico down the eastern side. Post-holes were discovered by the excavators between these columns, suggesting that the court could be fenced in – possibly to protect the spectators during the bull-jumping games. Behind the eastern portico are more storerooms, now under a canopy. In the centre of the court is a shallow pit which may have been used for sacrifices; if this was indeed its purpose then, along with Anemospília, these are the only such Minoan sacrificial areas to have been discovered.

On the west side of the courtyard are the remains of two important stairways. The first led to the upper floor beside what is termed the **Royal Lodge** or Throne Room, which overlooks the courtyard. The second, in the southwest corner, comprises the bottom four steps of what was the main ceremonial stair to the first floor, still impressive in its scale. Beside this is the curious *kernos*, or **altar**. The purpose of this heavy limestone disc, with 34 hollows around its rim and a single bigger one in the centre, is disputed: one theory has it as an altar where, at harvest-time, samples of the first fruits of the Cretan crops would be placed in the hollows as offerings to a fertility goddess, while other theories have it as a point for tax collecting or even an ancient gaming board.

The rooms along the west side of the court also merit exploration. Between the two staircases ran a long room which may have gone straight through to the upper floor, like a medieval banqueting hall. Behind this is the **Pillar Crypt**, where the double-axe symbol was found engraved on the two main pillars.

Behind that runs yet another corridor of **storerooms**; only accessible through areas which had some royal or religious significance, these would doubtless have been depositories for things of value – the most secure storage at the palace.

New discoveries

The excavations at Mália are by no means complete. Inside and beyond the fenced site to the north and west, digs are still going on, as an apparently sizeable town comes slowly to light. Beneath a canopy to the west of the northern end of the palace lies the **Hypostyle Hall**. This building consists of a number of storerooms and two interconnected halls of uncertain function. Benches run round three sides of the halls, leading some to speculate that this was some form of council chamber. New excavations west of here again have revealed another large section of the town now protected by a canopy. Due to open in 1998, a new approach will operate here as visitors will not be allowed to walk among the ruins of the town but will view it from a walkway suspended above. Interesting new **dwellings** and **streets** have been unearthed, some up to roof level which give a clearer idea of the considerable scale of the complex urban community that surrounded the palace. Five hundred metres to the north, close to the sea, is the *Chrysolakkos* or **Golden Pit**, which appears to have been a large, multichambered mausoleum dating from the Old Palace period. Its elaborate construction suggests a royal burial-place, as does the wealth of grave goods discovered here, among them the gold honeybee pendant (see p.105).

Back to town – the beach

Leaving the site and turning immediately right, you can follow a road west to a lovely stretch of clean **sand** which, if no longer the peaceful escape from Mália it used to be, is still a welcome place to bathe after a tour of the ruins. It was also a fine place to camp out, but the authorities may change their attitude to this as the strand begins to attract more mainstream tourists. The solitary makeshift **taverna** at the back of the beach serves decent fresh fish, though can be a little pricey considering the rather basic facilities. **Moving on**, you can easily walk back along the shore to Mália itself, or to the main road where buses pass every thirty minutes – either back to Iráklion or on towards Áyios Nikólaos.

Inland: the Pedhiádha

The hinterland east of Iráklion and south of Hersónisos consists mainly of hilly farm country, with large, widely scattered villages. Known as the Pedhiádha, this region is quietly prosperous but sees few visitors. Indeed if you're reliant on public transport, there's little opportunity to take in a great deal: most villages see just their daily market bus. But with your own transport, it makes for enjoyably aimless touring, and certainly the inland roads are far more attractive than the coastal one.

Kastélli and the frescoed churches

The area's chief village, **KASTÉLLI**, or Kastélli Pedhiádhos, is a pleasant place to pull over for a while, and perhaps even to stopover if you've an interest in seeking out some of the many nearby churches and ruins scattered. Chiefly an agricultural centre whose prosperity derives from the olive groves and vineyards spread across the surrounding hills, it has a number of tavernas and kafenía around the crossroads in the centre of town. There are even some comfortable modern **rooms**, the best of which – with bath and TV – are to be had at the newly opened and friendly *Hotel Kalliopi* (☎0891/32-685; ③), close to the centre where the bus drops you, which also has its own restaurant. Cheaper alternatives are *Taverna Lyttos* (☎0891/31-118; ②), opposite the bus stop, which does tasty *souvláki*, and *Rooms Veronica* (②), above a bar on the road which leads out to the east. Excitements, however, are few. The main attraction is the countryside itself, with its winding lanes traced by elderly oak and plane trees, and the many smaller satellite villages, often with frescoed medieval **churches**. As you drive, look out for signs to such churches, which are usually worth seeking out simply for the journey off the main routes, even if very often you can find no one to let you in.

One of the more famous is the fifteenth-century **Isódhia Theótokon**, with fine Byzantine frescoes, near the village of Sklaverohóri just a couple of kilometres west of Kastélli. The key is available from the house with a vine trellis about 50m before the church on the right. Six kilometres further west again, and down a side road beyond Apostolí, the **Moní Angaráthou** is another pleasant location. Although the monastery's church dates from the last century, the surrounding buildings are mainly sixteenth-century and include a picturesque white-walled courtyard with palms, orange trees and cypresses. Another church is **Áyios Yeóryios** at Ksidhás (confusingly also known as Lyttos), about 3km east of Kastélli, which has frescoes dated by an inscription to 1321.

Ancient Lyttos, Áyios Pandeleímon and potteries

Beyond Ksidhás the road climbs for 2km to the site of ancient **Lyttos**, a prominent city of Dorian Crete and mentioned by Homer as leading the Cretan contingent in the Trojan war. The ruins are located between the two small whitewashed chapels of Tímios Stavrós and Áyios Yeóryios, which serve as useful landmarks as you approach. Occupying a magnificent position in the foothills of the Dhíkti range, during the centuries prior to the Roman conquest, Lyttos was one of the most powerful city-states of Classical Greece and the bitter enemy of Górtys, Ierápytna (modern Ierápetra) and especially Knossós. When Lyttos engaged these three in a war for control of the island (221–219 BC), it overreached itself; whilst its army was launching an attack on Ierápetra, Knossós seized the opportunity to destroy the unguarded city, leaving it in ruins and taking its women and children into captivity. The historian Polybius vividly describes how on their return to Lyttos the troops broke down in tears at the sight, refused to enter their devastated homes and went for succour to Lappa (see p.210) near Réthimnon, one of its few allies. The city was, however, eventually rebuilt and enjoyed a small-scale renaissance under the Romans through to Byzantine times.

Sadly, what is visible above ground today in no way reflects the city's ancient status, as no systematic archeological exploration has yet taken place. However, what you can see underlines the fact that when the riches of Lyttos are finally excavated – including what was said by a Venetian antiquary to be the island's largest theatre, now lost – it will no doubt become one of the most important sites in Crete. Below the church of Tímios Stavrós, built over a large fifth-century basilica with stones from the ancient city, are the bastions and curtain of an enormous **city wall**. The church is believed to mark the centre, or agora of Lyttos. The church of Áyios Yeóryios (which has fragmentary frescoes) on the southernmost peak is also constructed from stones scavenged from Lyttos: incorporated into the outer wall is a fine fragment of carved acanthus foliage. Nearby, the ancient city's **bouleterion** or council chamber has been excavated, with visible platforms and benches. Spend half an hour roaming through the vines and olive groves on the surrounding slopes and you'll come across partially excavated dwellings, delicately carved tombstones, half-buried pillars and the enormous foundation stones of buildings waiting to be unearthed.

Should you decide to see only one of the many churches in this area then make it **Áyios Pandeleímon**, off the road back to Hersónisos just before the village of Piyí. To get there, set off north for a good kilometre out of Kastélli and you'll see a sign ("Byzantine Church and Paradise Tavern") directing you onto a dirt track to the right. There are several alternative trails but, providing you don't mind bumpy driving, it doesn't seem to matter which one you take: they all seem eventually to pass the church – just stick to the side of the valley, parallel with the paved road. The way is shaded with huge old trees and the church itself, which is surprisingly big, is set in a grove of oaks and planes around a spring which was very likely a sanctuary in ancient times. This idyllic spot shelters the small *Paradise Taverna* run by the eccentric Nikolaides family who hold the key to the church (March–Oct; at other times you'll need to ask in Kastélli) and feel that the effort of climbing the hill to open it at least obliges you to buy a drink from them. When you do enter the church, you'll find that the **frescoes**, although powerfully imposing, are weathered almost beyond recognition. Look out for images of the soldier saints on the north wall and an unusual scene of Ayía Ánna nursing the infant Mary. The structure of the church, probably early thirteenth-century, is interesting for the way it incorporates parts of the original tenth-century basilica and uses as columns some much older fragments, probably taken from Lyttos. The aqueduct that once transported water to the ancient city passes close by, and you may spot parts of it as you drive around looking for the church.

To the southwest of Kastélli is the large village of **Thrapsanó**, for centuries an important pottery-making centre in central Crete. Workshops still thrive in the village itself and towards Vóni and Evangelismós, and all welcome visitors if you want to admire the potters' skills although there's not a great deal on offer to buy. There is a good range of earthenware; *píthoi* are evident throughout Thrapsanó, not only in workshops but upturned in the main square and on the backs of parked pickup trucks.

Towards Lasíthi

The one inland route which visitors follow in any numbers is the drive up to **Lasíthi**. Once again the attractions are charmingly simple: scenery which becomes increasingly mountainous as you climb towards the plateau, spreading old trees beside the road, and still older churches in the villages. Starting from Iráklion, the normal route is to follow the coast road until just before Límin Hersonísou, where you turn inland towards Kastélli and then east through the Aposelémis valley to Potamiés and Goniés. Before reaching the turnoff on the right for Kastélli (you continue left), look out for the ruins of the **Roman aqueduct** which carried water from springs in the hills near ancient Lyttos to its port at Hersónisos, visible in a ravine below the road.

Approaching Potamiés you'll see the small Byzantine frescoed chapel of **Sotíros Christós** (locked) to the left; soon after this a signed track, also on the

The Lasíthi plateau itself is covered on pp.141–5.

left, heads for the tenth-century monastery of the **Panayía Gouverniótissa** (Assumption of the Virgin), one of the oldest in Crete. The track climbs through olive groves to a shaded parking space next to the deserted, partly ruined and rather eerie monastery buildings. The enormous ovens that once fed the brethren are still in evidence, and precarious staircases (not for the fainthearted) climb to the dormitories above. The tiny **chapel**, which still attracts visitors and the faithful, stands close by in a peaceful garden with a shady lemon tree. Inside are restored frescoes dating from the fourteenth century with a fine *Pantokrátor* in the dome. The chapel will probably be locked (key available from the kafeníon at the edge of the village), but a restricted view of the frescoes inside can be had through a small glassless window in the apse.

Five kilometres further on is **AVDHOÚ**, where there are more fine, if faded, frescoes from the fourteenth and fifteenth centuries in three churches: Áyios Andónios, Áyios Konstantínos and Áyios Yeóryios. The churches should be open; if not, enquiries in the village cafés should produce the necessary keys.

Mohós

Starting from Mália, or on a round trip from Áyios Nikólaos, you can take a short cut, turning inland at Stalídha and following the road signed for Mohós. This route is probably the most dramatic of the three approaches to the plateau (the third is from the other end, Neápoli – see p.140), with spectacular views back over the coast as the road climbs dizzily above the Gulf of Mália. After crossing a pass, you arrive at the village of **MOHÓS**, which boasts a pleasant leafy square edged by tavernas and cafés, and a major festival of the Panayía – albeit rather touristy – on August 15 every year. The late Swedish prime minister Olof Palme was a regular summer visitor here, and when he was cruelly murdered in Stockholm in 1986, Mohós was plunged into mourning. His simple house, just behind the church on the main square, has been turned into a shrine (ask to be directed to the **Villa Palme**), and the street in which it stands has been renamed Odhós Olof Palme. The mainly Swedish visitors to the house have filled two books with their heartfelt comments.

Krási and Panayía Kardhiótissa

Three kilometres beyond the point where the roads from Hersónisos and Stalídha join, a loop off the main route will bring you to the curiously named village of **KRÁSI**. Curious because Krási translates as "wine", but the village's fame is in fact based on water, in the form of a curative spring. This is situated under stone arcading in the shade of an enormous **plane tree**, which is claimed to be two thousand years old and the largest in Europe, with a girth that cannot be encircled by twelve men. The waters are reputed to be especially good for stomach complaints – worth noting if you have fallen foul of the Mália *souvláki* poisoner.

Not much further on, just before the village of Kerá, the convent of **Panayía Kardhiótissa** (Our Lady of the Heart; daily 8am–1pm & 4–8pm) lies immediately below the road and is one of the most important places of worship on Crete, with an annual celebration on September 8. The buildings date from the twelfth century, and though the outside of the monastery looks like whitewashed concrete, the interior is undeniably spectacular, with restored frescoes through-out. These came to light only in the 1960s, when they were discovered beneath accumulated layers of paint. There is also a copy of a famous twelfth-century icon of the Virgin, the original of which was taken to Rome in 1498. According to leg-end, successive attempts to steal the icon were thwarted when it found its way back to Kerá, despite being chained to a marble pillar; the pillar is now in the monastery yard, while the chain (kept inside the church) is believed to alleviate pain when wrapped around the bodies of the afflicted. In a peaceful garden out-side the church, one of the three remaining nuns will probably be on duty at the stone table in the shade of a mulberry tree or in the shop. If you wanted to try out your Greek, you could ask the sisters to tell you of how they came to "enter" the order at the age of ten – a story that reveals a darker side to the Orthodox Church in Greece.

The mountains

After the village of Kerá, the road winds on into the Dhiktean mountains, and the views become progressively more magnificent. To the left, **Mount Karfí** looms ominously, its summit over 1100m above sea level. This spire-like peak (*karfí* means "nail" in Greek) was one of the sites where the Minoan civilization made its last stand, following the collapse of the great centres after the twelfth century BC. In the face of Dorian advances, the last of the Minoans fled to remote refuges such as this, keeping alive shadowy vestiges of their culture. The solitary peak, now identified as a Minoan sanctuary, stands as a silent witness to the end of Europe's first great civilization.

The road continues to climb until, at Séli Ambélou, you approach a dramatic pass flanked by stone windmills on the ridges above. Beyond the rocky outcrops, the Lasíthi plateau suddenly unfolds before you. Almost straight ahead, the high-est peaks of the range dominate the landscape, including **Mount Dhíkti** itself – all 2148m of it. The *Séli* taverna here at the pass often serves barbecued roast lamb, and is a good place to stop and take in the sights – on clear days you can see as far as the island of Thíra (Santoríni), over 100km distant.

On the ridge behind the car-parking area, a couple of the windmills have been restored and pressed into use as souvenir shops. There's a path from here lead-ing to still higher viewpoints and eventually to the site of ancient **Karfí**, a five-kilometre hike away, but this is probably better approached from Tzermiádho (see p.143) on the plateau.

ACROSS THE ISLAND

There are a number of roads that run from Iráklion towards the **south coast**, but almost all the traffic seems to follow the one which heads slightly southwest, towards Festós and Mátala. Plenty of buses come this way too, leaving from the Haniá Gate terminal and heading for Festós, Mátala, Léndas or Ayía Galíni via Timbáki. Míres, in the heart of the Messará plain, is the southern junction for switching between these various routes. The only other regular bus service across the island from Iráklion runs southeast towards **Ierápetra**, via Áno Viánnos and Mírtos.

The southern half of the province is very different from the north: there's just one resort of any size, **Mátala** – and a day-trip route that takes in the major archeological sites of **Górtys**, **Festós** and **Ayía Triádha**. The rest is countryside with few concessions to tourism, which is not to say that the area is undeveloped: on the contrary, it represents the island's single most important location for agriculture. The **Messará plain**, in particular, has always been a vital resource, and its importance is reflected in widely distributed and wealthy villages.

The coast, with the exception of Mátala, is relatively little visited, and indeed a good part of it is quite inaccessible: east of **Léndas** (where there's excellent sand) is well over 30km of shore most of which can't be reached overland although a couple of rough tracks lead to a pair of likely bays and there's even a gorge to explore. To the west, the low-key resorts of **Tsoútsouros**, **Keratókambos** and **Árvi** have the only easily accessible beaches with facilities and places to stay. The first is reachable by a steep, rough track, and the last two are served by equally sheer asphalted roads.

Towards Festós

Crossing the island from Iráklion is not, on the whole, the most exciting of drives: you leave the city westwards (through the Haniá Gate) and on the outskirts turn south, under the highway, following the signs to Festós. From the beginning the road climbs, heading up to the island's spine, through thoroughly business-like countryside. This is more of what traditionally was the Malevísi, or Malmsey, wine-producing region: though some wine is still made, most of the grapes you'll see now are table grapes, grown for eating rather than pressing. With your own transport a more **scenic route** to Ayía Varvára (see below) is to take a right soon after leaving Iráklion along the route signed for Voutés, Áyios Míronas and Pírgou. This road skirts the eastern slopes of the valley and is a wonderful undulating ride through some pleasant out-of-the-way villages, which rejoins the main route just beyond the village of Priniás.

Moní Palianí and Ayía Varvára

Just beyond a turnoff for Dáfnes – noted for its wine – at the twenty-kilometre marker in the village of Veneráto, there's the option of a two-kilometre detour to the **Moní Palianí**, an ancient monastic foundation and now a nunnery. After leaving the road on the left (signed), keep your eyes skinned for another sign directing you right; the road then crosses a valley before climbing gently towards the nunnery gates. Founded as early as the seventh century, the place is an oasis of tranquillity where the nuns' cells surround a courtyard filled with oleanders, geraniums, vines and palms with a thirteenth-century church at its centre. Unlike many religious communities in Crete, this one is a viable concern, supporting itself through sales of lace and embroidery, which the nuns will be only too pleased to show you in their small shop.

AYÍA VARVÁRA, 8km further on, is the main village of this area, a place known as the *omphalos* (navel) of Crete. The great chapel-topped rock which you see as you arrive is held to be the very point around which the island balances, its centre of being. Not that this makes for any great tourist attraction. There are plenty of cafés and shops along the main street, but they cater mostly for local farmers in search of a bag of fertilizer or a tractor part.

Zarós and around

On the southern fringe of Ayía Varvára a turning takes off to the west, following the flank of the Psilorítis range towards **Kamáres** (see p.222) and eventually on to Réthimnon or down to Ayía Galíni. This is a beautiful drive and a relatively good, empty road: **ZARÓS** is a particularly attractive village famous for its spring waters, which are now bottled and sold all over Crete. Well-appointed hotels are rare inland, making the *Idi Hotel* (☎0894/31-302, fax 31-511; ④) a lovely place to get away from it all. Something of a retreat for German visitors – note the wooden bench by the swimming pool "made by German soldiers" based here during the wartime occupation – the hotel has information on several scenic walks on the Psilorítis range, and the taverna next door makes a speciality of the trout which splash around in the trout farm behind.

Along the way there are a number of ancient churches and monasteries, the first being **Moní Áyios Nikólaos**, 2km up a signed track on the right slightly west of Zarós (on foot there's a shorter route from the village – enquire at the supermarket). Not as picturesque as the Moní Vrondísi (see below) this monastery, set around a courtyard, is nevertheless very welcoming and the elderly monks will usually ask where you're from before offering some of their delicious homemade goat's cheese and coffee. To view the fourteenth-century paintings in the nearby church, visitors wearing shorts will need to cover their legs with an apron taken from a box at the entrance. There's also a great **gorge walk** to be had starting from here. Above the monastery is the cave of St Euthymios, an old hermitage. You can continue to climb, on foot, for a further 2km to the entrance to the Gorge of Zarós, whose three-kilometre length (now part of the E4 Pan-European walking route and signed accordingly) is negotiated by a path, including steps and bridges for the difficult bits, which takes much of the strain. The gorge is rarely visited, and your exertions will be rewarded by spectacular views of the Psilorítis range and – depending on the time of year – plenty of bird, plant and even animal life.

The fourteenth- to seventeenth-century **Moní Vrondísi**, above the road about 3km beyond the turn off for Áyios Nikólaos, is a gloriously peaceful foundation overlooking the Koútsoulidi valley. In a tranquil courtyard surrounded by monks' cells (mostly empty as the community now comprises one person) and fronted by two fig trees, is the monastery's simple limestone church. When you have found the monk or one of the guardians to open it, inside there are some fine fourteenth-century **frescoes**, including a moving depiction of the Last Supper in the apse; it is unique on the island, as this position is normally reserved for the *Pantokrátor* (Christ). Also on display is a collection of icons taken from the nearby church of Áyios Fanoúrios – Vrondísi itself has given up the finest of its artworks, including the six great panels by Dhamaskinós, to the icon gallery of Ayía Ekateríni in Iráklion (see p.70). Even without them, though, this is a wonderful setting, with its giant plane trees for shade, cool water gushing from a fifteenth-century Venetian fountain, with figures of Adam and Eve in the elaborate Italian style by the entrance, and views towards Festós and the Gulf of Messará. Most days the guardians will sell you their delicious *thimárisio* (thyme honey) gathered from hives in the nearby hills. Áyios Fanoúrios, all that survives of the **Moní Valsamónero**, is reached by a track from the next village, Vorízia. The **frescoes** in this church are among the best in Crete: painted in the fifteenth century by Konstantínos Ríkos, they depict scenes from the life of the *Panayía* (Virgin Mary) besides images of various saints and a fine *Pantokrátor*. The guardian is on site most weekdays (official opening hours 8am–3pm), but if not he can be found in the village.

The road continues 3km west of Vorízia to reach Kamáres and a possible ascent to the Kamáres Cave (see p.222).

The Messará plain

Continuing by the main road south from Ayía Varvára the way becomes genuinely mountainous, and after 7km you cross the Pass of Vourvoulítis (650m) and the watershed of the Messará. The **Messará plain**, a long strip running east from the Gulf of Messará, is the largest and most important of Crete's fertile flatlands. Bounded to the north by the Psilorítis range and the lower hills which run right across the centre of the island, to the east by the Dhiktean mountains, and to the south by the narrow strip of the Kófinas hills, it is watered, somewhat erratically, by the Yeropótamos. Heavy with olives, and increasingly with the fruit and vegetable cash crops that dominate the modern agricultural economy, the plain has always been a major centre of population and a mainstay of the island's economy. There is much evidence of this, not only at Górtys, Festós and Ayía Triádha but at a wealth of lesser, barely explored sites; today's villages exude prosperity, too, surrounded by neat and intensive cultivation.

As you descend to the plain by a series of long, looping curves, the main road heads west through Áyii Dhéka. A left turn eastwards takes you across far less travelled country and (see p.131) all the way to Ierápetra.

Áyii Dhéka

ÁYII DHÉKA, served by frequent buses from Iráklion, is the first village you reach on the Messará, and the most interesting. The place takes its name from ten early Christians who were martyred here around 250 AD, at the behest of the emperor Decius. The **Holy Ten** are still among the most revered of Cretan saints: regarded as martyrs for Crete as much as Christianity – the first in a heroic line of Cretans who laid down their lives to oppose tyrannical occupation. On the southwestern edge of the village are two churches associated with them: the older, originally Byzantine, has an icon portraying the martyrs and the stone block on which they are supposed to have been decapitated. Steps beneath the more modern chapel nearby lead to a crypt where you can see six of their tombs. Other reminders of the village's ancient past include the Roman statues, pillars and odd blocks of masonry scavenged from Górtys that are much in evidence: re-used in modern houses, propping up walls or simply lying about in yards. In the centre there are a number of roadside cafés and restaurants and a few signs offering **rooms** – it's a pleasant place to break your journey.

Górtys

The remnants of the ancient city of **GÓRTYS** (known traditionally as Gortyn or Gortyna) are scattered across a large, fragmented area, covering a great deal more than the fenced site by the road that most people see. The Italian Archeological Institute is currently carrying out extensive excavations that it hopes will eventually link the disparate elements of the ancient city. The best way to get some idea of its scale is to follow the path through the fields from the village. This heads off, more or less parallel to the road, opposite the chapel of Áyii Dhéka: it's an easy walk to the main site, and along the way you'll skirt most of the major remains.

Settled from at least Minoan times, when it was a minor subject of Festós, Górtys began its rise to prominence under the Dorians. By the eighth century BC, it had become a significant commercial power and, in the third century BC, it finally conquered its former rulers at Festós. The society was a strictly regulated one, with a citizen class (presumably Dorian) ruling over a population of serfs (presumably "Minoan" Cretans) and slaves. Even for the citizens, life was as hard and orderly as it was in Classical Sparta.

Evidence of early Górtys has survived thanks largely to the remarkable law code found here (see below) and to a lesser extent through treaties known to have existed between the Górtys of this era and its rivals, notably Knossós. Hannibal fled to Górtys briefly after his defeat by Rome, and the city also helped the Romans to conquer Crete, and it was during the ensuing Roman era that the city reached its apogee, from 67 BC onwards: as the seat of a Roman praetor it was capital of the province of Crete and Cyrenaica, ruling not only the rest of the island but also much of Egypt and North Africa. It was here that Christianity first reached Crete, when St Titus was despatched by St Paul to convert the islanders.

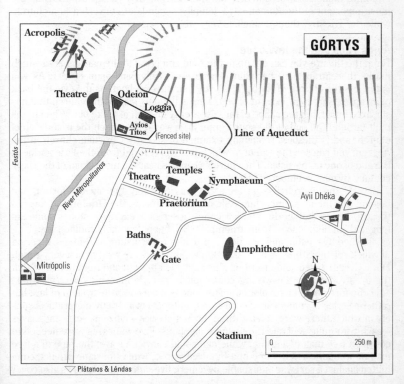

After the Saracen invasion in the ninth century, when much of the city was razed, Górtys was abruptly abandoned.

South of the road

In the fields en route to the site, it is the **Roman city** that dominates: this once stretched from the edges of Áyii Dhéka to the far banks of the Mitropolitanos (then known as the *Lethe*) and from the hills in the north as far south as the modern hamlet of Mitrópolis (where a small Roman basilica with good mosaics has been excavated). For most people, though, the ruins along the main path, others seen standing in the distance, and the tantalizing prospect of what lies unexcavated beneath hummocks along the way, are quite enough. In another setting, or individually, these might seem unimpressive, but with so many of them, abandoned as they are and all but ignored (fenced to keep souvenir hunters out, but not guarded nor advertised) they are amazing – you feel almost as if you have discovered them for yourself.

The **Praetorium** (governor's palace) has left the most extensive remains, a vast pile built originally in the second century AD, rebuilt in the fourth, and occupied as a monastery right up to the time of the Venetian conquest; within the same fenced area is a courtyard with fountains and the **Nymphaeum**. Somewhere near here, too, was the terminus of the main aqueduct that brought water from the region of modern Zarós. Further on, the **Temple of Pythian Apollo** was the most important of the Roman city's temples, again later converted to a church, while the **Theatre**, though small, is very well preserved.

Áyios Títos and the law code

From the theatre you can cut up to the road and cross to the parking area which marks the entrance to the main, fenced **site** (daily 8am–5pm; 800dr). As you enter, it is the church of **Áyios Títos** which immediately grabs the eye, the back of its apse rising high in front of you. This is the only part of the church that has survived intact, but the shape of the rest is easy enough to make out. When it was built (around the end of the sixth century), it would have been the island's chief church, and is the best remaining example of an early Christian church in the Aegean: you can see the extent to which it is still revered from the little shrine at the end of one of the aisles. The church's capitals bear the monogram of the sixth-century Byzantine emperor Justinian.

Beyond the church lies an area that was probably the ancient forum, and beyond this the most important relic of ancient Górtys, the **Odeion** (or covered theatre) and its **law code**. The law code – a series of engraved stones some 9m long and 3m high – dates from around 500 BC, but presumably codified laws long established by custom and practice. It provides a fascinating insight into a period of which relatively little is otherwise known; the laws are written in a very rough Doric Cretan dialect and inscribed alternately left to right and right to left, so that the eyes can follow the writing continuously (a style known as *boustrophedon*, after the furrows of an ox plough). The code is not a complete system of law, but rather a series of rulings on special cases, and reflects a strictly hierarchical society in which there were at least three distinct classes – citizens, serfs and slaves – each with quite separate rights and obligations. Five witnesses were needed to convict a free man of a crime, while one could convict a slave; the rape of a free man or woman carried a fine of a hundred *staters*, while the same offence committed against a serf was punishable by a mere five-*stater* fine. The laws also cover subjects such as property and inheritance rights, the status of children of mixed marriages (that is, between free people and serfs) and the control of trade.

The panels on which the law is inscribed are now incorporated into the round Odeion, which was erected under Trajan in around 100 AD and rebuilt in the third or fourth century (the brick terrace which protects the inscriptions from the elements is modern). The Odeion is just the latest incarnation of a series of buildings on this site, in which the code had apparently always been preserved – obviously this was a city which valued its own history. When they were discovered in the late nineteenth century, these ruins were entirely buried under eroded soil washed down from the hills behind.

In a small pavilion backing onto the site **cafeteria** there's a collection of **statuary**, demonstrating the high standard of work being achieved here during the city's halcyon days.

West of the river

Beside the fenced site the river runs by an abandoned medieval mill and on the far bank you can see a larger **Theatre**, in rather poor repair, set against the hillside. In Roman times the river ran through a culvert here and you could have walked straight across; nowadays, you have to go back to the roadbridge to explore this area. The guard at the site speaks no English, though he's very keen to encourage people to explore the outlying areas, and will give you directions to the easiest path up to the **Acropolis** on the hilltop above the river. Hardly anyone makes it up there, shying away from such a stiff climb in the heat, but the ruins are surprisingly impressive, with Roman defensive walls and a building known as the *kástro* (though apparently not a castle) still standing to a height of 6m in places. The lesser remains are among the earliest on the site, and include scant relics of a Greek temple that was later converted to a church. From this hilltop vantage point, you also get a fine overview of the layout of Górtys and can trace the line of the aqueducts coming in from the north.

Míres

From Górtys it's about 6km to **MÍRES**, a bustling farming town of some size, and the transport centre for the area. If you are changing **buses** – and you can get to Léndas or Mátala on the coast from here, to Zarós and Kamáres in the mountains (very occasionally), through Timbáki to Ayía Galíni or Réthimnon and even (once a day) to Réthimnon via the Amári Valley – these services depart from the "bus station" on the main street, actually a rather ramshackle bar. Buses for Festós continue directly to the site after a stop here to pick up and drop off passengers, so there's usually no need to change. Míres could hardly be described as attractive, but as a centre for local commerce as well as passing tourists, it at least has plenty of life, with scores of places to eat and drink, the only bank for miles around, and cheap **rooms** that are easy to find, if you happen to be stranded between buses. The *Hotel Olympic* (☎0892/42-777; ②) is characterless but clean; among a few places to eat nearby there's *Pizzeria Bambola*, where the chef leaves pizzas to cook in the oven while he leaps aboard a powerful Honda to deliver telephone orders. On Saturday mornings the town is enlivened by a busy market.

Three kilometres beyond Míres a turning on the right leads to the **Moní Kalivianí**, an impressive monastic complex which today serves as an orphanage, boarding school and sanatorium. Inside the gates, the buildings fronting the central avenue have cascades of magenta bougainvillea in summer, and everywhere there are plants sprouting more blooms. Behind the modern church there is a tiny fourteenth-century chapel, dedicated to the Panayía Kalivianís, with ancient frescoes. The nuns support themselves by weaving, embroidery and making handicrafts, which they sell at their store opposite the church.

Festós and Ayía Triádha

In a wonderfully scenic location on a ridge at the eastern end of the Messará plain with fine views towards the encircling mountains, the **palace of Festós** and its neighbouring "summer palace", the charming **Ayía Triádha**, are Minoan sites ranking second only to Knossós on the island.

Bus services to the Festós site are excellent, with some nine a day to and from Iráklion (the last leaves just before the site closes), but rather fewer on Sunday, five of which continue to, or come from, Mátala; there are also services direct to Ayía Galíni. All buses stop right by the Festós parking area. If you're arriving in the afternoon, plan to visit Ayía Triádha first, as it closes early. The **Tourist Pavilion** at Festós serves drinks and food and also has a few beds, though these are very rarely available (thanks to advance bookings) and pricey when they are. There are a few more **rooms** to be found in the nearby village of Áyios Ioánnis (see p.124) which also makes an ideal **lunch** stop after or between sites. There are also places offering **accommodation** along the road towards Mátala or, alternatively, you should be able to find something in the first larger place you strike in almost any direction – Míres, Timbáki or Pitsídhia.

Festós

The palace of **FESTÓS** (April–Sept Mon–Fri 8am–9pm, Sat & Sun 8.30am–6pm; Oct–March Mon–Fri 8am–6pm Sat & Sun 8.30am–6pm; 1200dr, students 600dr) was excavated by Federico Halbherr (also responsible for the early work on Górtys), at almost exactly the same time as Evans was working at Knossós. The style of the excavations, however, could hardly have been more different. Here, reconstruction has been kept to an absolute minimum, to the approval of most traditional archeologists: it's all bare foundations, and walls that barely rise above ground level.

As at Knossós, most of what survives is what the excavators termed the Second Palace, rebuilt after the destruction of c.1700 BC and occupied to c.1450 BC. But at Festós the first palace was used as a foundation for the second, and much of its well-preserved floor plan has been uncovered by the excavations. Fascinating as these superimposed buildings are for the experts, they help make Festós extremely confusing for more casual visitors to interpret. Combined with a distinct lack of elaboration, at least in the decoration of the palace, this adds up to considerable disappointment for many. Since much of the site is also fenced off, it becomes almost impossible to get any sense of the place as it once was.

Only Knossós was more important, and although there are major differences between Festós and the other palaces, these are in the end outweighed by the multitude of similarities. The rooms are set about a great central courtyard, with an external court on the west side and a theatral area north of this; the domestic apartments are, as usual, slightly apart from the public and formal ones; there are

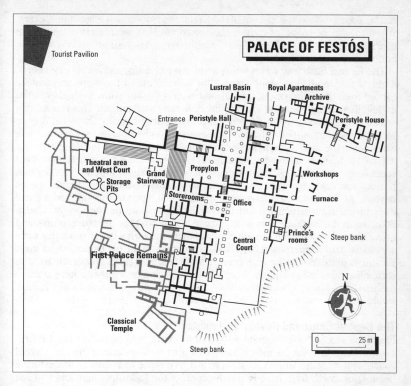

PALACE OF FESTÓS

Tourist Pavilion

Lustral Basin   Royal Apartments
                          Archive
Entrance Peristyle Hall   Peristyle House

Theatral area
and West Court   Workshops
        Grand   Propylon
Storage Stairway
Pits   Storerooms   Furnace
                      Office
                              Prince's
                    Central   rooms   Steep bank
First Palace Remains Court

Classical
Temple   N

0   25 m

Steep bank

the same lines of storage magazines and pits for grain; and on the east side are workshops for the palace craftsmen. While no traces of frescoes were found, this doesn't imply that the palace wasn't luxurious: the materials (marble, alabaster, gypsum) were of the highest quality, there were sophisticated drainage and bathing facilities, and remains suggest a large and airy dining hall on the upper floors overlooking the court. Bear in mind, as you explore, that part of the palace is missing: there must have been more outbuildings on the south side of the site where erosion has worn away the edge of the ridge and a corner of the central court itself has collapsed.

Entry: the West Court and Grand Stairway

You enter the palace from above, down steps leading past a **Tourist Pavilion** and approaching the northwest corner of the complex through the Upper Court. Step down first into the **West Court** and integral **Theatral Area**: as at Knossós there are raised walkways leading across the courtyard, and here one of them runs right up the steps that form the seats of the Theatral Area (accorded this title by archeologists who supposed it was used for viewing some kind of performance or spectacle). On the west side of the court are circular walled pits, probably for storing grain. The West Court itself is a rare survival from the original palace – the main walkway leads not up the stairs into the new palace but past them and into the entrance to the old palace. From there, much of the facade of the old palace can be seen as a low wall in front of the Grand Stairway which leads into the new. When the palace stood, of course, this would not have been apparent; then the court was filled with rubble and levelled (though not paved) at the height of the bottom step of the stairway.

The **Grand Stairway** was a fitting approach to Festós, a superbly engineered flight of twelve shallow stone steps, 14m wide. Some of the steps are actually carved from the solid rock of the hill, and each is slightly convex – higher in the middle than at the ends – in order to improve the visual impact. This remarkable architectural innovation anticipated similar subtleties of the Parthenon at Athens by twelve centuries. The entrance facade was no doubt equally impressive – you can still see the base of the pillar which supported the centre of the doorway – but it's hard to imagine from what actually survives. Once inside, the first few rooms seem somewhat cramped: this may have been deliberate – either for security purposes, to prevent a sudden rush, or as a ploy to enhance the larger, lighter spaces beyond. At the end would have been a blank wall, open to the sky, and a small door to the right which led out onto stairs down towards the Central Court. Standing in the entrance area now, you can look down over the **storerooms**, and going down the stairs you can get closer to them through a larger room that once served as an office. Exposed here is a storeroom from the old palace, with a giant jar still in place. At the far end, more *píthoi* stand in a room apparently used to store olive oil or other liquids; there's a stool to stand on while reaching in and a basin to catch spillage, while the whole floor slopes towards a hole in which slops would collect.

The Central Court and Royal Apartments

From the stores "office", quite an elaborate room, you pass into the **Central Court**, which is by far the most atmospheric area of the palace. In this great paved court, with its scintillating views, there is a rare sense of Festós as it must have been. Look north from here in the direction of the Psilorítis range and you can make out a black smudge to the right of a saddle between the two peaks. This marks the entrance to the Kamáres Cave (see p.222), a shrine sacred to the Minoans and the source of the great hoard of elaborate Kamáres ware pottery now in the Iráklion Archeological Museum. Even without the views – which would have been blocked by the two storeys to either side when the palace was standing – the courtyard remains impressive. Its north end, in particular, is positively and unusually grand: the doorway, flanked by half-columns and niches (possibly for sentries) covered in painted plaster, can be plainly made out. To the left as you face this are a couple of *píthoi* (left there by the excavators) and a stepped stone that some claim was an altar, or perhaps a block from which athletes would jump onto bulls; the equally unprovable counter-theory has it, more prosaically, as a base for a flowerpot.

Along each of the long sides of the courtyard ran a covered **portico** or veranda, the bases of whose supports are still visible. In the southwest corner are various rooms which probably had religious functions; beyond these, and hard to distinguish from them, are parts of the old palace which are mostly fenced off. Also here, right at the edge of the site, are the remains of a **Greek temple** of the Classical era, evidence that the site was occupied long after the Minoans and the destruction of the palace.

Heading up through the grand north door – notice the holes for door pivots and the guardroom just inside – a corridor leads through the **North Court** toward the

Royal Apartments. These have been covered and shut off to prevent damage from people walking through, and it's hard to see a great deal of the queen's rooms, or the king's rooms behind them. Above the king's quarters is a large **Peristyle Hall**, a colonnaded courtyard much like a cloister, open in the centre. On the north side this courtyard was open to take in the view of Psilorítis: it must have been a beautiful place, and perhaps also one of some religious significance. Staircases linked the hall directly with the Royal Apartments (and the **lustral basin** on the north edge of the king's rooms); nowadays it is easier to approach from the palace entrance, turning left up the stairs from the Propylon.

Palace dependencies

Continuing past the royal quarters on the other side, you come to the dependent buildings on the northeast side of the palace, which almost certainly predate much of the palace itself. Among the first of these is the so-called **Archive**, where the famous **Festós Disc** (see p.72) was discovered in one of a row of mudbrick boxes. A little further on is the **Peristyle House**, probably a private home, with an enclosed yard similar in style to the Peristyle Hall. From here, stairs lead back down to the level of the Central Court, into the area of the palace **workshops**. In the centre of another large courtyard are the remains of a furnace, probably used for metalworking or as a kiln. The small rooms roundabout were the workshops, perhaps even the homes, of the craftsmen. As you walk back to the central court, another suite of rooms – usually described as the **Prince's Rooms** – lies on your left, boasting its own small peristyle hall.

Ayía Triádha

AYÍA TRIÁDHA (daily 8.30am–3pm; 500dr, free on Sun) lies about 3km from Festós on the far side of the hill, an easy drive or a walk of about 45 minutes by a well-signed road around the south slope. Avoid the approach from the main road by car – the track up the hill is liable to rip your exhaust off. (There is also an old footpath around the north side, but it seems to have fallen into disuse: check with the guards at Festós about the current feasibility of the walk.) The site – discovered and excavated at the turn of the century by the Italian School – remains something of an enigma. Nothing exists to compare it with in what is known of Minoan Crete, nor does it appear in any records; even the name has had to be borrowed from a nearby chapel.

In sharp contrast with unadorned Festós, however, Ayía Triádha has provided some of the most delicate Minoan **artworks** found. From this site came the three vases of carved black steatite – the "Harvesters Vase", the "Boxer Vase" and the "Chieftain Cup" – on display in the Iráklion Archeological Museum (see p.74), as well as some of the finest works in the Fresco Hall there, including the unique painted sarcophagus. Yet again, the ruins enjoy a magnificent hillside site, looking out over the Gulf of Messará. The modern view takes in the coastal plain with Timbáki airstrip in the foreground (built by the Germans during the war, its runways are now more often used for motor races), but in Minoan times the sea would have come right to the base of the hill. Despite this beauty and wealth, Ayía Triádha is plainly not a construction on the same scale as the great palaces: the most commonly accepted explanation is that it was some kind of royal villa or summer retreat, but it may equally have been the home of an important prince or noble, or a building of special ceremonial significance.

You approach the site from the car park above. Predictably, the remains, in which buildings of several eras are jumbled, are confused and confusing. This matters much less here, however, for it is the atmosphere of Ayía Triádha that really makes the place – the absence of crowds, the beauty of the surroundings and the human scale of the villa with its multitude of little stairways and paved corridors between rooms.

The site

To your left as you climb down are the bare ruins of a Minoan house older than most of the other remains (the villa was broadly contemporary with the new palace at Festós) and beyond them a **shrine** which contained a frescoed floor and walls now on show in the Iráklion Archeological Museum. If you keep to the higher ground here you come into the courtyard of the villa, perhaps the best place to get an impression of its overall layout. The L-shaped building enclosed the courtyard only on its north and west sides, and the north side is further muddled by a much later hall – apparently a Mycenaean megaron – built over it. To the south of the courtyard is the early fourteenth-century chapel of **Áyios Yeóryios** (key available from the guardian), in which there are fragments of some fine frescoes.

The **Royal Villa** now lies mostly below the level of the courtyard, but in Minoan times it would not have appeared this way: the builders made use of the natural slope to create a split-level construction, and entrances from the court would have led directly into upper levels above those you see today. The finest of the rooms were those in the corner of the "L", looking out over the sea; here the best of the frescoes were found, including that of the famous stalking cat – now preserved in the Iráklion Archeological Museum. The quality of workmanship can still be appreciated in these chambers with their alabaster-lined walls and gypsum floors and benches. Beside them to the south is a small group of storerooms with a number of *píthoi* still in place; some bear scorch marks from the great fire which destroyed the palace about 1450 BC. From the hall and terrace out front you can walk around the **ramp** that runs beneath the north side of the villa. The Italian excavators named this the *Rampa dal Mare* and claimed that it once ran down to the sea, though there seems little evidence for this.

Follow it the other way instead and you can head down to the lower part of the site, the **town area**. By far the most striking aspect of this is the **market**, a row of stores which are once again unique in Minoan architecture. The stores, identically sized and fronted by a covered portico, run in a line down the hill; in front of them is an open space and, across that, the houses of the town. Only one problem mars the easily conjured image of the Minoan populace milling around the market while their rulers looked benignly on from above: this area apparently dates only from the declining years of the Minoan culture and is contemporary not with the villa, but with the megaron erected over it. Beyond the stores (and outside the fence) lies the **Cemetery**, where remains of two *thólos* tombs and many other graves were found, including the one containing the Ayía Triádha sarcophagus.

West towards Timbáki and Mátala

Continuing west from Festós, towards Ayía Galíni or Réthimnon, the final stretch of the Messará plain, with its acres of polythene greenhouses and burgeoning concrete sprawl, must be among the ugliest places in Crete. **TIMBÁKI** may also be the drabbest town. It's a place of some size, which means there are cafés and restaurants along the main street, stores and banks, and even a couple of hotels, but there's no reason to stay here longer than you have to. Just beyond, a turning leads to **KÓKKINOS PÍRGOS** on the coast. Here, too, plastic and concrete are the overwhelming images, and the place is barely redeemed by a plentiful supply of cheap **rooms** and the lack of crowds on the none-too-beautiful beach.

The more inviting beaches in this zone are in and around the developed resort of **MÁTALA** and the road which heads south from Festós will bring you there with a couple of sights to see along the way.

Inland: Vóri to Kamáres

Having dismissed this part of the island, it's worth remembering that – as is often the way on Crete – all you have to do is turn off the main road to escape altogether. **VÓRI** lies only a kilometre north of the turn-off to Festós and, despite being quite a big place, is a pleasant working village almost entirely off the beaten track. It even has places offering **rooms** as well as a couple of kafenía in the village square. That some tourists do come here is largely due to the excellent new **Museum of Cretan Ethnology** (daily 10am–6pm; 500dr), advertised by large signs along the main road. Hidden behind the church, it's worth seeking out for a comprehensive survey of traditional country life in Crete, and compares favourably with the equivalent museum in Réthimnon (see p.202); the museum won a special commendation in the European Museum of the Year award in 1992. The collection itself is a miscellany of agricultural implements, building tools and materials, domestic utensils, furniture, basketware, pottery, musical instruments, weaving and embroidery, all well labelled and fascinating. There are sections on the production of olive oil, wine-making and the distilling of *raki*, as well as a display of the myriad herbs and medicinal plants sought out by Cretans since ancient times. A collection of baskets is especially interesting, with 25 different designs reflecting their uses as beehives, eeltraps, cheese-drainers, animal muzzles and snail containers.

If you're heading for Ayía Galíni you have little choice but to return to the main road, but for the Amári Valley and Réthimnon it's also possible to take the new road up to Kamáres (see p.222) for another lovely, climbing drive.

Towards Mátala

The road south from the Festós site passes the Ayía Triádha turn-off and soon approaches the village of Áyios Ioánnis. Just before the village is the picturesque *Taverna Ayios Ioannis* on the main road, which serves excellent **lunch** on tables under a shady vine trellis; *kounéli*, the house speciality of charcoal-grilled rabbit, is recommended, and the lamb is tasty, too. The taverna also has simple but good-value **rooms** (☎0892/42-006; ②) in a garden at the rear.

Be sure to take in the tiny drum-domed church of **Áyios Pávlos**, five hundred metres beyond the taverna in a walled cemetery on the left side of the road close to a junction. Encircled by cypresses this delightful church is one of the oldest on the island with parts dating from the pre-Christian era, perhaps part of a Roman shrine to a water deity focused on the well at the rear of the graveyard. The area to the rear of the church is the most ancient, with the dome probably added in the fourteenth century and the narthex or porch – with its Venetian pointed arches – added in the sixteenth. Inside (the church is normally left open), some interesting **frescoes** are dated by a frieze to 1303, and have images of the Evangelists Matthew and Luke and a lurid representation of the punishments of Hell with souls being molested by serpents. This is one of the very few churches on Crete dedicated to St Paul who was none too taken with the islanders, describing them in one of his letters as "liars, evil beasts and lazy gluttons".

Almost opposite the church a road heads west for three kilometres through olive groves to **KAMILÁRI**, where you can see an early **Minoan tomb**, one of the oldest and best preserved in Crete. Dating from about 1900 BC, it was a circular structure with a large dome inside which communal burials took place, whilst cults were carried out in adjoining rooms. The stone walls still stand two metres high in parts; important clay models depicting worship at a shrine and a circular group of dancers unearthed here are now in the Iráklion museum. Incidentally, the design of these tombs is strikingly similar to tombs being constructed in southern Spain around the same time, but a link has not yet been proved. Head along the road into Kamilári and ask for directions to the tomb ("archaeológiki anaskafí" are the words you need), as it's a little tricky to find.

Otherwise, the main route continues for a couple of kilometres beyond Áyios Pávlos to take a right at a junction towards Pitsídhia (see p.127) and, 7km beyond the junction, rolls into Mátala.

Mátala

MÁTALA is much the best known of the beaches in the south of Iráklion province, and was once one of the chief ports of Górtys. You may still meet people who will assure you that, with its cave-dwelling hippy community, this is *the* travellers' beach on Crete. But that's now history – and bears about as much relation to modern reality as Mátala's role in legend as the place where Zeus swam ashore in the guise of a bull with Europa on his back.

The entry to the village should prepare you for what to expect; as you drive in past a couple of kilometres of new hotels, "Welcome to Mátala" signs and extensive car-parking areas line the roadsides all the way into town. It does get better, and development is still relatively small-scale, but the town never feels anything other than touristy: tourbus arrivals in the afternoon take up every inch of sand and prices (for rooms especially) are relatively high. For all practical purposes, Mátala consists virtually of a single street, the continuation of the main road into town as it curves round behind the beach. The "market" and many of the places to eat lie to the right, between the road and the beach, and the "old town", such as it is, is crammed against the rocks to the left. Almost every other practical need is easily taken care of: **car** and **bike rental** and **currency exchange** are all around the main square or up the single main street, and there are also a couple of **travel agents**. There's a **post office** van parked throughout the summer at the entrance to the beach car park, with competitive exchange rates as well as stamps for your postcards; the **OTE** also occupies a temporary building, this time in the middle of the car park behind the beach. The **bookshop** Kadianakis, near the main square, stocks foreign newspapers and a selection of English fiction and is a helpful source of information. The covered **market** still has a couple of authentic stalls selling fruit and veg, but these are rapidly being displaced by souvenir stores, general stalls and travel agents. Finally, if you want to escape, there are **boat trips** from the harbour (in addition to all the usual bus excursions on offer at the travel agents): a taxi service to Red Beach and Kómmos, and twice-weekly trips to Ayía Galíni and Préveli.

On the plus side, Mátala beach really is quite spectacular: a curving swathe of sand tucked under the cliff in which the notorious caves are carved; if you are prepared to walk, there are other beaches with far fewer people on them. The town crowds – there are always crowds – are relatively young, the atmosphere is boisterous and you will never be short of somewhere to enjoy a cocktail at sunset. If you enjoy that, Mátala has something to offer; if you're after solitude or a cheap room, try somewhere else.

Caves and beaches

The **caves** started it all. Nobody knows quite who started the caves, which are entirely man-made, but it seems likely that the first were Roman or early Christian tombs: they have since been so often reused and added to that it is virtually impossible to tell. The cliff in which they are carved, an outcrop of compacted sand, is soft enough to allow surprisingly elaborate decor: some caves have carved windows and doorways as well as built in benches or beds (which may originally have been grave slabs); others are mere scooped-out hollows. Local people inhabited the caves, on and off, for centuries, and during the war they made a handy munitions dump, but it was in the 1960s that they really became famous, attracting a large and semi-permanent foreign community. Name a famous hippy and there'll be someone who'll claim that he or she lived here too – Cat Stevens and Bob Dylan are only the most frequently mentioned. It has, however, been a very long time since the caves were cleared, and nowadays they're fenced off, open by day but searched by the police every night.

The **beach** below the caves is the focus for most of the town's activity, and during the day everyone hangs out either on the sand or in the tavernas overlooking it. The swimming is great – if surprisingly rough when the wind blows – with gently shelving sand in the centre, underwater remains of the Roman port around the base of the rocks on both sides (watch out for sea urchins), and multicoloured fish everywhere. If the crowds on this town beach get too much, you can head south, climbing over the rocks behind town in about twenty minutes, to another excellent stretch of sand known locally as **Red Beach**, but be warned that the track can be quite hard going and you may end up scrambling over loose scree on the way down. Usually half empty, this beach has curious dark reddish-brown sand and wonderfully clear water. On the way you pass more caves, many of which are in fact inhabited through the summer; indeed, when you know where to look, it turns out that there are a number of cave dwellings around, all some way from the village with the exact whereabouts of the better ones a closely guarded secret.

Accommodation

Finding a **room** should be no problem with so many alternatives, and travel agencies should be able to help if you can't face the trawl. Out of season, you may well be in a position to bargain, but Mátala does have a very long season – it's a popular Easter destination for Greek families. The most attractive place to stay is undoubtedly in the old town on one of the little backstreets, but there are very few places here. More realistic, and still right at the centre of things, is to take the little street to the left immediately after *Hotel Zafiria* (☎0892/45-112, fax 45-725; ④), along a road signed "Hotels and Rent Rooms", which is almost entirely lined with purpose-built rooms places. Among the best of these is *Hotel Nikos* (☎0892/45-375, fax 45-120; ③) with en-suite rooms around a charming plant-filled courtyard; try asking the eponymous proprietor for the cheaper rooms 25 and 26 which are furnished more simply. *Hotel Sofia* (☎0892/45-134, fax 45-743; ③) is also good, although rooms facing towards the town square can be very noisy. Quieter and mostly cheaper alternatives nearby include *Matala View* (☎0892/45-114; ②), *Iliaki* (☎0892/45-110; ③), *Fantastik* (☎0892/45-362; ③) and *Silvia* (☎0892/45-127; ②), which all have some rooms with bath. There's a **campsite** above the beach car park, *Matala Camping* (☎0892/45-340), which is fine and convenient if you like camping on sand. If you don't mind being further from the beach, then *Camping Kómmos* (☎0892/45-596) is a better bet, with an on-site swimming pool and taverna; buses between Pitsídhia and Mátala stop nearby.

Eating and nightlife

Finding something to **eat** is the least of your worries. Tavernas fringe the bay, with sufficient competition to keep prices reasonable; menus are generally very similar. The smallest and least pretentious is the *Skala* fish taverna with superb views across to the cliffs. It is also the furthest away and is approached through the bar of *Neosicos* – make sure of your steps across the cliffs, especially on the way back. *Kimata* and *Plaka* are other reliable possibilities near the beach. In town, *Minos Palace* is a reliable taverna close to the *Hotel Zafiria* while almost opposite the same hotel, *Kafeneío* is a stylish new bar which makes a pleasant breakfast venue and does cocktails in the evening. Takeaway food and ingredients for picnics can be found in the stalls of the "market".

The chief **entertainment** in the evening is watching the invariably spectacular sunset: almost every bar and restaurant has a west-facing terrace. Although there's a solitary **disco**, *Neosicos*, nightlife is generally low-key. The two most popular music bars are the *Marinero* and the *Rock Bar*, while the *Zwei Brüder* bar/taverna, in the main square as you arrive in town, is the longest-established meeting place, with music and reasonably cheap food. *Odysea* (near the *Skala* taverna) and the neighbouring *Sea Horse* are other likely places for a drink.

Pitsídhia, Kalamáki and Kómmos

An alternative base to Mátala, and a good way of saving some money and also enjoying rather more peace, is to stay at **PITSÍDHIA**, which sprawls around the main road about 5km inland. This is already a well-used option, so Pitsídhia is no unspoilt village, and nor is it quite as cheap as you might expect, but there are plenty of rooms, lively places to eat, and an affable young international crowd.

KALAMÁKI, which is right on the beach a similar distance from Pitsídhia as Mátala, is another possibility. At the moment it seems unfinished, a dusty, ugly place caught halfway between being a beach with a taverna on it and a full-blown resort, but there's plenty of accommodation in half-built rooms places, several bike rental companies with hardly any customers, a number of places to eat, and a long, empty, windswept beach. The road down there seems to run out halfway (unless they've finally completed the new paved one), but any of the dusty tracks seems to find its way to the coast eventually.

Kómmos

At the southern end of the long beach that starts in Kalamáki, almost halfway to Mátala, lies the archeological site of ancient **KÓMMOS**, a Minoan harbour town which was probably the main port for Festós and Ayía Triádha. The site can also be approached from Pitsídhia by a track signed "to *Camping Kómmos*" on the right, 1km west of the village.

Sir Arthur Evans was the first to report signs of Minoan occupation here, but real excavation started only a decade ago when Joseph Shaw began work, funded by the American School of Classical Studies. The work carried out in the seasons since then has made it clear that Kómmos is destined to become a major site of the future. Meanwhile, the excavations are fenced off and not strictly open to visitors – but this does not prevent you taking a look at what's been uncovered.

There are three main **excavation areas** to the north, centre and south none of them more than a stone's throw behind the beach. It is thought that the whole area will eventually yield evidence of occupation. The **northern area**, on a low hill close to the sea, contains **domestic dwellings** among which is a large house (on the south side) with a paved court and a **limestone wine press**. The **central group** – behind a retaining wall to prevent subsidence – has houses from the **New Palace era**, with well-preserved walls and evidence, in the fallen limestone slabs, of the earthquake around 1600 BC which caused much destruction here. A rich haul of intact **pottery** was found in this area, much of it in the brightly painted Kamáres style.

The most remarkable finds to date, however, came in the **southern sector** where what you see is partly confused by being overlaid by a Classical Greek sanctuary. Minoan remains here include a fine stretch of **limestone roadway**, 3m wide and more than 60m long, heading away inland, no doubt towards Ayía Triádha and Festós. The road is rutted from the passage of ox-drawn carts and would also have been pounded by the feet of countless Minoan mariners. Note the drainage channel on its northern side. To the south of the road one building contains the longest stretch of **Minoan wall** on the island: over 50m of dressed stone. The function of this enormous building isn't known but it may well have had a storage purpose connected with the port. Just south of this was another large building (now partly overlaid by a later Greek structure – probably a warehouse), 30m long and 35m wide, divided into five sections with its seaward end open to the sea. This was a shipshed or **dry dock** where vessels were stored out of the water during the winter (or non-sailing) season.

An interesting **temple** lies to the western side of this area, nearest the sea. Here an early tenth-century BC Dorian temple – one of the earliest in the whole of Greece – was replaced by a later one, apparently devoted to a pillar cult similar to that of the Phoenicians who had founded a trading empire based upon modern Lebanon. The excavators think that the Phoenicians may have erected the temple here for use by their sailors, who would have made frequent trading missions to Kómmos. The other remains and altars in this area date from the Hellenistic period when the site became a revered sanctuary. When fully excavated and opened to the public, Kómmos may well emerge as among the most important Minoan sites yet explored.

Léndas and Kalí Liménes

South of the Messará, two more beach resorts – Léndas and Kalí Liménes – beckon. Léndas has a couple of buses a day from Iráklion and in an undeveloped way is quite a busy place. Kalí Liménes, 20km south of Míres, for reasons which will become apparent, is hardly visited at all. If you have your own transport, the roads around here are all passable but mostly very slow: the Asteroússia Hills, which divide the plain from the coast, are surprisingly precipitous and even on the paved roads you have to keep a sharp eye out for sudden patches of mud, potholes and roadworks. The only halfway decent roads to the coast here are the 25km route from Górtys to Léndas via Mitrópolis, and the newly sealed 22km route from Míres to Kalí Liménes (follow the signs carefully). Both itineraries offer great views back over the Messará plain before toiling on through a quintessential mountainous Cretan landscape, where clumps of violet-flowering wild thyme cling to the verges in summer, and shepherds slow your progress as they herd their flocks of goats along the road at dusk.

Other than the direct Léndas–Iráklion service, public transport is very limited indeed – you'll almost always have to travel via Míres.

Léndas

Many travellers who arrive in **LÉNDAS** think they've come to the wrong place. The village is neat but not overly attractive, the beach is small and rocky; and the rooms are frequently all booked. Quite a few leave without ever correcting that first impression. For the real attraction of Léndas is not here at all but beyond the point to the west, a kilometre or so along the coast road. Here, at **Diskós Beach**, you come upon an enormous kilometre-long stretch of sand, where three good taverna/bars, each with a few basic rooms, overlook the beach from the roadside, and tents and makeshift shelters provide accommodation for many more down on the shore. This beach is almost entirely nudist, and largely caters to German tourists (all the menus are written in German). Once you've discovered why Léndas is so popular, the village itself begins to look slightly more welcoming. The bus drops you in a sandy yard which also serves as a car park for those who drive – from here you pick your way down to the beach as best you can although the few paths which look promising mostly end up in someone's back garden to the outrage of a barking dog or rooting piglet.

The village's focus is a not unpleasant platía with an ornamental plinth built around a tamarisk tree. Here most of the facilities you'll need are located, including Filophas's Store which sells newspapers and souvenirs, changes money and is a fund of local **information**, often doled out with a free *raki*. A **travel agent** on the square does **car** and **bike hire** and there's a **phone box** just off it. There are also couple of food stores, and numerous places to eat: the *Irini*, *Elpida* and *Vundulakis* tavernas are all reasonable. Nightlife is predictably laid back and confined to a handful of bars (the *Pink Panther* serves pizzas and cocktails). You'll see all the **accommodation** options pretty soon – *Lendas Bungalows* (☎0892/95-221, fax 95-222; ②) as you enter the village are relatively luxurious and good value, considering that you get a sea view, en-suite bungalow and use of a kitchen to prepare your own meals. Out at Diskós Beach (if you're walking, you can save time by cutting across the headland), *Villa Tsarakis* (☎0892/95-378, fax 95-377; ② with reductions for longer stays) has the best rooms, all with bath and circling a plant-filled patio a mere 50m from the sea. *Taverna Sifis* (②) further west, is slightly cheaper; both this taverna and the nearby *Odisseas* do decent food.

East of Léndas, you can also explore some smaller, near-deserted beaches, and the hilltop remains of ancient **Levín** (or Leben) overlooking them from immediately outside the village. This was an important healing sanctuary, with an *Asklepion* by a spring of therapeutic waters; people were still coming here for cures as recently as the 1960s when the spring was diverted and the site became neglected. At its height, from the third century BC onwards, the sanctuary maintained an enormous temple and was a major centre of pilgrimage. You can still see ruins spread over an extensive area, but sadly, little of their nature can be discerned. There's an arch through which the water once flowed, otherwise only the odd segment of broken wall survives, along with a few severed columns or statue bases, and isolated fragments of mosaic. Much closer in, just above the main part of the village, are the more substantial remains of an early Christian basilica, with a much smaller eleventh-century chapel still standing in their midst.

Lassaia, Krysóstomos and Kalí Liménes

Leaving Léndas **to the west**, past the beach, you can follow a mostly unpaved road along the coast all the way to Kalí Liménes. It's a very bumpy drive, but far from impossible, and on the way you'll pass a number of smaller beaches. The only one of these with any sort of permanent habitation is Platía Perámata, a sandy little village with a couple of stores, a few basic rooms and usually the odd camper. It's really not the best of beaches, though. In both the last two bays before Kalí Liménes small rooms places have recently opened above little beaches. The first,

KRYSÓSTOMOS, is a very basic affair with clean bungalow **rooms** with bath behind the *Taverna Ostria* (☎0892/42-204; ②), which also has an incongruous dancing bar above a pebbly beach. The second, **LASSAIA**, is slightly bigger. Tumbling down a hill to a bay with a good sandy beach, this is a village of holiday homes anarchically thrown up after the Greek fashion with little regard for planning or facilities. Hence the lack of good roads or electricity, as the rumbling chorus of generators which greets the dusk each evening reminds you. Surprisingly, there's a decent place **to stay**, *Taverna Lassaia* (☎0892/93-284; ②), where spotless rooms come with bath, fridge and TV although their sea view looks about to disappear behind the rising – and unplanned – edifice looming in front. The taverna also does excellent **food** and their generator is buried in a cellar, guaranteeing you a decent night's sleep.

KALÍ LIMÉNES itself was an important port in Roman times, the main harbour of Górtys and the place where St Paul put in, as a prisoner aboard a ship bound for Rome, in an incident described in the Bible in Acts 27. He wanted to stay the winter here, but was overruled by the captain of the ship and the centurion acting as his guard: setting sail they were promptly overtaken by a storm, driving them past Clauda (the island of Gávdhos) and on eventually to shipwreck on Malta.

Today Kalí Liménes is once again a major port, for oil tankers, which has rather spoilt its chances of becoming a resort, although it is peculiarly appealing. The constant procession of tankers gives you something to look at (they discharge their loads into tanks on an islet just offshore). There are **rooms** on the harbour at *Sea View Rooms* (①). The *Karavovrissi Beach* (☎0892/42-197; ②), a pension with bungalow rooms located in a garden behind a **taverna**, lies a kilometre or so east of the main village where the road from Míres/Pómbia arrives. The coastline is broken up by spectacular cliffs and, as long as there hasn't been a recent oil spill, the beaches – lined by shacks, a couple of which serve simple food and drinks – are reasonably clean and almost totally empty. But it has to be said that it's a long way from the postcard image of Crete.

There are, however, opportunities for some scenic **walking** around Kalí Liménes, and a little back from the village there's a dirt track heading 6km north to the **Moní Odigitria**. A wonderfully panoramic hike into the hills leads to this remote religious outpost where just two monks watch over an impressive collection of fifteenth-century icons in the fortress-like church. From here you can either hike back to Kalí Liménes or, more adventurously, head southwest from the monastery along a track leading to the Áyio Gorge. The gorge is walkable and marked on the *Heraklio Trekking and Road Map* produced by Petrákis (see maps section in Basics). Once on the beach (about 6km from the monastery or a 3hr walk), you'll need a boat (arranged at the harbour in advance) to get you back to Kalí Liménes as there is no route over the cliffs. Also make sure to take sufficient food and water and let people know where you are heading.

Back towards Míres

Heading **back to the Messará** you're in for a bit of mountain driving, and a total contrast once you hit the plain on the far side. Leaving Kalí Liménes, don't attempt to drive out of the west end of the village or you'll soon grind to a halt on precipitous rocks: the road inland heads off a short way east, back towards Léndas. The road is good and climbs beyond Pigaidákia to the pass over Mount Vigla, from where there's a very steep hairpin descent to Pómbia, a large agricultural centre. Beyond here you can either head straight on to Míres or take a left turn for Petrokefáli (where there's a simple pension should you want to stay) and the short route towards Mátala. Touring around here, through quiet and prosperous villages surrounded by their crops of oranges, pomegranates or olives, is a wonderfully peaceful contrast to the traffic of the main road.

Across the south: to Áno Viánnos and Árvi

The road east across the **Messará**, from Áyii Dhéka through Asími to Áno Viánnos in the shadow of the **Dhiktean mountains** is now paved all the way – a feat which has taken many years. Now an enjoyably solitary drive through fertile farming country – there are no buses across, very little transport of any kind, in fact – and, although there's not a great deal to stop for along the way, a visit to the secluded **monastic community** of the Moní Koudoumá is an escapist's dream. If you're looking for a slightly less spartan seaside stopover, the low-key coastal settlements of **Keratókambos** and **Árvi** each have their delights, while the more substantial village of **Áno Viánnos** has plenty of places for a lunch break plus a couple of churches and a folk museum to see.

From Iráklion the road cuts across the centre of the island, through Arkalohóri, to join this route at Mártha and continue through Áno Viánnos towards Ierápetra. In this direction there are a couple of daily buses, but you'll still have to change buses if you hope to hit the coast before Mírtos.

The coastal route

Coming across the island, access to the coast becomes a realistic proposal only beyond Pírgos, a sturdy farming village 10km down the road from Asími. However, for those looking for adventure there is a fine walk from here to the remote **Moní Koudoumá** set in a spectacular seaside location. The monastery nestles in a cove, surrounded by pinewoods, at the foot of a cliff down which descends a dizzying track with endless switchbacks. Arriving here is a distinctly end-of-the world experience and the few remaining monks have only a couple of nearby dwellings inhabited by elderly women for company. The monks see few visitors, but are extremely welcoming to those that do turn up, and will offer you food and a mattress in one of the dormitories set aside for "pilgrims". While the monks will not accept payment for their hospitality, a donation to "monastery funds" is unlikely to be refused. If you think the magic of the place may persuade you to prolong your stay, you should bring supplies with you. The nights here – illuminated by oil lamps in the absence of mains electricity – are exquisitely serene, broken only by the sound of the sea splashing against the rocks.

On foot, the easiest route from Pírgos (about 20km) is to leave the village by the Priniás road that winds down through the hamlet of Trís Ekklisíes, before it degrades into a dirt track. By road, your best bet is to double back to Stérnes and head south along a slightly better (but still unpaved) surface. Be warned, though, that the final cliff-face section is particularly hazardous – not the kind of thing to be attempted lightly in a rented car. Should you need to spend a night in **PÍRGOS** before setting out, *Rooms Tzaridakis* (☎0893/22-238; ①), just off the main street, is pleasant enough, and there are also a couple of decent tavernas nearby. At the eastern end of the main street lies the fourteenth-century church of Áyios Yióryios and Áyios Konstantínos: a Byzantine edifice with some interesting faded frescoes. The key is available from the house (no. 137) to the right of the church gate.

Tsoútsouros and Keratókambos

A much less arduous route to the sea comes 12km beyond Pírgos at Kató Kastilianá: 13km of trail which wind alarmingly down to Tsoútsouros. This is not an effort to be recommended, for **TSOÚTSOUROS**, despite its apparent isolation, is amazingly developed. The source of the crowds that flock here and how they reach it is a mystery; the small grey beach can barely cope.

It's far better to hold out for **KERATÓKAMBOS**, a tranquil fishing village 10km along a terrible coastal trail from here – or a similar distance by a much better route from the main road. The road down, via the highly picturesque village of Hondrós, is now paved – no doubt a portent of development. For the moment, though, Keratókambos remains tiny and quiet, very much a locals' resort. A single street of houses interspersed with cafés and tavernas faces a tree-lined sand and shingle beach with a shower on it. Two of the tavernas rent out a few **rooms** with bath (try *Morning Star* ☎0895/51-209; ②), and more places are signed in both directions along the seafront. You should however bear in mind that most rooms here are booked solid during July and August. For more luxury you could retrace your steps 2km or so to the point where the road emerges at the coast – this is Kastrí Keratókambos and here you'll find *V.E. Rooms* (②). If you do stay, or you want to **camp** in isolation, you could explore better patches of deserted sand along the coast road in either direction. For **food** both the excellent *Kriti* taverna and *Morning Star* on the seafront do good seafood and meat dishes.

Áno Viánnos

Moving on, the **coast road** gets better as you head towards Árvi, passing beneath a great crag of rock with a ruined castle perched upon it. Again, however, the direct approach is the turning off the main road, heading first through the large village of **ÁNO VIÁNNOS**, clinging to the southern slopes of the Dhíkti range. The air is much sharper up here, even in high summer, and the eating fare more substantial than on the sweltering beaches far below. The traditional centre of this part of southeastern Iráklion province, Áno (upper) Viánnos's importance has waned as the coastal settlements have grown. But it's still a substantial village with a couple of interesting **churches** containing well-preserved fourteenth-century frescoes. These, Ayía Pelayía (dating from the fourteenth century with a magnificent, if damaged, *Crucifixion* on the back wall) and Áyios Yeóryios, are located up a narrow, stepped side street close to the enormous plane tree on the village's eastern extremity. At the opposite end of the village is an interesting new **Folk Museum** (Mon–Sat 9.30am–1.30pm & 5.30–7.30pm; Sun 9am–1pm; 500dr) with displays of costumes, handicrafts and embroideries documenting Viánnos's social and cultural history from medieval times to World War II.

A snack bar uphill from the modern church has basic **rooms** (②) and there are a couple of places serving **food** in the centre, or you could head out along the main road east for 1km to the barn-sized *Taverna O Diabatis* which often puts on uproarious *lyra* concerts at weekends, drawing in farmers and their families from miles around for a wild night of singing and dancing.

Káto Sími

The Ierápetra road leads east out of the village, skirting an alarming precipice, and continues on through Amirás, where you turn off for Árvi by a giant memorial to the Cretans killed in World War II. With your own transport there's a scenic detour to the village of **KÁTO SÍMI** and its **ancient sanctuary** of Hermes and Aphrodite. To get there drive for 4km beyond the war memorial to take a signed road on the left to Káto Sími, a docile village 1km from the turn-off. Another war memorial on the edge of the village commemorates five hundred people put to death in 1943 in retaliation for an attack on a German patrol, when this and six other villages were destroyed. Continue through the village and when you reach a fork (with a modern house above), turn left to follow a rough track as it snakes up the mountain for 3km until you arrive at a wooded ravine filled with pines. Here, look out for a track off to the right. You will soon pass a waterfall and ford beyond which you should keep going for a further kilometre where the site lies above the road on the right, behind a fence. Laid out on a series of broad ledges on the mountainside, this remote location was first a Minoan shrine and then adopted by the later Greeks who perhaps transmuted the Minoan deities into their Hellenic equivalents, Hermes and Aphrodite. Some of the enormous quantity of votive offerings carried here by ancient pilgrims are now on display in the Iráklion museum. Turning off by the giant war memorial (see above), a paved road winds gradually down to sea level and emerges on the coast through the gorge of a stream which waters the exotic fruits grown around Árvi.

Árvi

Standing on the site of the ancient Roman town of Arvis, and hemmed in by rock cliffs which trap the heat – creating a microclimate among the hottest in Crete – **ÁRVI** has surprisingly not been overwhelmed by development. This may have something to do with a long but pebbly beach and the villagers' greater interest in the wealth to be made from growing bananas, oranges and pineapples in this near-tropical environment. There are **rooms**, but not always enough in high season: try the *Hotel Ariadne* (☎0895/71-300; ③), near the entrance to the village with balcony sea views, or the slightly cheaper *Gorgona* (☎0895/71-211; ②) or *Rooms Galaxy* (☎0895/71-373; ②), towards the centre. The most relaxing place to stay, however, is the friendly seafront *Rent Rooms Colibi* (☎0895/71-250; ②) with a delightful garden where balcony sea-view rooms come with bath, and there are breakfast tables beneath tamarisk trees, fronting a beach complete with showers. To get there, head west from the town for 1km until the road bends right; keep ahead here along an unpaved road next to the beach. Failing this, follow the usual street-corner signs. Once you've settled in there's not much else to do apart from baking in the sun, which is something you can often do comfortably here even when the rest of the island is too cold to contemplate it. When you need shade, there are numerous stores, bars, cafés and **tavernas** (try *Andigonia*) behind the beach; it's possible to **change money** at the *Hotel Ariadne* (see above).

On the hillside overlooking the village is the picturesque nineteenth-century monastery of **Áyios Andónios**, which now has only a couple of monks in residence. To get there – and it's a pleasant **walk** – go to the back of the village and you'll come to signposts guiding you to a track across a valley towards the monastery, on the side of a slope. It's especially tranquil here at dusk when the monks sit out on their terrace, happy to converse with passing visitors.

Along a bumpy track **to the east** lie more isolated beaches leading eventually to the tiny coastal hamlets of Faflángos and, after 6km, **AKROTÍRI SIDONÍA**, which has a superb **beach**, a couple of tavernas and a smart new **rooms** place (*Rooms Foráda* ☎0895/61-311; ③) where apartments come with kitchen and sea-view balcony. It should be possible to **camp** here at the far eastern end of the beach, but be aware of local sensitivities: these are not resorts but ordinary villages on the sea. Some maps don't mark it, but the dirt track continues to Tértsa and Mírtos (p.192), some 12km in all, which makes a pleasant walk.

GREEK PLACE NAMES

ΑΓ ΠΕΛΑΓΙΑ	Αγ Πελαγία	Ay. Pelayía
ΑΜΝΗΣΟΣ	Αμνήσος	Amnísos
ΑΝΩ ΒΙΑΝΝΟΣ	Ανω Βιάννος	Áno Viánnos
ΑΡΒΗ	Αρβή	Árvi
ΑΡΧΑΝΕΣ	Αρχάνες	Arhánes
ΒΑΘΥΠΕΤΡΟ	Βαθύπετρο	Vathípetro
ΓΙΟΥΧΤΑΣ	Γιούχτας	Yioúhtas
ΓΟΥΡΝΕΣ	Γούρυες	Goúrnes
ΓΟΡΤΥΣ	Γόρτυς	Górtys
ΗΡΑΚΛΕΙΟ	Ηράκλειο	Iráklion
ΚΑΛΟΙ ΛΙΜΕΝΕΣ	Καλοί Λιμένες	Kalí Liménes
ΚΕΡΑΤΟΚΑΜΠΟΣ	Κερατοκάμπος	Keratokámbos
ΚΝΩΣΟΣ	Κυωσός	Knossós
ΛΕΝΤΑΣ	Λέντας	Léndas
ΜΑΛΙΑ	Μάλια	Mália
ΜΑΤΑΛΑ	Μάταλα	Mátala
ΜΟΙΡΕΣ	Μοίρες	Míres
ΤΣΟΥΤΣΟΥΡΟΣ	Τσούτσουρος	Tsoútsouros
ΤΥΛΙΣΟΣ	Τύλισος	Tílissos
ΤΥΜΠΑΚΙ	Τυμπάκι	Timbáki
ΦΑΙΣΤΟΣ	Φαιστός	Festós
ΦΟΔΕΛΕ	Φόδελε	Fódhele
ΧΕΡΣΟΝΗΣΟΣ	Χερσόνησος	Hersónisos

travel details

Buses

Iráklion to: Áno Viánnos (2 daily; 6.30am & midnight; 2hr 30min/3hr); Anóyia (5 daily; 6.30am–4.30pm; 1hr); Arhánes (15 daily; 6.30am–8.30pm; 30min); Ay. Galíni (7 daily; 6.30am–4.30pm; 2hr 30min); Ay. Nikólaos (25 daily; 6.30am–10.15pm; 1hr 30min); Ay. Pelayía (6 daily; 8.15am–7pm; 30min); Festós (9 daily; 7.30am–5.45pm; 2hr); Fódhele (2 daily; 6.30am & 2.30pm; 1hr); Haniá (25 daily; 5.30am–8.30pm; 1hr 30min/3hr) Hersónisos (every 30min; 6.30am–10pm; 45min); Ierápetra (8 daily; 7.30am–6.30pm, via Ay. Nikólaos; 2hr 30min); Lasíthi plateau (2 daily; 8.30am & 3pm; 2hr); Léndas (1 daily; 1pm; 3hr); Mália (every 30min; 6.30am–10pm; 1hr); Mátala (7 daily; 7.30am–5.45pm; 2hr); Milátos (2 daily; 7am & 3pm; 1hr 30min); Omalós (daily at 5.30am; 4hr 30min); Réthimnon/Haniá (29 daily; 5.30am–8.30pm, a couple via the old road; 1hr 30min/3hr); Sitía (5 daily; 7am–4.30pm; 3hr 30min).

Mália/Hersónisos to: Lasíthi plateau (1 daily; 8.45am; 1hr 30min).

Some of these services are restricted on Sundays.

Ferries

To the Cyclades daily to Thíra, Íos & Páros; most days to Míkonos & Náxos; at least 2 weekly to Tínos, Skíros, Skíathos & Anáfi.

To Kárpathos/Rhodes Wed 8am, Sat 7am (10hr/12hr).

To Pireás 2 daily, at 7.15pm & 7.30pm; additional sailings Mon, Thurs & Sun (12hr).

To Thessaloníki Daily except Sun; times vary.

To Thíra 1–3 daily; all afternoon or evening sailings (2hr 30min fast boat/4hr).

These are summer timetables – schedules severely restricted in winter.

International ferries

To Ancona Wed 10pm & Sun 9pm (56hr).

To Çeşme and İzmir (Turkey) Mon midnight (39hr).

To Limassol (Cyprus) and Haifa (Israel) Tues 11am (28hr/36hr).

To Venice Every 8 days (63hr).

Flights

To Athens 7 daily (50min).

To Páros 3 a week (45min).

To Rhodes 4 a week (40min).

To Thessaloníki 3 a week (1hr 30min).

To Thíra/Míkonos 2 a week (40min/30min).

Summer timetables – no island flights and others restricted in winter.

CHAPTER TWO

LASÍTHI

Eastern Crete is dominated by **Áyios Nikólaos** and the mass tourism it attracts, and travellers who are interested in a more traditional face of the island tend not to look on the area with much favour. That said, Áyios Nikólaos itself is less crowded these days than it once was, though it still makes a lively and exciting base, whilst the surrounding countryside – the **Lasíthi plateau**, **Kritsá** and around **Eloúnda** in particular – is worth a few days of anyone's time.

Things improve, too, as you move towards the far east of the island, which is under the sway not of Áyios Nikólaos but of **Sitía**, a large and traditional town where tourism has had little outward effect. At the eastern tip, the Minoan palace at **Zákros** and the laid-back beaches around **Vái**, **Palékastro** and **Kserócambos** offer wildly contrasting escapes.

Along the south coast, there is generally far less development; **Ierápetra** is the major town and a decent stopover, although its immediate environs would win few beauty prizes. Not far away, however, at **Mírtos** and **Makriyialós** for example, there are beaches as good as any in the province.

THE LASÍTHI PLATEAU AND ÁYIOS NIKÓLAOS

The northwestern corner of Lasíthi may be the draw for almost all the province's visitors, but it's not just about resorts. Stay for a few days in the **Lasíthi plateau** and you experience a very different world; make your way east along the coast to **Goúrnia** and you can enjoy one of the best minor Minoan sites in near-isolation. And at **Áyios Nikólaos**, of course, there is genuine fun to be had, in what is perhaps Crete's most cosmopolitan enclave.

Transport, at least along the main roads, is excellent. There's a constant stream of buses between Iráklion and Áyios Nikólaos, stopping at major points en route, and good local services from both Áyios Nikólaos and the inland centre of Neápoli.

Mália to Áyios Nikólaos

Driving into Lasíthi from Mália there's a choice of routes. The wide, fast new road leaves the palace at Mália behind and embarks almost immediately on the long climb inland – rising at first through the **Gorge of Selinári** where travellers would traditionally stop at the chapel and pray to St George for safe passage. There's a truckstop here, but most traffic roars straight past and on through the tunnel blasted beneath the old pass. It's a tremendous engineering achievement, though beyond here – having bypassed **Neápoli** – there's little else to see until

---

you emerge high above Áyios Nikólaos to encounter spectacular views of the
Gulf of Mirabéllo.

Sísi

The old road follows the coast for a while longer, rolling on through Sísi with a
branch off to Mílatos (see below). **SÍSI** is becoming developed, but for the
moment this amounts only to scattered apartments, and the local beaches remain
quiet and small-scale. **Epáno Sísi**, the inland part of the village, has one or two
possibilities for rooms, but a more tempting stop is **Sísi Paralía**, 2km away on the
coast. Here a picturesque tiny harbour is overlooked by some traditional tavernas: try *Koursaras* or *Miramare* which have views of the harbour and sell fresh
fish. However, new construction has undermined the village's erstwhile tranquillity and as well as a large new holiday complex, *Kalimera Krita*, a couple of kilometres to the east, there's now also the usual array of bike rental offices, souvenir
stores and bars. Scattered around the village are numerous **rooms**; *Villa Asprogas*
(☎081/285-052; ④), a charming four-person villa with pool, is available for stays of
three days and longer. *Camping Sísi* (☎0841/71-247) is located just over 1km to
the west, and has its own swimming pool and plenty of shade.

Mílatos

MÍLATOS remains less developed, possibly because of its uncomfortable pebble
beach (though there are sun beds for hire). Once again **rooms** are available both
in the village and at the beach settlement 2km away. Here, tavernas, cafés and
stores cluster around a small church on the waterfront, the tavernas specializing
in fresh but expensive fish.

Although you'd never guess from what remains today, **ancient Mílatos** has a
distinguished story and the glory of a mention by Homer in the *Iliad* as one of the
seven Cretan cities that sent forces to fight at Troy. In mythology (backed up by
recent archeological finds) it was from Mílatos that Sarpedon, King Minos's

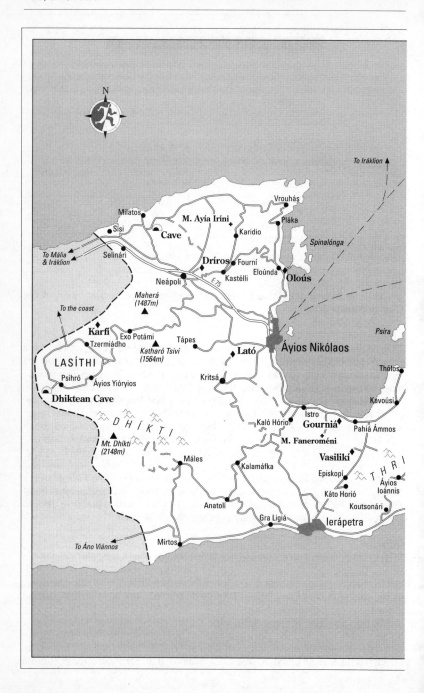

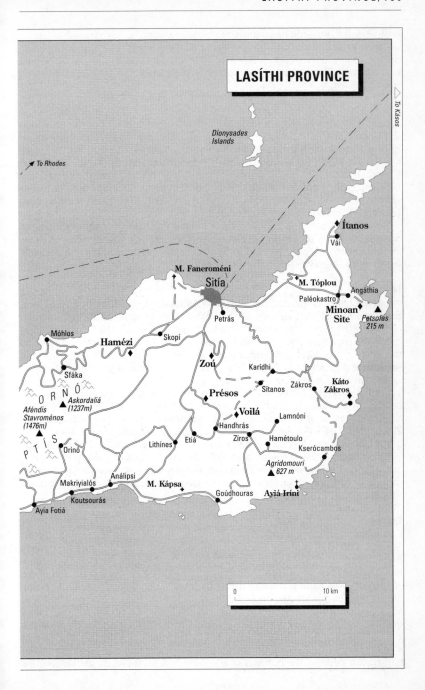

LASÍTHI PROVINCE

To Kásos

Dionysades Islands

To Rhodes

Ítanos
Vái

M. Faneroméni
Sitía
M. Tóplou
Angáthia
Paléokastro
Minoan Site
Petrás
Petsofás 215 m
Móhlos
Hamézi
Skopí
Karídhi
Zoú
Káto Zákros
Zákros
Sítanos
O R N Ó
Sfáka
Askordaliá (1237m)
Aféndis Stavroménos (1476m)
Présos
Lamnóni
Voilá
Handhrás
Ziros
Hamétoulo
P T Í S
Orinó
Lithínes
Etiá
Kserócambos
Agridomouri 627 m
Análipsi
Makriyialós
M. Kápsa
Goúdhouras
Ayiá Iríni
Koutsourás
Ayia Fotiá

0   10 km

brother whom the king had defeated to take the throne, sailed to found Miletus – destined to become one of the greatest of all the cities in Asia Minor. Unlike its namesake in modern Turkey, however, little has survived on the site to the east of the beach. The city faded into obscurity in antiquity and by Roman times no longer existed.

There's more recent history to be seen at the **Mílatos Cave**, 3km east of the village and signposted up a good dirt road. More a series of caverns than a single cave, this appears to go back for miles: with adequate lighting you might be able to discover just how far. Less adventurously, there's a small chapel to explore right at the entrance, a memorial to the events which earned the cave its notoriety. Here in 1823, during one of the early rebellions against the Turks, some 2700 Cretans (that at least is the number claimed) took refuge, were discovered and besieged in the cave. Eventually, having failed to break their way out, they were offered safe conduct by the Turkish commander – only to be killed or taken away into slavery as soon as they surrendered.

Beyond the cave, you could continue around the Áyios Ioánnis peninsula, or across to Neápoli, by a variety of dirt roads. Back through Mílatos village, however, the scarcely used paved road to Neápoli is an equally beautiful and certainly easier way to zigzag through the mountains.

Neápoli

NEÁPOLI, despite its size, history (Pope Alexander V was born here) and location, sees virtually no tourists other than those who stop for a coffee in the square between buses or as they drive through. A charming provincial town, it was formerly the capital of Lasíthi (a role now usurped by Áyios Nikólaos) and remains the seat of the local government and of the provincial courts; there's one **museum**, dedicated to folklore (Tues–Sun 10am–1pm & 6–9pm; 500dr), at the south end of the main square.

Facilities include a superbly restored **hotel**, the *Neapolis* (☎0841/33-966; ④), built in the Bauhaus style with fine views from some rooms. To get there, follow the street (Odhós Antistasis) facing the war memorial from the main square for 200m. There are signs for various other **rooms** to rent, and, around the square, a few tavernas and kafenía as well as a post office and banks. At *I Driros*, the zaharoplasteío facing the war memorial, you can try a *soumádha*, a refreshing almond drink highly popular with the locals. It's a peaceful place to stay, and it is from here that one of the roads up to the Lasíthi plateau (see following section) sets out.

Dríros

Continuing instead towards Áyios Nikólaos, there's soon a turning signed towards **DRÍROS**, a route that curls steeply up above the old and new roads (which here run almost exactly parallel). Following the signs you eventually come to a dead end beneath a rocky hillside, and scrambling up you'll find ruins of the ancient city – its earliest remains dating back to the eighth century BC. A canopy covers the **Temple of Apollo Delphinios**, one of the earliest known temples in all of Greece. It was dedicated to a cult that celebrated Apollo transformed into a dolphin, a guise the god used when guiding Greek sailors. That the chief sanctuary of Miletus in Asia Minor was devoted to the same cult is further evidence of a link between this area and the founding of the colony there. In the centre of the temple can be seen the remains of a sunken hearth. Amongst the discoveries were three hammered bronze statuettes, amongst the earliest known (now in the Iráklion museum), as well as two Eteocretan inscriptions – Greek letters used to write a Cretan, possibly Minoan tongue. It's hard to believe that this temple once lay on the edge of the bustling *agora*, or main square, and was approached by a flight of steps – visible in the gorge fronting the temple, now crammed with fig trees.

Finding anything else of note among the thorny bushes and ruined dry-stone walls roundabout is virtually impossible, and deciphering it once you do is even harder. Nevertheless, if you make it to the top of the hill – topped by a charming barrel-vaulted chapel – the views make the climb worthwhile, whilst the drab desolation all round is a startling contrast to the green country around Neápoli.

North and east of Dríros

To the north of Dríros, a series of twisting (mostly asphalt) roads link a string of remote farming villages which rarely see visitors. Many of the windmills you'll see perched along the heights are still functioning and used to grind flour. One, at Vrouhas, actually welcomes visitors.

If you want to continue east by the least arduous scenic route, however, take the road through **Kastélli**, **Fourní** – with its dramatic entry road lined with severely pruned eucalyptus trees – and **Pínes**, which winds down to Eloúnda with yet more wonderful views of the Gulf of Mirabéllo. The characteristic landscape of this part of Crete still remains, with its stone walls and windmills which hug the steep hillsides and summits.

Worth a detour, near the village of **Karídi**, is the impressive **monastery of Areti** which is currently being restored. Ask the builders if they mind you wandering around, and look out for the large cisterns where rainwater was stored (there was no spring in the area).

The Lasíthi plateau

Every day, scores of bus tours toil up to the **Lasíthi plateau** to view its famous sea of white cloth-sailed **windmills**. Most must leave disappointed, for few of the mills remain in operation, and those that do operate only for limited periods. Others are found next to tavernas and used as a feature to attract people. Nevertheless, even if you see no unfurled sails at all, the trip is still worth making for the drive alone.

From Neápoli a long and winding road, twenty slow kilometres of it, climbs into the mountains which ring the plain. When you think you have arrived, another village appears around the corner and the road climbs again. Before you reach **Amigdáli** there are a couple of roadside tavernas which have stunning views into the hills. Stock up on handmade wooden spoons which hang outside the craftsman's house at **Zénia**, or call in at the small taverna at **Éxo Potámi**. At **Mésa Potámi**, 4km further, you are almost on the plateau, but there are more tavernas to entice you, in addition to roadside stalls selling honey or whatever fruit is in season. When you finally come upon the plateau laid out below you, it seems almost too perfect – a patchwork circle of tiny fields enclosed by the bare flanks of the mountains. Closer to, it's a fine example of **rural** Crete at work, with every inch given over to the cultivation of potatoes, apples, pears, cereals and almost anything else that could conceivably be grown in the cooler climate up here.

The area has always been fertile, its rich alluvial soil washed down from the mountains and watered by the rains which collect in the bowl. In spring there can be floods, which is why the villages all cluster on the higher ground around the edge of the plain, but in summer the windmills traditionally come into use pumping the water back up to the drying surface. Although the plateau was irrigated in Roman times – and inhabited long before that – this system was designed by the Venetians in the fifteenth century, bringing the plain back into use after nearly a century of enforced neglect (during which time cultivation and pasture had been banned after a local rebellion). Where they survive, the windmills have barely changed, but in the past twenty years or so most have been replaced by more dependable petrol-driven pumps. The other windmills – the 26 stone ones standing guard on the ridges above the plain, also mostly ruined – were traditional grain mills. Today, only two of these are left in use.

Come on a day-trip and you will see all this. Stay overnight and you'll see a good deal more, as the tourists leave and a great peace settles over the plateau. The excesses of Mália or Hersónisos seem a world away as you climb into your cot to the sound of braying donkeys and a tolling church bell outside, and wake to the cock's crow the next morning. If you feel inclined to rise with the lark you'll see a diaphanous white mist floating over the plain and its windmills in the sparkling early morning sun. The winters are severe here – up to half a metre of snow is not unusual – so ideally you'd arrive at either end of the summer season: in late spring the pastures and orchards are almost alpine in their covering of **wild flowers**, an impression reinforced by the snow lingering on the higher peaks; in autumn the fruit trees can barely support the weight of their crop. Whatever time of year, though, bring some warm clothing as the nights get extremely cold.

A paved circular road links the villages on the plateau's edge. Whichever village you stay in you can catch the **bus** as it circles the plain, or more enjoyably walk through the fields from one to another. The path is rarely direct, but it's easy enough to pick your way by the trails – even right across the plain, from Psihró to Tzermiádho, is a bare ninety-minute walk. A good time to walk here in summer is the early evening when you'll encounter the villagers on their carts, donkeys and pick-ups making their way back home. Whichever point you arrive at on the circuit you'll be assailed by villagers encouraging you to buy their handmade **rugs** and **embroidered work**. If you're tempted to buy, don't jump at the first opportunity, and don't be afraid to bargain.

Tzermiádho

TZERMIÁDHO, the largest and most important village on the plateau's northern edge, comes complete with post office, OTE, bank, garage, a number of cafés and tavernas and even a couple of **places to stay**. The *Kri Kri* (☎0844/22-170; ②) in the centre is relatively comfortable, and there is also the more expensive *Hotel Kourites* (☎0844/22-194; ③) on the western edge of the village, though this is a rather soulless option. Both places have restaurants, and there's the bakery next to the *Kronia Taverna* in the centre, which sells extremely hot and fresh *tirópita*, some of the best to be had. The taverna itself is not a bad bet in the evening, but tends to be deluged with coach parties from the coast over lunch. A cheaper more authentic alternative is *Valentino*, along the road towards the *Hotel Kourites*.

From the road in the centre of Tzermiádho there's a sign up to the **Trápeza Cave**, in which Evans and Pendlebury discovered remains and tombs going back to Neolithic times. If you don't take up the offer from one of the many elderly "guides" who may accost you en route, you'll need to look out for a slope on the left where the track narrows. Follow this to the top and be alert for the narrow, unmarked cave entrance. As you wander in the murky darkness (a flashlight is essential) it's easy to imagine that this is where Crete began: Stone Age peoples huddled around fires no doubt telling stories in the manner of surviving tribal groups today. From these modest beginnings sprang the Minoans and then, under their tutelage, the Greeks.

The ascent to Karfí

From Tzermiádho there's also an ascent to the ancient Minoan site of **Karfí**, one of the most dramatic places in Crete, perched on the southeast slope of Mount Karfí, with an opportunity to see some spectacular birds of prey. The climb will take about an hour on foot – less if you drive the first part; you'll also need sturdy footwear and, in summer, plenty of water. There are a number of shady places for a picnic on the way up, or even at the site itself, but remember to take all rubbish away with you.

The start of the track up is located on the village's western edge at the side of the district health centre, opposite a blue sign marked in English "To the Tinios Stavros church". Follow this as it winds gently up to the Níssimos plateau (also accessible by car), a twenty- to thirty-minute walk offering fine views over the Lasíthi plain. Once on the plateau you will arrive at a fork where three dirt tracks diverge. Leave any transport here and take the left track, aiming for a saddle between two peaks. You will soon spot the red waymarks at the start of the ascent, followed fairly soon by the name, Karfí, daubed in Greek on various rocks. It's an easy and well-marked thirty-minute climb from here through a rocky landscape patrolled by agile goats.

At the end of the climb, after taking in the magnificent **views** over the coast and distant Hersónisos to the north, you'll come to the **archeological site** spread across a saddle between the summit of Mount Karfí (the location of an ancient peak sanctuary) to the west and the pinnacle of Mikre Koprana (topped by a trig point) to the east. Founded in the twelfth century BC, in this enclave Minoan refugees fleeing from the Dorian advance attempted to preserve vestiges of their ancestral culture. The settlement consists of a cluster of stone-built single-storey dwellings, a rather crude imitation of the site at Goúrnia. For the three thousand or so inhabitants who lived here prior to the site's peaceful evacuation around 1000 BC, life must have been a grim struggle, lashed by the winds and prey to the vicious winter elements. But this very inaccessibility was of great defensive value and preserved the settlement from attack, whilst the cultivation of the Níssimos plateau below provided food and pasture for livestock.

Among the ruins, excavated in the 1930s by John Pendlebury, the easiest building to identify is what the archeologist described as the **Great House**, an important building still retaining its walls and where a number of bronze artefacts were turned up. Behind this, just to the north, and in an area covered with a carpet of ancient potsherds, was a **shrine** with remarkable metre-high terracotta goddesses with arms raised in blessing, now in the Iráklion Archeological Museum. The remainder of this desolate village, intersected by a number of paved alleyways, isn't easy to make sense of, except for the dwelling thresholds and the odd evocative hand-grindstone lying among the collapsed piles of stones. But this remote eyrie, with all its historical associations, is one of the most haunting places on the island.

Whilst you're up here, there's a good chance you'll see the odd **griffon vulture** gliding majestically overhead; maybe even the much rarer **lammergeier**, or bearded vulture, now down to a handful of isolated pairs. There are few more dramatic sights than this raptor hoisting the leg bones of its victims into the air to dash them onto a rock below (nearly always the same one); once they are broken the bird extracts the marrow with its specially adapted tongue.

Áyios Konstantínos and Áyios Yeóryios

Clockwise from Tzermiádho, the next village of any size is **ÁYIOS KON-STANTÍNOS**, which is where the Neápoli road emerges on the plain. Here, too, you could find a **room** if you wanted one, and because it is the first (and last) village most people visit, it is packed with souvenir stores. Watch out particularly for a priest and his wife selling embroidered fabrics: these two could sell ice to Eskimos. You may also see a villager working her antique family "heirloom" in the doorway of her store. Natural dyes from onions, walnuts and other sources are still used by some.

ÁYIOS YEÓRYIOS, next in line, is larger and less commercial. There's a small and entertaining **Folk Museum** (summer only, daily 10am–4pm; 500dr), which also contains a fascinating photo-biography of Crete's great writer, Níkos Kazantzákis. Excellent-value **rooms** and **food** (and homemade wine) are to be had at the *Hotel Dias* on the village's main street (☎0844/31-207; ①), or try the *Hotel Rea* (☎0844/31-209; ①), further along the street, if this is full.

Psihró

Most people's main destination is **PSIHRÓ**, the base for visiting Lasíthi's other chief attraction, the Dhiktean Cave (see below), known as the birthplace of Zeus. The village itself is another simple plateau community strung out along a tree-lined main street. There are a couple of **tavernas**, and **rooms** can be found at the not overly-friendly *Hotel Zeus* (☎0844/31-284; ②), a little way beyond the village towards the Dhiktean Cave. If you find everything full – as is likely during the big local festival over the last three days in August – try the unofficial **campsite** by the *Taverna Panorama* (you're expected to eat there) at the western end of the village.

The Dhiktean Cave

The **Dhiktean Cave** (daily 8am–6.45pm; 800dr, students free) lies just past Psihró, up a trail for which you can hire a mule (a hefty 2000dr) but which is in reality neither particularly long nor dauntingly steep. According to legend it was in the Dhiktean Cave that Zeus was born to Rhea. His father, Kronos, had been warned that he would be overthrown by a son and accordingly ate all his offspring. On this occasion, however, Rhea gave Kronos a stone to eat instead and left the baby concealed within the cave, protected by the Kouretes, who beat their shields outside to disguise his cries. From here Zeus moved to the Idean Cave, on Psilorítis, where he spent his youth (see p.221). That at least is the version generally told here, and though there are scores of variations on the myth, it is undeniable that the cave was a cult centre from the Minoan period onwards, and that explorations around the turn of the century retrieved offerings, to the Mother Goddess and to Zeus, dating through to Classical Greek times.

If you resisted the guides at the bottom of the path you'll find them more persistent still at the entrance to the cave. Whatever they say, a guide is not compulsory, and in the middle of the day there are so many tours going through that there is plenty of light and commentary to be had without one. However, if you have neither flashlight nor an extremely lurid imagination, a guide is not a bad investment (around 2000dr for two people including lamps, or 500–600dr each if part of a larger group). It takes long experience and a Cretan eye to pick out such intimate details as the nipples the baby Zeus sucked on from the rest of the stalactites and stalagmites. Hokum aside, though, when you look back from the depths of the cave towards the peephole of light at the entrance, framed in a blue haze caused by the damp atmosphere, it's not hard to believe this to have been the infant Zeus's first sight of the world destined to become his kingdom.

A few general points. To avoid the crowds and savour the cave's mystical qualities to the full, try to arrive before noon. Also watch out for damp and extremely slippery stones underfoot on the way down: non-slip shoes are essential. Also note that new parking charges are enforced and don't attempt to avoid them by parking in the lane before the site. This is a no-parking zone and the tickets doled out are a nice earner for the local traffic police.

Further expeditions

If the cave has given you a taster for more of plateau countryside around, then one of the guides, the genial Petros Zárvakis, takes people into the hills for wild flower (mid-April to mid-June) and bird-spotting hikes (April to September). From May to September he also leads regular ascents to the summit of Mount Dhíkti which includes an overnight stay at a refuge and supper under the stars. It's not a terribly difficult climb, but you'll need to wear stout walking boots or shoes and bring a sleeping bag. The cost will depend on how many people there are (around 2000dr per person for a group of ten). For details contact the polyglot Petros at the café above the car park or ring him at his home in the village (☎0844/31-316).

Áyios Nikólaos

Sited on the picturesque Gulf of Mirabéllo, "Ag Nik", as **ÁYIOS NIKÓLAOS** is known to the majority of its English-speaking visitors, was originally the ancient port for Lató, one of the dominant cities of this area in Hellenistic times. This settlement faded in the Roman period and seems to have been abandoned in Byzantine times. The Venetians built a fortress here – of which nothing remains – and gave the surrounding gulf its name, Mirabéllo (lovely view). The town came slowly back to life, and by the nineteenth century the port was again busy. After union with Greece in 1913, Áyios Nikólaos was confirmed as the capital of Lasíthi province.

A quiet harbour town for most of this century, it was discovered in the 1960s by international tourism. The attractions were – and are – obvious: a setting on a small, hilly peninsula around a supposedly bottomless **lake**, now connected to the sea to form an inner harbour. It is wonderfully picturesque, and it knows it. The lake, the harbour and the coast all around are fought over by restaurants, bars and hotels, charging well above the odds. The town's reputation did take a nosedive some years ago when it became too crowded and too boisterous for its own good, but the worst of the holiday excesses now occur up the coast at Mália, and

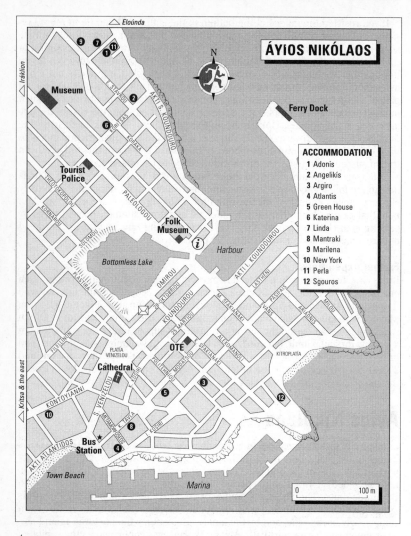

Áyios Nikólaos has emerged without any lasting damage. If you're looking for a beach, forget it – the few small patches of sand are either closely guarded by expensive hotels or have standing room only by the time you've finished breakfast.

Arrival, information and accommodation

You get the best impression of Áyios Nikólaos if you arrive by **ferry**; the dock is on a tiny peninsula, a couple of minutes' walk from the lake and the pretty town centre. The **bus station** is very much on the low-rent, southern side of town, where the concrete modernity is at its most apparent and the traffic noise never stops. Arriving here – or **driving** in on the one-way system – head up the hill to Platía Venizélou, and then down into the picturesque areas past the souvenir stores which line both Koundoúrou and 28-Oktovríou. The lake marks the centre of town in every way, and the narrow bridge over its channel is a notorious bottleneck for traffic and strolling visitors. From here, Aktí Koundoúrou curves around the sides of the harbour, and M. Sfakianáki strikes over a small hill to the cove of Kitroplatía. Almost all the action in Áyios Nikólaos takes place around these streets.

You'll probably want to visit the **tourist information** office (daily 8.30am–9.30pm; ☎0841/22-357) at some stage (see "Accommodation" below), situated between the lake and the port. The tourist police are at K. Paleológou 17 (☎0841/22-321), north of the lake. For departure information, and details of **bike rental** and **boat trips**, see "Listings" on p.150.

Accommodation

It's actually become much easier to find a **room** in Áyios Nikólaos in recent years, though in peak season you may still struggle for choice. Nevertheless, there are literally thousands of rooms scattered all over town, and the best move is to visit the tourist information office, which normally has a couple of boards with cards and brochures about hotels and rooms, including their prices. If the prices seem very reasonable it is because they are for the low season. There is no youth hostel and the nearest **campsite** (*Gournia Moon*) is 17km away (see p.159).

Adonis Pension, Salaminos 4 (☎0841/22-931). Overlooking the sea across the harbour, though a little noisy as it's above the road. Visit in low season and share a shower and the price drops by almost fifty percent. ②.

Angeliki's Guest House, Koritsas 39 (☎0841/26-946). Airy apartments in a flower-filled house with sea views. ④.

Argiro Pension, Solonos 1 (☎0841/28-707). Friendly place offering spotless and simple rooms with access to a garden. ②.

Atlantis Hotel, Metamorfoseos (☎0841/28-964). One block east of the bus station, this is nothing special but is handy enough, and has a snack bar below with breakfast for 500dr. ②.

The Green House, Modatsou 15 (☎0841/22-025). Probably the best cheap place to stay in town, this clean pension has shared bathrooms, and there's a garden. ②.

Katerina Pension, Stratigou Koraka 30 (☎0841/22-766). Another good and reasonable choice – some rooms have their own balcony and there's a pleasant garden. ②.

Linda Hotel, Salaminos 3a (☎0841/22-130, fax 26-433). This friendly place has 22 rooms all with shower, balcony and a partial sea view; it's located just off Akti Koundoúrou. ②.

Mantraki Apartments, Kapetan Tavla (☎0841/28-880). A possible choice in one of the town's quieter backstreets behind the bus station. Best for three or four people sharing, the apartments include a kitchen. ③.

Marilena Pension, Erithrou Stavrou 14 (☎0841/22-681). One of the main budget options, the *Marilena* is a clear winner, with a friendly proprietor and some rooms with sea view and balcony. ②.

New York Pension, Kontoyianni 23 (☎0841/28-577). Rough-and-ready place on a noisy street, close to the bus station – which is about the only reason for its popularity. ②.

Perla Pension, Salaminos 4 (☎0841/23-379). Basic family-run place, next door to the *Adonis*, on a hill to the north of the harbour. Front rooms have sea-view balconies. ②.

Sgouros Hotel, Kitroplatía (☎0841/28-931). Modern hotel next to one of the town's few beaches and close to loads of tavernas. ④.

The Town

Things to do in town by day are pretty limited – you're not supposed to have recovered from the night before so soon. A couple of **museums** (see below) hold some interest, but for most visitors the days are taken up strolling the area around **Lake Voulisméni** (allegedly over 60m deep), nosing around in the shops, and heading for the strips of **beach**. In the little cove at Kitroplatía there's a rocky foreshore from which you can swim, north of town by the *Dolphin* taverna you'll find a narrow length of gritty sand, or there's a municipal beach (with entry fee) beyond the bus station on the south side of town. This at least is clean and sandy, but again it's terribly crowded.

Most people simply end up diving off the rocks which line the foreshore north of town, or else they get out altogether: the sandy beach of Almirós is 2km south and there's a constant stream of people walking there; further in this direction by bus or bike there are good beaches around Kaló Hório, or in the other direction around Eloúnda (see following sections). The **boat trips** to beaches around the bay are also popular; see "Listings" for details.

The Folk Museum

The **Folk Museum** (daily except Sat 10am–1.30pm & 6–9.30pm; 200dr) is opposite the bridge and housed on the ground floor of the harbour master's office, across from the tourist office. It has a small but interesting display of handicrafts (especially embroidery), costumes, pottery, cooking utensils and old Cretan goat-leather bagpipes.

The Archeological Museum

There's more interest in the modern and well laid-out **Archeological Museum** (Oct–July Tues–Sun 8.30am–3pm; Aug–Sept 8.30am–5pm; 500dr, students free) on Paleológou, north of the lake, which as ever will mean a lot more after you've visited a few sites in the area.

Following some interesting Neolithic finds in Room 1, you come to Room 2 and the museum's star exhibit, the extraordinary **Goddess of Mírtos**. This goose-necked early Minoan (c.2500 BC) clay figurine – actually a jug – was found in the excavation of the superbly sited Bronze Age settlement at Fournoú Korifí, near Mírtos. Note the pubic triangle, breasts and the square panels thought to portray a woven garment. The beak-spouted jug she's holding (which is also the vessel's mouth) is similar to vases in the museum from the same period. Elsewhere in Rooms 1 and 2 some fine examples of **Vasilikí ware** are displayed, named after the early Bronze Age site on the isthmus of Ierápetra where it was first discovered. The lustrous mottled finish of this pottery was achieved by uneven firing, an effect which obviously pleased its creators. Even more remarkably, these flawless artefacts – including a "teapot" and a beak-spouted ewer dating from around 2500 BC – were made not on a wheel, but on the clay "turntables" exhibited in Room 2. The potter's wheel only reached Crete some six hundred years later; you can see an early example from a tomb at Kritsá in Room 4.

Room 3 displays some fine Marine-style pottery which, although found in a villa near Makriyialós, is thought to have come from the Knossós workshop. There's also some interesting **jewellery**, including a beautiful gold pin bearing an intricately crafted bramble motif and a tantalizingly long inscription in the undeciphered Linear A script on the reverse. In the same room is a wonderful collection of Late Minoan **clay sarcophagi** or *lárnakes* decorated with birds, fish and the long-tentacled octopus which seems to have so delighted Minoan artists. Archeologists assumed, when they turned up these items, that they were all burial chests. But when they found more of these painted tubs, with clearly identifiable plug-holes in the bottom, the Minoans had the last laugh – they were obviously avid bathers.

Room 4 contains a rare Minoan **infant burial** displayed exactly as found at its site at Kryá, near Sitía. Dating from the Late Minoan period, the transferring of the whole thing from site to museum by Costis Davaras "without displacing a single stone" must have been some headache. Finally, in Room 7, there's an eerie grinning skull from the Roman cemetery at Potamós, on the edge of Áyios Nikólaos, to send you on your way. A wreath of gold olive leaves is still in place about its crown; the silver coin originally in the mouth of the deceased is now displayed separately in the case. This was the traditional fare paid to the boatman Charon, who ferried the dead across the River Styx to the underworld.

Eating

There are tourist-oriented **tavernas** all around the lake and harbour with little to choose between them apart from the different perspectives you get on the passing fashion show. Have a drink here perhaps or a mid-morning coffee and choose somewhere else to eat. The places around the Kiroplatía are generally fairer value, but again you are paying for the location. The town's best **bakery** is Lambros, at the corner of Metamorfoseos and Venizélou near the bus station, where croissants, *karitigana* (Cretan sweet pastries) as well as the usual standards (*tirópita*, *spanakópita* and so on) are all delicious.

Taverna Auoas, Paleológou 44. On the way to the Archeological Museum, this serves good traditional Cretan food in and under a plant-covered trellised courtyard.

Avlí, Odhós P. Georgiou 12, two blocks behind the tourist office. Delightful garden ouzerí offering a wide mezédhes selection as well as more elaborate dishes. Open evenings only.

Casanova, Kitroplatía, east side. For a change from Greek food you could consider trying a meal here, where you'll find the usual Italian standards.

Du Lac, by the lake. Gets most plaudits (from locals as well as guidebooks) as the best on the lake for quality and service, and where the "fresh" fish usually is. Downside is that you pay through the nose for it.

Ellinikon, just off the northwest corner of Platía Venizélou, near the *Hotel Kronos*. A brilliant small café with loads of character that serves traditional mountain dishes, made fresh every day by the ebullient Yanni, and served with village *raki* or wine. The list of drinks and mezédhes available is chalked up inside on a board.

Itanos, Kyprou. On a side street off the east side of Platía Venizélou, this popular place serves typical Cretan food and wine and has a terrace across the road opposite.

La Strada, N. Plastira, slightly northwest of Platía Venizélou. Not bad pizzas and pretty good pasta at this popular Italian venue, although the meat dishes are overpriced.

Loukakis and **Ikaros**, Aktí S. Koundoúrou. Two good-value traditional tavernas, a few minutes' walk away from the port along the Eloúnda road, next to each other along the waterfront.

Ofou To Lo, Kitroplatía, last in line on the western side. The best of the tavernas fronting the beach here, offering well-cooked food at – for this area – reasonable prices.

Pelagos, Koraka, behind the tourist office. A stylish fish taverna housed in an elegant mansion. Great patio and excellent food, but at a price.

Sarris, Kyprou 15. Great little economical neighbourhood café-diner, especially good for breakfast and *souvláki* served on the leafy terrace.

Twins, fronting the harbour. Handy pizzeria, fast food outlet and coffee bar, open all hours. Their "small" pizzas measure 40cm in diameter.

Drinking, nightlife and entertainment

After you've eaten, you can start to get into the one thing which Áyios Nikólaos undeniably does well: **bars** and **nightlife**. Not that you really need a guide to this – the bars are hard to avoid, and you can just follow the crowds to the most popular places.

For a quieter **drink**, the *Hotel Alexandros* on Paleológou has a rooftop cocktail bar overlooking the lake and frequent live music sessions. Even better lake views are to be had from the terrace bars overlooking its western flank, reached by following Odhós Plastira from near Platía Venizélou – *Cafe Migomas* is a stylish place for breakfast and late drinks. The pleasantly old-fashioned *Asteria* café fronting the harbour is one of the oldest – and unlike many places in town you still get a bill and they trust you not to walk away without paying. The *Creta Café* and *Café Kastro*, among the disco bars on harbourside, are a surprisingly civilized havens of sanity, where Greek professionals unwind. Also, try *Yiannis* further down the harbour or, further still, the new bar *Porto*, where the ferry boats arrive. *Café du Lac*, 28-Octobriou, is similar stylish place near the lake. If you feel like a drink on the harbour itself then there is always the floating café-bar, the *Armida*, to consider. Finally, around midnight, when the crowds have gone, the cafés along the lakeside are pleasant places to linger – *Zygos*, on the north side near Paleológou, is a relaxing cocktail bar with a garden.

Quiet drinking, however, is not what it's all about in the **disco bars**. *Lipstick* and *Bolero* on Koundoúrou harbourside are very popular, as is *Studio* (above the *Creta Café*) although it doesn't get going until the small hours when the pubs and restaurants close. There are more bars to try at the bottom of 25-Martíou (known as "Soho Street") where it heads up the hill – *Rififi*, *Captain Sky*, *Scorpios*, *Royale*, *Tounel*, *Sixties* and *Sant Maria* get going at sunset; *Aquarius* across the harbour is the current hot-spot.

Each year Áyios Nikólaos mounts a summer-long **cultural festival**, "the Lato", which includes music, dance and theatre from Crete, Greece and elsewhere. Keep an eye out for posters advertising the various events, or ask at the tourist office.

Listings

Airlines Olympic Airways, Plastira 20 (Mon–Fri 8am–4pm; ☎0841/22-033).

Banks Banks and exchange places are mostly found along Koundoúrou (where there's also a cash-exchange machine) and 28-Octobriou. Visa and Mastercard cash dispensers are to be found here and beside the bridge near the harbour.

Boat trips Trips to points around the gulf mostly leave from the west side of the harbour, near the tourist office, and if you walk around here and along Akti Koundoúrou northwards you'll be accosted by their operators.

Books and newspapers Anna Karteri, Koundoúrou 5 near Platía Venizélou, has a good selection of books in English. Quick Film at no. 44 on the same street is the best source for foreign newspapers.

Bus station For route information, call ☎0841/22-234. Buy tickets on the bus for services to Eloúnda (220dr), Kritsá (220dr), Lasíthi (1050dr) and Vái (1900dr).

Car and bike rental Available from dozens of outlets, mainly in the harbour area – it's very expensive in high season, though outside the summer months shopping around might bring you a real bargain. Try the friendly and reliable Mike Manolis (☎0841/24-940), who has a pitch at the junction of 25-Martíou and Sfakianáki near the OTE and also rents mountain bikes. Other options are Bestrent (☎0841/23-405), Akti Koundoúrou 28, Scooterland, at the foot of Venizélou, and Clubcars (☎0841/25-868), 28-Octobriou 24. Wherever you rent make sure to check the insurance.

Ferries The main agents are Massaros Travel, Koundoúrou 29 (☎0841/22-267), Nostos Tours, Koundoúrou 30 (☎0841/22-819) and L.A.N.E (☎0841/26-465) near the OTE on the corner of 25-Martíou and Sfakianáki; there are many other travel agents for local tours.

Hospital The town hospital (☎0841/25-224) is at the northern end of Paleológou, one block beyond the Archeological Museum.

Laundry Nameless place on S. Davaki, off Paleológou; self and service washes.

Left luggage Facilities are available at the bus station from 6am to 9pm, but as there is little control of who goes into and out of the area reserved it's not really worth taking the risk.

Shopping Dimitri Spices along the Akti Koundoúrou waterfront, a little way past the *Loukakis* taverna, sells henna red and black sesame tea, along with the usual range of Cretan herbs. María Patsaki, Sfakianáki 2, sells a range of embroidery, textiles and antiques. Music Formula, Kontogianni 13, west of Platía Venizélou has a good selection of Cretan traditional music, including songs and *lyra*.

OTE On N. Sfakianáki just above 25-Martíou (☎0841/28-099 June–Oct daily 6am–midnight; Nov–May daily 6am–10.30pm).

Post office 28-Oktovriou, above the lake (Mon–Fri 7.30am–2pm; Sat 7.30–2pm; ☎0841/22-276).

Taxis There's a rank in the main square, Platía Venizélou, and another behind the tourist office, or call ☎0841/24-000.

The Gulf of Mirabéllo

North of Áyios Nikólaos the swankier hotels are strung out along the coast road – the flashest of them being the *Minos Beach* (☎0841/22-345, fax 22-548; ⑦) with its bungalows, private pools and jealously guarded beach – with upmarket restaurants, discos and cocktail bars scattered between them. Among them, and by way of contrast to this hedonistic beach life, a signposted road leads off to the right towards the sea and the Byzantine church of **Áyios Nikólaos**, from which the modern resort takes its name. To get in you'll need to ask at the nearby *Minos Palace Hotel* (☎0841/22-345, fax 23-816; ⑦) for the key, which will be handed over in return for the deposit of a passport. The trouble is worth it to see some of the earliest fresco fragments found in Greece, dating back to the eighth or ninth century. The geometric patterns and motifs that survive are the legacy of the Iconoclastic movement, which banned the representation of divine images in religious art.

Soon after this the road begins to climb above the **Gulf of Mirabéllo**: looking across, you can make out Psíra and Móhlos against the stark wall of the Sitía mountains, while nearer at hand mothballed supertankers are moored among the small islands sheltering in the lee of the peninsula. One of the largest of these islets, Áyios Pándes, is a refuge for the island's wild goat, the *kri-kri*. The animals have an elusive reputation, carefully avoiding the cruise parties from Áyios Nikólaos which put in to see them.

Oloús

The road drops back down to sea level as it approaches Eloúnda (see below). Before you reach the centre of the village, however, there's a track signed off to the right to the "sunken city" of **Oloús**. This leads down to a natural causeway which is the only link between the peninsula of Spinalónga (often known as "big Spinalónga" to distinguish it from the more famous island of the same name) and the mainland. All around the causeway on both sides you'll find people swimming from small patches of beach or basking on flat rocks. Protected by it are the remains of Venetian salt pans, now fallen into disrepair but which are worth checking for migrating birds in the spring.

Oloús itself lay around the far end of the causeway and along the coast to the right. Though it is known chiefly for having been the port of Dríros, what little remains is Roman: there's a fenced enclosure behind the popular *Canal Bar* in which you can see the floor of a Roman basilica with an odd, almost patchwork-style black and white mosaic, and among the rocks a little further round (watch out for sea urchins) are the sunken traces of harbour installations. The site has never been excavated, however, and this is about the extent of what is visible, but the excursion is worth it for the setting – the beaches, causeway, "French" canal and stone windmills. On the far side of the peninsula there are better beaches still – tough to get to except by boat.

Eloúnda

ELOÚNDA, though it's a fair-sized resort these days, with one very exclusive hotel (the *Elounda Beach*; ☎0841/41-412, fax 41-373; ⑦) and scores of new apartment developments, is a very different proposition from Ag Nik – low-key and slow moving. At its heart is an enormous square with cafés and restaurants, stores and hotels on three sides, the seafront promenade on the fourth. This is where you park if you've driven, it's where the bus stops, and it's also where the boats to Spinalónga (daily every 30min; 9.30am–4.30pm) leave from. Just about everything else in Eloúnda is in the immediate vicinity, including the post office, OTE (Mon–Sat 3–11pm, Sun 5–10pm), travel agencies, bookshop with foreign press and books, and car rental offices. There's also a **bank** with Visa and Mastercard cash dispensers and, just off to the south, an excellent bakery.

There are several **rooms** places close by, most at the far end of the village behind the church. A good place to start is the friendly *Pension Oasis* (☎0841/41-076, fax 41-128; ③), which has comfortable rooms with fans and fridges. If that's full, there are a couple more similarly priced places, *Athanais* and *Emilia* (both ③), a little further along the road. The central travel agencies can assist with finding rooms, studios and apartments: try the helpful Olous Travel (☎0841/41-324), next to the post office, which serves as a local information office. The bookshop (☎0841/41-641) also has details of the *Milos* and *Delfinia* apartments and studios a little along the road north (both ④), which come with pools and sea views. Sea-view rooms in a peaceful location can also be found at a couple of small places above bars along the track to Oloús, *Christina* and *Paradisos Taverna* (both ③).

Eloúnda has a good choice of **tavernas** and **restaurants** but many of them, particularly those along the seafront, tend to be rather pricey. Still, the overall standard is high and the food goes down well with the Sitian wines which seem to have cornered the market here. Good choices at the mid-to-upper end of the price scale include *Marilena*, which serves souped-up versions of traditional Greek dishes; *Vritomares*, in a plum spot in the centre of the harbour; and *Poulis*, on a floating pontoon on the Olous road. One of the best places for good fish is *Nikos*, bang in the centre of the square. For a change from the ubiquitous fish platters, the English-run *Bojos*, up the hill heading south, has a reasonably priced international menu (including satay and tandoori chicken) and enjoys pleasant surroundings. **Nightlife** in Eloúnda is low key, centred around café terraces and cocktail bars. The *Hellas* café is a good example of the latter, and has live Greek music at weekends.

Spinalónga

The great majority of people visiting the fortress rock of **Spinalónga** leave from Eloúnda (though there are also boats direct from Áyios Nikólaos and from Pláka) and it is certainly the most convenient way of getting there, with reasonably priced kaïkia making the trip every half hour or so.

The islet was fortified by the Venetians in 1579 to defend the approach to the gulf, and more particularly the sheltered anchorages behind the peninsula of Spinalónga. Like their other island fortresses it proved virtually impregnable and was handed over to the Turks only in 1715, by treaty – some fifty years after the rest of Crete had surrendered. The infamous part of the island's history is much more recent, however. For the first fifty years of this century, Spinalónga was a leper colony, the last in Europe. Lepers were sent as outcasts – long after drugs to control their condition had rendered such measures entirely unnecessary – to a colony primitive in the extreme and administered almost as if it were a detention camp. Its jail was frequently used for lepers who dared complain about their living conditions.

Even today there's an unnerving sense of isolation when the boat leaves you here, at a jetty from which a long tunnel leads up into the fortified centre. There are still just two easily sealed entrances: this tunnel, and a jetty on the seaward side (which you see if you approach from Áyios Nikólaos) which leads up to the old castle gate with its lion of St Mark. Around the base of the castle a real town grew up – Turkish buildings mostly, adapted by the lepers using whatever materials they could find. Although everything is in decay, you can still pick out a row of stores and some houses which must once have been quite grand.

Pláka

The colony's mainland supply centre was at **PLÁKA**, about 5km north of Eloúnda, and if you ask at *Manoli's Taverna* there you can still get someone to run you across to the island (1000dr). This is a better bet if you fancy having Spinalónga to yourself and don't want to share it with hundreds of others. Pláka itself remains a very quiet spot. Of the **tavernas**, *Manoli's* serves fresh fish at reasonable prices, whilst a few of the others – *Castello* (②), *Maria's* (②) and *Spinalonga* (②) – rent out basic **rooms**. There's beautifully clear water and a beach on which the pebbles are rather too large for comfort.

Only at weekends, when locals come to escape the crowds elsewhere, does the place lose its tranquillity – and even then it's quieter than anywhere else around. Walking, you could continue to the point of the cape in around ninety minutes, following the road which climbs almost as far as the next village, **Vrouhás**, before taking off along a track above the sea.

Kritsá and Lató

The other excursion everyone from Áyios Nikólaos takes is inland to Kritsá, a "traditional" village about 10km away. Despite the commercialization, this is a trip well worth making for a break from the frenetic pace of Ag Nik; buses run at least every hour from the main station. Along the way two sites delay you, each worthy of a visit.

Panayía Kirá

About 1km before Kritsá, the road runs straight past the lovely Byzantine church of **Panayía Kirá** (Mon–Sat 9am–3pm, Sun 9am–2pm; 800dr), inside which is preserved perhaps the most complete and certainly the most famous set of Byzantine frescoes in Crete. Of the three naves (the buttresses and lantern are later additions), the larger, central one is the oldest, though the frescoes have all been retouched and restored to such an extent that it is impossible to say with certainty which is the most ancient. All of them originate from the fourteenth and perhaps early fifteenth centuries. Those in the south aisle, through which you enter, depict the life of Anne, mother of Mary – her marriage to Joachim and the birth of Mary – and the early life of the Virgin herself up to the journey to Bethlehem. In the centre of the church Mary's story is continued and there are scenes from the life of Christ, including the Nativity, Herod's banquet and a superb Last Supper. And in the final aisle there are vivid scenes of the Second Coming and Judgement, along with the delights of Paradise and assorted interludes from the lives of the saints (especially St Anthony). Throughout, the major scenes are interspersed with small portraits of saints and apostles. Alongside the church are a couple of tavernas and a store selling excellent, but expensive, reproduction icons.

Lató

Just beyond the church you can turn off towards the archeological site of **Lató** (Tues–Sun 8.30am–3pm; free), about 3km up an asphalted road; the gate is often left considerably open after the official closing time. If the gate is locked however, scaling it isn't difficult, and since the guardian often locks up with people still inside, it doesn't seem to be a practice which is discouraged. Although there's as much to be seen here as in many of the more celebrated sites it's very little visited: presumably because most visitors' interests are directed to the Minoans, and this was a much later settlement, Doric in origin but flourishing through to Classical times. Even the archeologists shared this lack of curiosity, for systematic excavation of the site started only in 1967 under the French School.

The city's name derives from a Cretan Doric corruption of Leto, the mythical mother of Artemis and Apollo. Homer relates in the *Odyssey* how Eileíthyia (the Minoan goddess of childbirth) attended Leto when she gave birth to the god Apollo on the island of Delos: it is thus fitting that Eileíthyia became the patron goddess of Lató, as coins discovered here proved. That it was an important city is clear from the sheer extent of the ruins, which spread in every direction. It is a magnificent setting – this city of sombre grey stone sprawled across the saddle between the twin peaks of a dauntingly craggy hill – and standing on the peak you

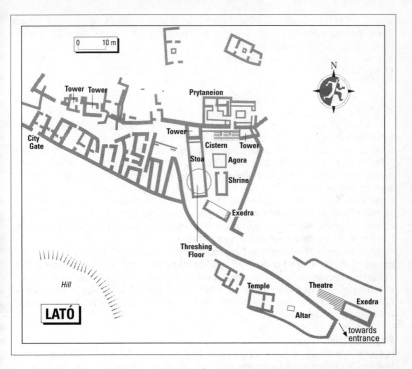

can look down onto the white cluster of Áyios Nikólaos (Lató's ancient port), with the bay and Oloús (a major rival of Lató in its heyday) beyond, or inland to the valleys and climbing peaks of the Dhiktean mountains. Ruins aside, these views would be worth the sweat getting up. The exposed position can't have been all that practical, however, and wearing a toga must have been a hazardous business in the fierce summer winds which gust from all directions.

You enter the site 200m or so below the ruins, then follow a rough path up to a rectangular area with a gateway, which would have been the original entrance to Lato. Continuing to climb up the street from here, you can see the stores and workshops abutting the city wall on the right with defensive towers and gateways into the residential areas on the left. Higher up still, the open area of the **agora** is an interesting fusion of early Greek and older Minoan influences. This pentagonal space was a meeting place for citizens but also incorporates a tier of steps on its northern side, reminiscent of the theatral areas at Minoan sites such as Knossós and Festós. The steps ascend between the remains of two towers to the **prytaneion**, or town hall, with small rooms at the rear which held the city's archives. In the centre of the agora is a deep square cistern and a shrine, flanked on the western side by a colonnaded **stoa**, a shady place to shelter from the elements. The southern end of this has been cut through by a relatively modern circular threshing floor. The **exedra** nearby was a sort of public seating area, and in the southeast corner of the site is another exedra with what is termed a "theatral area" beside it – a broad flight of steps again similar to the Minoan style – which leads to a raised terrace containing a well-preserved fourth-century BC temple with a stepped altar just before it.

Kritsá

If you wanted, you could retrace your steps from Lató to where the track divides, and then turn right to head down to Flamouri10aná on the Lakonía plain, from where there's a paved road (and buses) back to Áyios Nikólaos. Most people head for **KRITSÁ**, however. A sizeable place (known as "the largest village in Crete"), its popularity and fame as a handicrafts centre have not really spoilt it. Nowadays it feels more like a small town, with the main street lined with tourist stores selling (mostly) leather goods or embroidery. Despite the commercialism, prices are a great deal better than in Áyios Nikólaos – though you can still pay as much as £400/US$650 for some of the wonderful, elaborately woven rugs – and if you manage to avoid the tour-bus crowds (early morning and mid-afternoon are the best times) the place reverts to a friendly semi-somnambulance in which you're free to wander and browse under no pressure at all.

Kritsá's other chief claim to fame lies in its situation, with views back over the green valley up which you arrived and the mountains rising steeply behind. You get little impression of this at street level, other than an awareness that you are climbing quite steeply, so try to get out onto one of the balconies at the back of the cafés along the main street, where you can look back over the town and towards Áyios Nikólaos.

Practicalities

Staying in Kritsá is a surprisingly easy and attractive option. There are usually beds to be found – certainly more chance than on the coast – and it's an ideal place to experience something approaching a genuinely Cretan atmosphere.

A number of places offer **rooms**. One of the best is *Argyro*, on your way into the village (☎0841/51-174; ②), which is clean and friendly, has rooms with and without private shower, and its own café. *Pension Kera* (②), up the hill from the bus stop, is a slightly cheaper alternative; if this is full, any of the textile sellers opposite will put you in touch with family-run rooms nearby.

There are a number of **cafés** in the centre of Kritsá, including *Sareithakis*, a cool place to sit out under a plane tree. Otherwise, head for the bakers for tempting *tirópita* (cheese pies) or currant breads. One of the best-situated tavernas is *Castello*, in the centre, and there are a few others near where the bus stops.

As it is impossible to park in the village, car parks are provided at the top and bottom of the village.

Around Kritsá

If you want to explore further, you'll find more frescoed churches here and in the immediate surroundings. **Áyios Yeóryios**, for example, is on the edge of the village, signed uphill to the left as you walk through: the frescoes here are contemporary with those at the Panayía Kirá, though in a very much worse state of preservation. Further in this same direction, **Áyios Ioánnis** lies a kilometre or so down the road to Kroústas. These churches will probably be locked so you'll need to enquire as to accessibility from the guardian at the Panayía Kirá.

South to the isthmus

The main road south and then east from Áyios Nikólaos is not a wildly exciting one – a drive through barren hills dotted with villas above the occasional sandy cove. Beyond the reed-fringed beaches at Almirós and Amoudhára there's little temptation to stop until you reach the cluster of increasing development around **KALÓ HÓRIO**. Here there are several tavernas and mini-markets, an OTE and mobile post office. Below them paths wind down quite steeply, to a couple of excellent small beaches. On the first of them there's a taverna by the outflow from a small river. Immediately beyond is **ÍSTRO**, a burgeoning resort in its own right, just beyond which the exclusive *Istron Bay Hotel* (☎0841/61-303; ⑦) hangs from the cliff above a spectacular cove with a fine sandy beach. If you walk confidently through the hotel grounds you can get down to enjoy this and the hotel's beach bar: there's no such thing as a private beach on Crete, but apparently nothing to prevent all the approaches being privately controlled. Unfortunately, like all the beaches in this part of the bay, much rubbish is washed up although this is regularly cleaned away by the hotel.

Five kilometres further on, a track is signed on the right for the **Moní Faneroméni**. The track, concreted in its early stages, is a rough one and climbs dizzily skywards for 6km, giving spectacular views over the Gulf of Mirabéllo along the way. The **view** from the monastery itself, when you finally arrive there, must be among the finest on Crete. To get into the rather bleak-looking monastery buildings, knock loudly (and repeatedly if necessary). When you gain entry you will be shown up to the chapel, built into a cave sanctuary where a sacred icon of the Virgin was miraculously discovered, the reason for the foundation of the monastery in the fifteenth century. The frescoes, although late, are quite brilliant – especially that of the Panayía Theotókou, the Mother of God. The monk who unlocks the chapel has been known to be a little mean with the time (and electric light) you need to view the artworks – more time can usually be "purchased" with a discreet contribution to monastic funds.

Gourniá

Back on the coast road, another 2km brings you to the site of **Gourniá** (Tues–Sun 8.30am–3pm; 500dr), slumped in the saddle between two low peaks. A look at the map tells you much about ancient Gourniá's strategic importance, controlling the narrow isthmus with its relatively easy communication with the southern seaboard at modern Ierápetra. The overland route avoids a hazardous sea voyage around the eastern cape – a crucial factor in ancient times, especially in winter when sailing usually stopped because of rough seas.

This is the most completely preserved of the Minoan towns, and in its small scale contains important clues about the lives of ordinary people and perhaps about the nature of the communities from which the palaces evolved. The desolation of the site today – you are likely to be alone save for the sleeping guard – only serves to heighten the contrast with what must have been a cramped and raucous community three and a half thousand years ago.

There is evidence of occupation at Gourniá as early as the third millennium BC, but the remains you see today are those of a town of the New Palace period

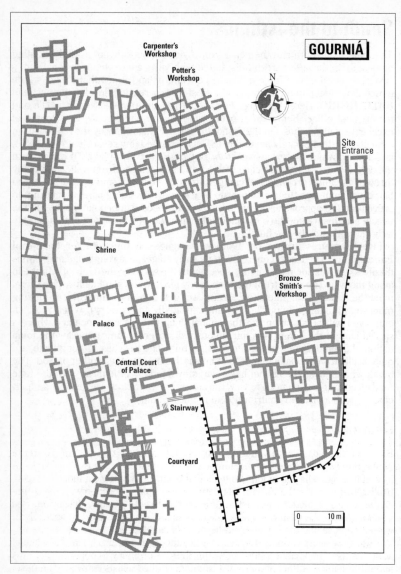

GOURNIÁ

Carpenter's Workshop

Potter's Workshop

Site Entrance

Shrine

Bronze-Smith's Workshop

Palace

Magazines

Central Court of Palace

Stairway

Courtyard

0   10 m

(c. 1500 BC). Around 1450 BC, as happened elsewhere, the town was destroyed by fire. Limited rebuilding occurred during the era of Mycenaean rule at Knossós, and the shrine may date from this late period. But the site was soon abandoned again and disappeared beneath the soil where it lay unsuspected until the awakening of archeological interest in the nineteenth century. Evans, as usual, was the first to scent Minoan occupation of this area and then a young

American, Harriet Boyd-Hawes, started digging in 1901. The site, a budding archeologist's dream, made her reputation.

The narrow, cobbled alleys and stairways – built for pack animals rather than carts – intersect a throng of one-roomed houses centred on a main square and the house of a local ruler or, more likely, governor. The settlement is not a large place, nor impressive by comparison with the palaces at Knossós and elsewhere, but it must have been at least as luxurious as the average Cretan mountain village of even 25 years ago. Among the dwellings to the north and east of the site are some which have been clearly identified, by tools or materials discovered, as the homes of **craftsmen**: a carpenter, a smith and a potter. It's worth remembering that the rooms may not have been as small as they appear – many of these are in fact basements or semi-basements reached by stairs from the main rooms above, and the floor plans of those did not necessarily correspond with what you see today. The houses themselves were mainly built of stone on the lower courses and mud brick above, with plaster-daubed reeds for roofing.

The **palace** (or governor's quarters) occupied the highest ground, to the north of a courtyard containing a familiar L-shaped stairway. With a smaller court at its heart, the whole is a copy in miniature of the palaces at Knossós or Festós. About 20m to the north of the palace a **shrine** was discovered. It is easily identified by the sloping approach path paved with an intricate pattern of evenly matched cobbles, and the shrine itself, up three steps, is a small room with a ledge for cult objects. Here a number of terracotta goddesses with arms raised were unearthed, as well as snake totems and other cult objects, now on display in the Iráklion Archeological Museum.

Across the island: Pahiá Ámmos and Vasilikí

It is tempting to cross the road from the Gourniá site and take one of the paths through the wild thyme to the sea and a swim. Don't bother – this seemingly innocent little bay acts as a magnet for every piece of floating detritus dumped off Crete's north coast. If you backtrack a little you could head instead to the **campsite** of *Gournia Moon* (☎0842/93-243), with its own small cove and beach; there's a bus stop directly above the campsite on the main road. There's almost as much junk washed up in the cove here, but at least the people who run the site make an effort to clear it up. The campsite has a taverna and store, and if you don't like the look of the sea, a swimming pool.

Pahiá Ámmos

There's a much larger beach, as well as rooms to rent and tavernas, at **PAHIÁ ÁMMOS** in the next valley. As you climb the road above Gourniá, be sure not to miss looking back over the site, its street plan laid out like a map. Even its best friends wouldn't describe Pahiá Ámmos as an attractive town, but this windswept mess of concrete does possess an eccentric Greek charm. However, the **pollution** problems mentioned above are, sad to say, even worse here. Local political battles have stymied a grand clean-up plan (with huge moles to keep out the junk) and much of the time it is positively dangerous to swim here. A close look at the sea should convince doubters. That said, should you still wish to stop over, Pahiá Ámmos at least has every basic facility you're likely to need, including a line of seafront **tavernas**. *Taverna Aiolos* is outstanding – one of the best fish restaurants at this end of the island – and you'll struggle to beat the locals to a table in high season. Their *kolokithokéftedes* (courgette balls), *achinosalata* (sea urchin's eggs) and fish dishes are highly recommended.

This is the narrowest part of the island, and from here a fast new road follows the ancient route through the Monastiráki gorge towards Ierápetra in the south. To the left the awesome slopes of the Thriptí range bear down on the road until some 3km along it you reach a turn-off for Vasilikí on the right.

Vasilikí

The archeological site of **Vasilikí** is visible from the main road, with an entrance from the side road a short distance down on the left. There is no obvious place to park off the road, and neither is the sign to the site apparent. Although Vasilikí is fenced the gate is always left open.

This Pre-Palatial settlement, dating from about 2650 to 2200 BC, may not be much to look at, but it's important for the light it throws upon the hazy millennium preceding the Minoan great period. Remains from this period occur at Knossós and other palaces but cannot be properly excavated because of the important buildings constructed on top of them. Vasilikí was the first of these early sites to be found in a pristine condition, due to its being abandoned after a fire about 2200 BC.

The site contains two main buildings, originally surrounded by numerous smaller (and simpler) dwellings. The remains of the edifice nearest to the entrance, on the lower slope of the hill, are slightly earlier than that on the crown. The **Red House**, as the former is named, has a number of interesting features. It is oriented with its corners towards the cardinal points of the compass, a practice normal in Mesopotamia and the Near East but alien to Egypt and the Aegean (a clue to Minoan origins?). In the southern corner deep basement rooms allow you to gain an idea of early Minoan building techniques: holes to support the absent wooden beams are visible as well as large patches of hard, red lime plaster, the forerunner of what later artists were to use as the ideal ground for the wonderful palace frescoes. This material gives the dwelling its modern name. The pottery known as Vasilikí ware, orange or red with dark, blotchy decoration, takes its name from this site where the fine examples on display in the archeological museums at Iráklion and Áyios Nikólaos were discovered. New excavations on the southern flank of the Red House have revealed a bath, a stretch of roadway and more dwellings.

Episkopí

Unless you wish to continue on up the lane into the village of Vasilikí (where you'll find a friendly bar) for another glimpse of rural Crete, the main road continues towards Ierápetra via **EPISKOPÍ**, almost exactly halfway across the isthmus. Here, below the road beside a pleasant raised platía where old men play *távli* in the shade of eucalyptus trees, lies a charming blue-domed **Byzantine church** with a double dedication to Áyios Yeóryios and Áyios Charálambos. The arched drum dome with elaborate blue-tile decoration, together with an unusual ground plan, make this church unique on the island. Entry to view a rather bare interior with a late *ikonostásis* is difficult due to the frequent absences of the *papás* who apparently possesses the only key, but anyway it's the church's exterior which gives it its standing in Byzantine architecture. The road's next stop is Ierápetra, 7km further on (see p.186).

> ### AN AIRPORT FOR THE EAST?
>
> The tranquil isolation of this strip may be about to end if plans for a new **international airport** – sited south of Vasilikí – are finalized. It's planned to take up a tract 5km long, and archeologists are worried about potential damage to as yet undiscovered sites in an important historical area; so far their opposition has managed to hold up the digging machines. There's also a rumbling row between the rival towns of Áyios Nikólaos and Sitía, the latter believing that it, and not Áyios Nikólaos/Ierápetra, should get the east's first major airport. Chaotically, Sitía is now going it alone and has started extending the runways on its own tiny airport to take wide-bodied jets – though whether they will ever land there is open to question. However, this move has not lessened the determination of Áyios Nikólaos and Ierápetra to go ahead with their own airport – once they've seen off the archeologists – which is intended to open up the east of the island to the development of package tourism.

THE FAR EAST

The far east of Crete marks yet another dramatic change in scenery and tempo. Although much of it is rocky, barren and desolate, it is an area of great natural beauty. With the exception of **Ierápetra**, the towns and villages are slower and quieter, life conducted at an easier pace. **Sitía**, in particular, seems a contented city unperturbed by its visitors. The north coast has few beaches, and in the main the mountains drop straight to the sea (the drive towards Sitía is as dramatic as any in Crete), but there are a couple of coves which are just about accessible, and beyond Sitía, as the heights tail away, there's more opportunity for swimming. The far east is much visited only in two spots – the overrated palm beach at **Vái** and the superb Minoan palace at **Zákros**. Away from these it's a great area for escapists. To the south of Zákros, isolated **Kserócambos** has deserted beaches by the score and along the south coast there are excellent strands at **Makriyialós**, **Ayía Fotiá**, the coast east of Ierápetra and at **Mírtos**.

Bus connections and main roads continue to be good: there are frequent rapid services from Áyios Nikólaos to Ierápetra, and good connections along the north coast to Sitía. Onwards from Sitía it's easy enough to continue to Vái or Zákros or to cut back south to Ierápetra; from Ierápetra, rather less readily if you're relying on public transport, you can carry on west, across the centre of Crete, to Iráklion.

The road to Sitía

Beyond the isthmus, the tawny bulk of the Sitía mountains makes a formidable barrier to further progress and the road at first is carved into the cliff face, teetering perilously above the gulf. The views become more expansive all the time, until at **PLÁTANOS** you reach a famous viewpoint, with a couple of tavernas – *Panorama* and *Skinoseli* further on – where you can look down on the island of Psíra, the site of a Minoan settlement, and west across the gulf to Áyios Nikólaos to watch the sunset. After this point the road runs further inland, emerging only occasionally to glimpses of the sea far below.

Of the tempting beaches you see, many are inaccessible, although **THÓLOS** (where there's a quiet beach and chapel but not much else, and similar pollution problems to Pahiá Ámmos, see p.159) can be reached 4km down an asphalted road. The *Tholos Beach* taverna, apartments and rooms are about halfway down. **Kavoúsi** with its Byzantine churches and main tree-lined street of oleanders and mulberry trees would be a better place to stay.

Móhlos and its islet

A more inviting alternative is **MÓHLOS** – though getting there involves tackling 5km or more of dusty hairpin bends. There is no bus connection down to the coast, which leaves you with the options of a taxi or walking. Shortest of the routes down is a road signposted soon after Plátanos, but you may have difficulty persuading the bus to stop here, at San Pandelémas, and although recently sealed it is also the least attractive route, past a large quarrying operation. There are equally obvious ways to follow down (in ninety minutes or less) from the villages of Sfáka, Tourlotí (a trail not marked on the maps) and Mirsíni, all of which are standard halts for the bus. The Sfáka road is also asphalted and the way to go if you have transport. You could also get to Móhlos by boat from Áyios Nikólaos – a regular trip in summer which includes a stop at Psíra: ask at the bus station in Áyios Nikólaos for details. Heading back from Móhlos to the main road involves a more serious walk, of two hours or more, which you might want to bypass by taking a taxi.

Tiny and out of the way as it is, Móhlos has plenty of **tavernas**: *Ta Kokilia* is the best on the seafront, while *Sta Limenária* in a cove to the west has interesting "specials" and vegetarian dishes. There are also two small **hotels**, *Sofia* (☎0843/94-179, fax 94-238; ③) and *Mochlos* (☎0843/94-205; ③) – the cheaper rooms at the latter don't have sea views – as well as numerous houses which rent out **rooms**. Try *Rooms Limenária* (☎0843/94-206; ②), close to the *Mochlos,* for pleasant rooms with bath, or the simpler *Pension Hermes* (☎0843/94-074; ②), just behind the *Mochlos.* Over the street from here *Rooms Fragiadakis* (☎0843/94-020; ②) offers good value apartments with kitchen, and, at the rear of the village, *Studios Hilaki* (☎0843/94-333) has new versions of the same. There are some new hotel developments, too, but fortunately these are far enough out not to affect the character of the village much.

Obviously, the place is not wholly unspoilt: rooms can be surprisingly expensive and often booked up in high season, and some of the bars and tavernas much fancier than you'd expect. This appears to be mainly because American and Greek teams are still excavating on the islet offshore, and they and their followers often spend whole summers here, occupying much of the available space. No matter, the atmosphere remains sleepy, there's plenty of space if you need to camp out, and plenty of rather rocky foreshore to swim off during the day. Keep an eye out for sea urchins while bathing here (the mini-market sells plastic shoes); they flourish in the clear, unpolluted water. In the mornings, you'll see divers collecting them for restaurants along the coast, which serve up the female ovaries as *achinosalata* – a much-prized delicacy.

The islet

The **islet** looks within swimming distance – and it is when the weather is calm – but it's easier to arrange a ride with a local fisherman if you want to go over. A return trip will cost around 2000dr for the boat – ask at *Ta Kokilia* taverna, where many fishermen hang around after work.

Early summer in Crete

The fortress and Venetian walls at Iráklion

The Lasíthi Plateau

The Palace of Knossós

Interior at Knossós

Storage jar at the Palace of Mália

The Dhiktean cave, "birthplace of Zeus"

Áyios Nikólaos

Vái beach

Windmill, Tóplou monastery

Elafonísi

Inhabited from the Pre-Palatial period, in Minoan times this barren rock was almost certainly a much less barren peninsula, and the sandy spit linking it to the mainland would have been used as a harbour (anchorages which could be approached from either side were a great advantage for boats that could sail only before the wind). You can see remains of late Minoan houses on the south side of the island, and there are more below the current sea level where recent excavations have also identified remnants of the ancient harbour. But the important discoveries at Móhlos were in the much more ancient tombs built up against the cliff. Here very early seal stones were found (including one from Mesopotamia), as well as some spectacular gold jewellery (now in the Iráklion Archeological Museum) and a fine collection of marble, steatite and rock crystal vases (in the Áyios Nikólaos and Sitía archeological museums).

Psíra

The larger island of **Psíra**, this time genuinely offshore, was also a Minoan port, and here the remains are of a town a little like Goúrnia but built amphitheatrically around a good natural harbour. It was first excavated in 1907 by an American, Richard Seager, who revealed a settlement which again was occupied from the early Minoan era. During the Neo-Palatial period, the community of merchants, sailors and fishermen shared in the general prosperity of the time.

A long, stepped street climbs away from the harbour; most of the dwellings here have a hearth in one of their rooms. No palaces or obvious public buildings were discovered but the site has produced rich finds of painted pottery. One jar, now on display in the Iráklion Archeological Museum, is noted for its decoration of bulls' heads interspersed with the double axe symbol. Trading with overseas areas such as Egypt and the Levant must have been necessary to import the essential requirements of life to such a parched, infertile place. The remains of what is thought to be an ancient well have been found – although the island is completely dry these days. The site was another of those destroyed about 1450 BC: later the Romans used the island for strategic and navigational purposes, and you can still make out the remains of their lighthouse and military settlement on the island's crown. As with the islet, you should be able to arrange a ride over to Psíra with a fisherman, or you could take a more organized visit from Áyios Nikólaos for around 500dr per person.

East to Mirsíni

From Móhlos to Sitía the road, lined with a riot of pink and white oleander flowers in summer, continues to toil through villages clinging to the mountainside, now high above a deserted bay, now enfolded by mountains, until the final approach to the city, and a descent in great loops through softer hills. As you progress, the familiar olive groves are increasingly interspersed with vineyards and there are some fine and highly regarded local wines to be had in the village cafés (especially in **Éxo Moulianá**). Wine under the Agrilos label is bottled in nearby Sitía. Most of the grapes, however, go to make sultanas: in late summer, when they are laid out to dry in the fields and on rooftops all around, the various stages of their slow change from green to gold to brown make a bizarre spectacle.

Mirsíni

Of the villages en route, **MIRSÍNI** has an attractive church built around, and entirely enclosing, a frescoed fourteenth-century chapel. You'll need to find the priest if you want to look inside, but no matter if you can't track him down – apart from the church, and a small pottery and weaving workshop, Mirsíni also has a **taverna** whose terrace has stunning views across the coast below.

Hamézi

Near to the ruined stone windmills on the final crest before the Bay of Sitía, a track is signed on the right for the ancient site of **Hamézi** (the village of the same name is further on). The track will eventually lead you to a Minoan site with a spectacular hilltop setting after about a fifteen-minute walk. Once on the track, take the second turning right, the one just beyond the windmills – this should bring you to a beekeeper's hut with hives stacked beside it. The fence circling the site on its conical hilltop is visible from here. Should you get lost on the way – which isn't difficult – head for the nearby village of Paraspóri (see below), where the boys at *Yiordanis' Bar* will be only too pleased to direct you. "Archaeológiki anaskafí" are the words you need, but make sure you are heading for the hilltop site or they may think you want Ahládia (see below).

Dating from the Pre-Palatial period (c.2000 BC), this grey stone ruin has a unique importance in Minoan archeology, for it is the only known structure to have had an oval ground plan, possibly dictated by the conical shape of the hill. It was thought at first to be a peak sanctuary, but the discovery of a cistern made a dwelling, or even a fortress, seem more likely. The ground plan sketched out by the walls – more than 1m high in places – consists of a number of rooms grouped around a central courtyard where the cistern is located. A paved entrance is visible on the south side. Whatever the building's function, it certainly had a commanding view over the surrounding terrain. While you're taking this in, keep an eye out for the rare Eleanora's falcon which breeds on the offshore island of Paximádha – the valley to the east is one of its favourite hunting grounds.

HAMÉZI proper is a sleepy little village spreading uphill to the north of the road, where plants are festooned over buildings and down white-washed steps. The village's **folk museum** (250dr) is worth a visit; it has a collection of ancient farm implements and rooms filled with furniture and utensils from the last century. To get there, head along the main street, passing the brilliant white church, and turn left up a charming stepped street. The museum lies at the top the street to the right; if it is closed, enquire at the kafeníon lower down and they'll usually locate a key.

Ahládia and Paraspóri

If you still have the appetite for more ruins, nearby at **Ahládia** are the remains of an impressive *thólos* tomb dating from the Mycenaean period, as well as a Neo-Palatial Minoan villa. The **tomb** lies 2km to the east of the village of **PARASPÓRI** up a track to the right, whilst the **villa** lies up another track (also on the right) 1km beyond Ahládia.

Moní Faneroméni

Further along the main Sitía road, just beyond Skopí, you'll come to a track signed left for the **Moní Faneroméni**. Partly asphalted, this five-kilometre track leads to a picturesque cove lapped by a turquoise sea. From here, the track climbs inland to the monastery, which can also be approached by another track 5km closer to Sitía.

What you'll find when you reach it is a charming monastic church overlooking a gorge near to the sea. Standing as a metaphor for more recent Cretan history, the church has been battered but still stands unbowed. In 1829 the monastery and tiny church were looted and burned by the Turks, and most of the frescoes destroyed. The beauty of what was lost is glimpsed in one scarred remaining fragment depicting a saint reading. The three indentations across his face are bullet holes, again Turkish. By the iconostasis hangs a curtain embroidered with a gold Greek cross which you may be tempted to peer behind; the remains of the founder here are not for the squeamish. The shoals of silver *taxímata* (ex votos) hung on the icon of the Virgin to implore her miraculous intervention attest to the importance of the shrine locally today – a tradition stretching back to Minoan times and probably beyond. There's a path from here, which would take you on foot to Sitía in less than two hours.

Sitía

After the excesses of Mália or Áyios Nikólaos, arriving in **SITÍA** can seem something of an anticlimax, even dull. But don't be fooled; Sitía's charms are subtle. Allow yourself to adjust to the more leisurely pace of life here and you may, like many other visitors before you, end up staying much longer than intended. The town certainly makes an ideal base from which to visit the other attractions in the region. Not even Sitía, of course, can entirely escape the tourist boom, and the increasing number of tourists attracted to the port has led to a great deal of new development at the fringes. Many of the new visitors are French or Italian, a legacy perhaps of the French troops who garrisoned the place under the Great Power protection at the end of the nineteenth century, and the Italians who occupied it during World War II.

This area was settled, as *Eteia*, in Classical times but may be identified with the Minoan *se-to-i-ja* inscribed on clay tablets found locally. That there was a substantial Minoan presence in the area is borne out by the excavations at Petrás, the town's southern suburb, where a settlement dating to the early second millennium BC has been unearthed and where, in the later Neo-Palatial period, there was a fine town with sophisticated buildings and roads. Details concerning the subsequent Greek and Roman settlements are sketchy and little tangible evidence, apart from some tombs and fish tanks (see p.167), survives. It was under the Venetians that the port really took off (they called it *La Sitia* – hence Lasíthi), as part of a conscious attempt to exploit the east of the island. For all their efforts, the area remained cut off by land from the rest of Crete and although what was in effect a separate fiefdom developed here, it never amounted to a great deal. Perhaps the most significant event of this era was the birth of Vitzentzos Kornáros, author of the epic Cretan poem, the *Erotókritos*. More physical remains are few, prey to earthquakes and the raids of Barbarossa. Where once there was a walled city, now you'll find only the barest remains of a fortress.

The town is set on a hill tumbling down towards the western end of the picturesque Bay of Sitía. Its oldest sections, hanging steeply above the harbour, look east over the bay and the long ribbon of new development along the coast. Life concentrates on the waterfront, around Platía Iroon Polytehniou in the corner of the bay. North towards the port and ferry dock is a seafront promenade crowded with the outdoor tables of rival tavernas. South, the main road runs behind the beach, flanked for miles by a rambling jumble of development.

Arrival, information and accommodation

The **bus station** is on Konstantinou Karamanli (aka the Beach Road) and though there's a left-luggage area of sorts, it's hardly secure. Leaving the station, turn left along the seafront which will bring you into the centre. **Ferry** arrivals from Áyios Nikólaos or the islands dock at the port at the northeastern end of town; it's a ten-minute walk (or two-minute taxi-ride) into the centre.

The tourist office has closed but the **Sitia Development Organization** (Mon–Fri 8.30am–3.30pm; ☎0843/23-590, fax 25-341) now performs the same role; its friendly office is located at Odhós Antheon 24, slightly west of the post office on the left. Other sources of information (and town maps) include a **hotel information kiosk** (☎0843/61-305, fax 28-644) at the start of the Beach Road, who can find and book you hotel rooms but have no information on cheaper places. The none-too-competent **tourist police** are at Mysonos 24 (daily 7.30am–2.30pm; ☎0843/24-200).

Accommodation

Rooms are rather scattered, but except at the busiest times you should be able to find something. Quiet and good-value places can be found in the older streets leading up the hill from the waterfront, especially behind the OTE and in the nearby streets off Kapetan Sifi. Odhós Kondhilaki, which runs down the side of the OTE, has numerous possibilities. If you are at a loss where to begin there are a number of helpful travel agencies around the centre who can suggest possible options; try *Porto Belis*, Karamanli 34, ☎0843/22-370.

Apollon, Kapetan Sifi 28 (☎0843/28-155, fax 22-733). One of the more reasonable of Sitía's clutch of unremarkable upmarket places. Rooms come with balcony, mini-bar and TV. ④.

Arhontiko, Kondhilaki 16 (☎0843/28-172). One of the most pleasant budget hotels, with a mature orange tree in the front garden. If it's full, the owner has a few other (more expensive) rooms with bath around the corner. ②.

Rooms Ariadne, Katapoti 49 (☎0843/22-418). Good, family-run place with rooms at the back overlooking a garden. It's three blocks north of the post office. ②.

El Greco, Arkadiou 13 (☎ & fax 0843/23-133). Charming small hotel a couple of blocks in from the seafront, with en-suite rooms, some with sea view. ③.

Rooms Elena, Kondhilaki 58 (☎0843/24-844). Try here if the *Venus*, next door, is full. ②.

Itanos, Platía Iroon Polytehniou (☎0843/22-146, fax 22-915). Smart, mid-range hotel on the town's main square. ③.

Kazarma Rooms, Ionias 10, near the fortress (☎0843/23-211). Excellent rooms with use of communal kitchen. ②.

Maria Hamilaki, Kondhilaki 35 (☎0843/22-768). Clean, simple rooms, overseen by friendly proprietress. ①.

Nora, Rouselaki 31 (☎0843/23-017). Near the ferry port, this is a small and friendly female-run hotel, with fine views over the harbour and bay; all rooms have balconies and showers. ③.

Sitía Beach, fronting the beach on Karamanlis (☎0843/528-821, fax 28-826). Sitía's "flagship" hotel is none too exciting as a building but extras include gardens, a restaurant, disco, tennis courts, two pools, a gym and a sauna. ⑥.

Pension Venus, Kondhilaki 60 (☎0843/24-307). Comfortable, recommended place, with an ebullient English-speaking owner. ②.

Youth Hostel, Odhós Therisou 4a (☎0843/22-693 or 28-062). One of the better ones around, at 1200dr a night – you pass it on the right as you drive into town. The very friendly proprietor is struggling to keep it afloat after assistance from the central organization has been withdrawn – which may mean higher prices.

The Town

Sitía is an absorbing place to wander around, doing no more than enjoying the atmosphere. The narrow streets behind the seafront feature the everyday scenes of a Cretan provincial town: villagers in to stock up on news and necessities and stores which cater to their every conceivable need, from steel drums to wooden saddles, seed to pick-up trucks. While you're people-watching, one thing not to be missed, especially on Sundays, is the volta, when the whole town puts on its finery to parade in front of the neighbours. To see the show, get a seat around six in the evening at a table adjacent to the road behind the waterfront.

You'll not be in town long, especially around the harbour area, before you bump into Níkos, a resident **pelican** who is also the town's pampered mascot. When he was first trapped in fishermen's nets some years ago, Níkos's wings were clipped to force him to stay. Now that his wings have grown again he shows no signs of wanting to leave; this may have something to do with the town council providing him with his own accommodation on the harbourside together with a daily supply of fresh fish. When not waddling proprietorially along the seafront greeting visitors, Níkos indulges a delinquent streak by dive-bombing bathers from a great height (he rarely hits them!), and flopping onto the sails of capsized windsurfers, making them impossible to right. In spite of the potential hazards posed by Níkos, the heat will eventually propel you towards the beach: the **town beach** is attractive and swimmable and windsurfers are on hire along the beach road. However, the better beaches are a few kilometres further east towards Ayía Fotiá – the bus to Vái will drop you off.

Aside from wandering the streets, sitting in the cafés or lying on the beach, there's a limited number of things to do. The **Folk Museum** at Kapetanios Sifi, near the OTE (Tues–Sun 9.30am–2.30pm, plus Tues & Thurs 6–8pm; 500dr), offers an entertaining look at traditional life: Adam Hopkins's book *Crete* includes a wonderful section on his stay with a family in Sitía, and reveals the extent to which the old lifestyle survives to this day. On the hill above the harbour lies the restored **Venetian fort**, now used as an open-air theatre. Climbing down towards the port from here, you can see the ruined remains of some **Roman fish tanks**, just along the harbour front from the pelican's house. Freshly caught fish were kept in these semicircular constructions until they were needed.

The Archeological Museum

To gain a clearer picture of the past, however, the **Archeological Museum** (Tues–Sun 8.30am–3pm; 500dr), on the Ierápetra road, sandwiched in between builders' yards, contains an interesting collection of finds from the surrounding area and the palace at Zákros. You enter the main room (proceeding clockwise), where finds from the early Minoan cemetery at nearby Ayía Fotiá are displayed, as well as some fine stone vases from Móhlos and its island neighbour, Psíra. A new case here contains recent finds from Petrás, Sitía's southern suburb, where important buildings from the Minoan Neo-Palatial period have been unearthed. One large building has a magazine for storing *píthoi* (the large earthenware jars),

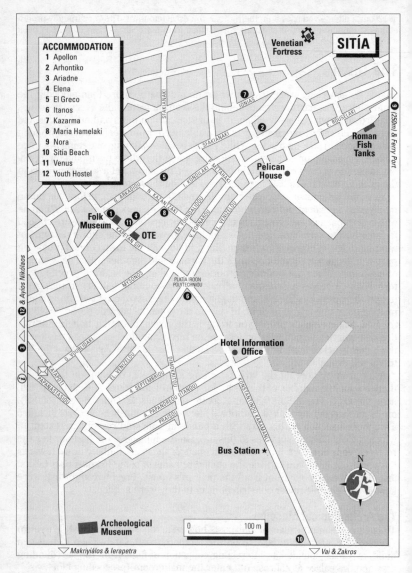

similar to that at Knossós. The archeologists are hesitant to describe this as a palace until more work has been done, but the early signs seem promising.

The **Zákros** section comes next: interesting exhibits here include a bronze saw, a wine press from a Minoan villa near the palace and a collection of seashells. Archeologists claim these had a sacred function, but it would be nice to think that the Minoans used them for decorative purposes as we do today – perhaps they even put them to their ears to listen to the sea.

Further on lies one of the museum's great treasures, a case full of rare **Linear A tablets**. They were discovered by archeologist Nikólaos Pláton in the archives room at the palace. Note how the Minoan characters have been delicately scratched into the soft clay. Some show evidence of being burned by the fire which destroyed the palace, and in fact it was the fire that preserved them, for as unbaked clay tablets they would have crumbled to dust. A nearby case illustrates the **domestic life** of the kitchen, the only one so far positively identified at any palace. Among the cooking pots and other utensils there's a superbly preserved terracotta grill, probably used for cooking some form of *souvláki* – a method used in the Greek world since pre-Mycenaean times and mentioned by Homer.

After the Hellenistic and Roman sections, don't miss the barnacle-encrusted tangle of Roman pots (probably from a wreck) which has been preserved by placing it inside a fish tank of salinated water. This artistically stunning idea was the brainwave of the museum's founder, the eminent Cretan archeologist Níkos Papadákis: his excellent guide to the monuments of Sitía and eastern Crete is on sale at the museum.

Eating

A line of enticing outdoor **tavernas** crowds the harbour front, many with a display of dishes and fresh fish to lure you in. Tempting as they are, eating at these seafront places can work out to be very expensive if you're not careful. Cheaper (and more interesting) eats are available away from the water, and there are a few good out-of-town possibilities too. If you're just looking for a **snack**, the *Paradosiaka* bakery at Kornárou 71, just behind the National Bank on Platía Iroon Polytechniou sells excellent *tirópita* and *spanakópita*, whilst the nearby *Picadilly* (in from *Zorba's*) sells delicious chocolate cakes. Bakeries and cake stores are something of a local attraction, and there are a couple more good ones along Venizélou: try the bakery at no. 49 or, for more mouthwatering delights, *Zacharoplasteion Kalambokis* at no. 95, east of the main square. The *Platía Café* on the central Platía Iroon Polytehniou does fancy (and pricey) **breakfasts**, but you do get the best people-watching site in town.

Creperie Mike, Venizélou 162. All kinds of authentic and delicious crepe, both savoury and sweet, served on their seafront terrace by the Belgian proprietor.

Creta House, Beach Road. Just along from the place below, this is a reliable traditional taverna with a harbourside terrace.

Itanos, Beach Road. The terrace bar of the hotel of the same name is renowned among locals for its mezédhes.

Kali Kardia, Foundalídhou 28. The "Good Heart", two blocks in from the waterfront, is an ouzerí where you can wash down a fish mezédhes with house retsina – a good place to mix with the locals.

Karnagio, ferry port. The ferry harbour's taverna is an excellent source of traditional fare; there's no menu, so you go in the kitchen and choose what you fancy. Great views over the bay from their terrace.

To Kyma, at the eastern end of the harbour near the pelican house. Well-prepared fish and meat dishes at reasonable prices.

Mixos, Kornárou 117. Traditional charcoal cooking on a spit in the street, served up with a very strong local wine.

Neromilos, off the road to Ayía Fotiá, 4km from Sitía. Housed in a converted ancient watermill high above the bay, this offers magnificent views as well as a good selection of mezédhes and grilled meat and fish. Take a taxi, as the road down can be pretty tortuous in the dark. Nearby in Roússa Ekklisía there's another village taverna which does great charcoal roasts and also has a superb terrace view.

Panorama, off the road to Ayía Fotiá. Further up the hill from the *Neromilos*, this taverna also serves up decent food from a charcoal grill.

Psistaria, Itanou (A. Papandreou). Opposite Knossos bike rental, this no-frills place is popular with locals for its *souvláki* and mezédhes. Good value.

Remezzo, at the harbour. One of the longest established places (1941), which serves decent food at above average prices on a terrace.

Sitia Beach, Karamanli 28 (Beach Road). Excellent pizzeria not far away from the bus station.

Zorba's, at the harbour. The biggest and most popular place on the seafront, and the only restaurant in town open all year round. It never changes and is good for standard dishes, like swordfish.

Drinking, nightlife and entertainment

Nightlife, mostly conducted at an easy pace, centres around drinking, disco-bars and a couple of clubs. These are mainly concentrated in two areas: up at the north end of Kornárou, and out along Beach Road (officially named Karamanli). In the first group there's the *Bisadio* – on the seafront after the pelican's house – whose terrace has a great view over the bay, and the stylish *Di Settia* nearby. Closer in along the harbour, try the *Time In* cocktail bar or *Skala*. At the other end of town, young Sitían professionals gather at their own open-air hideaway, *Status*, on the Ierápetra road, 100m past the Archeological Museum. Here, beneath a giant palm tree – which is spotlit at night – you can sip cocktails and dance to a disco on a crazy-paving floor; don't arrive before 10pm. Stealing *Status's* thunder is *Hot Summer* on the Beach Road which attracts a younger crowd for dance music around a garden (swimming) pool. But bigger than any of these is the monster *Planitarion* disco a couple of kilometres beyond the ferry port (take a taxi). It's got a sliding glass roof, state-of-the-art technological gadgetry and draws in crowds from all over the east: it can hold up to a thousand. Plays an eclectic mix of music including rock, jazz and Greek, all at frightening sound levels.

During the middle of August (16–20) the annual *Sultanina* or **sultana festival** marks the start of the grape harvest. The local export is celebrated with traditional music and dancing, and all the locally produced wine you can consume is included in the entrance fee to the fairground beyond the ferry port. Tickets for this are sold at a booth on the corner of the harbour, which also has tickets and information for the summer-long **cultural festival** – concerts, dance, theatre – the *Kornaria*.

Listings

Airlines Olympic are at Venizélou 56 (☎0843/22-270), just off the platía, for local flights to Kásos, Kárpathos and Rhodes; there's also a twice-weekly (Tues & Sat) service to Athens. The airport runways are being extended and it's worth checking on direct charters when this is completed in 1998.

Banks and exchange There's a branch of the National Bank (Mon–Thurs 8am–2pm, Fri 8am–1.30pm) at the bottom of Odhós Sífi, facing Platía Venizélou with a cash dispenser and cash-changing machines. There are also cash dispensers at two banks close to Venizélou: Ethniki Bank on the platía and, just south, Ionian Bank at Venizélou 47.

Bike and car rental Outlets for bikes are on Itánou (now renamed Odhós A. Papandreou) below the bus station, the best of the bunch being Petras Moto (☎0843/24-849), which provides helmets; nearby Knossos (☎0843/22-057) is another possibility. Club Cars, A. Papandreou 8 (☎0843/25-104) is reliable for car hire.

Books and newspapers Tsirilakis, Kornárou 49, close to the main platía, has English-language books (with a second-hand section) and newspapers.

Bus station At Karamo 4 (☎0843/22-272), at the southern end of the waterfront. This may be moving to a new site opposite the Archeological Museum, so enquire locally. Services to Áyios Nikólaos (8 daily; 2hr), Iráklion (5 daily; 3hr 15min), Ierápetra (5 daily; 1hr 30min), Vái (4 daily; 1hr) and Káto Zákros (2 daily; 1hr).

Ferries The ferry agent (for boats to Kásos and the Dodecanese) is Tzortzakis (☎0843/25-080, fax 22-731) Kornárou 150, behind the harbour front down towards the dock.

Hospital Herokamares, left beyond the youth hostel (☎0843/24-311).

Laundry Self-service laundry on A. Papanatasiou, just west of the post office.

OTE On Kapetan Sífi, 2 blocks west of Platía Iroon Polytechniou (Mon–Fri 7.30am–9.45pm).

Post office Platía Ethnikis Antistasis 2 (Mon–Fri 7.30am–8pm, Sat 7.30am–2pm).

The east: Vái and Palékastro

Vái beach, with its famous grove of palm trees and silvery sands, features alongside Knossós, the Lasíthi plateau and the Samariá gorge on almost every Cretan travel agent's list of excursions. For years it was a popular hang-out for backpackers, but repeated fires followed by a clean-up campaign to attract a more well-heeled crowd have resulted in a ring fence around the beach with a guard to enforce the new regulations, which prohibit overnight stays. People still claim to be able to sleep there, but it hardly seems worth the hassle. If you're looking for more to do than simply sizzle on the sands, there are a number of likely sights within striking distance of Vái – with your own transport, the beaches and archeological sites at Ítanos and Palékastro are within reach. The scenically sited ancient monastery at Tóplou, just to the north of Palékastro, is one of the most revered on the island.

Ayía Fotiá

From Sitía the road runs along the beach, tracking a rocky, unexceptional coastline past **Ayía Fotiá**, a small cove that now supports a cluster of new development. Here, in 1971, the largest Minoan graveyard yet found in Crete was excavated, revealing over 250 chamber tombs from the early Pre-Palatial period. Among the outstanding finds of vases, fish hooks, daggers and stone axes (now in the Sitía and Áyios Nikólaos archeological museums) were a number of lead amulets which suggest that these early Minoans regarded lead as well as silver as a precious metal. To reach the cemetery, keep your eyes skinned on the eastern edge of the village for a rough track descending sharply to the left immediately after the *Sitian Arts Pottery Garden* (blue sign). This leads (after 200m) to the fenced-off cemetery, close to the sea.

After some 7km the road turns inland, climbing into quite deserted, gently hilly country, the slopes covered in thyme, heather and sage with the occasional cluster of strategically sited beehives. In summer the sweet-scented, deep violet thyme flowers prove an irresistible attraction for the bees which feed on them almost exclusively, creating the much sought-after *thimárisio* (thyme honey).

Tóplou Monastery

Not long after you leave the coast, there's a road signposted up to the **Monastery of Tóplou** (daily 9am–1pm & 2–6pm), which is also the short way to Vái. As you approach, the monastery looks more like a fortress, standing defiant in landscape almost empty, save for a line of intrusive wind turbines along the ridge behind. The name Tóplou is Turkish for "with a cannon" – a reference to a giant device with which the monks used to defend themselves and uphold the Cretan monastic traditions of resistance to invaders. They needed it; the monastery was sacked by pirates and destroyed in 1498, and in the 1821 rebellion it was captured by the Turks, who hanged twelve monks from the gate as an example. In World War II it again served as a place of shelter for the resistance. The opening above the main gate harks back to these troubled times: the monks hurled missiles and boiling oil through it onto those attempting to gain entry.

Its forbidding exterior and grim history notwithstanding, Tóplou is startlingly beautiful within: a flower-decked, cloister-like courtyard with stairways leading up to arcaded walkways off which are the cells. The blue-robed monks keep out of the way of visitors as far as possible, but their cells and refectory are left discreetly on view. And in the church is one of the masterpieces of Cretan art, the eighteenth-century **icon** *Lord Thou Art Great* by Ioánnis Kornáros. This is a marvellously intricate work, incorporating 61 small scenes full of amazing detail, each illustrating, and labelled with, a phrase from the Orthodox prayer which begins "Lord, thou art great . . .". Outside in the shop you can buy enormously expensive reproductions of the icon, as well as postcards and books.

As you leave the church, take a look at the stone **inscription** set into the exterior wall. It records an arbitration by Magnesia, a city in Asia Minor, dating from the second century BC, concerning a territorial dispute between nearby Ítanos and Ierápytna (modern Ierápetra). At this time, when the Romans held sway over Crete, these deadly rivals clashed constantly, and finally Rome, unable to placate the two, called in the Magnesians to act as honest brokers. The inscription records part of their judgement (in favour of Ítanos) and was placed in the monastery wall at the suggestion of the English traveller and antiquarian Robert Pashley, who found it being used as a gravestone in 1834.

The monastery is reputed to be incredibly wealthy – it owns most of the northeastern corner of the island – and this is no doubt how they can afford the endless and extensive restorations which seem set to destroy the romance of the place (the sheer weight of visitor numbers doesn't help either). Latest tasteless additions include an over-restored windmill and an ornamental garden with crazy paving and ludicrous sculpture fronting the monastery entrance. The **museum** (700dr) – which now incorporates the church and the icon – has also been extended. Apart from a handful of superb icons, the main addition is a collection of tedious religious engravings which fill the wall space, alongside a niche devoted to weapons and battle paraphernalia dating from the Cretan War of Independence to World War II. Beyond Tóplou the road descends towards Vái through the same arid, rock-strewn landscape as before. This area is another where you might catch sight of the rare **Eleonora's falcon**, which breeds on the Dionysádes islands to the north – Tóplou and Cape Síderos (a closed military zone) are regular hunting grounds.

Vái

Vái beach makes for a thoroughly secular contrast to the spiritual tranquillity of Tóplou. Famous above all for its palm trees, the sudden appearance of what is claimed to be Europe's only indigenous wild date-palm grove is indeed an exotic shock. As you lie on the fine sand in the early morning, the dream of Caribbean islands is hard to dismiss. During the day, however, the sand fills to overflowing as buses – public ones from Sitía and tours from all over the island – pour into the car park in numbers which really can't be justified by a few palm trees. The board-walks laid out across the sand are not there only to protect feet from the burning sand, but also to guarantee a route through the mass of baking bodies. Even the adjoining beaches, where those in the know used to hide out to escape the swarm, get pretty crowded nowadays. Note that there is **no accommodation** here as this is a protected natural park; the nearest place for a bed is Palékastro (see below).

The buses are packed, the beach is worse, the café and taverna charge over the odds once you've endured the long queue, you pay to have a shower or use the toilet, and still people come here to camp rough. As everywhere, notices warn that "Camping is forbidden by law", and for once they really do seem to mean it – at least within the confines of the park which protects the palm trees. However, you can climb the steps cut into the rock behind the taverna to the cove to the south, or with rather more difficulty clamber over the rocks to that to the north, and join thriving little communities at either. If you do sleep here, watch your belongings: rip-offs abound. Having endured all this you may just, for a couple of hours at each end of the day, be able to enjoy Vái the way it ought to be. Alternatively, avoid the high season if you can.

Ítanos

The sand may be less good, but the emptiness of the three small beaches at **ÍTANOS**, 1.5km north of the turning to Vái, makes them far more enjoyable. There's still the odd palm tree scattered around, and if you're at a loss for something to do you can explore the remains of the ancient city here. Inhabited from Minoan times, Ítanos became important later, flourishing through the Classical Greek and Roman eras when she vied with Ierápytna (modern Ierápetra) for control of eastern Crete. One twenty-year squabble between these two led to the arbitration of Magnesia in 132 BC, part of the stone record of which is preserved at Tóplou Monastery (see p.172). The settlement here remained prosperous until the medieval Byzantine era when it was destroyed, most likely by Saracen pirates. All sorts of messy ruins strewn with potsherds survive beneath the twin acropolis, but little which retains any shape. There are two early basilicas you might be able to make out, as well as the beautifully cut lower courses of a Hellenistic wall on the western hill.

Palékastro and Angáthia

PALÉKASTRO, 9km south of Vái, is a pleasant little farming village and a good place to stay close to the beaches – with a couple of excellent tavernas on the main square which are worth breaking your journey for if you're simply passing through. However, the place is now starting to realize the potential of its position, and tourism is expanding – there's even a rather incongruous nightclub.

The **OTE** office (Mon–Fri 9.30am–9.30pm, Sat 9.30am–1.30pm), up a passage-way opposite the main door of the church, helps with finding rooms as well as having exchange facilities, stamps and phonecards. For **accommodation**, try *Hotel Itanos* (☎0843/61-205; ②) on the main square (not connected with the restaurant below it – ask instead at the supermarket next door), *Hotel Hellas* (☎0843/61-240, fax 61-340; ③; reduced rates for longer stays) or the *Hotel Palekastro* (☎0843/61-235; ②), 100m along the road to Sitía on the left. Don't be misled by a drab exterior here: the pleasant new rooms lie beyond a courtyard behind. There are also plenty of signs indicating **rooms**; along the road leading to Vái, *Rooms Mitsakakis* (☎0843/61-414; ②) and *Venus* (☎0843/61-267; ②) are worth a try, as is the good value *Vai* (☎0843/61-287; ①-②; open April–Sept): rooms above a taverna at the western end of the village on the Sitía road. The best place to eat in Palékastro is the **restaurant** at the *Hotel Hellas*. Next door to here, Motor Action (☎0843/61276) rents out **scooters** which provide a handy means of reaching some of the remoter beaches.

ANGÁTHIA, smaller in scale and even quieter, lies a kilometre nearer the beach. Just across the bridge leading into the village on the right you'll find *Taverna Vaios* (☎0843/61403; ②) which has a couple of pleasant sea-view balcony **rooms** with bath. The taverna also makes a good lunch stop if you're at the beach. **Chiona beach**, a good stretch of EU blue-flagged pebble and sand, is a kilometre beyond Angáthia and is the beach most people visit, probably because of its car park and nearby **tavernas**, the best of which is *Taverna Batis* with a beach-front terrace, at the northern end; there is no accommodation at Chiona. South of Chiona beach along a track running beside the sea, about 200m down on the right, a signed **walking track** will take you to the nearby Petsofas peak, a pleasant 3km hike.

The ancient site
The Minoan site of **Palékastro** lies towards the beach, about twenty minutes' walk from the village. Follow the signs to the *Marina Village Hotel* and then to the beach at Chiona. For archeologists this was a very significant place, the largest Minoan town yet discovered and the source of much information about everyday Minoan life. It is an obvious site to settle, a broad and fertile agricultural plain set on an excellent bay beneath the protection of a high, flat-topped bluff: and indeed the area was extensively inhabited both before and after the Minoan era. Much of the site is disappointing for the casual visitor, with only a few odd walls lost among the fields: many of the excavations were later infilled to protect them. Still, some of the latest excavations are open to view and offer fascinating glimpses of dwellings, stairways and streets. Try to resist entering the excavation areas through the broken fences as the delicate walls are still being made safe for posterity by the archeologists.

Local beaches
When you've had your fill of wandering among the olive groves seeking out some of the further-flung remnants, there are some excellent **beaches** not far beyond where you could easily camp out. The better sands are around the bay further to the south of Chiona, where for most of the year you can easily claim a cove to yourself. There's another around to the left, in the shadow of the bluff. Between Palékastro and Vái, a number of other good beaches are signed off the road, including **Kouremenos**, which is one of Crete's best **windsurfing** areas: in summer there are boards for hire.

Zákros and the far southeast

Palékastro is also the crossroads for the road south to **Zákros**, a beautiful drive through country where the soil is a strange pinkish-purple colour, as if indelibly stained with grape juice (although actually it's olives which grow around here). The few hamlets you pass on the way are so small that they make Zákros (or more properly Áno Zákros) seem positively urban when finally you get there.

Áno Zákros

A slow-moving little town, **ÁNO ZÁKROS** boasts three or four **tavernas** around its central square and a small **hotel**, the *Zakros* (☎0843/43-379, fax 93-379; ②) where the rooms at the back have good views over the gorge behind. It's also worth noting that guests here are entitled to free trips to Káto Zákros in the hotel's minibus. Throughout the summer at weekends the tavernas host numerous wedding feasts accompanied by dancing to *bouzoúki* and *lyra*; should you arrive then you'll most likely have a glass of wine thrust into your hand by one of the multitude of smartly dressed revellers filling the square. The little trade these establishments see the rest of the time, however, is almost exclusively passing through, since Káto (or lower) Zákros, and the palace, are on the coast 8km further on. Locally, Zákros enjoys a certain fame for its numerous **springs** which feed the lush vegetation hereabouts and which were also an attraction for the Minoans. If you follow the sign up to the right as you come into the town, or simply climb the hill from the centre, you'll reach a little chapel from where in five minutes a path leads beside the stream to its source and some pleasant, shady picnic spots. Information on how to get to it or to reach the start of the "Valley of the Dead" walk (see over) is available from the *Hotel Zakros*.

Leaving the village by the Káto Zákros road, you'll soon pass the remains of a **Minoan villa** dating from the late Neo-Palatial period (c.1500 BC); here a wine press was turned up which is now in the Sitía Archeological Museum. Pressing on towards the coast, a good new road winds spectacularly down to approach the small bay from the south. There are even better views if you turn left down the purple track which runs straight into the back of the village, past the palace.

Káto Zákros

From the first spectacular view as you approach along the clifftop road, **KÁTO ZÁKROS** is a delight. There's a pebbly sand beach, three good tavernas and a few places offering **rooms**, of which *Poseidon* (☎0843/93-316; ②) – on a rocky outcrop with spectacular sea views – is the best. A friendly new place for rooms and apartments with bath, *George Villas* (☎ & fax 0843/93-201; ③) is another pleasant haven with its eponymous and ebullient proprietor; follow the track heading inland from the palace entrance for 600m. *Rooms Alex* (☎0843/93-338; ②) is another possibility, though it's 2km (not 500m as their publicity says) back towards Áno Zákros. The *Taverna Akrogiali* (☎0843/93-316; ②) also has rooms with and without bath and acts as an agent for the nearby *Athena* (③) and *Sunrise* (②) rooms places. It's worth bearing in mind, however, especially if you're arriving by bus, that accommodation is severely limited (due to building restrictions surrounding the archeological site) and during high season you will rarely find a room on spec;

you may be able to sleep under the trees or on the beach but the patience of the villagers is wearing thin towards people who do this.

Along with a tiny harbour with a few boats, this is about all the place amounts to. Everything you really need you can find – they'll change money in the tavernas and you can even make long-distance and international phone calls from a kiosk – but there is absolutely nothing else, not even a store. However, the village now has its first ever cocktail **bar** – the aptly named *Amnesia* on the seafront – where the clientele have even been known to dance when the mood takes them. But this hardly causes a ripple, and if it's laid-back tranquillity you're after you've come to the right place.

Although in summer a couple of daily buses do run all the way to Káto Zákros, most transport still stops in the upper village. From here you could hitch the rest of the way quite easily, but it's also worth considering the **walk**, less than two hours to the palace via a beautiful ravine known as the **Valley of the Dead**. The easiest route traces the road for almost 2km, before turning left (curiously signposted "Dead's Gorge") onto a track which brings you out above the ravine. Getting to the bottom is something of a scramble, which may require hands as well as feet, but once you're down the trail is easy to follow along the left-hand side of the stream bed, marked by the usual red waymarks in case of confusion. It's a solitary but magnificent walk, brightened especially in spring by plenty of plant life. High in the cliff walls you'll see the mouths of caves: it is these, used as tombs in Minoan times and earlier, which give the ravine its name. At the bottom you rejoin the dirt road, which runs through groves of bananas and olives and into Káto Zákros past the palace. As an alternative you can follow the waymarked path all the way from Áno Zákros, avoiding the road altogether. To reach the path from the square take the road on the east side and to the right of the *Maestro Taverna* and small kafeníon next door, and fork right at the telegraph pole. The way descends along a path, passing beneath a stone arch. About 200m beyond this, you will come to a sign directing you to the gorge entrance. Should you experience any difficulties in finding the way enquire at the *Hotel Zakros*.

The Palace of Zákros

The valley behind Káto Zákros was explored by a British archeologist, David Hogarth, at much the same time as the other great Cretan palaces were being discovered, around the turn of the century. But Hogarth gave up the search, having unearthed only a couple of Minoan houses, and it was not until the 1960s that new explorations were begun by a Greek, Nikólaos Pláton. Pláton found the palace almost immediately, just yards from where Hogarth's trenches ended. The **Palace of Zákros** (Tues–Sun: July–Oct 8am–7pm; Nov–June 8am–3pm; 500dr; students free) thus benefited from the most modern of techniques in its excavation and, having been forgotten even locally, it was also unlooted. The site yielded an enormous quantity of treasures and everyday items, including storerooms with all their giant *píthoi* still in place and a religious treasury full of stone vases and ritual vessels.

For the amateur, Zákros is also full of interest, and a great deal easier to understand than many of the other Minoan sites. Here the remains are of one palace only, dating from the period between 1600 and 1450 BC. Although there is an earlier settlement at a lower level, it is unlikely ever to be excavated – mainly because this end of the island is very gradually sinking. The water table is already almost

PALACE OF ZÁKROS

Map labels: N, 0 25 m, Upper Town, Magazines, Portico, Light Well, Central Shrine, Archives Room, Latrine, Dye House, Kitchen, Storerooms, HARBOUR ROAD, Exit, Bathroom, Altar Base, Courtyard, Entry to West Wing, Queen's Megaron, Main Gate, Foundry, Treasury, Banquet Hall, Central Court, Light Well, Lustral Basin, Ceremonial Hall, Workshop, Cistern, Well, Workshops, Well, Portico, King's Megaron, To Entrance, Royal Apartments

at the palace level, and anything deeper would be thoroughly submerged. Even the exposed parts of the palace are marshy and often waterlogged – there are terrapins living in the green water in the cistern. When it is really wet you can keep your feet dry, and get an excellent view of the overall plan of the palace, by climbing the streets of the town which occupied the hill above it.

Though the palace is a small one, it can match any of the more important Minoan centres for quality of construction and materials. And it is unique in the way that so much of the town – a place very like Gourniá – can still be made out all around. The original destruction of the palace appears to have been a very violent one, with only enough time for the inhabitants to abandon it, taking almost nothing with them. This again contributed to the enormous number of artefacts found here, but more importantly the nature of the destruction, in which the palace was flattened and burnt, is an important prop in the theory that it was the explosion of Thíra which ended the Minoan civilization. Large lumps of pumice found among the ruins are supposed to have been swept there by the tidal wave which followed the eruption. However, many archeologists take issue with this hypothesis and question both its chronological accuracy and the type of destruction (for example fire), seeing the palace's demise as being more consistent with human rather than natural causes.

Entrance

A paved road led from the site to its **harbour**, the chief reason why a palace existed here at all. The harbour installations have disappeared beneath the sea, but two large houses excavated along the road are enough to show that this must have been a significant port: the first landfall on Crete for trade from Egypt, the Nile Delta and the Middle East. Among the ruins were found ingots of copper imported from Cyprus, elephant tusks from Syria and gold and precious materials from Egypt.

The **entrance** has been relocated on the site's south side and to follow the account below you will need to start from the **exit** – a white cabin visible to the far right – where you can pick up the ancient harbour road leading towards the palace. Starting from here enables you to follow the ancient road leading directly towards the main gateway of the palace in its eastern corner. Before entering the palace proper you pass various dwellings to the right and left as well as the remains of a foundry dating from the Old Palace period, beneath a protective canopy on the left. The road (a stretch has been reconstructed) then curves round into the town, passing the palace entrance to the left. Entering the palace, the **main gate** leads to a stepped ramp followed by a **courtyard** which may have served as a meeting place between the palace hierarchy and the townspeople. Here in the northeast corner beneath another canopy is a **bathroom** where visitors to the palace may have been required to wash or purify themselves before proceeding further. To the west of the courtyard lies the main or **Central Court**, a little over 30m by 12m, or about a third the size of that at Knossós. Crossing the north edge of the court you come to an **altar base**, with the lower courses of the west wing wall in grey ashlar stone beyond.

The west wing

The **west wing** (actually the northwest, as Zákros is not truly aligned north–south) is entered between two pillars and this is where, as usual, the chief ceremonial and ritual rooms were located. A **reception room** leads into a colonnaded **light well**, the hallmark of Minoan architecture. The light well's black stone crazy paving survives, as do the pillar bases and a drain in the northwest corner. It was here that the excavators unearthed what is arguably Zákros's single most important find: the **Peak Sanctuary Rhyton**, a carved stone vase depicting a peak sanctuary with wild goats, from which valuable information about Minoan religion was gleaned. The light well illuminated the **Ceremonial Hall**, beyond which lay the **Banqueting Hall**, originally a lavish room with frescoed walls and an elaborate floor. Pláton gave the room this name because of the large number of cups and drinking vessels discovered scattered about the floor.

At the heart of a complex of rooms behind the Banqueting Hall is the **Central Shrine** which contains a ledge and niche, similar to the shrine at Gourniá, where idols would have been placed. Nearby is the **lustral basin**, necessary for purification before entering the shrine. Here, too, was the **Treasury**, probably the most important discovery from the excavators' viewpoint as it is the only one so far positively identified. In a number of box-like compartments (which have been partially restored), almost a hundred fine stone jars and libation vessels were discovered, including the exquisite rock crystal rhyton – crushed into more than three hundred fragments – with its delicate crystal bead handle and collar that the Iráklion Archeological Museum is so proud of. Next to the Treasury, in the **Palace Archive**, hundreds of Linear A record tablets had been stored in wooden chests. Sadly, only a handful of the top layers survived the centuries of rain and flooding; the rest had solidified into a mass of grey clay, depriving the archeologists of potentially priceless clues in their attempts at deciphering the script. On the opposite side of the treasury is a **workshop** where pieces of raw marble and steatite were found. The remaining stone slabs most likely supported a craftsman's workbench. More workshops and storerooms lay to the west of the shrine, and one of these has been identified as a **dye-house**. And if you were wondering where the occupants of this end of the palace answered the call of nature, a lavatory with a cesspit outside the wall was found nearby. Further west, beyond the palace confines, new excavations are still going on.

North, south and east wings

On the north side of the Central Court was the palace **kitchen**, the first to be positively identified at any of the palaces. Bones, cooking pots and utensils were found strewn around the floor both here and in the storeroom or pantry next door. The south wing was devoted to **workshops**: for smiths, lapidaries, potters and even, according to Pláton, perfume-makers – possibly a borrowing from Egypt. The **well** that serviced this area still flows with drinkable water, and, close to the steps leading down into it, an offering cup was found, containing olives preserved by the waters. Pláton and his team devoured the three-and-a-half-thousand-year-old olives, which shrivelled upon contact with the air, and said that they tasted as fresh as those in the nearby tavernas.

Two large rooms regarded as **royal apartments** flank the east side of the Central Court behind a portico. The larger of the two, to the south, is called the King's Room and the smaller is claimed to be that of the queen. However, one of these may have been the throne room and there would have been elaborate rooms on the first floor, possibly with verandas overlooking the courtyard below, which might more realistically have been where the rulers lived. Next to a light well in the eastern wall of the King's Room lay the colonnaded **Cistern Hall** which, with its eight steps leading down to the water contained in a plaster-lined basin, may have served as a royal aquarium or even a swimming pool (if so, the only one known). It is ingeniously designed to maintain the water at a constant level with the excess draining into the well to the south, which lay outside the palace wall and was probably used by the townsfolk. The water from the spring was, as at Knossós, piped throughout the palace, and traces of the pipework are still to be seen around the site.

Beyond these royal apartments lay other **residential areas**, but much has been destroyed by centuries of ploughing combined with frequent waterlogging of the land here. In the steep **upper town** more survives and, close to the perimeter fence, a **narrow street** running east to west passes an impressive doorway to the left and gives you a some idea of how much of the town may have looked when twin-storey buildings overlooked these narrow thoroughfares. At nearby Pelekita, on the coast 3km to the north, the quarry from where the tufa limestone used to build the palace was taken was recently discovered.

Kserócambos and the coast

Hardly any tourist ever ventures south of Zákros, and indeed there's little in the way of habitation in the whole of the southeastern corner of the island, nor any public transport whatsoever. Even the boulder-strewn dirt roads seem to be left in this condition to discourage the adventurous, but these are a bonus for the walker. With your own transport, however, a little effort is rewarded with scores of excellent **beaches** – mostly deserted. There's a route by which you can circle back to Sitía, via a newly sealed road after Kserókambos, taking in an archeological site at Présos along the way.

Kserókambos

Leave Áno Zákros on the new road (towards Káto Zákros) and you'll shortly reach a track to the right, with a hand-painted sign for "Ambelos and Liviko View", next to another Minoan villa bisected by the road. It's not a bad surface, descending through olive groves and giant greenhouses to run along a deep ravine. After 10km, and just when you're convinced you're lost, a brilliant turquoise sea and white sandy beaches divided by rocky outcrops appear below.

Tucked in the lee of the foothills of the Sitían Mountains which rise away behind, the tiny hamlet of **KSERÓKAMBOS** is as tranquil a hideaway as you could wish. The settlement consists of one street with two tavernas, a couple of mini-markets selling basic food, and a few olive groves, strung out along its length. Both tavernas will provide information and keys for **rooms** and some nice apartments (if available, which they may not be in August). Try ringing ahead to secure space at the excellent *Liviko View* (☎0843/31-779; ②), run by a couple of Greek-Australians. The cooking here is recommended and at weekends they even put on the occasional *lyra* concert. **Camping** on the main beach is not allowed although you should be able to find secluded places away from here, but water may be a problem.

The **main beach** – a short walk away along the beach road and one of the best on the island – is a couple of kilometres of pristine shimmering sand that hardly sees a towel or sun bed all year, and if that isn't escapist enough, to the north and especially the south are wonderful isolated coves where you could never see a soul. The crystal-clear waters here are great for **snorkelling** too, which is why the mini-markets sell the basic equipment. Away from the sea there's little to do, but you could stretch your legs with a walk to the tiny chapel on a low hill to the south of the beach. Surrounding this are the ruins of an extensive **Minoan settlement** not yet fully explored or documented. Archeologists argue as to whether Kserókambos is the site of ancient Ambelos (in spite of a location of this name nearby) but artefacts discovered both here and at a looted peak sanctuary in the hills certainly suggest this was a settlement of some significance in ancient times, possibly connected with the Zákros palace to the north.

For a more ambitious **walk** you could follow a track (marked on the Harms Verlag map) which heads south behind the beach for 4km to the deserted village of Ayía Iríni, with plenty of opportunities for a dip along the way. Continuing inland from here along the same track would enable you to ascend to the peak of Agridomouri (630m), descending to Kaló Horió on the other side (6km from Ayía Iríni) with a possible return to Kserókambos via the new road (see below), and where there's the possibility of hailing a lift, a further 11km.

Kserócambos has nothing at all in the way of after-dark diversions – not even a bar – but the pitch-black nights here are magical with the opportunity for beach walking, a midnight swim or simply sipping *raki* beneath a dome of stars, trying to spot the various constellations.

Back to Sitía: via Zíros, Handhrás and Etiá

A new asphalted road now links Kserócambos with Zíros, so you can complete a circle back to Sitía. The road climbs out of Kserócambos to cross the northern shoulder of Mount Agridomouri; in early summer you'll see dense clumps of deep violet *thimári* (wild thyme) filling rock crevices and lining the roadside. This road is also populated by herds of goats who – despite the asphalt – still regard this as their traditional domain: quite a hazard should you come round a bend at speed. Take care when descending too, as there are sharp curves with steep precipices and no barriers (so far); errors of judgement have already led to accidents. Beyond the primitive hamlet of **Hamétoulo** – a piece of living Cretan folklore with twenty dwellings, a cobbled street and a church – all views are dominated by a giant radar dome on the mountain top, and the road itself is dotted with "No Photography" signs, alerting you that this is a military zone.

At the top of the climb the road levels to a plateau surrounded by rock cliffs, in the midst of which lies the fair-sized farming village of **ZÍROS**. Tumbling down a hillside towards a busy centre, it's a welcoming place, with a neat platía circled by willow and acacia trees with whitewashed trunks. There's even an occasional bus to Sitía (currently weekdays at 7.15am and 2.30pm). Along the main street, and facing a couple of palm trees, *Taverna Karkionakis* makes an excellent **lunch** stop, but there is no accommodation here at all. If you come in late July, you may be lucky enough to catch the annual festival – something not to be missed. Then the women of the village produce huge trays of delicacies, which are laid out on tables in the square and washed down with gallons of *raki* to the accompaniment of *bouzoúki* and *lyra*. For quieter times there are sixteenth-century frescoes to be seen in the church of **Ayía Paraskeví**, but you may prefer to soak up the atmosphere with a drink at a table in the square. In the early evening, when the rocky heights crowd in on all sides, it seems that places like Zíros are the real heart of Crete.

Gluttons for punishment could follow a rough dirt road down to the south coast at Goúdhouras (see over), but the easy way is via Handhrás, 4km to the west. The reasons for Zíros's size and prosperity are evident along the road out, as it cuts through olive groves and vineyards said to be among the best on the island.

Another tidy farming village, **HANDHRÁS**, is entered past its sail-less and derelict irrigation windmills. There's now a welcoming **taverna** here, *Tosteki*, signed from the main street. A turning southwest out of the village leads after 4km to **ETIÁ**, a hamlet where a ruined **Venetian mansion** stands in memorial to the glory days of the Italian city's power in Crete. Built by the Di Mezzo family (whose arms decorate the doorway) in the late fifteenth century, this once elegant edifice was badly damaged in 1828 when the local populace vented their rage on the Turks who had been using it as an administrative base; nowadays the ground floor, with its impressive entrance hall and vaulted ceiling, is all that remains of the three-storey building. Because few country houses of the Venetian period survive on Crete, however, the mansion has been declared a national monument under the care of the Greek Archeological Service and is currently being restored. The mansion lies 100m up a track, behind the roadside church with an elegant carved stone tower.

Continuing along the Handhrás–Présos road, a lane just outside Handhrás is signed on the right for **VOILÁ**, a ruined medieval village that you can just see at the foot of the hill. With its gothic arches and silent paved streets, this is a distinctly eerie place to wander round; two ornamental drinking fountains (one at each end of the village) with beautiful brass taps – a Turkish contribution to this Venetian stronghold – still function. The twin-naved Áyios Yeóryios church (usually locked) has an interesting sixteenth-century gravestone fresco in an interior recess; this and a tower of the Turkish period dominate the site. If you have the energy, you can climb to a ruined Venetian fort on top of the hill above the village.

Ancient Présos

The archeological site of **Présos** lies close to the modern village of the same name. This is another of those sites where what you see – in this case very little – cannot begin to match the interest and importance of the history. But even without ruins it would be worth taking the walk around the site for the scenery alone. From the centre of the village, opposite a kafeníon with a raised terrace, a dirt road is clearly signposted downhill. After about 1.5km you'll come to a signed gate for the "First Acropolis". This is where to leave your vehicle if you have one.

Présos first came to light in 1884, when the Italian archeologist Federico Halbherr turned up a large number of clay idols and some unusual inscriptions written in an unknown tongue – very likely the same as that of the Linear A tablets – using Greek characters. Set out with lines reading alternatively right to left and left to right, these Eteocretan (true Cretan) inscriptions are now believed to be evidence of the post-Bronze Age Minoans who fled the Dorian invasions to these remote fastnesses in the east of the island in an attempt to preserve their civilization. Présos seems to have been one of their principal towns, controlling the sanctuary of Dhiktean Zeus at Palékastro, probably an earlier Minoan shrine. With harbours on the north and south coasts of the island its power eventually led to conflict with the leading Dorian city of the region, Ierápytna (modern Ierápetra). Following final victory about 155 BC, Ierápytna razed Présos to the ground and the city was never rebuilt. With this defeat the long twilight of Minoan civilization, lasting more than a thousand years after the palaces had fallen, came to an end.

From the entrance follow the path west to a saddle between the two hills where the ancient city lay. On the summit of the **First Acropolis** you can make out the foundations of a temple. On the western slope of this hill are the remains of a substantial **Hellenistic house** excavated by the British archeologist Bosanquet at the turn of the century. Dating from the third century BC, the outer walls of superbly cut stone define the main living rooms at the front of the house with workrooms at the rear. In the largest workroom an olive press was found together with a stone tank for storing the oil. A stairway to the left of the main door led down to a cellar.

A hundred-metre walk across the saddle to the **Second Acropolis** reveals cuttings in the rock on the south side which formed the foundations of dwellings; the defensive wall which encircled these two hills can still be made out in places.

Sitía to Ierápetra

The main road across the island from Sitía to the south coast cuts between the east and west ranges of the **Sitía mountains**, giving some fine views in the hill country of the central section before descending towards the sea plain. There are a number of sturdy hamlets along the route, such as Áyios Yeóryios and Lithínes, good places to stop for a snack and a beer.

South to the coast

Just before Piskokéfalo, less than 2km out of Sitía, Minoan enthusiasts may want to pause at the remains of a **Minoan villa** (signed) cut through by the road. Dating from the late Neo-Palatial period (1550–1450 BC), it had two floors and is terraced into the hillside with the well-preserved staircase giving access to an upper floor. The villa's view would have encompassed the river valley below the road, where its farm lands were probably located.

At the entrance to Piskokéfalo itself a dirt road is signed to the left for **ZOÚ**, 6km further on, where there's another Minoan villa of the same period. Follow the road, which crosses a dry riverbed and then turns right (signed), eventually becoming asphalt as it winds up into the hills towards Zoú. The villa – not easily spotted and with no sign – lies on a high bank to the right of the road just before the village. Excavated by Nikólaos Pláton, the excavator of the palace at Zákros, this is more a farmhouse – cultivating the land in the valley to the east – than simply a country dwelling. The rooms seem to be divided between those for domestic life and others for work and storage of farm equipment. A pottery kiln (perhaps used for making olive oil containers) was discovered in one room, while two deep pits near the entrance probably stored grain.

Back on the main Sitía–Ierápetra road, it's a long climb to the island's spine, past Epáno Episkopí and the turning to Présos (see p.182), before the road dips towards **Lithínes**. Just after this the islands of Koufonísi, to the east, and Gaidhouronísi, to the west, become visible beyond the coastal plain out in the Libyan Sea. You emerge, eventually, on the south coast at **Pilalímata**. For empty beaches you should get off the bus just past here, where a road on the left is signed for the Moní Kápsa and Goúdhouras. There's a fair stretch of rather pebbly grey beach – known as **Kaló Neró**, with a couple of cafés – no more than 1km from the road. If you have transport, however, there are better strips of sand to be found scattered all along this rocky foreshore.

East: Moní Kápsa and Goúdhouras

Now served by a new asphalt road which somewhat diminishes the sense of isolation, the **Moní Kápsa** (daily 8.30am–noon & 4–7pm) enjoys a spectacular setting on a ledge in the cliffs just above the road and an abiding reputation for miracles. The original monastery, probably founded in the early Venetian period, was destroyed by Turkish pirates in 1471. It was rebuilt, but most of the present buildings were constructed in the nineteenth century, thanks to the energies of "Yerontoyiannis", a monk who earned himself a name as a Robin Hood-style hero as well as a healer. Locally he is revered as a saint, and although he never conducted a single service due to his illiteracy and is denied canonization by the Church, Cretans flock in to leave their offerings beside his silver encased cadaver and skull in the monastery chapel. You may also visit the cave behind the church to where he often retreated and from where there's a fine view towards the island of Koufonísi. As you enter the monastery, pairs of baggy trousers and other battered old items of clothing are hung on pegs by the door, for use by anyone who turns up in shorts or otherwise "unsuitably" attired. But most times of the year you will have the place to yourself, and the people around the monastery, lay workers mostly in addition to the two remaining monks, always seem to have time to sit you down for a chat and a cold drink.

Further along the same road, you come to the best beach of all, just before **GOÚDHOURAS**. There should be little problem camping around here, taking advantage of three or four tavernas in the village. It has to be said, though, that Goúdhouras itself is an exceptionally unattractive, plastic-wrapped little place.

West: Makriyialós and beyond

Westwards, the route to Ierápetra passes Análipsi and **MAKRIYIALÓS**, villages which have merged into each other along the road. Makriyialós has one of the best beaches at this end of Crete, with tavernas and sand which shelves so gently you begin to think you are going to walk the 320km to Africa. But while it is by no means overrun, heavy building has ensured that it's no longer exactly pretty either – and in any case it's not somewhere you're likely to find a very cheap room. Try *Irini Rooms* (☎0843/51-422; ②) on the main road, the quieter *Villa Stars* (☎0843/51-152; ③) or *Katerina* (☎0843/51-558; ③); both the latter offer attractive studio apartments in a garden setting. All three are within easy walking distance of where the bus drops you. The best place for **food** here is *Porfira*, on the main street, a taverna serving good traditional dishes.

As you leave Makriyialós, you pass yet another **Minoan villa** (signed only from the western approach), 200m inland from the road. Leave any transport and follow the level track starting to the west of the sign; this eventually climbs up to the site, behind a fence next to a house strewn with bougainvillea in summer. It was long suspected that such a tempting area would not have escaped the attentions of the ancient peoples, and in 1971 Costis Davaras began excavations which eventually unearthed an important villa of the late Neo-Palatial period (1550–1450 BC). As can be seen from the remains, it had strong outer walls and some fine stone-flagged floors. The ground plan is not unlike that of the palaces, with rooms situated around a central court, where an altar was also identified. The excavation also revealed that the house was destroyed by fire – yet more evidence for the endless debate over what caused the downfall of the Minoans.

There's a second bay immediately beyond Makriyialós, with a smaller, emptier beach, and the road then runs along what is for the most part an exposed and rocky coast littered with ugly plastic greenhouses, and only the occasional scrubby beach. **KOUTSOURÁS**, the main village hereabouts, has little to commend it, although *Pension Gorgona* (☎0843/23-935; ③) is a reasonable seafront place. There's also *Pension Dassenakis* (☎0843/51-203; ③), a little further east, which fronts the sea and is reached along a path which starts near a friendly kafeníon with pleasant terrace.

Koutsourás Communal Park and Orinó

Two kilometres further on, keep an eye out on the right for a small park. A great fire here in 1993 did enormous damage to a wildlife habitat once known as Dásaki, now renamed **Koutsourás Communal Park**. It was not the first time that it had been devastated by fire: during World War II it was burnt by the German army in order to root out resistance forces. The latest fire has reduced much of the pinewood covering the hills to blackened stumps, and devastated the flora and fauna in the gorge behind, including remarkable butterflies, which are, however, expected to return in numbers in the coming years. Many believe that the fire was not the accident it appeared (see box); many of the nearby villagers would prefer to see olives planted here or some other "sensible" use of the land.

Leave your vehicle by the café (currently closed) at the entrance and walk the 500m through the woods to the gorge. In late spring and summer, fluttering cardinal, Cleopatra and swallowtail **butterflies** drift past visitors. The gorge is (or was) also a haven for blue rock thrushes, griffon vultures, crag martins and other interesting bird life.

The energetic may wish to **walk** up the gorge into the mountains of the Thriptí range, ending up at the picturesque and isolated village of **ORINÓ** (6km; sturdy footwear required). Alternatively, there's a **scenic route** there, signed 2km further along the main road, which climbs steeply for 10km to reach the village, surrounded by lush greenery and wild flowers. At a height of nearly 1000m, it's quite cool up here even in summer, and locals tend to wear jumpers for most of the year. The three rustic **bars** along the main street don't always have beer (you're really off the beaten track here) but will happily serve up their home-produced *raki*, a fairly potent brew.

Ayía Fotiá and beyond

For a few kilometres after this there's a genuinely mountainous stretch, until the road dips down to a beach with a taverna, and in the following bay a poorly signed track leads down to **AYÍA FOTIÁ**. Hidden from the road in a wooded valley, Ayía Fotiá has its attractions: cheap **rooms** in the village, an excellent beach just a couple of minutes' walk away down the stream bed and cafés and tavernas with good music.

THE FIRES OF CRETE

Recent years have seen appalling **forest fires** throughout Crete, with devastations occurring in and around the hill villages to the north of Sóuyia and at the Ayía Iríni gorge in western Crete; terrific blazes in the hills surrounding Kalamáfka to the northwest of Ierápetra in the east also did enormous damage to the landscape.

Depressingly, these fires are not always the accidents they seem to be. Figures from the Greek Agricultural Ministry for the period 1968–93 attribute the cause of no less than 57 percent of all fires to unknown causes or arson. A survey of fires throughout Greece by the *I Koinonía* newspaper showed a dramatic increase in their number over the last decade and further sharp escalations prior to general elections. This, of course, is when the politicians – in a desperate scramble for votes – are willing to recognize the claims to land of those who may have started the fires in the first place. Under Greek law there is no organized system of land registry for publicly owned land, which means that if an area of woodland is burned down, the barren territory left behind becomes a no-man's-land which can be claimed under squatters' rights. Once olives or other crops have been planted, a foothold towards possession has been attained, with local politicians often smoothing over the obstacles to the ownership of the land being transferred. This callous attitude to the environment, where trees are little regarded for their beauty, has a long history. In his book *Wild Flowers of Crete*, biologist George Sfikas writes that "the Greek holds the deeply rooted view that a green wood is useless because the trees drink valuable water and don't produce anything". Until this attitude is combated and reversed the fires will continue to transform the island from one of the most fertile in the Mediterranean into one of the most barren.

Ayía Fotiá is, sadly, the last place from here to well beyond Ierápetra which could be described as inviting. The final 10km of road runs fast across a flat plain, unimaginatively developed for tourism along the coast and for hothouse agriculture inland. Neither **Férma** nor **Koutsonári** has much to offer, despite the latter's much vaunted "tourist village", a group of abandoned houses which have been restored to rent as holiday villas. As always though, head away from the coast and into the hills and you're back in timeless Crete. North out of Koutsonári, there's a scenic 8km drive to the hilltop hamlet of **Áyios Ioánnis** which has four churches.

Back on the coast road and just beyond the turnoff for the centre of Koutsonári is the village's **campsite** – *Camping Koutsounari* (☎0842/61-213) – which is the only campsite nearby if you want to be based at Ierápetra. It has a taverna and store, and although the campground is a bit gritty, there's a good beach and plenty of shade. This is also the beginning of the aptly named **Long Beach**, a windswept line of sand (and the wind can really blow here) which stretches virtually unbroken along the final 5km of shore to Ierápetra.

Ierápetra

IERÁPETRA has various claims to fame – the largest town on the south coast of Crete, the southernmost in Europe with the most hours of sunshine – but until recently charm was not one of them. Despite an excellent EU blue-flagged **beach**, it's a rather sprawling place and a major supply centre for the region's numerous and affluent farmers who have grown rich on the all–year cultivation of cucumbers, tomatoes and peppers in the plastic greenhouses which scar the landscape along this coast (see the box on p.191). The farming lobby's armlock on the town hall and its budget long stymied plans to make Ierápetra more attractive to its visitors who, they argued, only profited hotels, restaurants and related tourist businesses. The result was a relentless decline in the number of package tourists and a general malaise, symbolized by the closure of the tourist office in the late 1980s. But under a dynamic new mayor Ierápetra has begun to bounce back. Mayor Mastorakis has succeeded in persuading the farming lobby, and the town is now experiencing a resurgence, as buildings, streets and squares are refurbished and landscaped. Work has already started on an ambitious plan to revamp the whole seafront and harbour area with gardens and a swimming pool, and Ierápetra is at last starting to resemble what it actually is: one of the richest towns on the island. In tune with this renaissance, a new tourist office is set to open in 1998.

Although you'd hardly know it to look at the town today, Ierápetra has quite a history. Early knowledge is sketchy, but it's almost certain that there was a settlement, or at least a port, here in Minoan times. A look at the map suggests a link across the isthmus with Gourniá and it was probably from Ierápetra and other south-coast harbours that the Keftiu, as the Egyptians called the Cretans, sailed for the coast of Africa. However, it was as a Doric settlement that **Ierápytna**, as the place was then known, grew to real prominence. By the second century BC it occupied more territory than any other Cretan city.

Ierápytna became a bastion of the Greek Dorians against their bitter enemies the Eteocretans: the final victory over Eteocretan Présos in 155 BC ended the last Minoan presence in eastern Crete. Those Eteocretans not killed in battle or put to flight were sold into slavery, a sombre end to the last vestiges of a great

IERÁPETRA

KAZANTZAKIS
AFXENDIOU
BARITAKI
GIANNAKOU
KOKKINI
MASTORAKI
PORFIROGENI
KYPROU
EOKA
PLOUMIDI
ADRIANOU
HOUTA
ANAGNOSTAKI
GLINOU
KORNAROU
MELA
NEARCHOU
VASARMOU
MAMOUNA
DERE
MAKEDONOMACHON
LOUGIOUMOUTZAKI

Áyios Nikólaos

Bus
Station ★

MOUTZAKI

PLATÍA
PLASTIRAS

ZOURARI

LAKERDA
STAKIANAK
KOUNOUPARI
MILIARAKI

PLATÍA
VENIZÉLOU

OMIRIAS
OTE
KOTHRI
MARKOPOULOU

PLATÍA
ELEFTHERIAS

Archeological
Museum

Fruit
Market

PLATÍA
KANOUPAKI

Post
Office

Tourist
Police

Ayios
Ioannis

KYRBA

SAMOUIL

PAGOMENOU
KONDILAKI
KORAKA

Ferry
Terminal

Mosque

Napoleon's
House

Aféndis
Christos

Venetian
Fortress

N

0   200 m

Makriyialós

Mírtos

civilization. Only Ítanos, near Vái, now stood between Ierápytna and the complete domination of the eastern end of the island. Prolonged wars and disputes rumbled on for almost a century, and were finally brought to an end only by Rome's ruthless conquest of the entire island. Even then Ierápytna stubbornly resisted to the last, becoming the final city to fall to the invading legions. When Rome then joined Crete to Cyrene in northern Libya, forming the province of Cyrenaica, Ierápytna embarked on a new career as an important commercial centre in the eastern Mediterranean – trading with Greece and Italy as well as Africa and the Near East. During this period much impressive building took place – theatres, amphitheatres, temples – of which virtually nothing survives today, save for piles of fractured pillars and column capitals scattered in odd corners around the town. From the Romans to the tourists is a chronicle of steady decline. The Venetians (who favoured Sitía as their administrative centre in the east) left behind a small

fortress, now restored, defending the harbour entrance. The Turks, under whom Ierápetra languished as a backwater, are represented by a nineteenth-century **mosque** and nearby Ottoman fountain.

Arrival, information and accommodation

The **bus station** is just up from Platía Plastíra on Lasthenou – the Áyios Nikólaos road – around five minutes from the centre. It's convenient for a couple of the good budget places to stay (see below), though for a better impression of the town head down towards the water, past the souvenir stores and stalls selling German newspapers, to the seafront and promenade. Here, with a string of restaurants and bars stretching out in either direction – to the left behind the beach, right towards the fortress and the harbour – Ierápetra can be genuinely picturesque.

A new **tourist office** (☎0842/25-473; hours uncertain but probably closed weekends) is due to open in 1998 to the side of the town hall on Platía Kanoupaki, and will provide maps and help with accommodation. The **tourist police** (☎0842/22-560) are located on the waterfront, across the square from the Archeological Museum, though the most you'll get from them is a few blank looks and, if you're lucky, a town map. Another good place for **information** is the Ierapetra Express travel agency on Platía Eleftherías (☎0842/22-411, fax 28-330), who also rent out a number of excellent seaside apartments for longer stays.

Accommodation

Some new places have opened up recently, and the range of choices is decidedly better than it used to be. There are cheaper possibilities near the bus station and in the centre, though the hotels fronting and behind the north and easterly beach are more modern and pricey. There is no youth hostel and the only nearby **campsite** is *Camping Koutsounari*, 7km out of Ieráptera on the Sitía road (see p.186). If you camp, you'll have to come into town in the evenings for food and nightlife.

Coral, Ioannidou 12 (☎0842/22-846). Located behind the beach and tavernas along Samouil, to the north of the Venetian fort, these are pleasant rooms with bath in a restored house in the old quarter. ②.

Cretan Villa, Lakerda 16 (☎0842/28-522). Close to the bus station, and offering en-suite rooms in a beautiful 180-year-old house with a delightful patio for taking breakfast. ②.

El Greco, Kothri 6 (☎0842/28-471 fax 28-791). Best of the beachfront places with en-suite rooms, but it's only worth paying the extra if you get a room with balcony sea view. ③.

Ersi, Platía Eleftherías 20 (☎0842/23-208). Completely refurbished hotel where excellent rooms come with bath and balcony – the higher the better for sea views. The owner here also has some apartments nearby – which come with kitchen and lounge – for the same price. ②.

Four Seasons, Kazantzakis (☎0842/24-390). A couple of hundred metres up the road from the bus station, this is one of the older properties in the town, built in 1866. There's a friendly atmosphere; one of the rooms on the ground floor has lovely painted designs on its wooden ceilings. ③.

Pension Gorgona, Katsanevaki 9 (☎0842/23-935). Close to the church of Áyios Ioánnis, this well-run pension in the old quarter has simple but perfectly adequate rooms, some with bath. ②.

Livikon, Koundouriotou 25, just south of Platía Venizélou (☎0842/22-731). Charming small hotel on this now pedestrianized street; all rooms come with bath and balcony. ②.

The Town

Things to do in Ierápetra by day – apart from lie on the beach – are severely limited. The morning **fruit market** near the museum on K. Adrianou can provide a colourful and entertaining half hour; get there before noon on weekdays or come on Saturday for the rather bigger affair. The **Archeological Museum** itself – housed in the former Turkish school – is rather less colourful. Its dusty rooms (officially open Tues–Sun 8.30am–3pm; 400dr) are known to close at a moment's notice, but it's probably worth the effort if only to see a fine Minoan terracotta **larnax**, excavated at nearby Episkopí. Dating from the very end of the Neo-Palatial period (c.1300 BC) the *lárnax*, or clay coffin, has fascinating painted panels, one of which depicts a mare suckling her foal. Other scenes revel in the stalking of the *kri-kri* or wild goat by hunting dogs. If he's in the mood, the guardian (on request) will raise the *lárnax* lid to enable you to see the remains of the three corpses still inside. The Greek and Roman section contains a selection of statuary, mostly headless because iconoclastic Christians tended to regard the stone craniums as places where the spirit of the devil was lurking. One more recent discovery, however, managed to hang on to hers: a wonderful second-century statue of the fertility goddess, **Demeter**, holding an ear of corn in her left hand. Her head is crowned by a small altar encoiled by two serpents, symbols of her divinity. Incomprehensibly, for years the staff have gone to great lengths to prevent visitors taking photographs of her, so prepare to be bawled out if you try.

Elsewhere in town, two churches which stand out from a miscellaneous collection are the twin-domed **Aféndis Christós** (near the fort), a fourteenth-century building with a fine carved and painted wooden iconostasis (key from the house to the left of the entrance), and **Áyios Ioánnis**, an equally ancient, but now restored, former mosque. The Tzami, or **Turkish Mosque**, has now been painstakingly restored and retains a substantial chunk of its minaret and – inside – the original *mihrab*. There's also an old house in which locals claim that **Napoleon** spent the night of June 6, 1798, on his way to Egypt.

Out of town

If you're staying in Ierápetra and it finally becomes too much, there are a number of ways out. Simplest is the day-trip by kaïki to **Gaidhouronísi** (known as Chrissi or Donkey Island in much of the tourist literature), some 10km offshore. A real desert island, with a fine cedar forest and a couple of tavernas, Gaidhouronísi has some excellent sandy beaches and plenty of room to escape – although you wouldn't want to miss the boat back. Boats leave from the jetty on the seafront at 10.30am, returning at 4.30pm.

Alternatively, there are more **beaches** along the coast a few kilometres in either direction, with good bus services along the main road behind them.

Eating and entertainment

When it comes to **eating** and **drinking**, your only problem here is sifting out the quality from the quantity. For **breakfast**, *Veterano* is a stylish new terrace bar on Platía Eleftherías, which has rapidly become one of the most popular venues. Along Markopoulou, the seafront promenade stretching north of the tourist police office, there's a string of restaurants with outdoor seating but none are outstanding. Things are better on the Samouil promenade to the south of the ferry terminal where another line of **restaurants** faces the sea. The town's two best places are here: *Napoleon*, which is Ierápetra's oldest, is good for seafood and standards such as *moussaká*, whilst the nearby *Konaki* also does traditional dishes well. Here too, is *Kyknos*, which along with *Ouzeri Manos* and *Kafenion E. Manthourares* are the best places for mezédhes.

The **bars** and **discos** are concentrated in the streets immediately behind the seafront, mainly along Kyrba, which is also the area to find more basic food and takeaways. Music bars abound here, with those playing Greek music found on the beach road, and those favouring mainstream European sounds a street inland. Along and around Kyrba, *Seven Blue Notes*, *Medusa*, *Diagoras* and *Le Figaro* are popular, as is the disco *Zanadu* which is nearby on the waterfront. Three stylish new bars not far away which attract good crowds are *Lythos*, opposite the *Cretan Villa* pension with occasional (and restrained) live music, *Anna 1900* behind the post office, and the aptly named *Odeon*, housed in a former music school – a pleasant garden bar located along Lasthenou, above Platía Venizélou on the right.

On Sunday evenings in summer free performances of Cretan **lyra** and **dance** are staged at the small open-air theatre to the left of the town hall, starting at around 10pm.

Listings

Banks The National Bank on Platía Eleftherías and the Ionian Bank on Platía Venizélou both have cash dispensers.

Bike rental The best deal is at Moto Cross (☎0842/23-432) at Kothri 36, just behind the waterfront. They provide helmets and also goggles, which you'll appreciate when the sand starts to fly in the summer winds (the proprietor also has rooms to rent). Alternatives are Galaxie (☎0842/25-374) at Metaháki 1, and Omega Motors (☎0842/28-995) at Lampraki 1.

Books and newspapers Markou Frangouli, Koundoúriotou 5, just off Platía Eleftherías, has the best range of foreign press and magazines as well as a good selection of books in English.

Bus station On Lasthenou; for information call ☎0842/28-237. Services to Iráklion, Áyios Nikólaos, Sitía and Mírtos.

Post office Stilianou Hota 3; Mon–Sat 7.30am–2pm.

Shopping Hermés on Platía Eleftherías has a range of textiles and local handicrafts and there are more shops along Koundoúriotou selling embroidery. Eútsin, Kothri 12, just north of the National Bank on Platía Eleftherías sells Cretan herbs, teas and spices as well as cheeses, olive oil and honey.

Telephones OTE at Koraka 25; Mon–Fri 7.30am–10pm.

Travel agency Ierapetra Express (☎0842/22-411, fax 28-330) on the central Platía Eleftherías is a helpful source of travel information, and also provides general information about the town and local festivals and events. It also produces a rental apartments brochure which it will send out on request.

West to Mírtos

Heading west from Ierápetra, the first stretch of coast is grey and dusty, the road jammed with trucks and lined with drab ribbon development. Where the concrete runs out, the plastic greenhouses start. However, if you're travelling under your own steam, there are a couple of **scenic detours** worth taking at **Gra Ligiá**.

THE PLASTIC REVOLUTION

The plastic **greenhouses** that disfigure much of this coastline are a great source of wealth for the farmers of Ierápetra and its satellite villages. The system was introduced here in the 1960s by a Dutch farmer named Paul Coopers. He correctly surmised that the mild climate and fertile soil along this coast would perfectly suit greenhouse crops, which could be produced all year and sold to supermarkets in northern Europe in the depths of winter. The plastic tents were initially ridiculed, but once the canny Cretan farmers saw the size and quality of the tomatoes that emerged from them in the middle of January, the revolution began. Coopers died in a road accident in 1968 when the new system had hardly got going. However, in typically Cretan fashion the farmers did not forget who had brought them this horn of plenty – they erected a statue to Coopers on the site of his first greenhouse.

Into the hills

From **GRA LIGIÁ**, the first detour winds upwards past a dam, followed by an unsightly quarrying operation, before climbing again – with fine views over the Libyan Sea – to the charming hamlet of **KALAMÁFKA**, tucked into a mountain cleft. The bars along the tiny main street provide a good excuse to stop for a while. From here, you could reach the north coast and Áyios Nikólaos via the village of Prína or, by taking the road to Anatolí, pick up the second detour. This also starts from Gra Ligiá, a hundred metres beyond the first, and is signed for Anatolí, eventually climbing to **MÁLES**, a village clinging to the lower slopes of the Dhíkti range. Here would be a good starting-point if you wanted to take a **walk** through some stunning mountain terrain. Otherwise, the road down (signed for Míthi) has spectacular views over the Libyan Sea and eventually follows the Mírtos river valley down to Mírtos itself.

Two Minoan sites: Néa Mírtos and Pírgos

Continuing along the coast road at Gra Ligiá, it's 8km further to **NÉA MÍRTOS**, where a Minoan site excavated in the 1960s by a British team yielded important evidence concerning early Minoan settlements. Known locally as **Fournoú Korifí** (Kiln Hill), the site is located beyond the village on the peak to your right, just after a chapel on the coastal side of the road. Immediately after the hill you'll see a sign for the "Minoan Villa"; follow a level track 50m inland and leave your vehicle. A path to the right will eventually lead you up to the site; there are thorns for the last 50m.

The excavations – which are not always easy to make sense of – revealed not a villa but a much earlier stone-built village of nearly one hundred rooms, spread over the hilltop. Probably typical of numerous other settlements sited on the coast of eastern Crete during the early Pre-Palatial period (c.2500 BC), these rooms contained stone and copper tools, carved seals and over seven hundred pottery vessels. Some of these were Vasilikí-type jugs with their intriguing mottled finish, and many were no doubt used to store the produce of the surrounding lands, then less arid than today – olives, vines and cereals. In a room in the southwest corner of the site was located the oldest known Minoan domestic shrine which produced the most important of the finds: the goddess of Mírtos, a clay idol with a stalked neck carrying a ewer. (It's now in the Áyios Nikólaos museum, along with the rest of the finds from this site and Pírgos.) Around the goddess, broken offering vessels were strewn about the floor, many of them charred by the fire which destroyed the site about 2200 BC. The riddle of the fire, which seems to have left no casualties and provoked no rebuilding, is yet another of the unresolved Minoan questions. However, the site of Pírgos may offer a few clues.

Pírgos

PÍRGOS, just 2km further on, is considerably easier to get to and has a superb view over the coast. The sign to this Minoan villa comes immediately before a large bridge across the Mírtos river and leads into what appears to be a quarry, which makes it hard to work out the way up. Once you spot it though, the trail to the top (waymarked with whitewashed stones) is obvious and it's a bare ten-minute walk to the site.

The settlement here was inhabited at much the same time as Fournoú Korifí and was also destroyed by fire around 2200 BC. Unlike Fournoú Korifí, however, Pírgos was reoccupied and rebuilt following its destruction, when it appears to have incorporated the former's lands. By the time of the Neo-Palatial period (c.1600 BC), the community occupying the lower slopes was dominated by a two- or three-storey country villa spread over the crown of the hill. A **stepped street** flanked by some well-cut lower courses of the villa's outer wall leads into a **courtyard**, partly paved in the purple limestone of the region. At the rear of the villa (furthest away from the sea) on the west side, it's possible to make out a **light well** floored with the same purple limestone. Many of the walls carry marks of the ferocious blaze which destroyed the villa around 1450 BC, lending credibility to the Thíra explosion theory, especially when volcanic material was discovered amidst the rubble. But it now seems that whilst the villa was burned, the surrounding settlement was untouched – another puzzle to contemplate as you savour the magnificent sea view from the courtyard.

On your way down, take a left turn at the bottom of the stepped street and follow the hill around to see the remains of an enormous plastered **cistern**, the largest found in Minoan Crete, dating from the Pre-Palatial era (c.1900–1700 BC). When it burst over the northern side of the hill in ancient times it was not repaired. Beyond this a fine stretch of **paved road** survives from the early period: this led to a burial pit, now excavated.

Mírtos

Across the bridge, the main road turns sharply inland, while a turnoff cuts back down to the coast and **MÍRTOS**. Razed to the ground by the German army in 1943 as a punishment for resistance activities, Mírtos today is an unexpected pleasure after the drabness of what has gone before. This charming white-walled village is kept clean as a whistle by its house-proud inhabitants, and most of the summer you'll find space to breathe on the long shingle beach. In August, though, the place can get pretty full, often with young travellers who sleep on the beach to the irritation of the authorities. But Mírtos takes all this in its easy stride and refuses to be overwhelmed to the point where it is taken over – and so long as there are no big hotels it doesn't seem likely to be.

Most of the time there are plenty of **rooms** advertised throughout the village, on every street it seems. On the main street behind the beach there's a small and newly refurbished hotel, the *Mirtos* (☎0842/51-227, fax 51-215; ②) which is excellent value. Nearby, *Rooms Angelos* (☎ & fax 0842/51-106; ③) offers rooms with bath and kitchen, and *Cretan House* (☎0842/51-427; ②) has pleasant rooms near the church. At the west side of the village near the beach, *Big Blue*

(☎0842/51-094, fax 51-121; ③) has sea-view balcony rooms with bath, and there are many similar places close by. More economical options are provided by *Nikos Rooms* (☎0842/51-116; ②) with bath and kitchen, and the simpler *Rooms Despina* (☎0842/51-343; ①) at the back of the village near the bus station.

Information about rooms, villas for rent and lots more can also be had from Aris Rent-a-Car Travel (☎ & fax 0842/51-017), just up the street from *Hotel Mirtos*. The proprietor here also rents out **cars**, sells boat and plane tickets, changes money and operates a taxi service to Iráklion and Haniá airports. The village has a couple of **supermarkets** and bakeries to provide essentials for the growing number of visitors, and there are international **phone** and newspaper kiosks along the main street. The **bus station** – actually a couple of rickety stands on the main road at the rear of the village, is useful for frequent buses to and from Ierápetra and less frequent services to Iráklion and Mátala.

For **eating** and **drinking**, the short promenade behind the beach is lined with bars and tavernas: *Votsalo* is a good bet, while further along *Akti* does some vegetarian dishes. In the heart of the village, *Katerina's* is the oldest-established place and has a loyal band of customers. Once the sun goes down there's little to do but prolong your eating and drinking into the night, although the odd bar sometimes risks breaking the late night curfew with a blast of (soft) rock, and in summer there's the occasional *lyra* and *bouzoúki* concert on the beach.

There are more good **beaches** and a pleasant **walk** out along the dirt track which follows the coast west to **TÉRTSA**, 6km away, and then on to Árvi (see p.133); you could try **cycling** it, renting a bike from the *Hotel Mírtos*.

Inland, the character of the main road, now heading towards Áno Viánnos (see p.132) and Iráklion, changes immediately as it begins to climb around the south side of the Dhíkti range. Here you're back into the traditional Crete of small mountain villages and alarming precipices.

GREEK PLACE NAMES

ΑΓΙΟΣ ΝΙΚΟΛΑΟΣ	Αγιος Νικόλαος	Áyios Nikólaos
ΑΓΙΟ ΦΩΤΙΑ	Αγία Φωτιά	Ayía Fotiá
ΒΑΙ	Βάι	Vái
ΓΟΥΡΝΙΑ	Γούρνια	Goúrnia
ΕΛΟΥΝΤΑ	Ελούντα	Eloúnda
ΖΑΚΡΟΣ	Ζακρος	Zákros
ΙΕΡΑΠΕΤΡΑ	Ιεράπετρα	Ierápetra
ΚΡΙΤΣΑ	Κριτσά	Kritsá
ΛΑΣΙΘΙΟΥ	Λασίθιου	Lasíthi
ΜΑΚΡΥΓΙΑΛΟΣ	Μακρύγιαλος	Makriyialós
ΜΙΡΤΟΣ	Μίρτος	Mírtos
ΜΟΧΛΟΣ	Μόχλος	Móhlos
ΝΕΑΠΟΛΗ	Νεάπολη	Neápoli
ΠΑΛΑΙΚΑΣΤΡΟ	Παλαίκαστρο	Palékastro
ΣΗΤΕΙΑ	Σητεία	Sitía
ΣΠΗΝΑΛΟΓΚΑ	Σπηναλόγκα	Spinalónga
ΤΖΕΡΜΙΑΔΟ	Τζερμιάδο	Tsermiádho
ΨΥΧΡΟ	Ψυχρό	Psihró

travel details

Buses

Some of these services are restricted on Sundays.

Áyios Nikólaos to: Eloúnda (19 daily; 6.15am–9pm; 30min); Ierápetra (9 daily; 6.30am–8.30pm; 1hr); Iráklion (31 daily, 6 via Iráklion Airport; 6am–10.15pm; 1hr 30min); Kritsá (11 daily; 6am–6pm; 30min); Lasíthi plateau (1 daily; 2pm; 2hr returning 7am); Mália (25 daily; 6am–10.15pm; 30min); Sitía (6 daily; 6.30am–6pm; 2hr).

Ierápetra to: Áno Viánnos (Mon–Fri 2 daily; 6am and 4.30pm; 30min); Ay. Nikólaos (10 daily; 6.30am–9.30pm; 1hr); Iráklion (9 daily; 6.30am –9.30pm; 2hr 30min); Makriyialós (9 daily; 6.15am–8pm; 30min); Mírtos (6 daily; 6am–8pm; 30min).

Sitía to: Ay. Nikólaos (5 daily; 6.15am–5.15pm; 2hr); Ierápetra (5 daily; 6.15am–8pm; 2hr); Iráklion (5 daily; 6.15am–5.15pm; 3hr 30min); Kato Zákros (2 daily; 11am and 2.30pm; 1hr 30min); Makriyialós (5 daily; 6.15am–8pm; 1hr); Palékastro (5 daily; 6am–2.30pm; 45min); Vái (4 daily; 9.30am–2.30pm; 1hr).

Ferries

To the Dodecanese The *Sifnos Express* leaves Ay. Nikólaos on Wednesday mornings for Sitía, Kásos, Kárpathos, Hálki, Rhodes, Sími, Tílos, Nísiros, Kós, Kálimnos, Astipalía, Amorgós, Páros and Pireás; Saturday morning to Sitía, Kásos, Kárpathos, Hálki and Rhodes. *Lasithi* sails Saturday afternoon from Ay. Nikólaos to Rhodes. There is a sailing from Sitía to Pireás via Ay. Nikólaos and Mílos on Sunday, Tuesday and Thursday.

To the Cyclades *Sifnos Express* sails on Saturday afternoon from Ay. Nikólaos to Anáfi, Thíra, Folégandros, Mílos, Sífnos and Pireás.

These ferries operate very infrequently in winter.

Flights

From Sitía Once weekly to Kásos (summer only) and Kárpathos (summer only), twice a week to Athens (Wed and Sun all year).

CHAPTER THREE

RÉTHIMNON

éthimnon province is dominated by mountains, its borders defined to the east by the island's highest peaks, including the looming mass of Psilorítis, and to the west by the far reaches of the Lefká Óri. The towns, even the provincial capital Réthimnon, feel compact and hemmed in, and so do many of the beaches – especially along the often wild and inaccessible southern coast.

It's not surprising, then, that the **interior** offers the greatest attractions – in the villages ranged around the **Psilorítis massif** and in a series of wilderness hikes originating from them. A few days here are strongly recommended, for casual ramblers and committed hikers alike. The peaks themselves are approached most easily from **Anóyia**, a high mountain town with a reputation for weaving and embroidery. From here, you can hike across to the south side of the mountains or down, via the **summit of Psilorítis**, to the villages of the **Amári valley** – some of the least visited and most traditional places in Crete.

On the north coast, **Réthimnon** is at the centre of some of Crete's most drastic resort development, with hotels and apartments spreading ever eastwards along a narrow strip of plain. The town, though, has just about managed to keep its priorities straight, and a core of life continues relatively unaffected. To the west, a sandy coastline, still not greatly exploited, runs all the way to the borders of Haniá. And a little way inland you're on the fringes of the White Mountains (Lefká Óri), studded with traditional hill villages such as **Argiroúpolis** and **Asigonía**, and surrounded by more great **hiking** country. But for time by the sea, it's across the island on the **south coast** that the province has most to offer. Here there are just two resorts of any size, overblown **Ayía Galíni** and its rapidly emerging rival, **Plakiás**. Away from these enclaves is the Crete of old: little-known pockets of sand, hard to access but well worth it.

Réthimnon

Although it's the third largest town in Crete, **RÉTHIMNON** never feels like a city, as Haniá and Iráklion do. Instead, it has a provincial air; it's a place that moves slowly and, for all the myriad bars springing up along the seafront, preserves much of its Venetian and Turkish appearance. Arriving, especially if you approach from the east in the evening, it looks exactly as it does in old engravings or in Edward Lear's watercolours – dominated by the bulk of a Venetian fortress, the skyline picked out with delicate minarets.

All of this is increasingly under commercial threat, but for the time being it's an enjoyable place to spend some time, with a wide, sandy beach and palm-fringed promenade right in front of the tangled streets of the old town. There are hundreds of tavernas, bars, cafés and discos, but the big hotels are all out of town, stretching for miles along the shore to the east. Staying in town, away from the front, you'll find things relatively quiet at night, though noisily animated during the day.

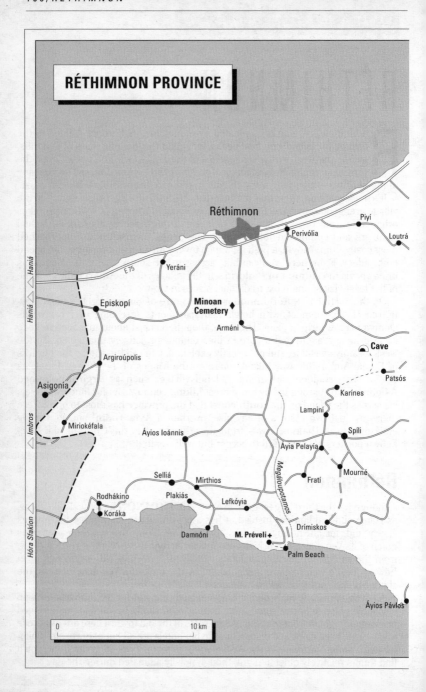

RÉTHIMNON PROVINCE

Réthimnon

Piyí

Loutrá

Perivólia

Haniá ◁ | ◁ Haniá

E 75

Yeráni

Episkopí

**Minoan
Cemetery** ◆

Arméni

◁ Cave

Argiroúpolis

Patsós

Asigonía

Karínes

◁ Imbros

Lampiní

Miriokéfala

Spíli

Áyios Ioánnis

Ayia Pelayía

Mourné

Selliá

Fratí

Mírthios

Rodhákino

Plakiás

Lefkóyia

Megáloupotamos

Koráka

◁ Hóra Sfakion

Damnóni

M. Préveli +

Drímiskos

Palm Beach

Áyios Pávlos

0   10 km

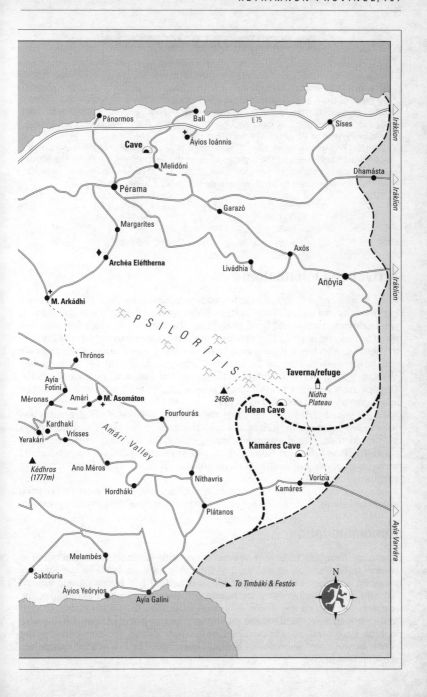

ACCOMMODATION PRICE CODES

All accommodation establishments in this book have been **price-coded** according to the scale outlined below. The rates quoted represent the cheapest available **double room** in high season. For rented apartments and villas, the price code refers to the price of the whole apartment, not just to a double room within the apartment. Out of season, room rates can drop by up to fifty percent, especially if you negotiate rates for a stay of three or more nights. Single rooms, where available, cost around seventy percent of the price of a double.

Rented private rooms usually fall into the ② or ③ categories, depending on their location and facilities, and the season; a few in the ④ category are more like plush self-catering apartments. They are not generally available from late October through the beginning of April, when only hotels tend to remain open.

① up to 4000dr	⑤ 12,000–16,000dr
② 4000–6000dr	⑥ 16,000–20,000dr
③ 6000–8000dr	⑦ 20,000dr upwards
④ 8000–12,000dr	

For more accommodation details, see p.35.

Arrival and information

Most people arrive in Réthimnon by road, turning off the main E75 north coast highway (known as the New Road) and descending the 1km into the town. If you're driving, you should head straight for the waterfront, which is the easiest place to find and to park. The new **bus station** is located to the west of the centre below the fortress. If you come in on the **ferry** you'll arrive more centrally still, at the western edge of the harbour; simply walk into the old town directly ahead of you. If you're leaving from the **airport** at Haniá, a bus leaves from the Olympic Airways office in town (see "Listings", p.205) to connect with flights, two and a quarter hours before they depart.

To get your bearings from the bus station, walk north along Sintagmatos and Riga Fereo before turning right along Melissinou, or one of the narrower alleys of the old town. You'll eventually emerge near the harbour, from where the **tourist office** (Mon–Fri 8am–5.30pm, Sat 9am–2pm; ☎29-148) is only a short walk away along the seafront. Here you can pick up maps, timetables and accommodation lists.

A bi-monthly English and German information paper, *Crete Summer* (free from hotels and shops), lists things to see and do in and around the town and province.

Accommodation

There are many places to stay in Réthimnon, with the greatest concentration of **rooms** in the tangled streets west of the inner harbour, between the Rimondi Fountain and the museums: there are also quite a few places on and around Arkadhíou. The higher-category **hotels** are all modern and businesslike; the cheap hotels are, on the whole, less good value than the rooms places, though more likely to have space – there are several along or just off Arkadhíou. If you're looking for central, rock-bottom budget accommodation, the only option is the **youth hostel** (see "Seafront and behind", opposite). The two nearest **campsites** are 4km east of town.

The phone code for Réthimnon is ☎0831.

Fortezza and harbour area

Anna, Katehaki 5 (☎25-586). Comfortable pension in a quiet position on the street which runs straight down from the entrance to the fortress to Melissinou. All rooms have bath, and some have a kitchen, too. A couple more new rooms places are very close by. ③.

Atelier, Himáras 32 (☎24-440). Pleasant rooms in a place run by a talented potter who has her studio in the basement and sells her wares in a store on the other side of the building. ②.

Barbara Dokimaki, Platía Plastíra 7 (☎22-319, fax 24-581). Strange warren of a rooms place, with one entrance at the above address, just off the seafront behind the *Ideon*, and another on Dambergi; ask for the newly refurbished top-floor studios. ②.

Fortezza, Melissinou 16, near the Fortezza (☎55-551, fax 54-073). Stylish, top-of-the-range hotel with everything you'd expect for the price, including a pool and restaurant. ⑦.

Rent Rooms Garden, Nikifourou Foka 82 (☎28-586). Good-value rooms with bath in an ancient Venetian building in the heart of the old town. ③.

Rooms George, Makedonias 32 (☎50-967). Decent rooms, some with fridge, near the Archeological Museum. ③.

Ideon, Platía Plastíra 10 (☎28-667, fax 28-670). Hotel with brilliant position just north of the ferry dock; the balcony rooms have a sea view. There's little chance of space in season, though, unless you've booked in advance. ⑦.

Rooms Isidora, Mavili 1 (☎26-293). Comfortable rooms in a quiet location, a couple of blocks below the Fortezza. ③.

Lefteris, Platía Plastíra 26 (☎51-735). Clean, pleasant pension rooms, with and without bath. They will allow one-night stays, but would rather rent by the week. ③.

Rent Rooms Makri Steno, Nikifourou Foka 54 (☎55-465, fax 50-011). Another rambling, but nicely renovated mansion, with light, fresh rooms and a huge roof terrace. ③.

Seeblick, Platía Plastíra 17 (☎22-478). On the seafront as you walk round from the inner harbour towards the outer wall of the fortress. Rooms with sea view cost more, but are good value for the position; some cheaper rooms are available without views. The owners prefer to rent by the week and won't even consider a single-night stay in season. ③.

Seafront and behind

Leo, Vafe 2 (☎26-197). This hotel has lots of wooden decor and a traditional feel. The price includes breakfast, and there's a good bar. ③.

Minoa, Arkadhíou 60 (☎22-508). Basic hotel rooms, but clean and central. ②.

Olga's Rooms, Souliou 57 (☎29-851 or 23-493). Nice old building on this touristy street with some very good rooms with bath overlooking the sea and some cheaper rooms without. Several other relatively upmarket rooms places can be found on Souliou. ②.

Rethimnon, V. Kornárou 1 (☎23-923). Very pleasant rooms of a high standard in an old building just off Arkadhíou; there's a bar downstairs. ②.

Sea Front Rent Rooms, Arkádiou 159 (☎51-981, fax 51-062). Some rooms with sea-view balconies (though can be noisy) in a nicely restored mansion, with lots of wood and ceiling fans. The owners have a number of apartments nearby. ③.

Youth Hostel, Tombázi 41 (☎22-848). The cheapest beds in town, either in dormitories or (illegally) on the roof. The hostel is large, clean, friendly and popular, and there's food, showers, clothes-washing facilities and even a library of books in an assortment of languages. ①.

Zania, Pavlou Vlastou 3 (☎28-169). A refurbished old house, right on the corner of Arkadhíou by the old youth hostel building, but with only a few rooms available. ③.

Near the Public Gardens

Brascos, Dhaskalaki 1, corner of Moatsou (☎23-721, fax 23-725). B-class hotel comfort and international blandness, but often *Brascos* has space when everywhere else is full. ⑤.

Byzantine, Vosporou 26, near the Porta Guora (☎55-609). Spotless rooms with bath in a renovated old Byzantine palace. The tranquil patio bar is open to all. ④.

Campsites

Camping Arkadia (☎28-825). Only a few hundred metres from *Elizabeth*, further east along the beach. Bigger and slightly less friendly, similar prices.

Camping Elizabeth (☎28-694). Pleasant, large site on the beach about 4km east of town; all facilities. Take the bus for the hotels (marked *Scaleta/El Greco*) from the long-distance bus station to get there.

The City

Réthimnon is a thoroughly enjoyable place to wander around. Although much of it has succumbed to fast-food outlets and supermarkets, the buildings themselves have changed little, and there's still the odd corner where English and German are not automatically spoken, a few curious old stores, and craftsmen working away in their traditional get-up of high boots, baggy trousers (*vrákes*) and black headscarves (*tsalvária*).

The monuments described below don't amount to a great deal on paper, but walking between them is often every bit as interesting as getting to them. The streets themselves are a fascinating mix of generations of architecture, the Venetian buildings indistinguishable most of the time from the Turkish and all of them adapted and added to by later generations. Ornate wooden doors and balconies are easily spotted, ancient stonework crops up everywhere, and there are a number of elaborate **Turkish fountains** hidden in obscure corners: one by the Kara Pasha mosque, another below the south side of the fortress at the corner of Smírnis and Koronaíou, two more on Patriárhou Grigoríou leading up from here towards the Public Gardens.

The harbour and the fortress

The impressive breakwaters, which are constantly being extended, reveal some of the problems with the **harbour**. Originally created by the Venetians, it has spent the centuries since constantly silting up, and until very recently had given up on trying to handle really big ships or ferries: when the locals decided to set up their own ferry service to Pireás (the *Arkadhi* was bought by public subscription) the whole thing had to be completely cleared out, and only a constant dredging operation keeps it open. Even now, the ferry is virtually the only large ship to call here; the inner harbour is for small fishing kaïkia and pleasure craft only, and the outer part is given over almost entirely to tourists.

If you follow the shoreline round to the west you'll emerge beneath the walls of the massive **Venetian Fortress** (Tues–Sun 8am–8pm; reduced hours in winter; 600dr). Said to be the largest Venetian castle ever built, this was a response, in the last quarter of the sixteenth century, to a series of pirate raids (by Barbarossa in 1538 and Uluch Ali in 1562 and 1571) which had devastated the town. Whether it was effective is another matter – the Venetian city fell to the Turks in less than 24 hours (they simply bypassed the fort), and when the English writer Robert Pashley visited in 1834 he found the guns, some of them still the Venetian

△ Haniá

RÉTHIMNON

★ Bus Station

SINTAGMATOS

RIGA FEREOU

Fortress

IGOUM GAVRIL

△ Spili

TRANTALIDHOU

DHIMITRAKAKI

Public Garden

10

MAVILI

KINONAKI YIANNI

ARMATOLON

MELISSINOU

KATEHAKI

1

Archeological Museum

13 7

NIKIFOROU FOKA

6

2

11

Historical and Folk Art Museum

Porta Guora

Nerandzes Mosque

ETHNIKIS ANDISTASIS

Rimondi Fountain

PETIHAKI

8 18

Centre for Contemporary Art

PLATÍA MARTIRON

SOULIOU

12

SALAMINOU

MESOLONGIOU

PLATÍA PLASTIRA

DHASKALAKI

5

Minaret

4

15

Loggia

PALEOLOGOU

3 9

Youth Hostel

Inner Harbour

MIATSOU

OTE

16

ARKADHIOU

Ferry Dock

19

17

DHIMOKRATIAS

V. KALERGI

ELEFTHERÍOU VENIZELOU

Veli Pasha Mosque

Kara Pasha Mosque

14

KOUNDOURIOTOU

YERAKARI K

EOT

HORTATZI G

PLATÍA IRÓON

K. GIAMBOUDHAKI

E. PORTALIOU

PAPANDREOU

SOFOKLI VENIZELOU

0   250 m

▽ Iráklion & campsites

ACCOMMODATION

1	Anna	11	Lefteris
2	Atelier	12	Leo
3	Barbara Dokimaki	13	Makri Steno
4	Byzantine	14	Minoa
5	Brascos	15	Olga's
6	Fortezza	16	Réthimnon
7	Garden	17	Seafront
8	George	18	Seeblick
9	Ideon	19	Zania
10	Isidora		

originals, to be entirely useless. Walk around the outside, preferably at sunset, to get an impression of its vast bulk; there are great views along the coast, and a pleasant resting point around the far side at the *Sunset Taverna*.

The **entrance**, however, is not on the seaward side but in the southeastern corner, opposite the new Archeological Museum. As you walk in through the walls there's a small café-bar in what must have been some sort of guardhouse within the bastion, and then you emerge into the vast open interior space, dotted with the remains of barracks, arsenals, officers' houses, earthworks and deep shafts. At the centre is a large domed building which was once a church and later a mosque, designed to be large enough for the entire population to take shelter within the walls. Although much is ruined now, the fort remains thoroughly atmospheric, with views from the walls over the town and harbour, or in the other direction along the coast to the west.

Among the most impressive remains are the **cisterns** where rainwater would have been collected: deep and cool, and dimly lit by slits through which shafts of sunlight penetrate. The church/mosque, recently restored, has a really fabulous dome and a pretty carved *mihrab* (a niche indicating the direction of Mecca and sadly defaced by graffiti), both of which are Turkish additions. Just to the north of this are some fine arched foundations and a stairway leading down to a gate in the seaward defences. This was in theory for resupplying the defenders, but in practice it was through here that the Venetians fled from the Turkish attack.

The archeological and historical museums

Réthimnon's **Archeological Museum** (Tues–Sun 8.30am–3pm; 500dr, students free) occupies a building almost directly opposite the entrance to the fortress. This was built by the Turks as an extra defence for the entry, and later served as a prison, but it's now entirely modern inside: cool, spacious and airy. It's worth a look, especially if you're going to miss the bigger museums elsewhere: there're Minoan pottery and sarcophagi, and lots of Roman coins, jewellery, pots and statues, all of them from Réthimnon province. Take a look beneath the central atrium at an unusual unfinished Roman **statue of Aphrodite**. The sculptor's chisel marks are plainly visible, allowing you to glimpse the goddess's features – never completed – emerging from the stone.

Even smaller, and a good deal more enjoyable, is the **Historical and Folk Art Museum** (Mon & Tues 9am–1pm & 6–8pm, Wed–Sun 9am–1pm & 7–9pm; 400dr, students 100dr), recently relocated to a beautifully restored seventeenth-century Venetian mansion at M. Venardou 28, close to the Nerandzes Mosque. Inside, in just two not particularly large rooms, are gathered musical instruments, old photos, basketry, farm implements, an explanation of traditional bread-making techniques, smiths' tools, traditional costumes and jewellery, lace, weaving and embroidery, pottery, knives and old wooden chests. Much of this looks as if it has just come out of someone's attic – as it sometimes has – and the displays include explanations (most of them translated) of how they've gathered the items, often as a result of a traditional craft workshop, farm or bakery closing down. It's a fascinating insight into a fast disappearing rural (and urban) lifestyle, which had often survived virtually unchanged from Venetian times to the 1960s.

Nearby is the town's newest museum, the **Centre for Contemporary Art** (Tues–Sat 10am–2pm & 6–9pm, Sun 10am–3pm; 500dr, students free), at the junction of Himaras and Melissinou, which you will see signposted throughout the town. It features a programme of rather hit-and-miss temporary exhibitions, from tribal art to modern Greek painting and installation.

The Rimondi Fountain and city centre; some mosques

The centre, at least as far as tourists are concerned, is probably the area from the Loggia to the Rimondi Fountain, with streets of shops, restaurants and bars radiating in every direction. The seventeenth-century Venetian **Loggia**, for many years the town museum, is now home to a shop, selling high-quality – and pricey – reproductions of classical art. The **Rimondi Fountain**, at the other end of Paleológou, is also seventeenth-century Venetian. Half-hidden under a blocked-off arcade, the fountain's lion-head spouts still splash water down to a marble bowl, and nowadays they look out over one of the liveliest areas in Réthimnon – Platía Petiháki. Straight up from the fountain, a line of cafés and tavernas leads into Ethníkis Andistásis, the **market** street. Turn right just before this and the back streets will lead you to the fine **Nerandzes Mosque** (currently closed for restoration), whose minaret, ascended by a steep spiral stair, has the best views in town. When the current works are complete the body of the mosque may return to its role as a meeting hall, often used for staging concerts.

Up through the market area, the old city ends at the only surviving remnant of the city walls, the **Porta Guora**. Through the gate you emerge into the Platía Tessáron Martíron with its ugly, unfinished modern church. Almost directly opposite are the quiet and shady **Public Gardens**, a former Turkish cemetery now laid out with a fine variety of palms and other trees. In July, the gardens play host to the festivities of the **Réthimnon Wine Festival** (see "Drinking, nightlife and entertainment" on p.204).

Wandering further afield into the newer parts of town, two more **mosques** complete the roll of Réthimnon's acknowledged "sights". **Veli Pasha**, up behind the bus station, has a fine minaret whilst **Kara Pasha** by Platía Iróon is older, but only part of the facade survives, with a small garden planted in front.

The beach

To find the **beach** you hardly need a guidebook: the broad swathe of tawny sand in the centre of town advertises itself. There are showers and cafés here, and the waters protected by the breakwaters are dead calm (and ideal for kids). Sadly they are also crowded and none too clean. Outside the harbour, less sheltered sands stretch for miles to the east, only marginally less crowded but with much cleaner water. Interspersed among the hotels along here is every facility you could need – travel agents, bike rental, bars and restaurants.

Eating

Immediately behind the town beach are arrayed the most obvious of Réthimnon's **restaurants**, all with illustrated menus out front and most with waiters who will run off their patter in English, German, French, Swedish or whatever else seems likely to appeal. These places are not always bad value – especially if you hanker after an "English breakfast" – but they are all thoroughly touristy. Look out, here and throughout town, for the wonderful fresh fruit juices and shakes which have become a local speciality: the melon is particularly good. Around the **inner harbour** there's a cluster of rather more expensive and intimate fish tavernas.

Although they lack the sea views, the cluster of kafenía and tavernas by the **Rimondi Fountain** and the newer places spreading into the streets all around generally offer better value. There are a couple of good **pizza** places here, too, and a number of old-fashioned kafenía, a couple of which serve magnificent yoghurt and honey.

Takeaway food means either *souvláki* – there are numerous stalls including a couple on Arkadhíou and Paleológou and *O Platanos* at Petiháki 52 – or buying your own. **Market** stalls are set up daily on Andistásis below the Porta Guora, and there are small general stores scattered everywhere, particularly on Paleológou and Arkadhíou; east along the beach road you'll even find a couple of mini supermarkets. The **bakery** *I Gaspari*, on Mesolongíou just behind the Rimondi Fountain, sells the usual *tíropita*, cakes and the like, and it also bakes excellent brown, black and rye bread. There's a good zakharoplasteío on Petiháki, and another at Koundouriotou 49, west of Platía Martíron.

Tavernas and restaurants

Agrimi, Platía Petiháki. Just one of the places touting for your custom as you walk up from the fountain. It's a good place to sit outside, and the food is usually reliable.

Alana, Salaminas 11. A romantic, tree-filled courtyard setting for candlelit tables and (mostly) non-Greek food. High prices.

Avli, Xanthoudidou 22, just west of the Rimondi Fountain. Upmarket but folksy place offering traditional meals (the lamb is good) in one of the prettiest and most romantic garden settings in town.

O Gounakis, Koronaíou 6, the old town. Hearty, no-frills cooking. The family running this bar/restaurant perform *lyra* every night, and when things get really lively, the dancing starts.

Kargaki Haroulas, Melissinou by Mesolongíou. Big, cheap Greek breakfasts plus standard taverna dishes at reasonable prices.

Kombou, edge of Atsipópolou village, 3km southwest of town. An excellent garden taverna, this is where the locals go. The Cretan specialities on offer include *spilogáradouma* (a type of lamb sausage) which should be eaten with *áfogalo*, a creamy sauce. Take a taxi there and back. Open evenings only.

Kyria Maria, Moshovitou 20. Pleasant, unassuming small restaurant tucked down an alley behind the Rimondi Fountain – after the meal everyone gets a couple of María's delicious *tiropitákia* topped with honey, on the house.

Minares, Odhós Vernadou. A little touristy, but very friendly, with reliable food and one of the nicest settings in the centre of town, right next to the Nerandzes Mosque.

Palazzo, the inner harbour. One of the nicest places on the harbour, with rooftop tables, but rather overpriced.

Taverna Petrino, junction of Salaminas and Diakou, behind the inner harbour. Small family-run neighbourhood taverna, less commercialized than those on the harbour.

O Pontios, Melissinou 34. A tiny place near the Archeological Museum and the Fortezza, this is run single-handedly by Katerina, the charming proprietor. A good lunchtime stop.

O Psaras (The Fisherman), corner of Nik. Foka and Koronaíou. Simple, economical and unpretentious fish taverna with tables beside a neighbourhood church.

Samaria, Venizélou, almost opposite the tourist office. One of the few seafront places patronized by locals; well-prepared food at fair prices.

Sunset Taverna, on the west side of the Fortezza. Mostly visited for its views rather than the food, but the meals aren't bad and the tables are right by the edge of the sea – the waiters have to cross the road to the kitchen.

O Zefyros, at the inner harbour. Less outrageously priced and among the more reliable of the fish tavernas here.

Drinking, nightlife and entertainment

Bars and **nightlife** are concentrated in the same general areas as the restaurants. At the west end of Venizélou, in the streets behind the inner harbour, pavements soon fill with the overflow from a small cluster of noisy **music bars** where party-goers gather before the nightly opening of the local discos. The café-cum-cocktail places around the Rimondi Fountain are great for people-watching, but the cacophony of late evening noise from competing bars is less than relaxing; a string of more subdued **cocktail bars** can be found up Salaminos towards the Fortezza. Larger **discos** are mostly out to the east, among the big hotels, but there are one or two in town as well.

Every August the town puts on its **Anagennisiakó** or **Renaissance Festival**. Held in the Fortezza, it includes classical and folk concerts and theatrical events, as well as performances of Classical tragedies and comedies. A full programme is available from the tourist office. There's more public entertainment on offer at the annual **Wine Festival**, staged in the Public Gardens in the second half of July. The entrance fee includes all the wine you can drink from barrels set up around the gardens, and there are also food stalls and entertainment laid on. You'll need to take your own cup or buy one of the souvenir glasses and carafes on offer outside. Although it's touristy, the locals go too, and as the evening progresses and the barrels empty the organized entertainments give way to spectacular displays of the local dance steps.

Cafés, bars and discos

Café Santan, Salaminos, west of the inner harbour. Most popular of several pleasant cafe-cocktail bars in this street.

Delfini Club, Venizélou, below the eastern harbour mole. Beachside open-air disco which incorporates a pool and features go-go dancers: all very Sixties.

Dimman, Arkadiou 220. One of the noisiest rock bars in this zone with a young clientele; provides people-watching possibilities and views from the first-floor balcony tables.

Fortezza, inner harbour. Big, glitzy disco-bar, where there's not much action till midnight.

Galera, Platía Petiháki. Large beers, toasted sandwiches and snacks. *Basiliko*, next door, offers the same sort of thing.

Metropolis, Nearchou. Just round the corner from the *Fortezza*, on an alley which connects with Arkadhíou. A loud rock-music bar with other bar-discos nearby.

Odysseas, Venizélou, right by the inner harbour. Touristy Cretan music and dancing place, with live performances every evening from 9.30pm.

Punch Bowl, Arambatzoglou 42. Obligatory Irish pub (complete with draft Guinness) which is pleasant and convivial.

Rouli's, Venizélou, behind the end of the beach. One of the cheapest and liveliest of several noisy bars here.

Venetsianako, close to the old harbour pier at the west side of the inner harbour. Stylish place where the in-crowd go for morning, noon, or afternoon coffee.

Xtreme, Nearchou. Just around the corner from the Fortezza, on an alley which connects with Arkadhíou. A loud rock-music bar with other bar-discos nearby.

Zanafoti, Platía Petiháki. Long-established kafeníon overlooking Rimondi Fountain. The prices are higher than average, but it's a great place to people-watch over a coffee; there's good yoghurt and honey too.

Listings

Airlines Olympic Airways, Dhimitrakáki 6 (☎24-333), facing the Public Gardens.

Banks National Bank is at the foot of Dhimokratias near the bus station and has a 24hr cash dispenser which takes Mastercard and Eurocard. Over the road, the Interamerican Bank has a cash-exchange machine. Credit Bank at Koundouriotou 29, and Ionian Bank at

Koundouriotou 134 all have Visa cash dispensers while the Commercial Bank on Platía Iróon, near the seafront, has a cash dispenser accepting Eurocard and Mastercard, as well as a cash-exchange machine.

Bike rental There are several competing bike rental outlets on Paleológou: try Stavros (☎22-858), which also rents out mountain bikes, or Arkadi (☎29-134) at Venizélou and Papandreou. Hellas Bike Rental (☎53-329) organizes one-day downhill (the bikes go "up" on a trailer) biking excursions to the White Mountains, Arkádhi, Kournás, Margarítes and Psilorítis.

Boat trips The *Dolphin Express* sails four times daily to Pánormos, Balí and the Skaléta "pirate" caves; there are also trips to Yeoryioúpolis, as well as evening cruises and fishing expeditions. The *Pirate* and its sister ship the *Popeye* make similar trips in more touristy "Jolly Roger" vessels, complete with sails, which are great for kids.

Car rental Direct (☎25-110, fax 21-260) at Platía Iróon 31 is reliable, and check the free paper *Crete Summer* (see below) for offers.

Cinema There are several, including the open-air Astoria on Melissinou beneath the south side of the Fortezza (lovely place, poor films) and Cinema Pandelis on the main road out towards Iráklion (new films, many in original version).

Ferries The agent for the Réthimnon–Pireás ferry, Rethymniaki, is at Arkhadíou 250 (☎55-518). Since the sister ship to the *Arkadí* (the *Préveli*) came into service, there are now daily sailings to Pireás at 7.30pm. In high season, there are sometimes additional morning sailings at 7am – usually on Saturday. For details and tickets for the Kastélli, Yíthio (Gythion), Kíthira and Kalamáta ferries, visit the very helpful Ellotia Tours at Arkadhíou 161 (☎51-062). The *Artemis* and *Minoan Prince* also make a one-day cruises to Santoríni (Thíra) several times a week.

Laundry Laundry at Tombázi 45, by the youth hostel (daily 9am–2pm & 5–9pm).

Left luggage The long-distance bus station has a small and chaotic office; Direct Cars also has an office at Platía Iróon 31, as does the Tourist Services travel agency opposite the Delfini Club, just east of Platía Iróon.

Mountain climbing and walking The local EOS is at Dhimokratias 12 (☎22-655); besides advice on climbing it also organizes walking tours (contact Sifis Spandidakis). Walking tours (from one day to two weeks) are offered by The Happy Walker, Tombázi 56 (☎52-920), a Dutch operation located near the youth hostel.

Newspapers and books Foreign newspapers are sold at several places along the seafront. Best for these, and for a wide selection of new books in English, is International Press at the junction of Venizélou and Petiháki. Good places for secondhand English-language books are Palaiobibliopoleío at Soulíou 43 in the old town, and Direct Cars on Platía Agnostou, which offers fifty percent of the cover price for unwanted paperbacks. The information paper *Crete Summer*, is free from hotels and shops.

Pharmacies Scattered about the main shopping streets, especially Koundouriótou and Arkadhíou. Check the rota on the door for late/weekend opening. The tourist office has a list of English-speaking doctors.

Post office The main post office (Mon–Fri 7.30am–8pm, Sat 7.30am–2pm) is in a smart new building on Moátsou, opposite the *Hotel Brascos*. There's also a temporary office, in season, just behind the beach at the bottom of the eastern breakwater (on S. Venizélou; Mon–Fri 8am–10pm, Sat 7.30am–2pm).

Shopping Most of the souvenir stores are along Arkadhíou, Paleológou and Souliou; the market is on Andistásis, while more general stores line Arkadhíou and Koundouriótou. There's also a market on Thursday along Dhimitrakaki, near the Public Gardens. Souliou has the most upmarket and varied tourist stores (including one that sells nothing but herbs and herbal remedies), but prices throughout town are markedly higher than in Haniá. For beach games and fishing or diving gear, try Spiros Spor on Petiháki. Official shop hours are Mon, Wed & Sat 8am–2pm, Tues, Thurs & Fri 8am–1pm & 5–8pm.

Taxis Ranks in Platía Tessáron Martíron and Platía Iróon. Call ☎24-316 for a radio taxi.

Telephones The OTE office at Koundourióti 28 (daily 7am–10pm).

Toilets Public toilets on the beach by the tourist office (clean!), opposite the Loggia and in the Public Gardens.

Travel agents Several along Paleológou, Arkhadíou and Koundouriótou, and also around Platía Iróon and along Venizélou. Creta Connection (Kallergi 15; ☎24-977), Creta Tours (Venizélou; ☎22-915), Caroline Tours (Platía Agnostou; ☎24-351, for boats from Kastélli Kissámou–Yíthio) and Creta Travel Bureau (Venizélou 3; ☎24-983) can all arrange excursions and ferry tickets. For flights home you'd be better off in Haniá or Iráklion.

The Monastery of Arkádhi

Of all the short trips which could be taken out of Réthimnon, the best known is still the most worthwhile. This is to the **Monastery of Arkádhi** (daily 8am–8pm), some 25km southeast of the city. Immaculately sited in the foothills of the Psilorítis range, Arkádhi is something of a national Cretan shrine. During the 1866 rebellion the monastery served as a Cretan strongpoint in which, as the Turks took the upper hand, hundreds of Cretan guerrillas and their families took refuge. Here they were surrounded by a Turkish army until, after a siege of two days, the defences were finally breached on November 9, 1866.

As the attackers poured in, the ammunition stored in the monastery exploded: deliberately fired, according to the accepted version of events, on the orders of the abbot. Hundreds (some sources claim thousands) were killed in the initial blast, Cretan and Turk alike, and most of the surviving defenders were put to death by the enraged assailants. The following year the British philhellene J. Hilary Skinner, fighting with the insurgents, could still describe "scores of bodies unburied, half-buried, sun-dried, and mangled, to be seen within the monastery". That he was here at all is proof of the international sympathy for the cause of Cretan independence which this ultimate expression of the cry of "Freedom or Death" did much to promote. Figures as disparate as Victor Hugo, Garibaldi and the poet Swinburne were moved to public declarations of support, and in Britain money was raised for a ship (the *Arkádhi*) to run the Turkish blockade. Though Crete's liberty was still some way off, the monastery remains the most potent symbol of the struggle. There are celebrations of the anniversary of the blast on 7–9 November.

The buildings

Nowadays you can peer into the roofless vault beside the cloister where the explosion took place, and wander about the rest of the well-restored grounds. Despite the carnage, the bulk of the monastery buildings, including the others around the central cloister, were relatively unscathed and Arkádhi is still a working monastery. Before its notoriety, indeed, it was one of the richest in Crete and already a well-known stopover for travellers (grouchy Edward Lear spent one of his better-tempered nights here), as well as being a centre of resistance. Pashley relates a story of events over forty years prior to the famous blast, when eighty Muslims, who had occupied the monastery to pacify local rebels, were captured and put to death: in retaliation, many of the buildings were burnt. More recently the monastery lent assistance to guerrilla fighters during World War II: George Psychoundákis, for example, describes handing over supplies from a parachute drop to the monks.

Of the surviving buildings the **church** is much the most impressive, with a rich mix of styles which places it among the finest Venetian structures left in Crete. Its highly decorative facade, dating from 1587, features on the 100-drachma note – isolated here in the Cretan countryside, it seems startlingly out of place. The rest of the monastery is mainly seventeenth-century (though it was originally founded as early as the eleventh) and more familiar in layout and style. Across the courtyard from the scene of the explosion a small **museum** (300dr) devoted to the exploits of the defenders of the faith contains a variety of mementos and tributes, blood-stained clothing and commemorative medals.

Getting there

Getting to Arkádhi is straightforward. In addition to all the tours, there are **buses** from Réthimnon at 6am, 10.30am, noon and 2.30pm, returning at 7am, 11.30am, 1pm and 4pm. Going up at 10.30am and back at 1pm gives you about the right amount of time, but these are the most popular buses, and consequently can be crowded; alternatively hitching a lift down should be no problem – the road ends here and the only place any traffic can go is back down to the coast. You could also try walking on to Thrónos in the Amari valley (see p.226) – get someone at the monastery to set you on the right track.

The **old road** up is attractive in itself: if you're driving take the route out of Réthimnon via Perivólia and then follow the signs at Plataniás which lead under the highway towards the monastery via Ádhele and Piyí. Five kilometres beyond Piyí you'll come to Loutrá where, on the right, the *Taverna Panorama* (☎0831/71-339; ①) makes a good lunch or drink stop; the panorama is at the back where a terrace looks out over groves of olives towards the sea. They make their own wine here in five-, ten- and even twenty-year-old vintages which you can buy, and should these ancient vintages prove too potent, they also have **rooms**.

As you climb into the lower reaches of the mountains, the road, and the valley through which it runs, gradually narrow until at the end it's a real ravine. This opens out quite suddenly into the small plain at whose centre stands the monastery: you'll pass a modern monument to the martyrs of independence – with displayed human skulls – and arrive at a huge spreading tree where the bus stops and cars park. There is **food** available at a rather unattractive cafeteria, but this is also a quiet place to picnic, either on benches around the outside of the monastery or walking out into the meadows which surround it.

With your own transport you could take an **alternative route** back to the coast through some picturesque wooded hill country dotted with interesting villages. Directly in front of the monastery a paved road cuts away to the northeast before it reaches Eléftherna, 5km away, and ancient Eléftherna (see p.216), followed by Margarítes (see p.215).

West towards Haniá

Heading west from Réthimnon the roads are easy and efficient, but they offer little in the way of diversion. As you leave the city, you immediately start to climb; within a couple of kilometres the **old road** peels off to head inland with opportunities to visit some charming villages such as **Argiroúpolis** and **Asigonía**, while the main **highway** carries on above the coast.

The E75 highway

Following the highway, you drop back to sea level at **YERÁNI**, 6km from Réthimnon, with a rocky cove good for swimming. There's a sign here to the Yeráni cave, site of a Neolithic cult rediscovered when the road was built, but the cave is not actually open to the public. Beyond, after another brief flirtation with the hills, the road finally levels out beside the **Gulf of Almirós**, from where it traces the shore, flat and straight, the rest of the way to Yeoryioúpolis (see p.269). A long and windswept sandy beach follows it all the way, separated from the road by straggling bushes of oleander: there are frequent spaces to pull over and park if you want a swim, and just a few new developments beginning to spring up. The beach itself is virtually deserted much of the way, but there can be dangerous currents so don't venture too far out: it gets further from the road and considerably more sheltered as you approach the development at Yeoryioúpolis.

The old road

The much more scenic **old road** is by comparison quite populous. You'll pass through five or six prosperous little villages before arriving, after 23km, at **EPISKOPÍ**, something of a local market centre. Here you're approaching the foothills of the White Mountains, which rise with increasing majesty ahead. To the left here a road runs up to some of the smaller villages, a rarely travelled route where the old life continues little affected, and where there are good opportunities for hiking in the surrounding hills.

Continuing west, beyond Episkopí, the old road soon divides, the main way descending steadily towards Yeoryioúpolis, a secondary route climbing through the village of Kournás (see p.271) and then dropping steeply to the lake.

Towards Argiroúpolis

A turn-off at Episkopí heads south towards Argiroúpolis. A couple of kilometres before you arrive at the village proper, the wonderful and friendly *Mikedaki Rooms* (☎0831/81-225; ②) is a strong candidate for best-value pension on the island. A splendid garden hides spotless rooms with bath, all of which have terrace balconies with fine views of the mountains and valley behind – you can even see the sea. Guests are also free to use a well-stocked kitchen to prepare breakfast to eat on their balconies.

At the back of the pension, where the land falls away beyond an orchard and an ancient stone threshing floor, tracks lead down into the Moussélas river valley. There's a fine **walk** to be had by following any of these, aiming for a small chapel directly west and easily visible across the valley. From a little beyond the chapel, a dirt track ascends diagonally to cross the shoulder of the Káto Agori peak. Following this in a north-west direction will lead you to the village of Pátima. From here it's possible to follow more tracks in a vaguely circular route – taking in the hamlets of Kástellos, Filakí and Arhontikí. From the latter village there's a track back along the east side of the valley which emerges near to the pension; in all about 10km. The tracks and villages are marked on the Petrákis *Réthimno Walking and Driving* map (see Basics p.30) as is the European E4 Footpath, which crosses the valley nearby to track the northern bank of the Moussélas to Asigonía, another fine walk.

Argiroúpolis

ARGIROÚPOLIS, 6km south of Episkopí, is a charmingly scenic village with a split personality. The **lower village**, reached by taking a right downhill (the Asigonía road) when you come to a fork, is effectively comprised of five **tavernas** in a spectacular wooded setting where gushing springwater cascades in every direction from the hill above. Vegetation is abundant in this fertile environment and, as well as great numbers of chestnut and plane trees, there are even exotic banana plants. The roar of water is impressive and there's so much of it here that it supplies the whole of the town of Réthimnon, as signs inform you. The tavernas have all incorporated water "features" into their terraces – walls of tumbling water, oriental wooden water bells as well as the more prosaic water wheel; the whole scene is especially magical at night with lights illuminating the foliage above. All the tavernas are good, but for added interest you might visit the *Vieux Moulin*, downhill from the others, which is run by Argiroúpolis' ebullient mayor, Stelios Manousakas, who is a voluble expert on all things to do with the village and frequently corrects visiting archeologists (see below) on their facts. Close to the *Vieux Moulin*, and accidentally discovered in 1994 by a British team, is a remarkable nineteenth-century fulling mill complete with a unique and rare **wooden fulling machine** once driven by water from the spring. It is hoped to restore this unique piece of Crete's industrial history and open it up to the public. Between the fulling mill and the springs are the remains of the **Roman baths** of ancient Lappa. Ask at the taverna for directions to both.

The **upper village**, reached by taking the left fork uphill (or by climbing a path which ascends from the spring), lies around its tranquil square overlooked by the elegant seventeenth-century Venetian church of **Áyios Ioánnis**, with an extended section to the south enjoying views over the river valley. The village is built over the prestigious ancient city of Lappa, parts of which have recently been revealed, and archeologists are currently busy excavating and documenting the city's ancient necropolis in the valley to the north, where they have unearthed a wealth of grave goods. A Dorian settlement in origin, Lappa was an ally of Lyttos (see p.108) in the latter's wars against Knossós. When it fiercely opposed the Roman invasion in 67 BC, the city was defeated and destroyed by the conquering legions. Later, when Lappa aided Augustus in his struggle against Antony for the control of the Roman world, the victorious Augustus permitted the Lappans to rebuild their town and gifted them a water reservoir in 27 BC which, incredibly, still supplies the village today. The city flourished for many centuries, even outlasting Roman rule, but was razed again by the Saracens in the ninth century. It recovered during the Venetian occupation and was an important centre, as is evidenced in the numerous villas left behind by Venetian landlords. Remnants of buildings from all periods of the village's history have been incorporated into most of the houses: you'll spot classical inscriptions, ancient columns and bits of Venetian stone carving in the most unlikely places.

A **tour** of the village is recommended. From the opposite side of the main square to the church, go beneath a stone arch where there is a store selling local wine and olive oil as well as the village's "beauty products" including avocado soap. Beyond the arch keep ahead to pass an elegant Venetian dwelling (left) with a **fine portal** bearing the legend "Omnia Mundi Fumus et Umbra" (All Things in This World are Smoke and Shadow). The street eventually climbs and the houses become brilliant white. This is not a "tourist village" however, and discreet glances inside open

Venetian houses on Réthimnon harbour

The Rimondi fountain, Réthimnon

Mountain village

MATTHEW HANCOCK

Arkhádi monastery, Réthimnon province   The mosque at Haniá

PETER WILSON

Haniá lighthouse

Sub-tropical palms, Kourtaliótiko gorge

Fisherman unloading his catch

Fresco, Church of Miháïl Arkhángelos

The Samarian gorge

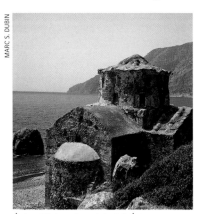

Áyios Pávlos chapel, Lefká Óri

Paleohóra bay

Departing ferry

doorways will reveal the everyday toil of the village women – rolling *bourekákia* pastries for the evening meal, peeling corncobs or embroidering and repairing family clothing. This route will lead you past more crumbling Venetian houses, some being refurbished, to a superb **Roman mosaic** floor beneath a canopy on a street corner. Part of a third-century bath house, its quality is not only an indication of the wealth of ancient town, but also of how much still lies buried beneath the modern village. Following the same street around the hill will lead back to the arch and the main square; heading **downhill** from the square along narrow, stepped streets, you come to a smaller square, with a couple of tiny churches en route. One of these, **Áyios Nikólaos**, dates from the eleventh century and holds fourteenth-century frescoes by Ioánnis Pagoménos (John the Frozen).

Ancient Lappa's **necropolis** lies to the north of the town at a site known as the Five Virgins, after a nearby chapel. Here hundreds of **tombs** – currently being investigated by archeologists – have been cut into the rock cliffs, many of them with elaborate interior and exterior decoration. The chapel takes its name from five young women put to death by the Romans in the third century for secretly practising Christianity in the tombs. The village commemorates their martyrdom on the first Tuesday after Easter when local shepherds bring their lambs to the shrine to be blessed and freshly milked sheeps' milk is boiled on site and drunk by those attending. Nearby is a gigantic 2000-year old **plane tree** (with a path cut through it and claimed by locals to be the oldest in Crete), by yet another spring.

Practicalities

In the midst of such spectacular walking terrain, anywhere else in Europe you would probably not be able to move for hikers. But here there's usually no problem finding a room – in fact you're spoilt for choice. Three excellent tavernas overlooking the Moussélas river valley to the south of the main square all offer **rooms** and are all excellent. *Morpheus* (☎0831/81-015; ②) has doubles and triples with and without bath, whilst *Arhea Lappa* (☎0831/81-004; ②) and *Agnantema* (☎0831/81-276; ②) both do en-suite doubles. With a fantastic view down the valley from its taverna terrace, the latter probably has the edge for location. **Buses** to Argiroúpolis leave from Réthimnon at 11.30am and 2.30pm and travel in the opposite direction at 7.30am, 12.30 and 4pm (all Mon–Fri only).

There are any number of superb **walks** to be had, many facilitated by the Petrákis *Réthimno* map (see p.209). The seriously adventurous can make a trek along the European E4 Footpath south along the Mousselás valley to follow the Kalikratiano Gorge, which reaches the sea at Frangokástello (see p.300), around 25km away.

Miriokéfala

The road south from Argiroúpolis allows visits to more villages and interesting churches. After 7km – with possible stops en route to explore the hamlets of Maroulou and Arolíthi just off the road to left and right – it arrives at **MIRIOKÉFALA**, whose former monastery church of the **Panayía Antifonitria** has ancient Byzantine frescoes, among the earliest on the island. The tiny drum-domed edifice – located in a courtyard at the bottom of the village – has **frescoes** depicting the Passion dating from the eleventh and twelfth centuries, and its **icon**

THE VENDETTAS OF THE LEFKÁ ÓRI

The **White Mountains of Crete** breed a race of men among the toughest in Greece; men whom, so the Cretan saying goes, neither know how to forgive – nor forget. **Blood feuds** are common in these mountainous regions, and resemble those of Sicily in the tight-lipped attitude adopted towards authority when outsiders from down below come prying. Fear of **retribution** is so great that no one wants to talk to the police when they attempt to investigate the acts of brutality these feuds entail. The latest chapter in one long-running vendetta saw a shepherd from Asigonía, Yiannis Mouzourakis, take to the hills with his rifle in 1994 threatening to avenge the rape and murder of his mother and the death of his brother; both had been killed in an inter-family feud over grazing rights. The brother, father and cousin of the murderers were later found shot dead. When pursued, Mouzourakis sent a message to the police saying that he would be willing to give himself up, but only when he had completed the vendetta by killing the remaining relatives on his list. The most notorious feud of all between the Sfakian Satzekakis and Pendaris families, started in the 1940s and left 150 people dead before it finally ended in 1988. In recent years riot police have been sent out from Athens to patrol the pastures here, where sheep rustling has provoked still more venomous disputes. There are few who believe that the vendettas will ever end, and in Sfakiá some villages have been completely abandoned because of them.

of the Virgin is held in great veneration locally. The church should be open, but the bar a little further along will be able to advise if not.

With your own transport there's a stunningly **scenic route** (also serving as the European E4 Footpath for this stretch) heading west from here, via the outlying hamlets of Kallikratís and Ásfendos, which eventually joins up with the main Hánia–Hora Sfakíon road, just north of the village of Imbros (see p.298). It's a rocky, unmetalled track through a desolate but picturesque landscape with spectacular climbs and descents in parts; if you take it sensibly the route is perfectly feasible, but you'd probably be unwise to attempt it outside summer or in bad weather.

Asigonía

Beyond the tavernas in the lower village at Argiroúpolis (see p.210), the road continues for 6km to **ASIGONÍA**, a ruggedly rustic settlement at the end of a perpetually cloudy cul-de-sac. A superb ride, the road winds through the verdant cleft of the Gipari gorge where trees thrust skywards from a riverbed flowing with water all winter, but which lies arid in the summer drought. This habitat breeds a profusion of birdlife: as well as blue rock thrushes, pipits and the ubiquitous tits, you may also spot griffon vultures and hawks hovering around the crags.

The road finally arrives in Asigonía's broad platía – ringed by busts portraying Venizélou and associated village heroes, but curiously not its most celebrated recent son, George Psychoundákis (see p.276), still alive and now in his late seventies. His story of perilous wartime treks over the mountains delivering messages to the various intelligence outposts has now become part of island legend.

From the square, the main street climbs uphill between simple stone dwellings, their yards piled with the firewood needed to stave off the bitterly cold winters here. Many of the men still cling to the traditional *saríki* black head-dress, baggy *vraka* trousers and high boots, and almost all still dress in black. The bars overlooking the square and along the main street – usually the haunt of card-playing farmers and shepherds at the end of the working day – are welcoming, although there are no places offering food or accommodation.

With an economy firmly based on stockbreeding, it's hardly surprising that the village's most important festival (on April 23) involves flocks of sheep being brought at dawn to the church to be milked, sheared and dedicated to Áyios Yeóryios, their patron saint and protector. Village girls then boil the milk on the spot and offer steaming cups of it to villagers and visitors.

The road south from Asigonía soon becomes a track, which snakes through a valley to Kallikrátis before doubling back towards Miriokéfala (see p.211) and its frescoed church. This is a fine **walking route** (about 20km) with a possibility of returning to Asigonía by way of Maroulóu, but with your own transport the more direct and convenient way is from Argiroúpolis.

East by the coast road

Leaving Réthimnon to the east, you can strike almost immediately onto the new road, which runs fast, flat and dull along the coastal plain, or follow the old road, squeezed into the narrow gap between this and the sea. This way you'll pass through a string of **village suburbs**, connected now by an almost continuous string of hotel development for some 10km. At Stavroménos the old road cuts under the highway and heads inland; the new road continues to hug a featureless coastline, now with barely any development at all, past the odd rocky beach. A little further along the coast, the cheerful resorts of Pánormos and Balí are both welcoming places to rest up for a while, but are probably a bit too crowded in high season.

Pánormos

PÁNORMOS marks a distinct break (still more marked if you are coming the other way, suddenly to emerge on the flat): the end of the level ground and the start of a spectacular, swooping mountain drive which continues virtually all the way to Iráklion. Here, too, is the last of the large hotels for some time, curving round a headland above a small bay and beach.

The tiny village of Pánormos is just a short detour off the road, a pretty little place with a couple of bars and tavernas perched above the harbour and a small, sandy beach. Surprisingly, this is an ancient settlement (a minuscule river runs through to the sea) with the ruins of what was once a large sixth-century basilica, probably destroyed in the ninth-century Saracen invasion, and of a later Genoese castle. There are also quite a few new **rooms** places as well as the large hotel, so the beach can become crowded in midsummer, particularly when the day cruises from Réthimnon stop here. However, development is low key and the village has managed to retain a sleepy and relatively authentic Cretan ambience, making it a relaxing place to spend a few days. The *Taverna Restaurant* (☎0834/51-209; ③) which has rooms and serves good, fresh fish, and *Lucy's Pension* (☎0834/51-212, fax 51-434; ④) are both decent places to stay.

SAVE THE TURTLE

This stretch of coast is one of the main breeding areas of the **loggerhead sea turtle**, now on the list of endangered species. Until recently the turtles were common throughout the Mediterranean, but the demands placed on the environment by both tourism and industry have led to many of their breeding habitats being developed or polluted. A sea-going creature for most of its life, the turtle must return to a beach – always the same one – in order to lay its eggs, and the stretch of coastline between the city of Réthimnon and Skaléta is now the second largest nesting area for loggerheads in the Mediterranean. Once these beaches are developed, the turtles, governed by powerful homing instincts, are unable to relocate to another and will die infertile. Unfortunately, nesting also occurs from early June to the end of August, coinciding with the high point of the tourist season. Once the female has buried her eighty to a hundred eggs on a nocturnal visit to the beach, the eggs must then remain undisturbed for a period of two months, before the hatchlings emerge to head for the sea. But even should they avoid being skewered by a beach umbrella or crushed by the feet of bathers – both common hazards – further dangers lie ahead for the newborn turtles. When they emerge, many of them, instead of heading for the sea, guided by the brightness of the horizon, are instead lured inland by artificial lights from hotel and tourist developments and perish from exhaustion or dehydration. Emblematic of Crete's and Greece's problem of balancing tourist development and the needs of the natural environment, it remains to be seen whether the loggerhead turtle will avoid the fate of the dodo.

Balí

The next stop you might consider making is at **BALÍ**, a small resort set around a series of little coves. Here the road drops down briefly from the heights to a desolate patch of low ground behind a bay. There's a large garage (where the bus will drop you), opposite which a road runs around the bay towards the village. On foot, this last stretch is further than it looks – a couple of kilometres to the village, more to the best beach. What you see first, though, is a fair-sized pebbly beach at the end of the bay: this often shelters a considerable collection of camper vans and tents. Sadly, it's no longer really worth the effort of walking any further; although the beaches are still spectacular, they're very much overrun, and Balí has become a package resort too popular for its own good. Only well out of season, when there are bound to be bargains given the number of rooms here, is it worth staying; you could try *Mira Mare* (☎0834/94-256; ③) which has a sea view.

Balí proper consists of three coves. The first has a pebbly beach and a couple of tavernas and rooms places: here, too, is the *Bali Beach Hotel* (☎0834/94-210, fax 94-252; ④), the first and still much the most luxurious hotel. In the second cove is the original village, with most of the local stores as well as more hotels, rooms and tavernas. One side of this cove has been concreted to form a harbour (there are day-trips by boat from Réthimnon), and on the other you can swim, though rarely with much space. The third cove is known as Paradise Beach, and though it's still much the best for swimming – with a patch of sand and, on either side, crags of rock with level places to sunbathe – it's too crowded and overlooked really to deserve the name any more. Two shady **tavernas** just above the beach make reasonable lunch stops however, and there are a couple of rooms places, including the *Sunrise Apartments* (④), with good sea views. If you stay overnight you could have this beach all to yourself in the early morning sun, when you may just be able to appreciate why it got its name. Slightly outside the cove, but still well sheltered within the larger bay, are a couple of rocks to dive from. It's a beautiful place to splash about, surrounded by mountains which seem to rise direct from the sea to impressive heights.

A good viewpoint to appreciate Bali's setting, and a more peaceful place to break your journey, is the tiny part-ruined, part-restored seventeenth-century **Monastery of Áyios Ioánnis** (daily 9am–noon & 4–7pm) reached by a good track to the north of the coast road, about five minutes west of the resort by car. The monastery church has some late frescoes, but its reputation among Cretans today is for an energetic role in the struggle against Turkish rule, for which it was bombarded by the Turkish navy.

Beyond Balí

After Balí, the next access to the coast is at Ayía Pelayía (see p.94), 25km further on. Nor is there much else to stop for: **SÍSES** has wonderful views from its perch beside the highway, and a few rooms, but little else. From the village a track with an appalling surface cuts up to the old road. Don't be deceived by maps which show some kind of way through above Balí – there is no other practicable route inland between Pánormos (from where there's a good road to Pérama) and Fódhele.

East on the mountain roads

Taking the old roads east, inland through the fringes of the Psilorítis range, there are a variety of routes and a number of interesting detours. The old main road, through Dhamásta, has least to offer, though it's a pretty enough drive. Striking higher into the **mountains** is more rewarding. For a combination of relatively easy driving and interest, perhaps the best option is the road up through Garázo and Axós to **Anóyia**, though you can also reach Axós on the even higher, stunningly scenic road from Pérama.

Margarítes

Whichever route you follow, you'll leave the coast at Stavroménos and head up through Viranepiskopí. The first potential detour comes some 5km further on, a right turn to **MARGARÍTES**, 4km beyond the turnoff, which has a long tradition of pottery manufacture and is scattered with workshops; along the steep main street you can buy the results. Truth to tell, though, most of the output is fairly unsophisticated, but one of the most authentic places is the workshop of Níkos Kavgalákis on the village's southern edge. Jovial Níkos not only turns out pots, but also the enormous Ali Baba jars similar to those found in the Minoan palaces and still used throughout agricultural Crete today.

There are cafés at the top of the village where *Taverna Gianousakis* (☎0834/92-255; ②) offers **rooms** with bath. Further down, on the village's pleasant platía, the shady terrace of the main bar overlooks the Margeritsanos valley, a good place to sit and rest awhile.

Ancient Eléftherna

Beyond here the road climbs for 4km to the village of **ARCHÉA ELÉFTHERNA** where, opposite a fountain, a paved way on the right leads after 200m to a parking place by the *Acropolis Taverna* (a good lunch stop) perched on the edge of the archeological site. From here a track leads to the spectacularly sited acropolis of **ancient Eléftherna**. The city that stood here in ancient times was one of the most important of eighth and seventh century BC Dorian Crete. When the Romans came in search of conquest in 67 BC it put up a stiff resistance, and later flourished as the seat of a Christian bishop. The Saracen invasions finished it off, however, and only recently has excavation of the site recommenced (by the University of Crete) after British archeologists packed up and left in 1929.

Beyond the taverna the path leads across a stretch of level rock, part of the original approach, carved in ancient times to resemble paving stones. Imposingly situated on a high promontory between two watercourses, the acropolis proper lies beyond a hefty *pírgos* or **tower** (which in large part still stands). Soon after this follow a path which descends to the left to reach the remarkable **Roman water cisterns** carved into the hill's west side, where enormous supporting pillars of solid rock support a cavernous interior as large as a church; nearby are the remains of the aqueduct which fed them. Proceeding north along a path which climbs back to the acropolis you will find significant fragments of massive walls and ancient buildings – not always easy to make sense of – and the roofless ruined church of **Ayía Ánna**, still revered as a shrine by locals who come to light candles here. Almost certainly located on the site of an earlier church, the tiny shrine still retains some poignant fresco fragments, sadly exposed to the elements, as well as a couple of ancient altars, once witnesses to pagan sacrifices but now with a Christian function. More remains lie still further north on the acropolis' tip where, by looking east into the valley, you can see the remarkable **new excavations** of the ancient town below.

Directly beneath the northern edge of the acropolis in Eléftherna's recently excavated **necropolis** on the valley floor, archeologists made a potentially very significant discovery: traces of a human sacrifice made in front of the funeral pyre of some local magnate. It apparently dates from the late eighth century BC, about the same time that Homer was describing very similar sacrifices of Trojan prisoners in front of the funeral pyre of Achilles. The victim, who was bound hand and foot and had died in a ritual during which his throat was cut, may well have been expected to serve the dead man in the next world – also found in front of the pyre were sacrificed animals and offerings of perfume and food. Other cremations on the site (some twenty have been found, though only one human sacrifice) had offerings including gold, jewellery and fine pottery, as well as four tiny, superbly crafted ivory heads which are among the best work of their time (c.600 BC) yet discovered anywhere. These and other finds from the necropolis are displayed in the archeological museum at Réthimnon.

Although there's a **path** from here down to the new excavations and the Hellenistic bridge (see below), the way isn't always clear: if you would rather avoid scrambling through the olive groves, the routes described below are probably more practicable.

The New Excavations and Hellenistic Bridge

The new excavations below the acropolis to the east have uncovered a significant part of Hellenistic and Roman Eléftherna; many dwellings and a fine **Roman villa** with well-preserved mosaics fragments are already visible. One house has a curious "garden seat" covered with mosaic decoration, and between the houses run paved streets complete with drains and sewers, and dotted with numerous altars. The excavations will continue in the coming years and this is set to become a site of major importance. To reach the new excavations return to the turnoff before the taverna and backtrack slightly (in the direction of Margarítes) to take a signed road ("archeological site") on the left just before the tenth-century Byzantine chapel of **Ayía Iríni**. Incidentally, this beautiful little church dominated by a massive cypress tree is worth a look: inside there's a fine twelfth-century *Pantokrator* in the dome, the only surviving **fresco** of what must once have been a glorious painted interior. Following the dirt road to the archeological excavations, keep ahead downhill until you come to a white cabin used by the site's guardian. You should leave any transport here; the site is a short distance beyond this.

An impressive stone-built **Hellenistic bridge** lies in the valley below the acropolis. With your own transport you should head 2km west to Arhéa Eléftherna's twin village, Eléftherna, where a track on the right at the edge of the village will bring you – after about 700m – to the bridge. Villagers will direct you should you have difficulty locating it.

There's said to be a practicable walk from Eléftherna to the monastery of Arkádhi (see p.207), less than 5km southwest as the crow flies, but you'll have to check out the route locally. There is also a newly asphalted road to the monastery from here, and is the way to go with transport. Otherwise, to continue east, you've little choice but to retrace your steps to the main road.

Pérama to Axós

PÉRAMA is a substantial place, an agricultural centre which also has a little light industry: its businesslike main street is lined with banks, stores and cafés. The chief interest in this is the rarity value of seeing a town of such size in Crete that owes nothing whatever to tourism. Even if you do no more than drive through it's a refreshing sight, and you may well find yourself passing this way more than once if you take one of the local detours available.

The Melidhóni Cave

The most obvious of these is to **MELIDHÓNI**, 5km northeast of Pérama. The village itself is unremarkable, but a thirty-minute walk (or a short drive, signed from the village) leads to a great **cave**, whose series of chambers are thick with stalactites and stalagmites. This was the legendary home of Talos, a bronze giant who protected the coasts of Crete by striding around the island thrice daily (or perhaps only three times a year) hurling rocks at unfriendly ships: the Argonauts were greeted thus when they approached the island. Far more infamously, however, the Melidhóni cave was also the setting for one of the most horrific atrocities in the struggle for Cretan independence. Here, in 1824, around three hundred local villagers took refuge, as they had often done before at time of war, in the face of an advancing army. This time, however, the Muslim commander demanded that they come out: when the Cretans refused, and shot two messengers sent to offer safe conduct, he tried to force them out by blocking the mouth of the cave with stones, and cutting off the air supply. After several days of this, with the defenders opening new air passages every night, the troops changed their tactics, piling combustible materials in front of the cave and setting light to them. Everyone inside was asphyxiated.

The bodies were left where they lay for the cave to become their tomb, and ten years later Robert Pashley became one of the first to enter since the tragedy, to find in places "the bones and skulls of the poor Christians so thickly scattered, that it is almost impossible to avoid crushing them as we pick our steps along". This grisly event was far from unique – numerous other caves around the island have similar histories, although none claimed so many victims.

A shrine near the entrance to the cave today commemorates the dead. There's also a small **bar**, run by a Greek couple who previously lived in the States, where you can pick up a map of the cave before you visit.

Garázo, Axós and the Sendóni Cave
Back through Pérama, the main road wends along the valley of the Yeropótamos all the way to the turning for **Garázo**, a small village where hardly anyone seems to stop. If you do, you'll find that the simple roadside cafés are friendly and exceptionally good value.

Seven kilometres further on, **AXÓS**, especially if you arrive at lunchtime, makes a surprising contrast to Garázo. Where the main road passes through, it is lined with weaving and embroidery for sale (mostly rather poor) and with tavernas crowded with tourists. This is largely because the village serves as a lunch stop for "Photo-Safari" day-trips from Iráklion and Réthimnon. If you catch it without the crowds, Axós is undeniably attractive; the small church of **Ayía Iríni** (try ringing the priest on ☎0834/61-311 if locked) dates from the fourteenth century and contains significant frescoes, and the site of a **post-Minoan settlement** (signed from the centre), also called Axós, is barely accessible on a ridge above the village.

The upper road from Pérama, emerges in Axós by the church, first passing through **Livádia** and **Zonianá**, two rather tumble-down, straggly but atmospheric villages, as traditional as any you'll find in Crete. Should you pass through either in the early evening, you're likely to find what seems to be the entire population out in the streets, the elders in traditional dress and the young keen for a chance to try out their English. Just beyond Zonianá you can visit another spectacular cave, the recently opened **Sendóni Cave** (April–Oct daily 9am–7.30pm; Nov–March 10am–4pm) with a magnificent display of stalactites, stalagmites and petrified waves. A vast tunnel-like cavern, it has been fitted with a series of walkways extending some 500m or so into a spur of Mount Ida. Local legend has it that the cave was discovered by an eight-year-old girl who, lured away by fairies, was later found dead in its darkest recesses. The hefty entrance fee is intended to finance more walkways penetrating still deeper into the cave, which is thought to extend at least another kilometre beyond what is already on view. This will also allow the somewhat spooky pleasure of viewing some miniature bats which are known to breed there.

Anóyia

The focus of this route is **ANÓYIA**, a small town perched beneath the highest peaks of the Psilorítis range. It is the obvious place from which to approach the Idean Cave and, for the committed, the summit of Psilorítis itself. The weather, refreshingly cool when the summer heat lower down is becoming oppressive, is one good reason to come, but most people are drawn by the proximity of the mountains or by a reputation for some of the best woven and embroidered work in Crete. The last is greatly exaggerated but the town still makes a very pleasant break from the coast. The impression gleaned as you look around is of a prosperous place, a fact underlined by the many pricey bars along the main street, something not usually seen this far from the coastal strip. The source of all this wealth is stockbreeding; the sheep farmers here are some of the richest in Greece, which is why you'll find a gentlemen's club in the upper town, where the wealthiest of these barons do their wheeling and dealing in opulent surroundings.

As you drive through, it seems that Anóyia has two quite distinct halves: from what appears to be the older, lower part, the road takes a broad loop around, to re-emerge near the modern-looking platía (**Platía Meídani**) of the upper town. In many ways this appearance is deceptive. A series of steep, sometimes stepped alleys connect the two directly, and however traditional the buildings may look, closer inspection shows that most are actually concrete. This reflects a tragic recent history – the village was one of those destroyed as reprisal for the abduction of General Kreipe (see p.343) and at the same time all the men who could be rounded up here were killed. The local handicrafts tradition is in part a reflection of this history, both a conscious attempt to revive the town and the result of bitter necessity with so large a proportion of the local men killed. At any rate it seems to have worked, and large numbers of these surviving elderly widows (accompanied now by their daughters) are anxious to subject any passing visitor to their terrifyingly aggressive sales techniques.

The impression of an old and a new town persists even when you know it to be false. The upper half of the village has almost all the **accommodation** as well as the **bank** (no foreign exchange) and **post office** (reluctant foreign exchange), police, most of the non-tourist stores and the large **Platía Meídani**, lined with bars where the younger residents hang out. The more antique feel of the lower half is reinforced by the elderly men, baggy trousers tucked into their black boots, moustaches bristling, who sit at the kafenía tables, and by the black-clad women sitting outside their textile stores nearby. In the square (Platía Livádhi) in the lower half of town stands a statue, and next to it a wooden carving of Venizélos, arm in a sling with a curious bird sculpture dangling from the tree overhead – the strange works of a revered local sculptor (see below). Walk the lanes between the two halves of town and there's a real country feel: empty houses and garages closed up with wire and used to stable livestock; goats grazing in vacant lots; and more workshop/homes where the craftswomen have set up showrooms in their front parlours.

The curious **sculptures** in the lower square are the work of Algiliadi Skoulas, who died in 1996 aged ninety-two. Yéorgos Skoulas has now opened a **museum** (open daily 9am–7pm) to his father, reached by turning right behind the Venizélos statue and continuing along the line of textile shops to turn left uphill; the museum is on the right. The exhibits are a collection of Skoulas senior's bizarre sculptures and paintings, whose naive simplicity his son will explain with enthusiasm. Skoulas junior usually treats visitors to a performance on the *lyra* – on which he's a deft exponent – and he may even throw in a *mantináda* vocal. There's not a great deal else in the way of sights here, although enthusiasts may wish to see the fourteenth-century church of **Áyios Ioánnis** on the main street, which has some well-preserved wall paintings.

Incidentally, Anóyia is a noted centre of **lyra music**; many of the greatest performers on the instrument have come from the town. The late Níkos Xylouris was a shepherd who made his own *lyra* and taught himself to play, and whose performances and compositions turned him into a Cretan legend. The house where he was born is now *Kafenion Xylouris*, on the lower square. His brother, Psarantonis, is also a great talent and continues to live here.

Practicalities

Anóyia sees a lot of day-trippers, but most stay only an hour or so. Linger a while, or stay overnight, and it's surprisingly uncommercial. It shouldn't normally be hard to find a **room** in the upper half of town, where you'll see signs leading off all along the main street. A couple of the best places are located on the road that swings left (east) from the lower square, Odhós Pándidoni. About 500m along the road as it climbs you'll come to the flower-bedecked *Rooms Aris* (☎0834/31-460, fax 31-058; ②), quickly followed by the friendly *Hotel Aristea* (☎0834/31-459; ②) which has en-suite rooms with sensational balcony views. *Rooms Idi* (☎0834/31-021; ②) and *Rent Rooms Pasparaki* (☎0834/31-048; ②) are a couple more simple options along the main street (Kendriko Dhrómos) but aren't really that much cheaper.

The one drawback to staying overnight is that there are limited places offering **food**: one taverna on the main road where it loops out of the lower village (*Prásini Foliá*, with a large open-air space for dancing and which occasionally hosts "Cretan Evening" tours) can be depressing when it's full with rowdy coastal revellers and just as depressing when it's cavernously empty. Then, you'd be best off going to the grill places on the lower square, where the choice will most likely be limited to whatever happens to be on the spit (usually succulent lamb). In the upper village beyond the *Hotel Aristea* on the right, *Taverna Mitato* is a decent restaurant, but also plagued by the bus tours from the coast. Your best bet for some peace and a fantastic view from its terrace is *Taverna Skalómata*, which is thankfully too small for bus parties and where barbecued lamb is again the thing to go for. It's on the upper edge of town on the road out to Mount Psilorítis and the Idean Cave, an easy hop by car but a bit of a hike on foot. Wherever you eat, ask to sample the **local cheese** which is excellent.

One **bar** on the main street you shouldn't miss is that of Níkos Manousos, a Communist patriot who has turned his kafenío into a shrine to the now derided ideology. In the dusty old bar, fading framed photos of Communist heroes such as Marx and Lenin, Castro and Che Guevara, interspersed with heroes of the Cretan war against the Turks, gaze down on the ageing imbibers below. The quietly spoken Níkos always serves a small mezé with whatever you order, and the *raki* is recommended.

Psilorítis and its caves

Heading for the mountains, a smooth road swiftly ascends the 21km from Anóyia to an altitude of 1400m, to reach the **Nídha plateau** at the base of **Mount Psilorítis**. It's a steady climb most of the way, and a road travelled little except by the shepherds who pasture their sheep up here (and who nowadays travel back and forth by pick-up). Along the way in late spring, as the snow recedes, you'll see myriad wild flowers and, at all times, quite a few birds including vultures and magnificent golden eagles, a stirring image as they glide imperiously across their mountain domain. The *mitáta* or stone huts close to the roadside – many of them ruined – are former shepherds' dwellings where traditionally the sheep's milk yoghurt and cheese would be made, although many are now used as dog kennels and even chicken coops. Somewhere near the highest point a track leads off right to the **ski area**: an unlikely thought in summer, although it does see plenty of snow in season. Soon after, the small plateau and its bare summer pastures fan out below you, and the road – the last section unpaved – drops to skirt around its western edge.

The Idean Cave

At what is effectively the end of the road (shortly beyond, it peters out in a network of trails across the plateau), a modern **taverna** stands looking over the plain. *Taverna Nida* (☎0834/31-141; April–Sept daily; Sat & Sun only in winter) serves hearty taverna standards and has a couple of **rooms** (②) sharing a bath. Stelios Stavrakakis, the friendly proprietor, is a fount of information on the plateau and the viability of walking routes in the vicinity, and given a couple of days' notice he can also arrange explorations on **horseback**, either guided or independent.

Opposite the taverna, a path (about a fifteen-minute walk) leads up to the celebrated **Idean Cave** (Idhéon Ándhron), a rival of that on Mount Dhíkti (see p.144) for the title of Zeus's birthplace. Although scholarly arguments rage over the exact identity of the caves in the legends of Zeus, and over the interpretation of the various versions of the legend, locals are in no doubt that the Idean Cave is the place where the god was brought up, suckled by wild animals.

Certainly this hole in the mountainside, which as Cretan caves go is not especially large or impressive, was associated from the earliest times with the cult of Zeus, and at times ranked among the most important centres of pilgrimage in the Greek world. Pythagoras visited the cave, Plato set *The Laws* as a dialogue along the pilgrimage route here, and the finds made within indicate offerings brought from all over the eastern Mediterranean. Current excavations have revealed that the cave cult had a much longer history than this, too. First signs of occupation go back as far as 3000 BC, and though it may then have been a mere place of shelter, by the Minoan era it was already established as a shrine, maintaining this role until about 500 AD.

Something of a disappointment when you finally get there, the cave and the area around it has more the feel of a mining operation than an important historical site. A major – and prolonged – archeological dig is going on inside the cave behind a fence constructed across its mouth, and a number of railway tracks leading away from it are used to carry the tons of rock and rubble from these

---

THE MEMORIAL TO PEACE

At the northern end of the plateau, German artist Karen Raeck has constructed a **rock sculpture** titled *Immortal Freedom Fighter of Peace*, commemorating the suffering of the town of Anóyia at the hands of the German army in 1944 (see p.219). A one-woman reconciliation mission between her homeland and Anóyia, Raeck has spent most of the last fifteen years living in the town and has gained the respect and trust of its inhabitants. The monument, measuring 30m by 9m, consists of a large number of huge boulders laid out in an impressionistic image of a winged figure when viewed from the air. The shepherds of the plateau assisted Raeck in carrying and positioning the stones, and during the work's assembly she lived in one of their stone huts. The sculpture is visible from the terrace of the *Taverna Nida* who have information about it and will point it out if asked; an excursion to see it at close quarters makes for a very pleasant stroll across the plateau.

excavations. Many visitors clamber over the fence, but when you've descended the steps on the other side it turns out to be fairly shallow affair, devoid of even natural wonders and certainly not a patch on the dramatic interior of the Dhiktean Cave.

To the summit

The taverna also marks the start of the way to the summit of **Psilorítis** (Mount Ida), at 2456m the highest mountain in Crete. Though it's not for the unwary or unfit, the climb should present few problems to experienced, equipped climbers (see Thrónos, p.227 for a possible guided ascent). The route, which diverts from the path to the cave just beyond the small spring and chapel, is marked with red dots: a guide who knows the mountain would be useful, since it's not always obvious which is the main trail, but is by no means essential. Don't attempt it alone, however, as you could face a very long wait for help if you ran into trouble. If you do make the climb, it should be a seven-to-eight-hour return trip to the chapel at the summit, though in spring thick snow may slow you down. It's wise to carry enough food, water and warm gear to be able to overnight in one of the shelters should the weather turn – in any event a night at the top, with the whole island laid out in the sunset and sunrise, is a wonderful experience.

For the first thirty minutes or so **the climb** trails south across the mountainside, a gradual ascent until you reach a gully where it starts in earnest. Head west here, away from the plain, on a rocky path up the left-hand side of the gully. After about an hour-and-a-quarter of this you reach an open height with a stone shelter and good views back the way you came: do not follow the most obvious trail at this point, which leads only to one of the lesser peaks (Koussákas, 2209m), but follow the ridge downhill and south instead, unlikely as this may look. After barely fifteen minutes you reach a basin where several trails meet, and where there is spring water and stone **huts** for shelter. Turn right, northwest, and an obvious uphill trail will take you all the way to the summit, though it is only in the last twenty minutes that the peak itself becomes visible and the ground starts to fall away to reveal just how high you are. The summit itself is marked by another shelter and the chapel of **Tímios Stavrós** (a name by which the peak is sometimes known locally and in which Níkos Kazantzákis famously claimed to have lost his virginity); nearby there's water in a cistern, which you are advised to boil or purify before drinking. When it's clear, the panoramas from the top make the climb well worthwhile. Usually, though, conditions are very cold and windy and the views are spoilt by cloud or heat haze.

Other routes: the Kamáres Cave

While the route outlined above is probably the easiest to follow without a guide, there are any number of **alternate routes** up and down. From the west you can climb from virtually any of the Amári villages below the peak (especially Fourfourás, p.228), but although this is relatively straightforward in the sense that you can see the peak almost all the way, there are no real trails and you may run into difficulty with patches of thorny undergrowth or loose scree. South, Vorízia and Kamáres also make possible starting/finishing points. If you want to descend towards **KAMÁRES**, the trail divides in the basin mentioned above, about halfway from Nídha to the summit. It's not hard to follow, heading south from the basin, but is a good deal steeper and longer than anything outlined above: perhaps six hours down to Kamáres, and seven to eight hours for the ascent. About halfway, there's a junction with a trail to the huge **Kamáres Cave**, in which the first great cache of the elaborate pottery known as Kamáres ware was found (it's now in the Iráklion Archeological Museum). From the cave you either backtrack to this trail to continue to the village or carry on east to another trail, equally steep.

If you're prepared to camp on the plateau (there's plenty of water but conditions can be very cold) or stay at the taverna, an even more attractive option is to tackle the peak in one day, and continue south next day from the **Nídha plateau**. This is a beautiful hike – as long as the road they're blasting through here is out of sight – and it's also a relatively easy one, four hours or so down to **VORÍZIA**, five or six to Kamáres. For either, track around to the southern edge of the plateau, where a gully (soon to become a considerable ravine) leads off. Large red arrows direct you towards Kamáres on the trail which passes east of the cave. For Vorízia, you follow the ravine for about an hour until a faint trail climbs out on the left (soon after this, the stream bed becomes impassable). Above the ravine there are fine views and a heady drop for another hour, when you must turn left (east) again. This is not obvious, but you should begin to see signs of life – goat trails and shepherds' huts. You cut past the top of a second, smaller ravine to a stone hut and then descend, zigzagging steeply, to a dirt road and Vorízia. Vorízia and Kamáres both have **rooms** and **food** and at least one **bus** a day to Míres.

Across the island

Heading south across the island, towards Plakiás or Ayía Galíni, the road takes off from the very centre of Réthimnon, running along the side of the Public Gardens and then climbing rapidly above the town. Look back from the final bend and you have the city, its castle and harbour laid out like a map below you, with the sea behind. Once you've passed the large service station which marks the end of the populated north

THE WILDEST CAT IN CRETE

In Cretan myth and legend there have long been told tales of the *fourokattos* ("furious cat"), a centuries-old name which refers to a **wild cat** living in the mountains of Psilorítis. Although in 1905 two skins from such a beast were purchased at the market in Haniá by a British woman attached to a scientific mission, for most of this century scientists have regarded the existence of such a beast as impossible. They also dismissed the stories of shepherds and goatherds – who claimed to have seen this wild cat – as incredible. Then, in 1996, an Italian university team studying the carnivores of the Cretan mountains were astonished when they returned to their traps one morning to find they had snared a five-and-a-half-kilo wild cat . The news created a sensation as the beast was taken to the University of Crete for study. Tawny in colour and with a snarl like a tiger, the cat does not belong to the species of cats on the mainland of Greece and the rest of Europe; its nearest relative is a species inhabiting North Africa and Cyprus. Scientists believe that it is an extremely reclusive and fully nocturnal animal, which explains why it is so rarely seen. However, the cat's discovery has not only proven generations of Cretans to have been right, but has turned the zoological history of the island upside down. The scientists are now getting to grips with some conundrums. Just how did it get to Crete in the first place? Was it perhaps brought over as a domesticated beast by the ancestors of the Minoans, or has it been on the island since it became separated from the mainland? And, the question that the Cretan media have been asking ever since the discovery: are there any more?

coast, the road winds into the back country of rural Crete. It's a scenic ride, and whilst settlements are few, both Arméni, with a fascinating Minoan cemetery, and Spíli, tucked into the folds of Mount Kédhros's foothills, are inviting places to make a break.

Arméni Minoan cemetery

A little under 10km from Réthimnon, just before the village of **ARMÉNI**, a sign to the right points the way to a remarkable **Minoan cemetery** (Tues–Sun 8.30am–3pm; free). Important discoveries have been made here in over two hundred rock-cut tombs dating from the Late Minoan period, after the fall of the great palaces. Pleasantly sited today in a shady oak wood, most of the tombs are of the *drómos* (passage) and chamber type. One large tomb on the south side of the site which the guide will point out has a spectacular *drómos* and finely cut chamber and may well have belonged to a royal personage. Some other tombs had only the *drómos* cut, and work on them seems for some reason to have been abandoned. Many *lárnakes* (clay coffins) and grave goods found in the tombs – including weapons, jewellery, vases and a rare helmet made from boar's tusks – are now on display in the archeological museums at Réthimnon and Iráklion. One mystery yet to be solved regarding the cemetery remains: the location of the no doubt sizeable settlement which provided this necropolis with its customers.

Onward routes

Another 10km takes you to the first of the turnoffs **towards Plakiás**: this one on a new road through Áyios Ioánnis and down the Kotsifoú gorge. Just by this turning there's a café/truck stop which is the best place to change buses if you are travelling between Ayía Galíni and Plakiás or vice versa (there's a timetable posted outside). There's also a good chance here of a lift with passing tourists or a local truck. Only a little further the alternative route to Plakiás takes off – through Koxaré and the Kourtaliótiko gorge. Either way, the drive is a pretty spectacular one.

Spíli

Sticking to the main route south, **SPÍLI** is 30km from Réthimnon; it's the one place on this road where you might spend some time for its own sake. The town doesn't look much as you drive through, though the mountainside which hovers over the houses is impressive, but if you get off the main road, into the alleys which stagger up towards the cliff, it is wonderfully attractive. A sharp curve in the road marks the centre of town, by a small platía overlooked by lofty plane trees. Just above there's a charming Venetian fountain, with a long row of lions' heads splashing cold water into a trough, and above this begins a steep mosaic of flowered balconies, cobbled lanes, shady archways, giant urns and chimneypots. On occasion, Spíli can become quite crowded – many of the bus tours passing along the road make a brief stop here, usually for lunch – but between times and in the evenings it is quiet and rural. Stay overnight and you'll be woken early by the sounds of the farmyard and an agricultural community starting work.

Practicalities

There are numerous places offering **rooms** spread out along the main road – the flower-decked *Green Hotel* (☎0832/22-225; ②) at the north end of town is good, although not the oasis it once was since its discovery by organized tour groups. Just behind, however, is a delightful smaller pension, *Heracles* (☎0832/22-411; ③), with spotless balcony rooms with bath. The genial and eponymous proprietor here also rents out **mountain bikes**, is an authority on walking in the area and will exchange money. Just along the road from these two lies *Sun Set Rooms* (☎0832/22-306; ②), another good place with pleasant balcony rooms.

Of the few **eating** places, *Taverna Stratidakis*, between the fountain and the *Green Hotel*, is a good bet, as is *Taverna Giannis* (50m beyond the fountain on the Ayía Galíni road); *Café Babis*, over the road from the fountain is good for **breakfasts** (local yoghurt and honey are excellent) and evening drinking. Almost everything else you're likely to need is clustered around the fountain square, including most of the local stores and businesses: there's a **post office** and **bank** on the main road, and a metered phone in the souvenir/newspaper store on the corner by the fountain (although there are also cardphone kiosks along the main street).

Walks around Spíli

If you can stay longer there are some challenging **hikes** which start in Spíli – across to Yerakári in the Amári valley for example. However, the new road (spectacular drive though it is) linking the two places makes this seem less of an achievement than it once was.

A less taxing four-kilometre hike brings you to the pretty village of **LAMPINÍ**, to the northwest, and its domed Byzantine **church of the Panayía**, sited above a valley. This was the scene of a terrible massacre in 1827 (marked by a plaque) when the Turks locked the congregation inside the church before setting fire to it. All perished, and only fragments of the fourteenth- and fifteenth-century frescoes survived the blaze. To get there follow the main road back to Mixórrouma, turning right in the village on a road signed for Karínes.

To extend this walk, you could continue 5km beyond Lampiní to **KARÍNES** itself, another attractive village with a friendly kafeníon in the midst of gently terraced hills. A further 7km brings you to **Patsós** with a turn on the left 1km before it (and a 10min walk) to the Áyios Andónios **cave** and a beautiful gorge with trees and water, a Minoan and later Dorian and Roman sanctuary. From Patsós, Thrónos (see p.226), 9km away and reached via the hamlets of Pandánasa, Apóstoli and Kalóyeros, becomes a realistic end destination with the possibility of a bed and a meal (but ring ahead to make sure in high season).

Heading in the other direction from Spíli, a **walk** encompassing Mourné, Fratí and Ayía Pelayía takes in some superb scenery with views of the Psilorítis and Lefká Óri ranges besides four ancient churches (fine frescoes at the last one) and offers opportunities for birdspotting. Take the road from Spíli to Mourné, beyond which a track – along which you'll see the churches – heads southwest in the direction of Fratí, approached by a stiff descent. From here there's an easy route above the Kissanos river valley to Ayía Pelayía and the main road back to Spíli.

Another fine **trail** is the 15km from Spíli to Moní Préveli (see p.237). Take the road west to Mourné and then follow a track heading south. After about three kilometres and just before Drímiskos, follow a cross track heading west towards the Megapótamos river. When you reach the river valley, head south to arrive at the Palm Beach (see p.237). At the sea turn right (west) to cross the river and keep ahead along a track to reach the monastery. To save yourself the journey back you could arrange to be picked up by taxi from here to return you to Spíli; it should be arranged in advance, will cost about 4000dr and can be booked through the proprietor of the pension *Heracles*, who will also answer any queries relating to the above hikes. All the above routes are marked on the Petrákis *Réthimno* map (see Basics, p.30).

Beyond Spíli, the road towards Ayía Galíni follows a long valley between Mount Kédhros and the lesser summit of Sidhérotas. Apart from the odd patch of extremely bad road surface it holds few excitements.

The Amári valley

An alternative route south from Réthimnon, and a far less travelled one, is the road which turns off on the eastern fringe of town to run via the **Amári valley**. Amári is one of those areas, like Sfakiá, which features large in almost everything written about Crete – and especially in tales of **wartime resistance** – yet which is hardly explored at all by modern visitors. Shadowed by the vast profile of Psilorítis, its way of life survives barely altered by the changes of the last twenty, or even fifty, years. Throughout the valley, isolated hamlets subsist on the ubiquitous olive, with the occasional luxury of an orchard of cherries (especially around Yerakári), pears or figs, and throughout there are a startling number of richly frescoed churches. It's an environment conducive to slow exploration, with a climate noticeably cooler than the coast: in midsummer the trees, flowers and general greenery here make a stunning contrast to the rest of the island.

Three **buses** a day run from Réthimnon to the crossroads at Ayía Fotiní: onwards from there the service is sporadic to non-existent. It's best to explore on foot – in which case a water bottle and the best map you can find are essential equipment – but the main roads are fine if you have your own transport. As for staying in the valley, there are officially **rooms** only in Thrónos and Yerakári, but don't let this deter you from asking in other villages: villagers are often only too happy to have a paying guest for a night or two, and traditional hospitality here has not yet been extinguished by abuse.

Whenever you come, but in July or August especially, you may be lucky enough to stumble on a village **festival** in honour of the local saint, the harvest or some obscure historical event; they're worth going out of your way for, so keep an eye out for notices pasted in kafeníon windows. Beginning in a distorted cacophony of overamplified Cretan music, the celebrations continue until the participants are sufficiently gorged on roast lamb and enlivened by wine to get down to the real business: the dancing. Cretan dancing at an event such as this is an extraordinary display of athleticism and, as often as not, endurance. If the party really gets off the ground locals will dig out their old guns and rattle off a few rounds into the sky to celebrate. It should prove an experience not swiftly forgotten.

The eastern side

There are two roads through the Amári valley, one following the eastern side and clinging to the flanks of the Psilorítis range, the other tracing the edge of the lesser Kédhros range on the western side. Both are scenically spectacular, but the **eastern route** probably has the edge in terms of beauty and places of interest.

Thrónos

Going this way, the first of the real Amári villages is **THRÓNOS**, situated just off the main road at the head of the valley on the site of ancient Sbritos, whose port was modern Áyia Galíni. Like so many others here, Thrónos seems lost in the past, with its beautifully frescoed **church of the Panayía** and majestic views across the valley and up to the mountains. There are more ancient remains, too. In the Byzantine era this was the seat of a bishop (hence *thrónos*, throne) and these early Christian days are recalled by the remains of a mosaic which spreads under the village church and spreads beyond its walls, with traces both inside and out. The new building, in fact, is only about a quarter the size of the original church, whose floor-plan, guarded by a low rail, can be clearly seen. The elderly keeper will usually appear with the key as soon as you start to take an interest in the church; if not, ask the local kids, who will no doubt be watching your every move, or in the café/store alongside. On the hill above the village are still earlier remains of the **acropolis** of ancient Sybritos, easily reached by following a path beyond the church on the village's eastern edge. The hill is topped by a radio mast and if you make it clear where you want to go, the villagers will show you the way. Besides plenty of ancient ruins, there are spectacular **views** from the top.

If you want **to stay**, simply follow the crude "Rent Rooms" signs through the ramshackle streets to *Rooms Aravanes* (☎0833/22-760; ②), a modern concrete structure with pink cinderblock balconies. The building is an aberration, but once inside it's out of sight and the balconies have the best view in the village. The rooms are pleasant and there's a taverna on the ground floor, which is just as well for the only other place in the village offering food is a basic *kafepantopolíon*. The owner here also acts as agent for a beautifully restored **stone-built house** in the village where en-suite rooms (②) come with more spectacular balcony views. The proprietor, Lambros Papoutsakis, is a man of diverse talents: besides constructing *lyras*, he is quite a player, too. He also gathers herbs in the mountains (on which he's an expert), conducts walks to the top of Mount Dhíkti (see below), finds fossils and distills his own *raki*. The *Aravanes*'s yard outside is also pressed into use for periodic big *bouzoúki* get-togethers, with dozens of tables put out and fires lit for barbecuing; keep an eye out for the posters, as these are well worth attending.

Hikes from Thrónos include a relatively easy path leading north through the foothills in a couple of hours to the monastery of Arkádhi (see p.207) where you can pick up buses again, but get directions from *Rooms Aravanes*, as the way divides more than once. South, a paved road runs back into the main valley via Kalóyeros, also an extremely easy stroll from Thrónos. Fifteen minutes' walk beyond this village, a narrow path on the left leads uphill to the small stone church of **Áyios Ioánnis Theológos**, whose fine frescoes date from 1347 – ask about the key in the village on the way.

The ascent of Psilorítis

The proprietor of *Rooms Aravanes* (see above) also conducts guided treks to the peak of Mount Psilorítis, Crete's highest peak at 2456m. Although he does guide groups up in the daytime, his preferred approach is during the full moons of June, July and August, which avoids the heat of the day. Then, the group starts out by Landrover in the early evening to reach the start point on the mountain. After a meal cooked in the open and a short nap, the ascent begins in moonlight almost as bright as daylight. When the summit is reached at around dawn the sunrise is always spectacular, and on clear days the mountain offers a breathtaking view of the whole island and its four seas spreading in all directions. Ring in advance for details; it's not a difficult climb, but you'll need sturdy footwear and a sleeping bag.

The Moní Asomáton and Amári

From Thrónos, back on the main road, the **Moní Asomáton** is only 1km further south. The buildings are Venetian, though the monastery itself is older; having survived centuries of resistance and revolution, it finally became an agricultural school in 1931. It's not open to the public, but no one seems to mind if you wander in and look over the lovely old buildings, with a weed-infested central courtyard containing a church, a fountain and – at the rear – a prodigious plane tree.

Outside and beside a friendly taverna – a line of fir and eucalyptus marks the beginning of the five-kilometre paved road to the village of **AMÁRI**, the chief village of the valley. This is another beautiful drive or manageable walk, although the second half climbs quite steeply up the hill of Samítos, which rises right in the middle of the valley. On the way you pass through two picturesque villages, Monastiráki and Opsigiás, but Amári itself outdoes them: it looks like nothing so much as a perfect Tuscan hill village – note the steeply sloping roofs to cope with the winter snows and the chimneys for wood fires. There's really nothing to do here – even the couple of kafenía seem to close for a siesta in the afternoon – but there are scintillating views across to Psilorítis. For a bird's-eye view, climb the Venetian clock tower which dominates the narrow alleyways (the door is always open). It's not immediately obvious how to get here, but keep climbing and circling the hill until you reach the church; enter the churchyard through some wrought-iron gates and then climb a flight of steps behind. Just outside town, the church of **Ayía Ánna**, reached down a lane opposite the police station, has some extremely faded frescoes – and well they might be: dating from 1225, they have a fair claim to being the oldest on Crete. As well as a police station, Amári also boasts an OTE and **post office**, and there's a daily bus at about 4pm for Réthimnon.

Fourfourás and beyond

Continuing south to **FOURFOURÁS** and beyond, there are more lovely villages, with the peak of Psilorítis now almost directly above and the softer lines of Mount Kédhros behind the Samítos hill on the other side. Fourfourás is a traditional place to begin the climb of Psilorítis, although no one seems to tackle the peak from here any more (Anóyia and Kamáres are more convenient); it is also the trailhead of some arduous hikes to the lesser peaks. At **NÍTHAVRIS** the road divides. South, with the coast coming into view, you can head down to Ayía Galíni (see p.230) or follow the flank of the mountains around through Kamáres (see p.222). Turn off west and you can curve round to complete a circle of the valley through the villages on the lower slopes of **Kédhros** (1777m).

The western side

The villages on the western side of the valley look little different, but in fact they are almost entirely **modern** – rebuilt after their deliberate destruction during World War II. George Psychoundákis (see p.276) watched the outrage from a cave on the slopes of Psilorítis:

I stayed there two or three days before leaving, watching the Kedros villages burning ceaselessly on the other side of the deep valley. Every now and then we heard the sound of explosions. The Germans went there in the small hours of the twenty-second of August and the burning went on for an entire week. The villages we could see from there and which were given over to the flames were: Yerakari, Kardaki, Gourgouthoi, Vrysses, Smiles, Dryes and Ano-Meros. First they emptied every single house, trans-

porting all the loot to Retimo, then they set fire to them, and finally, to complete the ruin, they piled dynamite into every remaining corner, and blew them sky high. The village schools met the same fate, also the churches and the wells, and at Ano-Meros they even blew up the cemetery. They shot all the men they could find.

Officially these atrocities – other villages around Psilorítis, from Anóyia to Kamáres, were also burned – were in reprisal for the kidnap of General Kreipe, four months earlier. But Psychoundákis, for one, believed that it was a more general revenge, intended to destroy any effective resistance in the closing months of the German occupation. Today the villages of Méronas, Elénes, Yerakári, Kardháki and Vrísses mark the southward progress of the German troops with etched stone **memorials** dated one day apart. Áno Méros has a striking war memorial of a woman wielding a hammer.

Even here, a number of frescoed **churches** survived the terror. Between Vrísses and Kardháki one such lies off to the right of the road, lying low in a field of grain and apparently forgotten. Push the door aside, however, and the gloom gradually reveals beautiful Byzantine paintings around the altar.

Yerakári

YERAKÁRI is a bigger, more modern and prosperous-looking village than most, with several places to stop for a drink or some food, and **accommodation** at *Taverna Rooms Gerakari* (☎0833/51-013; ①) on the main street. Bubbly Kiría Déspina Bolioudáki is the proprietor here, and her rooms seem to be only a sideline. The taverna's kitchen is a veritable pickling and bottling factory for the fruits of the region – especially cherries, for which the village is famous – which she spreads out to dry on every available neighbour's rooftop during the picking season. Her cheeses, *thimarísio* (thyme honey) and pickled cherries are all for sale and recommended, although the cherry brandy is probably an acquired taste.

With transport you have the option of taking the spectacular **new road** heading west from Yerakári to Spíli (see p.224) with tremendous views along a valley between the heights of Kédhros and Sorós towards the distant and magnificent Lefká Óri. The way to the road lies up the hill at the end of Yerakári's main street. Starting out unpromisingly as a rough dirt track, almost before you know it you're bowling along a superb asphalted highway thoroughly out of synch with what has gone before.

Áyios Ioánnis Theológos

Just to the south of the Yerakári you'll pass the unusual **Monastery of Áyios Ioánnis Theológos**, with a spreading oak tree in front providing shade for a tapped spring. There are thirteenth-century frescoes in an exposed side chapel, and slightly later ones as you enter the church, all very battered and exposed to the elements. Traces of the medieval stone road or track on which the church was originally aligned can still be made out behind it.

Méronas

Continuing along the road north to complete the Amári valley's western flank, beyond Mesonísia and Elénes comes **MÉRONAS** where, to the right of the road, a soft pink Venetian-style **church of the Panayía** shelters frescoes from the fourteenth century; you'll need to ask for the key across the road. Again, it takes time to adjust your eyes to take in the painstaking detail of the artwork, darkened with age; a torch would allow you to see a great deal more than the candles or night-lights which usually provide illumination.

Ayía Galíni

Twenty years ago **AYÍA GALÍNI** must have been an idyllic spot: an isolated fishing community of some five hundred souls nestling in a convenient fold of the mountains which dominate this part of the south coast. Although this was the port of ancient Sybritos (see p.226), the modern village is barely a hundred years old, its inhabitants having moved down from the mountain villages of Mélambes and Saktoúria as the traditional threat of piracy along the coast receded. Catch it out of season and the streets of white houses, crowded in on three sides by mountains and opening below to a small, busy harbour, can still appeal. But this is a face which is increasingly hard to find. Packed throughout the season with package tourists, and confined by the limits of its narrow situation, the village's old houses are rapidly being squeezed out by ever larger apartment buildings and concrete hotels. Since the beach was never up to much anyway, there's little reason to stay here long in summer. The lack of a decent beach is a shame, as is the use of the potentially picturesque harbour area as a parking lot, for otherwise there's something appealing about Ayía Galíni's relatively staid and respectable brand of tourism. It's a nicer place than it looks, or than you'd expect from first impressions, largely because the people have stayed friendly and the atmosphere Cretan despite the development.

Practicalities

Buses to Ayía Galíni terminate at the bus station by the church, in the village proper. It's a handy spot to get your bearings since few of the streets are named and such names as there are seem rarely used. The nucleus of the place is built around three streets which run down to the harbour. The first of these (technically Venizélou) is a continuation of the main road into town: along it you'll find post office, bakery, doctor and a couple of car rental places. In the narrow street parallel to this to the east is the garage and stores; the next street along is packed with tavernas (and known locally as "Taverna Street"). All of this falls within an extremely small area where nothing is more than a couple of minutes' walk away.

Many places near and including the post office (below the bus station towards the harbour) **change money**; when the latter is closed try Creta Exchange opposite, which gives bank rates. Soulia Car Rental (☎0832/91-347), a little nearer the harbour, is a good place for **car rental**, and Monza Travel (☎0832/91-004), on Taverna Street, also hires out cars and **bikes**. Travel **information** and **tickets** are available here, too. The OTE has a phone cabin on the harbour (daily 8am–2pm & 4–10pm) and card **phones** can be found throughout the centre. A **bookshop** with a decent selection of English fiction and books about the island is Le Shop Kalliopi just in from the harbour road close to the post office, and international **newspapers** are available from the shops on the road in from Réthimnon.

Accommodation

There are so many **rooms** that you can usually find something – though for much of July and August all but a handful are pre-booked by tour operators. Prices are very closely linked to demand: for most of the summer both are high, but not alarmingly so, and away from peak seasons you can often get an exceptional bargain.

Probably the best place to start looking is at the top of the town, either walking down to the left from the main road, or up Taverna Street and round to the right.

The latter way is best to the friendly *Hotel Minos* (☎0832/91-292; ②), an excellent-value place with sea-view rooms, all with bath and use of a kitchen, and open all year. Next door to here, *El Greco* (☎0832/91-187, fax 91-419; ④) is a pleasant upmarket possibility with air-conditioned balcony rooms; be sure to ask for the air-conditioning remote control. Opposite the *Minos*, *Hotel Idi* (☎0832/91-152, fax 91-082; ③) has pleasant balcony en-suite rooms. A little further towards town from here and on a bend *Hotel Hariklia* (☎0832/91-350, fax 91-257; ②) is another delightful, small, spotless and Scandinavian-run pension with good harbour views and en-suite rooms; guests also have use of a kitchen to prepare breakfasts and snacks. Nearby is *Rent Rooms Acropol* (☎0832/91-273; ①), a very basic place with an unbeatable location right on the edge of the cliff. The daughter of the people here runs the *Hotel Acropolis* (☎0832/91-234; ②), not far away on the main road, which is much more likely to have a room but also less well positioned. Between these you'll pass dozens of other possibilities – *Rooms Candia* (☎0832/91-203; ②) and *Rooms Dedalos* (☎0832/91-214; ②) are promising – and you'll need to ask at each one. One economical possibility nearer the sea is *Akteon* (☎0832/91-208; ②), reached by turning left off the end of Taverna Street; the rooms are simple but have great views.

There's also a **campsite**, *Camping Agia Galini* (☎0832/91-386), to the east near the mouth of the river, reached either by a road which takes off from the main road about 1km outside the village, or by walking out along the beach.

Eating

One major and undeniable benefit which the crowds have brought to Ayía Galíni is a vast range of **food** and **drink**: much of it excellent and, thanks to the competition, not overpriced. The bulk of the tavernas are located, surprisingly enough, along Taverna Street, which in the evening is choked with pedestrian traffic. There are plenty of economical – if rather unexciting – places here with tables spilling out into the street. Perhaps the best value of all for wholesome traditional food and a great setting is the *Restaurant Onar*, overlooking the harbour from a rooftop at the bottom of the street. Near here, to the east side of the harbour, the slightly pricier *Madame Ordans* is another rooftop place serving well-prepared international food on a terrace. *Zeferos* is one of the best places along the harbour for the usual standard dishes. Close to the north end of Taverna Street, *La Strada* does good pizzas; the brothers who run it are accomplished performers on the *lyra* and *laoúto* (lute), often treating their customers to an impromptu concert.

Other places which are not on Taverna Street, and hence less easy to find, include *Charley's Place* opposite the bus stop, quiet and out of the way, and *Stelios Café*, on the square below this on the main road, where they occasionally serve freshly made *loukoumádhes* (honey puffs); at night the *Stelios* transmutes into a cocktail bar. The town's traditional kafeníon, *Miro*, just off Taverna Street a little way down, stubbornly clings to its identity in the face of the surrounding mayhem. Not far away on the street proper, *Milestone* is a place serving fancier breakfasts, with prices to match.

Drinking and nightlife

There are plenty of **bars** and **discos** where you can carry on after you've eaten, mostly around the bottom of Taverna Street and near the harbour. *Zorba's*, where dancing starts after midnight, is a long-established favourite and *Escape* and *Juke Box* at the foot of Taverna Street are other options, whilst the nearby *Paradiso* is currently the resort's most popular venue.

Beaches and day-trips

The **beach** at Ayía Galíni is astonishingly small when you consider the number of people who expect to use it. It's not even very sandy or attractive – once the few patches of soft sand have been claimed you have to rent a chair if you hope to lounge in any comfort. It lies to the east of the village, reached by a narrow path that tracks around the cliff from the harbour front, or by one that descends from the top of the town (or you can drive round and park by *Camping Agia Galíni*). Walking round by the cliffs, you'll pass caves which in World War II served as gun emplacements. You can get food and drink at a number of places behind the beach; among the **tavernas**, *Kostas* is probably the best value, but both *Sunset* and *Acropol* are good.

Further afield to the west are some much better patches of sand. **Boats** from the harbour (details from any travel agent, or get your tickets when boarding) make daily day-trips to the beaches of Áyios Yeóryios and Áyios Pávlos (around 3000dr per person) as well as to the Paximádhia islands 12km offshore, which have wonderful fine sand beaches but little shade, making a sun umbrella a must.

ÁYIOS YEÓRYIOS is also fairly easily reached on foot: take the main road up past the bus station, and at the crown of the first bend follow a left turn (signed) towards a group of apartments. Just beyond these, cross a dry river bed and head up the hillside on a well-worn path marked with splashes of red paint. The beach is almost two hours away, a shingle cove with two tavernas, one of which, *Nikos*, has rooms (②); there are a couple of other, less attractive coves along the way.

ÁYIOS PÁVLOS is even further, but also much more attractive, with some striking rock formations around a sheltered bay, and excellent snorkelling. The main **beach** here can make for difficult bathing due to slippery rocks and, in summer, strong winds. Both of these problems can be dealt with by going west over the headland, where there's fine sand and a more sheltered beach. In addition to the people arriving by boat from Ayía Galíni, Áyios Pávlos has now attracted a colony of New Age yoga practitioners who fly in stressed-out executives for two weeks of muscle-stretching at their centre, the *Practice Place*. The boat is perhaps the most pleasant way to get here, but you can also drive via Saktóuria, on a recently sealed road. This is now the quicker route, but another scenic way there (or back) is to take the old main road out of town towards Spíli and through Mélambes, turning left (signed) after about 12km to go through upper and lower Saktóuria, an excitingly winding route with great views. Once you get there, you'll find two **taverna/rooms** places, *Áyios Pavlos* (☎0832/41-555; ③) and *Mama Eva* (☎0832/41-557; ②), immediately above the beach, and the *Livikon* (☎0832/41-551; ②) a little way back up the road, as well as a couple of modest apartment developments.

Plakiás and around

Thirty kilometres west of Ayía Galíni, Plakiás is beginning to rival it as a south-coast resort. Commercialized as it is though, it still has a very different feel: the accommodation is simpler, less of it is booked in advance, the nearby beaches are infinitely better and it attracts a younger crowd.

There are two main approaches to the area, both off the Réthimnon–Ayía Galíni road. The first is on a newly surfaced road down through the **Kotsifóu gorge**; the second, just a few kilometres further on, via the even more impressive

Kourtaliótiko gorge. Either way, it's worth pulling over in the gorge to take time to appreciate the scenery and the wildlife (from snakes by the water to birds of prey soaring above). On the first route the gorge eventually opens out to leave you on the main coast road west of Plakiás: turn right for Sellía, left for Mírthios and Plakiás. On the second there are parking places about halfway through the gorge and steps leading down to the chapel of Áyios Nikólaos near the bottom. Further on, you have a choice of turning right for Lefkóyia and Plakiás or continuing to follow the course of the stream all the way down to Préveli.

Mírthios

MÍRTHIOS hangs high above the Bay of Plakiás, with wonderful views down over it. It's a small village but, thanks to a large and friendly **youth hostel** (☎0832/31-202; ①), one which sees a fair number of young travellers. The hostel is hard to miss, lying just above the road in the very centre of the village with a fantastic view that any five-star hotel would envy. Facilities are pretty basic (though you can cook), but it's a popular meeting place and a good source of local information; if you want more luxury, several other places offer **rooms**. Along the road opposite the hostel are a few tavernas with terraces hanging over the hillside, and a general store. *Plateia Taverna*, right under the youth hostel, is particularly good and friendly.

There's a **post office** for changing money, but for other facilities you have to go down to Plakiás (see below), about twenty minutes' steep downhill walk on a path which sets off from the platía/car-parking space opposite the hostel. The long walks to the beach (and much longer climbs back) are the chief disadvantage of staying here, but you are rewarded with considerably lower prices and a friendlier atmosphere – locals still just about outnumber visitors. And, of course, if you're a keen walker it's heaven: ask at the youth hostel about some of the more substantial hikes, to almost entirely deserted coves to the west, or up into some of the gorges. The Plakiás bus usually comes up to Mírthios after it has dropped most of the passengers, but check with the driver. You may get left by the junction, about ten minutes' walk away, on the way in.

Plakiás

PLAKIÁS itself is growing all the time, and it's no longer the unspoilt village all too many people arrive here expecting. Even so, it's still some way from the really big league, and if it's not that attractive in itself it does make a good base for **walks** in the beautiful surrounding countryside and trips to excellent **beaches** all around. The road comes in from the east, behind the beach, and heads straight into the heart of things along the harbour front. There's basically just a single street that runs inland, rapidly deteriorating into paths which wind up towards Sellía and Mírthios; otherwise everything is strung out in a line facing the sea or in tiny new streets, no more than three or four houses long, built off the main road. The coast road very rapidly becomes an extremely rough track west of the last houses, eventually ending altogether at Soúda Beach after 3km or so.

There are relatively few facilities in Plakiás, but there's at least one of everything you could need. A **post office** van is parked by the harbour, and although there's no bank you can **change money** here or at many of the travel agents – such as Monza Travel on the seafront next to the *Hotel Lamon* – or supermarkets. Also along the seafront are a few **car** and **bike rental** places: try the reliable

Moto Auto Plakias (☎ & fax 0832/31-632) who deal in both, or Odyssia (☎0832/31-596) for higher-potency bikes as well as **mountain bikes**. There's a **laundry**, Saloon Wash, across from the Christos Taverna at the western end of the seafront, which will get your clothes back to you washed and dried in ninety minutes. International press is available at shops on the seafront, whilst Monza Travel (☎0832/31-433) is good for information and **travel tickets** and has a **used book exchange** where you can recycle your holiday reading. Some of the tackiest souvenirs in all Crete can be bought at the Forum **supermarket**, in the new development on the road in; it also sells books, sunscreen and some food. Fast **taxis** to Iráklion (about 15,000dr one way), Réthimnon and Haniá are available; call ☎0832/31-287.

Numerous travel agencies can sell you tickets for **boat trips** to Souda Beach, Damnóni, Préveli and even Loutró; the *Venus* leaves for Préveli's Palm Beach daily at 10.30am and 1.30pm (returning at 2 and 4pm). Other diversions to keep you from beachtime boredom include **scuba diving** with the Aegean Dive Centre (☎0832/31-206; April–Sept), slightly inland at the west end of the seafront, who rent equipment, lead **snorkelling** expeditions and give lessons. To follow walks in the attractive country surrounding Plakiás there are a couple of excellent walking guides and a map of the area by Lance Chilton (see Contexts, p.369) which should be on sale in the Plakias Market, to the right of the *Livikon Hotel* on the seafront.

Accommodation

There are loads of new **hotels** and **rooms** in Plakiás. Indeed there's little else, but even so you may have difficulty finding a vacancy in high season. As ever, it's a question of wandering around and asking everywhere: the places up the backstreets lack the sea views but are quieter and usually the last to fill. The relaxed **youth hostel** (☎0832/31-560; ①) has moved to the rear of the town (follow the signs from the road heading inland next to Monza Travel) where its buildings are surrounded by an olive grove. There's also a **campsite**, *Camping Apollonia* (☎0832/31-507, fax 31-607) on the right as you enter the town, which although small and cramped has good facilities and a pool.

When things get tight or you simply fancy a quieter location, the beaches to the east and west (see below) can be great places to escape the crowds. Wherever you stay, be warned that Plakiás is periodically plagued with **mosquitoes**: the pyrethrin coils or electric devices sold locally are the most effective deterrent.

Pension Afroditi (☎ & fax 0832/31-266). A charming pension in a gleaming white building with spotless en-suite rooms and lots of cascading bougainvillea. Located at the back of the village, near the youth hostel, it also rents apartments. ③.

Ammoudi Hotel (☎0832/31-355). Friendly and good-value place 3km east at Amoúdhi Beach; isolated, with a good taverna and balcony rooms 100m from the shore. ②.

Christos Taverna (☎0832/31-472). Balcony rooms with bath overlooking the west end of the beach above the taverna of the same name. Try for rooms on the sea side as those at the rear overlook the noisy road. ②.

Eolus (☎0832/31-287). Tempting fate by naming their good-value rooms place after the god of the winds, the hospitable couple here have some rooms with bath, just in from the sea along the road running inland from Monza Travel. ①. The nearby *Rooms Nefeli* (②) is another possibility for rooms with bath and fridge.

Ippokambos (☎0832/31-525) Delightful new rooms place at the back of the town on the street running behind the sea. All rooms come with bath and balcony. ②.

Hotel Livikon (☎0832/31-216). Right by where the buses stop along the seafront, the sea view rooms overlook the road and can be noisy. ②.

Hotel Paleos Alianthos Beach (☎0832/31-851, fax 31-197). On the sea at the eastern end of the beach. Not a bad option if you're looking for something more upmarket. All en-suite rooms have air conditioning and there's a pool, bar and a taverna on site; don't confuse this with the similarly named and overpriced place behind. ③.

Hotel Phoenix (☎0832/31-331, fax 31-831). Two kilometres west near Soúda Beach, this modern hotel has sea-view balcony rooms with breakfast included. ④.

Secret Nest Taverna, on the main street which heads inland from near the bridge (☎0832/31-235). This restaurant has a few pleasant rooms upstairs. ②.

Stefanakis Rooms, the west end of the beach (☎0832/32-027, fax 31-632). Simple, good-value balcony rooms. Enquire at the nearby *Bar Smerna* if there's nobody around. ②.

Eating and drinking

Right on the seafront at the centre of town is a growing strip of **tavernas** and bars with tables right out by the water, none of them terribly cheap (in fact food is generally costly here by Cretan standards); for **breakfast**, the *Argo Fourno* does excellent *tirópita* and *spanakópita*. *Sofia's* here is almost the longest-established place in town, serving huge portions of reasonably good food; *Gorgona* next door is very similar. Slightly further west the veteran *Christos*, opened in 1949, is a bit cheaper, with a pleasant tamarisk-shaded terrace and usually at least one vegetarian dish. Near the bridge at the entrance to the town, *Lysseos* strives for a more romantic atmosphere. The ambience and food seem rather more authentically Cretan at another cluster of places round the corner from *Christos*, facing west along the shore: *Kedros*, *Glaros* and *Taverna Sunset* each have their devotees and all make a fair stab at the usual staples. There are also a few places worth seeking out behind the seafront; at the eastern end, *Taverna Medusa* is a great little place serving meat and fish dishes on a terrace; to get there take the street leading inland from Monza Tours, and turn right. On the way here you'll pass *Nikos Souvlaki*, which dishes out the cheapest meals in town often with some impromptu *bouzoúkia* thrown in. Finally, behind the seafront, the *Secret Nest Taverna* (see "Accommodation" above) offers fish dishes served on a pleasant terrace.

Bars and nightlife

Nightlife in Plakiás is best described as sedate, especially when compared to the excesses of the north coast or even neighbouring Ayía Galíni. The few **bars** don't take much finding, since the music will lead you there. Most are lined up on the waterfront, keeping people who stay here awake. *Smerna*, a new cocktail bar at the western end of the seafront is run by an ebullient Austrian scuba diver – the house special, "Blue Moon", is recommended. *Ostraco* is another lively place operating on two tiers with a balcony to ogle the passing crowds. Real late-nighters can move on to the fancy *Club Bahalos* on the seafront, or to the far less pretentious *Meltemi* dancing bar, in a wooden hut out near *Camping Apollonia*. Things don't start to liven up here till midnight or so.

Beaches

Getting to the **beach** need involve no more than a two-minute walk. The town is set at the western end of the bay, and east of the paved harbour grey sand curves around in an unbroken line to the headland 1km or more away. Unfortunately this beach is not as good close up as it appears from a distance. The long open sweep of the bay means it can be exposed and windy, and the strong summer **winds** do seem to affect Plakiás more than other places along this coast. Peaceful rooms places in this zone include *Panorama* and *Finikas* (both ①); look for the signs to each on the main road in from Réthimnon. There's plenty of space – especially towards the far end where there's a large hotel and a beach bar – but you'll find much better sands beyond the headland at Damnóni (see below), or to the west at Soúda Beach.

Soúda Beach is just over half an hour's walk west of town, past signs of encroaching development, and there are places to stop for a swim along the way. The sand is grey and coarse, but there's plenty of room and the water at the far end is reasonably sheltered. Above the very end of the beach, the *Galini* taverna enjoys a lovely position in a miniature palm grove.

Damnóni and Lefkóyia

Just to the east of Plakiás Bay, beyond a headland riddled with caves and wartime bunkers and gun emplacements, lie some of the most tempting beaches in central Crete, albeit a very poorly kept secret. Three splashes of yellow sand, divided by rocky promontories, go by the general name of **Damnóni**. The easiest way to get there without transport is **by boat** which leaves the harbour at Plakiás daily (April–Oct) at 10.30am. To get there on foot, follow the main road east and turn right along a track which leads through the olive groves. After a while you'll see the beach below you and a path which runs down to it – about thirty minutes in all. Alternatively, but slightly longer, you can walk right to the end of the beach, past the big hotel, and on over the headland. Driving, you have to go much further round: follow the road towards Lefkóyia and turn down at the sign for Damnóni or, much further on, for Amoúdhi.

Damnóni Beach itself is the first you reach, and the only one that has so far really seen the beginning of the development: work on a big new hotel, the *Minoan Prince*, going up on the heights behind, has been stalled for years whilst the western half of the beach has been colonized by a Swiss-owned holiday village, and piles of concrete boxes are now stacked up the hill overlooking what was once a beautiful bay. On the road in, the beach's original rooms place, the charming *Pension Sokrates* (☎ & fax 0832/31-480; ②) is still going strong and maintains its serenity by means of a dense surrounding garden filled with palms, jasmine and bougainvillea. Whether you want to make use of the other undeniably pleasant rooms, studios and more expensive apartments here will depend on your attitude to the concrete invasion. There are still two **tavernas** on the beach, a wonderfully long strip of yellow sand and super-clear water. The *Taverna Damnoni*, fronting the sand, always seems very unfriendly; they also have some particularly dank rooms to rent. The *Taverna Akti*, just behind, is a better bet for food and service.

At the far eastern end of Damnóni Beach you'll still find a few people who've dispensed with their clothes, and the little cove which shelters the middle of the three beaches (a scramble over the rocks, or there's a just-passable track) is entirely nudist. This little enclave can get very crowded, and at times looks like an illustration from *Health and Efficiency* magazine – blow-up beach balls and all – but it's a good-humoured crowd and, exceptionally, there are usually quite a few Greek naturists, too. Again, the water is beautiful and there are caves at the back of the beach (around which people camp) and rocks to dive from. There's some great snorkelling to be had around these rocks with their caves and passages. Continuing over the rocks you pass another tiny pocket of sand (also nudist) before **Amoúdhi Beach**, where there's a rather more sedate atmosphere and another taverna (very friendly, with much better rooms for rent; see Plakiás "Accommodation" on pp.234–5). Further west still you can reach **Skínaria Beach** – another fine strip of sand – now also approachable from the main road and along a track signed to the *Skinaria Beach Hotel* (☎0832/31-295; ③). There's a **taverna** here too, the *Lybian Star*.

If lying on beaches was your only plan, you'd have less far to walk, and probably spend less, staying in the village of **LEFKÓYIA** rather than Plakiás. Lefkóyia is barely twenty minutes' walk from Amoúdhi and has a couple of supermarkets, four or five pleasant rooms places, and a couple of tavernas (try *Stelios*) by the main road; its chief disadvantage is that it is not itself on the coast, and that it has no other facilities. For the people who stay here, these are also its chief advantages. Don't, incidentally, try to walk to the *Beach Hotel* signposted from the village – it is an extremely long way.

Moní Préveli and Palm Beach

Some 6km southeast of Lefkóyia the celebrated **Monastery of Préveli** (daily 9am–2pm & 4–7.30pm; winter 9am–5pm; 500dr) perches high above the sea. In World War II the monks here provided shelter for Allied troops stranded on the island after the Battle of Crete, feeding the soldiers and organizing them into groups to be taken off nearby beaches by submarine. There's a monument commemorating the evacuations and, alongside the icons in the church, a number of offerings from grateful individuals and governments. The church also houses a cross said to contain a fragment of the True Cross; there's a small museum with other relics and religious vestments; and a fountain in the courtyard with the Greek inscription "Wash your sins, not only your face". There are also fine views out to sea towards the distant and chunky-looking Paximádhia islands which have lent their name to the tooth-cracking lumps of twice-baked bread served up with mezédhes in the island's kafenía.

The road to Préveli turns off the main road between Lefkóyia and Asómatos, now a paved surface which descends into the fertile valley of the Megapótamos river – which, unusually for Crete, flows throughout the year – before it eventually climbs towards the monastery. A couple of kilometres before the Préveli monastery you pass the ruined **Monastery of Áyios Ioánnis** (called Káto, or lower, Préveli) the site of the original sixteenth-century monastery. It was used by the community prior to Abbot Prévelis' decision during the following century to seek out the greater safety of the monastery's present site. It was torched by the Turks in the last century and long abandoned; only the church now stands complete amid the broken walls, cattle mangers and derelict dwellings once used by the monks. Nevertheless it's an atmospheric place to wander around: the church is open and retains its wooden *ikonostásis*, and nearby there's a beautiful courtyard with a vine trellis which provides plenty of shade.

Palm Beach

Earlier still you'll have passed an ancient-looking bridge (actually a nineteenth-century copy of a Venetian original), where a sign indicates a left turn to a taverna and Palm Beach. Almost immediately you turn right, shortly crossing another cobbled Venetian bridge, beyond which the track leads eventually (after perhaps twenty minutes' tortuous, rough driving) to *Amudi* rooms/taverna (②), one of two on a not terribly attractive beach alongside Palm Beach. From here it's a ten-minute scramble around the cliff, a narrow, slippery path for which you need decent shoes and at least one hand free to hold on with – though once you've managed the first bit it gets a lot easier. Alternatively, you can head down the cliffs from Préveli, which is even tougher: a track (barely driveable, or a 15min walk) takes off about 1km before the monastery, and at the end a marked path clambers steeply down over the rocks, for about thirty minutes. If you don't feel confident of climbing, the boat will get you here with a great deal less fuss.

Sadly, **Palm Beach** is no longer worth all this effort – at least not if you're here in the middle of the season. It still looks beautiful – a sand-filled cove right at the end of the Kourtaliótiko gorge, where a freshwater estuary feeds a little oasis complete with palm grove and cluster of oleanders – but too many visitors have ruined it. If you do come (and at the beginning of the season it's still lovely), take all your rubbish away with you. Behind the beach, you can walk up the palm-lined riverbanks or paddle through the icy water upstream. Lots of people camp along the banks, a lovely setting, but again they have no way of disposing of their rubbish and sewage. Further upstream, before the gorge becomes too steep to follow, are a couple of deep pools nice to swim in. On the west edge of the beach, a small bar sells drinks and a few basic provisions, mostly tinned. A strange thought as you lie on the crowded sands here is that it was from here, fifty years ago, that many of the soldiers who sought refuge at the monastery were eventually evacuated by submarine.

West of Plakiás: Sellía and Rodhákino

Heading west from Plakiás, towards Frangokástello, it's a stiff climb up towards Mírthios and then round, hugging the mountainside, to **SELLÍA**. Looking up from Plakiás or across from Mírthios you would imagine that Sellía had the best views of all over this area, but if you do no more than drive through you see nothing – it is the backs of the houses which face out towards Africa. If you want to stop and take a look it's easy enough to find a path through or, better still, head for the church and cemetery at the western edge of town. There's a track from the centre of the village down to Plakiás, about thirty minutes' walk steeply below, and there's a pleasant long circular hike from Plakiás up here and then back down via Mírthios. Drivers and bikers heading west from here would be advised to check their fuel as there is no official garage before Hóra Sfakíon.

Beyond Sellía the nature of the country changes and there's a real feeling of the approach of western Crete. The road runs high above a series of capes and small coves, quite a good surface all the way apart from a brief unpaved section just outside Argoulés. The only village of any size is **RODHÁKINO**, set on steep streets above a ravine which leads down to the small, grey sand and shingle beach of Koraka, where General Kreipe was finally taken off the island after his kidnap in 1944. There are a couple of good **rooms** places here, both offering studio-style facilities with kitchenette. One, *Rooms Yiannidakis* (☎0832/31-663; ②), is set back from the beach near a new chapel, whilst the other, *Sunrise* (☎0832/31-787; ②) has a **taverna** with a rooftop terrace and fine view. A little to the west of here, Polirizio beach in the next bay along has another rooms place, *Panorama* (☎0832/31-788; ①), together with a taverna.

Beyond Rodhákino on the main road west, a number of beaches look incredibly tempting far below, but only one is at all easy to get to: heading down a vertiginous dirt track just before the tarmac on the main road runs out near to Argoulés.

GREEK PLACE NAMES

ΑΓ ΓΑΛΗΝΗ	Αγ Γαλήνη	Ay. Galíni
ΑΝΩΓΙΕΑ	Ανώγεια	Anóyia
ΑΣΙΓΩΝΙΑ	Ασιγωνία	Asigonía
ΑΞΟΣ	Αξός	Axós
ΕΠΙΣΚΟΠΗ	Επιοκοπή	Episkopí
ΘΡΟΝΟΣ	Θρόνος	Thrónos
ΚΑΜΑΡΕΣ	Καμάρες	Kamáres
ΛΕΥΚΟΓΕΙΑ	Λευκόγεια	Lefkóyia
Μ. ΑΡΚΑΔΙΟΥ	Μ. Αρκαδίου	Arkádhi monastery
ΜΠΑΛΙ	Μπαλί	Balí
ΜΥΡΘΙΟΣ	Μύρθιος	Mírthios
ΠΕΡΑΜΑ	Πέραμα	Pérama
ΠΛΑΚΙΑΣ	Πλακιάς	Plakiás
ΠΡΕΒΕΛΙ	Πρέβελι	Préveli
ΡΕΘΥΜΝΟ	Ρεθυμνο	Réthimnon
ΣΠΗΛΙ	Σπήλι	Spíli
ΦΟΥΡΦΟΥΡΑΣ	Φουρφουράς	Fourfourás
ΨΗΛΟΡΕΙΤΗΣ	Ψηλορείτης	Psilorítis

travel details

Buses

Ayía Galíni to: Festós (6 daily; 7.45am–4.15pm; 30min); Hóra Sfakíon (1 daily at 7am; 2hr 30min); Iráklion (7 daily; 8am–8pm; 2hr); Plakiás (daily at 6.30am, 9am and 2.30pm; 1hr 30min); Réthimnon (daily at 6.30am, noon, 2.30pm and 4pm; 1hr 30min).

Plakiás to: Ayía Galíni (daily at 10.30am and 7pm; 1hr 30min); Réthimnon (6 daily; 7am–5pm; 45min).

Réthimnon to: Amári (2 daily; 1hr); Anóyia (2 daily; 5.30am and 2.30pm; 1hr 30min); Arkádhi (daily at 6am, 10.30am and 2.30pm; 50min);

Ay. Galíni (4 daily at 7am, 10.30am, 12.45pm, and 2.15pm; 1hr 30min) ; Haniá (20 daily; 7am–10pm; 1hr 30min–3hr); Iráklion (20 daily; 6.30am–9.45pm; 1hr 30min–2hr); Omalós (daily at 6.15am and 7am; 2hr 30min); Plakiás (6 daily; 6am–4pm; 45min); Spíli (daily at 7am, 9am, 10.30am, 12.45pm, 2.15pm; 40min). *Some of these services are restricted on Sunday.*

Ferries

To Pireás Daily at 7.30pm.
To Thíra Seasonal day-trips (Tues & Thurs).

CHAPTER FOUR

HANIÁ

Haniá, Crete's westernmost province, is still its least visited, which is alone a significant part of its attraction. And although tourist development is spreading fast, and has already covered much of the coast around Haniá, the west is likely to remain one of the emptier parts of the island, partly because there are no large sand beaches to accommodate resort hotels, partly because the great archeological sites are a long way from here. In their place are some of the most classic elements of the island: scattered coves, unexploited rural villages, and a spectacular vista of mountains.

The city of **Haniá**, island capital until 1971, is reason in itself to come; unequivocally the most enjoyable of Crete's larger towns, it is littered with oddments from its Venetian and Turkish past, and bustles with harbourside life. To either side, almost along the whole **north coast** of the province, spreads a line of sandy beach – at times exposed, and increasingly developed, but still with numerous reaches where you can escape the crowds. The expanse of sand is broken by three peninsulas: **Akrotíri**, enclosing the magnificent natural harbour of the **Bay of Soúdha**; **Rodhópou**, a bare and roadless tract of mountain; and, at the western tip of the island, **Gramvoúsa**, uninhabited and entirely barren. Akrotíri is overshadowed by NATO, with air bases on land and naval installations in the bay, but it's still worth a day-trip, with a couple of excellent beaches, **Stavrós** above all, and two beautiful monasteries. Most of the region's tourists stay to the west, on the coast between Haniá and Rodhópou, in one of a number of villages now joined together by a string of low-key development through **Ayía Marína** and **Plataniás**, with the villas and apartments thinning out as you head further from the city.

The south is overshadowed by the peaks of the **Lefká Óri** – the White Mountains – whose grey bulk, snowcapped from January through to June, dominates every view in western Crete. Although marginally less high and considerably less famous than the Psilorítis range, they're far more rewarding for walking or climbing. Along the south coast the mountains drop straight to the Libyan Sea and the few towns here lie in their shadow, clinging to what flat land can be found around the bays. Through the heart of the massif there's no road at all, nor is there any driveable route along the south coast: unless you want to travel back and forth across the island you'll have to rely on boats here, or on walking. Despite the summer hordes who thunder through the National Park in the **Gorge of Samariá**, Europe's longest gorge, the hike is still a stunning experience. With a little spirit of adventure and preparation there are scores of other, deserted **hiking** routes to take.

The south-coast communities beneath the mountains see plenty of visitors, mostly gorge-trippers passing through, but none could really be described as a resort. **Ayía Rouméli** and **Loutró** can be reached only on foot or by boat, although this hasn't prevented Ayía Rouméli, the end-point of the Samariá gorge walk, from becoming crowded and somewhat overdeveloped; if you want somewhere to unwind after your exertions, the serenity of Loutró is a much better bet. **Hóra Sfakíon**, the capital of the wild region known as Sfakiá, is a pleasant enough place to stay if you can handle the influx of day-trippers; far more peace is to be found down the coast a little, at the superb beaches by the Venetian castle of **Frangokástello**.

The west end of the island, beyond Rodhópou, is very sparsely populated. The port of **Kastélli** is the only town of any size, and there's a growing resort at **Paleohóra** in the south. **Soúyia** may be the next in line, but for the moment it seems in a rather charming state of limbo. The whole of the mountainous south-western corner, an area known as **Sélinos**, is worth exploring, with rough roads leading to untouched mountain villages and little-known ruins and churches. On the west-facing coast – hard to get to but well worth the effort – are two of Crete's finest beaches, **Falásarna** and **Elafonísi**.

THE NORTH COAST

Using **Haniá** as a base, getting around the **north coast** is easy enough: it's a heavily populated region with excellent roads and a stream of buses along the main routes. Trying to get off the beaten track presents more of a problem if you're dependent on public transport. On Rodhópou, for example, there are no services at all, and while most inland villages are served by at least a couple of daily buses, it can be frustrating if you want to get to several in a day.

Renting a vehicle or motorcycle, then, is a good investment, and there are plenty of outlets in Haniá (see "Listings" on p.260). Just remember that this is mountainous country – the smaller mopeds are (more or less) all right for one person but with two people on board they simply won't make it up many of the hills.

Haniá

HANIÁ, as any of its residents will tell you, is the spiritual capital of Crete, even if the title is now officially bestowed on Iráklion's urban sprawl. With its shimmering waterfront, crumbling masonry and web of alleys, it is an extraordinarily attractive city, especially if you can catch it in spring when the Lefká Óri's snowcapped peaks seem to hover above the roofs. The permanent population – fast expanding into hill and coastal suburbs – always outnumbers the tourists, although in August visitors seem to run them pretty close. It all adds up to a city worth getting to know, where you'll almost certainly stay longer than you intended, making use of plentiful accommodation, excellent markets, stores and nightlife, and most other facilities.

Some history

Haniá's recent history, in which it featured as a hotbed of nationalist sentiment under the Turks, as well as its proximity to the scene of most of the heavy fighting in the Battle of Crete, has left it with little in the way of monuments. Yet it's one of the longest continuously inhabited city sites anywhere in the world, and remains an enticing place to wander round, with odd reminders of the past at every pace and antiquities in the most unlikely settings.

As **Kydonia**, it was a Minoan community of obscure status: only scattered remnants have so far been brought to light, but many believe that there's a major **palace** still to be discovered somewhere in the vicinity, perhaps beneath modern buildings on the Kastélli hill overlooking the harbour, where

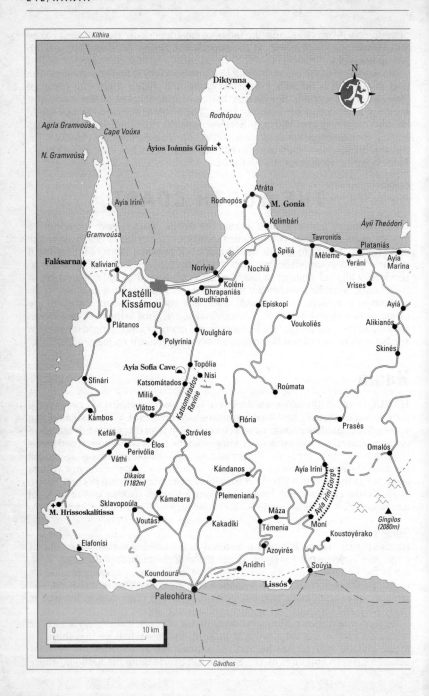

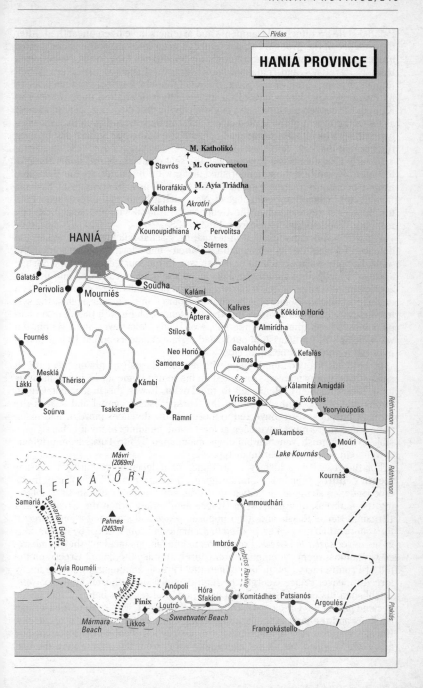

HANIÁ PROVINCE

Piréas

M. Katholikó
Stavrós
M. Gouvernetou
Horafákia
M. Ayía Triádha
Kalathás
Akrotíri
HANIÁ
Kounoupidhianá
Pervolítsa
Stérnes
Galatás
Perivolia
Soúdha
Kalámi
Mourniés
Kalíves
Kókkino Horió
Aptera
Almirídha
Stílos
Fournés
Gavalohóri
Kefalás
Neo Horió
Vámos
Mesklá
Samonas
Thériso
E 75
Lákki
Kámbi
Kálamitsi Amigdáli
Vrísses
Exópolis
Soúrva
Tsakístra
Ramní
Yeoryioúpolis
Alíkambos
Moúri
Máyri
(2069m)
Lake Kournás
LEFKÁ ÓRI
Kournás
Samariá
Ammoudhári
Pahnes
(2453m)
Imbrós
Ayía Rouméli
Anópoli
Hóra
Sfakíon
Komitádhes
Patsianós
Argoulés
Fínix
Loutró
Mármara
Beach
Likkos
Sweetwater Beach
Frangokástello

Réthimnon
Réthimnon
Plakiás

Palatial-style architectural fragments and artefacts have been unearthed. After the collapse of the Minoan palace culture, it grew into one of the island's most important cities – well enough known for its citizens to warrant a mention in Homer's *Odyssey* – and remained so through the Classical Greek era. When Rome came in search of conquest, the city mounted a stiff resistance prior to its eventual capitulation in 69 BC, after which it flourished once more. The Kastélli hill served as the Roman city's acropolis, but dwellings spread at least as far as the extent of the walled city which can be seen today. Roman mosaics from this era have been discovered beneath the Cathedral Square and up near the present market.

In early Christian times Kydonia was the seat of a bishop, and under the protection of Byzantium the city flourished along with the island. As the Byzantine Empire became increasingly embattled however, so its further outposts, Kydonia (and Crete) included, suffered neglect. Not much is heard of the place again until the thirteenth century, when the Genoese (with local support) seized the city from the Venetians and held it from 1263 to 1285.

When the Venetians finally won it back they acted quickly to strengthen the defences, turning the city – renamed **La Canea** – into a formidable bulwark in the west. The city walls were built in two stages. In the fourteenth century Kastélli alone was fortified: within these walls stood the original cathedral and the city administration. Later, in the sixteenth century, new walls were constructed as a defence against constant raids by pirate corsairs – in particular against the systematic ravages of Barbarossa. It is these defences, along with the Venetian harbour installations, that define the shape of Haniá's old town today. Within the walls, meanwhile, a flourish of public and private construction left La Canea perhaps the island's most beautiful city.

In 1645, after a two-month siege with terrible losses (mostly on the Turkish side – their commander was executed on his return home for losing as many as forty thousand men), Haniá fell to the **Turks**. It was the first major Cretan stronghold to succumb, becoming the Turkish island capital and seat of the pasha. Churches were converted to mosques, the defences more or less maintained, and there must have been at least some building: today it is barely possible to distinguish Venetian buildings maintained by the Turks from originals of Venetian or Turkish workmanship.

For the rest, it is a history of struggle: for independence during the **nineteenth century**, then in **resistance** against the Germans in World War II. In the independence struggle, the city's most dramatic moment came in 1897, following the outbreak of war between Greece and Turkey, when the Great Powers (Britain, France, Russia and Italy) imposed peace and stationed a joint force in the waters off Haniá – an event used to dramatic and comic effect by Kazantzákis in his novel *Zorba the Greek*. From here, in one famous incident, they bombarded Cretan insurgents attempting prematurely to raise the flag of Greece on the hill of Profítis Elías (see p.261). When the Turkish administrators were finally forced to leave, Prince George, the high commissioner chosen by the powers, established his capital here for the brief period of regency before Crete finally became part of the Greek state. During **World War II**, with most of the German landings and the bulk of the fighting on the coast immediately west of the city, Haniá suffered severe bombardment, the destruction eventually compounded by a fire which wiped out almost everything apart from the area around the harbour. In the final six months of their occupation of the island, the Germans withdrew to a heavily defended perimeter centred on the city. In the postwar period, the town was rebuilt, and sprawling, traffic-congested suburbs now encircle the ancient core. The arrival of **tourism** has inspired the will – if not the resources – to save and restore much of the city's crumbling architectural heritage, and Haniá is currently enjoying a period of peace and prosperity unrivalled in its modern history.

Arrival and information

Arriving by **boat**, you'll anchor at the port and naval base of **Soúdha**, at the head of the magnificent Bay of Soúdha, an approach which offers unparalleled views of the Lefká Óri as you near the island. Soúdha itself is about 10km from Haniá and city buses run approximately every fifteen minutes from here to Haniá market-place, although these can be swamped when the ferries arrive – you might be better off taking a taxi (about 1500dr) from the square right by the dock. You wouldn't choose to stay in Soúdha – the hotels are sited right above the constant traffic of the main road and it's a grubby, dusty, concrete little place. Fortunately there's no real need to stay: most ferries arrive first thing in the morning and leave in the evening. If you are stuck you'll find just about everything on the square right by the ferries: stores, a bank, a post office, a couple of bars and restaurants and two inexpensive hotels.

The city's brand new **airport** is about 15km out, in the middle of the Akrotíri peninsula. There are only two buses from here to the centre (currently 5.40am & 6pm), so you'll probably need a taxi if you're not being picked up by a package-tour bus. Plentiful taxis meet the flights and the journey to Haniá costs about 2500dr; the official prices to other popular destinations are listed at the rank.

The **bus station** is on Odhós Kidhonías, within easy walking distance of the centre. There's a left-luggage facility here if you want to leave your bags while you find a room.

Arriving by **car** can be a nightmare once you hit the harbour area and get tangled up in the one-way system and no-parking zones. In fact, finding anywhere to park at all within the walls of the old town can verge on the impossible in high season – besides which many of the more attractive hotels simply can't be reached by car, though some of the bigger places will provide you with porter's trolleys. The least stressful solutions are to park outside the old town and walk in to find accommodation, or opt for a place such as the *Xenia* or *Argo* hotels (see below) which have their own car parks. As a car is near useless inside the old walled city and distances are easily walkable anyway, there's a lot to be said for parking it up for the duration of your stay. Longer-term parking places can usually be found along Aktí Kanári to the west of the Naval Museum, near the seafront: make sure not to leave any valuables in the car.

The combined and very helpful **EOT** and **Municipal Tourist Office** (Mon–Fri 8am–2.30pm; ☎ & fax 92-624) is at Kriári 40, just east of Platía 1866, on the ground floor of the Mégaro Pántheon building. For ticket and **departure** information, see the relevant entries in "Listings", pp.260–1.

The phone code for Haniá is ☎0821.

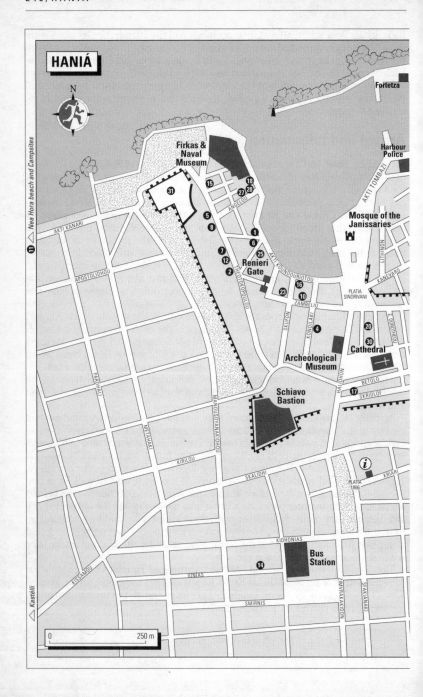

HANIÁ

N

11 ◁ Nea Hora beach and Campsites

Fortetza

Firkas & Naval Museum

Harbour Police

AKTI TOMBAZI

Mosque of the Janissaries

AKTI KANARI

31

15

18

27 28

ANGELOU

5

8

1

6

25

7

12

2

THEOTOKOPOULOU

Renieri Gate

23

16

10

ZAMBELIU

MOUNDOURIOTOU

PLATIA SINDRIVANI

NONIMITI

KANEVARO

E.DOROTHEOU

APOSTOLIOHOU

SKUFON

KONTILAKI

4

20

30

Cathedral

PARDHALI

METAHAKI

MANDUSOYANAKIDHOU

Archeological Museum

HALIDHON

BETOLO

17

SKRIDLOF

Schiavo Bastion

KIRILOU

SKALIDHI

i

PLATIA 1866

KRIARI

KISSAMOU

IONIAS

KIDHONIAS

14

Bus Station

ZIMVRAKAKIDHON

SFAKIANAKI

SMIRNIS

◁ Kastélli

0   250 m

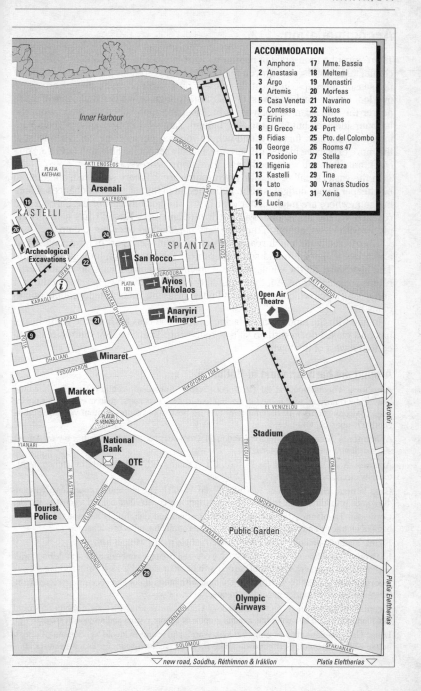

ACCOMMODATION

1	Amphora	17	Mme. Bassia
2	Anastasia	18	Meltemi
3	Argo	19	Monastiri
4	Artemis	20	Morfeas
5	Casa Veneta	21	Navarino
6	Contessa	22	Nikos
7	Eirini	23	Nostos
8	El Greco	24	Port
9	Fidias	25	Pto. del Colombo
10	George	26	Rooms 47
11	Posidonio	27	Stella
12	Ifigenia	28	Thereza
13	Kastelli	29	Tina
14	Lato	30	Vranas Studios
15	Lena	31	Xenia
16	Lucia		

Inner Harbour

PLATIA KATEHAKI

Arsenali

AKTI ENOSEOS

KALERGON

KASTÉLLI

SIFAKA

SPIANTZA

Archeological Excavations

San Rocco

VOURDOUBA

PLATIA 1821

Ayios Nikolaos

KARAOLI

SARPAKI

Anaryiri Minaret

FOTIE

DHALIANI

Minaret

TSOUDHERON

Market

YIANARI

PLATIA S. VENIZELOU

National Bank

OTE

N. PLASTIRA

Tourist Police

VELOUDHAKIDHON

APOKORONOU

SARPDONA

SIFAKA

IKAROU

MINOOS

AKTI MIAOULI

Argo

Open Air Theatre

KIPRIU

NIKOFOROU FOKA

EL VENIZELOU

Stadium

TRIKUPI

KORAI

DIMOKRATIAS

TZANAKAKI

Public Garden

HONDAK

Olympic Airways

KORNAROU

SOLOMOU

SFAKIANAKI

Akrotíri

Platía Eleftherías

Accommodation

There must be thousands of **rooms to rent** in Haniá and, unusually, quite a few comfortable **hotels**, though you may face a long search for a bed at the height of the season. Perhaps the most desirable rooms (with prices to match) are those overlooking the **harbour**, west of Hálidhon, though be warned that some of those nearer the water can be noisy at night. Most are approached not direct from the harbourside itself but from the alley behind, Zambelíu, or from other streets leading off the harbour further round (where you may get more peace). The nicest of the more expensive places are here too, usually set back a little way (and thus quieter), but often still with good views from upper storeys.

In the eastern half of the **old town** rooms are far more scattered, and tend to be cheaper if your budget is tight. In the height of the season your chances of finding somewhere are much better over here. Immediately east of the harbour and reached via the alleys that lead north off Kanevaró, **Kastélli** has some lovely places with views, although they are very popular and often booked up.

There's really not much reason to stay in the modern part of town, unless you arrive late and need to find somewhere near the bus station on your first night. The hotels are, on the whole, soulless business establishments, and many of the rooms are uninspiring. Another possibility is close to the town beaches at the east and west fringes which are quiet and often pleasant: we've listed a couple of bargains here.

In line with the funding crisis facing Greek hostels as a whole, the youth hostel has now closed down with no sign of reopening. There are two **campsites** located to the west of the town.

Around the harbour: west of Hálidhon

Amphora, Theotokopóulou 20 (☎ & fax 93-224). Fourteenth-century Venetian building, beautifully renovated with some interesting features such as spiral staircases and four-poster beds. Balcony rooms with harbour view are the best value; rooms without view are significantly cheaper. ⑤.

Apartments Anastasia, Theotokopóulou 21 (☎88-001, fax 46-582). Worth a try for longer stays or if you want to self-cater. ④.

Artemis, Kondiláki 13 (☎ & fax 91-196). Clean rooms with bath and use of kitchen in this touristy street running inland from Zambelíu. ④.

Casa Veneta, Theotokopóulou 57 (☎90-007, fax 75-931). The charming proprietor offers studio rooms with kitchenette in a new building cunningly constructed behind a Venetian facade.

Contessa, Theofánous 15 (☎98-566). Another small and delightfully renovated hotel with bags of character and harbour views from some rooms. Includes breakfast. ⑤.

Eirini, Theotokopóulou 13 (☎93-909). Clean, simple rooms without bath. ②.

El Greco, Theotokopóulou 49 (☎90-432). Ivy-covered frontage conceals comfortable hotel with decent rooms in a quiet street; roof garden with harbour view. Will assist with parking. ④.

George, Zambelíu 30 (☎88-715). Old building with steep stairs and eccentric antique furniture – rooms vary in price according to position and size. ②.

Ifigenia, Theotokopóulou 15 (☎ & fax 94-357). Good-value rooms with bath in another restored Venetian mansion. The owner has a small empire of similar rooms and studios nearby. ③.

Lena, Theotokopóulou 60 (☎ & fax 72-265). Wonderful rooms in an old wooden-built Turkish house with a charming German owner. Has its own café downstairs for lazy breakfasts. ③.

Lucia, Aktí Koundouriótou (☎90-302). Harbourfront hotel with balcony rooms. Less expensive than you might expect for one of the best views in town, although the rooms at the back are less inviting. ③.

Meltemi, Angélou 2 (☎92-802). First in a little row of possibilities well located on the far side of the harbour, this pension may be noisier than its neighbours, but has en-suite rooms with fabulous views and a good café downstairs. ③.

Nostos, Zambelíu 42 (☎94-743, fax 94-740). Stylish studios with fridge and kitchenette in converted Venetian mansion. Some rooms with sea view and charming roof terrace overlooking the harbour. ⑤.

Porto del Colombo, Theofánous and Moschon, near the Renieri Gate (☎ & fax 70–945). Similar to the *Amphora*, though slightly darker and more old-fashioned, this hotel occupies a building they claim was once the French Embassy and later home of Eleftheríos Venizélos. All rooms with TV and mini-bar. ④.

Stella, Angélou 10 (☎73-756) Creaky, but charmingly eccentric old house close to the *Hotel Piraeus*, with plain, clean rooms with bath above a ceramics shop. ③.

Thereza, Angélou 8 (☎92-798). Beautiful old pension in great position with stunning views from its roof terrace and some rooms; classy decor too. More expensive than its neighbours but deservedly so; you'd be well advised to book ahead in high season. ⑤.

Xenia, Theotokopóulou 88 (☎91-238). This rather anonymous contemporary building is typical of the state-owned Xenia chain, but modern rooms all come with fully functioning facilities, balcony and sea view, and there's a car park. ⑤.

The old city: east of Hálidhon

Fidias, Sarpáki 8 (☎52-494). Signposted from the cathedral. This pension is a favourite backpackers' meeting place: rather bizarrely run, but extremely friendly and with the real advantage of offering single rooms or arranging shares. ①.

Kastelli, Kaneváro 39 (☎57-057, fax 45-314). Not the prettiest location, but comfortable, modern, reasonably priced, and very quiet at the back. The proprietor is exceptionally helpful and also has a few apartments and a beautiful house (for up to five people) to rent. Will assist with parking. ③.

Madame Bassia, Betolo 51, near the cathedral (☎56-440). An unpromising exterior conceals renovated rooms with bath and balcony. The sprightly, eponymous proprietor speaks fluent French, but has never been off the island. ③.

Monastiri, Ay. Markou 18, off Kaneváro (☎54-776). Simple rooms, some with sea view and bath, in the restored ruins of a Venetian monastery. Roof terrace with view and car park. ③.

Morfeas, Isódhion 15 (☎40-619). Between the Cathedral Square and Platía Sindrívani, in first street parallel to Hálidhon. Rather dark, but good value for so central a position. ②.

Navarino, Sarpáki 67 (☎71-083). Pleasant, good-value rooms with shared bath. ②.

Nikos, Dhaskaloyiánnis 63 (☎54-783). Níkos's hotel is the only one in Haniá built directly on top of a Minoan ruin – visible through a basement window as you enter – with a beautiful and rare 3500-year-old painted pillar. Good-value relatively modern rooms, all with shower. ②.

Port, near the Arsenali (☎59-484, fax 42-797). Pleasant and efficient rooms with bath and balcony. ③.

Rooms 47, Kandanoléon 47 (☎53-243). Quiet, traditional rooms place on street leading up from Kaneváro into Kastélli. Some rooms have balconies with great sea views. ②.

Vranas Studios, Ay. Dhéka & Kalinákou Sarpáki, near the cathedral (☎58-618). Pleasant spacious studio rooms with TV and air-conditioning, fridge and kitchenette. ④.

The modern city

Argo, Míaouli Beach at the start of Aktí Míaouli near the eastern wall (☎40-980). Truly charming and good-value old-style hotel with great sea-view rooms with bath, in a vibrant area away from the tourist maelstrom. There's a car park too. ③.

Lato, Ionías 8 (☎95-088). Hotel with good rooms and very handy for the bus station. Easy parking. ③.

Posidonio Moní Gonías, corner of Aktí Papanikóli (☎ & fax 93-572). A new hotel right on the beachfront road, behind the town beach, which means some way from everything else. A good deal for seafront location and easy parking. ③.

Tina, Boniali 3 (☎41-195). Functional hotel in a backstreet location just off Tzanakáki near the Public Gardens. Quiet and comfortable, and may have rooms when other places are full. Easy parking. ③.

Campsites

Camping Hania (☎31-138). Behind the beach, 4km west of Haniá, just about walking distance if you follow the coast around, but more easily reached by taking the local bus (see p.255). There's a large sign to tell you where to get off; walk down towards the sea for about five minutes through a patch of new development. The site itself is rather basic, but lovely: small, shady, and just a short walk from a couple of the better beaches.

Camping Ayía Marína (☎68-596). A much bigger and more expensive site, 4km or so further west on an excellent beach at the far end of Ayía Marína village. This is beyond the range of Haniá city buses, so to get here by public transport you have to go from the main bus station.

The city

The **old city** clusters around the harbour, and most tourists rightly confine themselves to this area or the fringes of the new town up towards the bus station. You may get lost wandering among the narrow alleys, but it's never far to the sea, to one of the main thoroughfares or to some other recognizable landmark. The best way to get around the city is to walk, but the terminus for most **city buses**, especially those heading west, is at Platía 1866: for Sóudha and the eastern side of town you may find it easier to get on at one of the stops by the market.

The major junction at the south end of Hálidhon, as much as anywhere, marks the centre of town. To the east, Odhós **Yianári** leads past the market and, if you follow it round, either to the main coast road or out onto the Akrotíri peninsula. **Skalídhi**, westwards, leads eventually out of town towards Kastélli Kissámou. North, straight ahead, Hálidhon descends to the harbour and into the heart of the old town. As you stand at this junction, everything in front and below you is basically the old, walled city – behind and to either side lie the newer parts. Much of your **shopping** and other business will take place around the border of the old and new represented by the main Hálidhon junction: down towards the market you'll find pharmacies, newspaper stores and banks. **Tzanakáki** (Apokóronou on some maps) and, opposite, **Konstantínou** (which later becomes Dhimokratías) represent modern Haniá, full of clothes stores, car-rental places and more banks.

Hálidhon is perhaps the most commercially touristy street in Haniá: walk down here and you pass the Cathedral Square, about halfway down on the right, and the Archeological Museum, just beyond on the left, before reaching a square by the harbour – officially called Platía Sindriváni, it is known by everyone simply as **Harbour Square**. To the left, Aktí Koundouriótou circles around the outer harbour, crowded with outdoor cafés and tavernas. Straight ahead is the strange, squat Mosque of the Jannissaries, while on the little bluff that rises behind is the area known as **Kastélli**, site of the earliest habitation in Haniá.

Carry on past here and you'll curve round to the right to the **inner harbour**, where ruined Venetian arsenals look out towards the breakwater. Behind is the most rundown, and in some ways the most atmospheric part of the old town –

alternatively approached by turning right off Hálidhon before reaching the harbour. To the left of Hálidhon, in the relatively narrow strip between the outer harbour and the wall, the alleys are narrower, and the houses older and more attractive, though they have been very much taken over by the tourist trade.

The harbour and around

The **harbour** comes into its own at night, when the lights from bars and restaurants reflect in the water and the animated crowds – locals as much as tourists – parade in a ritualistic volta of apparently perpetual motion. There are stalls set up on the waterside selling everything from seashells to sketches, and buskers serenading the passers-by. By day, especially in the hot, dozy mid-afternoon, it can be less appealing: deserted and with a distinct smell of decay from the rubbish washing up against the quayside. You could always escape on a carriage ride around town behind one of the poor nags that stand waiting in the square all day, sweating beneath their straw hats.

Walk straight on from Platía Sindriváni, past the *Plaza Bar*, and you chance upon the curious, domed profile of the **Mosque of the Janissaries**. Built in 1645, the year Haniá fell to the Turks, it is the oldest Ottoman building on the island, and has been well restored – apart from the jarring concrete dome.

KASTÉLLI

The buildings on the height above the mosque occupy the site of **Kastélli**, the oldest part of the city. Favoured from earliest times for its defensive qualities, this little hill takes its name from a fortress which originally dated from the Byzantine era. Later it was the centre of the Venetian and of the Turkish towns, but very little survived a heavy bombardment during World War II.

Walking up Kaneváro from the harbour square you'll pass various remains, including – at the corner of Lithínon – the fenced-off site where a **Minoan house** is being excavated. Further up Lithínon, towards the top of the rise, are various Venetian doorways and inscriptions and, at the end of the street, a fine old archway. On the next corner, with Kandanoléon, is a larger area of excavation identified simply as "Minoan Kydonia". Neither of these digs is open to the public, though you can see a fair amount through the fence. Swedish archeologists excavating here have traced the outline of a substantial building engulfed by a violent fire about 1450 BC, like that which destroyed Knossós. Many believe that this is the **palace** long thought to have existed here and, if so, would complete a pattern across the island. It was later rebuilt after the fire and, given its proximity to the mainland, may well have been the focus of Mycenaean power on Crete. Among pottery finds here were some dating back to the Neolithic era, but the greatest prize uncovered was an archive of clay tablets bearing Minoan Linear A script (see Contexts, p.336), the first to be found so far west in Crete.

THE INNER HARBOUR

Back at the bottom of the hill the waterfront curls round to the right along Aktí Tombázi, into the **inner harbour**, where pleasure boats, private yachts and small fishing vessels are moored. Much of it, including the sixteenth-century Venetian arsenals and various traces of the ancient defensive bastions, has recently been refurbished, and in the evenings this is now a fashionable part of town. Just on the corner past the Mosque of the Janissaries is the local **handicraft co-operative** (Mon–Sat 9.30am–10.30pm), with a permanent exhibition of goods for sale, though not everything is of particularly high quality. (Just nearby and behind the Harbour Police office is a very clean public toilet, something of a rarity in Crete.)

Beyond all this are the Venetian arsenals, a cluster of restaurants and bars, and the modern *Porto Veneziana* hotel. From here you can follow the sea wall round as far as the minaret-style **lighthouse**, where there's a bar and an excellent view back over the city.

THE OUTER HARBOUR AND CITY WALLS

In the other direction from Platía Sindriváni is the **outer harbour**, with its broad promenade fronted by pavement restaurants and bars. The hefty bastion at the far end houses Crete's **Naval Museum** (daily 10am–4pm; 500dr, students 300dr), which is of little interest unless you're heavily into naval warfare or seashells (one small room is full of them). A somewhat confusing presentation of shipping over six thousand years, it consists mainly of models and pictures of ships, diagrams of naval battles, and assorted memorabilia going back to the times of Classical Greek triremes. A recent reorganization has brought in all kinds of maritime gear from engines to lighthouse parts as well as the setting up of a new section on the **Battle of Crete** of 1941, perhaps the best reason for a visit. The photographic display here is especially poignant and graphically depicts the sufferings of the Haniá villagers at the hands of the Nazis (the English translations are ludicrous however – men in one photo are lined up before a German "biting squad"). Whether visiting the museum or not, it's worth going through the main gate to visit the compound of the small naval garrison (open museum hours, but no need to pay the admission fee). Here you can climb onto the seaward fortifications of the **Fírkas**, as this part of the city defences is known. It was on this spot that the modern Greek flag was first raised on Crete – in 1913 – and there are more fine views.

Carrying on round the outside of the Fírkas, which has been well restored, you can peer through loopholes at the great vaulted chambers within. On the far side is the *Hotel Xenia*, itself raised up on part of the fortifications, and beyond this you can cut inland alongside the best-preserved stretch of the **city walls**. Following the walls around on the inside is rather trickier, but worth a try for the chance to stumble on some of the most picturesque little alleyways and finest Venetian houses in Haniá. Keep your eyes open for details on the houses, such as old wooden balconies or stone coats of arms. The arch of the **Renieri Gate**, at the bottom of Moschón, is particularly elegant. There are also a number of good craft stores around here: a couple of the best, along with an expensive antiques store, are on Angélou just round from the Naval Museum entrance; several newer ones line Theotokopóulou, the delightfully old-fashioned street that runs behind.

The rest of the old city

South from the harbour square, up Hálidhon, lie the less picturesque but more lively parts of the old city. First, though, just a short way up on the right, is Haniá's **Archeological Museum** (Mon 12.30–7pm, Tues–Fri 8am–7pm, Sat & Sun 8.30am–3pm; 500dr), housed in the Venetian-built church of San Francesco. Though it doesn't look much now, with its campanile gone and a crumbling facade, this building was once one of the island's grandest: inside, where there has been substantial restoration, you get a better sense of its former importance. The Turks converted the church into a mosque, from which a beautiful fountain and the base of a minaret have survived in the pungent, flowery garden alongside.

Large quantities of Minoan pottery, including a few of the huge Minoan storage jars or *píthoi*, dominate the front part of the museum. In the centre is a collection of Minoan clay coffins (*lárnakes*), some wonderfully decorated, and one still containing two small skeletons. For archeologists, the most important items are the **inscribed tablets** excavated in Kastélli: this is the only place other than Knossós where examples of Linear A and Linear B script have been found together. Towards the back of the church, the collection is arranged chronologically, progressing through a large group of Classical sculptures, a case full of Greco-Roman glassware and some recently discovered third-century Roman **mosaics** reassembled on the floor. These are really lovely, particularly those of Dionysos and Ariadne, and of Poseidon and Amymone. Outside in the garden courtyard (often enlivened by classical music drifting over the wall from a café outside) are other assorted sculptures and architectural remnants, including a lovely one-legged, headless lion.

Almost next door to the archeological museum and signed down an alley is the **Cretan House Folklore Museum** (Mon–Sat 9am–3pm & 6–9pm; 500dr) a charming collection of artefacts, tapestries and traditional crafts equipment. The old traditions are continued, and embroidered cloths and tapestries made on the premises are offered for sale. On your way out, take a look at Haniá's Roman Catholic church in the same courtyard, an elegant building and quite a culture shock after so many Orthodox churches.

CATHEDRAL SQUARE AND "LEATHER STREET"

Just past the museum, on the other side of Hálidhon, the **Cathedral** sits at the back of a small square. Given Haniá's history and importance, you might expect this to be rather impressive: in fact it's a singularly unattractive little building, dating only from the last century. Nor is the square, which must once have been at the heart of life in Haniá, particularly lively any more except as a taxi rank; to one side, above a *períptero* (street kiosk), are the ramshackle domes of a former Turkish bath. The rebel Dhaskaloyiánnis (see p.295) was tortured to death in the square around 1770.

The street just above, **Odhós Skridlóf**, is considerably more interesting and animated. Here traditional leathermakers still ply their trade, and although many are now geared to tourists, prices for leatherware remain the best in Crete. There are still a few shops which ignore sandals and bags in favour of traditional high Cretan boots and hefty work shoes.

As a final gesture to Hálidhon, take the last right before the top and walk down beside a high stretch of wall into the vicinity of the **Schiavo Bastion**. There's not a great deal to see here, but it's strange to find yourself so suddenly out of the crowds and among the scruffy yards and inquisitive dogs of the backstreets.

THE MARKET AND POINTS NORTHEAST

In the other direction, continuing to the end of Skridlóf or up behind the cathedral, you reach the back of the **market**, a wonderful kaleidoscope of bustle and colour when in full swing. Installed in an imposing and rather beautiful cross-shaped structure, this dates from the beginning of the century, when it was supposedly modelled on the market at Marseilles. At the back is a small shaded square where locals sit outside a couple of kafenía. As you wander round these streets, a minaret keeps appearing above the rooftops, only to disappear when you head towards it: actually located on Dhaliáni, it seems to be part of a carpenter's workshop, but is fenced off and closed to visitors.

A second minaret (this one missing its top) adorns the church of Áyios Nikólaos in **Platía 1821**, further over to the east. Built by the Venetians, the church was converted to a mosque under Sultan Ibrahim and reconverted after Crete's reversion to Greek authority, but has been so often refurbished that there's nothing much to see. The square itself, whose name recalls the date of one of the larger rebellions against Turkish authority, after which an Orthodox bishop was hanged here, is another pleasantly shaded space set with café chairs. Nearby are two more old churches: San Rocco, just a pace towards the harbour, is small and old-fashioned, while Áyii Anáryiri, which retained its Orthodox status throughout the Turkish occupation, has some very ancient icons. Again the area as a whole, known as **Spiantza**, is full of unexpected architectural delights with carved wooden balconies and houses arching across the street at first-floor level. Many of the streets between here and the inner harbour have recently been recobbled and generally refurbished, and they're among the most atmospheric and tranquil in the old town.

Continue **eastwards**, past another section of ruined wall stretching round from the inner harbour, and you'll hit the sea again along the Aktí Míaouli. From here you can follow the coast round into the smarter areas of the modern city.

The new town

Modern Haniá sprawls in every direction, encircling the old town: with time on your hands, there are parts that are worth the walk. Starting in front of the market, the areas to the southwest, on the way to **Platía 1866** and the bus station, have an attractively old-fashioned commercialism about them, full of general stores stocking the essentials of village life.

Heading southeast from the market, Tzanakáki leads to places of more specific interest. First of these is the **Public Gardens**, a few hundred metres up on the left. Laid out by a Turkish pasha in the nineteenth century, they include a few caged animals (not really enough to call a zoo, but there are *kri-kri*, ponies, loud monkeys and birds), a café where you can sit under the trees, a children's play area and an open-air auditorium. The latter, often used as a cinema, is also the setting for local ceremonies and folklore displays which can be really enjoyable – look in to see what's on.

Carry on down the street, then take the second left onto Sfakianáki and you come to the **Historical Museum and Archives** (Mon–Fri 9am–1pm; free), which consists of a couple of gloomy rooms in a small and undistinguished grey building, with poorly labelled photos, a few revolutionary arms from the struggle against the Turks and relics of Venizélos, and many more rooms filled with musty papers and books.

At the end of Tzanakáki is **Platía Eleftherías**, with a statue of Venizélos in the centre and an imposing court building along the south side. This court house was originally the government building built for Prince George's short-lived administration. From here Dhimokratías leads back to the centre, running past the rear of the Public Gardens and ending (as Konstantínou) opposite the market again. Alternatively, follow **Iróon Politehníou**, which runs due north from Platía Eleftherías down to the sea. A broad avenue divided by trees and lined with large houses, interspersed with several (expensive) garden restaurants and a number of fashionable café/bars where you can sit outdoors, it makes for an interesting walk in a part of the city very different from that dominated by the tourist crowds of Hálidhon.

The beaches

Haniá's beaches all lie to the west of the city. The **bus** for the beaches leaves Haniá from the east side of Platía 1866, about halfway up, and runs along the main road towards Kastélli. This means that if you get off anywhere much before Kalamáki you face quite a walk down to the sea. It's easier to hang on, and get off either by the large Oasis Beach sign or at Kalamáki itself, the next stop. Buses run every twenty minutes or so throughout the day, from around 8am to 9pm.

NÉA HÓRA TO GOLDEN BEACH

The **city beach** at Néa Hóra is about a ten-minute walk from the harbour along Aktí Koundouriótou, round past the Fírkas and the *Hotel Xenia*, and on by the city's open-air swimming pools (often drained) and a small fishing-boat harbour. The beach starts in a very crowded section with showers, cafés and restaurants, among these an outstanding fish taverna, *Akrogiali* (see "Eating and drinking, p.256). Offshore is a tiny islet with a sandy beach large enough for about five people at a time, but it's an unnervingly long swim – it's better to rent a pedalo or canoe if you want to explore.

If you continue west you can walk – for some twenty minutes – over a stony, scrubby stretch of sand where quite a few people camp or seek isolation for nude sunbathing. It's a dirty and rather exposed length of gritty beach, though new apartment buildings behind are beginning to provoke a clean-up. **Áyii Apóstoli**, at the end of this walk, amid a clutch of restrained development, is much more agreeable: there's an excellent bungalow/hotel development (*Aptera Beach Bungalows*) with a beachside bar, a restaurant which serves a delicious lunchtime buffet, and a good long stretch of yellow sand. The only drawback is the crashing breakers, which can become vicious at times. At the end of Apóstoli's beach a barbed-wire fence attempts to prevent you getting onto the next section, but if you want to continue on foot it's worth clambering over the rocks: going round to the road involves a long detour and something of a climb over a low hill. At the next section, known as **Hrissí Aktí** (Golden Beach), there's more good sand which has attracted the apartment-builders. But it's not yet overcrowded, has a good taverna and is popular with locals.

To get to either of these sections from the road, head down the track signed to the *Aptera Beach Bungalows* (for the beginning of the first beach) or past *Camping Hania* to approach from the other end. There's quite a bit of new development around, mostly apartments but also a number of **restaurants** – *Jetée*, to which you'll see signs, is good, if a little pricier than most. At the far end, as the beach curves round to a little headland, another taverna is set out on stilts over the water.

OASIS BEACH TO KALAMÁKI

Beyond the Golden Beach headland lies a tiny sand cove, another small promontory, and then the long curve of **Oasis Beach** running on round to **Kalamáki**. This is crowded, and justly so – the swimming is probably the best in the area, with a gently shelving sandy bottom and a fossil-covered (and very sharp) rocky islet/reef that fends off the bigger waves. There's also a string of cafés and tavernas, and other facilities including windsurf rental and lessons. Kalamáki is the furthest beach accessible by city bus, and it's right by the road. To walk this far would probably take a little over an hour non-stop, but it makes far more sense to dawdle and enjoy the empty beaches along the way, arriving at Kalamáki in time to get the bus back.

Eating and drinking

Evenings in Haniá centre around the harbour, and you need not stray far from the waterfront walk to find a cocktail before dinner, a meal, a late-night bar and an all-night disco, although you may be put off by the enormous crowds in high summer. The most fashionable waterfront area these days, particularly with locals, is towards the far end of the inner harbour, around Sarpidóna, but many attractive new places have now opened up in the heart of the old town too, a few in tastefully and partially restored ruined buildings. If you're on a tight budget, however, you'll probably need to steer clear of the harbour altogether.

Tavernas and restaurants

For **eating** by the waterfront, Platía Sindriváni is a good starting-point: spanning out from here, in a circle round the **harbour**, is one restaurant, taverna or café after another. They all have their own character and irritating greeters, but there seems little variation in price or what's on offer, although the inner harbour is a little less frantic. Places in from the water are generally a little cheaper, with plenty of possibilities on Kondiláki, Kaneváro and most of the streets off Hálidhon. Alternatively, striking out a little further afield can take you off the tourist trail altogether and the more local restaurants to the east and west of the centre can make a refreshing change from the touting and brashness of many harbourfront places.

Aeriko, Aktí Míaouli, on the bay to the east of the inner harbour. You'll be eating with mainly locals at this excellent place, which offers a wide selection of well-prepared dishes on a pleasant seaside square.

Akrogiali, Aktí Papanikoli 19 on the Néa Hóra seafront. It's worth taking a taxi-trip to this excellent and fair-priced fish taverna with friendly service, a pleasant terrace and outstanding seafood – which explains why it's always packed.

Amphora, Aktí Koundouriótou, outer harbour. The restaurant of the hotel of the same name (restaurant entrance on the harbour) is one of the more reliable places to eat fish on this strip; serves a range of Cretan specialities.

Anapolous, Sífaka 37, east of Platía Sindrivani. Stylish new restaurant inside a roofless period building. You can eat mezédhes or go for their more substantial dishes; there's often tasteful live guitar accompaniment.

Ciao, Hálidhon, opposite the Archeological Museum. Italian-style restaurant with reasonably priced pizzas and spaghetti.

To Dhiporto, Betolo 31, above Skridhlóf. Very long-established, very basic place amid all the leather stores whose multilingual menu still offers such delights as Pigs' Balls – or, more delicately, *Testicules de Porc*.

Dino's, inner harbour by bottom of Sarpidóna. One of the best choices for a pricey seafood meal with a harbour view.

To Hani, Kondiláki 26. Claims to be a "garden restaurant" aren't strictly accurate, but there are tables at the back in a very quiet dead-end alley (as well as less inviting ones out front in Kondiláki); the food is run-of-the-mill, but reasonably priced.

Kariatis, Platía Keteháki 12. Pricey place serving a sleek blend of Greek and Italian food on a terrace. Also does pizzas.

Karnáyio, Platía Keteháki 8, set back from the inner harbour near the port police. Not right on the water, but one of the best harbour restaurants nonetheless; its touristy looks belie very good food, a friendly atmosphere and prices certainly no higher·than surrounding restaurants. *Faka*, on the other side of the square, is also good.

Le Bistro, Kondiláki 17. French-run place serving up sweet and savoury crepes plus a few more elaborate dishes with a Gallic flavour.

Mathios, inner harbour by bottom of Sarpidóna. Haniá's oldest fish taverna and another good choice.

Nikteridha, 5km east of town in the village of Korakiés. Head for Akrotíri and, at the top of the hill after the Venizélos tombs, follow the signs to the left for the village. This traditional taverna has a delightful garden setting and is especially worthwhile at weekends when there's often music and dancing. You'll pass a couple of other places with outdoor grills and views over Haniá – as well as more music and dancing – as you climb up the road out of town.

Pafsilipon, El. Venizélou 89. A 5min walk from the market along Venizélou, this new-town restaurant is in a stylish Neoclassical mansion with garden and often music. The house speciality is *toúrta*, a cheese and meat pie.

Pension Lito, Epískopou Dorothéou 15. Café-taverna with live music (usually Greek-style guitar), one of several in this street.

To Pigadi To Tourkou ("The Well of the Turk"), K. Sarpáki 1, just north of the market. Greco-Moroccan restaurant with an interesting menu combining the two cuisines. Has small terrace and is fairly expensive,

Spicy Restaurant, Potie 19, slightly east of the cathedral. Friendly and economical no-frills place serving up decent taverna standards at all hours of the day.

Sultana's, Moschón 2, close to the Renieri Gate. Pleasant little restaurant inside a fifteenth-century Venetian palace, this time with a roof and a courtyard. Good but pricey.

Tamam, Zambelíu 49, just before the Renieri Gate. Young, trendy place with adventurous Greek menu including much vegetarian food. Unfortunately, has only a few cramped tables outside, and it can get quite hot inside.

Taverna Ela, top of Kondiláki. Standard taverna food in a roofless ruin, with live Greek music to enliven your meal.

Tholos, Ay. Dhéka 36. In a small street a stone's throw north of the cathedral, this is yet another recycled Venetian ruin. Good restaurant though, and *moskári tis yiágas* (baby veal) is a house speciality in addition to lots of seafood options.

Cafés, bars and snacks

The abundant **cafés** round the harbour tend to serve cocktails and fresh juices at exorbitant prices, though breakfast (especially "English") can be good value. There are more traditional places around the market (including a couple of zaharoplasteía, one on Tsoudherón, the other on Mousoúron, down the steps from the side entrance) and along Dhaskaloyiánnis, where Platía 1821 is a delightfully tranquil oasis. **Fast food** is also increasingly widespread, with numerous *souvláki* places and even a couple of burger joints (on Kalergón by the top of Sarpidóna). *Souvláki* places congregate on Karaolí, round at the end of the outer harbour near the Naval Museum, and around the corner of Plastíra and Yianári across from the market.

If you want to get stuff together for a **picnic**, head for the market, which offers vast quantities of fresh fruit and vegetables as well as meat and fish, bread, dairy stalls for milk, cheese and yoghurt, and general stores for cooked meats, tins and other provisions. Several small stores down by the harbour square sell cold drinks and a certain amount of food, but these are expensive (though they do open late): it's better to head for the shops in the new town where locals go. A couple of large **supermarkets** can be found on the main roads running out of town – particularly *Nea Agora* and *Inka* on the way to Akrotíri. A specialist **mountain-cheese** shop can be found on Sífaka, near where it joins Karaolí.

To Avgo Tou Kokora ("Egg of the Rooster") corner of Ay. Dhéka and Sarpaki near the cathedral. Pleasant modern bar with a good line in pancakes, salads and imaginative snacks.

Bougatsa, the start of Apokoronou, near the market. Tiny place that serves little except the traditional creamy cheese pie – *bougátsa* – to eat in or take away.

Café Byzantio, Yianári, opposite the market. A good breakfast bar over the road from the market's main entrance.

Cosy Roof Garden, Cathedral Square. Pleasant roof terrace bar overlooking the square for breakfast or cocktails and late drinks.

Fortetza, sea wall, near the lighthouse. Strange hybrid restaurant/café on the far side of the harbour near the lighthouse. A free ferry shuttle takes people across from outside the port police – a good gimmick, saving you a lengthy walk. Wonderful place to have an apéritif at sunset, but most popular late at night; there are queues for the boat at midnight.

I 5n Epohi ("The Fifth Season"), Afendoúlief, tucked in a small street behind the harbour opposite the Fortetza (see above) quay. This curiously named bar is a refreshingly traditional kafeníon serving mezédhes and breakfast staples just yards from the crowded harbourfront.

To Haniotiko, Platía 1821. Great little kafeníon on this delightful square. Among their mezédhes choices *kalitsoúnia hórta* (vegetable pie) and *ktapódi krasáto* (octopus in wine) are tasty. The bar also has a great *lyra* and *rembétika* tradition and stages live performances during the winter months. *Kafenion Platanos*, opposite, with tables under the trees is one of the most tranquil breakfast bars in town.

Meltemi, Angélou 2. Slow, relaxed place for breakfast with harbour view and easy chairs; later on, locals (especially ex-pats) sit whiling the day away or playing *távli*.

Mitropolitikon, Cathedral Square. Pleasant setting with tables out on the square in front of the cathedral. Serves good juices.

Neorion, Sarpidóna. The place to sit and be seen in the evening, in an area packed with bars where everyone is doing the same; some tables overlook the harbour. Try an expensive but sublime lemon *granita*.

Oblomov, Kondiláki. Touristy, trendy little cocktail bar/café with classical music and a laid-back atmosphere.

Pili Tis, Porta Sabioyera. A superb outdoor bar sited in a garden on top of the eastern harbour bastion, near to the *Porto Veneziano Hotel* and reached through a deceptively small doorway. Great in the evening with lights dangling from the tamarisk trees and views over the Sarpidóna district, as well as out to sea.

Synagogi, running between Kondiláki and Skúfon. Reminding the world that synagogue is a Greek word for getting together, this is a pleasant drinks bar with good music inside a Venetian mansion bombed in World War II.

Singanaki, Dhaskaloyiánnis. Traditional bakery serving *tirópita* and the like, with a cake store next door.

Tasty Souvlaki, Hálidhon 80. Always packed, despite being cramped for space – a testimonial to the quality and value of the *souvláki*. Take-away might be a better option.

Vasilis, Platía Sindriváni. Reasonably priced breakfasts (for this area).

Zaharoplasteio 13, Platía 1866. Excellent breakfast café in the real heart of town, with an outdoor terrace to watch the action.

Nightlife and entertainment

Haniá's nightlife is frenetic throughout the summer, and if you want to dance until dawn there are plenty of possibilities. The local crowd tend to cruise the **bars** around the harbour and the old quarter before heading out around midnight to the large **discos** and **clubs** along the coast to the west, particularly Plataniás. However, if you find that too much of a long haul there are plenty of places in town to work up a sweat. The smartest clubs in Haniá are on and around Sarpidóna.

A few places offer more authentic entertainment, including **rembétika**, which approximates to Greek blues, and traditional **dancing**. If this appeals, it's worth checking for events at the open-air auditorium in the Public Gardens and for performances in restaurants outside the city, which are the ones locals go to. The hoardings in front of the market usually have details of these, together with programme information for the couple of **open-air cinemas** that show English-language films with subtitles (rather than dubbed versions): the *Kipos* in the Public Gardens, and the *Attikon* on Elefthérias Venizélou out towards Akrotíri, about 1km from the centre. The latter has a great atmosphere, but be sure to sit near a speaker since they reduce the sound level as the evening progresses so as not to offend the neighbours.

The main annual **festival** in Haniá is the commemoration of the Battle of Crete in the last week of May, with folklore and other events mostly in the Public Gardens. Also celebrated is June 24, St John's Day. Check with the tourist office for details of these and other celebrations in the nearby villages.

Late bars and discos

Anayennisi, Schiavo Bastion, junction of Skalídhi and Hálidhon. Tucked down a passage near the bastion, this is Haniá's biggest disco playing loud techno with lots of lights; gets pretty frenetic after midnight.

Ariadne, inner harbour just off Aktí Tombázi. Live modern Greek music venue: standing room only.

Berlin Rock Café, Radimanthus. Round the corner at the top of Sarpidóna, a late-night disco-bar.

Fagotto, Angélou 16. Very pleasant laid-back jazz bar, often with live performers in high season.

Fedra, Ay. Dhéka. Near the *Tholos* restaurant (see p.257), this is another good jazz place.

Fraise, Sarpidóna. Sit inside for the music, or outside and watch the crowds go by.

Four Seasons, inner harbour. Very popular music bar by the port police, where the town's youth gather to size each other up.

Millenium, Tsoudherón behind the market. Big, bright and brash place playing Greek music.

El Mondo, Kondiláki. A survivor from the days when this street was very rowdy, and still popular with servicemen in from the bases.

Platía, outer harbour. Quayside bar converted from former landmark hotel, with live Greek music.

Remember, outer harbour, behind the *Plaza*. "English-style pub", quite pleasant if you like that sort of thing.

Rudi's Bierhaus, Sífaka 24, east of Platía Sindriváni. Haniá's beer shrine: Austrian Rudi Riegler stocks almost a hundred of Europe's finest beers and will explain the story behind each one if you have the time and inclination. Serves good mezédhes, too.

Sebax, Kanerváro 15, slightly east of Platía Sindriváni. Off-beat late night café with its own clientele, a pleasant garden and funky sounds.

Traditional music

Café Kriti, Kalergón 22, at the corner of Andrógeo. Basically an old-fashioned kafeníon where there's Greek music and dancing virtually every night.

Skala, Kalergón 12. Haniá and Crete's only *rembétika* venue. This place opens at midnight and the performance goes on with the same musicians right through until dawn without a break – when the show lifts off the audience are something else. A memorable experience.

Haniá by Night, on the new Iráklion road. An enormous modern dance hall that attracts many of Greece's best singers.

Vareladiko, in Ayía, 7km to the southwest. Another regular stage for big-name events; at other times it's a popular club venue.

Listings

Airlines Olympic, the only airline with scheduled flights to or from Haniá, has an office at Tzanakáki 88 (Mon–Fri 9am–4pm; ☎57-701, 57-702 or 57-703), opposite the Public Gardens.

Airport There's a bus from the Olympic office, connecting with their flights. For airport information phone ☎63-264.

Banks The main branch of the National Bank of Greece is directly opposite the market and has a 24hr cash dispenser that accepts Mastercard. Credit Bank, Hálidhon 106, and the Ionian Bank on Yianári, at the junction with Hálidhon, also have cash dispensers (Visa and American Express); more cash dispensers are now being installed throughout the town. Smaller banks offering exchange facilities are next to the bus station, and there are a couple of after-hours exchange places on Hálidhon.

Bike and car rental For cars try Hermes, Tzanakáki 52 (☎54-418) or Tellus, Kaneváro 9 (☎50-400), both friendly and efficient; for bikes Kavroulakis, Hálidhon 91 (☎43-342) is reliable. Other options for cars include Cornaros, Hálidhon 86 (☎73-131), and Summertime, Dhaskaloyiánnis 7 (☎28-918). Avis, Hertz and other big companies mostly have offices on Dhimokratías in the modern town.

Boat trips Various boat trips are offered by travel agents around town, mostly round Soúdha Bay or out to beaches on the Rodhópou peninsula; Domenico's (☎55-019) at the start of Kaneváro offers some of the best of these. The *Aphrodite* sails daily in summer at 12.30pm from the Old Harbour to the offshore island of Áyii Theódori, for swimming and *kri-kri* spotting. For details of trips (one to three days) on a small yacht with an English skipper, call at the jewellery shop at Hálidhon 3 or at E. Barbopoulos (Tsoudherón 1; ☎22-244, 23-394).

Diving The Diving Centre, Kissámou 121 (☎93-616). Scuba diving for beginners and experienced divers on day-long trips around the nearby coast. They have a pitch on the Old Harbour in summer.

Ferry tickets The ANEK line office is on Venizélou, right opposite the market (☎27-500).

Hospital On the east side of town at the junction of Dragoúmi and Kapodístriou (☎27-000).

Laundry Speedy Laundry (☎88-411), junction of Koroneou and Korkidi, just west of Platía 1866 is highly efficient and charges 2000dr for a load; will also collect and deliver. There are others at Kaneváro 38 (9am–10pm), Epískopou Dorothéou 7 and Áyii Dhéka 18; all do service washes.

Mountain climbing and walking The local EOS, at Tzanakáki 90 (☎44-647), provides information about climbing in the Lefká Óri and takes reservations for the mountain refuge at Kallergi, near the Samarian gorge. Trekking Plan, Karaolí Dimitríou 15 (☎44-946) organizes pricey one- to five-day guided treks into the Lefká Óri and also hire out mountain bikes.

Newspapers and books English and other foreign-language newspapers are sold at two places on Odhós Yiánari, one right by the corner of Hálidhon, the other towards the market. There are two bookshops on Hálidhon which stock a fair range of foreign material: one (Pelekanakis) near the top, the other at the bottom in the square. The town's best bookshop with a good English selection is Petraki, Yianári 68, facing Platía 1866 at the top of Hálidhon. For guides and maps you could also try the kiosk in the market or the one by Cathedral Square.

Pharmacies Several on Yianári between the market and Platía 1866; more up Tzanakáki.

Post office The main post office is at Tzanakáki 3 (Mon–Fri 8am–8pm, Sat 8am–2pm); they also change money and cheques.

Shopping Stores aimed at tourists are found in the old town, especially jewellery and souvenirs on Hálidhon and all around the harbour. The leather goods on Skridlóf are excellent value. At Potié 51, Mat sells nothing but chess and *távli* sets in all shapes and sizes and near-by, at no. 43, Yiakoumaki has Cretan lutes and *lyras*. Other interesting places to look include the handicraft centre and antique stores on the inner harbour, and various art-craft stores on Zambelíu, Kaneváro and Theotokopóulou. Apoyeio, Yianári 80, above the news-stand mentioned above facing Platía 1866, does a good line in used books and CDs of all categories. A good selection of Greek folk and foreign CDs is stocked by CD House, near the market at the junction of Dimokratías and Nikoforou Foka, and Stathopoulos, opposite the market next to the National Bank.

Taxis The main taxi ranks are in Platía 1866. For radio taxis, try ☎98-700.

Telephones OTE at Tzanakáki 5, just past the post office (daily 6am–11pm); you can still phone from any *períptero* (street kiosk), which can be pricey for long distance. Cardphones are a better bet and are all over town.

Tourist police Kareskáki 44 (☎73-333). The town and harbour police are on the inner harbour.

Travel agencies Bassias Travel, Skridlóf 46 (☎44-295) is a good outlet for cheap bus tickets, flights and standard excursions. Other agents for tours and day-trips are everywhere – one of the biggest is Interkreta, Kaneváro 9 (☎52-552), and Omalos Tours, Platía 1866 2 (☎97-119) is also reliable.

Work If you're looking for work picking oranges or on other harvests, join everyone else in Costa's on the harbour square first thing in the morning.

Akrotíri and the Bay of Soúdha

The hilly peninsula of **Akrotíri** loops round to the east of Haniá, protecting the magnificent anchorages of the Bay of Soúdha. It's a somewhat strange amalgam, with a couple of developing **resorts** on the north coast, several ancient **monasteries** in the northeast, and military installations and the airport dominating the centre and south. Leaving town, the roads are good, but as you progress the surfaces become worse and the signs more confusing: heading for the more distant monasteries you wind up on a really narrow track and, eventually, are reduced to walking.

The Venizélos Graves

Following the Akrotíri signs east out of Haniá you embark on a long climb as you leave the city. At the top there's a sign to the **Venizélos Graves**, the simple stone-slab tombs of Eleftheríos Venizélos, Crete's most famous statesman, and his son Sophocles. The setting, looking back over Haniá, is magnificent and also historic – the scene in 1897 of an illegal raising of the Greek flag in defiance of the Turks and the European powers. The flagpole was smashed by a salvo from the European fleet, but the Cretans raised their standard by hand, keeping it flying even under fire. Two stories attach to this: one that the sailors were so impressed that they all stopped firing to applaud; the second that a shell fired from a Russian ship hit the little church of Profítis Elías, which still stands, and that divine revenge caused the offending ship itself to explode the very next day.

The beaches: Stavrós

The road divides by the graves: straight ahead takes you to the airport and to Korakiés, very close by, where there's an excellent taverna, *Nikteridha*; the northern branch, to Horafákia and Stavrós, is the road to the **beaches**. This is pleasant country to drive around, gently rolling and dotted with villages that are clearly quite wealthy – many city workers live out here or build themselves country villas. About 5km along the northern road, past the village of Kounoupidhianá, the road suddenly plunges down and emerges by the beach at **Kalathás**, two little patches of sand divided by a rocky promontory, with a couple of tavernas on the road behind. This makes a fine place to spend a lazy day, marred only slightly by the proximity of the road. Two kilometres beyond Kalathás on the Áyia Triádha road out of Horafákia, there's an excellent zaharoplasteío called Stavros Bakery, whose *baklavá* variations are terrific: try their *karída baklavá*, made with coconut.

Taking a left at Horafákia along a road heading west leads, after a kilometre, to **TERSANAS** where there's a decent little beach, a couple of tavernas and a few apartment blocks within a craggy cove. This makes a pleasant enough stop for a swim and a bite to eat, but if you're planning on lingering awhile it's best to carry on to the end of the road, another 3km beyond Horáfakia, where you'll find a near-perfect beach at **STAVRÓS**, an almost completely enclosed circular bay. The sea is dead calm with a gently shelving sand underfoot, making it ideal for kids. It's an extraordinary-looking place, too, with a sheer, bare mountainside rising just 100m away from you on the far side of the bay. This is where the cataclysmic climax of *Zorba the Greek* was filmed (the hill is known locally as Zorba's Mountain) and is also the site of a cave, whose entrance can just about be seen from the beach, in which there was an ancient sanctuary.

The beach is often crowded – it doesn't take many people to fill it up – but even so it's a pleasant place to bask for a few hours, and is the one place near Haniá that's easily accessible by bus (6 daily). There are **tavernas** behind the beach, one makeshift the other a little more formal, if you want to make it a meal break. Nearby **Blue Beach**, with a tiny sand beach in a cove that is largely artificial (though you wouldn't know it), has one of the best **apartment/rooms** places, *Blue Beach* (☎0821/39-404, fax 39-406; ④); pricey but worth it for its spotless rooms and clifftop position. Next door, there's a decent taverna, predictably named *Zorba's* (a more tranquil lunchtime alternative to Stavrós) which also rents out apartments (☎0821/39-010; ④). Otherwise, accommodation is scattered in the flat plains lining the coast between Stavrós and Tersanas which generally needs to be booked in advance – you'll need your own transport if you plan to stay here. A good contact for apartments close to the sea in the Stavrós area is a shop in Haniá at Tsoudherón 1 (☎0821/41-174, fax 53-743; ask for Kírios Barbopoulos); stays are for a minimum of three days. They don't seem to mind if you ring them from on the spot and can have a place sorted out pretty quickly.

The monasteries

For the **monasteries** at the northern end of the peninsula the most direct approach is to branch right in Kounoupidhianá and follow the signs to Ayía Triádha, though there's also a road up from the airport and a dusty track which cuts across from the Stavrós road. If you follow the signs, you should make it eventually.

Ayía Triádha

Ayía Triádha (daily 8am–2pm & 5–7pm; 300dr), sometimes known as Moní Zangarólo after its founder, was established in the seventeenth century and built in Venetian style. Today, while not exactly thriving, it is one of the few Cretan monasteries to preserve real monastic life to any degree. Its imposing ochre frontage is approached through carefully tended fields and olive groves – all the property of the monastery. Close up, though, some of the buildings themselves are distinctly dilapidated and, despite an ongoing programme of renovation, at least half of the premises lie redundant and empty. Some of the halls at the back have been given over to the stabling of the monks' goats, and skinny cats wander seemingly at will.

You can walk right through the complex, though the monastic cells are locked, and sit on benches shaded by orange trees on the patio. The **church**, which appears strangely foreshortened, contains a beautiful old gilded altarpiece and, around the walls, ancient wooden stalls; like most of the monastery it is built from stone that glows orange in the afternoon sun. By the entrance is a small museum with vestments, relics and ancient manuscripts, mostly dating from the eighteenth or nineteenth centuries, and a few icons which are considerably older. Above, you can climb up beside the campanile to look out over the monastery's fields and beyond. In the courtyard there's a water cooler, and if you're lucky the traditional hospitality will extend further, to a glass of *raki* and a piece of *loukoúm* in the hall where you sign the visitors' book. The monks will also sell you their olive oil, intended to raise funds for the restoration programme.

Gouvernétou and Katholikó

Outside Ayía Triádha a sign directs you towards **Gouvernétou** (daily 9am–12.30pm & 4.30–7pm) – about 4km away, first on dirt track ascending through a biblical landscape of rocks and wild olives, and then up a paved but twisting and rutted road through a rocky gully; a spectacular but not a particularly easy drive. The monastery itself is a simple square block of a building, older than Ayía Triádha, with the usual refreshingly shaded patio and ancient frescoes in the church; there's a tiny museum, too. Despite its more remote location, Gouvernétou, with its carefully tended flowerbeds and chapel, feels like a thriving community. Nevertheless, the few visitors here, and the stark surroundings, help to give a real sense of the isolation that the remaining monks must face for most of the year.

Beyond you can follow (on foot) a path which leads towards another monastery, Katholikó, and the sea. After about ten minutes you reach a **cave** in which St John the Hermit is said to have lived and died – a large, low cavern, stark, dank and dripping, with hefty stalactites and stalagmites. Small outbuildings surround the entrance.

Thus far the walk has been easy, along an obvious path, but as you continue to descend the going gets steeper, rockier and sharper, and in places you have to look for the red paint daubed on the rocks to confirm that you are still on the right trail. In a further fifteen minutes you reach the amazing ruins of the **Monastery of Katholikó**, built into the side of, and partly carved from, a craggy ravine of spectacular desolation. This is older still – it was abandoned over three hundred years ago when the monks, driven by repeated pirate raids, moved up to the comparative safety of Gouvernétou. The valley sides are dotted with caves which formed a centre of still earlier Christian worship, at least one of which (just before the buildings) you can explore if you have a torch.

Spanning the ravine by the ruins is a vast bridge leading nowhere. Cross it and you can scramble down to the bottom of the ravine and follow the stream bed all the way to the sea – about another fifteen minutes. There's a tiny natural **harbour**, a fjord-like finger of water pushing up between the rocks, where remains of a port can still be made out. Hewn from the rock, and with part of its roof intact, is what appears to be an ancient boathouse or slipway. There's no beach, but it's easy enough, and delightfully welcome, to lower yourself from the rocks straight into the astonishingly clear green water.

The walk **back up** takes considerably longer – perhaps an hour in all – and is much more strenuous than it might have seemed on the way down.

Soúdha Bay

On the **south side of Akrotíri** there are beaches near Stérnes, but in practice it's not worth the effort to get there. Almost all of this part of the peninsula is a military zone and the only coast you can reach is a small and rather scrubby stretch of sand. The one consolation is the view of the bay as you go down towards Maráthi: above all of the little island (Néa Soúdha) bristling with Venetian and Turkish fortifications which, from a distance at least, appear miraculously well preserved. It proved as impressive a defence as it looks, holding out as a Venetian stronghold for over thirty years after the rest of the island had fallen, before eventually being voluntarily abandoned.

For an alternative route back, you can cut around the other side of the neck of the peninsula, following the road which curves round to Soúdha town. This again affords spectacular views of the bay (there are signs prohibiting photography of the military secrets therein), down over the villas built into the hillside.

The Allied war cemetery

Just before Soúdha, at the water's edge, you pass the superbly sited **Allied war cemetery**. Surrounded by eucalyptus trees, it lies 1km before the town, down a lane signed "Soúdha cemetery" close to the *Paloma* taverna (which is good and cheap). With its row upon row of immaculately tended headstones, many of them to unknown soldiers and very young men, the serene and dignified cemetery brings home with some force the scale of the calamity of the Battle of Crete in which most of them perished. Grave 10E on the cemetery's northern side holds the remains of the distinguished archeologist John Pendlebury (see p.352), who took over at Knossós after Evans retired; he died fighting alongside Cretans during the German assault on Iráklion in 1941.

From here the main Soúdha road heads back to Haniá or you can join the E75 highway and continue east.

East to Yeoryioúpolis

Heading directly east out of Haniá you can either pick up the main E75 road where it starts, on the south side of town, or follow the buses and most of the other traffic to Soúdha and join it there. As it climbs above the edge of the **Bay of Soúdha** the E75 follows the track of the old road; at the point of the bay stands an old fortress, originally the Turkish bastion of **Izzedin**, now pressed into service as a prison.

The new road is fast, but you'll see little through the screen of trees and flowering shrubs until you emerge on the coast just past Yeoryioúpolis. Once you set off down the hill past Izzedin there are a couple of turnoffs to villages but just one junction of any size, between Vrísses and Yeoryioúpolis, signed to both of them.

If you're in no hurry, or you simply want an attractive circular drive, then the minor roads that head inland or out onto the Dhrápano peninsula have much more to offer.

Áptera and inland

Shortly before the fort, roads lead off left and right: left is signed to Kalámi (just a few hundred metres away, immediately below the prison) and Kalíves (which you can see on the coast way below); turn right and you climb to Megála Horáfia and, turning off again, ancient **ÁPTERA** (daily 8.30am–3pm; free). Áptera occupies the table top of this mesa-like mountain, about 3km from – and a good climb above – the new road. From the fifth century BC well into early Christian times this was one of the island's most important cities: substantial ruins remain, although since their excavation early this century they have deteriorated considerably and are hard to interpret. This should all be about to change, however, as the Ministry of Culture has bought up all the surrounding lands and there are now plans to remove many of the fences which currently impede understanding and enjoyment of the excavations. It is also planned to plant information boards and maps around the site. In the meantime a leaflet containing a site plan and historical outline is available from a kiosk in the car park. A new phase of excavation work is already under way which has uncovered some impressive remains.

Among the more obvious relics revealed in the first phase of work are the massive **walls**, almost 4km long, which predate everything else at the site. The large L-shaped Roman **cisterns** and the remains of a small theatre to the south of these are just a couple of the numerous other buildings scattered around the abandoned monastery which marks the centre of the site; here also are the remains of a Classical Greek **temple** constructed from ashlar blocks and excavated by German archeologists in 1942. Highlights of the **new excavations** (reached by following a track west from the car park) are the foundations, flagstones, water ducts, intricately carved capitals and fallen (but otherwise perfectly preserved) Doric columns of a communal **atrium** thought to date from 500 BC and completely destroyed in the earthquake of 700 AD, which sounded the final death knell of this formerly mighty and prosperous city.

Another attraction of the site is a crumbling Turkish **fort** – substantially shored up with reinforced concrete – on the lip of the hilltop, with the best of all the **views** across Soúdha to the Akrotíri peninsula. Immediately below is the Izzedin fortress, and below that the three small islands, including heavily fortified Néa Soúdha, which protect the narrow entrance to the bay. From here its superb strategic qualities are plain, with the deep-water anchorages accessible only by running the gauntlet of these forts and fortified islands. According to legend the islands were formed after a musical contest between the Muses and the Sirens on the height near the ancient city: defeated, the Sirens plucked off their wings, flung themselves into the bay, and were transformed into the islands. Áptera, literally translated, can mean "featherless" or "wingless" – one derivation of the city's name.

If you're looking for **food** before or after visiting the ruins, at the foot of the hill which ascends to the site, the *Taverna Áptera* (☎0825/31-313) makes up with its fine culinary skills for what it lacks in shade. Run by an Anglo-Greek couple, the taverna also acts as a noticeboard for a few pleasant **villas** (some with pool) in this area which, although usually intended for longer lets, can be taken for the odd day or two.

Stílos and Samonás

From Áptera you can retrace your steps back to the main road, or continue inland to circle round via the Dhrápano peninsula, a very attractive drive. In Megála Horáfia, right opposite the Áptera turnoff, there's a large taverna which is frequently the venue of *bouzoúki* nights – look out for posters.

The first place of any size south of here is **STÍLOS**, which is where the Australian and New Zealand rearguard made their final stand during the Battle of Crete (this was then the main road south), enabling the majority of Allied troops to be evacuated while they themselves were mostly stranded on the island. Many found refuge in the villages in the foothills around here and were later smuggled off the island – some of these villages were destroyed in retribution. Today Stílos is an unremarkable agricultural centre, but there are a couple of kafenía with shady tables beside the road where you can pull over for a drink.

Not far beyond comes the turning to **SAMONÁS**, a narrow road winding steeply up through 180-degree hairpins, with better views at every turn. The reason to take this detour is to visit the isolated Byzantine church of **Áyios Nikólaos** at Kiriakosélia, signed beyond Samonás, which, for location and artworks, is one of the most beautiful on the island. The church, nestling in a valley, has recently been restored and contains fantastic **medieval frescoes**, as good as any on Crete. Painted in the thirteenth century, these have not been touched by the restorers – at least not recently – and are patchy and faded against their deep-blue background, but parts still seem as vivid as the day they were created: in particular a *Madonna and Child*, at eye level on the left-hand side and a dramatic Christ *Pantokrátor* in the drum dome. You really need a car to see them, because the keyholders (Kostas or Roussa) live in Samonás – you pick them up there and drive on to the church, a couple of hilly kilometres further. Head for the kafeníon in Samonás – preferably in the afternoon – and they'll ring for someone to take you, and cheerily overcharge for a drink while you wait. By contrast Kostas or Roussa (or one of their daughters) always seem to refuse money for their time.

The Dhrápano peninsula and Vrísses

A multitude of roads crisscrosses the **Dhrápano peninsula**, almost all of them scenic and well surfaced. This is rich agricultural land, a countryside of rolling green, wooded hills interrupted by immaculately whitewashed, and obviously wealthy, villages. Nowhere are there individual attractions to detain you long, but all these settlements have kafenía where you can sit awhile and wonder at the rural tranquillity away from the main-road traffic. Coming from Stílos you can either head through Néo Horío to Kalíves on the coast, or turn off later for Vámos at the centre of the peninsula. The direct approach, however, is from the E75 highway below Áptera.

Kalíves, Almirídha and the coast

From Kalámi, the old road drops rapidly down to the coast at **KALÍVES**, an agricultural market centre of some size. Approaching, you pass a long sandy beach in the lee of Áptera's castle-topped bluff which looks attractive but is hard to reach. The main beach stretches west from the centre of the village, curving round at the far end by a small harbour where it's more sheltered. The village itself, a rather straggly development lining the main beach road for over 2km, is very much a resort these days, and the plethora of low-rise apartments and studios strung out along both sides of the road, have now been joined by a largish, though pleasant enough hotel, the rather pricey *Kalíves Beach* (☎0825/31-285, fax 31-134; ⑥). The apartments can be great value, but since they tend to be spread out at either end of the village it's easiest to start at one of the travel agencies in the centre – they should know where the vacancies are. You'll find several places to eat on the main road through, but the best spot is occupied by the *Mini-Golf Bar* (which really does have crazy golf as well as overpriced cocktails and snacks), overlooking the western (town) end of the beach.

ALMIRÍDHA, the next village along the coast, is smaller, marginally more of a resort, and considerably more attractive. Again there are far more apartments than rooms (but less chance of finding space here), and there's a row of tavernas behind a couple of small patches of sand in a sheltered little bay. The lovely beach is a popular spot for windsurfing, with a fairly reliable breeze once you're slightly offshore. When the breeze blows inland, seafront dining becomes a somewhat risky experience – though on a hot day its always a welcome refresher; like Kalíves, Almirídha is popular with local families who drive down to swim and enjoy a leisurely lunch. The fish tavernas, *Dimitri's* and *Manoli's*, as well as the more expensive *Thalami*, offering standard Greek dishes, are all worth a try. The *Enchanted Owl* is an English-run newcomer with an international menu and serves – if you can face it – a "real English breakfast". If you can't find an apartment in the resort's centre, *Pension Katerina* (②) about a ten-minute walk up the hill to the east, has lovely views and pleasant enough rooms.

Beyond Almirídha the coast becomes increasingly rocky, with cliffs almost all the way round to Yeoryioúpolis denying access to the sea. The roads also deteriorate if you go this way, but as you climb the views become increasingly worthwhile. There are more beaches below **PLÁKA**, a picturesque hamlet (with rooms) which, like Kókkino Horió on the steep height above it, served as a set for the filming of parts of *Zorba the Greek*. **Kefalás**, with views over the sea on both sides, is a prettier village still.

Gavalohóri and Vámos

An excellent new road runs inland from Almirídha towards Vámos. Immediately inland you pass below **Aspró**, a tiny, ancient hamlet looking down over the coast. This is the old Greek village as you've always imagined it: a couple of lucky foreigners have snapped up the only empty houses.

GAVALOHÓRI, further on, offers something more tangible to stop for, in the shape of a small but excellent **folklore museum** (daily 9am–8pm; 400dr; when closed, enquire at the women's co-operative mentioned below) in a beautifully restored Venetian building with Turkish additions. The history and culture of the village is documented in the various rooms, with items clearly labelled in English as well as Greek. Of particular interest are the examples of stone-cutting, wood-carving and *kopanéli* (silk lace made by bobbin-weaving), which is now being revived in the village. The mulberry trees planted around the village by the Turks still produce silk from the silkworms that feed on their leaves. Evidence that this is an ancient settlement is scattered throughout the village's narrow, winding streets: there are Byzantine wells on the outskirts, and on the corner by the museum you can see the remains of a Turkish coffee shop with inscriptions and old jars. In the central square there is a store run by the Women's Agrotourism Co-operative, an organization dedicated to reviving many of the disappearing arts and crafts of the region, and the results of their work – glass, ceramics and *kopinéli* – are on sale. At nearby **Kálamitsi Amigdáli**, 8km to the south, another women's craft co-operative has been set up and they are also weaving silk to sell. Watch out for signs directing you to the workshop as you drive through. If it's closed seek out Maria Kakotisláki (currently acting as their "marketing manager") at the kafeníon on the main square.

VÁMOS is the chief village of the north Apókoronas region, complete with a big new health centre. Only size really distinguishes it from all the other villages, however, and the kafenía round the crossroads are as peaceful as any you'll find. An interesting new venture here is Vamos S.A., a co-operative promoting ecotourism. They currently have a good **taverna** near the centre of the village, *I Sterna Tou Bloumosifi*, to the right as you enter from Haniá. The co-operative also has a grocery store selling the cheeses, herbs, honey, oil and wine of the region and even a tourist office which changes money and offers motorcycle and mountain bike rentals, in addition to organizing **walks** to Byzantine monasteries and churches nearby. If you're tempted to stay they have also tastefully restored a number of traditional houses around the village rented out as furnished **guesthouses** (☎0825/23-350, fax 23-100; ⑤), complete with bath and TV.

Vrísses

Almost whichever route you follow, you'll end up approaching **VRÍSSES**, a major junction of the old roads and still, though bypassed by the new, the crossroads for the route south. If you're travelling between Hóra Sfakíon and Réthimnon or anywhere else to the east, you usually have to change buses here. Set on the banks of the Almirós (or Tris Almiri) river, Vrísses is a wonderfully shady little town, its streets lined with huge old plane trees. On the riverside are a couple of tavernas by a bridge and a monument to the independence settlement of 1898; plenty of smaller cafés line the main street, many of them offering good local honey and yoghurt said to be the best on the island. There are also **rooms**, should you want one, though they're not desperately attractive.

Heading back towards the coast from Vrísses, the road cuts under the E75 once again, following the river valley down to Yeoryioúpolis. This is another lovely stretch, through well-watered fields and woods. About halfway you can pull over to a picnic spot shaded by cypress trees, with a whitewashed chapel by the roadside, fresh spring water and huge picnic tables.

If you're **driving** to Sfakiá, incidentally, it's a good idea to fill up here: fuel is available at a couple of villages en route, but there are only sparse, expensive supplies in other villages along the south coast. About 4km along the road to Hóra Sfakíon, and worth a look if you're passing, the village of **ALÍKAMBOS** lies just off the road. In the nave of its **church of the Panayía** there are outstanding **frescoes** by the fourteenth-century master, Ioánnis Pagomenos; they depict the Virgin and Child, Áyios Yeóryios and Áyios Dimítrios, and are remarkably well preserved, which is surprising in view of the way the locals prod them vigorously with their fingers when pointing out images or the names of the saints. The paintings in the bema are by a later artist. The church lies down a track off to the left just before the village and near a Venetian fountain. Should you miss the unsigned turnoff, the kafenío in the village square, fronted by a couple of unexploded bombs from World War II, will provide directions. At Máza, 3km northeast of here, there's another frescoed church, although this is not quite so good nor as well preserved.

The rest of the route south to Hóra Sfakíon is covered on pp.297–8.

Yeoryioúpolis

YEORYIOÚPOLIS (or Georgioupolis) lies at the base of Cape Dhrápano where the Almirós flows into the sea. Like Vrísses it's a beautiful old place, with a tree-lined approach and ancient eucalyptuses shading the huge square in the centre. Unlike Vrísses it's now an established resort, although on a small enough scale to remain an extremely pleasant place to spend a few days.

The main course of the river runs into the Gulf of Almirós on the northern edge of Yeoryioúpolis, by a small harbour protected by a long rocky breakwater, and there are numerous smaller streams running into the sea all around. This is another favoured nesting ground of the loggerhead sea turtle (see p.214); information about the animals is to be had from the seafront kiosk of the Sea Turtle Protection Society of Greece which also runs trips up the river in small boats to visit colonies of their diminutive relatives, the terrapin. The main town **beach** heads off to the south, curving round to join the continuous stretch which runs alongside the Réthimnon road for miles. Close to town it shelves very gently and enjoys the protection of the breakwater, and is popular with Greek families. Showers are provided here, and there are more showers further round, by *Mike's Oasis* (good ice cream and cocktails). At the far end, there are new hotels and beach bars, but there are also **dangerous currents** offshore: don't venture too far out, and take heed of any warning notices on the beach. Windsurfers can be rented by the *El Dorado* hotel. Streams crossing the beach create little quicksands in places (only knee-deep), but most of these have wooden bridges to let you cross without getting your feet wet.

A second, much more sheltered beach lies to the north of the river in a small bay. Swimming here is safer and there are generally fewer people, but the water can be extremely cold, owing to the rivers emptying at each end of the sand. There are a couple of simple bar/tavernas behind this beach. At the far end, beyond the smaller stream, you can follow a path over sharp rocks, past an old chapel and various caves, but in the end it leads only to more sharp rocks and eventually peters out above the cliffs. Blue Adventures at the *Georgioupolis Beach* hotel (at the town end of the main beach), organizes diving and snorkelling trips, and gives a weekly free introduction to scuba diving (☎0825/61-012, fax 61-034 for details).

Arrival, information and services

Buses drop you on the main road, just a couple of minutes' walk from the square and crossroads at the centre of town. There are several local **travel agents** and **car-rental** places: Geo Travel (on the square near *Sun Set* bar, ☎0825/61-370) is one of the best, with services including **money exchange** at decent rates. They can also arrange **horse-riding** excursions, and sell tickets for the Samariá gorge trip. You can buy newspapers and attempt to make **phone calls** from a *períptero* (kiosk) on the square, although there are now cardphone kiosks nearby; a couple of small **stores** and a fruit stall here stock all the basics, and just off the road to the beach there's an excellent bakery, *To Pikaniko*, selling the usual *tirópita* and *spanakópita* as well as filled croissants and other temptations. Another good bakery lies along the road south from the square leading to the main E75 highway where a kiosk at the bus stop (opposite the *Crystal Palace* disco-bar) also sells inclusive tickets for the **Samariá gorge** return trip; buses leave daily at 6.30am and 7.20am.

If you want to do some **walking** in the area (in addition to the walks mentioned below), *Six Walks in the Georgioupolis Area* by Lance Chilton is a great little guide to getting into the local countryside; it comes with an accompanying route map and may be available from shops in the village, but you're best getting hold of it in advance (see Contexts, p.369).

Accommodation

There are **rooms** to rent everywhere, it seems, and only at the height of season are you likely to have any trouble finding a vacancy; even then you should be all right if you arrive early in the day.

Some of the better places to stay, the first to fill up in high season, are to the right from the square, down the lane which heads towards the beach. *Zorba's Taverna* (☎0825/61-381, fax 61-018; ②) and *Andy's Rooms* (☎0825/61-394; ②) are possibilities here, located on a side road behind the *Sun Set* bar. Further along the beach road itself are places where the views and sounds are of the sea rather than the street – *Rooms Irine* (☎0825/61-313; ③) and *Pension Cretan Cactus* (☎0825/61-027; ③) for example. Another good option nearby is the friendly, clean and plant-packed *Rent Rooms Stelios* (☎0825/61-308; ③) where studio rooms come with kitchen. Another cluster of rooms places lies inland, to the west of the square: *Taverna Paradise* (☎0825/61-313; ③) has rooms with bath above a restaurant and nearby, surrounded by lofty plane trees, the pleasant *Hotel Drosia* (☎0825/61-326, fax 61-636; ③) has en-suite rooms with fridges and tea-/coffee-making facilities. Off the square's southern end to the left is the cheaper *Rooms Voula* (☎0825/61-359; ②) above a souvenir store, which also allows use of a kitchen. To the north of the square across the river are a few more secluded places: *Anna*, *River House* and *Irini* (all ②). Mosquitoes can be a problem by the river, but the wildlife on the banks is some compensation. Kingfishers are regular visitors here.

If you still have trouble finding space, two basic hotels right on the square, the *Amfimala* (☎0825/61-362; ①) and the more recently renovated *Penelope* (☎0825/61–370; ②), are often the last to fill, probably because of the noise at night. With your own vehicle, you could consider a trip to the charming hill village of Exópolis, 3km out of town to the west, where excellent-value studio rooms with a pool and spectacular view are to be had at *Marika Studio Apartments* (☎0821/58-831, fax 58-831; ④); in high season you'd be advised to ring ahead as this has now been discovered by tour operators. There are also a couple of tavernas nearby with more stunning terrace views along the coast. At the **taverna** on the corner, the friendly Georgia will probably call you over for a chat if she spots you from her kitchen; she does some hearty dishes and is popular with walkers in the area.

Eating, drinking and nightlife

Restaurants in Yeoryioúpolis are concentrated round the square, and there are plenty to choose from. The *Café Georgioupolis Pub* is a fine place for breakfast or to sit over a long drink, watching the world go by; nearby *Samaria* is similar. *Hotel Amfimala* has the square's most authentic kafeníon with outdoor tables and, just west of the square, *Taverna Paradise* is another good place, with tables in a garden. Overlooking the river, *O Fanis*, serves deliciously fresh and well-presented fish dishes at reasonable prices. East of the square and out a bit to where the E75 passes the village's edge, *Taverna Georgis* cooks excellent meat and fish dishes on a charcoal fire and in a wood-fired oven; it's set slightly back from the street, approached through a bower, and not to be confused with the dreary place next door. Another good alternative, away from the rush, is *To Arkadi*, on a point by the mouth of the river, on the far side. The *Hotel Gorgona* on the town beach also has a decent taverna looking out to sea.

Bars crowd around the square and out towards the main road – *Sun Set* serves poor cocktails but has good music and atmosphere. Alternative entertainment is on offer at a tiny, open-air **cinema**, where they show a different film every night, usually subtitled; programme details are pinned to a tree in the square. There's a choice of two **discos**: the raucous *Time*, across the river bridge and then right after 500m, with a free mini-van service from the square; or the *Crystal Palace* disco-bar in the opposite direction, on the E75 highway. When you've tired yourself out on the dance floor, you can recuperate on their floodlit mini-golf course outside. Live **Cretan music** shows are held every Saturday night at the *Georgioupolis Beach Hotel*.

A small **land train** transports visitors along the seafront and to various places of interest inland, such as Lake Kournás (see below).

Lake Kournás

Four kilometres inland from Yeoryioúpolis, the island's only freshwater lake, **Lake Kournás**, shelters in a bowl of hills – an easy if unexciting walk. It's worth noting that there are more rewards in hiking up the Almirós valley towards Vrísses or tackling the steep climb to Exópolis (see opposite) on the road to Vámos, where there are two wonderfully sited tavernas – try *Georgia's* – with magnificent views.

As lakes go, it's small and shallow, but it nevertheless makes for an interesting afternoon's excursion. The appearance of the lake varies greatly according to when you visit: during the day its colours change remarkably as the sun shifts around the rim of the bowl, and its size alters over the course of a year. In late summer the level drops to reveal sand (or dried mud) beaches all around, and a number of popular camping spots. Earlier in the year, the water comes right up to the tidal ring of scrubby growth and it's much harder to find anywhere to camp or to swim from. The lake and the hills around it are also a good place to seek out some of the more unusual island wildlife (see Contexts p.364). There's a path which makes a circuit of the lake, about an hour's walk. On the bank where you arrive there are a few simple **tavernas** – popular with the locals for outings, with lamb barbecued on spits – and a few pedaloes and canoes for rent. Most of these tavernas, including the *Korissia* (☎0825/96-367; ③), have a few **rooms** upstairs, somewhat overpriced and gnat-infested but immaculately sited looking out over the water, and very comfortable if you have insect-repellent coils to burn. If these are full, you could try for rooms at the village of Mourí, which is straight up from the junction with the path that leads down to the banks. To get to the lake you could take the touristy land train from Yeoryioúpolis, or hire a bicycle. Walking there (about 4km from Yeoryioúpolis) is also feasible, preferably via the hamlet of Mathés from where there's a waymarked rambling route to the lake's northern edge – which links in nicely with the route around it mentioned above. Once you're beyond the E75 highway it's a pleasant stroll – ask the villagers at Mathés to direct you to the path, should you have difficulty.

The village of **KOURNÁS** is another 4km beyond the lake, a stiff climb which reveals a charming hill settlement fanning out around its inclined main street.

You may not find a room here, but one place definitely worth a lunch stop is the *Káli Kardiá* **taverna** at the top of the main street. Here some of the best lamb and sausages in the area are cooked up, together with tasty *souvláki* and super salads – and don't forget to try their noted *galaktoboúreko* dessert, a lemony egg-custard pudding. After you've eaten you could take a look at the church of **Áyios Yeóryios**, downhill and signed to the right from the square. A fine old church with Venetian additions, it has some impressive fresco fragments. If it's locked, enquiries nearby should produce a key.

From here you could follow the poorly maintained road to rejoin the old Haniá–Réthimnon road somewhere before Episkopí (see p.209).

Inland: walks and Venizélos country

The country behind Haniá, a small agricultural plain into which the foothills of the White Mountains intrude, is not the most thrilling in Crete, but with a day to spare it does deserve exploration – especially if you're prepared to embark on some serious hiking. For the most part they grow oranges here, which are the best in Crete and hence, as any local will tell you, the finest in the world. Many of the villages are also associated with **Eleftheríos Venizélos**, the revered Cretan statesman who, as prime minister of Greece for most of the period from 1910 to 1932, finally brought Crete into the modern Greek nation.

Thériso
Perhaps the most attractive journey is the fourteen-kilometre drive up to **THÉRISO**, hometown of Venizélos's mother and one of the cradles of Cretan independence. Here in 1905 the Revolutionary Assembly was held (all baggy black shirts and drooping moustaches, as depicted in so many Cretan museums) that ousted Prince George and did much to precipitate union with Greece. The trip out to the little house, with its plaque commemorating the famous son, is an all but obligatory one for Cretans, and the village is frequently crowded with busloads of battling schoolkids. There's actually little to see apart from a traditional country village, but it's worth going anyway for the drive up **Thériso gorge**. In terms of spectacle this can't, of course, compare with Samariá and, in any case, the bed of the ravine is given over to the (mostly paved) road. But it is exceedingly pretty in the lower reaches, gentle and winding with the stream crossed and recrossed on rickety bridges, and surprisingly craggy towards the top where the walls are cracked and pocked with caves.

If you want to continue and complete a circle round to Mesklá (see below), you face a heady climb into the foothills of the mountains and over what feels like an impressively lofty ridge. This road is narrow, rocky and punctuated by gates to prevent livestock straying, and it's not always obvious which way to go, but it's not too bad a drive. Alternatively, it makes a wonderful long hike, occasionally traversed by organized rambling groups but quite possible on your own – as long as you check the route beforehand, ask the way if in doubt, and check bus times to get you home again. There are **buses** to both Thériso and Mesklá from Haniá, and the walk between the two takes less than three hours. Given the vagaries of the timetable though, the trip is liable to take all day if you do it by bus.

On to Mesklá

Right at the top lies **SOÚRVA**, a cluster of whitewashed houses with stupendous views over the surrounding valleys. There's nothing to do here – a lone kafeníon is tended by a menacing guard dog – but it is a hell of a setting. From Soúrva the way spirals slowly down to **MESKLÁ**, another beautiful village, set on a swift-flowing brook and surrounded by lush agricultural land and orange groves; there are several small café/tavernas here. Under the Venetians, Mesklá was a place of considerably more importance than it is now, as indicated by the tiny chapel of **Metamórphosis Sotírou** (Transfiguration of the Saviour) at the bottom of the village (a turn up to the left if you are approaching from the Fournés end) containing the remains of fourteenth-century **frescoes**. The chapel itself is unprepossessing, and many of the paintings have been severely damaged by damp and mould, but parts remain clearly visible and are all the more remarkable for their ordinary surroundings. At the top of the village there's another chapel dedicated to the **Panayía** (next to a large modern church of the same name) which was constructed in the fourteenth century over a basilica of the fifth century which had, in its turn, been raised over a Roman temple to Aphrodite: yet another Cretan holy place which has attracted worshippers for well over two millennia to precisely the same spot. The Roman mosaic floor that had served all three shrines was recently removed to protect and preserve it. Enquiries in the village should produce a key if you wish to see the interior.

Mesklá was also the centre of one of the great legends of Cretan resistance, the **Kandanoleon revolt**. According to the story (which is certainly not historically accurate, though it probably has some basis in fact), much of western Crete rose against the Venetians early in the sixteenth century. They elected as their leader one George Kandanoleon, who established a base in Mesklá and from here ran a rebel administration, collecting taxes and effectively controlling much of the west. It was only by treachery that he was finally brought to heel. In order to legitimize his authority, Kandanoleon arranged for his son to marry the daughter of a Venetian aristocrat, Francesco Molini (see p.320). The marriage took place and the celebrations began, with Kandanoleon and several hundred of his supporters eating and drinking themselves to a stuporous standstill. At which point, by pre-arranged signal, a Venetian army arrived and captured the Cretans as they slept; their leaders were hanged at villages around the countryside, and the revolt was over.

Fournés and Mourniés

Continuing on foot you could tackle the steep climb to Lákki (see p.281) on the main road to Omalós and the Samariá gorge. The road, however, and the direct route to Haniá, head down to **FOURNÉS** and join the main road there. Fournés is a very much larger place, with stores lining the road (good for stocking up if you're doing this circuit in reverse), heavily cultivated fields round about and a large producers' co-operative.

If you want to complete your Venizélos pilgrimage you should also visit **MOURNIÉS**, where the great man was born in 1864. Immediately south of Haniá, this is easiest reached by heading out towards the main E75 highway. Mourniés is just a couple of kilometres southwest off this and, Venizélos's birthplace aside, has little to see, but it's another pleasant drive out of the city, along a road lined with ancient plane trees.

The coast west of Haniá

West from Haniá the main road (now the E65) follows the coastline more or less consistently all the way to the base of the Rodhópou peninsula. Occasionally it runs right above the water, more often 100m or so inland, but never more than easy walking distance from the sea. The coastal route is well served by buses, running every thirty minutes between Haniá and Kolimbári, early morning to late evening. As always, though, you'll really need your own transport to explore the remoter areas inland.

In the early stages the various villages have merged into an almost continuous string of ribbon development – not exactly ugly, but not particularly attractive either. There are villas, hotels and sporadic pensions or rooms to rent all the way, though little in the budget range, and vacancies are often scarce in season. As you leave the city behind, this development thins, giving way between towns to orange groves protected from the *meltémi* by calamus-reed windbreaks, where only the occasional path penetrates down to the sea. There is **beach** of sorts almost all the way, though much is windswept, dirty and subject to crashing breakers; for secure swimming you're better off closer to Haniá – at the city beach of Kalamáki, at Ayía Marína or at Plataniás.

This coastline was the scene of the fiercest fighting in the **Battle of Crete**, and the bridgehead from which the Germans established their domination. There's a reminder of this almost immediately you leave the city, in the form of an aggressive swooping eagle, erected beside the road by the Germans as a memorial to their paratroops. Passing this, you're into the stretch of coast along which the town beaches are ranged (p.255), though the road here actually veers away from the sea as much as it does anywhere. Frequent minor roads run either down to the beach or up into the hills, where there are some pleasant villas and small hotels looking down over the coastline, and a great deal of development going on.

Galatás and around

Villages like Dharátsos, **GALATÁS** and places even less well defined, seem thoroughly unattractive as you drive along the main road, but in most cases there is a real village, up in the hills inland. Galatás actually turns out to be a fair-sized place, in whose village hall is a small Battle of Crete museum, basically a collection of rusty guns and helmets. Outside is a memorial to those who died here, including 145 New Zealand soldiers. *Uncle John's*, opposite, is a good place for a snack if you're passing.

Four kilometres to the southwest of Galatás village, **Ayía Reservoir** is renowned for its **birdlife**. Despite being flanked by a couple of unsightly factories, the watery marshland is home to a rich variety of species, including crakes, avocet, marsh harrier, spotted flycatcher and squacco heron in season. The kingfishers here are a delight and not at all put off their diving tricks, it seems, by human visitors. The best approach is by a track which descends to the left of the *Beautiful Helen* café about a hundred metres before a church on the village's eastern perimeter. Once you've descended along this, veer right to reach an area with two gates. Go through the right hand gate (which should be open) to follow a path flanked by tall rushes to pass an electricity generating station (right). Soon after this another small rough track through trees on the left will lead you to the edge of the lake where the low, bevelled concrete roof of an old building makes an ideal "hide". The best sightings should be in the early morning or a couple of hours before dusk, and binoculars are essential.

Ayía Marína and Plataniás

Kalamáki, where the road finally comes in sight of the beach, marks the limit of the local bus service from Haniá and also the end of this strip of sand. Beyond, low hills drop straight to the sea round a couple of bends and then you emerge at Káto Stalós, which runs into **AYÍA MARÍNA**, the first substantial village along this stretch. In fact, there's virtually no break in the development from Káto Stalós to Plataniás, creating the most built-up strip in the west of the island, with stores, restaurants, hotels, rooms for rent, travel agents, tavernas, discos and bike-rental places coming one after the other. This is better than it sounds: it's all fairly low-rise, there's a decent beach almost all the way along (with facilities including jet-skis, windsurfers and parascending) and, by resort standards, it's all pretty quiet.

Ayía Marína's coastal half – the older village lies a little inland – is distinguished by a small brick factory and, towards the end of the village, *Camping Ayia Marina* (☎0821/68-596), proudly guarding a beautiful sector of **beach**. Curving round a little promontory, this has a fine view of the sunset and of **Áyii Theódori**, the island offshore which is now a sanctuary for *kri-kri* or wild goats (you're not allowed to land on the island). From the west of the islet a great cave gapes like the jaws of a beast; indeed, legend has Áyii Theódori as a sea-monster which, emerging from the depths to swallow Crete, was petrified by the gods. Remains found in the cave suggest that it was a place of Minoan worship in antiquity, while in more recent times the Venetians turned the whole island into a fortress against the threat of piracy and Turkish invasion.

Heading west again, **PLATANIÁS** follows seamlessly, boasting a delightful old quarter perched high on an almost sheer bluff above the road. There are a number of **tavernas** which attract evening and weekend trippers from Haniá, notably *O Milos*, a restaurant of repute towards the west end of the village (evenings only). Specialities here, and elsewhere in the village, are *yíros* and *kokorétsi* – meat or offal cooked on huge spits over charcoal – but the *Milos* has extra attractions in the form of an old millstream which runs through a walled garden where you eat. *The Carob Tree*, halfway up the hill to the old village, has a more varied menu and views way along the coast, while the *Margarita*, a little way back down the hill, serves a memorable tuna steak. The best location, though, has to be the eagle's eyrie occupied by the *Vigli* taverna whose spectacular terrace view over the coast makes the climb worth the sweat, and which serves the usual taverna standards.

Just along the main street are a number of **rooms** places should you want to stay – try *Filoxenia* (☎0821/48-502; ②) – as well as a **post office** and **banks** and **supermarkets**. On the main street at the western end of town and almost opposite the post office, *Oinopantopouleo* is a friendly little shop selling olive oil, honey, herbs and wine from the region; they'll let you taste before you buy.

For most young people in Haniá, however, Plataniás means **clubs** and **discos**, and a great exodus from the city takes place in summer at around midnight when the clubs here begin to lift off. Almost opposite its namesake restaurant, *Mylos*

Club is one of the current favourites and in addition to its nightly disco has a day-time beachfront music bar with pool, and a scene all of its own. *Portocali* is one of the biggest discos on the island and blasts off at midnight, spilling out wild sounds and techno pyrotechnics until morning. *Utopia* is another place nearby where inebriates are encouraged to cross a rope bridge suspended high above the ground – a feature which should provide plenty of work for insurance lawyers.

Yeráni to Tavronítis

Beyond Plataniás, things change little all the way to the Rodhópou peninsula, though signs of tourism get fewer the further you go, with lots of isolated villas and one or two slightly more concentrated developments in places such as **Yeráni**. These on the whole are pleasantly low-key, but the beach is rarely that great, being very open to wind and waves and with rather gravelly, grey sand. Frequent paths and tracks lead down from the road to the sea.

MÁLEME is perhaps the place you're most likely to stop. Just beyond lies the airfield which saw much of the early fighting in the Battle of Crete and where the German invasion began on May 20, 1941; the loss of this airfield in controversial circumstances was crucial to the German success. Although it's a restricted military zone no one seems to mind if you wander just inside the gate to have a peek. Just before the airfield, the giant *Creta Princess* hotel lies to the right of the road, dominating the only bit of sandy beach around. If you're feeling brazen you can walk through to this: the hotel also has a pool and a couple of bars in luxurious grounds.

Almost directly opposite the hotel, a narrow lane leads up to the **German war cemetery**, set on a hillside below the ridge known as Hill 107, which played a crucial role in the defence of, and the battle for, the airfield. Overlooking the battleground where so many of the four and half thousand buried here lost their lives, the lines of flat headstones, each marking a double grave, lend a sombre aspect to an otherwise peaceful scene. In a piece of almost grotesque irony, until recently its keepers were George Psychoundákis, author of *The Cretan Runner*, and Manóli Pateráki, who played a leading role in the capture of General Kreipe (see p.343). When offered the job, Psychoundákis was allegedly told, "You looked after the Germans while they were alive, why not look after them now they're dead?"

In a bizarre twist of fate, the discovery in 1966 of a splendid **Late Minoan tomb** nearby demonstrated that this area had already been a graveyard for over three thousand years. To reach it, follow the lane leading down from the cemetery to the first left bend, where a track signed on the right leads 100m along a terraced hillside to the tomb, again on the right. The *dhrómos* or entrance passage of the stone-built tomb and its heavy lintel are well preserved.

There's a final reminder of Máleme's significance in the Battle of Crete as you cross the River Tavronítis on a long modern bridge: beside it, twin pontoon bridges survive from the war. **TAVRONÍTIS** itself is still a traditional farming centre, with fruit for sale at stalls beside the road; it marks the junction with the road across the island to Paleohóra (p.314).

Kolimbári and Moní Gonía

Continuing west, **KOLIMBÁRI**, at the base of the Rodhópou peninsula, has far more appeal than anything that has preceded it along this coast. If there were a sandy beach, it would be a perfect resort: as it is there's a long strip of pebbles and clear water looking back along all the coast towards Haniá in the distance. It's little spoiled, and behind the narrow main street with a few tavernas there's a concrete promenade lined with more tavernas and a small harbour. The place is tranquil and, should you want to stay, there are a few places offering **rooms**: for rooms with bath try the good-value *Hotel Dimitra* (☎0824/22-244; ②) at the end of the village, set slightly back from the sea. A good place for a drink is *Mylos*, a stylish bar converted from an old olive oil mill, with a pleasant sea-view terrace. The best **taverna** in the village is *Argentina* on the main street, which is noted for its fish. More tavernas also cluster around the seafront and at the top of what used to be a 500-metre-long avenue lined with magnificent plane trees, separating the village from its junction on the main road: in a breathtaking act of municipal vandalism the planes were all felled to allow the road to be widened into the soulless asphalt highway it has now become. At the junction there's a cluster of hotels, bars and restaurants serving the passing trade, as well as a couple of grill tavernas that are favourites with the locals. *Lefka* (☎0824/22-211; ②) is reliable and also offers rooms.

Out onto the peninsula, it's only a few minutes' walk to the **Moní Gonía** (closed from 2–5pm; the strict "no shorts" signs outside apply only to beachwear). The monastery occupies a prime site, with stupendous views and a scramble down to what appears to be a sandy cove – rumoured to be the monks' private beach. Founded at the beginning of the seventeenth century, the monastery perhaps has less to show than some, but has stirring tales to tell of resistance to the infidel Turk. Here they can point to the cannonball still lodged in the walls to prove it – a relic they seem far more proud of than any icon. Which is not to say there are no worthwhile icons: the church has a fine series of post-Byzantine ones dating from the seventeenth and eighteenth centuries (plus a few modern ones), of which Áyios Nikólaos, in a side chapel, is particularly fine. More are kept in the small **museum** (300dr), along with assorted vestments and relics. Although there are (or were) only six monks left, they remain very hospitable and there's even a "tourist monk", Brother Andónios, who has been pointing things out to visitors for years, often treating them to a glass of *raki* and a look at his treasured stamp collection (all contributions welcome).

Opposite the monastery and beside a fountain, a steep track climbs the cliff in five minutes to the tiny fourteenth-century church that was attached to the original monastery. The church has fragmentary frescoes, and from its terrace there's a wonderful **view** over the monastery and the Gulf of Haniá beyond.

The Rodhópou peninsula

The road that extends onto the **Rodhópou peninsula** goes nowhere in particular, petering out into a dirt track beyond Afráta and then circling back, but the first part at least is a superb drive. Just beyond the monastery is a modern Orthodox academy and from here the road follows the coast for a short way and then begins to climb, hairpinning its way to a dizzy height above the sea before turning inland. The views are magnificent – not only back along the coast you have traversed but also down into the translucent green sea.

AFRÁTA is a tiny place, little visited, with a few simple kafenía. Carry on down the hill past the first two of these and you'll come to *Taverna Roxani*. The charming Roxani speaks no English, but she serves good, simple food in a lovely setting with a shady terrace – try the *fagrí* (sea bream) if available.

Below *Roxani's*, keep right on a paved track which drops steeply, and after little more than 1km you'll reach a rocky cove at the far end of the gorge you can see from the village. The exceptionally clear water here offers great swimming, often with no one else about, though you need to watch out for sea urchins and sharp rocks. In the other direction from Afráta, an unsurfaced road is signed to Astrátigos and Áspra Nerá. This is not too bad a drive, and shortly after Áspra Nerá you can rejoin the paved Rodhopós road to head down to the base of the peninsula again.

Towards the tip of the peninsula you'll find no more driveable roads, though there are a couple of sites you might consider undertaking a major hike or a boat trip to reach. The latter is certainly the easier option – in summer the terrain is frighteningly hot, barren and shadeless for walking – especially as day-trip boats from Haniá quite often make for **Diktynna**, almost at the top of the peninsula above a little bay on the east side. An important Roman sanctuary to the goddess of the same name, this was probably built over more ancient centres of worship, and though it has never been properly excavated there's a surprising amount to be seen. The boats come here mainly because it's a sheltered spot to swim (when the sea is rough, fishing boats often shelter here too), but they allow plenty of time to explore.

On the other side of the peninsula, the isolated **Church of Áyios Ioánnis Giónis** can make a challenging hike and, on August 29 (commemoration of the death of St John the Baptist), is host to a major pilgrimage and a mass baptism of boys called John, marking one of the most important festivals of the Cretan religious calendar. At this time the two- to three-hour walk (each way) among crowds of people, is definitely worth it. Although you can approach from Afráta, the main path up the spine of the peninsula starts in Rodhopós, which you reach via the first turn off the main road after Kolimbári, and to where there is an occasional bus (from Kolimbári).

Inland from Kolimbári

A road south from Kolimbári towards Episkopí tracks the valley of the Spiliakos river and offers an opportunity to see an impressive cave and a trio of superb churches, one of which is unique on the island.

The road arrives, after just over three kilometres, at the pleasant rural village of Spiliá. On a hill above the village is located the **Cave of Áyios Ioánnis Xénos** (St John the Stranger), a sizeable grotto with a church – dedicated to the eleventh-century evangelist – built inside it. To reach it follow the signs from the centre of the village or consult locals; it's a popular picnicking place with villagers. On the village's southern edge lies the charming fourteenth-century frescoed church of the **Panayía**, raised on the lower slope of a hill and ringed by pines. Inside, the dark interior (a torch is useful) is decorated with fine frescoes from the same period.

Just over a kilometre to the south of Spiliá a sign on the right indicates the church of "Holy Stephen". Leave any transport here and follow a wooded path for fifty metres to the **chapel of Áyios Stéfanos**, a tiny tenth-century white-walled chapel squatting beneath overhanging oak trees. It should be open, and inside you'll find the heavy stone walls decorated with exquisite **frescoes** dating from the period following the Arab conquest, when the Christian faith was being triumphantly restored.

The church of Miháil Arhángelos Episkopí

A further kilometre towards Episkopí (and signed on the right) lies the remarkable church of **Miháil Arhángelos Episkopí**, one of the oldest churches in Greece, which, with its unique concentric stepped **dome**, is unique in Crete. This feature gives the structure its local name "The Rotunda". The church was, as its official name suggests, a bishop's seat during the Venetian period. But the edifice is much older than this, and just how old archeologists are now trying to discover as they excavate the graveyard surrounding it. It is believed that the present church was built over the remains of an early Christian basilica. Earlier research suggests that the core rotunda section dates to the first Byzantine period, completed perhaps as early as the sixth century, and originally stood alone; the rest of the building was added after the end of the Arab occupation in the tenth century. The excavations in the graveyard have revealed various layers of burials from all periods of the church's history.

The interior is just as fascinating, with **frescoes** dating back to the tenth century including a poignant fragment with the head and partial wing of Áyios Miháil, the church's patron. Take a look also at mosaic floor fragments (thought to date to the earliest period), and an impressive double-seated marble **font**. Father Melchizedek, the guardian monk, lives in a cell at the rear of the church and is an authority on its history and construction, which he will relate to you (in impeccable English) if you can lure him away from his plant-filled garden.

SFAKIÁ AND THE LEFKÁ ÓRI

South of Haniá loom the **Lefká Óri**, or White Mountains – a formidable barrier to progress. Just a couple of metres short of the highest point of the Psilorítis range (trekkers are building a cairn in an attempt to overtake it), these are in every other way more impressive mountains: barer, craggier and far less tamed. There is just one road into the heart of the mountains, climbing up to the cold, enclosed plateau of Omalós. From here any further progress southwards is on foot – most obviously the spectacular, and spectacularly popular, descent through the great cleft of the **Samariá gorge**. Famous as it is, this is just the largest of a series of ravines by which streams make their escape to the coast. Far less beaten tracks lead, for example, down the **Ímbros gorge** towards Hóra Sfakíon, or from Ayía Iríni to Soúyia. With more preparation you could also go climbing among the peaks – there's a mountaineering hut above Omalós – or undertake an expedition right across the range.

Walks also thread their way along the south coast, although it's a great deal easier to get around by boat. Regular summer services link **Ayía Rouméli**, at the bottom of the Samariá gorge, with **Loutró** and Hóra Sfakíon; in the other direction, there are less frequent connections to Paleohóra and Soúyia. **Hóra Sfakíon** is the capital of this region – **Sfakiá** – which for all its desolation and depopulation is perhaps the most famous, and certainly the most written about, in Crete. It is an area notorious for its fierceness: harsh living conditions, unrelenting weather and warlike people. Most men here, it is claimed, still carry a weapon of some kind concealed about their person.

Historically the region was cut off and barbaric, almost a nation apart which, as occupying armies came and went, carried on with life – feuding, rustling, rearing sheep – pretty much regardless. Most of the great tales of Cretan resistance, of *pallikari* fighters and mountain guerrillas, originate in Sfakiá or in Sélinos, west of the mountains. The local version of the Creation reveals much of the Sfakiot spirit. As recounted in Adam Hopkins's book (see p.367), it begins:

> . . . *with an account of all the gifts God had given to other parts of Crete – olives to Ierapetra, Ayios Vasilios and Selinou; wine to Malevisi and Kissamou; cherries to Mylopotamos and Amari. But when God got to Sfakia only rocks were left. So the Sfakiots appeared before Him armed to the teeth. "And us Lord, how are we going to live on these rocks?" and the Almighty, looking at them with sympathy, replied in their own dialect (naturally): "Haven't you got a scrap of brains in your head? Don't you see that the lowlanders are cultivating all these riches for you?"*

Stealing was a way of life and so was feuding and revenge – with vendettas on a Sicilian scale continuing well into this century, and occasionally even now (see p.212).

The Venetians had plans to pacify the region, but their castle on the coast at **Frangokástello** was rarely more than an isolated outpost. The Turks did more, imposing taxation on Sfakiá, for example, but they also provoked more violent revenge, notably in the revolt of Dhaskaloyiánnis (see p.295) and many which succeeded it. The mountains were always a safe refuge in which bandits and rebels could conceal themselves while armies took revenge on the lowlands. In World War II Sfakiá resumed this traditional role: when the Germans invaded, King George of Greece was rushed across the island and down the Samariá gorge to be evacuated, and it was from Hóra Sfakíon that the bulk of the Allied forces were evacuated (see p.299). Throughout the war, the mountain heights remained the realm of the resistance, and in the late 1960s two ex-civil war guerrillas were found still hiding out here, twenty years on.

Nowadays all of this seems distant. There are frequent buses to Hóra Sfakíon and Omalós and a constant stream of people trekking between the two, but you don't have to get far off this path to realize how the reputation grew, and why it still holds such sway.

Omalós and the heart of the mountains

The little plateau around **Omalós** lies pretty much at the heart of the Lefká Óri, surrounded by the highest peaks of the range. Between several hundred and a couple of thousand people head up here daily to join the stampede down the Gorge of Samariá, but only a handful stop to see anything on the way, and very few indeed take any of the more venturesome routes into the mountains. The gorge route is described in detail on the following pages, and while mountaineering doesn't really fall within the scope of this book, a few starter suggestions are also included. Bear in mind that this is a genuinely wild mountain zone – venture nowhere alone or without adequate equipment.

The road up

The road up to Omalós turns inland from Haniá's western outskirts, heading at first across a rich but rather dull countryside of orange groves and vineyards interrupted by large modern villages. Shortly before Alikianós (see p.320), the big white building bristling with TV aerials is a prison with a fairly open regime

THE GEOLOGY OF THE LEFKÁ ÓRI

The **Lefká Óri** take their name from the pale-coloured **limestones** of which they are formed. These rocks were laid down between 150 million and 40 million years ago, when the region which is now Greece and the Aegean Sea featured a different pattern of land and water, dominated by a large landmass called Apulia.

Material eroded from Apulia was transported southwards and deposited in the sea as a series of limestones which are now seen over much of western Crete: they are known as the **Plattenkalk** or Ida limestones. The nature of the limestone varied according to the distance from the Apulian coast: those deposited close to the coast were coarse and contained quite large pebbles, while those further away were much finer and were often arranged in thin layers alternating with a flint-like rock called chert.

To understand how these limestones were formed into the mountains seen today it is necessary to understand something of the theory of "plate tectonics". This states that the earth's crust is composed of a number of large, very slowly moving plates, which are added to at "mid-ocean ridges" and destroyed again in ocean trenches at "subduction zones". About 35 million years ago the plate containing Africa began to move northwards relative to the plate containing Europe, forcing the Plattenkalk limestones up, and eventually causing slices of the Apulian rocks from the north to be pushed over them. This buried and deformed the Plattenkalk limestones – the results of which can now be clearly seen in the walls of the Samariá gorge, where bands of light limestone and dark chert are intensely folded.

Eventually the movement of African plate caused some of the old sea floor to the south to be pushed under all these rocks and initiated a "subduction zone" running along the southern margin of Crete; further movement has since been taken up by subduction of the sea floor. This process has caused continued slow uplift of Crete, particularly in the south close to the subduction zone. As the Lefká Óri have been pushed up in this manner the slices of Apulian rocks on top of them have been eroded away. (Although old Apulian rocks can still be seen to the north of the mountains where the uplift has been less pronounced.)

As the mountains move upwards only very slowly, streams flowing from the centre of Crete have been able to follow their original courses and cut through the mountains, causing the spectacular gorges now seen. This process has been going on for about the last 25 million years and is still continuing – hence gorges such as that at Samariá are getting deeper as the White Mountains continue to rise at the rate of about two metres every thousand years.

(its inmates work in the fields). This is the building after which the Battle of Crete's "Prison Valley" was named, and at the Alikianós turnoff there's a large memorial to local members of the wartime resistance.

Soon after Fournés (see p.273) you begin to climb in earnest to the Lefká Óri through a series of sweeping great loops with increasingly alarming drops. **LÁKKI**, the only village of any size you pass, has stupendous views from its leafy churchyard, to the rear of a small platía. A bracingly green-and-white place looking back down over the plain in one direction and over the valley of the River Vrísi in the other, it makes an ideal base for walking in the surrounding hills, especially in spring when wild flowers abound. A couple of **rooms** places straddle the main road through, both offering more views; *Kri-Kri* (☎0821/67-316; ①), covered with an avalanche of scarlet bougainvillea in summer has perfectly adequate simple rooms, and doubles as one of the village's two **tavernas** which cater heartily for appetites generated by mountain air and whetted with the prospect of strenuous activity. The proprietor here, Gregorios Stamatakis, is extremely friendly and despite speaking limited English will do his best to point out **walking routes** in the vicinity; some of these are marked on the Petrákis *Haniá Trekking and Road Map* (see "Maps", p.30). The paths are easy to follow and none too taxing. *Rooms Nikolas* (☎0821/67-232; ①) over the road has similar rooms with superbly modern shared bathroom facilities. If you encounter honey being sold around the village snap it up: it's made by local producers and is delicious.

Omalós and the plateau

Leaving Lákki the road climbs on, past another memorial at the spot where Kapetan Vasilios (Sergeant Major Dan Perkins) and a Cretan colleague were ambushed (a story recounted in *The Cretan Runner* – see p.367), to a pass at a little over 1200m, before dropping suddenly to the flat expanse of the **Omalós plain**. If you've caught the dawn bus up from Haniá, it's only now that there's enough light properly to take in the eerily deserted, enclosed little world – and to acknowledge your gratitude at being spared the details of your bus's flirtations with the void at every curve of the ascent. At over 1000m the Omalós plateau is cold, its vegetation stunted, and its enclosing ring of stone is clearly visible all around.

Omalós

There's just one small village on the road, **OMALÓS** itself, sited at the centre of the plain. The place is largely unaffected by the daily dawn procession in summer when up to fifty buses pass through (usually without stopping, to the local traders' annoyance) carrying the gorge walkers from all over the island. And once the hordes have gone it settles back into the tranquil rustic settlement it remains for most of the year. A couple of brand new **hotels** look very out of place alongside the chapel and few crude stone houses of the original settlement. The *Hotel Exari* (☎0821/67-180, fax 67-124; ②) in particular, is a large, modern building entirely out of keeping with its surroundings and has en-suite rooms. The nearby *Hotel Neos Omalos* (☎0821/67-269, fax 67-190; ②) has more rooms with bath, and is marginally less flash, while relatively ordinary rooms are available at the friendly *Samaria* (☎0821/67-168; ①), to the right as you enter the village. The revamped *Hotel Gingilos* (☎0821/67-181; ②) has modern rooms with bath and is run in an eccentric style by an entertaining farming family. Note that all the places listed above are fully open during the April to October season; outside of this period they open weekends only. For **eating** and **drinking**, each of the accommodation places has its own bar and taverna serving up hearty mountain fare.

Scattered about the plain are other settlements, but none has the aura of permanent habitation: in winter everything is deep in snow and deserted. In spring the land is marshy and waterlogged – almost becoming a lake if there's a sudden melt. Only in summer do people live here full-time, moving up from Lákki and other villages on the lower slopes round about (Ayía Iríni, Zóurva, Prasés) to pasture sheep and goats or to cultivate, on a small scale, cereals and potatoes.

Walk out into the plain in almost any direction and within five minutes you'll have left all traces of modern life behind, with only the jingling of the occasional goat's bell or the deliberate piling of stones to remind you of human presence. If you do spend the night, there are fabulous starry skies up here.

With your own transport, if you are not planning to walk the gorge, there's a spectacular surfaced road which cuts west through the mountains to link up with the Haniá road to Soúyia just north of Dimitrianá and Ayía Iríni (see p.321) and is a possible route to Paleohóra as well (see p.315).

Scaling the peaks

If you need more of a reason to stay at the top, you could hike the couple of hours (7km) up to the EOS (Greek Mountain Club) **Kallergi Hut** (April–Oct; occasional winter opening for determined skiers; ☎0821/54-560). At 1677m, this acts as the base for climbing into the peaks, and is reached by following the road on from Omalós for about thirty minutes, then turning left onto the dirt track signed to the hut, a further hour's walking; you can also take a path from the top of the Samariá gorge, which cuts the hike to a little over 3km (about 1hr 15min). The hut itself – with no prizes for a friendly welcome – is probably the best source of information on tackling the peaks. Beds are cheap (①), but **meals**, served morning and evening, are not (and you're pretty much obliged to eat at least one). In common with the gorge itself this place is very popular with hikers in summer, and if you do set out with the intention of overnighting, ring ahead first to reserve a place. Sleeping out is an option, but even in high summer the nights can be bitterly cold at this altitude.

For adventurous walkers, there's a two-day hike from here through the heart of the range to Anópoli and Hóra Sfakíon. This would take you right past **Páhnes**, the highest summit in the west and, at 2453m, just 3m short of Psilorítis for the title of loftiest in Crete: Haniot mountaineers regularly add stones to the cairn on the peak in an attempt to catch up. With less commitment you could follow the beginning of this trail for two or three hours for some scintillating views down into the gorge and across the seas to the south and west. The hut itself is perched high over the gorge, but it looks even more impressive from the isolation of these bare stone peaks, a slash of rich green in an otherwise unrelenting landscape of grey and brown.

You'll get more of a sense of achievement – and certainly impress others more – if you tackle the climb to the peak of **Mount Gíngilos** (2080m), beginning from the top of the Samariá gorge. Its north face, the one everyone sees, is a near-vertical slope of solid rock; round the back though, you can reach the summit with only a little scrambling. It's hard work and you need confidence with heights, especially if it's windy, but no special mountaineering skills are necessary. A large yellow sign points the way from the back of the *Tourist Lodge* at the top of the gorge and the path, though not marked with the usual paint splashes, should be easy enough to follow for the two and a half hours to the top. At first you track around to the west, climbing above the plain, before cutting south, downhill slightly, towards the back of the mountain. Here, almost exactly halfway, amid bizarre rock formations which include an arch across the path, there's a spring of ice-cold water (drinkable). Beyond, you begin to climb in earnest for the final thirty minutes. The ascent is signalled with red paint – stick to the path as there are hidden hazards and even the official route needs hands as well as feet. The rewards are an all-round panorama from the summit and, with luck, the chance to spot some of the rarer animal life which crowds have driven from the gorge itself.

The Gorge of Samariá

The one trip that every visitor – even those eminently unsuited to it – feels compelled to make is the hike down the **Samariá Gorge**, since 1962 a national park. At 18km in length, the gorge (or *farángi*) is the largest in Europe. Descending dramatically from the Omalós plateau, this natural wonder was formed by a river which flows between Mount Volakiás to the west and the towering bulk of the Lefká Óri to the east which, over time, has sliced a steep, cavernous ravine between the two. In summer the violent winter torrent reduces to a meek trickle and this is when the multitudes descend. So if you're expecting a wilderness experience, an opportunity to commune peacefully with nature, think again. On the other hand, this is not a Sunday afternoon stroll to be lightly undertaken; especially in spring when the river is roaring, or on a hot midsummer day, it can be a thoroughly gruelling test of fitness and stamina. The mules and helicopter standing by to rescue the injured are not mere show: anyone who regularly leads tours through the gorge has a stack of horror stories to regale you with – broken legs and heart attacks feature most frequently. To undertake the walk you need to be reasonably fit and/or used to lengthy walks, and you should have comfortable, sturdy shoes that will stand up to hot, sharp rocks.

Gorge **wildlife** means most famously the *kri-kri* (variously the *agrimi*, *Capra aegagrus*, the Cretan wild goat or ibex), for whose protection the park was primarily created. You are most unlikely to see one of these large, nimble animals with their long backswept horns, though you may well see ordinary mountain goats defying death on the cliff faces. More likely candidates are the local birds and reptiles. Almost four hundred varieties of **birds** are claimed to have been seen here, including owls, eagles, falcons and vultures; bird-watchers after a coup should look out for the endangered lammergeier (or bearded vulture). On the ground lizards abound, there's the odd snake and you may just spot the beech marten, spiny mouse and weasel, species of which are unique to Crete. The multifarious **trees** – Cretan maple, pine and cypress – are remnants of ancient forests and provide the backdrop to an often dazzling array of **wild flowers**, perhaps the most rewarding finds when in season; the purple *Tulipa saxatilis* and rock plants such as aubretias, saxifrages and anemones stand out, and there are wild irises and orchids here too. **Herbs** are also to be seen in abundance; besides the intoxicatingly aromatic thyme and rosemary and common sage and oregano, there are half a dozen species which exist exclusively in the gorge and nowhere else. Also to be found here – and usually growing in the most inaccessible places – is **Cretan dittany**, a celebrated medicinal herb referred to by Aristotle and Hippocrates and taken by women in ancient times as a method of abortion; indeed modern science has shown the ancients to have been correct in believing that the herb acted as an abortifacient when taken in large quantities in early pregnancy.

Two books on the gorge can prove useful in identifying most of the flora and fauna and are portable enough to take along. *The Samaria Gorge Yesterday and Today* (Toubis, Athens) documents the history of the gorge from the Romans to World War II, and includes an illustrated guide to the flora and fauna along its length, whilst *The Gorge of Samaria and its Plants* by Albertis Atonis (Albertis, Iráklion) provides a step-by-step description of the flora. Both titles are widely available from bookshops in Haniá and Réthimnon.

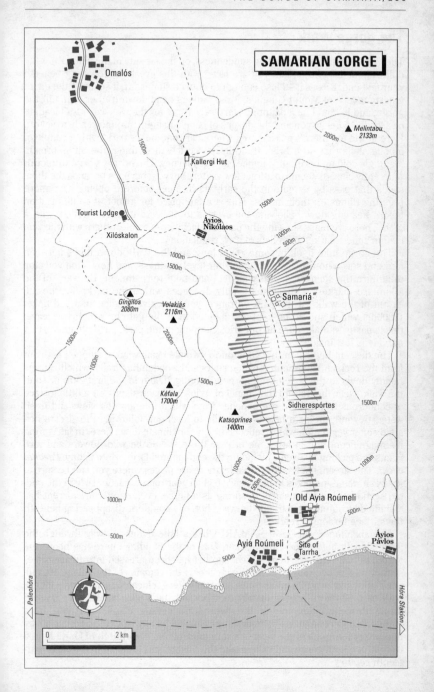

SAMARIAN GORGE

Omalós

Melíntaou
2133m

2000m

Kallergi Hut

1500m

1500m

Tourist Lodge

Xilóskalon

Áyios
Nikólaos

1000m

1000m

500m

1500m

Gíngilos
2080m

Volakiás
2116m

Samariá

2000m

Kéfala
1700m

1500m

1500m

Sidherespórtes

1500m

Katsoprínes
1400m

1000m

1000m

1000m

500m

Old Ayia Roúmeli

500m

Áyios
Pávlos

1000m

Ayía Roúmeli

Site of
Tarrha

500m

500m

N

Paleohóra

Hóra Sfakíon

0   2 km

The gorge walk

The gorge begins, with startling suddenness, on the far side of the plain. After the dull tranquillity of the plain you are faced with this great cleft opening beneath your feet and, across it – close enough to bounce stones off, it seems – the gaunt limestone face of Mount Gíngilos. Most walkers head down (rather than up) the gorge, and it would be a daunting start were it not for the well-worn trail leading clearly down below you and the dozens of people hanging around ready to set off. Here at the top there's a large area where cars and buses park, with a couple of mobile stalls that do a brisk trade in hot coffee (first thing, the air is breath-foggingly cold up here) and supplies for the journey. The nearby gorge **museum** (currently closed) seems to attract few visitors anyway, perhaps because the thousands that pass by its gate in the early dawn, long before it opens, have more pressing things on their minds. This is a fine place for a spot of contemplation before heading down, allowing the crowds to disperse if you've arrived with a mob. There are maps showing the path and facilities en route, others with the vegetation zones marked, and lists of park regulations.

The gorge hike itself is some 16km long and the **walk** down takes between four and seven hours, depending on your level of fitness, and how often you stop to admire the scenery, bathe your feet and take refreshment. Be wary of the kilometre markers – these mark only distances within the park, not the full extent of the walk. At the park entrance, you'll be given a date-stamped ticket (1200dr) which should be kept and handed in at the gate by which you leave; this is partly to make sure no one tries camping in the park, partly to check that nobody is lost inside.

The descent begins on the **Xilóskalon** (wooden stairway), a stepped path cut from the rock and augmented by log stairs and wooden handrails, which zigzags rapidly down to the base of the gorge, plunging 1000m in the first 2km or so of the walk. Near the bottom the chapel of Áyios Nikólaos stands on a little terrace of coniferous trees: there are benches from which to enjoy the view, and fresh water. Beyond, the path begins gradually to level out, following the stream bed amid softer vegetation which reflects the milder climate down here. In late spring it's magnificent, but at any time of year there should be wild flowers and rare plants (no picking allowed), including the endangered large white peony, *Paeonia clusii*. The stream itself is less reliable: there are places where you can be sure of icy fresh water and pools to bathe sore feet all year round (particularly in the middle sections), but what starts in spring as a fierce, even dangerous torrent has dwindled by autumn to a trickle between hot, dry boulders, disappearing beneath the surface for long stretches.

The abandoned village of **SAMARIÁ** lies a little under midway through the walk, shortly before the 7km marker. One of the buildings here has been converted to house the wardens' office, another has been pressed into (inadequate) service as a public toilet, but for the most part the remains of the village are quietly crumbling away. Its inhabitants, until they were relocated to make way for the park in 1962, were predominantly members of the Viglis family, who claimed direct descent from one of the twelve aristocratic clans implanted from Byzantium. Certainly this settlement, as isolated as any in Crete and cut off by floodwater for much of the year, is a very ancient one: the church of Óssia María, from which both gorge and village take their name, was founded in the early fourteenth century.

After Samariá the path is more level, the walls of the gorge begin to close in and the path is often forced to cross from one side of the stream to the other, on stepping stones which at times may be submerged and slippery. Beside you, the contorted striations of the cliffs are increasingly spectacular, but the highlight comes shortly after the Christós resting point with the Sidherespórtes (**Iron Gates**) where two rock walls rise sheer to within a whisker of a thousand feet: standing at the bottom, one can almost touch both at once. For this short stretch, there's a wooden walkway raised above the stream, whose swirling waters fill the whole of the narrow passage. Almost as suddenly as you entered this mighty crack in the mountain you leave it again, the valley broadens, its sides fall away, and you're in a parched wilderness of rubble deposited here by the spring thaw.

Before long – 8km beyond Samariá – you reach the fringes of Ayía Rouméli, where there's a gate by which you leave the park and a couple of stalls selling cool drinks at crippling prices. Frustratingly, however, this is not the end of the walk: old Ayía Rouméli has been all but deserted in favour of the new beachside community, a further excruciatingly hot, dull twenty minutes away. Arriving finally in **Ayía Rouméli** proper (see p.289), you face the agonizing choice between plunging into the sea or diving into one of the tavernas for an iced drink – though in the event it takes a strong will to walk past the rows of enticingly dew-dropped cans of chilled fruit juice and ice-cold beers set out to divert you from your course to the water. Once your senses adjust, Ayía Rouméli is a pretty unattractive place – but that drink, and the first plunge in the sea, are likely to live in the memory as the most refreshing ever.

Walking up the gorge

Starting from the bottom, the hike up to **Omalós** is not as hard as some imagine, though it will take rather longer – six to seven hours at a reasonable, steady pace. Few people do it all the way, which means that at the top you may well find the gorge almost empty; on the way up, however, you'll have had to pass all the hordes charging down. You could also walk a short way up and come back – an outing offered as a day-trip known as "Samariá the Lazy Way". This will show you the Iron Gates, the most spectacular individual section, but it means a lot of walking in the dullest parts down by the coast and none of the almost alpine scenes nearer the top.

Gorge practicalities

Conditions permitting, the gorge is open between the hours of 6am and sunset, from April 10 to October 31 inclusive; however the first three weeks after opening and the final two weeks before closure will entirely depend on weather conditions and you're advised to ring ahead to save a wasted journey. Entrance to the national park costs 1200dr and should you enter after 4pm, you're only allowed into the first couple of kilometres from each end. During winter the hike is dangerous and often impossible, and even early and late in the season flash floods are a real possibility and not to be taken lightly; in 1993 a number of walkers perished when they were washed out to sea. If in doubt, the Haniá Forest Service has a **gorge information** number (☎0821/67-140) and the gorge office (☎0821/67-179) at the entrance will also provide advice. Outside the official season, and at the discretion of the wardens, you may be allowed through if the weather is good, but there will be very little transport.

There are a whole series of national park rules (posted at the entrance), but the most important are **no camping**, no fires (or smoking outside the designated areas), no alcohol, no hunting and no interfering with the wildlife or collecting plants. There are wardens who patrol to ensure these are obeyed, that no one wanders too far from the main path (another breach of regulations unless you have a permit obtained in advance from the Haniá Forest Service) and that no stragglers are overtaken by nightfall.

As for **supplies** for the walk, you want to carry the minimum possible. On a day-trip you needn't necessarily carry anything, though a water bottle and something to munch on the way are probably worthwhile (there are springs at regular intervals and ice-cold water in the stream, but for long periods you'll find neither – especially over the last, hottest hour) as is some means of carrying clothes you discard en route (7am at the top feels close to freezing; 1pm at the bottom may hover around 100°F – approximately 38°C). If you plan to stay a day or two at the bottom you'd do better to leave your pack at Haniá's bus station for collection later, taking only what's essential. As far as **food** is concerned, you needn't worry about starving: you can find enough for breakfast in the stalls at the top (or sit down properly for a meal in the *Tourist Lodge* with a fine terrace view), and Ayía Rouméli is more than equipped to feed everyone arriving at the bottom.

Buses and boats

The vast majority of people who walk through the gorge do so as part of a **day-trip**: a very early bus to the top, walk down by early afternoon, boat from Ayía Rouméli to Hóra Sfakíon and bus from there back home. Most go with one of the **guided tours** offered by every travel agent on the island – certainly if you're staying in a hotel anywhere in the east of Crete this is much the simplest method, and probably the only way of doing it in a single day. Most tours will include all bus and ferry connections, but not food or the entrance fee to the park itself. (If you're planning to stay on the south coast, the tour bus can save you the effort of carrying your bags; simply stow them underneath and retrieve them in Hóra Sfakíon. Do let them know your plan, though, both to guard against an unexpected switch of bus and to prevent search parties being sent out.) If, however, you are staying in Haniá, or marginally less straightforwardly in Iráklion or Réthimnon, you can save money and avoid having to walk in a large group by taking the **public bus**.

From Haniá there are four departures a day, at 6.15am, 7.30am, 8.30am and 1.30pm (this latter service changes to 4.30pm outside school term time), arriving at the top about ninety minutes later. You'll normally be sold a return ticket, including the return leg from Hóra Sfakíon (which needn't necessarily be used the same day), so if you don't want this you'll have to make your intentions very clear; the bus station is in total chaos when the first buses leave. There's a lot to be said for taking the earliest bus: more of the walk can be completed while it's still relatively cool, there's no need to force your pace, and if you're planning to stop over anywhere at the bottom you've more chance of being among the first to arrive. On the other hand, everyone now does this – there's often a procession of as many as five full buses leaving Haniá before dawn, the bus station is in turmoil, there are queues and confusion when you arrive, and you're unlikely to escape from crowds the whole way down. It may be hotter, but it's also quieter if you set out later. The first buses of the day **from Iráklion** (5.30am) **and Réthimnon** (6.15am and 7am) to Haniá continue direct to Omalós.

Heading back, at least five **boats** a day leave Ayía Rouméli for Hóra Sfakíon through most of the summer, with four of them calling at Loutró; there's a slightly reduced service from April to mid-June and from mid-September to the end of October, and hardly any boats from November to April when the gorge is closed. The trip takes around an hour and you should check current times when you arrive: at the time of writing there were two boats at 3.45pm and the **last ferry** at 6pm. You'll need to leave by 6pm anyway to be sure of connecting with the last Haniá bus. For Soúyia and Paleohóra there's a daily sailing at 4.30pm between May and September. **Buses** from Hóra Sfakíon back to Haniá leave at 7am, 11am, 4pm, 6pm and 7pm; for Réthimnon there's a direct one at 6.30pm (otherwise you change at Vrísses); for Plakiás and Ayía Galíni at 5.30pm.

Accommodation

If you want to make the gorge part of a longer excursion, there are several accommodation options. The option of staying at the top, in the *Tourist Lodge* (☎0821/67-237) is no longer a possibility since it closed its rooms, although their **taverna** is a still great place for a meal later in the day, with spectacular mountain **views** from its terrace. The nearest bed you can get to the entrance is now at one of the places in Omalós (see p.282), or you could simply sleep out (there are usually quite a few people trying to find a flat space for their sleeping bags around the entrance). This has few real advantages; you'd have to be up very early to steal a march on the first arrivals from Haniá (for much of the year this would mean setting off before daylight) and from Omalós you face an extra five-kilometre walk to reach the top of the trail, but it does make quite a change to stay up here and freeze for a night and of course it gives you the opportunity to explore more than just the gorge.

Staying on the **south coast** for a night or more after your exertions makes more sense: there are rooms at Ayía Rouméli (see below), Loutró (p.290) and Hóra Sfakíon (p.298) or westwards in Soúyia (p.322) and Paleohóra (p.314).

Ayía Rouméli

Once you've drunk and eaten your fill, plunged into the sea and out again, lain on the pebbles for a while and rested, **AYÍA ROUMÉLI**'s attractions soon begin to pall. It's a singularly unattractive example of over-rapid development, with a rash of concrete tavernas and rooms for rent spreading over a shingly beach. By local standards it's expensive too, although given the difficulties of transport this is perhaps not altogether surprising. Ayía Rouméli does have its good points though – mainly the sheer number of places to eat and to stay – and at night it's very peaceful. Should you be tempted, try the tranquil *Livikon* (②) at the rear of the village, or the sea-view rooms attached to tavernas *Tara* (☎0825/91-231; ②) or *Zorba's* (②); you can also book ahead at the *Hotel Agia Roumeli* (☎0825/91-241, fax 91-232; ③). The village is even attempting to be environmentally conscious: the pile of huge concrete tank traps behind the beach shields an experimental solar energy plant; at night, or other times when this system can't cope, a diesel generator cuts in.

The kiosk which sells **boat tickets** is plainly marked down by the beach: if you're catching the bus back from Hóra Sfakíon, get a ticket when you emerge from the gorge for the last connecting boat, and spend the afternoon on the beach; if you plan to stay elsewhere on this coast, take the first boat available for the best chance of finding a room at your destination. Given the choice, Ayía Rouméli is the least attractive of the places you could stay, though it does at least have a fair number of rooms and a surprisingly large beach if all you want to do is crash out on the pebbles (a couple of the tavernas have showers which they'll let you use if you eat there). Just to the east of the village (near the solar plant) is a clump of trees among which a few people are usually camped, and on the beach in this direction are some caves, also sometimes used to sleep out in.

Finding anything much to do apart from laze on the beach takes some ingenuity. Although there was an ancient settlement here – Tarra, inhabited probably from the fifth century BC through to the fifth AD – and more or less constant later habitation, very little remains to be seen. The ruined Turkish fort, under which you pass as you emerge from the gorge onto the beach, doesn't really justify the scramble up to see it. Tarra straddled the stream where it ran into the sea, just to the east of the present village – the only obvious remains are the foundations of an early Christian basilica by the present church of Panayía, around which you may also spot a few tiny fragments of mosaic. This, supposedly, was the site of a much earlier temple of Apollo.

Loutró and south-coast walks

Of all the south-coast villages, **LOUTRÓ** perhaps best sums up what this coast ought to be all about. It's an incredibly soporific place, where there's absolutely nothing to do but eat, drink and laze – and where you fast lose any desire to do anything else. The big excitements of the day are the occasional arrivals and departures of the ferries. The days start bright and are soon lost in an overpowering heat shimmer; evening comes cool and darkness falls fast – by 10pm the place is virtually asleep. All this despite the fact that it has been almost entirely taken over by tourists. Little happens all summer long to interrupt this easygoing idyll, but if you're here for the great feast of the Panayía on August 15 the small church is the place to head for, From the early dawn, the formidable local priest conducts the service which lasts until after midday. The small churchyard then fills up with all those who had intended to come earlier – and each of whom receives a disapproving glare from the *papás* – as biblical quantities of *arní* (roast lamb), *psomí* and *krasí* are doled out and everyone enjoys a great feast.

The short waterfront arching around a beautiful little bay consists of a row of perhaps six tavernas and a similar number of rooms places plus one small hotel; the mountains rise immediately behind the waterfront. There's no road in, and everyone here has either come on the boat or walked, which helps to keep things very low-key, prices reasonable, big groups rare, and the people genuinely friendly. Although the transparent blue water here is always inviting, perhaps Loutró's main drawback is its lack of a real **beach**. There's a small stretch of pebbles in front of the eastern half of the seafront, with large signs asking bathers to remain respectable. Try lying topless here and you'll be told none too politely to cover up; those who persist risk being catcalled by the village children. But the sheltered bay is otherwise ideal for swimming, clear and warm, and people bask nude on the rocks around the point, far enough out to avoid offence. The good news is that there are other beaches in walking distance (see below), with small boats (or even your own hire canoe) ferrying visitors to the best, at Sweetwater and Mármara.

Rooms in Loutró seem uniformly basic and comfortable, though to be sure of finding one you should arrive as early as possible – an increasing number seem to be pre-
booked through enterprising travel agencies and foreign holiday firms. Try for one
with a balcony (the *Porto Loutro* and *Blue House* offer top-floor rooms with huge roof
terraces); the quietest places are generally the furthest round to the east, such as
Keramos (☎ & fax 0825/91-356; ②) and *Ilios* (☎0825/91-160; ②) both with rooms over
tavernas, but nowhere is exactly loud or stays open late. The only place with preten-
sions is the *Hotel Porto Loutro* (☎0825/91-433, fax 91-091; ③), right in the middle of
the village above the beach, whose white cubes fit in surprisingly well with the surroundings; it's lovely and not outrageously expensive, though since the rooms are
pretty accurate reproductions of a simple Greek room you may question whether it's
worth paying the extra. Even here you may find yourself showering in salt water if
there's a shortage (as there is most summers these days). A cheaper option is the
Blue House (☎0825/91-127; ②), whose en-suite rooms are also pretty good. Other
cheaper places (but not by much in high season) are to be found further into the village, around the church. Here the good-value *Rooms Manousoudaki* (☎0825/91-348;
②) and *Rooms Patrudakis* (☎0825/91-351; ③) are pleasant places for rooms with bath.
If you can't find anywhere at all to stay, you could hike or take a boat over to Fínix or
Líkkos (see pp.292–3). You could also consider **camping** out by the castle, on the
headland or on Sweetwater Beach (see p.292) but you should be aware that freelance
campers are not very popular in the village after years of problems.

When it comes to **eating** and **drinking**, *The Blue House*, recognizable from its
blue-checked tablecloths rather than a sign, is also arguably the best restaurant in
Loutró, and the owner one of the friendliest characters. There's usually a fair vegetarian selection here, and at several other places. Good fish is on offer too, at
Keramos and *Ilios* further round the bay. The only place open late is the *Café Bar
Maistrali*, the westernmost building in Loutró (alongside the concrete jetty), where
everyone heads in the evening. Its cocktails and music – they also serve exotic
breakfasts – may seem a bit slick in this setting, but it's certainly a pleasant way to
wind up your day. The **practicalities** are easily taken care of: you can change
money and buy supplies at the mini-market, and a second store a little further on
(immediately before the beach) has a good selection of second-hand books and also
changes money. *The Blue House* has a public phone, and **canoes** can be rented from
waterfront owners for expeditions to the nearby coves and beaches. The *Keramos*
taverna operates a taxi-boat to Hóra Sfakíon (6000dr) and elsewhere, and they can
arrange one- to three-day cruises aboard a nine-metre boat complete with skipper.

Boat tickets are sold from a kiosk at the end of the dock, but they only go on
sale a few minutes before departure; try to have the right change. The smaller
boats tie up at this dock, but the *Samaria* sails straight up to the beach, lowering
its bow onto the pebbles. (Occasionally it comes to the dock to unload supplies –
a truck drives off onto the jetty, which is barely large enough to contain it, is
unloaded and filled with empties and drives back onto the next ferry. There are
no more than a few feet of space for it to drive up and down.)

The coast around Loutró: Sweetwater to Mármara

Anyone who spends any time at all in Loutró is eventually taken with the urge to
explore – even if it's just climbing up to the ruins on the headland. There are plenty of long, tough walks available (see the following section), but there are also easier hikes to nearby beaches. Some of these can also be reached by boat.

Sweetwater Beach

Sweetwater Beach lies approximately halfway between Loutró and Hóra Sfakíon, in the middle of a barren coastline. From the sea, as you pass on one of the coastal boats, it appears as a long, extremely narrow slice of grey between sheer ochre cliffs and a dark, deep sea. Closer up, the beach seems much larger, but there's still a frightening sense of being isolated between unscaleable mountains and an endless stretch of water.

The beach takes its name from the small springs which bubble up beneath the pebbles to provide fresh, cool drinking water. You can dig a hole almost anywhere to find water; there are plenty already made, but you should take care not to pollute the groundwater with soap. For years there was a little enclave of nudist campers here, their idyll interrupted only by the occasional intrepid cliff walker. Over the last couple of years, though, daily boat services have started from both Loutró and Hóra Sfakíon, bringing a lot more people. So far these have not spoilt the place – the beach is easily big enough to absorb everyone – and the campers are still here, for once doing a good job of keeping the place pristine: there are signs up warning against leaving rubbish, and people regularly make an effort to pick up any junk that is left behind. The long-term residents tend to monopolize the only shade, in the caves at the back of the beach, but you can always escape the sun at the small bar/taverna which sits on a lump of concrete just off the western end of the beach, reached by a rickety plank. You can get cold drinks and simple meals here and they also rent out sun umbrellas. There are no other facilities beyond the boats, which come once in the morning and again in the late afternoon. Walking here is also a possibility, though a very hot and shadeless one: about 45 minutes to Loutró, an hour to Hóra Sfakíon (see following section). On a calm day, you could even paddle a canoe over from Loutró. The path runs along behind all the houses in Loutró – to join it from there, climb up behind the beachside kiosk and church.

Fínix

Immediately to the west of Loutró, in the little bay on the other side of the promontory, stood **ancient Fínikas**, now known as **FÍNIX** or Phoenix. This was a major town during the Roman and Byzantine periods, and a significant port long after that: it was the harbour at Fínix, a more comfortable place to wait out the winter storms than Kalí Liménes, which St Paul's ship was hoping to reach when it was swept away (see p.130). A local story has the saint actually landing here and being beaten up by the locals he tried to convert: given the attitude to Cretans revealed in Paul's epistle to Titus, it is, as Michael Llewellyn Smith points out, "safe to say that if he *had* landed here they *would* have beaten him up".

Yet again there is very little to be seen. These days the bay, with its rocky beach, has just one **taverna**, the *Finix* (☎0825/91-257; ②), an exceptionally languid place, with simple food and **rooms** with bath – the epitome of a tranquil hideaway. It's hard to believe there could ever have been a population of any size. Up on the headland, though, there's certainly evidence of later occupation, principally in the form of the Venetian fortification on the point and from where – on clear days – it's possible to glimpse the island of Gávdhos, 50km out to sea. Nearby are traces of a Byzantine basilica and other scattered remains; most curiously, however, there's a building, very much in the form of a Venetian church, sunk entirely below ground level. Its arched roof is intact, the interior entirely full of water. Nowadays it is deliberately flooded and used as a storage cistern, but its original purpose remains a mystery. It could always have been a cistern, of course, but it seems too elaborate for that; an alternative theory suggests it was an underground arsenal attached to the castle.

To get to Fínix by the most direct route, join the path – now part of the E4 European Footpath – that runs behind Loutró, up behind the beachside kiosk and the church. This will lead you straight up, past the castle and directly over the headland, in around fifteen minutes; if you're continuing beyond Fínix, you don't have to go down to the water as a path continues straight past the back of the bay, but it's only marginally shorter. It's also possible to get there by walking out past the last house in Loutró and simply following the rocky coast around. This is a much longer and tougher walk, but it does have the compensation of passing plenty of good rocks to swim from, and extensive remains of old buildings which you can imagine are, and may indeed be, ancient Fínikas. Boats to Mármara also regularly call in at Fínix, bringing supplies.

Líkkos and Mármara

Beyond Fínix, the path continues to another, much longer bay, **LÍKKOS**, with three rather poorly patronized **taverna/rooms** places, making it another escapist's paradise. The economical *Rooms Yeóryios* (☎0825/91-457; ①), the last of these, right in the middle of the beach, has a pleasantly eccentric (eponymous) owner and is very friendly and quiet. Now that electricity has finally reached here, the place is also very comfortable – and there's plenty of fresh water too, which there may not be in Loutró. If you ring him, Yeóryios will come and pick you up from Loutró or Fínix (free) with his boat. Unfortunately Líkkos is not a very attractive **beach**, with rocks and pebbles, and is awkward to swim from unless you wear shoes. Behind, you can look up and see the village of Livanianá, perched on the eastern flank of the Arádhena gorge (see over p.295).

The gorge emerges at the sea in the next bay along, **Mármara** (or marble) **Beach**. This is another fairly small cove, with a sandy beach surrounded by interesting rock formations full of caves and slabs to dive from or sunbathe on. Unfortunately it also sees at least three boats a day from Loutró, which in summer bring more people than can comfortably be accommodated. So although out of season it might be more attractive than Sweetwater, at peak times it is far less so – and it has the additional disadvantages of no one to keep it clean and no fresh water (or anything else, so bring plenty to drink with you). Some people do camp here, but to do so you have to make a very long hike for supplies, or regularly take the boats to and from Loutró. Walking to Mármara takes a little over an hour in all, and the second half, from the far end of the beach at Líkkos, is hot and exposed, climbing high onto the cliff.

More challenging hikes

Loutró lies close to the heart of the network of coastal paths linking Ayía Rouméli to Hóra Sfakíon (see p.298) and, in the absence of a road, is an important junction. Most real traffic nowadays goes by boat, of course, and the last inland hamlets have finally had a driveable track built to them. But the paths and tracks remain, to give a variety of possible **hikes**, even the easiest of which can be demanding in the heat of high summer. You'll need, at the very least, decent shoes to cope with rough, rocky terrain and a water bottle, which you should fill at every opportunity. You should also have a companion, since some of these paths are pretty isolated, and outside help cannot be relied upon.

Coastal routes from Loutró

The **coastal path** – still serving as the E4 (see above) – is the most obvious, the most frequently used by tourists and, in terms of not getting lost, the simplest to follow. There's not a great deal to see en route, however, nor is it an easy walk – the path is often frighteningly narrow and uneven as it clings to the cliff face, and in summer it is very, very hot, offering no shelter at all from the sun, so headwear and protection are advised.

From **Loutró to Hóra Sfakíon** this is barely a problem: it's the most heavily travelled part, the whole walk takes less than two hours (8km), and there's a rest stop at Sweetwater Beach halfway. Loutró to Sweetwater is straightforward and fairly well beaten: beyond here the path clambers over a massive recent rockfall and then follows the cliffs until it eventually emerges on the Hóra Sfakíon–Anópoli road about thirty minutes' walk above Hóra. This is easy to find in the other direction too, the path (to the left) leaving the road at the first hairpin bend.

In the other direction, **Loutró to Ayía Rouméli** is an altogether tougher proposition. For a start you can expect to be walking for four hours solid, and for seconds there's no chance of refreshment between the tavernas at Líkkos and Ayía Rouméli. The path has already been described as far as Mármara Beach (see previous pages). Afterwards you climb again to track along the exposed cliff face for around an hour before reaching the first sign of civilization, a solitary cottage and a few trees. In about another hour, you'll arrive at the eleventh-century chapel of **Áyios Pávlos**, yet another site where St Paul is supposed to have landed. Here he allegedly christened locals in a nearby spring. The chapel itself is ancient and rather beautiful, set on a ledge above the water, and surrounded by dunes. Inside are fresco fragments dated to the thirteenth century. You could cool off in the sea here before setting out on the final hour to Ayía Rouméli.

Coming from Ayía Rouméli this path is well marked, heading east out of the village. Ten to fifteen minutes after Áyios Pávlos it splits, left to climb inland to Áyios Ioánnis and Anópoli (for more on these, see the following sections), right to continue along the coast.

To Anópoli

If you're hiking for its own sake, or for that matter if you want to take the easiest way from Ayía Rouméli to Hóra Sfakíon without necessarily calling at Loutró, then the **inland routes** centring on Anópoli have a great deal to be said for them (see "Anópoli to Ayía Rouméli", opposite).

ANÓPOLI itself is a quiet country village, not much used to visitors, dominating a small upland plain with a few, rare vestiges of forest. Another wonderful location to sample the simple delights of rural Crete, it has a couple of kafenía and a small general store on the square which lies at the end of a long road in, after the way levels following the climb. Outside of holiday periods such as the festival of Panayía on August 15, if you wanted to stay away from all the hustle of the coast you should be able to find somewhere here. The village also makes a good base for an exploration of the Arádhena gorge (see opposite). There are several **rooms** places along the road as you approach from Hóra Sfakíon; the friendliest is the excellent-value *Panorama* (☎0825/91-100; ①) for en-suite rooms where you'll get a warm Sfakiá welcome. The other good place is in the village proper, a couple of kilometres further, where *Rooms Kopasis* (☎0825/91-169; ①) has rooms with bath fronting the statue of Dhaskaloyiánnis (see below) on the main square. Both places have good **tavernas** and any of the goat, lamb or sausage dishes here are mouthwatering. *Ta Tria Adelfia* (☎0825/91-150; ①) half way between the two is another possibility for simpler (but not cheaper) rooms if these are full.

Anópoli was the home of the first of the great Cretan rebels against the Turks, **Dhaskaloyiánnis** – the subject of a celebrated epic poem. To cut a very long story extremely short, Dhaskaloyiánnis, a wealthy ship-owner, was promised support by Russian agents if he raised a rebellion in Sfakiá, support which in the event never materialized. (The Russians hoped only to create a diversion for their campaigns against the Ottoman Empire elsewhere.) The revolt, in 1770, was short-lived and disastrous for Sfakiá, which for the first time was brought well and truly under the Turkish heel: Dhaskaloyiánnis gave himself up and was executed. There's now a statue of him in the square.

Getting to Anópoli, which is high above the coast more or less directly above Loutró, is not easy unless you have a car. **From Hóra Sfakíon** it's 12km up a very steep, winding road with alarming hairpin bends and few barriers, making meeting a bus or truck coming in the opposite direction a pretty nerve-wracking experience if you happen to be on the outside. You probably wouldn't want to drive this at night, nor would you really want to walk it up either, but you might not have much choice, since the one daily **bus** drives up at 4pm and down again at 6.30am. The walk up **from Loutró** also looks terrifying – you can see the path tracking back and forth across an almost vertical cliff – but is in fact far less bad than it seems: about ninety minutes, climbing steeply most of the way. This is best done very early, before the sun gets too powerful; at the top you're on the fringes of Anópoli – turn left for the centre.

Anópoli to Ayía Rouméli

To head for Ayía Rouméli from Anópoli, follow the road through to the far end of the village, where it becomes a little-used, dusty jeep track, signed to Arádhena. There may be shorter ways on the old paths than this track (ask around if you're determined), but there's so little traffic that following the road makes little difference. It takes about thirty minutes to the edge of the **Arádhena gorge**, 3km away, on the far side of which is the virtually abandoned hamlet of Arádhena. Adam Hopkins claims that the people left to escape with their lives from a series of Sfakiot vendettas. He's probably right, but in the light of what is happening elsewhere, such depopulation seems commonplace. With the new road, one or two people have moved back and started to restore some of the crumbling buildings.

The first thing to grab your attention when you reach the gorge is the steel **bridge** – a remarkable construction, all the more remarkable when you discover that it's a bridge to nowhere, as the road on the far side soon peters out at nearby Áyios Ioánnis. Constructed in 1986 by the local Vardinoyiannís family, controllers of a international business empire, the bridge was a gift to provide a lifeline to the outside world without which their home village would probably have died. Rumble across it in a car and the terrifying crack of the wooden boards against metal thunders around the gorge below. The **views** from the bridge down into the gorge – one of Crete's most precipitous – below are vertiginously spectacular.

Across the bridge and right on the opposite rim of the gorge is the romantically picturesque Byzantine church of **Mihaíl Arhángelos**, with its curious "pepper-pot" dome standing proud against the Lefká Óri's heights. The white-walled church dates from the fourteenth or fifteenth century and was constructed on the ruins of a much earlier basilica, of which the central nave and apse may be a part. Inside, are some outstanding **frescoes** (torch useful) depicting the life and crucifixion of Christ as well as the church's patron saint. A fairly ancient *ikonostásis* stands in the church's porch. The church is now permanently locked following a number of thefts and to obtain a key to view it you should make enquiries at Anópoli (try *Rooms Kopasis* on the square). Scattered round about and beyond the nearly deserted village are a few traces of ancient Araden, a still unexcavated Greco-Roman town from whose stones the church is said to be built. Looking inland from the churchyard or the bridge you can see the old path, negotiable on foot or by pack animals only, zigzagging down to the bottom and back up the other side which for well over two millennia was the only way across the gorge. Incidentally, this is still the path you take to follow the gorge down to the sea (see below).

The road from the bridge now ends at **ÁYIOS IOÁNNIS**, beneath the massed peaks of Páhnes, Troharís and Zaranokefála, 5km or another hour or so beyond. A more substantial and outwardly prosperous place since the construction of the bridge, it goes so far as to have a **taverna** on the way in where you can rest up for a while or have a beer at tables beneath shady pines. Close to the taverna (below the road to the left) are a couple more **Byzantine churches** with fourteenth-century frescoes; the taverna should have keys. There are also several impressively large caves nearby. You should ask to be put on the right track from here, the way isn't immediately obvious. Generally, you have to head to the left, between two chapels, after which the path becomes hard to follow for a while until it emerges on top of the cliffs. From here it loops down as a rough but obvious path to join the coast trail before the chapel of Áyios Pávlos. You should be able to complete the approximately seventeen-kilometre walk from Anópoli to Ayía Rouméli in about five hours, though with rest stops and wrong turnings it could well take much longer; leave plenty of leeway if you need to catch a boat back. If you are undertaking this walk in reverse, start early so as to complete the climb of the cliffs before it becomes too hot.

The Arádhena gorge

A return trip from Loutró, up to Anópoli and down to Mármara Beach (where you can get a trippers' boat back; last at 4pm, or there's taxi-boat available from the *Yeóryios* taverna at Líkkos Beach, a short walk to the east) via the **Arádhena gorge** makes a challenging excursion. You must be reasonably fit to tackle this, as the gorge involves some scrambling and climbing – although metal ladders bolted to the rock have now replaced the rather precarious ropes and rope-ladders previously provided to help you over the worst parts. Although this doesn't really need any special mountaineering skills, it can be pretty scary – and not helped by the ominous presence of picked-clean skeletons of goats, which presumably have either fallen from the top or been washed away in spring floods.

The sense of achievement, however, is immense, and the gorge, though far smaller, is in physical terms almost as impressive as that of Samariá. There isn't much in the way of wildlife, but the rocky river bed is forced into an extremely narrow gap between sheer walls almost all the way down – and there'll be hardly anyone else around. Allow five hours at least from Loutró to Mármara (two and a half to the top of the gorge, two and a half down it) adding on an extra ninety minutes if you walk back to Loutró; even taking a boat back, in the heat of high summer eight hours may be more like it once you've stopped a few times. An **alternative starting-point** is Anópoli (see p.294) which would allow you to get the gorge completed early on in the walk, although once back at Loutró you would still have the ninety-minute ascent back to the village, with the possible option of a taxi (about 1200dr) from Hóra Sfakíon if it all becomes too much.

To reach the start of the **descent** into the gorge you set off by turning right off the road and onto the old path, 600m before you reach the gorge and just before the bridge comes in to view. Heading half right across a stony stretch of ground with a small pinewood to the right leads you to the recently repaired stepped path down to the bottom (and this side should be used rather than the track on the other side which is deteriorating fast now it's not used much). This and the first stretch, with its relatively flat bottom as you head under the bridge through an impressively deep section, conspire to lull you into a false sense of security: as it gets steeper further down, you find yourself jumping from rock to rock or lowering yourself carefully down dry cascades. Look out as you go for the paint marks indicating the route – these often seem to take you over unnecessarily tricky terrain, but you usually discover the reason further on when you reach an impassable portion. Fill up with water at every opportunity, as there's none towards the end of the gorge or at the beach.

If all this sounds too tough there is an **easier alternative**, though not tried and tested. Head out past Fínix (follow the upper path, bypassing the cove) and you'll come to a fork in the path: the lower one goes to Líkkos, the upper to Livaniáná, which you can see above you. From here a path leads down into the gorge, emerging fairly near the bottom having bypassed all the really difficult bits. The Ímbros ravine (see below) is another slightly softer option, with more wildlife but less dramatic terrain.

The road south: to Hóra Sfakíon and Frangokástello

The easy way **into Sfakiá** is by a good road which cuts south from Vrísses (p.268), almost immediately beginning to spiral up into the mountains, towards the plateau of Askífou. The climb seems straightforward from a bus or car, but the country you drive through has a history as bloody as any in Crete: you pass first through a little ravine where two Turkish armies were massacred, the first during the 1821 uprising, the second in 1866 after the heroic events at Arkádhi (see p.207); the road itself is the one along which the Allied troops retreated at such cost in the final stages of the Battle of Crete. This chaotic flight has been described in detail in just about all the books covering the battle (and also in Evelyn Waugh's *Officers and Gentlemen*) – it makes for strange reading from the comfort of a modern journey.

Askífou Plateau

The **Plateau of Askífou** offers the relief of level ground for a while, now as it did then. The plain is dominated by a ruined Turkish castle on a hill to the left of the road – a hill so small and perfectly conical it looks fake, put there expressly to raise the castle above its surroundings. There are several small villages up here, chief of them **AMOUDHÁRI**, with a couple of small tavernas and the chance of a room if you wanted to stay (one place, over the bakery, tends to be noisy in the morning; the only other disturbance to the peace here is the twice-daily convoy of buses, arriving empty and returning with sated gorge-walkers).

For keen walkers, a path leads from Petrés, immediately south of Amoudhári to Anópoli, a long day's hike (18km) through the mountains via the hamlet of

Kalí Láki, beyond where the path follows a rough track to reach Anópoli. Though detailed on the Petrákis *Haniá Trekking and Road Map* (see "Maps", p.30) it's not a terribly easy route to follow and you should attempt to get thorough directions locally before trying this, though this may not be easy unless you speak fluent Greek. Less taxing hikes are to be had by following any of the tracks which climb westwards from the village into the foothills of the Lefká Óri (with good opportunities for birdspotting) or, in the other direction, east of the nearby village of Goní where a track leads for 10km to the hamlet of Asigonía (see p.212).

The Ímbros ravine

On the far side of the Askífou plateau lies the village of **ÍMBROS**. Beyond, the road climbs briefly again out of the plain and then begins gradually to descend to the south coast. This stretch is lovely: an excellent, winding track which follows dramatically one side of the **Ímbros ravine**, tracking high through conifer-clad slopes with the cleft always dizzily below. As you approach the coast, still high above it, you begin to glimpse distant sparkles of water until finally the road breaks out of its confinement, way above the sea, with a broad plain to the east (and Frangokástello hazy in the distance), steeper drops to the west, and immense vistas out towards Africa ahead. Hóra Sfakíon is out of sight until you are almost upon it, an alarming plunge down through hairpin bend after hairpin bend. Driving, you need to watch out for buses: it can be alarming in the evening meeting the vast convoy coming the other way on these relatively narrow curves, and in the afternoon you'll pass them parked in every available spot since they can't all squeeze into Hóra Sfakíon.

It is also possible to walk down the Ímbros ravine, following a track which, until the completion of the new road, was the district's main thoroughfare. This is easily enough done – in less than three hours – and it's a wonderfully solitary walk, a spectacular contrast to the crowds at Samariá. The only problem is that you miss the wonderful views from above. In its own way the ravine is as interesting as its better-known rival, albeit on a smaller scale: narrow and stiflingly confined in places, speckled with caves in others and at one point passing under a monumental, natural stone archway. The path starts from the southern fringe of Ímbros village, close by a blue shrine near a kafeníon (serving excellent cheese omelette with honey), where a well-trodden trail leads down to the stream bed. Through the ravine you simply follow the stream until, emerging at the lower end, an obvious track leads away again towards the village of Komitádhes. Unfortunately, the last 5km west to Hóra Sfakíon makes a hot, boring anticlimax to your walk. It's also easy enough to walk the gorge as a half-day trip from Hóra Sfakíon (or Loutró, by getting the first boat from there): simply take the early bus to Haniá, and get off at Ímbros.

Should you be arriving here by car and the needle is quivering around empty, a **garage** is sited just after where the road turns west along the coast towards Hóra Sfakíon.

Hóra Sfakíon

Squeezed between the sea and the mountains, **HÓRA SFAKÍON** (often known simply as Hóra meaning "chief town") couldn't grow even if it wanted to. Nevertheless it's a surprise to find the capital of Sfakiá quite so small. It is, too, a thoroughly commercial centre these days: restaurants cram the seafront promenade between the square where the buses stop and the pier where the boats dock, and every house in town seems to display a large "Rooms" sign. Although it is cheap and pleasant enough if you do decide to stay, and relatively quiet by the end of the day, the beach is small and pebbly and there is little else to distract you.

Supposedly, Hóra once had as many as a hundred churches and chapels, built for one reason or another by devout Sfakiots, but few survived the wartime bombardments. There are a couple of ancient-looking examples on the road as you curve down into Hóra, but all seem permanently locked. As for other monuments, a plaque on the waterfront, between the restaurants, commemorates the Dunkirk-style wartime evacuation when some ten thousand men were taken off the island: almost as many were left behind to be bombed as they waited to be taken prisoner or to escape as best they could. Many of the inhabitants who aided the operation were later dealt with brutally by German execution squads. A memorial opposite *Rooms Panorama* on the bend above the town commemorates their bravery; as is the custom here, the skulls of the dead are visible behind a window in the monument's base.

If you have time to kill you're probably best off getting out, to Sweetwater Beach (see p.292) an hour along the coast path west (or accessible by twice-daily boat), or to Frangokástello (see p.300), 14km east. The coast road to the east runs some way from the sea through a series of small, little-visited villages: Komitádhes has a couple of tavernas and even a few rooms, but Vraskás and Voúvas can offer no more than a kafeníon and a general store each. It's also possible to visit the **Cave of Dhaskaloyiánnis**, one of several large caves in the cliffs to the west of Hóra. Always a hideout in times of trouble, this was where the rebel leader (see p.295) set up a mint to produce revolutionary coinage. The tourist office (see below) will provide directions on how to reach it, and also has information about local boats which can take you there if you don't fancy the hike.

Practicalities

Rooms are better and cheaper if you avoid the obvious places right on the front or the main road. Good places to try for rooms with bath are *Panorama* (☎0825/91-296; ①) on the bend as you descend into the town, and with some rooms overlooking the eastern harbour, or the central *Hotel Stavris* (☎0825/91-220, fax 91-152; ②) at the top of the street behind the waterfront tavernas, where you can also change money.

There are a couple of good **supermarkets**, which even sell new and secondhand books in English, and some decent **restaurants** along the seafront promenade: *To Limani* is worth trying for its seafood special which includes five kinds of fish; it also has a good array of vegetarian food, such as *bouréki* and vegetable-stuffed aubergines. The backstreet parallel to the waterfront is also where almost all the other facilities are. Practically the first building is an excellent bakery, and there's also a large supermarket with better prices than those on the front, a dairy shop for local cheese, yoghurt and honey, several exchange places, the post office and a small **tourist office**. The **OTE** (7am–3pm) is on the main square.

Boat tickets for the coastal ferries and also to the island of Gávdhos are sold from a hut at the bottom of the jetty: check which boat you'll be getting as the *Samaria* is too big for the dock and comes in instead right on the other side of town, quite a long way to run if you're waiting in the wrong place. **Bus tickets** are sold from a wooden hut on the square: for Haniá, most people already have tickets and the important thing is to get on the bus in order to secure a seat.

The south-coast bus to Plakiás leaves at 4.30pm, and this is often even more crowded. If you should miss the boat to Loutró, there's a **taxi-boat** available from the *Samaria* taverna on the waterfront.

Frangokástello

FRANGOKÁSTELLO lies 3km off the main road, just under 10km from the junction with the Hóra–Vrísses road (buses divert along the new road through the village). A series of isolated dwellings dotted across a plain between the mountains and the Libyan sea, it's a curious place to arrive in as there's no real centre or square as such, leaving you with little option but head for the castle, the imposing silhouette of which comes into view long before anything else. Despite its lack of a focus, for peaceful lassitude the **beach** at Frangokástello is still among the best spots in Crete, with fine sand, crystal-clear water (with good snorkelling opportunities) and very little effort required either to get here or to find food and drink once you've arrived.

Once on the beach, if you want company you'll find it around the castle where the best part of the sand is, sheltered and slowly shelving; for solitude head westwards along the shoreline – less soft sand and more wind, but still very pleasant. There are beaches to the east too: follow the coastal path for ten to fifteen minutes and you'll arrive at the top of a low cliff overlooking perhaps a kilometre of beautiful, deserted sand and rocks. Lying in the sun here the only thing to disturb the afternoon tranquillity is the occasional muffled crump of an explosion offshore, emanating from the home-made depth charges of local fishermen going about their business in the time-honoured and highly illegal way. Watch closely, and you'll see the sudden spout of water near the boat before the noise of the explosion reaches you.

The **castle**, so impressively four-square from a distance, turns out close up to be a mere shell. Nothing but the bare walls survive, with a tower in each corner, and over the seaward entrance an escutcheon, which can just be made out as the Venetian lion of St Mark. Still, it's some shell. The fortress was originally built in 1371 to deter pirates and in an attempt to impose some order on Sfakiá: a garrison was maintained here throughout the Venetian and Turkish occupations, controlling the plain as surely as it failed to tame the mountains (even today, the orange-pink walls look puny when you see them with the grey bulk of the mountains towering behind). In 1828, Frangokástello was occupied by Hadzimihali Daliani, a Greek adventurer attempting to spread the War of Independence from the mainland to Crete. Instead of taking to the hills as all sensible rebels before and since have done, he and his tiny force attempted to make a stand in the castle. Predictably, they were massacred and their martyrdom became the fuel for yet more heroic legends of the *pallikari*. Locals will claim that to this day, on or around May 17, the ghosts of Daliani and his army march from the castle: they are known as *dhrossoulítes*, or dewy ones, because they appear in the mists around dawn.

Just below the castle, before the beach, there's a patch of greenery which shades a taverna, *Fata Morgana*, and a tiny freshwater creek with thoroughly incongruous ducks on it: between the road and sea to the west are more little streams and marshy patches like this, home to terrapins and some type of water snake or eel.

Practicalities

The first turning off the road takes you straight down to the sea where a left turn along the shore leads past just about all the places which offer **rooms**. At the western end approaching from Hóra, *Studios Stavris* (☎0825/92-250, fax 91-152; ③) has beach-front rooms with bath and cooking facilities; soon after this, down a left turn, *Blue Sky* (☎0825/92-095, fax 92-090) is an agency run by a friendly Greek-German couple who rent out luxury apartments which sleep up to six (⑤) besides renting **cars** and **mountain bikes** and acting as a local **information** centre. Nearer the castle, the tavernas *Oasis* (☎0825/92-136, fax 92-244; ②), *Korali* (☎0825/92-033, fax 92-310; ②) *Flisbos* (☎0825/92-069, fax 92-042; ③) and the friendly *Koukounari*, also known as *Babis & Poppi* (☎ & fax 0825/92-092; ②), all have rooms with bath and sea views. This can be a **mosquito zone** so make sure to come prepared if this is likely to bother you. There's also good **camping** among the dunes, both right by the castle and along the longer beach to the west, with plenty of ruined walls and bamboo groves for shelter – if you do camp here, respect local sensitivities and take your rubbish away with you.

For **eating** and **drinking**, most of your options lie within a few minutes' walk of the castle. Just west of here is the village's kafeníon, *Kale Kardia*, for **breakfast** drinks and snacks. **Tavernas** cluster around the beach to the right, on the promontory, while others straggle along the road. None are particularly sophisticated, but they're friendly and pleasant enough places to spend a few hours. *Flisbos* is the best for fish and although the service can often be tortuously slow, what you get is usually worth the wait. *Taverna Babis & Poppi* on the road is another reliable place, whilst *Korali* is good for mezédhes and does more elaborate stuff too. *Oasis* is a bit fancier, with prices to match.

Nightlife mostly consists of stretching supper well into the night, or perhaps taking a bottle of *raki* down to the beach to contemplate the stars. However, Frangokástello does have a new **disco-bar**, *By Panos*, serving up a wide range of drinks and cocktails and an eclectic mix of sounds; it's on the seafront near to the *Blue Sky* turnoff.

There are also a couple of **mini-markets**, selling most things you're likely to want. An early morning **bus** (6.30am) runs to Hóra Sfakíon to connect with the first bus from there, and buses running between Plakiás and Hóra Sfakíon also pass through. For a description of the road **east to Plakiás**, see p.238.

THE FAR WEST

Crete's far west has, to date, attracted surprisingly little attention from tourists or developers, though inevitably that is beginning to change. The one town of any size west of Haniá is **Kastélli Kissámou**, a port with a twice-weekly ferry service to the Peloponnese, very regular buses to Haniá and little else to attract visitors. Beyond, Crete's west-facing coast remains remote: west of a line between Kastélli and Paleohóra there's little public transport, no more than a handful of rooms to rent, and absolutely nothing in the way of luxurious facilities. Yet here you'll find two of the finest beaches on the island – **Falásarna** and **Elafonísi** – both of them, sadly, beginning to suffer from overexploitation. For longer stays in this part of Crete it's important to carry all the money and most of the supplies you'll need – there are some facilities at the beaches, but the villages are few and far between, and have only the most basic of shops.

On the **south coast**, good roads and several buses a day run to **Paleohóra** and **Soúyia**. The former is already a resort of some size – surprisingly large given its isolation, but far from totally despoiled – the latter is smaller and not as immediately attractive but still inexpensive and friendly. Regular boats connect the two places, or there's a footpath by way of the ruins of ancient **Lissós**, on the coast just west of Soúyia. Moving between them by road is rough and sometimes impossible unless you're prepared to backtrack most of the way to the north coast; the only properly paved roads are those which run north–south. Along the way, there's spectacular mountain scenery in which frescoed medieval churches are liberally scattered.

Kastélli Kissámou and the north coast

Kastélli lies some 20km beyond the crossroads at Kolimbári (p.276), and the new E65 highway which runs across the bottom of the Rodhópou peninsula has now cut journey times considerably. It has also left the **old road** – always a beautiful drive – as a delightful backwater. Going this way you wind steeply up a rocky spur thrown back by the peninsula and emerge through a cleft in the hills to a magnificent sunset view of the Gulf of Kissámou, with Kastélli in the middle distance. With the sun setting behind the craggy heights of **Cape Voúxa** at the far west of Crete, this is a memorable panorama. There's a roadside restaurant from which you can enjoy the view, and further along a number of quite large, entirely unvisited villages, such as Nochiá, Koléni or Kaloudhianá, where you could also stop for a drink or a bite to eat at a number of inviting tavernas.

As it leaves the height, the road loops back out of the hills onto the fertile plain of Kastélli. Almost as soon as you hit level ground there's a sign to a **campsite**, *Camping Mithymna* (☎0822/31-144), on the coast about 1km from the road. It takes its name from the ancient town of *Mithymna*, thought to have been approximately where the nearby village of Noríya now stands. Well-equipped and reasonably priced, it is generally to be found fairly empty since a new campsite opened up in Kastélli itself (see below). The village of Kaloudhianá, 4km further along, is also the place to turn for the inland route to Topólia and Elafonísi.

Kastélli Kissámou

Heading for the west coast, you'll pass through **KASTÉLLI KISSÁMOU** (mostly known simply as Kastélli), which at first sight seems to offer little to get excited about. It's a busy little town and port with a rather rocky beach. But this very ordinariness has real charm once you get over your initial reaction: it's also a working town full of stores used by locals and cafés not entirely geared to outsiders. "Kissámou" was appended to plain "Kastelli" in 1966 to avoid confusion with the town of the same name in Iráklion province. *Kísamos* was the prestigious Greco-Roman city-state which once occupied the site in ancient times; exciting new excavations (see p.303) are now revealing just how important this city was.

On the western outskirts the old and new roads join forces to head straight through the town, bypassing the centre: parallel to this road, towards the sea, runs the main street – Odhós Skalidi – with stores and banks, leading into the central square, Platía Kastellioú. A block to the southwest of this is another square where the **buses** pull in. There's a second cluster of development along the **waterfront**, a five-minute walk directly down from the main square, with a short promenade and a small **folklore museum**, housing an interesting collection of household miscellany.

The town

Kastélli hasn't got much in the way of sights, but a couple of locations are worth a visit. The first are some fascinating new **archeological excavations** near to the bus station which have revealed remains and mosaics from the Roman city of Kisamos, originally the port of nearby Polyrínia (see p.305). To get there, cross the main road from the bus station and head one block south where, to the west of the hospital, the excavations are visible behind a fence. On view are some richly decorated **dwellings** with striking **mosaics**. One particularly fine example fills a room and portrays foods and fruits, various birds and a wonderful depiction of a hunter out with his fierce hound, straining at the leash. Just around the corner and one block west of here, trial excavations are in progress and seem set to reveal more remarkable finds. The only problem for modern Kastélli is that once its ancient predecessor is revealed it will be impossible to contemplate any new building taking place in what is, after all, the centre of the town. It is planned to display finds from the excavations plus the town's small archeological collection in a refurbished **museum** on the main square.

The town's other feature worth a visit is a beautiful old **Venetian fountain** (inscribed with the date 1520). It lies about 100m east of the main square along a small street (Odhós Kampouri); beyond a plane tree, it stands in a small courtyard to the left.

Practicalities

All the facilities you're likely to need lie on or near the main square. **Ferry tickets** for boat connections with Kíthira, Yíthio and Monemvassía are on sale at Xirouchakis Travel (☎0822/22-655) one block inland from the main square, or from nearby Horeftakis Tours (☎0822/23-888); the **ferry dock** is a good 2km west of town – a significant walk if you're heavily laden, or a cheap taxi-ride. **Boat trips** to the island of Gramvoúsa (daily at 9am; 5000dr) also leave from here and tickets are available from the agents above or from an office on the quayside. The **post office** (Mon–Fri 7.30am–2pm), which also changes money, and the **OTE** (same hours) are both on the main street to the east of the square, and there are phonecard kiosks near the bus station and around the centre. For **bike rental**, try the reliable Motor Fun (☎0822/23-440) on the main square; **car hire** is available from Kissamos Travel (☎0822/23-740) with an office next to the bus station. One shop worth a visit is Fotografias Anifandakis, slightly east of the main square along Skalidi, where veteran photographer Yeóryios Anifandákis has his shop and studio. He's photographed most of the island during his long career and sells his photos here, including some excellent ones of the stunning Roman mosaics (see above) unearthed in the new excavations in the town.

ACCOMMODATION

Kastélli has an abundance of **accommodation**, even in high season rarely filled to capacity. Options in the town centre include the *Castelli Hotel* (☎0822/22-140; ②), on the main square, with rooms at the cheaper end of this price band, although it's not the friendliest of places. Across the square, *Rooms Koutsounakis* (☎0822/23-416; ②) is another possibility for rooms with bath and balcony sea views. Nearby there's *Rooms Vergerakis* (☎0822/22-663; ②) which has (only slightly) cheaper rooms without bath. Places on the **seafront** include, at the western end, *Maria Kastanaki Beach* (☎0822/22-610; ①) for en-suite balcony rooms with and without private bath; similar facilities are on offer at the nearby *Argo* (☎ & fax 0822/23-563; ②). Slightly to the east, the more expensive but efficiently run *Manty Apartments* (☎0822/22-830, fax 22-825; ③) also has balcony rooms with separate kitchen/diner, worth considering for a longer stay – those on higher floors tend to escape the late-night noise from the terrace bar downstairs. An excellent-value hotel fronting the sea at the eastern end of the beach beyond the football ground, is the very friendly *Galini Beach* (☎0822/23-288, fax 23-388; ③), with sparkling en-suite rooms, bounteous breakfasts and a good restaurant.

A tranquil option away from the sea is the *Hotel Playies* (☎0822/23-404; ③), set on a hill above town along the road to Polyrínia (see opposite); all rooms have private bath and balconies with good sea views, there's a pool, and it should be possible to bargain when business is slack. Although it's easily reached with your own transport, they have a minibus and if you give them a call are willing to pick guests up from the port or bus station. West of the square, 150m down the main street, you'll find the town's **campsite**, *Camping Kissamou* (☎0822/23-443), with some shade and a nice pool, although this does tend to be an obvious first stop for people who bring cars and campervans across on the ferry from Yíthio.

EATING AND DRINKING

The best **restaurants** are somewhat less obvious than you might imagine. Along the seafront there are a couple of places where the food is worth a try: the reasonably priced *Papadakis* at the western end for seafood, or the nearby *Makedonas*. However, the best places for quality rather than location lie in the heart of town. Here, the *Stork Taverna,* along the main highway just to the west of the bus station, offers an excellent selection of traditional Cretan dishes. Further west still, as you head out to the port, *Taverna Stimadoris* (on the right) is another good place for fish and often hosts lively wedding parties at weekends, when you'll get a free traditional music concert with your meal. Fish is also the main item on the menu at *Katerina's*, a taverna on the picturesque small fishing harbour a kilometre west of the centre. One of the best places of all lies about a kilometre inland along the road to Lousakiés; *Taverna Agatho* (☎0822/22-844; evenings only) is a little family-run village restaurant where they speak not a word of anything other than Greek, but where you are guaranteed the warmest of welcomes and a delicious spread that you won't forget. Finally, *To Akrogiali* (☎0822/31-410) is one more fish restaurant worth seeking out for excellent fresh seafood served on a terrace with the waves almost lapping your table legs; it lies 1km beyond the *Galini Beach* hotel at the eastern end of the waterfront. It's not easy to miss as it's located immediately east of a seafront soap factory whose chimney stacks are visible from some distance; give them a ring if you still have problems finding it, but don't let the location put you off.

Wherever you eat, you'll probably be offered some of the local **red wine**. Made from the *roméïko* grape, which is believed to have been brought to the island by the Venetians, it is as good as any produced on Crete.

Although the seafront area often has a listless, end-of-season air by day, it comes to life at night when the locals pile in to drink at the numerous **bars**.

Polyrínia

Kastélli Kissámou's name is taken from ancient *Kísamos*, which once stood here and served as a port for the sizeable ancient city of **Polyrínia**. About 7km inland, above the village of Paleókastro (confusingly also known as Polirinía), vestiges of the ancient settlement can still be seen. There are **buses** up from Kastélli Kissámou (Mon, Wed & Fri 7am & 2pm; returning 30min later), but the walk is perfectly feasible; your best bet is to take a bus or taxi up, and walk back down.

It's something of a climb from the village to the hilltop site, where ruins are scattered across two horns of high ground which seem to reach out to enclose the Gulf of Kissámou. Originally an eighth-century BC Dorian colony from the Peloponnese, Polyrínia – a name meaning "rich in lambs" – remained a prosperous city down to Roman times and beyond. One of its main claims to fame, however, would not endear it to most Cretans: an inscription found here and dated to 69 BC tells of how the Polyrinians created a statue in honour of the Roman conqueror of Crete, Quintus Metellus, referring to him as the "saviour and benefactor of the city". It seems that Polyrínia did not join in the resistance put up by Haniá and other cities to the Roman invasion, and as a result was spared destruction.

The most obvious feature when you reach the site is the **Acropolis** (stunning **views** of the coast from the top), which is in fact almost entirely a Venetian defensive structure, but there are all sorts of foundations and obscure remains scattered about, including the vestiges of an aqueduct and miscellaneous Roman and Greek masonry incorporated into the church that now stands on the site. The church is itself constructed on the base of what must have been an enormously impressive Hellenistic building, possibly a fourth century BC temple. The sheer amount of work involved in cutting and dressing these stone blocks and transporting them to places as inaccessible as this makes you wonder at the phenomenal scale of manpower at the service of these towns in antiquity. The unsightly breeze blocks used for the cemetery wall of the modern church makes a starkly ironic contrast.

On the way back from the site, the pleasant *Taverna Polyrinia* in the village of Áno Paleókastro has views almost as good as those from the top.

The west coast: Falásarna

Leaving Kastélli Kissámou for the west, the road climbs back into the hills again, cutting south across the base of the Gramvoúsa peninsula. The paved road now continues all the way down to the beautiful beach at **FALÁSARNA** (reached by turning off the road at Plátanos), with two buses a day direct from Haniá. The last part snakes down a spectacular series of hairpin bends before turning north onto the narrow coastal plain, where farmers have discovered the benefits of plastic greenhouses for forcing tomatoes, melons and the like. The end of the asphalt is marked by two tavernas just above a sublime beach, a broad crescent of yellow sand edged by turquoise waters. Although the beach can occasionally be afflicted by washed-up oil, tar and discarded rubbish, this doesn't detract from the overall beauty of the place. Besides, if it gets too crowded here, there are two more beaches within easy walking distance, as well as others further south which can be reached along rough tracks.

There are an increasing number of **rooms** places here, some of them quite good; try *Sun Set* (☎0822/41-204; ③), which has excellent balcony rooms with sea views and private bath as well as a good **restaurant** below; they also rent out apartments (④) for longer stays. On the way here you'll also pass the slightly cheaper *Rooms Kalami* (☎0822/41-461; ③), with similar rooms above a seafront taverna. Many of the people who stay here **camp** at the back of the beach, either in a couple of small caves or beneath makeshift shelters slung between a few stumpy trees; take your rubbish away with you.

Ancient Falásarna and Gramvoúsa

The **ancient city** and port of Falásarna lies just to the north of the beach. If you follow the main dirt track for 1km past the tavernas and through the olive groves, at the edge of the archeological site you will pass the large stone "**throne**" that has puzzled experts for decades – there is still no satisfactory explanation for its function.

The westernmost of the cities of ancient Crete, and now undergoing systematic excavation, Falásarna was founded prior to the sixth century BC and remained the sworn enemy of nearby Polyrínia (see p.305). What you are now able to see are the scattered remains of a city built around a large depression (its inner harbour) and the bed of a canal that once joined this to the sea. All of the site is now high and dry, offering conclusive proof that Crete's western extremities have risen at least 8m over the last 24 centuries or so. The excavators discovered large stone blocks thrown across the entrance to the old harbour; current thinking suggests that this was carried out in the first century BC by the Romans to prevent ships using the port as the base for a "pirates' nest". The harbour was defended by part of the city wall linked by a number of towers to a harbour mole, with the **South Tower**, the nearest to the sea, a formidable bastion built of huge sandstone blocks. More ruined structures are to be seen ascending the acropolis hill behind, and near to the chapel of Áyios Yeóryios a recently excavated building (beneath a canopy) revealed a number of well-preserved **terracotta baths**.

Continue on the best of the roads past the throne and you pass under Cyclopean walls to emerge above another small bay. Tempting as it is, this is too sharp and rocky for you to be able to get to the sea, but it does give you views to the north, over **Cape Voúxa**, which are shielded from Falásarna itself. Towards the top you can see the island of **Gramvoúsa** (not to be confused with the uninhabitable rock of Pontikonísi, a more distant islet which can sometimes be seen from the beach at Falásarna) on which the Venetians built an important castle. Along with the fortified islands of Néa Sóudha and Spinalónga, this was one of the points that held out against the Turks long after the Cretan mainland had fallen. When the Venetians left, the fort was allowed to fall into disrepair until it was taken over by Greek refugees from other Turkish-occupied islands (notably Kásos) who used it as a base for piracy. It took a major Turkish campaign to wrest the fortress back, and thereafter they maintained a garrison here. In the War of Independence it became a base for the Turkish ships attempting to maintain a blockade of the coastline. Another slightly larger and wilder island, Agría Gramvoúsa, lies to the north just off the cape.

It's possible to visit these islands by organized **boat trips** from Kastélli (see p.303), where you can also rent a boat for a cruise of several days, and there are also rumours that you can wade across to one of them if you hike up the peninsula. This seems unlikely, but certainly if you fancy some wild and lonesome walking, **Gramvoúsa peninsula** fits the bill – being extraordinarily barren and quite unpopulated. A path of sorts runs up the eastern side from the village of Kaliviani and about three hours' walk will take you to a really spectacular white-sand beach (sadly with an even worse tar problem than Falásarna) more or less opposite Gramvoúsa island. Bear in mind that there are no tavernas or shops at Kaliviani and, although the friendly *Kafenion Siponitakis* (facing the start of the path) will make you a tasty potato omelette and salad, provisions for the hike should be purchased ahead. In high summer, you'll also need water – which can be replenished at a spring near to the chapel of Ayía Iríni, about 6km out.

Routes to the southwest

Heading for the **southwest**, the normal way is to follow the inland route by turning off the north-coast highway at Kaloudhianá, before Kastélli. This is a lovely rural drive up the valley of the Tiflós, and follows a reasonably good road as far as Váthi. In the sturdy farming villages of this unusually green part of Crete there are plenty of opportunities to take in the local wildlife, or to do some walking in the oleander- and chestnut-wooded hills and along numerous gorges. Alternatively, the **coast road** southwest of Plátanos, although lacking greenery, is often spectacularly scenic and a perfectly easy drive now that it is entirely paved. Both roads eventually end up at the romantically sited monastery of **Hrissokalítissa** and the idyllic beaches of **Elafonísi**, a little to the south. If you have your own transport, try to go out one way and return the other.

A direct route to **Soúyia** (see p.320) leaves Haniá along the road to Omalós and the start of the Samariá Gorge. Branching off at Alikianós, it follows the valleys through the western foothills of the White Mountains, passing the **Ayía Iríni gorge** and a string of Sélinos villages before sweeping down the Herokténa valley into Soúyia.

The inland route

The area of the far west between Topólia in the northeast and Váthi to the southwest includes some of the most fertile lands on the island. Here, lush woodland watered by tumbling streams emanating from the mountains is a haven for a rich variety of flora and fauna. Water is so plentiful around places such as Élos and Kefáli, in fact, that tourism comes a very poor second to agriculture. Everyone it seems has a *kípos* (smallholding), with a couple of dozen olive trees or a vegetable patch. The life of these villages is dictated by the needs of the farmers, a hardworking and laconic bunch who dress in sturdy boots and lumberjack shirts and greet one another with gruff cries of "*yia!*" (abbreviated from *yia sou*) from the open windows of Japanese pickup trucks – the ultimate status symbol around these parts, as only bona fide farmers owning above a certain hectarage get a government subsidy to buy one.

Following the **inland route**, after some 4km of ascent you reach the village of **VOULGHÁRO**, where you could stretch your legs in search of two ancient frescoed churches, Áyios Yeóryios and Áyios Nikólaos – in the satellite villages of Mákronas across the valley and Mourí along a track 2km further south, respectively. Just south of Mourí you could also descend into the ravine (see below) making for the village of Koutsoumátados, a **walk** of about 5km. This walk (in reverse) is described in *Landscapes of Western Crete* (see Contexts, p.369).

By road you'll continue climbing to **TOPÓLIA**, 3km after Voulgháro, whose church of Ayía Paraskeví has more frescoes, this time from the late Byzantine period. You could also take in the village of Kalathenes, 3km along a turnoff on the right to the south of here, where there are the remains of a fine sixteenth-century **Venetian villa** known as the Rotonda.

The direct route south from Topólia, however, soon enters a tunnel before skirting the edge of the dramatic **Katsamátados ravine**, one of the most imposing on the island. Nearing the middle of the ravine you'll come to a signed stairway cut into the rock on the right, and a muscle-taxing short climb to the **cave of Ayía Sofía**. This is one of the largest caves on Crete and remains found here date its usage back to Neolithic times; it now shelters a small chapel, along with stalactites, stalagmites and its present residents, a colony of bats.

Proceeding along the ravine, you will soon reach the hamlet of **KATSOMÁTADOS** where the roadside *Rooms Taverna Panorama* (☎0822/51-163; ②) is a possible stopping-place for a meal (excellent *hórta* from its own *kípos*), coffee and Dutch cakes, or even **rooms**, should you decide to get into more detailed exploration of the area. Its friendly proprietor Manolis Motakis and his Dutch wife Antonia are keen to put up walkers, and will advise on various hiking routes around the ravine as well as climbing Koproula, the highest peak hereabouts.

Miliá and the eastern Enneachora

Three kilometres south of Katsomátados you enter an area known as the Enneachora where – with your own transport – a turning on the right allows to you follow a beautifully scenic drive through the leafy hills and farming villages on the western flank of the Tiflós valley. Soon after the turnoff, a sign on the left indicates a turning to the *Platania* **taverna**. A path through woods leads to the taverna's terrace, close to a gigantic thousand-year-old **plane tree** which gives the place its name. It's a friendly hideaway which serves up good meat and mezédhes to the passing trade, but makes its money from mammoth wedding feasts.

On the edge of the first village you meet, **Vlátos**, there's a road signed on the right to **MILIÁ**, a remarkable "eco-tourist" village which is unique on the island. The precipitous unmetalled track climbs dizzily along the shoulder of Mount Kefáli for 5km offering magnificent **views** over the chestnut- and olive-clad valley below. You will eventually reach a car park, from where a rough track leads into a stunningly picturesque hamlet of stone houses, once occupied by farmers and shepherds. The isolation of the village eventually led to its abandonment almost a century ago until, in the early 1980s, a relative of a former inhabitant proposed to restore the whole place as a working village, welcoming visitors. Other families who owned ruined houses joined in and they formed a co-operative, backed by EU money. Stonemasons used to building traditional dwellings were brought over from the Peloponnese and helped the villagers to recreate what you now see: an almost too perfect village with solid stone houses on many levels overlooking a verdant cleft brimming with chestnuts, oaks, planes and olives.

You should soon locate one house which now serves as the community centre and **bar/taverna** (open daily) offering organic food and vegetables all produced on the village's land, as well as freshly baked bread. Visitors are welcome to become involved in the ongoing farming activities which include planting and sowing as well as chestnut, olive and apple harvesting (Miliá means "apple tree" in Greek); you can even help in making *raki* at the village's own still. Otherwise you can walk in the nearby hills or simply contemplate the natural surroundings;

the nights up here are truly magical. The en-suite **rooms** (actually your own house) are a delight and contain appropriate rustic furnishings and ancient fittings such as huge fireplaces and stone ovens but positively no telecommunications, save one mobile phone link with the outside world. To stay, you can simply turn up or ring ahead (☎ & fax 0822/51-569; on-site mobile 093/543-383; ③) to make a reservation. This kind of imaginative enterprise is perhaps a pointer to the future for the development of tourism on the island.

The road continues through the simple villages of Vlátos, Rogdiá and Límni each with its own bar but little else, until it rejoins the direct road just over a kilometre before Pervólia.

Élos and Pervólia

The direct route from Katsomátados tracks the lower slopes of the Tiflós valley and, shortly after the turnoff to Vlátos, a turning on the left heads southwest to pick up the road to Paleohóra (see p.314). The way then passes slopes covered with magnificent stands of chestnut, plane and other deciduous trees. Chestnuts, in fact, are a major local crop around here and **ÉLOS**, 4km along, is the centre of the chestnut-growing region known as the Enneachora (nine villages). This is a wonderfully refreshing place, even at the height of summer, and it's easy to forget just how high you are here – the mountains to the south rise to about 1200m. In the village's square, shaded by plane, eucalyptus and, of course, chestnut trees, *Rooms Kastanofolia* ("chestnut den", ☎0822/61-258; ②) is a clean and simple place with en-suite **rooms** above a good **taverna**, run by the young and tireless Kiría Kokolákis who serves a daily special fresh from the oven. There are ducks in a pool filled by a stream running beside the taverna's terrace and, directly opposite over the road, you can stroll along a track that leads a couple of kilometres into the chestnut forests. Behind the taverna there is also an impressive old arch which was probably once part of a Turkish aqueduct, and just beyond this lies a fourteenth-century **Byzantine chapel**, with frescoes (key available from the taverna). The great event in Élos's year is the annual **chestnut festival** in late October.

Five kilometres further, a turn on the left indicates a sharp descent to the picturesque hamlet of **PERVÓLIA** tucked into the folds of a high gorge beneath the northern flank of Mount Áyios Díkeos Ióv (Job the Just). The village is another verdant oasis with charming narrow streets punctuated by simple whitewalled dwellings and smallholdings overflowing with vigorously sprouting vegetables. Park any transport where you cross a bridge at the foot of the descent, and continue on foot to the bottom of the village and a fountain, near a recently erected bust to one of the noted local *pallikári* (guerilla fighters) of the last century, Anagnostis Skalidis. At the house opposite you will find a small **museum** assembled by one of his descendants, Zácharia Skálidis. An amiable man who speaks only Greek, he will be delighted to show you around his collection, which includes lots of atmospheric photos from a Crete long gone, as well as old guns, letters and coins.

Kefáli and Váthi

Barely 2km beyond Pervólia, another charming Enneachora village, **KEFÁLI**, has a fine fourteenth-century frescoed **church**, Metamórphosis tou Sotirís (Transfiguration of Christ), down a track on the left as you enter the village. Inside, the church has some interesting and apparently genuine early graffiti, scratched across the paintings. An Englishman, Francis Lerfordes, has marked his contribution with the date 1553, while Turks later inscribed their blasphemous thoughts along with the crescent symbol – to the further detriment of the art works. The main street has **rooms** with and without bath above *Taverna Polakis* (☎0822/61-260; ②), with a splendid balcony view over the Bay of Stomíou. The owner, Yeorgos Polakis, is a fount of local knowledge and will direct you to the church should you encounter difficulties. The aptly named *Panorama* taverna, opposite, provides meals with a view.

Nearby **VÁTHI**, 1km or so after Kefáli, is another of the Enneachora villages with two more ancient **churches** for enthusiasts: the thirteenth-century Áyios Yeóryios off the central square, and Mihaíl Arhángelos, just to the south, with fourteenth-century frescoes.

The coast road

If you were to carry straight on in Kefáli, you'd be on the coast road back around to Plátanos. Just out of Kefáli magnificent coastal **views** unfold, with the distant beaches of Elafonísi shimmering mirage-like in a turquoise sea. The recently sealed road then winds laboriously on towards the coast, with yet more stunning views over the Mediterranean. Around you, olives ripen on the terraced hillsides and the villages seem to cling desperately to the high mountainsides, as if miraculously saved from some calamitous slide to the sea, glittering far below.

By **KÁMBOS**, 14km from Kefáli, you've descended enough for there to be an excellent beach below the village, albeit an hour's hike down a superb gorge inhabited by colonies of doves. Should you want to try this at a more leisurely pace, **accommodation** and **food** are available at *Rooms Hartzulakis* (☎0822/41-445; ②) where the friendly owner, Lefteris Hartzulakis, will advise on walking the gorge and seeking out the *dictamus* herb (Cretan dittany) that grows there – used as a panacea by the Cretans since ancient times. **SFÍNARI**, a tortuous 7km north and slightly inland from a quiet pebble beach, is more developed, but the **beach** – slightly west of the village – is somewhat spoiled by greenhouses and derelict buildings a bit too close to the sand for comfort. The southern end of the strand, however, is less cluttered and here a cluster of tavernas gather beneath shady tamarisks. Among the **tavernas**, *Captain Fidias* (☎0822/41-107; ②) is worth a try and also offers **rooms** with bath; shady **camping** is available behind.

Beyond Sfínari the route climbs again and there are some terrific **views** from high above the coast as the road twists and turns for 10km to cross the shoulder of Mount Manna, before dropping towards Plátanos and the turning for Falásarna (see p.305); after this it's an easy descent to the coast on the Gulf of Kissámou and the main E65 to Kastélli (see p.302).

Hrissoskalítissa

HRISSOSKALÍTISSA lies some 10km southwest of Váthi, on a road which deteriorates rapidly. There are a couple of tavernas on the way down here, but otherwise little beyond the weathered, white-walled monastery (now, in fact, a nunnery) of the Virgin of the Golden Step, beautifully sited on a rocky promontory above the sea. Today barely functioning, it has reduced from some two hundred residents to just one often grumpy nun and one monk, whose main task seems to be keeping the place acceptable for tourists. The present church – containing a much-venerated thousand-year-old icon of the Virgin – dates only from the last century, but the monastery building is an ancient foundation: the first church was built in a cave here in the thirteenth century and recent investigations have turned up evidence of a much earlier Minoan settlement (or shrine) as well. Look out for the ninety steps that lead to the top of the crag around which the place is built: one of them appears golden (*Hrissí skála*) to those who are pure in spirit – a fact which the authors are unable to verify.

Elafonísi

For **ELAFONÍSI** you've another 5km of very dusty, bumpy road to traverse, but it's possibly still worth it. The almost tropical lagoon of white-sand beaches tinged pink by shells, aquamarine waters, salt-encrusted rock pools and bright red starfish is still, despite increasing exploitation, as idyllic a spot as any in Crete. The water is incredibly warm, calm and shallow and Elafonísi – actually an island just offshore – is a short wade across the sandbar. There are more beaches on its far side (with waves), along with the odd ruined wall, seashells and a monument to Australian sailors shipwrecked here in 1907. A couple of simple **cafés** stand on the edge of the beach as you arrive.

Not surprisingly, all this has not gone undiscovered, and there are now two **boats** a day from Paleohóra, a daily **bus** from Haniá and Réthimnon, at least one bus tour as well as scores of day-trippers who often fill an improvised car-parking space to bursting. The arrival of the crowds has brought lines of sun umbrellas and loungers to the beach, but there's an almost total lack of any infrastructure to cope with their needs. The chief result of this is that there are often piles of rubbish on the mainland beach and a solitary Portaloo is all there is in the way of sanitary arrangements. Next to this stands a somewhat incongruous phone kiosk, and that's it. Rather than make a coherent plan to protect this uniquely beautiful place, many believe that the authorities have deliberately left the final 5km of track to the beach unpaved in an attempt to discourage the hordes who would descend on the place if it was tarmac all the way.

The area itself is privately owned and as no permanent structures are allowed to be built nearer than 1km to the beach, the only **accommodation** is set well back. If you wanted to stay, *Rooms Elafonisi* (☎0822/61-274; ③) is a pleasant enough place and has its own **taverna**, but you may feel that the best thing to do here is to have a look and a swim, before heading on your way. Rumours persist that there are plans for a major tourist development of the waterfront, but for the moment things trundle along in the anarchic Greek fashion. It's to be hoped that something of the natural beauty of this place will survive the impending concrete mixers.

Moving on

Continuing south from Elafonísi is no easy matter, though you could catch the boat if you were heading for Paleohóra. There's a **coastal path**, reasonably well marked, via which you should be able to reach Paleohóra in about six hours. Be sure to get some accurate directions before setting out, however, as this coastline is barely inhabited and a wrong turn could lead you a very long way astray in hostile terrain.

Another **walk** is the 7km along a track heading inland to **SKLAVOPOÚLA** and its satellite hamlets. Set at an altitude of 640m, this is one of the remotest communities in the Sélinos (see p.312). Pashley made it here and identified

Sklavopoúla as the site of Doulópolis, a Dorian city renowned for its military prowess. The village's present name ("village of the Slavs") may stem from a resettlement of Slavs here by Nikiforas Fokas (see Contexts p.339) following his reconquest of Crete from the Saracens in 961, the settlers being perhaps Armenians from Bulgaria. There are no fewer than seven **churches** in the vicinity of the village, all with **wall paintings**; those of the Panayía, Áyios Yeóryios and Sotíros Christós – are extremely fine (enquire for keys at the kafeníon in the main square). The tracks to reach Sklavoupoúla are clearly marked on the Petrákis *Haniá Trekking and Road Map* and also on the Harms-Verlag map (see "Maps", p.30). By continuing east through Kalamiós, after 8km you reach the main surfaced road at Voutás, where there is no chance of a bus but you may be able to pick up a lift to Paleohóra, a further 13km.

If you're **driving**, there is a sealed road which turns off the inland route between Élos and Topólia, cutting down to Paleohóra by way of Aligí and Drís to meet the main road at the village of Plemenianá. An alternative route, also recently asphalted, goes west at the fork before Aligí and proceeds through some lonely, if spectacular, mountain country via Arhondikó and Voutás to approach Paleohóra from the west. Along the way scores of little streams cascade beside, under, or sometimes across, the road. You'll find hardly any traffic passes on both routes, and the rare villages are ancient and rustic; their inhabitants stand and stare as you drive through, but are extremely welcoming if you stop.

The southwest

The direct route from the north coast to **Paleohóra** is a well-surfaced road and takes the line of least resistance across the mountains: consequently it feels a great deal less intimidating. However, the scenery is always enjoyable with dramatic vistas, plenty of greenery and the advantage of numerous villages along the way, meaning that you're never far from a place to stop for a drink or a bite to eat. From the turning at Tavronítis, the road traces a long valley fingering its way beneath the hills as far as Voukoliés, a large village with a crowded Saturday morning market (all over by about 10am). Hereafter you begin to climb in earnest, through several much smaller villages, towards the **eparchy (province) of Sélinos**.

Sélinos

Sélinos, the southwestern corner of Crete has, despite its isolation from the north and centre of the island, played a significant role in its history since ancient times, and as early as the third century BC several of the communities here were important enough to form a confederation with Górtys (see p.114) and Magus, king of Cyrenaica, in Libya. Under the Romans cities such as Lissós, Elyrós and Syia (modern Sóuyia) prospered greatly. This distinguished past laid the foundations for the communal pride which created the scores of **churches** constructed during the Byzantine period, the main cause of Sélinos's fame today. Every village seems to offer at least one example, while some have as many as three or more.

Flória, Anisaráki and around
Sited at an altitude of 580m **FLÓRIA**, almost exactly halfway across the island, is divided into two halves: Apáno (or upper) Flório and Kato Flório straddling the road. The upper village has the church of Áyii Patéres (the Holy Fathers),

although only fresco fragments remain. The lower village has the more important
Áyios Yeóryios with thirteen panels of fine fifteenth-century frescoes. To reach
it, go down a lane to the right of the second taverna you pass on the right. After
about 600m you'll come to a small footbridge over a dry streambed; cross this and
after 50m veer left at a fork to follow the path leading to the church. Near to the
first taverna (the better of the pair), two war memorials – one German, one Greek
– face each other across the road, serving as grim reminders of the terrible atrocities that happened here during World War II when, locals will tell you, they saw
their parents and relatives gunned down in the self-same road.

If you take the short detour from Kándanos (see below) up to **ANISARÁKI**
you'll find more fine frescoes in the fifteenth-century churches of Ayía Ánna,
Panayía and Ayía Paraskeví. Nearby, the hamlet of **KOUFALOTÓS** has, half way
between the two, the chapel of **Áyios Mihaíl Arhángelos**, with fourteenth-century paintings by the Cretan master, Ioánnis Pagoménos (see p.319) The chapel
is located down a track on the right (coming from Anisaráki), and across a stream.

Kándanos
KÁNDANOS, approached along a verdant valley planted with olives, is the chief
village of the eparchy (though it's a great deal smaller than Paleohóra), and
makes a pleasant, quiet place to stop for a coffee or even a meal. Despite pre-
serving its ancient name going back to Dorian times and the existence of as many
as fifteen Byzantine churches in the vicinity (it was the see of the Orthodox
Church in the Byzantine period and the see of the Roman Church under the
Venetians), the village buildings are almost entirely new, for the place was razed
to the ground by the Germans for its role in the wartime resistance. In 1941, after
the German army had taken Máleme (see p.276) troops were dispatched urgent-
ly along this road to prevent the Allies landing reinforcements at Paleohóra. The
resistance fighters of Kándanos determined to stop them, and despite a ferocious
pitched battle the Germans could not break through for two crucial days; their
progress was frustrated by the Cretans who also shot a number of German soldiers in the action. In retribution the Germans utterly destroyed the village and a
sign was erected on the spot. The original sign set up then is today preserved on
a war memorial in the square. In German and Greek it reads: "Here stood
Kándanos, destroyed in retribution for the murder of 25 German soldiers, and
never to be rebuilt again."

The village that arose defiantly from the ashes is a pleasantly easygoing place
today with two Byzantine **churches**, Mihaíl Arhángelos and Áyios Ioánnis, and a
couple of bars and tavernas. On the outskirts is a waterworks, given to the village
by the Germans after the war as an act of reconciliation.

Plemenianá, Kakodhíki and Kádhros
Beyond Kándanos the next few villages on or close to the main road are also
worth a look and all have frescoed churches: Áyios Yeóryios in **PLEMENIANÁ**
has paintings dating from the fifteenth century, while **KAKODHÍKI**, known for
its curative springs, has several churches nearby. These include the very ancient
chapel of Mihaíl Arhángelos, probably early thirteenth-century, beside the modern church of Ayía Triádha, and the hilltop Áyios Isidhóros, with magnificent
views and frescoes defaced by the Turks. Just off the road to the left **KÁDHROS**,
some 9km from Kándanos, has the churches of Ioánnis Chrysóstomos and the
Panayía, whose fine frescoes are almost complete. Many more small churches

can be found throughout the area, particularly if you get off the road into the smaller villages. Few, if any, of them will be open when you arrive – but express an interest at the nearest kafeníon or to a local passer-by and it rarely takes long to hunt out the priest or someone else with a key.

The road now tracks the Kakodikianós valley for 10km, crossing to the river's west bank for the approach into Paleohóra.

Paleohóra

PALEOHÓRA was known originally as Kastél Selínou – the castle of Sélinos – and for much of its history was no more than that, a castle. Built by the Venetians in 1279, the fort was destroyed by Barbarossa in 1539 and never properly reconstructed even when the small port grew up beneath it. The ruins are still perched at the bulbous end of the headland now occupied by the settlement of Paleohóra – at its narrowest a bare four blocks across from the harbour on one side to the beach on the other.

The village is rapidly growing into a small town, and its facilities can barely cope with the increasing volume of visitors. For the time being, though, it retains an enjoyably laidback, end-of-the-line feel, helped out by superb and extensive sands. Warm right through the winter, this out-of-season backwater makes an excellent place to rent an inexpensive apartment long-term. A eucalyptus-lined avenue leads into the single main street, Venizélos, lined with taverna after café after bar. The **bus** will drop you at the northern end of here; coming in by **car** will necessitate a tangle with the town's confusing one-way system. Although not particularly attractive by day, Venizélos is the vibrant soul of the village, and on summer evenings it is brightly illuminated and filled to overflowing as the bar and restaurant tables spill across the pavement and encroach onto the road. From the main street, nothing is further than a five-minute walk away, and you have a choice of heading south towards the castle and yacht marina or east and west to the beaches.

The better **western beach** (called "Sandy Beach"), magnificently broad and sandy, lined with tamarisks and supplied with showers, faces a bay with excellent easy windsurfing (good boards for rent). People still try to camp along here under the trees, but these days you're likely to be moved on in high summer to the official campsite (see p.316). The **eastern beach** (called "Pebble Beach") is a much less attractive proposition – pebbly at first but sandy further north, at the base of the peninsula. However, it is this eastern side which has the livelier promenade and most of the action and eating places away from the main street, and is also the **harbour** where the Gávdhos boat ties up. You won't be in Paleohóra long before you encounter Yeros and Aris, two more of Crete's urbanized delinquent **pelicans**. Whenever they get a sniff of fish in any passing shopping basket, it's a cue to attempt a mugging: you'll often see harassed village women fighting off the big birds as they close in for the heist.

The oldest parts of town, if you want to explore, are also on the east side, to the south of the harbour: from here you can clamber up into the **castle**, for the views back over town, or walk right around the end of the promontory to return to the beach on the other side. Neither of these options is as appealing as it might be, since the fortress itself is little more than a hillock ringed with broken walls, while a new marina dominates the point; there are some very much more attractive **walks** to be had inland, to charming villages like Ánidhri and Azoyirés (see p.319), or along the coast in either direction.

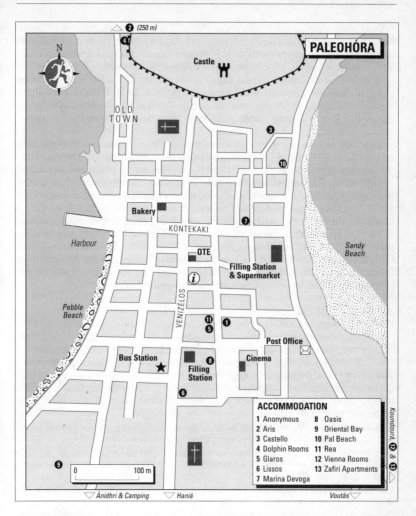

PALEOHÓRA

Castle

OLD TOWN

Harbour

Bakery

KONTEKAKI

OTE

Filling Station & Supermarket

Sandy Beach

Pebble Beach

VENIZÉLOS

Post Office

Bus Station

Filling Station

Cinema

Koundourá

ACCOMMODATION

1	Anonymous	8	Oasis
2	Aris	9	Oriental Bay
3	Castello	10	Pal Beach
4	Dolphin Rooms	11	Rea
5	Glaros	12	Vienna Rooms
6	Lissos	13	Zafiri Apartments
7	Marina Devoga		

0   100 m

Ánidhri & Camping   *Haniá*   *Voutás*

Practicalities

The municipal **tourist office** (daily except Tues 10am–1pm & 6–9pm; ☎0823/41-507) on Venizélos can give you a copy of their town map, and advise about likely rooms places, as well as apartment lets should you be interested in a longer sojourn.

Several **travel agents** are dotted around the town: Interkreta Travel (☎0823/41-393, fax 41-050), close to the junction of Kontekáki (the other main thoroughfare running east–west) and Venizélos, is the best for boat tickets and timetables, and gives out information on just about everything else, as well as changing money. It also sells tickets for local **ferries** – to Elafonísi (daily at

9.30am returning at 4pm), Gávdhos (Mon, Tues & Thurs 8am, Wed & Sat 8.30am) and along the coast to Soúyia and Ayía Rouméli (both daily 8.30am), Loutró and Hóra Sfakíon (both daily 8.30am). You can also pick up tickets at the ferry company offices, on the road down to the jetty. A reliable place for **car** and **bike rental** as well as **mountain bikes** is Sirocco (☎0823/42-105) on Venizélos, opposite the town hall, with Notos Rent a Car (☎0823/42-110), a few doors along, a possible alternative. A new bus service to Omalós has been inaugurated to enable the **Samariá gorge walk** to be done from here; it leaves the bus station at 6am daily throughout the summer.

There are two **banks** (Mon–Fri 8am–2pm) on Venizélos, just north of the town hall, and the **OTE** (Mon–Fri 7.30am–10pm) is immediately south. There are also cardphones next door, at the nearby kiosk, down by Sandy Beach and around the main junction. The **post office** (Mon–Sat 7.30am–2pm), which also changes money, is out on the road behind Sandy Beach, and there's a **health centre** in the street parallel to Venizélos to the west (Mon–Fri 8am–2pm) and a **pharmacy** on Kontekáki. A **laundry** offering service washes, Tsisaki (daily 8am–2pm & 4.30–10.30pm), is located on Venizélos close to the tourist office. Speed Film on Kontekáki does fast **film processing** and the photographer/proprietor Kóstas Paterákis sells his own postcards taken around Sélinos. If you have a car running low on fuel, the town has three **filling stations**; the one behind the Sandy Beach has the longest hours, where Petrakis is also the biggest and best-stocked **supermarket**.

ACCOMMODATION

Finding a **room** is unlikely to be a major problem outside August. Inexpensive places are mostly found in the backstreets behind Venizélos, but you'll see signs everywhere. We've also listed a couple of pleasant places behind the beach a few kilometres to the west, possible options with your own transport. Paleohóra's **campsite**, *Camping Paleohora* (☎0823/41-120) lies 2km northeast of the centre, reached along the road running behind the pebble beach. Sited in an olive grove close to the beach with plenty of shade, its only drawback is the bonehard terrain.

Anonymous (☎0823/42-509). Simple but pleasant rooms off a charming and unusual garden just behind Venizélos, on the street heading inland to the cinema. ②.

Aris (☎0823/41-502, fax 41-546). Charming and peaceful garden hotel at the south end of the peninsula on the edge of the old town beyond the castle. Pleasant en-suite balcony rooms, most with sea view. ③.

Castello, south end of Sandy Beach (☎0823/41-143). Charming and good-value little rooms place for rooms with bath and balcony sea views. ②.

Dolphin Rooms, near the seafront below the east side of the castle (☎0823/41-703). Good-value simple rooms with friendly proprietors in an atmospheric part of the old town. ①.

Glaros, north end of town (☎0823/41-635, fax 41-298). A possible upmarket alternative to the nearby *Rea* and *Oasis*. En-suite rooms with balconies and fans. ④.

Lissos Apartments, north end Venizélos (☎0823/41-266). Pleasant studio rooms with kitchen. ③.

Marina Devoga Rooms, Kontekáki, the street heading west from the lower end of Venizélos (☎0823/41-564). Clean, budget rooms with bath within easy distance of Sandy Beach. ②.

Oasis (☎0823/41-328). Balcony rooms with bath overlooking a garden to the north of town. ③.

Oriental Bay (☎0823/41-322), Pleasant en-suite rooms over a seafront taverna at the northern end of the Pebble Beach. ③.

Pal Beach, Sandy Beach (☎0823/41-512, fax 41-578). The town's priciest hotel with air-conditioned en-suite sea-view rooms fronting the Sandy Beach, although you're not getting a great deal more for your money than elsewhere, not even a pool. ④

Rea, north end of town (☎0823/41-307, fax 41-605). Friendly place with air-conditioned balcony rooms close to Venizélos. ④.

Vienna Rooms, Koundourá, 5km west along the coast (☎0823/41-478). A modern, good-value place near the sea with tranquil en-suite rooms and pool and garden. ③.

Zafiri Apartments, 2km west of town on the road to Koundourá (☎0823/41-0280, fax 41-367). Pleasant apartments and studios near the sea in a detached building with garden. ③.

EATING AND DRINKING

There are plenty of places to choose from for meals, and prices here are generally reasonable. By the Pebble Beach there are several places specializing in **breakfast**, although the "all-in" breakfasts tend to be a severe rip-off. *Elxis*, a new place slightly south of the junction of Venizélos and Kontekáki is a new-style kafeníon with a younger feel, serving breakfast snacks, juices and mezédhes. Incidentally just around the corner from here the town's best **bakery**, *Bakakis*, offers the usual breakfast standards as well as tempting treats.

When it comes to more substantial fare, Paleohóra's **tavernas** and restaurants cater for all tastes. One of the most interesting places is a rare **vegetarian** restaurant, *The Third Eye*; run by a friendly Greek/New Zealand couple, it serves all kinds of local dishes, as well as Asian specialities, and offers some imaginative specials. It's located close to the Sandy Beach one block above Kontekáki, and signed from this street. Close by, *Pizzeria Niki*, just off Kontekáki, is a town favourite situated in a pleasant courtyard and offers excellent pizzas cooked in a wood-fired oven. Along the main street, Venizélos, is another bunch of places: *Savas* serving hearty traditional staples and takeaways is good, whilst further along *Dionisos* is a bit fancier with prices to match. One block west of the town hall, *Amnesis* is a pleasant restaurant in a restored town house and uses its patio as a children's play area. *Rena*, slightly south in the same street is another nice little garden place serving good casseroles and *moussaká* prepared by its eponymous proprietor.

At the northern end of the Pebble Beach seafront, the *Oriental Bay* taverna is a good bet for seafood served on a pleasant shady terrace. The rest of the places along here are much of a muchness, although *Pelican* fronting the boat jetty is not bad and a slightly pricier, meal-with-view option is *Fortezza Bar-Restaurant*, just below the fort, with excellent views over the bay and decent food. Also on the Pebble Beach promenade is the *Seagull Snack Bar*, serving up excellent salads and omelettes (try the "special omelette"). Close by, and facing the same beach, is *The Wave*, a tranquil place serving good seafood, enhanced by an evening view of the moon rising behind the mountains. The Sandy Beach's solitary taverna is *Galaxy*, near the main supermarket which provides a live guitar accompaniment to the usual taverna staples. Along the road to the campsite is *Vrissali*, a pleasant taverna which serves traditional Greek dishes on a shady garden terrace, but often suffers from a lack of customers. One highly recommended place and perhaps the area's most authentic Cretan restaurant is *Taverna Grameno*, 3km west towards Koundourá along the coast road, fronting Grameno beach; it's a friendly garden taverna with a play area for kids, and the cooking here is excellent – try the *saligkári* (snails) or *volví* (pickled wild onions).

BARS AND NIGHTLIFE

Holding on firmly to its village roots, Paleohóra promotes itself as a docile seaside resort with family appeal: if you're looking for all-night discos and raucous bars you've come to the wrong place. Most bars keep their music volume well down after dark and even the liveliest part of town, the Pebble Beach promenade, is a pretty tame affair when compared to most other resorts on the island. After a day at the beach, entertainment in Paleohóra is confined mainly to the **bars**. Many of the most popular of these are shoe-horned into the Venizélos-Kontekáki junction. There are better choices along the main street, Venizélos, where a couple of old-fashioned café/ouzería serve good-value drinks. One of the most entertaining is the central *Kafenion Extra Prima Turbo* whose name reflects the personality of its ebullient owner. The **old town**, sandwiched between the castle and the sea on the peninsula's east flank makes for a pleasant evening stroll and its friendly (and only) bar, *Hania Bar*, provides an opportunity for a quieter drink.

For more stylish (and pricier) drinking, the bars along the Pebble Beach promenade are where the action tends to be. Here *Skala* near the harbour, *Sunrise* and the German-run *Titanic* (the latter two serving cocktails) are complemented by the *Nostos Disco-Bar* where you can join locals dancing in an outside courtyard bar. The town's only true **disco**, imaginatively named the *Paleohora Club*, lies at the north end of the Pebble Beach close to the campsite. **Bars** along Sandy Beach on the west side of town are few and not popular with locals, perhaps because of the extra 300m walk from the centre, though the fancy places here, like *Jetée*, are good for lingering over a sundowner.

Nightly showings at the open-air **cinema**, *Cine Attikon*, tucked away in the northern backstreets, are also worth knowing about; most of their films are in English and programmes (advertised near the harbour and in the tourist office) change daily.

Around Paleohóra

Follow the coast either way from Paleohóra and you'll find more beaches. To the **west** it's not a terribly pretty coastline, marred by plastic greenhouses, but there are some excellent beaches along the way. A paved road along the coast leads after 5km to **Grameno Beach** on a small peninsula which, although pebbly, has trees for shade. On the landward side of the road here, *Taverna Grameno* (see p.317) is a good place to eat. Continuing along the road will quickly bring you to **KOUNDOURÁ**, which also has rooms but is spoiled by more greenhouses: you could try *Vienna Rooms* (see p.317). The paved road peters out 4km beyond Koundourá at **Kríos** ("cold"), another pebble beach where the water can be incredibly chilly due to underwater springs. The dirt road from here on continues to several shingly, deserted bays, where some people camp beside beautifully clear water. In theory you can continue on foot right around this coast to Elafonísi (see p.311), but check first for an exact route and ascertain the state of the path – there have been tragic incidents involving walkers getting into difficulties on this stretch. However, this route has recently been upgraded as part of the E4 European Footpath (tracking the west coast all the way to Kastélli Kissámou) and should now be clearly waymarked.

To the **east**, things are simpler: a footpath traces the shore for miles beyond the campsite, passing a succession of grey pebble strips with fewer people clad in fewer clothes the further you venture. This path continues to Lissós (14km/3hr) and Soúyia (18km/4hr), and if you time it right you can return to Paleohóra by boat (currently leaving around 5.30pm in summer). Again you should carefully check out both the route and the boats beforehand, as the service deteriorates rapidly out of high season. The path is waymarked, but it doesn't simply follow the coast all the way, and there are one or two steep scrambles. Since the most scenic section is through the gorge between Lissós and Soúyia, it might be easier to do it from there (see p.324). An alternative, easier walk takes you down from Prodhrómi, inland, but you'd have to take a taxi to the starting-point. The village of **ÁNIDHRI**, en route, is particularly beautiful, with a fourteenth-century church, **Áyios Yeóryios**, which has an unusual double altar and fine **frescoes** depicting the lives of Christ and Áyios Yeóryíos by Ioánnis Pagoménos (John the Frozen), the most prolific of several painters whose signatures appear frequently around Sélinos. The village **bar** (actually the old village school, recently converted) makes a good place to pause for a drink, and has a pleasant terrace with views.

Finally, with your own transport, you could follow a **spectacular drive** along the road which heads northwest from the town and tracks the valley of the River Pelekaniotikós, calling at a string of charming Sélinos hamlets such as Voutás – with the possibility of a detour to Sklavopoúla (see p.311) and its frescoed churches – Kámatera and Arhondíko, en route to Stróvles and Míli 25km on, where it joins up with the road south to Elafonísi. Now completely surfaced, it's an exhilarating ride through some dramatic mountain scenery. To join the road, head west out of Paleohóra along the coast, turning right after 500m into the hills in the direction of Voutás; it's worth bearing in mind that **filling stations** are non-existent in these remote regions.

The interior: Azoyirés and Teménia

Other villages in **the interior** are equally unspoilt and, if you have transport, almost any of the tracks into the hills are fascinating. Heading north out of Paleohóra on the main road, you'll soon reach a couple of signs to **AZOYIRÉS**, one official, the other extolling the virtues of "Azoyires, Paradise Village", with its museum and caves. The eight-kilometre road up to the village – set amidst woods of cypress and pine – is paved until the last couple of kilometres. Head straight for the centre (ignoring the sign for the museum, which will almost certainly be closed), where there are two **taverna/rooms** places, *Mikailis* and *Alpha* (both ①), though neither is that special and a better alternative would be to take a packed lunch to enjoy under the trees on the banks of the nearby stream.

The **museum** (officially Sat & Sun 9am–2pm) is a single-room record of the Turkish occupation, full of fascinating old stuff. Outside the opening hours, the curator can usually be found if you ask at *Alpha*, right at the bottom of the village, by a chapel built into a cliff and the old olive-oil factory: a pretty path leads down there, above a lovely tree-filled ravine where pine, cypress, olive and maple grow. The **cave** is in the other direction, on an easy-to-miss road which sets off left just before the tavernas, and winds steeply upwards for nearly 2km (keep climbing and turning where there's any doubt about the way). At the top you have to park and there's an obvious path leading on – look up and you'll see a cross, which marks your destination. Approaching the cave, some 200m above, you may disturb quail (sometimes on the menu at *Alpha*); the eerie sounds in the cave itself emanate from more birds, mostly pigeons, bizarrely amplified by the cave. Going down, there's a steep metal stairway and rock-cut steps descending 50m or so to a little shrine lit from above by dim, reflected light. If you have a powerful torch, you can continue a fair way, although there's no proper path here: frankly, it's not that impressive. By the way, it's worth remembering the route you take to the cave, and to return by the same route, as a wrong turning can lead you into prickly gorse.

Beyond Azoyirés you can continue for a further 10km or so – on a reasonable unpaved road and following the indicated turns – to **TEMÉNIA**, where, as you enter there's an ancient chapel atop a low hill to the left and, a little further on a sign on the right for the thirteenth-century monastery church of **Sotíros Christós**. Sited at the end of a kilometre-long paved drive, you will soon see the charming drum-domed church occupying a low hill and surrounded by trees; the entrance has some curious stone steps built into the sides of a shallow porch. The church contains a number of fine **frescoes** and should be open, but if not, enquire at the later monastery buildings nearby. Above the village proper – located off the road and between the two churches – are scant traces of the ancient city of Hyrtakína with remains of fourth-century BC houses and a sanctuary. At Teménia you rejoin a good, newly surfaced road which cuts through from Kandános to the Soúyia road at Rodováni. A couple of kilometres in this direction leads to the particularly attractive village of **MÁZA**, with its frescoed church of **Áyios Nikólaos**, containing more stunning fourteenth-century paintings by Ioánnis Pagoménos, depicting scenes from the life of the saint.

Haniá to Soúyia

Although you can cut through by the route outlined above, the main road to Soúyia (see pp.322–3) is the one which runs right across the island from Haniá. This follows the route to Omalós for about 13km before turning off through Alikianós to skirt west of the highest mountains. Beside this turning there's a large **war memorial**. The Cretans it remembers were mostly local members of the irregular forces which defended the area known as "Prison Valley" in the Battle of Crete (you've already passed the prison, see p.280). Cut off from any other Allied units – who indeed believed that resistance here collapsed on the first day of the battle – the Greeks fought on even as everyone else was in full retreat. By doing so they prevented the Germans getting around the mountains to cut the road and guaranteed that the evacuation from Hóra Sfakíon could go ahead. In much earlier history, Alikianós was also the site of the wedding massacre which ended the Kandanoleon revolt (see p.273).

Alikianós

Right in the centre of an area known as the Portokalahória ("the orange villages"), a huge orange-growing district, **ALIKIANÓS** itself has couple of churches worth a look. Once in the village, follow the Koufós road (signed) for a short distance to reach the small fourteenth-century church of **Áyios Yeóryios** on the right and close to the road. It used to have some fine fifteenth-century frescoes, but lost them as a result of damage in World War II. In an orange grove behind houses over the road from this church lie the ruins of the **Da Molini castle** (some locals refer to it as Da Moulin) which may have been the scene of the Kandanoleon wedding massacre. To reach it, head in along the nearest street and, when you ask the way, you'll be conducted over back-garden fences to reach the weed-festooned ruin with impressive walls. The entrance lintel (which is now overgrown) carries the inscription *Omnia Mundi Fumus et*

Umbra ("All in the World is Smoke and Shadow") a sentiment to which the Venetians were particularly attached, and which ultimately turned out to be grimly accurate regarding their Cretan possessions.

Continue along the same road for a kilometre to reach the best of Alikianós's churches, **Áyios Ioánnis**, 50m down a signed track into more orange groves on the right. A beautiful fourteenth-century building on the site of at least two previous churches dating back to the sixth century, the church is currently undergoing long-overdue restoration to protect it from the elements. Employing bits of the previous basilica in the construction of its apse, the church has surviving **frescoes** depicting the Ascension as well as a number of saints.

Ayía Iríni gorge and Moní

Back on the route south, after **SKINÉS**, a large village with several tavernas and kafenía set among extensive orange groves, the road starts to climb out of the valley into the outriders of the Lefká Óri. Here the citrus trees give way to leafier, deciduous varieties – chestnuts and planes especially – and the villages are a great deal smaller. Just over halfway across the island, near Ayía Iríni, there's a road signed to Omalós (see p.283); recently sealed along its entire length, it is now an effortless and exhilarating drive over extremely high mountains, with wonderful views and plenty of vegetation. **AYÍA IRÍNI** is also a very green village, with lots of old chestnut trees, although it is still suffering the aftermath of a **great fire** in the late summer of 1994, which devastated a vast tract of land between the Ayía Iríni gorge and Soúyia, and set fire to many villages en route. The gorge can be **walked**, via Moní (see below), as far as the coast at Souyía, roughly 12km distant: it's about a five-hour trek. The route down into the gorge can be picked up on the south edge of the village and is marked on the Petrákis *Haniá Trekking and Road Map* (see "Maps", p.30). The walk can also be carried out using Souyía as a base (see p.324).

Continuing south by road, you start gradually to descend, looping down to occasional views of the Libyan Sea and, in the last few kilometres, tracing a gorge with Soúyia framed at the far end. Beyond Rodhováni are the remains of ancient **Elyrós**, the most important city in southwest Crete in Roman times and earlier; there's now very little to see. In **MONÍ**, the last village before the coast, the delightful fourteenth-century **church of Áyios Nikólaos** has frescoes by Ioánnis Pagaménos, including a huge and striking image of St Nicholas himself. Outside the church, take a look at the **campanile** or free-standing bell tower – it's an architectural curiosity and the only one known on the island. Before setting out for the church, ask in the first bar you pass on entering the village for the key: it's actually kept at a house a few doors along but they'll sort you out. The church lies along a track which descends from the road on the right about 50m beyond the bar.

Koustoyérako

Only about 5km short of Soúyia, a road cuts back to the ancient Sélinos villages of Livadás and Koustoyérako, some 8.5km away at the end of the road. Reached by a climb up a hillside still covered with blackened tree stumps – vestiges of the fire mentioned above – **KOUSTOYÉRAKO** is a very ancient village that was, and still is, the home of the Paterákis family, famed in the annals of resistance to German occupation. Manóli Paterákis was one of those who took part in the capture of General Kreipe (see p.343). He died some years ago, at the age of 73, when he fell while chasing a wild goat through the mountains.

The village, like so many, has a long history of resistance to foreign occupation, and was destroyed by Venetians, Turks and Germans alike. In 1943, German troops entered the village, which the men had deserted, and rounded up the women and children in the village square:

They lined them all up, and, as they refused to speak, prepared to execute the lot. But, before they could press the trigger of their heavy machine-gun, ten Germans fell dead. For some of the village men – about ten – had taken up position along the top of a sheer cliff above the village, from where they could watch every detail, and, at just the right moment, had opened fire. Not a bullet went wide. Terrified, the Germans took to their heels. . . .

George Psychoundákis, *The Cretan Runner*

Next day the Germans returned, but by then the village was deserted; they blew up the empty houses in frustration. Cóstas Paterákis, now in his late seventies, who fired the first shot and killed the machine-gunner (Patrick Leigh Fermor has described this as one of the most spectacular moments of the war), still lives here.

While the villagers have no desire to become tourist attractions, the village itself is a lovely and very friendly one, set beneath the heights of the Lefká Ori looking out over the Libyan Sea. At the entrance to the village there's a striking modern war memorial, and a simple taverna, next to the school and village playground. Further along, you reach the square, with a couple of kafenía. The famous shot was fired from the rocky cliffs above, to your right as you face inland. At the top of the village, to your left from the square, is a tiny Byzantine chapel, **Áyios Yeóryios**; inside are some beautiful remains of frescoes, with sixteenth-century graffiti carved into them. The chapel itself may be as early as tenth-century in origin: the inscription inside the door dates from sixteenth-century restorations and records various generations of the Kandanoleon family – the last named is one María Theotokópoulos. From this tenuous connection comes the claim that El Greco (Doménico Theotokópoulos) came originally from Koustoyérako. In the graveyard is the tomb of another Kandanoleon, George. One of Crete's great revolutionary leaders, he led the sixteenth-century revolt against Venetian rule (see p.273) and his body was returned to his birthplace following his execution by the Venetians. Before setting out for the church (which is kept locked) you'll need to enquire at the kafenío on the square; they should be able to turn up someone to take you to the church, where the key will be retrieved from its hiding-place whilst you turn your back.

In summer French groups frequently camp by the school, and from here climb – with a guide – to Omalós and the gorge. If you ask permission, and take your meals at the taverna, you'd probably be allowed to **camp** here, too.

Soúyia

SOÚYIA is a small village slowly on its way to becoming a resort. For the moment, though, there are no big hotels and no major tour operators, just lots of rooms, simple restaurants and bars, and general stores which double as travel agents, phone offices and banks. In front there's an enormous swathe of bay and sparklingly clean, clear sea, and a long pebbly beach. Not immediately attractive at first sight, the place does tend to grow on you, and is very welcoming with plenty of room to spread out. You could camp here under a few scraggly trees if you wanted, although you'd be advised to get as far away from the central beach as possible to be left in peace. Around at the east end of the bay there's something of a nudist community – known locally as the Bay of Pigs.

The village **church**, down by the beach at the western end of an avenue flanked by tamarisks, is the village's only feature. The story goes – in typical Cretan fashion – that it was built after a local man slept here and dreamt that an ancient church lay beneath him and that he was being summoned to erect a new one on the site. Sure enough the ancient church was found and the new one built. Unfortunately the new building was far smaller than the old and at a different angle: as a result the sixth-century Byzantine mosaic which formed the floor of the original stuck out beyond the walls of the new one. Although much of the original mosaic has been taken away for "restoration" and seems unlikely to return, you can still see where it was. The original church was a part of ancient Syia, a port for Elyrós (see p.321) which flourished through the Roman and early Christian eras: other remains can be seen in the village and around to the east of the bay.

Practicalities

There are **rooms** are everywhere in Soúyia, although there's a distinct lack of low budget places, particularly in high season. Along the main street as you come in are *Pension Galini* (☎0823/51-488; ③) and the friendly *Captain George* (☎0823/51-133, fax 51-194; ③) which both offer en-suite rooms in a pleasant setting. Over the road from these two, *Idomeneas Apartments* (☎0823/51-540, fax 0821/51-539; ④)) has modern studio singles and doubles with kitchen and balcony. Up a short track close to the entrance to *Captain George*, are the friendly *Rooms Irtakina* (☎0823/51-130; ③) where you are welcomed with a *raki*, and *Pension El Greco* (☎0823/51-026; ③), both tranquil possibilities for rooms with bath at the back of the village. On the same street there are also more basic, but perfectly adequate rooms places such as *Paradisos* (☎0823/51-359; ②), *Lissos* (☎0823/51-244; ②) and *Filoxenia* (②). On the seafront the good-value *Hotel Santa Irene* (☎0823/51-342, fax 0821 /90-047; ③) has spotless en-suite balcony rooms (some with sea view) around a garden. Nearby is *Zorba's* (☎0823/51-353; ③) with more en-suite rooms, and a slightly cheaper option for rooms with bath just west of here is *Rooms Syia* (☎0823/51-476; ②).

Places to eat include the *Hotel Pikilassos*, just off the main street, with taverna-style dishes served on a little terrace, or *Rembetiko*, just inland on the main street, a newcomer serving well-cooked traditional dishes on a pleasant garden terrace. Further inland, and off the main street to the right near the police station *Polifimos* is another decent place. There's also *Paradisos* café/pizzeria, in the same building as the eponymous rooms place. Among several waterfront places *Oceanis* is good for traditional Greek standards and there's the popular *Liviko*. At the eastern end of the seafront, the pricier, German-run *Omikron* has a more north European flavour, and some vegetarian choices.

At night, there are a couple of **disco-bars** which sometimes attract a crowd: the first, *Alabama*, is sited among the trees on the far side of the stream to the east of the village, whilst the other, *Fortuna*, is at the northern edge, on the left as you come in. Other more centrally located **bars** include *Raki Bar* next to Polifimos Travel and *Bla Bla Bla*, behind the *Omikron* taverna, both with music after dark.

The local **travel agent**, Polifimos Travel (☎ & fax 0823/51-022; 9am–2pm & 4.30–11pm) on the main street just before the beach is very friendly and has piles of information on everything to do in the area. It also **changes money**, **rents cars**, sells **boat tickets** for Paleohóra, Hóra Sfakión, Elafonísi, Gávdhos and other destinations and has a **taxi-boat** which does day-trips for small groups to Lissós (see below), Loutró and Gávdhos. Just over the road is a **mini-market** stocking plenty of food and essentials which also has a public **phone**; and there's a card-phone kiosk nearby.

To walk the Ayía Iríni gorge (see p.321) back to Souyía you could take the early morning bus from here to the village of Ayía Iríni (7am) which allows you to com-plete the walk back down the gorge before it becomes too hot. The bus for walk-ing the Samariá Gorge leaves daily at 7am in summer and there are also daily buses to Haniá at 7am and 3.30pm.

Lissós

The archeological site of **Lissós** is a great deal more rewarding than anything you'll see in Soúyia itself. The four-kilometre walk there, a little over an hour (90min if you dawdle), is part of the pleasure: you set out on the road which heads west, behind the beach, and at the harbour turn right (there's a rusty old sign marked "Lisos") onto a track leading slightly inland. The route is well marked once you're on it, leading up a beautiful echoing gorge, which you follow for about thirty minutes, and then climb steeply out of towards the sea. Make sure to take this climb left out of the gorge which is easily missed. After a short level stretch the sea comes into view, followed almost immediately by Lissós, below you at the back of a delightful little bay with the chapel of Áyios Kiriákos and the archeo-logical site further inland. An alternative way of seeing the site and saving a walk both ways is to book Yiánnis's **taxi-boat** (about 5000dr for up to six people) at Polifimos Travel (see above). Ideally in summer you'd get him to drop you at Lissos's pebble beach between 5–6pm which would leave you with plenty of time for a look around the ancient site (you'll very likely have it all to yourself) before the cool walk back to Souyía through the gorge. To gain the path back to Souyía follow the track (now waymarked as part of the E4 Pan-European Footpath) which climbs the steep hill on the east side of the archeological site.

The site
Originally a Dorian city, Lissós grew through the Hellenistic and Roman eras and continued to thrive, along with its neighbours Syia and Elyrós, right up to the Saracen invasion in the ninth century, when they were all abandoned. These places have little history, although it is known that they joined together around 300 BC – along with Hyrtakína in the hills behind, Pikilássos on the inaccessi-ble coast between here and Ayía Rouméli, and Tarra, at modern Ayía Rouméli – to form the Confederation of Oreioi, and were later joined by Górtys and Cyrenaica (the latter in North Africa). The remains at Lissós are mostly Classical Greek and Roman.

The most important survival is an **Asklepion**, or temple of healing, built beside a curative spring against the cliffs on the east side of the site. The temple proba-bly dates from the third century BC, although the **mosaic floor** which is its most obvious feature was added later, in the first century AD; it's a poignant ancient relic, however, depicting images of polychrome birds in its central section (includ-ing a quail) and elaborate and beautifully crafted geometric patterns on its outer borders. The excavations here revealed a hole dug through the floor which con-tained numerous broken statues and a headless image of Asclepius, the Greek god of healing; this was probably the work of fanatical early Christians who destroyed the temples, decapitated the statues (where they believed the spirit of the devil resided) and defaced the walls. Notice also the marble altar-base which would have supported a statue, and the "snake pit" (or hole to place sacrifices) next to it. On the gentler, western slope of the valley, opposite, are a group of tombs that look like small stone huts, with barrel-vaulted roofs – hardly the best advertisement for the healing temple. You'll also find a small ruined theatre and two thirteenth-century churches, Áyios Kiriákos – with a nearby **spring** – and Panayía, which reused older material from the site.

When you've completed your explorations, the small pebble **beach** provides solace in the form of a swim, and at a cabin, sometimes occupied by the site's guardian, you may be able to beg a cool drink. Ask here if you find the site locked or if you need directing onto the continuation of the path westward towards Paleohóra.

Gávdhos

Gávdhos, the southernmost point of Europe, is the largest of Crete's offshore islands and the only one with any significant population. Plain and somewhat barren, its attraction lies in its enduring isolation. The 50km of rough sea separating it from the coast of Crete frequently prove too much for the kaïkia, and the ports they serve have themselves only begun to see tourists in the last few years. Consequently – and despite the fact that it's now possible to get a very basic package tour to Gávdhos – the trip to the island remains one more talked about than done. Not that you can expect complete solitude: in summer, there's a semipermanent community of beach-campers who often outnumber the local population of little over fifty.

In the north and east, the low coast features a number of deserted beaches; in the southwest the island rises to 384m, its shoreline rocky and barely accessible. The interior, with four distinct settlements, is carpeted with pines and scrub and rich with the scent of wild thyme, but it can still be a pretty inhospitable environment, with summer temperatures which frequently climb well beyond 38°C (100°F).

To the northwest of Gávdhos (and passed en route from Paleohóra) lies the flat little islet of **Gavdhopoúlo**, inhabited only in summer by the occasional shepherd taking advantage of the grazing. If you want to visit, you'll have to arrange a trip with one of the local fishermen.

Practicalities

Ferry connections aren't bad in summer: from Paleohóra via Soúyia (May–Oct leaves Paleohóra 8am Mon, Tues & Thurs, passing Soúyia at 9am, returns at 2.45pm, Wed & Sat 8.30am, returns at 2.45pm); from Hóra Sfakíon (June–Sept, Fri 6pm, Sat & Sun 9am, returns 4pm); from Gávdhos to Hóra Sfakíon (July–Sept, Sat 6am & 4pm, Sun 4pm; June, late Sept & Oct, Sat only at 4pm). Outside these months things are much less certain – there are occasional sailings all year round by the postboat taking essential supplies across (mostly from Paleohóra) but these are dependent on the weather (unpredictable even in high summer) and other circumstances. The only accurate information can be had on the spot or by contacting Interkreta Travel in Paleohóra (p.315). Whatever time of year, this crossing can be rough, so take precautions if your seaworthiness is in doubt.

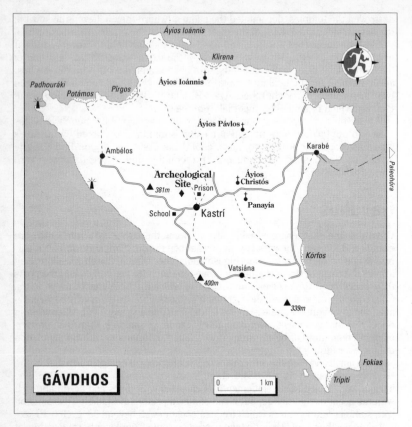

GÁVDHOS

0   1 km

Rooms are most obviously available in Karabé where *Calypso* (☎0823/42-118;
②) and *Rooms Tsigonakis* (②) both have rooms with showers (when the water's
on), or there's the simpler *Rooms Yiorgos* (①). Accommodation can also be had in
Kastrí and elsewhere if you ask around, and there are now a couple of rooms
places on each of the main beaches, Sarakiníkos (try *Manolis*; ①) and Kórfos (see
p.328). It's even possible to book ahead from Paleohóra (try Interkreta Travel,
p.315). If you're prepared to **camp** you can pick your spot just about anywhere,
on the beaches or in any number of sheltered locations inland, though be aware
of local sensibilities and take your rubbish away.

The most obvious sign of the hardship of Gávdhos life is the paucity of **food**
available. With the exception of a few basic vegetables, and the occasional feast
when someone slaughters a sheep or goat, almost everything has to be imported
from the mainland and there is little choice in any of the island's stores or eating
places. (Karabé and Sarakiníkos have the best options, with at least a chance of
fresh fish.) It makes sense to bring some supplies with you, especially fresh bread
and fruit, although visitors who fail to spend anything at all not surprisingly irri-

tate locals somewhat. The local *thimárisio* (thyme honey) is wonderful, and watch out for the island wine, which is vicious.

Water is also in short supply. There is very little springwater and most fresh water has to be drawn from wells or collected in rainwater cisterns; check with locals before drinking from any of them. Don't expect to find too many showers or modern plumbing, and don't join those thoughtless visitors who insist on contaminating the limited fresh-water supply with soap. There is no mains electricity either, though generators are fairly widespread, as can be seen from the number of TV aerials.

In **emergencies** there should be a doctor in Kastrí during the summer and there's also a telephone line to the mainland, with a phone in each of the four main settlements. The best advice, however, is not to tempt fate – especially as an accident could mean being airlifted by army helicopter, incurring a hefty bill which your insurance may not cover. At least a few words of Greek would be extremely useful, though locals try their best with all visitors.

Around the island

As you approach, the harbour is hidden behind a headland, and the island looks totally uninhabited – only with the aid of binoculars might you pick out one or two isolated homes. The port at **Karabé** is minute. Lost in a drab expanse of rock and scrub, two kafenía sit alongside a stubby concrete breakwater, and a few ramshackle houses and a church squat behind in silent support. Add in a couple of very basic **rooms** places (see p.326) and that's about it. If you want to get to one of the **beaches** the easy way it's normally possible to find a boat here, or you could take one of the vehicles (tractors with trailers or a minibus to Sarakiníkos) that usually meet the ferry. If you do hire a boat make sure to take along sufficient drinking water and make sure the boatman understands when you want to be picked up. Some people bring rented scooters and bikes across on the ferry with them – it certainly facilitates island exploration.

Forty minutes' stiff walk will take you north across the headland, past the pretty little church of Áyios Yeóryios, to **Sarakiníkos**, one of the best of the strands, a broad strip of golden sand where there are eight or nine very basic tavernas. It's a fair-sized track that leads here, but the only real road – a dirt track built in 1980 for the benefit of Gávdhos' four vehicle-owners – runs inland from Karabé. A five-kilometre hike to the west of Sarakiníkos, passing close to the church of Áyios Ioánnis and the sandy Klirena beach, leads to another fine isolated beach, **Áyios Ioánnis**, which has become a summer hangout for a permanent hippy occupation, despite (or because of) the fact that there are no facilities and little fresh water. You could also head south from Karabé, a similar distance, to Kórfos beach, the second most popular. This is also served by a frequent boat service (see above).

Kastrí

KASTRÍ, the island capital, is an hour's walk along this steadily climbing dirt track – a ghostly sort of place where only a handful of houses remain inhabited while the majority gradually crumble away to become one with the weathered and fissured rock on which they stand. Depopulation here has been acute and constant. In the Middle Ages Gávdhos is said to have had eight thousand residents and had a bishop of its own: even in 1914 there were 1400 souls living here. Given the isolation and the stark severity of island life the drain is hardly surprising, but it has undoubtedly made conditions even harder for the members of the six families who remain. Not far from the village there is a minor (unfenced) archeological site from which some derive proof that the island was settled as far back as Neolithic times. What is certain is that Gávdhos was inhabited in the Classical Greek era (some claim that this was the island of Calypso visited by Odysseus) and was well known to the Romans, who christened the place Clauda or Kaudos – St Paul was blown past Clauda in the storm which carried him off from Kalí Liménes (see p.130).

In Kastrí you'll find the island **post office** incorporating the telephone office (although there are now cardphone kiosks in all the villages), store and occasional taxi service which along with a number of other very basic stores also serves as a café and meeting place. On the outskirts stands a substantial two-storey building where political prisoners were incarcerated between the wars; there have been attempts since to convert it to a hotel and a sanatorium, but currently it stands empty.

Ámbelos and Vatsianá

Climbing out of Kastrí the track reaches the ridgeline and divides. Close to this junction is the old island school, now redundant. The left branch leads to the tiny settlement of **VATSIANÁ**, the right to the equally sparse hamlet of **ÁMBELOS**. From the latter there's a particularly fine view towards North Africa, a sealane ploughed constantly by enormous supertankers. A track north from here leads to the isolated beaches of Potamós, where there are no facilities and you'll need to take along water. From either village you can continue by narrow paths to some great beaches: north from Ámbelos to Potamós – behind which you can explore a couple of spectacular ravines – and nearby Pírgos. There are no facilities at either beach and you'll need to take along water. Heading south or east from Vatsianá will bring you to Kórfos or Tripití.

Kórfos and Tripití

A twisting track east from Vatsianá leads to **KÓRFOS**, 2km away, where there's a good beach (known locally as Yeorgo's beach, after the man who lives here with his family over the summer at the taverna on the hill behind). They have a couple of basic **rooms** (①) to rent or you can camp nearby (but ask first). Depending on the water situation, it may also be possible to use the showers here. Yeorgo's **boat** ferries visitors to and from Karabé and you might even be able to persuade him to make a boat trip to **TRIPITÍ** (rather a long hike from Vatsianá), the most southerly point of Europe. The beach here is pebbly with no shade but the water is brilliantly clear and a snorkeller's paradise, with lots of aquatic life to be seen. When you need a break, you can climb the famous **three-holed rock** and sit on the edge of a continent.

GREEK PLACE NAMES

ΑΓ ΜΑΡΙΝΑ	Αγ Μαρίνα	Ay. Marína
ΑΓ ΡΟΥΜΕΛΗ	Αγ Ρουμέλη	Ay. Rouméli
ΑΚΡΩΤΗΡΙ	Ακρωτήρι	Akrotíri
ΑΛΙΚΙΑΝΟΣ	Αλικιανός	Alikianós
ΑΠΤΕΡΑ	Άπτερα	Áptera
ΑΛΜΥΡΙΔΑ	Αλμυρίδα	Almirídha
ΑΝΟΠΟΛΗ	Ανόπολη	Anópoli
ΒΑΜΟΣ	Βάμος	Vámos
ΒΡΥΣΕΣ	Βρύσες	Vrísses
ΓΑΥΔΟΣ	Γαύδος	Gávdhos
ΓΕΩΡΓΙΟΥΠΟΛΗ	Γεωργιούπολη	Yeoryióupoli
ΕΛΑΦΟΝΗΣΗ	Ελαφονήση	Elafonísi
ΕΛΟΣ	Έλος	Élos
ΘΕΡΙΣΟ	Θέρισο	Thériso
ΚΑΛΑΜΙ	Καλάμι	Kalámi
ΚΑΛΥΒΕΣ	Καλύβες	Kalíves
ΚΑΝΤΑΝΟΣ	Κάντανος	Kándanos
ΚΑΣΤΕΛΛΙ	Καοτέλλι	Kastélli
ΚΟΛΥΜΒΑΡΙ	Κολυμβάρι	Kolimbári
ΚΟΥΡΝΑΣ	Κουρνάς	Kournás
ΛΑΚΚΟΙ	Λάκκοι	Lákki
ΛΟΥΤΡΟ	Λουτρό	Loutró
ΜΑΛΕΜΕ	Μάλεμε	Máleme
ΜΕΣΚΛΑ	Μεσκλά	Mesklá
ΜΟΥΡΝΙΕΣ	Μουρνιές	Mourniés
ΟΜΑΛΟΣ	Ομαλός	Omalós
ΠΑΛΑΙΟΧΩΡΑ	Παλαιοχώρα	Paleohóra
ΠΕΡΙΒΟΛΙΑ	Περιβόλια	Perivólia
ΠΛΑΤΑΝΟΣ	Πλάτανος	Plátanos
ΠΟΛΥΡΡΗΝΙΑ	Πολυρρηνία	Polirinía
ΡΟΔΩΠΟΣ	Ροδωπός	Rodhopós
ΣΑΜΑΡΙΑ	Σαμαριά	Samariá
ΣΟΥΓΙΑ	Σόυγια	Sóuyia
ΣΟΥΔΑ	Σόυδα	Sóudha
ΣΤΑΥΡΟΣ	Σταυρός	Stavrós
ΣΦΑΚΙΑ	Σφακιά	Sfakiá
ΣΦΗΝΑΡΙΟ	Σφηνάριο	Sfinári
ΦΑΛΑΣΑΡΝΑ	Φαλάσαρνα	Falásarna
ΦΟΥΡΝΕΣ	Φουρνές	Fournés
ΦΡΑΓΚΟΚΑΣΤΕΛΛΟ	Φραγκοκάστελλο	Frangokástello
ΧΑΝΙΑ	Χανιά	Haniá
ΧΡΥΣΟΣΚΑΛΙΤΙΣΣΑΣ	Χρυσοσκαλίτισσας	Hrisoskalítissa
ΧΩΡΑ ΣΦΑΚΙΩΝ	Χώρα Σφακίων	Hóra Sfakíon
ΧΩΡΑΦΑΚΙΑ	Χωραφάκια	Horafákia

travel details

Buses

Haniá to: Ayía Marína (every 15min; 8.15am–11am & 4pm–8pm); Elafonísi (1 daily; 7.30am return 4pm; 3hr); Falásarna (2 daily; 8.30am and 3.30pm; 2hr); Fournés (7 daily; 6.45am–8pm; 30min); Gavalohóri (2 daily; 11am & 2.30pm; 45min); Horafákia/Stavrós (6 daily; 6.50am–8pm; 30min); Hóra Sfakíon (3 daily; 8.30am, 11am, and 2pm; 2hr); Iráklion (20 daily; 5.30am–8.30pm; 3hr), one via the old road at noon (5hr); Kalíves (5 daily; 7am–7.30pm; 45min); Kastélli (15 daily; 6am–8.30pm; 1hr 30min); Kolimbári (29 daily; 6am–10.30pm; 1hr); Máleme (every 15min; 8.30–11.30am & 4–11pm); Omalós/Samariá Gorge (4 daily; 6.15am, 7.30am, 8.30am and 4.30pm; 90min); Paleohóra (5 daily; 8.30am–5pm; 2hr); Réthimnon (20 daily; 5.30am–8.30pm; 1hr 30min), one via the old road at noon (2hr); Skalóti (for Frangokástello) (1 daily; 2pm; 2hr 30min); Soúyia (2 daily; 8.30am and 1.30pm; 2hr); Vámos (4 daily; 7am–8pm; 30min).

Hóra Sfakíon to: Plakiás/Ayía Galíni (2 daily; 11am & 5pm; 1hr 30min–3hr).

Kastélli to: Elafonísi (1 daily; 8.30am; 1hr 30min); Omalós (3 daily; 5am, 6am and 7am; 3hr).

Paleohóra to: Omalós (for Samariá Gorge; 1 daily; 6am); Haniá (5 daily; 7am–6pm).

Souyía to: Omalós (for Samariá Gorge; 1 daily; 7am).

Yeoryióupolis to: Omalós (for Samariá Gorge; 2 daily; 6.30 & 7.20am).

Ferries

Gávdhos to: Hóra Sfakíon (July to mid-Sept, Sat at 7am and 4pm, Sun 4pm; June, late Sept and Oct, Sat only at 4pm).

Hóra Sfakíon to: Gávdhos (July to mid-Sept Fri 6pm, Sat and Sun 9am, returning 4pm; June, late Sept and Oct Sat only at 9am).

Kastélli to: Kalamáta (2 weekly; Wed 8am, Sat noon); Kíthira (4 weekly; Tues 8am, Thurs 1pm, Sat noon, Sun 7pm); Monemvassía (2 weekly; Thurs 5pm, Sun 9am); Neápoli (2 weekly, Thurs 5pm, Sun 9am); Pireás (1 weekly; Thurs 7pm); Yíthio (2 weekly; Tues & Sat 8am).

Paleohóra to: Gávdhos (June–Sept Mon, Tues & Thurs 8am; Wed & Sat 8.30am returning 2.45pm; May and Oct Fri and Sun 8.30am, returning 2.30pm); all weather permitting.

Sóudha to: Pireás (ANEK Line daily at 8pm).

Kaïkia (caiques) also run along the south coast, daily from Paleohóra to Soúyia and Ayía Rouméli (depart 8am, return 5.30pm); at least 4 times a day in season (May–Oct) from Ayía Rouméli to Loutró and Hóra Sfakíon.

Flights

To Athens 4 daily (45min).

To Thessaloníki 2 weekly; Tues 12.50pm & Fri 2.35pm (1hr 15min).

PART THREE

THE
CONTEXTS

THE HISTORICAL FRAMEWORK

The people of Crete unfortunately make more history than they can consume locally.
Saki

The discovery of the Minoan civilization has tended to overshadow every other aspect of Cretan history. And indeed it would be hard for any other period to rival what was, in effect, the first truly European civilization. It was in Crete that the developed societies of the east met influences from the west and north, and here that "Western culture", as synthesized in Classical Greece and Rome, first developed.

Yet this was no accident or freak one-off: Crete's position as a meeting place of east and west, and its strategic setting in the middle of the Mediterranean, has thrust the island to the centre stage of world history more often than seems comfortable. Long before Arthur Evans arrived to unearth Knossós, and for some time after, the island's struggle for freedom, and the great powers' inactivity, was the subject of Europe-wide scandal. The battle for the island when the Turks arrived had similarly aroused worldwide interest, and represented at the time a significant change in the balance of power between Islam and Christianity. In fact from Minoan times to World War II, there has rarely been a sustained period when Crete didn't have some role to play in world affairs.

THE STONE AGE

Crete's first inhabitants, **Neolithic cave dwellers**, apparently reached the island around 7000 BC. They came, most probably, from Asia Minor, or less likely from Syria, Palestine or North Africa, bringing with them the basics of Stone Age culture – tools of wood, stone and bone, crude pottery and simple cloth. A possible clue to the origins of these peoples may lie in the importance of bull cults at certain centres in Neolithic Anatolia.

Development over the next three thousand years was almost imperceptibly slow, but gradually, whether through new migrations and influences or internal dynamics, advances were made. Elementary agriculture was practised, with domestic animals and basic crops. Pottery (the oldest samples of which were found beneath the palace at Knossós) became more sophisticated, with better-made domestic utensils and clay figurines of humans, animals and, especially, a fat mother goddess or fertility figure. Obsidian imported from the island of Mílos was used too. And though caves continued to be inhabited, simple rectangular huts of mud bricks were also built, with increasing skill and complexity as the era wore on. One of the most important of the Neolithic settlements was at Knossós, where two remarkable dwellings have been revealed below the Central Court, and there is abundant evidence that many other sites of later habitation were used at this time – Mália, Festós, Ayía Triádha, the Haniá area – as were most of the caves which later came to assume religious significance.

THE BRONZE AGE: MINOAN CRETE

Minoan Crete has been the subject of intense and constant study since its emergence from myth to archeological reality at the beginning of the twentieth century. Yet there is still enormous controversy even over such fundamental details as who the Minoans were and what language they spoke. No written historical records from the time survive (or if they do, they have not yet been deciphered) so almost everything we know is deduced from physical remains, fleshed out somewhat by writings from Classical Greece, almost one thousand years after the destruction of Knossós. Nevertheless it is not hard to forge some kind of consensus from the theories about the Minoans, and this is what is set out below: fresh discoveries may yet radically change this view.

One of the central arguments is over **dating**. The original system, conceived by Sir Arthur Evans, divided the period into Early, Middle and Late Minoan (see p.350), with each of these again divided into three sub-periods – a sequence that has become extremely complicated and cumbersome as it has been further qualified and subdivided. Arcane distinctions between the pottery styles of Early Minoan IIa and IIb have no place in a brief history and a simpler system is used here (following the archeologist Nikólaos Pláton) of four periods: **pre-palatial**, proto-palatial or **First Palace**, neo-palatial or **New Palace**, and **post-palatial**. This has the additional advantage of avoiding many of the niceties of exact dating and of uneven development across the island. However, as many archeological texts and guides, as well as numerous museums on the island use the Evans system, the approximate corresponding periods – Early, Middle and Late Minoan – are given in brackets below.

PRE-PALATIAL: 3000–1900 BC (EM–MMI)

Among the more important puzzles of Minoan society is its comparatively **sudden emergence**. During the centuries before 2600 BC, there were important changes on the island, and thereafter very rapid progress in almost every area of life. Villages and towns grew up where previously there had been only isolated settlements, and with them came craft specialists: potters, stonecutters, metalworkers, jewellers and weavers. Many of these new settlements were in the east and south of the island, and there was significant habitation on the coast and near natural harbours for the first time.

It seems safe to assume that these changes were wrought by a new **migration** of people from the east, bringing with them new technologies, methods of agriculture and styles of pottery, but most importantly perhaps, a knowledge of seafaring and trade. The olive and the vine – which need little tending and therefore help free a labour force – began to be produced alongside cereal crops. Copper tools replaced stone ones

and were themselves later refined with the introduction of bronze. Art developed rapidly, with characteristic **Vasilikí ware** and other pottery styles, as well as gold jewellery, and stone jars of exceptional quality, based originally on Egyptian styles. Significantly, large quantities of **seal stones** have been found too, almost certainly the mark of a mercantile people. They were used to sign letters and documents, but especially to seal packets, boxes or doors as proof that they had not been opened: the designs – scorpions or poisonous spiders – were often meant as a further deterrent to robbery.

At the same time new methods of burial appear – *thólos* and chamber **tombs** in which riches were buried with the dead. These appear to have been communal, as, probably, was daily life, based perhaps on clan or kinship groupings.

THE FIRST PALACES: 1900–1700 BC (MMI–MMII)

Shortly before 1900 BC, the first of the palaces were built, at **Knossós**, **Festós**, **Mália** and **Zákros**. They represent another significant and apparently abrupt change: a shift of power back to the centre of the island and the emergence of a much more hierarchical, ordered society. The sites of these palaces were also no accident: Festós and Mália both dominate fertile plains, whilst Zákros had a superbly sited harbour for trade with the east. Knossós, occupying a strategic position above another plain to the south and west of Iráklion, was perhaps originally as much a religious centre as a base of secular power. Certainly at this time religion took on a new importance, with the widespread use of mountain-top peak sanctuaries and caves as **cult centres**. At the same time much larger towns were growing up, especially around the palaces, and in the countryside substantial "villas" appeared.

The palaces themselves are proof of the island's great prosperity at this period, and the artefacts found within offer further evidence. Advances were made in almost every field of artistic and craft endeavour. From the First Palace era came the famous **Kamáres ware** pottery – actually two distinct styles, one eggshell-thin and delicate, the other sturdier with bold-coloured designs. The true potter's wheel (as against the turntable) was introduced for the first time, along with a simple form of hieroglyphic writing. Elaborate jewellery, seals and bronzework were also being produced.

Cretan bronze was used throughout the Mediterranean, and its production and distribution were dependent on a wide-ranging **maritime economy**. For though Crete may have produced some copper at this time, it never yielded tin, the nearest significant sources of which were as distant as Iran to the east, central Europe in the north, Italy, Spain, Brittany and even Britain in the west. While some claim that Minoan ships actually sailed as far afield as the Atlantic, it seems more likely that the more exotic goods were obtained through middlemen. Nevertheless, Crete controlled the trade routes in the Mediterranean, importing tin, copper, ivory, gold, silver and precious stones of every kind, exporting timber from its rich cypress forests, olive oil, wine, bronze goods and its fine pottery, especially to Egypt. Minoan **colonies** or trading posts were established on many Cycladic islands as well as the island of Kíthira off the Peloponnese, Rhodes and the coast of Asia Minor; a fleet of merchant vessels maintained regular trade links between these centres and, above all, with Egypt and the east.

Around 1700 BC, the palaces were destroyed for the first time, probably by earthquake, although raiders from the early Mycenaean Greek mainland may also have seized this opportunity to raid the island whilst it was temporarily defenceless; this may well account for the wealth of gold and other treasure – much of it obviously Cretan – found in the later royal shaft graves at Mycenae.

THE NEW PALACES: 1700–1450 BC (MMIII–LMI)

Though the destruction must have been a setback, Minoan culture continued to flourish, and with the palaces reconstructed on a still grander scale the society entered its golden age. It is the **new palaces** which provide most of our picture of Minoan life and most of what is seen at the great sites – Knossós, Festós, Mália, Zákros – dates from this period.

The **architecture** of the new palaces was of an unprecedented sophistication: complex, multistorey structures in which the use of space and light was as luxurious as the construction materials. Grand stairways, colonnaded porticoes and courtyards, brightly frescoed walls, elaborate plumbing and drainage, and great magazines in which to store the society's accumulation of wealth, were all integral, as were workshops for the technicians and craftsmen, and areas set aside for ritual and worship.

Obviously it was only an elite which enjoyed these comforts, but conditions for the ordinary people who kept Minos and his attendants in such style appear to have improved too: **towns** around the palaces and at sites such as Gourniá and Palékastro were growing as well. (It was Arthur Evans who named Minoan society after the legendary King Minos, but there is little doubt that Minos was in fact the title of a dynasty of priest/kings, a word rather like pharaoh.)

Very little is known of how the **society** was organized, or indeed whether it was a single entity ruled from Knossós or simply several city-states with a common cultural heritage. However, in an intriguing reference to Crete in his *Politics*, Aristotle implied that a caste system had operated in the time of Minos. Clearly, though, it was a society in which **religion** played an important part. The great Corridor of the Procession fresco at Knossós depicted an annual delivery of tribute, apparently to a Mother Goddess; bull-leaping had a religious significance too; and in all the palaces substantial chambers were set aside for ritual purposes. Secular leaders were also religious leaders.

That Minoan society was a very open one is apparent too. There are virtually no **defences**, internal or external, at any Minoan site, and apparently the rulers felt no threat either from within or without, which has lead scholars to emphasize a military strength based on seapower. As far as internal dissent goes, it seems safe to assume that the wealth of the island filtered down, to some extent at least, to all its inhabitants: the lot of a Minoan peasant may have been little different from that of a Cretan villager as little as fifty years ago.

Externally, **maritime supremacy** was further extended: objects of Cretan manufacture turn up all over the Mediterranean and have even been claimed as far afield as Britain and Scandinavia (amber from the Baltic certainly found its way to Crete). Behind their seapower the Minoans clearly felt safe, and the threat of attack or piracy was further reduced by the network of colonies or close allies throughout the Cycladic islands – Thíra most famously but also at Mílos, Náxos, Páros, Mikonós, Ándhros and Dílos – and in Rhodes, Cyprus, Syria and North Africa. Nevertheless, this appears to have remained a trading empire rather than a military one.

Cultural advances

If the New Palace period was a high point of Minoan power, it also marked the apogee of **arts** and **crafts** in the island: again, the bulk of the objects you'll admire in the museums dates from this era. The **frescoes** – startling in their freshness and vitality – are the most famous and obviously visible demonstration of this florescence. But they were just the highly visible tip of an artistic iceberg. It was in intricate small-scale work that the Minoans excelled above all. Naturalistic **sculpted figures** of humans and animals include the superb ivory bull-leaper, the leopard-head axe and the famous snake goddesses or priestesses, all of them on show in the Iráklion Archeological Museum. The carvings on seal stones of this era are of exceptional delicacy – a skill carried over into beautifully delicate gold jewellery. Examples of **stone vessels** include the bull's head rhyton from Knossós and the three black vases from Ayía Triádha, which are among the museum's most valuable possessions. And **pottery** broke out into an enormous variety of new shapes and design motifs, drawing inspiration especially from scenes of nature and marine life.

The other great advance was in **writing**. A new form of script, **Linear A**, had appeared at the end of the First Palace period, but in the new palaces its use became widespread. Still undeciphered, Linear A must record the original, unknown language of the Minoans: it seems to have been used in written form almost exclusively for administrative records – stock lists, records of transactions and tax payments. Even were it understood, therefore, it seems unlikely that the language would reveal much. The pieces which have survived were never intended as permanent records, and have been found intact only where the clay tablets used were baked solid in the fires which destroyed the palaces. It is possible that a more formal record, an abstract of the annual accounts, was kept on a more valuable but also more perishable material such as imported papyrus or even a paper produced from native date-palm leaves.

Destruction

Around 1600 BC the island again saw minor earthquake damage, though this was swiftly repaired. But in about 1450 BC came destruction on a calamitous scale: the palaces were smashed and (with the exception of Knossós itself) burned, and smaller settlements across the island were devastated. The cause of this disaster is still the most controversial of all Minoan riddles, but the most convincing theory links it with the explosion of the **volcano** of Thíra in about 1500 BC: a blast which may have been five times as powerful as that of Krakatoa. The explosion threw up great clouds of black ash and a huge tidal wave, or waves. Coastal settlements would have been directly smashed by the wave, and perhaps further burnt by the overturn of lamps lighted on a day made unnaturally dark by the clouds of ash. Blast, panic and accompanying earth tremors would have contributed to the wreck. And then, as the ash fell, it apparently coated the centre and east of the island in a poisonous blanket under which nothing could grow, or would grow again, for as much as fifty years.

Only at Knossós was there any real continuity of habitation, and here it was with **Mycenaean Greeks** in control, bringing with them new styles of art, a greater number of weapons and above all keeping records in a form of writing known as **Linear B**, an adaptation of Linear A now used to write in an early Greek dialect. In about 1370 BC, Knossós was itself burnt, whether by rebellious Cretans, a new wave of Mycenaeans or perhaps as a result of another natural disaster on a smaller scale.

Such at least is the prevailing theory. But it has its problems – why, for example, should Festós have been burnt when it was safe from waves and blast on the south side of the island? And why should the eruption that vulcanologists now date to 1500 BC have had such a dramatic effect only fifty years later – indeed there are signs that away from the worst effects of the devastation many areas on Crete experienced comparative prosperity after it. As the debate continues, the best that can be said currently is that the volcano theory fits the available evidence better than most of its rivals. But many scholars still claim that the facts are more consistent with destruction by human rather than natural causes. The main counter-theory assumes an **invasion** by the Mycenaeans, and points to some evidence that Linear B was in use at Knossós before 1450 BC. But if the Mycenaeans came to conquer, they would have gained nothing by destroying the society already flourishing on Crete; nor would they have subsequently left the former population centres deserted for a generation or more.

A third theory attempts to answer these inconsistencies, suggesting that an **internal revolt** by the populace against its rulers (possibly in the wake of the chaos caused by the Thíra eruption) could provide an explanation. This theory would fit the evidence from sites such as Mírtos Pírgos on the south coast, where a villa dominating the site was burned down whilst the surrounding settlement remained untouched. Needless to say this theory does not find favour with those who see Minoan civilization as a haven of tranquil splendour, but it does fit with the later Greek tradition of a tyrannical Minos oppressing not only his own people but those abroad as well. Further archeological investigation both on Crete and other islands in the Aegean may ultimately resolve this Minoan mystery.

POST-PALATIAL: 1450–1100 BC (LMII–LMIII)

From their bridgehead at Knossós, the Mycenaeans gradually spread their influence across the island as it became habitable again. By the early fourteenth century BC they controlled much of Crete, and some of the earlier sites, including Gourniá, Ayía Triádha, Tílissos and Palékastro, were **reoccupied**. It is a period which is still little-known and which was written off by the early Minoan scholars almost entirely. However more recent excavations are revealing that the island remained productive, albeit in a role peripheral to the mainland.

In particular **western Crete** now came into its own, as the area least affected by the volcano. **Kydonia** became the chief city of the island, still with a considerable international trade and continuing, in its art and architecture, very much in the Minoan style. But Kydonia lies beneath modern Haniá and has never been (nor is ever likely to be) properly excavated – another reason that far less is known about this period than those which preceded it. In **central Crete** the main change was a retreat from the coasts, a sign of the island's decline in international affairs and trade and perhaps of an increase in piracy. Even here, however, despite the presence of new influences, much of the art is recognizably Minoan. Most of the famous clay and stone *lárnakes* (sarcophagi) – which were a distinctly new method of burial – date from this final Minoan era.

More direct evidence of the survival of Crete comes in Homer's account of the **Trojan War**, when he talks of a Cretan contingent taking part under King Idomeneus (according to him, the grandson of Minos). The war and its aftermath – a period of widespread change – also affected Crete. In the north of Greece the Mycenaeans were being overrun by peoples moving down from the Balkans, in particular the **Dorians**. Around 1200 BC the relative peace was disrupted again: many sites were abandoned for the last time, others burnt. Briefly, Mycenaean influence became yet more widespread, as refugees arrived on the island. But by the end of the twelfth century BC, Minoan culture was in terminal decline, and Crete was entering into the period of confusion which engulfed most of the Greek world. Some of the original population of the island, later known as **Eteo-Cretans** (true Cretans), retreated at this time to mountain fastnesses at sites such as Présos and Karfí, where they survived, along with elements of Minoan culture and language, for almost another millennium.

THE IRON AGE: DORIAN AND CLASSICAL CRETE

The bulk of the island, however, was taken over by the **Dorians**: there may have been an invasion, but it seems more probable that the process was a gradual one, by settlement. At any event, over the succeeding centuries the Dorians came to dominate the central lowlands, with substantial new cities such as **Láto** near modern Áyios Nikólaos.

Dorian Crete was not in any real sense a unified society: its cities warred with each other and there may, as well as the Dorians and Eteo-Cretans, have been other cultural groupings in the west, at Kydonia and sites such as Falásarna and Polyrínia. Nevertheless the island saw another minor **artistic renaissance**, with styles now mostly shared with the rest of the Greek world; in the making of tools and weapons iron gradually came to replace bronze.

Much the most important survival of this period, however, is the celebrated **law code** from Górtys. The code (see p.116) was set down around 450 BC, but it reflects laws which had already been in force for hundreds of years: the society described is a strictly hierarchical one, clearly divided into a ruling class, free men, serfs and slaves. For the rulers, life followed a harsh, militaristic regime similar to that of Sparta: the original population, presumably, had been reduced to the level of serfs.

As mainland Greece approached its **Classical Age**, Crete advanced little. It remained a populous island, but one where a multitude of small city-states were constantly vying for power. Towns of this period are characterized by their heavy defences, and most reflected the Górtys laws (Górtys remained among the most powerful of them) in tough oligarchical or aristocratic regimes. At best, Crete was a minor player in Greek affairs, increasingly known as the den of pirates and as a valuable source of mercenaries unrivalled in guerrilla tactics. The island must have retained influence though, for it was still regarded by Classical Athenians as the source of much of their culture, and its strict institutions were admired by many philosophers. In addition, many Cretan shrines and caves show unbroken use from Minoan through to Roman times, and those associated with the birth and early life of Zeus (the Dhiktean and Idean caves especially) were important centres of pilgrimage.

The multitude of small, independent **city-states** is well illustrated by the Confederation of Oreoi, an accord formed around 300 BC between Élyros, Lissós, Hyrtakina, Tarra, Syia (modern Sóuyia) and Pikílassos: six towns in a now barely populated area of the southwest. They were later joined in the Confederation by Górtys and Cyrenaica (in North Africa). Meanwhile Roman power was growing in the Mediterranean, and Crete's strategic position and turbulent reputation drew her inexorably into the struggle.

ROME AND BYZANTIUM

From the second century BC onwards, **Rome** was drawn into wars in mainland Greece, and the involvement of Cretan troops on one or often both sides became an increasing irritation. Hannibal was staying at Górtys at the time of one Roman attempt to pacify the island, around 188 BC. More than a century passed with only minor interventions, however, before Rome could turn its full attention to Crete – the last important part of the Greek world not under its sway.

In 71 BC Marcus Antonius (father of Mark Antony) attempted to invade but was heavily defeated by the Kydonians. A fresh attempt was made under **Quintus Metellus** (afterwards called Creticus) in 69 BC. This time a bridgehead was successfully established by exploiting divisions among the Cretans: Metellus was supported in his initial campaign against Kydonia by its rivals at Polyrínia. The tactic of setting Cretan against Cretan served him well, but even so it took almost three years of bitter and brutal warfare before the island was subdued in 67 BC. It was a campaign marked by infighting not only among the Cretans – Górtys was among those to take Metellus's side – but also between Romans, with further forces sent from Rome in an unsuccessful bid to curb Metellus's excesses and his growing power.

With the conquest complete, peace came quickly and was barely disturbed even in the turbulent years of Julius Caesar's rise and fall. Perhaps this was in part because there was little immediate change in local administration, which was simply placed under Roman supervision. At the same time, the end of the civil wars brought much greater prosperity: Crete was combined with Cyrenaica (in North Africa) as a single province whose capital was at **Górtys**, and though there was little contact between the two halves of the province, both were important sources of grain and agricultural produce for Rome.

Through the first and second centuries AD, important **public works** were undertaken throughout Crete: roads, aqueducts and irrigation systems, important cities at Knossós, Áptera, Lyttos and others, as well as considerable grandeur at Górtys. **Christianity** arrived with St Paul's visit around 50 AD; soon after, he appointed Titus as the island's first bishop to begin the conversion in earnest. Around 250 AD, the Holy Ten – *Áyii Dhéka* – were martyred at Górtys, probably during the first great persecution of the Christians initiated by the emperor Decius.

With the split of the Roman empire at the end of the fourth century, Crete found itself part of the eastern empire under **Byzantium**. The island continued to prosper – as the churches which were now built everywhere would testify – but in international terms it was not important and Byzantine rule, here as everywhere, imposed a stiflingly ordered society, hierarchical and bureaucratic in the extreme. Of the earliest churches only traces survive, in particular of mosaic floors like those at Sóuyia or Thrónos, though there are more substantial remains at Górtys, of the basilica of Áyios Títos.

Then in 824 Crete was invaded by a band of **Arabs** under Abu Hafs Omar. Essentially a piratical group who had been driven first from Spain and then Alexandria, they nevertheless managed to keep control of the island for well over a century. There was not much in the way of progress at this time – for its new masters the island was primarily a base from which to raid shipping and launch attacks on the Greek mainland and other islands – but there was a fortress founded at al-Khandak, a site which later developed into Iráklion. At the same time Górtys and other Byzantine cities were sacked and destroyed.

After several failed attempts, the Byzantine general **Nikifóras Fokás** reconquered Crete in 961, following a siege at Khandak in which he catapulted the heads of his Arab prisoners over the walls. For a while the island revived, boosted by an influx of colonists from the mainland and from Constantinople itself, including a number of aristocratic families (the *Arhontopouli*) whose power survived throughout the medieval era. By now, however, the entire empire was embattled by Islam and losing out in trade to the Venetians and Genoese. Frescoed churches continued to be built, but most were small and parochial.

Ironically enough it was not Muslims who brought about the final end of Byzantine rule, but Crusaders. The **fourth Crusade** turned on Constantinople in 1204 (at the instigation of the Venetians) sacking and burning the city. The leader of the Crusade, Prince Boniface of Montferrat, ceded Crete to the Venetians for a nominal sum.

VENETIAN CRETE

Before Venice could claim its new territory, it had to drive out its chief commercial rivals, the **Genoese**, who had taken control in 1206 with considerable local support. By 1210 the island had been secured, though for more than a century thereafter the Genoese pursued their claim, repeatedly siding with local rebels when it looked like there was a chance of establishing a presence on the island.

The **Venetians**, however, were not going to surrender the prize lightly. Crete for them was a vital resource, both for the control of eastern Mediterranean trade routes which the island's ports commanded, and for the natural wealth of the agricultural land and the timber for shipbuilding. The Venetian system was rapidly and stringently imposed, with Venetian overlords, directly appointed from Venice, administering what were effectively a series of feudal fiefdoms.

It was a system designed to exploit Crete's resources as efficiently as possible, and not surprisingly it stirred up deep resentments from the beginning. There were constant **rebellions** throughout the thirteenth century, led as often as not by one or other of the aristocratic Byzantine families from an earlier wave of colonization. Certainly the wealthy had most to lose: it was their land which was confiscated to be granted to military colonists from Venice (along with the service of the people who lived on it), and their rights and privileges which were taken over by the new overlords. The rebellions were in general strictly noble affairs, ended by concessions of land or power to their Cretan leaders. But there were more fundamental resentments too. Heavy taxes and demands for feudal service were widely opposed – by the established colonists almost as much as by the natives. And the **Orthodox Church** was replaced by the Roman as the "official" religion, the senior clergy expelled and much Church property seized. Local priests and monasteries which survived helped fuel antagonism: even from this early date the monasteries were becoming known as centres of dissent.

In the mid-fourteenth century, one of the most serious revolts yet saw the Cretans and second-generation Venetian colonists fighting alongside each other, in protest at the low fixed prices for their produce, steep taxes and the continued privileges granted to "real" Venetians. Although on this occasion the revolt was put down in a particularly fierce repression, the end result of this and the other rebellions was a gradual relaxation of the regime and integration of the two communities – or at least their leaders. The **Middle Ages** were perhaps the most productive in Crete's history, with exports of corn, wine, oil and salt, the ports busy with transhipment business and the wooded hillsides being stripped for timber.

After 1453, and the final fall of Constantinople, Crete saw a spectacular **cultural renaissance** as a stream of refugees arrived from the east. **Candia** – as the island and its capital were known to the Venetians –

became the centre of Byzantine art and scholarship. From this later period, and the meeting of the traditions of Byzantium and the Italian Renaissance, come the vast majority of the works of art and architecture now associated with the Venetian era. The great icon painter Dhamaskinós studied alongside El Greco in the school of Ayía Ekateríni in Iráklion; the Orthodox monasteries flourished; and in literature the island produced, among others, what is now regarded as its greatest work – the *Erotókritos* (see Books, p.368).

But it was the growing **external threat** which stimulated the most enduring of the Venetian public works – the island defences. Venice's bastions in the mainland Middle East had fallen alongside Constantinople, and in 1573 Cyprus too was taken by the Turks, leaving Crete well and truly in the front line. Large-scale pirate raids had already been common: in 1538 Barbarossa had destroyed Réthimnon and almost taken Haniá, and in the 1560s there were further attacks. Across the island, cities were strengthened and the fortified islets defending the seaways were repaired and rebuilt. As the seventeenth century wore on however, Venice itself was in severe decline; Mediterranean trade was overshadowed by the New World, a business dominated by the Spanish, English and Dutch.

Finally, in 1645 an attack on an Ottoman convoy provided the excuse for an all-out **Turkish assault** on Crete. Haniá fell after a siege which cost forty thousand Turkish lives, and Réthimnon rapidly followed. By 1648 the Turks controlled the whole island except **Iráklion**, and they settled down to a long siege. For 21 years the city resisted, supplied from the sea and with moral support at least from most of Europe. The end was inevitable, though, and from the Turkish point of view there was no hurry: they controlled the island's produce, they were well supplied, and they enjoyed a fair degree of local support, having relaxed the Venetian rules –for example they allowed Orthodox bishops back into Crete. By 1669 the city was virtually reduced, and in a final effort the pope managed to persuade the French to send a small army. After a couple of fruitless sorties involving heavy losses, the French withdrew in an argument over the command. On September 5, the city surrendered, leaving only the three fortified islets of Soúdha, Spinalónga and Gramvoúsa in Venetian hands, where they remained until surrendered by treaty in 1715.

TURKISH CRETE

It is arguable whether the **Turkish occupation** was ever as stringent or arduous as the Venetian had been, but its reputation is far worse. In part this may simply be that its memory is more recent, but Turkish rule was complicated too by the religious differences involved, and by the fact that it survived into the era of resurgent Greek nationalism and Great Power politics.

If on their arrival the Turks had been welcomed, it was not a long-lived honeymoon. Once again Crete was divided, now between powerful pashas, and once again it was regarded merely as a resource to be exploited. The Ottoman Empire was less strictly ordered than the Venetian, but it demanded no less: rather than attempt to take control of trade themselves, the Turks simply imposed crippling **taxes**. There were fewer colonists than in the Venetian era, and they took far less interest in their conquest so long as the money continued to come in. Very little was reinvested: outside the cities there was hardly any building at all, and roads and even defences fell into gradual disrepair. As far as local administration went, it was left to local landlords and the mercenary **Janissaries** they controlled to impose. At the local level, then, there was a further level of exploitation as these men too took their cut. Stultified by heavy taxes and tariffs, slowed by neglect, the island economy stagnated.

One way to avoid the worst of the burden was to become a Muslim and, gradually, the majority of the Christian population was converted to **Islam** – at least nominally. Conversion brought with it substantial material advantages in taxation and rights to own property, and it helped avoid the worst of the repression which inevitably followed any Christian rebellion. These Greek Muslims were not particularly religious: even among the Turks on the island, Islamic law seems to have been loosely interpreted, and many continued to worship as Christians in secret, but the mass apostasies served to further divide the island. For those who remained openly Christian the burden became increasingly heavy as there were fewer to bear it. Many took to the mountains, where Turkish authority barely reached.

As the occupation continued, the Turks strengthened their hold on the cities and the fertile plains around them, while the mountains became the stronghold of the Christian *pallikáres*. The first major **rebellion** came in 1770, and inevitably it was centred in Sfakiá. Under **Dhaskaloyiánnis** (see p.295) the Cretans had been drawn into Great Power politics: drawn in and abandoned, for the promised aid from Russia never came. With the failure of this struggle, Sfakiá was itself brought under Turkish control for a while. But a pattern had been set, and the nineteenth century saw an almost constant struggle for independence.

At beginning of the century the Ottoman Empire was under severe pressure on the Greek mainland, and in 1821 full-scale revolution, the **Greek War of Independence**, broke out. Part of the Turkish response was to call on the pasha of Egypt, **Mehmet Ali**, for assistance: his price was control of Crete. By 1824, in a campaign which even by Cretan standards was brutal on both sides, he had crushed the island's resistance. When in 1832 an independent Greek state was finally established with the support of Britain, France and Russia, Crete was left in the hands of the Egyptians, reverting to Turkish control within ten years.

From now on guerrilla warfare in support of union with Greece – *énosis* – was almost constant, flaring occasionally into wider revolts but mostly taking the form of incessant raids and irritations. The Cretans enjoyed widespread support, not only on the Greek mainland but throughout western Europe, and especially among expatriate Greek communities. But the Greeks alone were no match for the Ottoman armies, and the Great Powers, wary more than anything of each other, consistently failed to intervene. There was a major rising in 1841, bloodily suppressed, and in 1858 another which ended relatively peacefully in the recall of the Turkish governor and some minor concessions to the Christian population.

In 1866 a Cretan Assembly meeting in Sfakiá declared independence and union with Greece, and Egyptian troops were recalled to put down a further wave of revolts bolstered by Greek volunteers. Again the Egyptians proved ruthlessly effective, but this campaign ended in the explosion at **Arkádhi** (see p.207), an act of defiance which aroused Europe-wide sympathy. The Great Powers – Britain above

all – still refused to involve themselves, but privately the supply of arms and volunteers to the insurgents was redoubled. From now on some kind of solution seemed inevitable, but even in 1878 the Congress of Berlin left Crete under Turkish dominion, demanding only further reforms in the government. In 1889 and 1896 there were further violent encounters, and in 1897 a Greek force landed to annexe the island. Finally, the Great Powers were forced into action, occupying Crete with an international force and dividing the island into areas controlled by the British, French, Russians and Italians.

INDEPENDENCE AND UNION WITH GREECE

The outrage which finally brought about the expulsion of Turkish troops from Crete in 1898 was a minor skirmish in Iráklion which led to the death of the British vice-consul. A **national government** was set up, still nominally under Ottoman suzerainty, with Prince George, younger son of King George of Greece, as high commissioner: under him was a joint Muslim-Christian assembly, part elected, part appointed.

Euphoria at independence was muted, however, for full union with Greece remained the goal of most Cretans. A new leader of this movement rapidly emerged – **Eleftheríos Venizélos**. Born at Mourniés, outside Haniá, Venizélos had fought in the earlier independence struggles, and become a member of the Cretan Assembly and minister of justice to Prince George. Politically, however, he had little in common with his new master, and in 1905 he summoned an illegal Revolutionary Assembly at Thériso. Though the attempt to take up arms was summarily crushed, the strength of support for Venizélos was enough to force the resignation of Prince George. In 1908, the Cretan Assembly unilaterally declared *énosis* – much to the embarrassment of the Greek government. For meantime the "Young Turk" revolution looked set to revitalize the Ottoman Empire, and the Great Powers remained solidly opposed to anything which might upset the delicate balance of power in the Balkans.

The failure of the Greek government to act decisively in favour of Crete was one of the factors which led to the Military League of young officers forcing political reform on the mainland. With their backing, Venizélos became premier of Greece in 1910. In 1912 Greece, Serbia and Bulgaria declared war on the Ottoman Empire, making spectacular advances into Turkish territory. By the peace of 1913, Crete finally and officially became part of the **Greek nation**.

Though Greece was politically riven by World War I, and succeeding decades saw frequent, sometimes violent changes of power between Venizelist and Royalist forces, Crete was little affected. On just one further occasion did the island play a significant role in Greek affairs before the outbreak of war in 1940: in July 1938 there was a popular uprising against the dictator Metáxas and in favour of Venizélos, but it was swiftly put down.

The island was, however, hit hard by the aftermath of the disastrous Greek attempt to conquer Istanbul in pursuit of the "Great Idea" of rebuilding the Byzantine Empire. As part of the peace settlement which followed this military debacle, there was a forced **exchange of populations** in 1923: Muslims were expelled from Greece and Orthodox Christians from Turkey. In Crete many of these "Turks" were in fact Muslim Cretans, descendants of the mass apostasies of the eighteenth century. Nevertheless they left – some thirty thousand in all – and a similar number of Christian refugees from Turkey took their place.

WAR AND OCCUPATION

In the winter of 1940 Italian troops invaded northern Greece, only to be thrown back across the Albanian border by the Greek army. Mussolini's humiliation, however, only served to draw the Germans into the fight, and although an Allied army was sent to Greece, the **mainland** was rapidly overrun.

The Allied campaign was marked from the start by suspicion, confusion and lack of communication between the two commands. On the Greek side Metáxas had died in January, and his successor as premier committed suicide, leaving a Cretan – **Emanuel Tsouderós** – to organize the retreat of king and government to his native island. They were rapidly followed by thousands of evacuees, including the bulk of the Allied army, a force made up in large part of Australian and New Zealand soldiers. Most of the native Cretan troops, a division of the Greek army, had been wiped out in defence of the mainland.

According to the Allied plan, Crete should by now have been an impregnable fortress. In practice, though, virtually nothing had been done to improve the island defences, there were hardly any serviceable planes or other heavy equipment, and the arriving troops found little in the way of a plan for their deployment.

On May 20, 1941 the **invasion** of the island began, as German troops poured in by glider and parachute. It was at first a horrible slaughter, with the invaders easily picked off as they drifted slowly down. Few of the first wave of parachutists reached the ground alive and many of the gliders crashed: the main German force was smashed before it ever reached the ground. In the far west, however, beyond the main battle zone, they succeeded in taking the airfield at Máleme. Whether through incompetence (as much of the literature on the Battle of Crete suggests) or breakdown of communications, no attempt to recapture the field was made until the Germans had had time to defend it and, with a secure landing site, reinforcements and equipment began to pour in. Not long before the battle, the German codes had been cracked, and General Freyberg therefore knew in detail exactly where and how the attacks would come. Whether because he didn't trust the information, however, or because of the need to keep secret the intelligence breakthrough, he did not redeploy his troops. From now on the battle, which had seemed won, was lost, and the Allied troops, already under constant air attack, found themselves outgunned on land too.

Casualties of the **Battle of Crete** were horrendous on both sides – the cemeteries are reminiscent of the burial grounds of World War I victims in northern France – and the crack German airborne division was effectively wiped out. No one ever attempted a similar assault again. But once they were established with a secure bridgehead, the Germans advanced rapidly, and a week after the first landings the Allied army was in full retreat across the mountains towards Hóra Sfakíon, from where most were evacuated by ship to Egypt. On May 30, the battle was over, leaving behind several thousand Allied soldiers (and all the Cretans who had fought alongside them) to surrender or take to the mountains.

THE RESISTANCE

One of the first tasks of **the resistance** was to get these stranded soldiers off the island, and in this they had remarkable success, organizing the fugitives into groups and arranging their collection by ship or submarine from isolated beaches on the south coast. Many were hidden and fed by monks while they waited to escape, most famously at the monastery of Préveli. In this and many other ways the German occupation closely mirrored earlier ones; opposition was constant and reprisals brutal. The north coast and the lowlands were, as in the past, easily and firmly controlled, but the mountains, and Sfakiá above all, remained the haunt of rebel and resistance groups throughout the war.

With the boats which took the battle survivors away from Crete came intelligence officers whose job it was to organize and arm the resistance: throughout the war there were a dozen or so on the island, living in mountain shelters or caves, attempting to organize parachute drops of arms and reporting on troop movements on and around the island.

How effective the sporadic efforts of the resistance were is hard to gauge: they had one spectacular success when in 1944 they kidnapped the German commander **General Kreipe** outside Iráklion, and succeeded in smuggling him across to the south coast and off the island to Egypt. Among this group were the author Patrick Leigh Fermor and Stanley Moss (whose *Ill Met by Moonlight* describes the incident in detail). The immediate result of this propaganda coup, however, was a terrible vengeance against the Cretan population, in which a string of villages around the Amári valley were destroyed and such menfolk as could be found slaughtered (see p.228). Harsh **retribution** against Cretan civilians, indeed, was the standard reaction to any success the resistance had.

At the end of 1944, the German forces withdrew to a heavily fortified perimeter around Haniá, where they held out for a final seven months before surrendering. In the rest of the island, this left a **power vacuum** which several of the resistance groups rushed to fill. Allied intelligence would no doubt claim that one of the achievements of their agents in Crete was the virtual avoidance of the civil war which wracked the rest of Greece. On the mainland the organization of the resistance had been very largely the work of Greek Communists, who emerged at the end of the war as much the best organized and armed group. On Crete,

groups in favour with the Allies had been the best armed and organized, and certainly in the latter stages of the war, Communist-dominated organizations had been deliberately starved of equipment. There were only a few, minor incidents of violence on the island, and these were swiftly suppressed.

MODERN CRETE

In avoiding the civil war, Crete was able to set about **reconstruction** some way in advance of the rest of Greece, and since 1945 it has become one of the most prosperous and productive regions of the nation. The really spectacular changes, however, date from the last 25 years, fuelled above all by a tidal wave of tourism.

Politically, postwar Crete remains a place deeply mistrustful of outside control, even from Athens. At the local level above all, loyalties are divided along clan and patronage lines rather than party political ones, and leaders are judged on how well they provide for their areas and their followers. This was exemplified by **Konstantine Mitsotákis**, former head of the right-wing Néa Dhimokratía (ND) party and prime minister until his defeat by PASOK (the socialist party) in the 1993 election: a Cretan, many islanders respected his ability to get things done on Crete even if his party was not much liked.

Cretan politicians at the local level (there is no overall island government, only a regional administration controlled by appointees from Athens) continue to take an almost universal joy in standing up to central authority. In one famous incident the mayor of Iráklion organized a sit-in at the Archeological Museum to prevent artworks being taken abroad for an exhibition: fifty thousand turned out to support him, and though President Karamanlís ordered his arrest, the national government was eventually forced to back down.

Rivalries within Crete are fierce, too, most notably between Haniá, which was nominated as capital for a short period at the beginning of the century, and Iráklion the traditional and present capital and nowadays the richer and politically more important city. This factionalism results in all sorts of anomalies and compromises: symptomatic was the rather impractical decision to spread the University of Crete across three campuses, at Iráklion, Réthimnon (which has always considered itself the most cultured town in Crete) and the autonomous polytechnic of Haniá.

In **national politics**, the island presents a more unified front as the upholder of the **liberal tradition** of Venizélos . After the overthrow of the Colonels in 1974, Crete voted heavily against a restoration of the monarchy and for a republican system; in the presidential election which followed, support for the right-winger Karamanlís was less than half as strong on Crete as it was in the rest of Greece. This has been an abiding pattern: PASOK has consistently polled twice as many Cretan votes as ND.

Increasingly, however, the hold of the powerful old families (Mitsotákis is a member of one such long-established clan) and traditional loyalties are crumbling as their power-broking becomes less effective. The day-to-day reality of control from Athens cannot be denied even by the most fervent Cretan nationalist. It first flexed its muscles under the Colonels, when the major tourist developments were got underway, brushing aside local qualms over planning or the desirability of mass tourism. Nowadays the EU, through directives and grants, has also started to affect Crete, above all its farmers. But central power – and the increasing importance of issues over personalities – perhaps manifests itself most clearly with regard to **NATO**.

Crete is home to numerous American and NATO bases, many now officially "deactivated", plus a couple of which are believed by local activists to store **atomic weapons**. The missile base on Akrotíri is the chief suspect – its missiles (you can see them test-firing most Wednesdays) are certainly capable of carrying nuclear warheads. At Sóudha, as well as extensive naval installations, the US marine corps has its Mediterranean ammunition store in submarine pens. On a slightly crazier level, Crete is earmarked as a potential emergency landing site for the space shuttle. None of this is popular locally, and again the extent of it is a legacy of the Colonels: the Americans are singled out as the butt of most protests because of their part in the 1967 coup and their role (or lack of one) in the Cyprus affair. Crete's all-too-recent history of military occupation does nothing to make the presence of foreign troops easier.

Andreas Papandreou's PASOK, which won sixty percent of the total Cretan vote in 1985, promised that all US bases in Greece would be closed by 1988. In 1993 the base at Goúrnes shut down but there seems little prospect of all the bases closing: too much has been invested. Around $1000 million annually in rent and military aid is hard to give up, to say nothing of the other pressures applied. Above all is the fear that if they were thrown out, both bases and aid would simply be transferred to Turkey. But at least plans for expansion seem to have been shelved: there was to have been another base on the Méssara plain, possibly at Timbáki where the Germans had a big wartime base and which operates as a Greek military airport; new barracks were built but never occupied.

THE NINETIES

In the late Eighties and early Nineties Crete shared in the Greek and European economic downturn as a split developed between state employees (of which there are two-thirds more than in any other EU country) and the Mitsotákis government armed with a Thatcherite austerity programme to cut public expenditure. Strikes and mass protests ended with Nea Dhimokratía's crushing defeat in the general election of October 1993, and the return to power of a **PASOK government**, still led by the ageing and ailing Andreas Papandreou. The austerity programme of Mitsotákis was halted, but as Papandreou's health deteriorated there came no answers as to how the nation with the lowest productivity, highest inflation and largest external debt in the EU was to raise its living standards, a major election promise. The political crisis was compounded when the 76-year-old prime minister fell ill again at the end of 1995 and went into intensive care where he remained for two months, obstinately refusing to resign while the government of the country became paralyzed. Finally, his hands were prised off the levers of power (though not the PASOK party leadership) and he was succeeded by **Kóstas Simitis** in January 1996 five months before his death. Papandreou's demise was described by the Greek press as the end of the reign of the dinosaurs – the geriatric politicians who had ruled Greece since the end of the Colonels' regime. The rather dull technocrat Simitis surprised many by leading PASOK to another victory in the **general election** of 1996. Fuelled by a desire to take Greece into the EU mainstream, in the years since becoming premier Simitis has overturned the "gravy train" politics of Papandreou to make another assault on the bloated public sector in order to meet the

Maastricht criteria for monetary union. He was assisted in this goal in late 1997 when the IOC awarded the **2004 Olympic Games** to Athens and Greece. As a result, enormous funds are flooding into the country and some of the EU's biggest infrastructure projects are now under way, which are set to catapult much of the country's transportation system straight from the nineteenth into the twenty-first century, with new railways, roads and airports.

In Crete itself the age of mass-market tourism is beginning to pall as the attractions of sun, beach and cheap drinks along much of the coast attract mainly younger holidaymakers, who will move on when prices rise. There is also a dawning realization that whilst the island has until recently been winning the "numbers war" in terms of the legions of package tourists who visit, a considerable price has been paid in terms of environmental damage as natural resources and infrastructure are stretched to breaking point in high summer. As tourist numbers have declined in recent years, efforts to build a market in "green tourism" are in their infancy, held back by an indifference to environmental concerns by politicians, farmers and a populace which has yet to realize that environmentally organized tourism – for which the island, with its extended season, picturesque landscape and rich variety of flora and fauna is an ideal location – can be enormously profitable. Another major problem has been the lack of an autonomous Cretan tourist authority with the capacity to raise standards and promote the island and its attractions worldwide and not simply as part of the "Sunny Greece" image promoted by the inefficient and largely uninspiring EOT (Greek National Tourist Organization) in Athens. And for too long Cretans have adopted a part-time approach to the tourist industry – treating it as a summer sideline before returning to the farm to get in the olive and fruit harvests in the winter. This has led, barring a few commendable exceptions, to a lack of professionalism and consequent low standards in food, hotel management and tourist development, all areas where training and career possibilities are minimal or non-existent.

The island has faced up to invaders throughout its history, but the tourist invasion presents it with a new dilemma: to submerge its traditional ways in the pursuit of ever greater numbers or to try to raise the quality of development and at the same time preserve Crete's unique character. In a major policy speech in 1997, the head of the EOT encouragingly suggested that Crete should do more to cater for "the ramblers who visit the island to enjoy the paths which take them past the island's gorges, caves, mountain villages and archeological sites". More worryingly, and somewhat paradoxically, he also urged the development (with government subsidies) of marinas, conference centres with golf courses and luxury hotels with casinos. How Crete tackles these challenges in the years ahead will significantly determine the island's economic and social prosperity well into the next millennium.

MONUMENTAL CHRONOLOGY

	EVENTS	BUILDINGS AND MONUMENTS
STONE AGE 6000 BC	First inhabitants arrive from east.	Neolithic habitation of caves, and later more settled centres at Knossós and elsewhere.
PRE-PALATIAL 2600 BC	New migration brings more sophisticated culture and larger settlements: first Minoans.	Settlements especially in the south. Vasilikí, Móhlos and Mírtos among the best known.
PROTO-PALATIAL 2000 BC 1700 BC	Evidence of a more formally structured society. Earthquake destroys the palaces.	First palaces built at most of the famous sites.
NEO-PALATIAL 1700 BC 1450 BC	Beginning of the Minoan Golden Age Final destruction of the palaces.	Great palaces at Knossós, Festós, Mália, Zákros; thriving towns at Gourniá, Palékastro. Most of the Minoan remains date from this era. Many earlier sites reoccupied. Kydonia the island's chief city.
POST-PALATIAL 1100 BC	Gradual revival under Mycenaean influence. Mycenaean control giving way to Dorian.	Eteo-Cretans keep Minoan culture alive at Présos and Karfí.
DORIAN 300 BC 71 BC 69–67 BC	Island divided between rival groups, gradually emerging as constantly warring city-states. Cities on south coast form Confederation of Oreoi. Failed Roman invasion. Romans subjugate the island.	Dozens of small towns: Láto, Falásarna, along the south coast, Knossós and, above all, Górtys.
ROMAN 395 AD	Empire split, Crete ruled from Byzantium.	Górtys the chief Roman city. Others include Lyttos, Áptera, Knossós. Public works across the island.

BYZANTINE		Traces of early churches at Górtys, Soúyia, Thrónos
824	Arab invasion.	
ARAB		Górtys sacked; al-Khandak, later Iráklion, the Arab base.
961	Liberation by Nikifóras Fokás.	
BYZANTINE		Small churches throughout Crete.
1204	Fourth Crusade, Byzantium sacked, Crete sold to Venice.	
VENETIAN		Very extensive building. Early remains are mostly in the form of churches and monasteries.
1453	Fall of Constantinople, renaissance of Byzantine art on Crete.	Later works include the shape of most major towns and defences all over the island: e.g. at Iráklion, Réthimnon and Haniá; castles include Frangokástello and the fortified islets; other reminders in the shape of saltpans (for example Olóus) and deforested hillsides.
1645	Turks capture Haniá.	
1669	Iráklion surrenders.	
TURKISH		
1770	Revolt of Dhaskaloyiánnis.	Mosques and fountains in the cities, especially Haniá and Réthimnon, but few public works undertaken in the rest of the island.
1821	Greek War of Independence.	
1866	Explosion at Arkádhi.	
1897	Great Powers occupy Crete.	
1898	Independence under Prince George.	
INDEPENDENT		
1905	Revolutionary Assembly at Thériso, prince abdicates.	New government buildings at Haniá.
1908	Crete declares *Enosis*.	
1913	Union of Greece and Crete formally declared.	
1941	German invasion.	
1945	Liberation.	Cemeteries and war memorials.
1960s		Tourist boom starts.
1967–74	Dictatorship of the Colonels	
1986	Greece becomes full member of the EU.	

THE DISCOVERY OF BRONZE AGE CRETE

The story of the discovery of Bronze Age Crete – dominated by two larger-than-life characters in Heinrich Schliemann and Arthur Evans – is almost as fascinating as that of the Minoans themselves. Long before the appearance of these two giants, however, others had taken soundings and laid the foundations for their discoveries.

Already ancient in antiquity, Crete had disappeared into the mists of Greek mythology and Homeric legend, and it was only during the Venetian period that curiosity about the island's illustrious past was reawoken. In 1422 a Florentine monk, **Buondelmonte**, visited Crete and reported that he had seen over two thousand columns and statues at Górtys. More monuments and inscriptions were recorded by **Honorio de Belli** in 1596. In 1675, the Dutchman **Johann Meursius**, in his book *Creta*, sifted through the Classical references relating to the island.

In the eighteenth century a French explorer and botanist, **Joseph Tournefort**, described Crete in his *Voyage au Levant* of 1717; the English navigator **Richard Pococke** also took an interest, documenting his findings in the second volume of his *Description of the East* published in 1745. But these were largely superficial observations, and early in the nineteenth century it fell to another Dutchman, **Karl Hoeck** (who never actually visited the island), to write the first scholarly account of ancient Crete.

THE NINETEENTH CENTURY: TRAVELLERS AND TRADITION

A more genuinely first-hand record, and the best description of Crete's monuments and sites so far, was provided by Cambridge scholar **Robert Pashley** who, in the early 1830s, travelled extensively throughout the island; it can only have been a rugged journey. Pashley allied a Classical education with a keen eye, and seems to have had an uncanny knack for identifying ancient sites, written up in his entertaining *Travels in Crete* (1837). A century later, Pendlebury, the eminent British archeologist, paid Pashley fulsome tribute when he credited the traveller-scholar with identifying most of the important Cretan sites, including Knossós.

It was probably as well for those who were to come after him that it never occurred to Pashley to take up the spade. That he came near to doing so is borne out by his prophetic comments on Knossós: "The mythological celebrity and historical importance of Cnossus, demand a more careful and minute attention than can be bestowed on them in a mere book of travels."

During the years 1851–3 **Captain Spratt** (later Admiral) surveyed the Cretan coastline for the British admiralty. Taking an interest in the island's archeological remains, Spratt imperiously shipped quite a few of these back to the British Museum – often against the wishes of the local population. In an attempt to move a stone sarcophagus on board ship at Ierápetra he describes how one of his officers had to sleep in the sculptured coffin on the beach overnight "...to prevent it being injured wantonly or by local enemies (there were a party there who were opposed to our removal of the relic) . . . yet it did not wholly escape mischief, for some wanton hand destroyed what remained of the face of Hector."

Spratt also studied the island's natural history and geology, and it was the latter pursuit which earned him a footnote in Cretan archeology. His work for the British navy enabled him to demonstrate that, as a result of a geological convulsion in the sixth century AD, the whole island had been tilted upwards at its western end by as much as 8m, while the eastern end had sunk down. Spratt was probably wrong about the cause, but his observations remain valid, the tilting being clearly evident in the marshy swamps at the eastern site of Zákros.

THE AGE OF SCHLIEMANN

None of these early visitors to Crete, however, was concerned with pre-Classical history. The discovery of the great **Bronze Age** Minoan civilization was the almost single-handed achievement of Arthur Evans.

An important clue had been found as early as 1878. Digging at Knossós, a Cretan merchant, with the appropriate name of **Minos Kalokairinos**, had uncovered a number of large storage jars mixed in with Mycenaean pottery fragments – something that was to confuse later investigators. This find attracted the attention of **Heinrich Schliemann**, who had already excited world interest by his excavation of ancient **Troy** in northwest Turkey, followed by the fortresses at **Mycenae** and **Tiryns** in the Greek Peloponnese. The son of a poor German pastor who filled his head with the fabulous tales of Homeric Greece, Schliemann left school without completing his studies, to set up in business. In the course of a highly successful commercial career in which he amassed a fortune based on military contracts in the Crimean war and participation in the California gold rush, Schliemann never lost sight of the goal that he had set himself as a boy: to prove that the world of Homer was not mere myth as the majority of scholars then believed, and to discover the fabulous places mentioned in the *Iliad* and the *Odyssey*.

When he finally embarked on this quest in his late forties, Schliemann taught himself Latin and Greek which he used to dissect his Homer before setting out for Turkey and then Greece. To the chagrin of the professional classicists, he was later to claim that it was a thorough reading of Homer which had led him to his discoveries. In fact, Schliemann became so besotted with his Hellenic vision that he not only took a Greek wife, but did so after a public competition in which the celebrated archeologist offered his hand in marriage to the first Greek girl who was able to render a faultless recitation of the entire *Iliad* from memory. Given Schliemann's luck it was inevitable that the first woman to achieve this feat was also an outstanding beauty; **Sofia Schliemann** became as enthusiastic as her husband in the pursuit of Greece's Bronze Age past.

Schliemann arrived in Crete in 1887, made a visit to the site at Knossós, and became convinced that a substantial palace, equivalent to those that he had discovered on the mainland, lay waiting to be unearthed. But Crete was still under the subjection of Turkey and the authorities were often indolent and obstructive. In addition, when Schliemann attempted to negotiate the purchase of some land at Knossós, the Turkish owners proved impossible to deal with and finally, with his patience exhausted and his health declining, Schliemann departed. A chill, caught after an ear operation in Naples, led to his sudden death in 1890. It was this twist of fortune which was destined to make Arthur Evans the discoverer of Knossós and Minoan Crete.

THE FIRST EXCAVATIONS

Meanwhile, others had also begun to take an interest in the island's past. During the twilight period of Turkish rule there was some relaxation of the iron grip, and the sultan gave permission to a Cretan archeologist, **Joseph Hatzidhákis**, to set up the **Cretan Archeological Society**, the forerunner of the Iráklion Archeological Museum. In 1884 an Italian scholar arrived in Crete, became friends with Hatzidhákis, and the two men began to search for ancient sites.

The scholar was **Federico Halbherr**, whose name was also destined to become prominent in Cretan archeology. It was on one of their expeditions in 1885 that the first recorded discovery of **Bronze Age artefacts** was made at the **Psihró Cave** above the Lasíthi plateau. The following year the chance unearthing of a tomb near **Festós** gave Halbherr the idea that there was probably a settlement nearby. Preliminary excavations revealed substantial buildings as well as prehistoric pottery, but the political turmoil leading up to the end of Turkish rule postponed further progress.

Another important clue to what was to come had also been found on the volcanic island of **Thíra** in the 1860s. During quarrying operations for the enormous amounts of pumice needed to make cement for the construction of the Suez Canal, a buried settlement was revealed. Here whole rooms had been preserved intact, their walls covered with remarkable fresco paintings. Although it's now understood to be a colony or outpost of Minoan civilization, this was long before any comparable Minoan remains had been discovered on Crete itself.

ARTHUR EVANS

In 1882 a meeting occurred at one of Athens's most elegant mansions which was to have an enormous importance for Cretan archeology. The host was the famous archeologist Heinrich Schliemann, his guest a young scholar and journalist – **Arthur Evans**. Born in 1851, the son of a wealthy and distinguished numismatist, Evans's upbringing could hardly have differed more from that of the self-made German businessman. Educated at Harrow and then Oxford, Evans was always to have the time and the financial security to pursue his interests wherever they might lead him.

Schliemann was digging again at Troy and regaled his guest with the story of his excavations both there and at Mycenae. But Evans displayed more interest in Schliemann's extensive collection of ancient artefacts, particularly some **engraved seals** bearing an octopus design which he felt must be of Aegean, possibly Cretan, origin. Schliemann then announced to Evans that his next project was to be the excavation of another Mycenaean fortress at Tiryns, following which he would dig at the site in Crete from where, as Homer put it in the *Iliad*, "came forth the men from Knossós". Little can he have realized the frustration of this goal that lay ahead, or that his attentive guest would himself be the recipient of this great archeological prize.

For the time being Evans returned to England to take up a post as keeper of the Ashmolean Museum at Oxford, although he continued to pay visits to the Balkans and Greece. Evans's studies during this period, allied to the discovery of more seal stones bearing **pre-alphabetical writing**, led him to the proposition that Crete had been an important centre of Mycenaean culture, possibly even its birthplace. When, in 1893, a great hoard of **painted pottery** was discovered by Italian archeologists at the **Kamáres Cave** on Mount Ida (Psilorítis), Evans's mind was made up: he would visit Crete to search for more seal stones and, if circumstances allowed, make a fresh attempt to carry out the excavations at Knossós which had been denied to Schliemann.

Evans arrived in Crete for the first time on March 15, 1894. Typically, in spite of an horrendously rough voyage from Pireás lasting 24 hours, no sooner had he set foot on the island than, he recorded in his diary, he toured the Candia bazaar and purchased "twenty-two early Cretan stones at about one and a half piastres apiece". Evans had started out as he meant to continue and, once the initial obstacles had been overcome, the pace was hardly to slacken over the next thirty years.

With the assistance of Joseph Hatzidhákis, now curator as well as president of the Cretan Archeological Society, Evans began to negotiate for the purchase of the land at Knossós with its Turkish owners. He became bogged down in the same protracted wrangles that

had forced Schliemann to despair. But Evans was a man who usually got what he wanted. Even so it took five years, some valiant efforts from Hatzidhákis and a stroke of the kind of luck that some people seem to attract. In this case it was the lifting in 1898 of the Turkish yoke which had burdened Crete for 230 years. Evans, possessing a liberal political outlook, had worked with Hatzidhákis to raise funds in Britain and Crete for the victims of the insurrections during this period. Finally the major obstacle to starting excavations at Knossós had been removed.

KNOSSÓS: THE EARLY YEARS

In 1899 the new government changed the law and most of the restrictions on foreign excavators were cleared away. Evans's purchase of the land at **Knossós** went through and work started on March 23, 1900; interestingly for the future, the team that Evans assembled for the dig included an architect, **Theodore Fyfe**, from the British School at Athens. As the excavations progressed Evans soon realized that he was dealing with a site far older than the Roman, Greek or even Mycenaean periods. Then out of the earth came **frescoes**, **pottery** and what came to be known as **Linear B** tablets bearing the ancient Minoan script. On April 10 the Throne Room was discovered with its elegant **gypsum throne** – named at first the "throne of Ariadne" by Evans who thought it too dainty to hold the manly posterior of Minos himself – flanked by stone benches and frescoed walls.

During the first five years of the excavations, in which most of the palace was revealed, Evans made a number of innovations. In his magisterial style he named the new civilization **Minoan** after the legendary Cretan king. He then proceeded to delineate his division of the island's Bronze Age into **Early**, **Middle** and **Late Minoan** based on pottery styles found at Knossós:

Early Minoan 3000–2000 BC
Middle Minoan I & II 2000–1700 BC
Middle Minoan III + Late Minoan I & II 1700–1400 BC
Late Minoan III 1400–1100 BC

In spite of problems later encountered with this system – for example, not all contemporary sites went through the same artistic developments in similar timescales – Evans's system remains the one used by archeologists and scholars if only because no one has yet bettered it.

RESTORATION AND CONTROVERSY

Another of Evans's early decisions was to prove far more controversial: he determined that he would not only reveal the palace of Minos but that he would also **restore** large parts of it (he insisted on the word "reconstitute") to the splendour prior to its final destruction around 1400 BC. That Evans was able autocratically to decide this rested on his personal ownership of one of the major sites of antiquity – something that would be unthinkable today. "I must have sole control of what I am personally undertaking . . . my way may not be the best but it is the only way I can work," he wrote revealingly to his father.

What Evans had now embarked upon was one of the most expensive enterprises in the history of archeology, and in the early years funds were often stretched. But fortunately or otherwise for Knossós – depending on your viewpoint – two large legacies fell into Evans's lap eight years into the mammoth task, as a result of the deaths of both his father and his uncle (John Dinkinson the paper millionaire) within months of each other in 1908. Evans's plans for Knossós, destined to last for a further 23 years, were now financially secure.

With the assistance of architects Theodore Fyfe and later **Piet de Jong**, Evans first roofed the Throne Room and then reconstructed the **grand staircase**, replacing the **tapered columns** with his speculative concrete reconstructions (none of the wooden originals was ever found). Two Swiss artists then began to repaint the reconstructed walls with copies of the **frescoes** now in the Iráklion Archeological Museum. In 1930 the almost entirely conjectural upper storey (or **Piano Nobile** as Evans fancifully termed it) was added, using reinforced concrete. Next, the **Central Court** was extensively restored as the archeological site became a building site. Evans attempted to deflect criticism of his methods as he imposed his own grand design on the work of architects and artists by saying that he wanted to recreate the "spirit" of the palace structure and decor rather than create a literal reconstruction. This was where many scholars parted company with him. Pendlebury, who was to be

Evans's successor at Knossós (see p.352), put aside earlier reservations and defended Evans in a guidebook to the site stating that "without restoration the Palace would be a meaningless heap of ruins". Others furiously disagreed, and the debate is no less heated today. One thing, however, is certain: no professional archeologist would be allowed or would expect to carry out such a work again.

In his views on Minoan scholarship Evans could be equally autocratic and blinkered. When **Alan Wace**, director of the British School at Athens, excavated a number of tombs on the site of Mycenae in the Greek Peloponnese in the early 1920s, his findings led him to conclude that Mycenae had not only been a culture independent of that of Crete – Evans stated that it had been a colony of Crete ruled by Cretan overlords – but that in the later period Mycenaeans had been in control at Knossós. For Evans this was heresy, and he used his considerable influence to attack Wace, get him sacked and stop him carrying out any further work at Mycenae. Evans went to his grave believing he was right, but in the light of the decipherment of Linear B and later investigation, it is Wace's views that are generally accepted today.

THE END OF AN ERA

During the long periods that Evans spent working at Knossós, he lived in some style at the villa he had constructed for himself overlooking the palace site. The **Villa Ariadne**, as he typically named it, became the focus of scholarly life of a slightly stuffy Victorian kind. Evans revelled in the stream of distinguished visitors to Knossós, who were met at the harbour by his chauffeur-driven limousine and then plied with French champagne following a guided tour of the site. His relationship with the Greeks, not to say the native Cretans, seems to have been scratchy by comparison. A crusty, aloof man by nature, he seems never to have been able to relax with them and certainly would never be seen around a table at the kafenío, as later Pendlebury was. Evans's lack of fluency in modern Greek – in spite of the time he spent on the island – was also taken by many as a sign of his disdain for the degenerate latterday occupants of such ancient lands.

In 1924 Evans donated the Knossós site and the Villa Ariadne to the British School at Athens – it was only in 1952 that the site was to become the property of the Greek government – and in the early Thirties, approaching his eightieth year, he handed over the reins at Knossós to a young English archeologist, **John Pendlebury**, and retired to his home near Oxford to complete the final volumes of his monumental work *The Palace of Minos*. It was the end of an era. Sir Arthur Evans (as he was now titled) paid his last visit to the site with which his name remains inextricably linked in 1935, when he attended the festivities surrounding the unveiling of his **bronze bust** in the palace grounds. He died six years later, in 1941.

EVANS'S CONTEMPORARIES AND SUCCESSORS

Although Evans stole the headlines for forty years, much important work was meanwhile being carried out elsewhere. Above all, Federico Halbherr was excavating **Festós** and later **Ayía Triádha**. In 1900, the same year that Evans began digging at Knossós, Halbherr started work on the beautifully situated palace at Festós. He soon acquired legendary status among the country people, thanks to his custom of riding around on a coal-black Arab mare. The bulk of the palace – including a dramatic **staircase** – was laid bare in three seasons of work. Although some restoration was done on the site, it was nothing resembling Evans's efforts at Knossós – in fact Halbherr and his colleagues pursued a far more rigorously **scientific excavation**, the first carried out on Crete. The Italian School has continued its work at Festós, Ayía Triádha and Górtys throughout the century.

In the east **British teams** worked at **Zákros** (where Hogarth narrowly failed to uncover the palace) and the Minoan settlements at **Paleókastro** and **Présos**. John Pendlebury also made a great impression in this period. A man with great affection both for Crete and the Cretans, he covered vast tracts of the island on foot in his search for evidence of ancient sites. He found countless numbers of these and made many friends along the way. Besides his work at Knossós he also excavated the late Minoan refuge at **Karfí** above the Lasíthi plateau. Pendlebury was killed in the early years of World War II, fighting alongside the Cretans during the German attack on Iráklion in 1941. Work by the British School has continued at

Knossós as well as more remote sites such as the Minoan settlements at **Mírtos Pírgos** and **Mírtos Foúrnou Korifí**.

The **Americans** were also active in eastern Crete from the earliest days of exploration. A woman – in a field dominated by men – staked out her claim at **Gourniá** on the Gulf of Mirabéllo. **Harriet Boyd** (later Mrs Boyd-Hawes), a young classics scholar from Massachusetts, visited Athens in 1900 and was gripped by the excitement surrounding the archeological excavations then getting under way. She went to Crete, received the almost obligatory encouragement from Evans, and the following year set off by donkey for the east with her foreman, the Zorba-like Aristides, and his mother, her constant companions. After a number of false starts she alighted on Gourniá and to her own, and the world's, surprise there uncovered the **workers' village**. The telegram she sent to the American Exploration Society, after three days' digging, says it all: "Discovered Gourniá Mycenaean site, streets, houses, pottery, bronzes, stone jars." It was, of course, a Minoan site, but the archeologists were still feeling their way back into a past much more ancient than anyone then realized.

Another skilled American archeologist working in the east was **Richard Seager**. In the early 1900s he excavated the important early Minoan settlement at **Vasilikí**, with its famous pottery, before moving on to the islands of **Psíra** and then **Móhlos** where substantial settlements were found. Seager was a good friend of Evans, who attended the funeral following Seager's sudden death at Iráklion in 1925. "He was the most English American I have ever known" was Evans's quintessential epitaph. The North American contribution (now a joint venture with Greek scholars) continues at Móhlos, as well as at **Kómmos**, where Joseph Shaw is excavating an impressive Minoan port to the north of Mátala.

The **French** have also contributed some excellent work at **Mália**. After initial investigations by Joseph Hatzidhákis and during the years of World War I from 1915 on, the French School at Athens were awarded the site in 1922. Having excavated the **Minoan palace** they are now at work on unearthing the extensive settlement which surrounded it.

RECENT DEVELOPMENTS: ZÁKROS

The discovery of ancient Crete has continued steadily throughout this century – barring wartime interruptions – if not always as spectacularly as it began. The outstanding exception was **Nikólaos Pláton's** excavation at **Zákros** which, from 1962 onwards, finally revealed the palace long suspected to have been there. Sixty years earlier Hogarth had missed the palace by a few yards, and in one of his treks around eastern Crete in 1938 the voracious Pendlebury, accompanied by his archeologist wife Hilda, had combed the area. "We must have been sitting on the very site – and we saw nothing" said Hilda Pendlebury later. Fittingly, one of Crete's greatest archeological prizes of all fell to a Cretan.

Prior to Hogarth and Pendlebury, Zákros had also been visited by Captain Spratt in 1852, as well as Halbherr, and Evans himself. **Hogarth** did expose parts of the surrounding settlement, with houses containing rich pottery, clay seals and bronze tools. The site then lay dormant until after World War II. Nikólaos Pláton became convinced that because of the submerged but excellent harbour – in a prime position for trade with the Near East – there had to be a palace here. With funds from the Greek Archeological Society and two wealthy American backers, he started work in 1962 where Hogarth had left off. The **unlooted palace**, never reoccupied after its destruction by fire around 1450 BC, was now revealed, together with a rich yield of artefacts, including over three thousand vases. Pláton continued to supervise the excavations at Zákros until his death in 1992, and work on uncovering the town surrounding the palace is still in progress.

In the recent excavations, Greek and Cretan archeologists have finally been able to play a more equal role than in the early days, when foreign archeological teams often treated them with patronizing high-handedness. Some, like Hatzidhákis and Marinátos, were there from the start but unable to compete with the wealthy foreigners in what was very much a private enterprise affair. Now, with mainly state funding, Greek archeologists such as **Yannis and Efi Sakellarakis** (at Arhánes, Anemóspilia and the Idean Cave), **Davaras** (Móhlos, Psíra and many more), **Alexiou** (Leben), **Zois** (Vasilikí), **Tzedakis** (Arméni), **Papadakis** (Koufonísi), **Karetsou** (Mount Yioúhtas), **Kanta** (Monastiráki) and **Tsipopoulou** (Petrás) are contributing greatly to the island's archeological discoveries. These continue to be added to as each season passes and, although it is unlikely that another Knossós will come to light, there are indications – such as those in the work continuing at **Haniá** – that many more sites, particularly in the west, lie awaiting the spade.

A once neglected area of Cretan archeology – the post-Bronze Age, Dorian and Roman – is also now being given more attention than ever before at sites across the island. These Minoan and post-Minoan sites today stand as a tribute not only to the dedicated archeologists who discovered and exposed them, but also to the work of the nameless thousands of Cretans who laboured with spade, trowel and barrow to uncover the past of their illustrious ancestors.

CRETE IN MYTH

Crete is intimately associated with much of ancient Greek mythology, and in particular with Zeus, who was not only brought up on the island, but according to some ancient Cretans was buried here as well. The Dhiktean Cave (see below), a gash on the face of Mount Dhíkti which soars above the Lasíthi plateau, has most claims to be the birthplace of the greatest god in the Greek pantheon, and symbolizes the potent influence of Minoan Crete on the land to the north.

THE BIRTH OF ZEUS

According to the earliest accounts of the myth, **Zeus** was the third generation of rulers of the gods. The original ruler, Uranus, was overthrown by his youngest son Kronos. In order to prevent such a fate overtaking him, too, Kronos ate his first five children at birth. When she was bearing the sixth child, his wife, Rhea, took refuge in a Cretan cavern (a site much argued over, but most commonly assigned to the Dhiktean Cave, p.144). Here Zeus was born, and in his place Rhea presented Kronos with a rock wrapped in blankets, which he duly devoured. Zeus was brought up secretly in the cave, his cries drowned by the **Kouretes**, who kept up a noisy dance with continuous clashing of shields and spears outside. The Kouretes, believed by Cretans to be the sons of the Earth Mother, were especially revered on the island as the inventors of beekeeping and honey as well as the hunting bow, and an inscription found at Palékastro suggests that they may well have a Minoan origin. The baby fed on milk from a mountain goat-nymph, Amalthea, one of whose horns he later made into a miraculous gift which a wish would fill with whatever was desired (hence the horn of plenty).

Having grown to manhood on Crete, Zeus declared war on Kronos and the Titans, a struggle which lasted ten years. Eventually, however, Zeus emerged as supreme ruler of the gods on **Mount Olympus**, and Kronos was banished to the Underworld. This myth has a precedent in Hittite texts of the second millennium BC which themselves had taken it over from the earlier Hurrians, a people who had settled in Syria and northern Mesopotamia. The Minoans passed it on to the Greeks.

THE ORIGIN OF THE CRETANS

The sexual prowess of Zeus led him into a bewildering number of affairs, one of which led to his best-known return to the island of his birth – with Europa – and the founding of the Cretan race. **Europa** was a princess, the daughter of King Phoenix (after whom Phoenicia was named), and Zeus lusted after her mightily. Approaching the shore of Phoenicia, Zeus saw her gathering flowers, and came to her in the guise of a **white bull**. Fascinated by the creature's docility Europa climbed onto its back, at which he leapt into the sea and carried her off across the sea to Crete. They landed at Mátala, travelled to Górtys (where one version has it Zeus ravished her beneath a plane tree which has never lost its leaves since) and were married at the Dhiktean Cave. One of the presents of Zeus to his bride was **Talos**, a bronze giant who strode round the island hurling boulders at approaching strangers. Jason and the Argonauts were greeted by a hail of stones from Talos when they approached Crete: aided by their companion, the sorceress Medea, they brought about the giant's fall by piercing a vein on his ankle – his single vulnerable spot – thus allowing the *ichor*, a divine fluid which served as blood, to drain from his body.

MINOS AND THE MINOTAUR

The Zeus of the Europa tale, taking the form of a **bull**, is almost certainly mixed up with earlier, native Cretan gods. The sun god of Crete also took the form of a bull, and the animal is a recurrent motif in the island's mythology. In the story of Minos, a bull once again has a prominent role. Europa bore Zeus three sons – Minos, Rhadamanthys and Sarpedon – before eventually being deserted. Later she married the king of Crete, Asterios, who adopted her children. Upon reaching manhood the three brothers quarrelled for the love of a beautiful boy named Miletos – a reflection of the mores and customs of the time. When Miletos chose Sarpedon, an enraged Minos drove him from the island. However, before boarding a ship to Asia Minor, Miletos killed King Asterios. Legend associates both Miletos and Sarpedon – who joined him in Asia Minor – with the founding of Miletus (see p.137), later an important city in Greek and Roman times. With Sarpedon removed, **Minos** claimed the throne and settled upon Rhadamanthys a third of Asterios' dominions. Rhadamanthys became renowned as a law-maker, appears in some tales as ruler at Festós, and every ninth year visited Zeus's cave on Mount Dhíkti to bring back a new set of laws. So great was Rhadamanthys's fame as a law-giver that Homer tells of how Zeus appointed him one of the three judges of the dead along with Minos and Aeachus.

Minos, meanwhile, was another ruler driven by lustful passions. He liaised with a succession of lovers including the Minoan goddess **Britomartis**, whom he chased relentlessly around the island for nine months until she threw herself into the sea off the end of the Rodhópou peninsula to escape his attentions. Rescued from drowning by the net of a fisher-man, she became known as Diktynna ("of the net"), and a great temple to her was erected on the site (see p.278). Minos's wife and queen, **Pasiphae**, incensed by her rakish husband's infidelities, put a spell on the king: whenever he lay with another woman he discharged not seed but a swarm of poisonous serpents, scorpions and insects which devoured the woman's vitals. News of his affliction (which bears a striking resemblance to venereal disease) apparently got around, and one of his bedmates Prokris, daughter of the Athenian king Erechtheus, insisted that he should take a prophylactic draught before their tryst which apparently pre-vented her invasion by serpents and scorpions.

Earlier, when he had gained the throne of his father, Minos prayed to Poseidon (or perhaps his father Zeus) to send a bull from the sea which he could offer as a sacrifice, thus signifying the god's recognition of the justice of his claim to the throne. When the radiant bull emerged from the sea, Minos was so taken by its beauty that he determined to keep it, sacrificing in its place another from his herds. Punishment for such hubris was inevitable, and in this case the gods chose to inflame Minos's wife, Pasiphae (a moon goddess in her own right – again the bull symbolizes the sun), with intense desire for the animal. She had the brilliant inventor and craftsman **Daedalus** construct her an artificial cow, in which she hid and induced the bull to couple with her: the result was the **Minotaur**, a beast half man and half bull (probably human

with a bull's head). To hide his shame, Minos had Daedalus construct the **labyrinth** in which to imprison the monster.

THESEUS AND ARIADNE

Meanwhile Minos had waged war on Athens after Androgeous, one of his sons by Pasiphae, had gone off to that city and won every event in the Panathenaic games, only to be slain on the orders of the outraged Athenian king, Aegeus. Part of the settlement demanded by the victori-ous Minos was that an annual tribute of seven young men and women be provided as sport or sacrifice for the Minotaur. The third time the tribute was due, **Theseus**, the son of King Aegeus, resolved to end the slaughter and him-self went as one of the victims. In Crete he met Minos's daughter **Ariadne**, who fell in love with him and resolved to help him in his task. At the instigation of the sympathetic Daedalus, she provided Theseus with a ball of thread which he could unwind and, if he succeeded in killing the Minotaur, follow to find his way out of the maze.

At first everything went to plan, and Theseus killed the beast and escaped from the island with Ariadne and the others. On the way home though, things were less successful. Ariadne was abandoned on a beach in Náxos (where she was later found by the god Dionysos and carried off to Olympus). Approaching Athens Theseus forgot to change his black sails for white – the pre-arranged sig-nal that his mission had succeeded. Thinking his son dead, King Aegeus threw himself into the sea and drowned.

Back on Crete, Minos imprisoned Daedalus in his own labyrinth, furious at Ariadne's deser-tion and his part in it, and at the failure of the maze. Locked up with Daedalus was his son, **Ikarus**. They escaped by making wings of feathers – from birds devoured by the Minotaur – held together with wax. Daedalus finally reached Sicily and the protection of King Kokalos: Ikaros, though, flew too close to the sun, the wax melted and he plunged to his death in the sea. Still set on revenge, Minos tracked Daedalus down by setting a puzzle so fiendishly difficult that only he could have solved it: a large reward was promised to the first person who could pass a thread through a triton shell. When Minos eventually arrived in Sicily he posed the problem to Kokalos who said it would be easy. He then consulted secretly with Daedalus who drilled the shell at its point and tied a thread to the leg of an ant which was sent into the shell. When the insect emerged through the hole, Kokalos took the shell to show Minos. Now certain that Daedalus was hidden in the palace, Minos demanded that Kokalos hand him over. Kokalos appeared to agree to the request and offered Minos hospitality in the palace. There Minos met an undignified end when he was scalded to death in his bath by the daughters of the king, urged on by Daedalus.

The postscript to all this concerns **Zeus's death**. According to the Cretans, and reflecting the older Minoan idea of a fertility god who annually died and was reborn, Zeus was buried beneath Mount Yioúhtas near Knossós, in whose outline his recumbent profile can still be seen from the palace site. It was a purely local claim, however, and clashed with the northern Greek concept of Zeus as an immortal and all-powerful sky-god. The northern Greeks regarded the islanders' belief in a dying Zeus as blasphemy, and their contempt for the Cretan heresy gave rise to the saying "all Cretans are liars."

WILDLIFE

Although the south coast of Crete is closer to Libya than it is to Athens, the island's wildlife owes much more to mainland Greece than it does to Africa. This is because Crete lies at the end of the long range of drowned limestone mountains which make up most of the Balkan peninsula: the range peters out in Libya and Egypt, and you need to go a long way south into the Sahara before you again find mountains as high as the Cretan ones. Crete, then, has typically northern Mediterranean fauna and flora.

Islands tend to be short on wildlife because of their isolation from the main bulk of species on the mainland. Not so Crete – it's rich in flora and fauna, and provides the full range of Mediterranean habitats. In fact, there are over two thousand species of **plants** in Crete, nearly a third of the Greek flora, and about as many as in the whole of Britain; richer partly because it went relatively unscathed through the Ice Ages, and partly because botanical variety tends to increase the nearer you go to the equator. With the wealth of plant life come far more **insects** than you get further north. The survival of Cretan wildlife in all its richness and diversity has been facilitated by the fact that agriculture remains fairly "undeveloped". Much of the land is steep and rocky with only a thin capping of soil, and you'll see modern intensive agriculture only on the lowland plains – although the pressures are mounting, in the form of wide-

spread use of chemicals, increased water abstraction and tourist development. You won't find many birds or wild flowers among the hectares of polytunnels around Timbáki, but you will in the mountains where such methods remain uneconomic.

The only feature really lacking, as elsewhere in Greece, is **trees**. The Minoan civilization was a seafaring one, so as early as the Bronze Age there was a high demand for timber for shipbuilding. Some of the lower hills were perhaps deforested four thousand years ago, a process completed by the Venetians. Today, native forests exist only in remote uplands and gorges.

Crete's chief drawback, at least if you hope to combine nature with the rest of the island's sights and life, is the pattern of its **climate**. Because it's so far south, the summers are long and dry, and that period equates to our northern winters, when many plants shut down or die, with a corresponding decline in activity from all other wildlife. Trying to see wild flowers or birds in lowland Crete in August is a bit like going out for a nature ramble in Britain in January. For flowers, the best time to go is March: the season continues through to late June in the mountains, while around the coasts many plants keep flowering right through the winter.

MAJOR HABITATS

Rarely in Europe do you find such a wide range of habitats so tightly packed, or real "wilderness" areas so close to modern towns and resorts, as in Crete. Broadly speaking, you can divide the island into four major **habitats**: the coast, cultivated land, low hillsides less than 1000m, and mountains above 1000m. Crete is the only Greek island which is mountainous enough to have all four of these habitats.

Along the **coast**, sandy beaches and low rocky cliffs are the norm. Marshy river deltas or estuaries are rare (simply because Crete is a dry country and there aren't too many rivers) but where you can find them, these wetland habitats are among the best places to look for birds.

Cultivated land is very variable in its wildlife interest. Huge wheatfields, or huge olive groves for that matter, have little to offer, but where the pattern is smaller in scale and more varied, it can be very good. This is especially true of the small market gardens – *perivólia* – often found on the edge of towns and villages, which are particularly good for small birds. Small hayfields can be a colourful mass of annual flowers and attendant insects in spring and early summer.

Low hillsides to 1000m comprise much of Crete. Scrubby hillsides, loosely grazed by goats and sometimes sheep, are the most typical Mediterranean habitat, extremely rich in flowers, insects and reptiles. Botanically, they divide into two distinct types: the first is *phrígana*, the Greek word for the French *garigue*, and consists of scattered scrubby bushes, always on limestone, especially rich in aromatic herbs and wild flowers. You can often find *phrígana* by looking for beehives: Cretan beekeepers know where to find the thyme and rosemary that gives the local honey its wonderful flavour. The other hillside habitat is *maquis*, a dense, very prickly scrub with scattered trees. Of these two hillside habitats, *phrígana* is better for flowers, *maquis* for birds.

Mountains over 1000m are surprisingly common: three separate ranges go over 2000m, and they are responsible for much of the climate, creating rain and retaining it as snow for a large part of the year. The small upland plateaux amongst the mountains – Omalós or Lasíthi most famously – are a very special feature, with their own distinctive flora and fauna. Although the Cretan mountains don't as a rule have the exciting mammals of the mainland, they are very good for large and spectacular birds of prey.

FLOWERS

What you will see, obviously, depends on where and when you go. The best time is **spring**, which generally starts in mid-February in the southeast corner of the island, is at its peak during March over most of the lowlands (but continues well into April), and in the mountains comes later, starting in late April and going on through to June. In **early summer**, the spring anemones, orchids and rockroses are replaced by plants like brooms and chrysanthemums; this ranges from mid-April in southern Crete to late July in the high mountains. These timings vary from year to year, too, exceptionally by as much as a month – in early April 1986 it was too hot to lie on the beach at Yeoryióupoli at midday, but at the same time in 1987 there was snow on the beach at Réthimnon, just 30km away.

Things are pretty much burnt out over all the lowlands from July through to the end of September, though there are still some flowers in the mountains. Once the hot summer is over, blooming starts all over again. Some of the **autumn-flowering** species, such as cyclamens and autumn crocus, flower from October in the mountains into December in the south. And by then you might as well stay on for the first of the spring bulbs in January.

Year round, the best insurance policy is to be prepared to move up and down the hills until you find flowers – from the beginning of March to the end of June you are almost guaranteed to find classic displays of flowers somewhere on the island, and you'll see the less spectacular but still worthwhile displays of autumn-flowering species from October to early December. If you have to go in July, August or September, then be prepared to see a restricted range, and also to go high up the mountains. The four habitats all have their own flowers, though some, of course, overlap.

On the **coast** you might find the spectacular **yellow horned poppy** growing on shingled banks, and **sea stocks** and **Virginia stocks** growing amongst the rocks behind the beach. A small pink **campion**, *Silene colorata*, is often colourfully present. Sand dunes are rare but sometimes there is a flat grazed area behind the beach; these are often good for **orchids**. **Tamarisk trees** often grow down to the shore, and there are frequent groves of Europe's largest grass, the **giant reed**, which can reach 4m high. In the autumn, look for the very large white flowers of the **sea daffodil**, as well as **autumn crocuses** on the banks behind the shore. The **sea squill** also blooms in autumn, with very tall spikes of white flowers rising from huge bulbs.

On **cultivated land** avoid large fields and plantations, but look for small hay meadows. These are often brilliant with annual "weeds" in late spring – various **chrysanthemum** species, **wild gladiolus**, **blue** and **purple vetches**, and in general a mass of colour such as you rarely see in northern Europe. This is partly because herbicides are used less, but mostly because the hot summers force plants into flowering at the same time.

The trees and shrubs on **low hillsides** are varied and beautiful, with colourful brooms flowering in early summer, preceded by bushy rockroses – *Cistaceae* – which are a mass of pink or white flowers in spring. Dotted amongst the shrubs is the occasional tree; the **Judas tree** flowers on bare wood in spring, making a blaze of pink against green hillsides which stands out for miles. Lower than the shrubs are the **aromatic herbs** – sage, rosemary, thyme and lavender – with perhaps some spiny species of **Euphorbia**. Particularly attractive is *Euphorbia acanthothamnos*, a rock-hugging species which forms low humps with small green leaves and delicate golden flowers. Because Crete is dry and hot for much of the year, you also get a high proportion of **xerophytes** – plants that are adapted to drought by having fleshy leaves and thick skins.

Below the herbs is the ground layer; peer around the edges and between the shrubs and you'll find a wealth of **orchids**, **anemones**, **grape hyacinths**, **irises**, and perhaps **fritillaries** if you are lucky. The orchids are extraordinary; some kinds – the *Ophrys* species – have especially fascinating and unusual flowers. Each *Ophrys* species is pollinated by a particular insect, which they attract by sight and smell: sight by having a flower which imitates the female insect and so deludes the male into "mating" with it; smell by imitating the particular sex pheromone which the insect uses. They're much smaller and altogether more dignified than the big blowsy tropical orchids you see in florists' stores. But beware of orchids – they're addictive, and you can easily become an orchid freak and spend your entire holiday face down on a hillside.

The **irises** are appealing, too; one of them, a small blue species called *Iris sisyrinchium*, only flowers in the afternoon, and you can actually sit and watch them open at around midday. Once spring is over, these plants give way to the early summer flowering of the brooms and aromatic herbs, as well as a final fling from the annuals which sense the coming of the heat and their own death. When the heat of the summer is over, the autumn bulbs appear, with species of **crocus** and their relatives, the **colchicums** and the **sternbergias**, and finally the **autumn cyclamens** through into early December.

Mountains are good to visit later in the year. The rocky mountain gorges are the home of many familiar garden rock plants, such as the **aubretias**, **saxifrages** and **alyssums**, as well as **dwarf bellflowers** and **anemones**. Look for dwarf **tulips** in fields on the upland plateaux in spring. The mountains are also the place to see the remaining Greek native **pine forests**, and in the woodland glades you will find **gentians**, **cyclamens** and **violets**. Above 1500m or so the forests begin to thin out, and in these upland meadows glorious **crocuses** flower almost before the snow has melted in spring – a very fine form of *Crocus seiberi* is a particularly early one. Autumn-flowering species of crocus and cyclamen should reward a visit later in the year.

BIRDS

There are fewer endemic **bird species** in Crete than there are flowers, because birds can move around. However, Greece has a good range of the resident Mediterranean species, plus one or two very rare ones such as the **Ruppell's warbler** or the **lammergeier vulture**, which have their European breeding strongholds in Greece. The great thing about birdwatching in Crete is that, if you pick your time right, you can see both resident and migratory species. Crete is on one of the main flypast routes for species that have wintered in East Africa, but breed in northern Europe. They migrate every spring up the Nile valley, and then move across the eastern Mediterranean, often in huge numbers. This happens from mid-March to mid-May, depending on the species, the weather, and where you are. The return migration in autumn is less spectacular because it is less concentrated, but still worth watching out for.

One drawback is that until recently the "sport" of shooting songbirds was common, and although things have improved, the birds remain understandably cautious. Some are still caught for the cagebird trade, as you will realize from looking at the goldfinches and others hung in cages from the front of houses and apartments. Birds of prey get a rough deal, too, as witness the dusty cases of badly stuffed eagles in many tavernas and kafenía.

A general point about watching birds is that they're active at a pretty antisocial time – just after dawn is the peak activity time for most small birds. On a walk before breakfast you can see heaps of birds, yet you can walk the same area a few hours later and see almost nothing. Exceptions to this are water birds and wading birds, which are often visible all day, and big birds of prey, which frequently use the rising thermals of early evening to soar and gain height.

On the outskirts of **towns** and in the **fields** there are some colourful residents. Small predatory birds such as **woodchat shrikes**, **kestrels** and migrating **red-footed falcons** can be seen perched on telegraph wires. The dramatic pink, black and white **hoopoe** and the striking yellow and black **golden oriole** are sometimes to be found in woodland and olive groves, and **Scops owls** (Europe's smallest owl) can often be heard calling around towns at night. They monotonously repeat a single "poo", sometimes in mournful vocal duets.

Look closely at the **swifts** and **swallows**, and you will find a few species not found in northern Europe: **crag martins** replace house martins in the **mountain gorges**, for example, and you may see the large **alpine swift**, which has a white belly. The **Sardinian warbler** dominates the rough scrubby **hillsides** – the male with a glossy black cap and an obvious red eye. These hillsides are also the home of the **chukar**, a species of partridge similar to the red-legged partridge found in Britain.

Wetlands and **coastal lagoons** are excellent for bird spotting, especially at spring and autumn migration, although this habitat is hard to find. There's a wide variety of **herons** and **egrets**, as well as smaller waders such as the **avocet** and the **black-winged stilt**, which has ridiculously long pink legs. **Marsh harriers** are common too, drifting over the reedbeds on characteristic raised wings. Scrubby woodland around coastal wetlands is a good place to see migrating smaller birds such as **warblers**, **wagtails** and the like. They usually migrate up the coast, navigating by the stars; a thick mist or heavy cloud will force them to land, and you can sometimes see spectacular "falls" of migrants.

The **mountains** hold some of the most exciting birds in Crete. Smaller birds like the **blue rock thrush** and **alpine chough** are common, and there is a good chance of seeing large and dramatic birds of prey. The **buzzards** and smaller **eagles** are confusingly similar, but there are also **golden eagles** and **vultures**. One very rare species of vulture, the **lammergeier**, is more common in Crete than anywhere else in Europe; you may be lucky enough to see it soaring above the Lasíthi or Omalós plateaux. It's a huge bird, with a wingspan of nearly 3m, and with narrower wings and a longer wedge-shaped tail than the other vulture you are likely to see, the **griffon vulture**.

MAMMALS

Cretan mammals are elusive, generally nocturnal, and very hard to see. Islands tend to have fewer species than the mainland, because mammals can't swim or fly to get there, and in this Crete is no exception, with about half the species that you could expect to see on mainland Greece. Even such common animals as red squirrel and fox have never made it across the water, nor will you find large exciting mammals like wolves or lynxes in the mountains, as you might (although very rarely) on the mainland.

However, there are some compensations. Islands often have their own endemic species, and the one in Crete is the **Cretan spiny mouse**, which is found nowhere else; if you happen to be on a rocky hillside at dusk you may see this largish mouse with very big ears and a spiny back fossicking around. The other compensation in Crete is the ancestral **wild goat** or *kri-kri*; a small population still exists in the White Mountains around the Samarian gorge, and also on some offshore islands – but you'll be very lucky if you see one outside the zoos. Apart from those, Crete has quite a few **bat** species, as well as **weasels**, **badgers**, **hares** and **beech martens**.

One recent addition to the zoological record was the remarkable discovery in 1996 of the **Cretan wild cat** (see p.223), long thought to be either extinct or a folktale. The single captured specimen is currently being studied, but the numbers and habitat of the animal are still unknown.

REPTILES AND AMPHIBIANS

The hot, rocky terrain of Crete suits reptiles well, with plenty of sun to bask in and plenty of rocks to hide under, but the island's isolation has severely restricted the number of species occurring: fewer than a third of those that are found on the mainland. Identification is therefore rather easy. If you sit and watch a dry stone wall almost anywhere you're bound to see the small local wall lizard, **Erhard's wall lizard**. A rustle in the rocks by the side of the road might be an **ocellated skink** – a bit like a lizard, but with a thicker body and a stubbier neck. In the bushes of the *maquis* and *phrígana* you may see the **Balkan green lizard**, a truly splendid bright green animal up to 50cm long, most of which is tail – usually seen as it runs frantically on its hind legs from one bush to another.

At night, **geckoes** replace the lizards. Geckoes are small (less than 10cm), have big eyes and round adhesive pads on their toes which enable them to walk upside down on the ceiling. Sometimes they come into houses – in which case welcome them, for they will keep down the mosquitoes and other biting insects. Crete has three out of four European species. The island is also one of only a handful of places where the **chameleon** occurs in Europe, although it is nowhere common. It lives in bushes and low trees, and hunts by day; its colour is greenish but obviously variable.

Tortoises, sadly, don't occur in Crete, but the stripe-necked **terrapin** does. Look out for these in any freshwater habitat – Lake Kournás, for example, or even in the cistern at the Zákros palace. There are also **sea turtles** in the Mediterranean: you might be lucky and see one while you're swimming or on a boat, since they sometimes bask on the surface of the water. The one you're most likely to see is the **loggerhead turtle**, which can grow up to 1m long. Crete has important breeding populations on beaches to the west of Haniá, around Mátala, and the largest (over 350 nests) at Réthimnon, but tourism and the development associated with it are threatening their future. Each year, many turtles are injured by motorboats, their nests are destroyed by bikes ridden on the beaches, and the newly hatched young die entangled in deckchairs and umbrellas left out at night on the sand. The turtles are easily frightened by noise and lights too, which makes them uneasy cohabitants with freelance campers and discos.

The Greek government has passed laws designed to protect the loggerheads, and the Sea Turtle Protection Society of Greece now operates an ambitious conservation programme but, in addition to the thoughtlessness of visitors, local economic interests tend to prefer a beach full of bodies to a sea full of turtles.

The final group of reptiles are the snakes, represented by four species, only one of which is poisonous – the **cat snake**. Even this is back fanged and therefore extremely unlikely to be able to bite anything as big as a human. So you can relax a bit when strolling round the hillsides

– though most snakes are very timid and easily frightened anyway. One species worth looking out for is the beautiful **leopard snake**, which is grey with red blotches edged in black. It's fond of basking on the sides of roads and paths.

Only three species of amphibian occur in Crete. The **green toad** is smaller than the common toad, with an obvious marbled green and grey back. The **marsh frog** is a large frog, greenish but variable in colour, and very noisy in spring. And **tree frogs** are small, live in trees, and call very loudly at night. They have a stripe down the flank, and vary in colour from bright green to golden brown, depending on where they are sitting – they can change colour like chameleons.

INSECTS

Insects are a much-neglected group of animals, which is a shame because many of them are beautiful, most lead fascinating lives, and they are numerous and easy to observe. You need to adjust your eyes to their scale to see them best: sit down for half an hour in the countryside by a bit of grazed turf, a patch of long grass, or a shrubby bush, and think small. You'll be surprised at the variety of shapes and colours of insects that will slowly come into focus.

There are around a million different species of insects in the world, and even in Crete there are probably a few hundred which have yet to be scientifically described or labelled. About a third of all insect species are **beetles**, and these are very obvious wherever you go. You might see one of the **dung beetles** rolling a ball of dung along a path like the mythological Sisyphus. If you have time to look closely at bushes and small trees, you might be rewarded with a **stick insect** or a **praying mantis**, creatures that are rarely seen because of their excellent camouflage.

The **grasshopper** and **cricket** family are well represented, and most patches of grass will hold a few. Grasshoppers produce their chirping noise by rubbing a wing against a leg, but crickets do it by rubbing both wings together. **Cicadas**, which most people think of as a night-calling grasshopper, aren't actually related at all – they're more of a large leaf hopper. Their continuous whirring call is one of the characteristic sounds of the Mediterranean night, and is produced by the rapid vibration of two cavities, called tymbals, on either side of the body.

Perhaps the most obvious insects are the **butterflies**, because they're large, brightly coloured and fly by day. Any time from spring through most of summer is good for butterflies, and there's a second flight of adults of many species in the autumn. Dramatic varieties in Crete include two species of **swallowtail**, easily identified by their large size, yellow and black colouring, and long spurs at the back of the hind wings. **Cleopatras** are large, brilliant yellow butterflies, related to the brimstone of northern Europe, but bigger and more colourful. Look out for **green hairstreaks** – a small green jewel of a butterfly that is particularly attracted to the flowers of the asphodel, a widespread plant of overgrazed pastures and hillsides. One final species typical of Crete is the **southern festoon** – an unusual butterfly with tropical colours, covered in yellow, red and black zigzags. It flies in the spring, its caterpillars feeding on *Aristolochia* (birthwort) plants.

SITES

You don't need to go that far to see Cretan wildlife – even in Iráklion, patches of **wasteland** hold interesting and colourful flowers, and nearby Knossós is good for flowers, insects and reptiles. In general, though, people and wildlife don't go together too well, so it's best to get away from the towns and into the villages.

A good site is a good site at any time of the year, except in high summer when everything is burnt out anyway. It's also usually true that a good flower site will yield plenty of other wildlife, and vice versa: a wide variety of plants leads to a wide variety of insects, which in turn implies that birds and reptiles will be numerous. So you can often use a blaze of plants as an indicator for a spot that would be worth exploring.

One possible exception to this is birds. Birds are mobile and fickle, often choosing to congregate in unprepossessing places such as windswept estuaries or smelly sewage farms. Birds adapt well to small-scale agriculture, too, even though the native plants may have been out-competed by olives, artichokes or melons.

LASÍTHI

The **eastern end** of Crete is the driest part, and also the part where **spring** comes first. So it

would be good to base yourself here if you were planning a trip early in the year, say February. The extreme eastern coast is dry and rocky, although Vái boasts a much-photographed grove of the Cretan **date palm** – one of only two native European palm species. Further west, the scenery is dominated by the Dhíkti mountains and the big bay of Áyios Nikólaos: even close by the development here, some good sites for flowers and birds survive.

The nearest of these is **Láto**, overlooking plains of olives and fruit trees that run down to the sea. It's a mass of colour with flowers in the spring, and, in common with other ancient sites, its old walls and ruins are a perfect habitat for lizards. **Mália**, similarly, has good flowers in spring and early summer, and the added advantage of being close to seacliffs where you can find many of the typical Mediterranean seashore flowers. Between the ancient site and the shore are the remains of a marsh, which is likely to hold interesting birds, including herons, harriers and migrating small warblers. **Gourniá** is also worth a trip for its flowers: they're particularly good at all of these sites because goats are excluded. Look for anemones in the spring; although there's only one spring species, *Anemone coronaria*, it comes in a bewildering range of colours from white to purple and scarlet. An Asiatic buttercup species which grows round here (*Ranunculus asiaticus*, a common plant over much of Crete) is quite unlike the buttercups of northern Europe, being much larger and with colours including white, pink and yellow. Around the walls of Gourniá you'll also find a large yellow and white daisy, *Chrysanthemum coronarium*, a species which is attractive to butterflies.

Just north of Áyios Nikólaos is the island of **Spinalónga**, and nearby, the disused saltpans at **Eloúnda**. The island is good for flowers, and the saltpans are always worth checking out for birds, especially during spring and autumn migration time.

Later in the year, the uplands of **Mount Dhíkti** and the **Lasíthi plateau** come into their own. The plateau is at 850m, so its spring flowers come later than those in the lowlands – April or early May would be a good time, with the summer flowers going on into June. The plateau itself is well cultivated, but the areas round the edge are rich in flowers, including many orchids. Try exploring a bit off the well-worn track from Psihró to the

Dhiktean Cave. Here you may find two varieties in particular: *Ophrys tenthredenifera*, one of the largest and most dramatic of the insect-imitating orchids, with beautiful pink sepals and a brown lower lip fringed with pale yellow; and the butterfly orchid *Orchis papilionacea*, which has a compact spike of pink florets, each with a large lip spotted and streaked with darker pink. Keep your eyes on the skies, too, since you are close to the mountains: sightings of eagles and vultures, including lammergeiers, are always possible.

Mount Dhíkti goes up to over 2000m, and boasts most of the dramatic flowers of the Cretan mountains. Look for early-flowering crocus species on the edge of the melting snowfields in April and May, and maybe you'll find cyclamens and peonies under the mountain woodland as well. Rocky gullies amongst the mountains are rich in specially adapted plants called chasmophytes, including endemic Cretan species.

IRÁKLION

Although **Iráklion** is the only one of the four Cretan provinces that doesn't have a major mountain range, it includes the foothills of both the Dhíkti range to the east and the Psilorítis massif in the west.

The ancient Minoan site of **Festós** is an excellent start. The ruins are only average for wildlife, but the hills around are excellent for flowers, insects and reptiles, and the river running through Ayía Triádha is always worth checking out for birds. The site of Festós itself is also a good place to look for bird migration; since it's high up, you stand a good chance of seeing migrating birds of prey coming over the plain and up into the hills.

If you walk from the car park heading north, you find yourself on a lovely hillside. There are scrubby bushes of rockroses – *Cistus* species – and round these a wonderful display of anemones, irises, orchids and the whole panoply of Cretan spring flowers. *Anemone heldreichii*, a delicate blue and white variety, is one of Crete's 130 or so endemic species. Another plant with a very restricted distribution is *Ophrys cretica*, one of the insect-imitating orchids with distinctive white markings on its maroon lip. In spring, *Orchis italica* is the most obvious orchid – tall shaggy spikes of small pink florets, each looking like a small

man with a cap. I say "man" advisedly, as you will realize if you look closely at the plant! One final flower to look out for is familiar as an annual garden flower, love-in-a-mist *Nigella arvensis*. With blooms varying from deep blue to pale pink, it's best known for its extraordinary inflated fruit, surrounded by a crown of deeply dissected bracts.

There are butterflies here too, including the scarce swallowtail, attracted by the nectar. Keep your eyes open, too, for Balkan green lizards in the bushes. Further on towards Ayía Triádha the river holds passage migrants including herons, terns and sandpipers – and the bushes are often full of migrating passerines, hotfoot from Africa. As always, a careful scrutiny of bushes and grasses will produce a horde of beetles, spiders and other invertebrates – with a chance of a praying mantis to brighten things up.

RÉTHIMNON

The two areas selected in **Réthimnon** are both on the south coast. That doesn't mean that you should ignore the rest: three other extremely promising sites are the Nídha plateau above Anóyia, the foothills of Mount Kédhros above Spíli, and the Amári valley.

Ayía Galíni, for all its summer crowds, is a great spot in spring, with some excellent walks on the headlands and hills roundabout, small-scale hayfields and olive groves, and a riverbed with some marshy areas. In other words, a really good range of the typical Cretan lowland habitats, and all within easy walking distance.

The river flows into the east of the village. On the far side is a range of hills, worth exploring for spring flowers, and the caves and cliffs overlooking the river have breeding colonies of lesser kestrels and Alpine swifts. The small reedbeds and marshy areas around the river have warblers and nightingales, too, and there are hoopoes in the olive groves.

A series of tracks leads away to the north and along the cliffs to the west. Any of these go through typical *phrígana* habitat, in which are scattered small meadows with wild gladioli and tassel hyacinths. The latter species is related to the grape hyacinth which is often used in boring clumps by British gardeners, but is far more attractive growing wild. Look for Jerusalem sage *Phlomis fruticosa*, a downy shrub whose golden flowers are attractive to bees. Another plant that grows around here (and many other places in Crete) is the unmistakeable giant fennel, a huge plant over 2m tall. Its scientific name is *Ferula communis*, which implies that it was once used as a walking stick, and, seeing the size of the stems, you can see why. There are orchids growing on the hillsides, including a Cretan speciality that rejoices in the name of *Ophrys fuciflora maxima*; a large orchid, it has a "face" on its lower lip that looks rather like a Minoan bull.

Further along the coast to the west, **Moní Préveli** has a similar range of habitats and fewer people. Again, there is a river valley that repays exploration for migratory birds, open hillsides with flowers and aromatic herbs, and some rugged coastal scenery. If you see a small scrub warbler around here with a black cap and throat, a red eye, and a white "moustache" then you may have seen Ruppell's warbler, probably the rarest warbler in Europe. The whole coastline from Préveli to Ayía Rouméli, some 75km to the west, is wild and rugged, punctuated by gorges, and a good place to look for large eagles and vultures.

HANIÁ

Haniá, at the western end of Crete contains some of the wildest and least developed scenery in the whole of the Mediterranean. Yeoryióupolis on the north coast and the famous Samariá gorge are described in detail here – but there are lots of other opportunities.

Yeoryióupolis has a wide range of habitats within easy reach – a marsh, a river with reedbeds, dry hillsides along the coast to the north, Crete's only freshwater lake – and an excellent beach as well. Between the main road and the sea are low sand dunes, often a good place for colourful flowers like Virginia stocks, sea stocks and the yellow horned poppy. Close to the east of the village is a marshy area, with birds like reed (and other) warblers, and marsh harriers floating overhead. There's a very pleasant walk along the River Almirós, branching up through olive groves and scrubby slopes to the hilltop village above. Here you'll find numerous small birds, attracted by unusually dense and lush woodland. Inland a bit is the small lake at **Kournás**, where a paddle round the lake may reveal stripe-necked terrapins poking their heads out of the water.

The **Samariá gorge** is rightly famous for wildlife as well as scenery, but remember that you'll find very similar flora and fauna at Imbrós and the other less-known ravines. The best flowers and other wildlife all come in the higher reaches, where you have the marvellous combination of rocky cliffs coming down into upland woods.

Still better, if you have time, is to take more than a day over this trip and spend some time on the **Omalós plateau** before heading down. This is especially rewarding later in the year, when the plateau and the slopes around it will have spring and summer flowers long after everything is burnt out on the coast. The plateau is renowned for its mountain flowers, including the very variable *Tulipa saxatilis*, a small pink or purple tulip endemic to Crete. Other endemic species found here include Cretan dittany *Origanum dictamnus*, a low shrub with furry rounded leaves and pink flowers, regarded by locals as a medical panacea (you may be offered it as a tea) and *Daphne sericea*, an evergreen shrub, with very unusual two-tone flowers of pink and yellow. There are also rare birds and mammals – watch the sky for golden eagles, griffon vultures, lammergeiers and falcons, and the distant cliffs and surrounding mountains for wild goats.

The start of the gorge takes you down the wooden staircase through light woodland. There are rock thrushes on the cliffs – the male has a striking orange breast, blue head and* white rump. Rock plants like *Aubretia* grow on the cliffs, along with *Linum arboreum*, a low perennial flax with brilliant yellow flowers. Two endemic cliff plants to watch for are the Cretan rock lettuce *Petromarula pinnata*, which looks nothing like a lettuce and isn't even related, with long spikes of deep blue flowers, and *Ebenus cretica*, a bushy pea with grey foliage and pink flowers.

Under the trees at the sides of the paths are orchids, including the handsome yellow *Orchis provincialis*, with a tight flowerhead of spiked yellow florets. Cyclamens and anemones grow here, and you may find a fritillary *Fritillaria messanensis*, with a drooping purple and green bell-shaped flower. Perhaps the most stunning flower is a white peony with huge, yellow-centred flowers: called *Paeoni clusii*, it grows in profusion around a ruined chapel about 3km down the gorge. There are more lovely flower meadows round the village of Samariá, about halfway down, but as you drop lower the cliffs tower above you until it is hard to see anything else, and once you are through the famous gates at the end, the walk is less interesting in every sense. Around the base of the cliffs at the bottom of the gorge are colonies of crag martins – a drab-looking bird, but a dramatic flier.

Pete Raine

BOOKS

Where separate editions exist in the UK and USA, publishers are detailed below in the form "UK publisher; US publisher". Where books are published in one country only, this follows the publisher's name. O/p signifies an out-of-print – but still highly recommended – book.

Many of the more popular titles below are widely available in Crete, but local editions tend to be shabby, and imported ones expensive. The more specialist titles might be more easily found at a dedicated travel **bookstore** (some are included under Map Outlets on p.30) or a Greek-interest bookshop: in London try the Hellenic Book Service, 91 Fortess Rd, London NW5 1AG (☎0171/267 9499, fax 267 9498) or Zeno's Greek Bookshop, 6 Denmark St, London WC2H 8LP (☎0171/240 1968, fax 836 2522).

ARCHEOLOGY AND ANCIENT HISTORY

There is a vast body of literature on ancient Crete, especially on the Minoans, but a lot of it is very heavy going. Below are some of the more widely available, accessible and useful books. Other names to look out for include **Nikólaos Pláton** and **Stylianós Aléxiou**, whose books you may find available in local translations. There are also local guide booklets on all the major museums and sites, often with nice pictures, but usually very poor text.

Gerald Cadogan *Palaces of Minoan Crete* (Routledge). Complete guide to all the major sites, with much more history and general information than the name implies.

John Chadwick *Linear B and related scripts* (British Museum Publications; University of California Press). A short version of *The Decipherment of Linear B* by one of those closely responsible. In *The Decipherment of Linear B* (Cambridge UP), the whole fascinating story of the decipherment of Linear B is graphically told by Chadwick who collaborated with Ventris, the English architect who made the crucial breakthrough. The same author's *Mycenaean World* (Cambridge UP) vividly describes the society revealed by the tablets.

Leonard Cottrell *The Bull of Minos* (Bell & Hyman o/p; Amereon Aeonian Press; Efstathiadis, Athens). Breathless and somewhat dated account of the discoveries of Schliemann and Evans; easy reading.

Costis Davaras *Guide to Cretan Antiquities* (Noyes Press, US; Eptalofolos, Athens). A fascinating guide by the distinguished archeologist and former director of the Áyios Nikólaos museum to the antiquities of Crete (ancient through to the Turkish era). Cross-referenced in dictionary form, it has authoritative articles on all the major sites as well as subjects as diverse as Minoan razors and toilet articles, the disappearance of Cretan forests and the career of Venizélos.

Arthur Evans *The Palace of Minos* (o/p). The seminal work, still worth a look if you can find it in a library.

Reynold Higgins *Minoan and Mycenaean Art* (Thames & Hudson; OUP o/p). Solid introduction to the subject with plenty of illustrations.

J. D. S. Pendlebury *The Archaeology of Crete* (Methuen o/p; Norton o/p). Still the most comprehensive handbook, detailing virtually every archeological site on the island. Pendlebury's *Handbook to the Palace of Minos* is still an excellent guide to the Knossós site by someone who – as curator after Evans's retirement – knew it inside out. A local edition has been reprinted in Crete.

Nikos Psilakis *Monasteries and Byzantine Memories of Crete* (locally published). Self-explanatory title: readable and well-illustrated.

Ian F. Sanders *Roman Crete* (Aris & Phillips; Humanities Press). Very dry, and hard to come by, but a total record of all Roman remains on Crete.

Peter Warren *The Aegean Civilizations* (Phaidon o/p; Peter Bedrick o/p). Illustrated introduction by one of the leading modern experts; it's essentially a coffee-table book, but informative and easy on the eye. Warren's other publications tend to the technical.

R. F. Willetts *The Civilization of Ancient Crete* (Barnes & Noble, US), *Cretan Cults and Festivals* (Greenwood Press), *Aristocratic Society in Ancient Crete* (RKP o/p; Greenwood Press). Rather heavy, scholarly accounts of the social structure of ancient Crete. His *Everyday Life in Ancient Crete* (Batsford o/p; John Benjamins) is a more accessible read for the layman.

H. G. Wunderlich *The Secret of Crete* (Efstadhiadis, Athens). The secret is that the palaces were really elaborate tombs or necropoli. Sensationalist nonsense widely sold on Crete.

HISTORY

By contrast with the proliferation of ancient history, there is no book in English devoted to modern Cretan history: good general accounts are included in Hopkins's and Smith's books on the island; otherwise you're forced to wade through Greek or Ottoman history, selecting the relevant portions.

Richard Clogg *A Concise History of Greece* (Cambridge UP). More rigorously historical account of Greek history from its emergence from Ottoman rule to the present day, covering the wider aspects of Crete's struggle for independence and union with Greece.

Adam Hopkins *Crete, its Past, Present and People* (Faber & Faber, o/p). Excellent general introduction to Cretan history and society. Recommended.

John Julius Norwich *Byzantium: the Early Centuries, Byzantium: the Apogee* and *Byzantium: Decline and Fall* (all Penguin; Knopf). The three volumes of Norwich's history of the Byzantine Empire are terrific narrative accounts, and much can be gleaned from them about Crete in this period.

James Pettifer *The Greeks: the Land and People since the War* (Penguin, UK). Excellent introduction to contemporary Greece – and its recent past. Pettifer roams the country and charts

the state of the nation's politics, food, family life, religion, tourism and all points in between. Only passing reference to Crete, however.

Oliver Rackham and Jennifer Moody *The Making of the Cretan Landscape* (Manchester UP). A fascinating study of the Cretans in their environment, from antiquity to the present day.

Michael Llewellyn Smith *The Great Island* (Allen Lane, UK o/p). Covers much of the same as Hopkins's book, but with more emphasis on folk traditions, and a lengthy analysis of Cretan song.

WORLD WAR II

Antony Beevor *Crete: The Battle and the Resistance* (Penguin; Westview Press o/p). Relatively short study of the Battle of Crete, with insights into the characters involved. Beevor looks at recent evidence to conclude that defeat was at least in part due to the need to conceal Allied intelligence successes.

Alan Clark *The Fall of Crete* (NEL, UK o/p; terrible Efstadhiadis edition widely sold on Crete). Racy and sensational – but very readable – military history by a maverick English politician. Detailed on the battles, and more critical of the command than you might expect from a former cabinet minister.

W. Stanley Moss *Ill Met by Moonlight* (Buchan & Enright; Lyons). An account of the capture of General Kreipe by one of the participants, largely taken from his diaries of the time. Good *Boys' Own* adventure stuff. Moss also translated Baron von der Heydte's *Daedalus Returned* (o/p) which gives something of the other side of the story.

George Panayiotakis *The Battle of Crete* (local edition). Pictorial history of the battle and its aftermath using contemporary photos. Available from major bookshops on the island.

George Psychoundákis *The Cretan Runner* (Penguin; Transatlantic Arts, US; Efstadhiadis, Athens). Account of the invasion and resistance by a Cretan participant; Psychoundákis was a guide and message-runner for all the leading English-speaking protagonists. Great.

Tony Simpson *The Battle for Crete, 1941* (o/p). A very different way of looking at the subject, putting the campaign into an international context and relying heavily on oral history for details of the combat. Uncompromisingly critical of the command, and far more interesting than straight military history.

I. McD. G. Stewart *Struggle for Crete: A Story of Lost Opportunity* (Oxford UP o/p). Authoritative detail on the battle from someone who was there. Rather dry military historian's approach.

Evelyn Waugh *Officers and Gentlemen* (Penguin; Little, Brown), *Diaries* (Phoenix; Little, Brown). Both include accounts of the battle, and particularly of the horrors of the flight and evacuation.

TRAVEL WRITING

Anonymous *Greek Men Made Simple* (MUC, Athens). Everything you ever wanted to know plus everything you never thought to ask is the subtitle of this hilarious dissection of the Greek male and his sexual ego by a Greek-resident English woman (hence the anonymity) with plenty of experience of both. Despite clumsy editing, it's an invaluable *vade mecum* for would-be Shirley Valentines and is widely available at bookshops on the island.

Robin Bryant *Crete* (o/p). Thematic interweaving of the author's observations during his stay on Crete with aspects of the island's history, folklore and festivals, immediately prior to the arrival of package tourism.

David MacNeill Doren *Winds of Crete* (John Murray UK o/p; Efstathiadis, Athens). An American and his Swedish wife find enlightenment on Crete – between times, quite an amusing and well-observed travelogue documenting many of the island's customs and curiosities in addition to some hair-raising brushes with Cretan physicians.

Edward Lear *The Cretan Journal* (Denise Harvey, Athens). Diary of Lear's trip to Crete in 1864, illustrated with his sketches and watercolours. He didn't enjoy himself much.

Henry Miller *The Colossus of Maroussi* (Minerva o/p; New Directions). Miller's idiosyncratic account of his travels in Greece on the eve of World War II includes a trip to Crete where diarrhoea, biting flies and Festós palace all get bit-parts in the epic.

Robert Pashley *Travels in Crete* (John Murray o/p). The original nineteenth-century British traveller, full of interesting anecdotes and outrageous attitudes. Try the library.

Dilys Powell *The Villa Ariadne* (Hodder & Stoughton, UK; Efstadhiadis, Athens). The story of the British in Crete, from Arthur Evans to Paddy Leigh Fermor, through the villa at Knossós which saw all of them. Good at bringing the excitement of the early archeological work to life, but rather cloying in style.

Pandelis Prevelakis *Tale of a Town* (Doric Publications, Athens). English translation of a native's description of life in Réthimnon.

J. E. Hilary Skinner *Roughing it in Crete* (1868 o/p). Great title for account of another Englishman's adventures, this time with a band of rebels. Interesting on the less glamorous side of the independence struggle, since he spent the whole time searching for food or dodging Turkish patrols.

Capt. T. A. B. Spratt *Travels and Researches in Crete* (Coronet Books, US). Another nineteenth-century Briton who caught the Cretan bug whilst surveying the island's coastline, and left behind this account of its natural history, geology and archeology.

Christopher Thorne *Between the Seas* (Sinclair Stevenson o/p; Trafalgar Square o/p UK). The account of a walk along the length of the island with observations on Cretan country life, past and present.

Jackson Webb *The Last Lemon Grove* (o/p). Published in 1977, an account of an American living in the then-remote village of Paleohóra. Wonderfully atmospheric.

FICTION

Níkos Kazantzakís *Zorba the Greek, Freedom and Death, Report to Greco* (all Faber & Faber; Simon & Schuster; local editions available in Crete). Something by the great Cretan novelist and man of letters is essential reading. Forget the film: *Zorba the Greek* is a wonderful read on Crete which provides the backdrop to the adventures of one of the most irresistible characters of modern fiction. *Freedom and Death* is if anything even better.

Ioannis Kondylakis *Patouchas* (Efstathiadis, Athens). The story of a Cretan shepherd on a journey of self-discovery is a wonderfully observed and humorous fictional sketch of Turkish Crete in the last century by a little-known Cretan author. Widely available on the island.

Vitzentzos Kornaros *Erotokritos* (tr. Theodore Stefanides, Merlin Press; Humanities). A beautifully produced English translation of the massive sixteenth-century Cretan epic poem.

Mary Renault *The King Must Die* (Sceptre o/p; Vintage), *The Bull from the Sea* (Penguin; Vintage). Stirring accounts of the Theseus legend and Minoan Crete for those who like their history in fictionalized form.

WILDLIFE

Michael Chinerey *Collins Guide to the Insects of Britain and Western Europe* (Collins, UK). This doesn't specifically include Greece (there's no comprehensive guide to Greek insects) but it gives a good general background and identification to the main families of insects that you're likely to see.

Stephanie Coghlan *Birdwatching in Crete* (Snails Pace Publishing, UK). Slim booklet detailing the best birdwatching sites and what you may see there, with checklists. No pictures for identification though, so you'll need a guide too.

Anthony Huxley and William Taylor *Flowers of Greece* (Hogarth Press o/p; Trafalgar Square o/p). The best book for identifying flowers in Crete.

Christopher Perrins *New Generations Guide to Birds of Britain and Europe* (HarperCollins; University of Texas Press). An alternative look at bird ecology as well as pure identification.

Peterson, Mountfort and Hollom *Field Guide to the Birds of Britain and Europe* (HarperCollins; Houghton Mifflin). There's no complete guide to Cretan birds; this is probably the best general tome – ageing but excellent.

George Sfikas *Wild Flowers of Crete* (Efstathiadis, Athens). Comprehensive illustrated guide to the island's flora. Widely available at bookshops on the island.

Paul Whalley *The Mitchell Beazley Pocket Guide to Butterflies* (Mitchell Beazley; published in the US as *Butterflies* by Transatlantic Arts). A useful identification guide.

HIKING AND TRAVEL GUIDES

Bruce and Naomi Caughey *Crete off the Beaten Track* (Cicerone Press, UK). Details a large number of walks throughout the island; available in many bookstores in major towns.

Lance Chilton, *Ten Walks in the Plakiás Area* and *Six Walks in the Georgioupolis Area* (both Marengo, UK). Well-described rambles and treks ranging from half an hour to half a day in these two scenic zones, by an experienced guide. *More Challenging Walks in the Plakiás Area* is a recent new addition. Available from bookshops in the UK or direct from the publisher: 17 Bernard Crescent, Hunstanton, Norfolk PE36 6ER (☎ & fax 01485/532710).

Marc Dubin *Trekking in Greece* (Lonely Planet o/p). An excellent walkers' guide, expanding on some of the hikes covered in this book and adding others. Includes day-hikes and longer treks, plus extensive preparatory and background information. Look for a new version with a UK publisher in 1999.

Jonnie Godfrey and Elizabeth Karslake *Landscapes of Eastern/Western Crete* (Sunflower, UK). Full of hiking and touring suggestions which make a useful adjunct to this guide.

Stephanos Psimenos *Unexplored Crete* (Road Editions, Athens). Bible-sized (motor) biker's guide to the island packed with loads of biker information and bonding lingo, related in an often quirky translation from the original Greek. Still, if you want to bike around the island using routes known only to goats, this is the book for you. Widely available at bookshops in all major towns in Crete.

FOOD AND DRINK

Miles Lambert-Gócs *The Wines of Greece* (Faber & Faber, UK only). Comprehensive survey of the emerging wines of Greece with plenty of fascinating historical detail; a chapter is devoted to Cretan wines.

George Sfikas *Fishes of Greece* (Efstathiadis, Athens). Pictorial guide to all the fish you're likely to encounter in the island's tavernas. Widely available in Crete.

Sofia Souli *The Greek Cookery Book* (Toubi's, Athens). One of the best books to start you cooking Greek food when you get back home. Everything from *tzatzíki* to *kataïfi*, including a few Cretan specialities. Profusely illustrated and widely available on the island.

LANGUAGE

So many Cretans have been compelled by poverty and other circumstances to work abroad, especially in the English-speaking world, that you'll find someone who speaks some English in almost any village. Add to that the thousands attending language schools or working in the tourist industry – English is the lingua franca of the north coast – and it's easy to see how so many visitors come back having learnt only half a dozen restaurant words between them. You can certainly get by this way, even in quite out of the way places, but it isn't very satisfying.

Greek is not an easy language for English-speakers, but it is a beautiful one, and even a brief acquaintance will give you some idea of the debt western European languages owe to it. More important than that, the willingness and ability to say even a few words will transform your status from that of dumb *tourístas* to the honourable one of *ksénos*, a word which can mean stranger, traveller and guest all rolled into one.

On top of the usual difficulties of learning a new language, Greek presents the added problem of an entirely separate **alphabet**. Despite initial appearances, this is in practice fairly easily mastered; a skill that will help enormously if you are going to get around independently (see the alphabet and transliteration box opposite). In addition, certain combinations of letters have unexpected results. This book's transliteration system should help you make intelligible noises but you have to remember that the correct **stress** – marked in the book with an accent – is absolutely crucial. With the right sounds but the wrong stress people will either fail to understand you, or else understand something quite different from what you intended.

Greek **grammar** is more complicated still: nouns are divided into three genders, all with different case endings in the singular and in the plural, and all adjectives and articles have to agree

LANGUAGE-LEARNING MATERIALS

TEACH YOURSELF GREEK COURSES

Breakthrough Greece (Pan Macmillan; book and 2 cassettes). Excellent, basic teach-yourself course – completely outclasses the competition.

Get By in Greek (BBC Publications, UK; book and two cassettes). One of the BBC's excellent crash-course introductions which gets you to survival-level Greek (bars, tavernas, asking the way) in a couple of weeks.

Greek Language and People (BBC Publications, UK; book and cassette available). An in-depth study course which, whilst more limited than the *Breakthrough* course in scope, is good for acquiring the essentials, and gets you using the Greek alphabet from the start.

Anne Farmakides *A Manual of Modern Greek* (Yale; McGill; 3 vols). If you have the discipline and motivation, this is one of the best course for learning proper, grammatical Greek; indeed, mastery of just the first volume will get you a long way.

PHRASEBOOKS

The Rough Guide to Greek (Rough Guides). Practical and easy-to-use, the Rough Guide phrase-books allow you to speak the way you would in your own language. Feature boxes fill you in on dos and don'ts and cultural know-how.

DICTIONARIES

The Oxford Dictionary of Modern Greek (Oxford UP). A bit bulky but generally considered the best Greek–English, English–Greek dictionary.

Collins Pocket Greek Dictionary (Harper Collins). Very nearly as complete as the Oxford and probably better value for money.

Oxford Learner's Dictionary (Oxford UP). If you're planning a prolonged stay, this pricey two-volume set is unbeatable for usage and vocabulary. There's also a more portable one-volume Learner's Pocket Dictionary.

with these in gender, number and case. (All adjectives are arbitrarily cited in the neuter form in the following lists.) Verbs are even worse. To begin with at least, the best thing is simply to say what

you know the way you know it, and never mind the niceties. "Eat meat hungry" should get a result, however grammatically incorrect. If you worry about your mistakes, you'll never say anything.

THE GREEK ALPHABET: TRANSLITERATION

Set out below is the Greek alphabet, the system of transliteration used in this book and a brief aid to pronunciation.

Greek	Transliteration	Pronounced
A, α	a	a as in f*a*ther
B, β	v	b as in v*e*t
Γ, γ	y/g	y as in *y*es when before an e or i; when before consonants or a, o or ou it's a breathy, throaty g as in *g*asp
Δ, δ	dh	th as in *th*en
E, ε	e	e as in g*e*t
Z, ζ	z	z sound
H, η	i	ee sound as in f*ee*t
Θ, θ	th	th as in *th*eme
I, ι	i	i as in b*i*t
K, κ	k	k sound
Λ, λ	l	l sound
M, μ	m	m sound
N, ν	n	n sound
Ξ, ξ	ks	ks sound
O, o	o	o as in t*o*ad
Π, π	p	p sound
P, ρ	r	rolled r sound
Σ, σ, ς	s	s sound
T, τ	t	t sound
Y, υ	i	ee, indistinguishable from η
Φ, φ	f	f sound
X, χ	h	harsh h sound, like ch in lo*ch*
Ψ, ψ	ps	ps as in li*ps*
Ω, ω	o	o as in toad, indistinguishable from o

Combinations and dipthongs

AI, αι	e	e as in g*e*t
AY, αυ	av/af	av or af depending on following consonant
EI, ει	i	ee, exactly like η
OI, οι	i	ee, identical again
EY, ευ	ev/ef	ev or ef depending on following consonant
OY, ου	ou	ou as in t*ou*rist
ΓΓ, γγ	ng	ng as in a*ng*ie
ΓΚ, γκ	g/ng	g as in *g*oat at the beginning of a word, ng in the middle
ΜΠ, μπ	b	b at the beginning of a word, mb in the middle
NT, ντ	d/nd	d at the beginning of a word, nd in the middle
ΤΣ, τσ	ts	ts as in hi*ts*
ΣΙ, σι	sh	sh as in *sh*ame
ΤΖ, τζ	ts	j as in *j*am

Note: An umlaut on a letter indicates that the two vowels are pronounced separately, for example Aóös is Ah-oh-s, rather than A-ooos

GREEK WORDS AND PHRASES

Essentials

Yes	*Né*	Sorry/excuse me	*Signómi*	Hot	*Zestó*
Certainly	*Málista*			Cold	*Krío*
No	*Óhi*	Today	*Símera*	With	*Mazí*
Please	*Parakaló*	Tomorrow	*Ávrio*	Without	*Horís*
Okay, agreed	*Endáksi*	Big	*Megálo*	Quickly	*Grígora*
Thank you (very much)	*Efharistó (polí)*	Small	*Mikró*	Slowly	*Sigá*
		More	*Perisótero*	Mr/Mrs	*Kírios/Kiría*
I (don't) understand	*(Dhen) katalavéno*	Less	*Ligótero*	Miss	*Dhespinís*
		A little	*Lígo*		
Excuse me, do you speak English?	*Parakaló, mípos miláte angliká?*	A lot	*Polí*		
		Cheap	*Ftinó*		
		Expensive	*Akrivó*		

Other Needs

To eat/drink	*Trógo/píno*	Stamps	*Gramatósima*	Toilet	*Toualéta*
Bakery	*Foúrnos, psomádhiko*	Petrol station	*Venzinádhiko*	Police	*Astinomía*
Pharmacy	*Farmakío*	Bank	*Trápeza*	Doctor	*Iatrós*
Post office	*Tahidhromío*	Money	*Leftá/hrímata*	Hospital	*Nosokomío*

Requests and Questions

To ask a question, it's simplest to start with *parakaló*, then name the thing you want in an interrogative tone.

Where is the bakery?	*Parakaló, o foúrnos?*	How many?	*Póssi/pósses?*
Can you show me the road to . . . ?	*Parakaló, o dhrómos ya . . ?*	How much?	*Póso?*
		When?	*Póte?*
We'd like a room for two	*Parakaló, éna dhomátio ya dhío átoma?*	Why?	*Yatí?*
		At what time . . . ?	*Ti óra . . . ?*
May I have a kilo of oranges?	*Parakaló, éna kiló portokália?*	What is/Which is . . . ?	*Ti íne/pió íne..?*
		How much (does it cost)?	*Póso káni?*
Where?	*Pou?*	What time does it open?	*Tí óra aníyi?*
How?	*Pos?*	What time does it close?	*Tí óra klíni?*

Talking to People

Greek makes the distinction between the informal (*esí*) and formal (*esís*) second person, as French does with *tu* and *vous*. Young people, older people and country people nearly always use *esí* even with total strangers. In any event, no one will be too bothered if you get it wrong. By far the most common greeting, on meeting and parting, is *yá sou/yá sas* – literally "health to you".

Hello	*Hérete*	My name is . . .	*Me léne . . .*
Good morning	*Kalí méra*	Speak slower, please	*Parakaló, miláte pió sigá*
Good evening	*Kalí spéra*	How do you say it in Greek?	*Pos léyete sta Eliniká?*
Good night	*Kalí níkhta*		
Goodbye	*Adhío*	I don't know	*Dhen kséro*
How are you?	*Ti kánis/ti kánete?*	See you tomorrow	*Tha se dho ávrio*
I'm fine	*Kalá íme*	See you soon	*Kalí andhámosi*
And you?	*Ke esís?*	Let's go	*Páme*
What's your name?	*Pos se léne?*	Please help me	*Parakaló, na me voithíste*

Greek's Greek

There are numerous words and phrases which you will hear constantly, even if you rarely have the chance to use them. These are a few of the most common.

Éla!	Come (literally) but also Speak to me! You don't say! etc.	*Po-po-po!*	Expression of dismay or concern, like French "O la la!"
Oríste?	What can I do for you?	*Pedhí mou*	My boy/girl, sonny, friend, etc.
Bros!	Standard phone response	*Maláka(s)*	Literally "wanker", but often used (don't try it!) as an informal address
Ti néa?	What's new?		
Ti yínete?	What's going on (here)?		
Étsi k'étsi	So-so	*Sigá sigá*	Take your time, slow down
Ópa!	Whoops! Watch it!	*Kaló taxídhi*	Bon voyage

Accommodation

Hotel	*Ksenodhohío*	Cold water	*Krío neró*
A room . . .	*Éna dhomátio . . .*	Can I see it?	*Boró na to dho?*
for one/two/three people	*ya éna/dhío/tría átoma*	Can we camp here?	*Boróume na váloume ti*
for one/two/three nights	*ya mía/dhío/trís vradhiés*		*skiní edhó?*
with a double bed	*me megálo kreváti*	Campsite	*Kamping/kataskínosi*
with a shower	*me doús*	Tent	*Skiní*
Hot water	*Zestó neró*	Youth hostel	*Ksenodhohío neótitos*

On the Move

Aeroplane	*Aeropláno*	Where are you going?	*Pou pas?*
Bus	*Leoforío*	I'm going to . . .	*Páo sto . . .*
Car	*Aftokínito*	I want to get off at . . .	*Thélo na katévo sto . . .*
Motorbike, moped	*Mihanáki, papáki*	The road to . . .	*O dhrómos ya . . .*
Taxi	*Taksí*	Near	*Kondá*
Ship	*Plío/Vapóri/Karávi*	Far	*Makriá*
Bicycle	*Podhílato*	Left	*Aristerá*
Hitching	*Otostóp*	Right	*Dheksiá*
On foot	*Me ta pódhia*	Straight ahead	*Katefthía*
Trail	*Monopáti*	A ticket to . . .	*Éna isistírio ya . . .*
Bus station	*Praktorío leoforíon*	A return ticket	*Éna isistírio me epistrofí*
Bus stop	*Stási*	Beach	*Paralía*
Harbour	*Limáni*	Cave	*Spiliá*
What time does it leave?	*Ti óra févyi?*	Centre (of town)	*Kéndro*
What time does it arrive?	*Ti óra ftháni?*	Church	*Eklissía*
How many kilometres?	*Pósa hiliómetra?*	Sea	*Thálassa*
How many hours?	*Pósses óres?*	Village	*Horió*

Numbers

1	*énos éna/mía*	12	*dhódheka*	90	*enenínda*
2	*dhío*	13	*dhekatrís*	100	*ekató*
3	*trís/tría*	14	*dhekatésseres*	150	*ekatón penínda*
4	*tésseres/téssera*	20	*íkosi*	200	*dhiakóssies/ia*
5	*pénde*	21	*íkosi éna*	500	*pendakóssies/ia*
6	*éksi*	30	*triánda*	1000	*hílies/ia*
7	*eftá*	40	*saránda*	2000	*dhío hiliádhes*
8	*okhtó*	50	*penínda*	1,000,000	*éna ekatomírio*
9	*enyá*	60	*eksínda*	First	*próto*
10	*dhéka*	70	*evdhomínda*	Second	*dhéftero*
11	*éndheka*	80	*ogdhónda*	Third	*tríto*

The time and days of the week

Sunday	*Kiriakí*	What time is it?	*Ti óra íne?*
Monday	*Dheftéra*	One/two/three o'clock	*Mía/dhío/trís óra/óres*
Tuesday	*Tríti*	Twenty to four	*Tésseres pará íkosi*
Wednesday	*Tetárti*	Five past seven	*Eftá ke pénde*
Thursday	*Pémpti*	Half past eleven	*Éndheka ke misí*
Friday	*Paraskeví*	Half-hour	*Misí óra*
Saturday	*Sávato*	Quarter-hour	*Éna tétarto*

GLOSSARY

ACROPOLIS Ancient, fortified hilltop.

AGORA Market and meeting place of an ancient city.

AMPHORA Tall, narrow-necked jar for oil or wine.

ÁNO Upper; as in upper town or village – Áno Zákros.

APSE Curved recess at the altar end of a church.

ARCHAIC PERIOD Late Iron Age from around 750 BC to the start of the Classical period in the fifth century BC.

ARSENALI Arsenals – a term used rather loosely for many Venetian defensive and harbour works.

ASKLEPION Sanctuary dedicated to Asclepius, the Greek god of healing, where the sick sought cures for their ailments.

ATRIUM Central altar-court of a Roman house.

ÁYIOS/AYÍA/ÁYII Saint or holy (m/f/pl), common place-name prefix (abbrev. Ag. or Ay.): Áyios Nikólaos, St. Nicholas; Ayía Triádha, Holy Trinity.

BASILICA Colonnaded "hall-type" church.

BYZANTINE EMPIRE Created by the division of the Roman Empire in 395 AD, this was the eastern half, ruled from Byzantium or Constantinople (modern Istanbul). On Crete, Byzantine churches of the fifth to the twelfth century are almost commonplace, and Byzantine art flourished again after the fall of Constantinople in 1453, under Venetian rule, when many artists and scholars fled to the island.

CENTRAL COURT Paved area at the heart of a Minoan palace.

CLASSICAL PERIOD Essentially from the end of the Persian Wars in the fifth century BC to the unification of Greece under Philip II of Macedon (338 BC).

DHIMARHÍO Town hall (modern usage).

DHOMÁTIA Rooms for rent in private houses.

DORIAN Civilization which overran the Mycenaeans from the north around 1100 BC, and became their successor throughout much of southern Greece, including Crete.

EPARHÍA Greek Orthodox diocese, also the smallest subdivision of a modern province.

ETEO-CRETAN Literally true Cretan, the Eteo-Cretans are believed to have been remnants of the Minoan people who kept a degree of their language and culture alive in isolated centres in eastern Crete as late as the third century BC.

GEOMETRIC PERIOD Post-Mycenaean Iron Age named for the style of its pottery: beginnings are in the early eleventh century BC with the arrival of Dorian peoples – by the eighth, with the development of representational styles, it becomes known as the Archaic period.

HELLENISTIC PERIOD The last and most unified Greek empire, created by Philip II and Alexander the Great in the fourth century BC, finally collapsing with the fall of Corinth to the Romans in 146 BC.

HÓRA Main town of a region; literally it means "the place".

IKONOSTÁSIS Screen between the nave of a church and the altar, often covered in icons.

JANISSARY Member of the Turkish Imperial Guard: in Crete under the Turks a much-feared mercenary force, often forcibly recruited from the local population.

KAFENÍON Coffeehouse/café: in a small village the centre of communal life and probably the bus stop, too.

KAΪKI A caique, or medium-sized boat, traditionally wooden. Now used for just about any coast-hopping or excursion boat.

KÁMBOS Fertile agricultural plateau, usually near a river mouth.

KAPETÁNIOS Widely used term of honour for a man of local power – originally for guerrilla leaders who earned the title through acts of particular bravado.

KÁSTRO Medieval castle or any fortified hill.

KÁTO Lower; as in Káto Zákros.

KERNOS Ancient cult vessel or altar with a number of receptacles for offerings.

KRATER Large, two-handled wine bowl.

LARNAKES Minoan clay coffins.

LUSTRAL BASIN A small sunken chamber in Minoan palaces reached by steps: perhaps actually some kind of bath but more likely for purely ritual purification.

MEGARON Principal hall of a Mycenaean palace.

MELTÉMI North wind that blows across the Aegean in summer and can be vicious in Crete. Its force is gauged by what it knocks over – "tableweather", "chairweather" etc.

MINOAN Crete's great Bronze Age civilization which dominated the Aegean from about 2500 to 1400 BC.

MONÍ Monastery or convent.

MYCENAEAN Mainland civilization centred on Mycenae c.1700–1100 BC: some claim they were responsible for the destruction of the Minoans, and certainly Mycenaean influence pervaded Crete in the late and post-Minoan periods.

NEOLITHIC The earliest era of settlement in Crete, characterized by the use of stone tools and weapons together with basic agriculture.

NÉOS, NÉA, NÉO New.

NOMÓS Modern Greek province: Crete is divided into four.

ODEION Small amphitheatre used for performances or meetings.

PALEÓS, PALEÁ, PALEÓ Old.

PALLIKÁRI Literally "brave man": in Crete a guerrilla fighter, particularly in the struggle for independence from the Turks, also a general term for a tough young man.

PANAYÍA The Virgin Mary.

PANIYÍRI Festival or feast – the local celebration of a holy day.

PANTOKRATOR Literally "The Almighty", a stern figure of Christ or God the Father frescoed or in mosaic on the dome of many Byzantine churches.

PARALÍA Seafront promenade.

PEAK SANCTUARY Mountain-top shrine, often in or associated with a cave, sometimes in continuous use from Neolithic through to Roman times.

PERÍPTERO Street kiosk.

PERISTYLE Colonnade or area surrounded by colonnade, used especially of Minoan halls or courtyards.

PÍTHOS (pl. PÍTHOI) Large ceramic jar for storing oil, grain etc, very common in the Minoan palaces and used in almost identical form in modern Cretan homes.

PLATÍA Square or plaza. KENTRIKÍ PLATÍA is the main square.

PROPILEA Portico or entrance to an ancient building.

RHYTON Vessel, often horn-shaped, for pouring libations or offerings.

STELE Upright stone slab or column, usually inscribed.

STOA Colonnaded walkway in Classical era marketplace.

THEATRAL AREA Open area found in most of the Minoan palaces with seat-like steps around. May have been a type of theatre or ritual area, but not conclusively proved.

THÓLOS Conical or beehive-shaped building, especially a Mycenaean tomb.

ACRONYMS

ANEK Anonimí Navtikí Evería Krítis (Shipping Co of Crete, Ltd), which runs most ferries between Pireás and Crete, plus many to Italy.

EA Greek Left (Ellenikí Aristerá), formerly the Greek Euro-communist Party (KKE-Esoterikoú).

ELTA The postal service.

EOS Greek Mountaineering Federation, based in Athens.

EOT Ellinikós Organismós Tourismoú, the National Tourist Organization.

KKE Communist Party, unreconstructed.

KTEL National syndicate of bus companies. The term is also used to refer to bus stations.

ND Conservative (Néa Dhimokratía) party.

OSE Railway corporation.

OTE Telephone company.

PASOK Socialist party (Pan-Hellenic Socialist Movement). Currently the government party.

SEO Greek Mountaineering Club, based in Thessaloníki.

INDEX

the perfect getaway vehicle

low-price holiday car rental.

rent a car from holiday autos and you'll give yourself real freedom to explore your holiday destination. with great-value, fully-inclusive rates in over 4,000 locations worldwide, wherever you're escaping to, we're there to make sure you get excellent prices and superb service.

what's more, you can book now with complete confidence. our £5 undercut* ensures that you are guaranteed the best value for money in holiday destinations right around the globe.

drive away with a great deal, call holiday autos now on **0990 300 400** and quote ref RG.

holiday autos
miles ahead

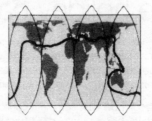